UTILITY AND DEMOCRACY

The Political Thought of Jeremy Bentham

Utility and Democracy

The Political Thought of Jeremy Bentham

PHILIP SCHOFIELD

OXFORD
UNIVERSITY PRESS

OXFORD
UNIVERSITY PRESS

Great Clarendon Street, Oxford OX2 6DP

Oxford University Press is a department of the University of Oxford.
It furthers the University's objective of excellence in research, scholarship,
and education by publishing worldwide in

Oxford New York

Auckland Cape Town Dar es Salaam Hong Kong Karachi
Kuala Lumpur Madrid Melbourne Mexico City Nairobi
New Delhi Shanghai Taipei Toronto

With offices in

Argentina Austria Brazil Chile Czech Republic France Greece
Guatemala Hungary Italy Japan Poland Portugal Singapore
South Korea Switzerland Thailand Turkey Ukraine Vietnam

Published in the United States
by Oxford University Press Inc., New York

First published 2006

British Library Cataloguing in Publication Data
Data available

Library of Congress Cataloging in Publication Data
Data available

Typeset by Newgen Imaging Systems (P) Ltd., Chennai, India
Printed in Great Britain
on acid-free paper by
Biddles Ltd., King's Lynn, Norfolk

ISBN 978–0–19–820856–3

Preface

In writing this book, which takes the political thought of Jeremy Bentham for its subject-matter, and approaches it through the discipline of the historian, I have aimed to present Bentham on his own terms. I have not seen it as my role to attempt to contribute directly to contemporary debates about the strengths and weaknesses of utilitarianism, or about the explanatory power of legal positivism, or about whether Bentham is best interpreted as a liberal or an authoritarian, and so forth. These are the tasks of the philosopher, of the legal theorist, and of that variety of historian of political thought who studies the past in order to shed light on the present. Nevertheless, providing it is not the case that no one ever learns anything from history, it is possible that the contents of this book may be of some interest to participants in those debates. If Bentham is invoked by philosophers, legal theorists, historians of political thought, and scholars from other disciplines such as political science, economics, and literary and cultural studies (as he increasingly is), then it may be of service to have a more detailed historical account, and in turn a clearer understanding, of what it was that Bentham himself thought, and of the circumstances which prompted him to think it. My ambition has been to provide a more satisfactory narrative of the historical development of Bentham's political thought—or at least of some aspects of Bentham's political thought—than has hitherto appeared, and thereby to provide a framework for future research, where that may be appropriate.

It is the central thesis of this book that in or around 1804 the notion of sinister interest emerged in Bentham's thought, and had a major impact on his understanding of the political process. It is the presence of sinister interest which, crudely speaking, distinguishes 'the radical Bentham' of the nineteenth century from 'the enlightenment Bentham' of the eighteenth century. Having said that, I also contend that, in certain key elements, Bentham's thought remained remarkably stable. Those elements included not only the principle of utility, but also, and more fundamentally, his theory of real and fictitious entities. Bentham's philosophy began with the physical world, and the way in which the human mind experienced that world, and then represented it in discourse. When Bentham had explained the nature of the physical or the real, he found himself in a position to explain the nature of the moral. Pleasure and pain were real, and if sentient creatures who had the capacity to experience pleasure and pain did not exist, nothing would matter.

While this is not a short book, it suffers from a number of lacunae. The vast amount of material which Bentham printed and published during his lifetime, together with that which has been published since, and the near impossibility of reading with ease the great mass of his manuscripts which remain untranscribed, make it very difficult to study, let alone to integrate into one's account, more than a small proportion of his corpus. This book would have benefited, for example, from a more systematic consideration of Bentham's general jurisprudence; from a more detailed account of the four sub-ends of the principle of utility—abundance, subsistence, security, and equality—and their relationship to his politics; from a more extensive consideration of his religious manuscripts; from a study of the writings on Prize Law, which Bentham regarded as one more element in the system of misrule; and from a deeper appreciation of his economic thought. Considerably more might have been said on specific aspects of his mature political thought, for instance, on his analysis of the different forms of government, on his insights into the nature of corruption and corruptive influence, and on his opposition to titles of honour. An extremely pertinent chapter might have been written on Bentham's attitude towards the reward of officials, in particular his preference for remuneration by salary instead of by fee—a subject to which he devoted an enormous amount of attention throughout his career. It is my hope that it will be found possible to incorporate studies of these topics within the framework which this book provides.

All this points to the sobering thought that any study of Bentham is necessarily more provisional than that of many other past thinkers. A 'definitive' study of Bentham, or at least of more than some narrowly defined area of his thought, is still some way off. This is due to the lack of a reliable and complete edition of his works, though the situation is being progressively remedied by the Bentham Project at University College London. By the time this book is published, twenty-six volumes will have appeared in the new, authoritative edition of *The Collected Works of Jeremy Bentham*, though forty or so more will be needed to finish the job. When the vast amount of manuscript which is still unexplored is brought to the attention of scholars, much more will be discovered not only about the historical development of Bentham's thought, but also about the philosophical content of that thought. For the present, I have based my narrative on what I consider to be the most authentic sources available, and have tried to be sensitive to the date at which the material in question was written. This approach reveals the continuities and discontinuities in Bentham's thought, and helps to achieve the goal of presenting an account of what Bentham himself said, rather than what his editors and interpreters have had him say. I have avoided any reliance on the recensions of Bentham's works produced by Étienne Dumont, brilliant though they are, and of outstanding importance in terms of the diffusion of Bentham's ideas to a Francophone audience. An exception is *Political Tactics*, for which I have relied on the English retranslation of Dumont's French translation of Bentham's original English manuscripts (themselves lost in the 1810s). In another instance—*Analysis of the Influence of Natural Religion on the Temporal Happiness of Mankind*—I have relied on a text published in Bentham's lifetime by an editor (George Grote) commissioned by Bentham, but over whose work he did not exercise much control. In short, I have adopted a hierarchy of preferred sources, choosing to rely, where possible, first on texts which have been published in *The Collected Works of Jeremy Bentham*; second, on texts which Bentham himself printed or published in his lifetime; and third, on Bentham's original manuscripts. Fortunately, things will only get better for the Bentham scholar as more texts appear in the new, authoritative edition.

A few words need to be said in explanation of Bentham's working methods, and the different categories of manuscript into which his papers may be conveniently divided, since, at various points in this book, mention is made of the category of manuscript from which some particular quotation is taken. Bentham tended to compose his works on sheets of foolscap (double sheets earlier in his career, single sheets later), ruled with a wide margin and with a double line at the top for the date and heading. Many of these 'text sheets' contain numerous additions (usually interlinear, but sometimes marginal), deletions, and emendations. Bentham's habit was to write a sequence of several sheets of text, to read it over and make corrections, and then to write summaries of the content in the margin. The marginal summaries were written in the form of short paragraphs and numbered consecutively. These marginal summaries were often copied onto separate sheets ('marginal summary sheets') by one or other of Bentham's amanuenses. The marginal summary sheets, written on single sheets of foolscap ruled into four columns with a double line at the top for the date and heading, also bear occasional corrections and emendations in Bentham's hand. A further category of sheets, which Bentham termed rudiment sheets, contain notes, aphorisms, general principles, and plans, and usually consist of double sheets of foolscap, each sheet being ruled into four columns.

I joined the Bentham Project in 1984, and in that sense this book has been over twenty years in the making. In that time, I have accumulated an enormous intellectual debt to colleagues at the Project. In the first place, I must express my deep sense of gratitude to Frederick Rosen and William Twining—for many years General Editor of *The Collected Works of Jeremy Bentham* and Chair of the Bentham Committee, respectively. Their vision and leadership, their intellectual integrity and curiosity, their rigorous standards of scholarship, and their commitment to the 'Benthamic' enterprise, have been truly inspirational. Without their encouragement, guidance, and support, I would probably be sweeping the platforms on Preston Station. I am similarly compelled to acknowledge my debt to the two other former General Editors of *The Collected Works of Jeremy Bentham*, both great historians: the late John Dinwiddy, who introduced me to the Bentham Project, and J. H. Burns, the doyen of Bentham scholars. I want to thank the current staff of the Bentham Project—Catherine Fuller, Kate Barber, Michael Quinn, Catherine Pease-Watkin, Deborah McVea, Irena Nicoll, Oliver Harris, and Tony Draper—for being such marvellous friends and colleagues, and for creating a climate in which collaborative research is able to flourish. They are a pleasure to work with, and have supported me unstintingly in the preparation of this book. Past members of the Project, including the late

Janet Semple, Stephen Conway, Jane Desmarais, Marilyn Morris, Cyprian Blamires, Jonathan Harris, Colin Tyler, Alan Pitt, and Luke O'Sullivan, have all contributed, albeit unwittingly, to this book, as have the students who, over the years, have taken our MA/LLM course on Jeremy Bentham and the Utilitarian Tradition.

I have profited from the writings, lectures, papers, and conversation of the worldwide community of Bentham scholars, which includes David Lieberman, Stephen Engelmann, James Crimmins, Douglas Long, Gerald Postema, Hugo Bedau, Ross Harrison, Paul Kelly, Oren Ben Dor, Marco Guidi, Emmanuelle de Champs, Gunhild Hoogensen, and Allison Dube. I need to make a special mention of Donald Jackson, whose unpublished paper on sinister interest pointed me in the right direction. I also wish to thank the growing coterie of Japanese scholars with an interest in Bentham and utilitarianism—and in particular Yoshio Nagai, Michihiro Otonashi, Naobumi Hijikata, Daisuke Arie, and Yasunori Fukagai—for giving me several opportunities to present my work to Japanese audiences.

I wish to express my thanks to three historians who have been responsible for nurturing my interest in eighteenth-century Britain: W. H. Snow, my teacher at Chorley Grammar School and Runshaw Sixth Form College; Frank O'Gorman, whose special topic I was privileged to attend at the University of Manchester; and the late I. R. Christie, who supervised my Ph.D at University College London.

I am very grateful to my colleagues in the Faculty of Laws, University College London, for so graciously welcoming a historian into their midst. I would like to make especial mention of Andrew Lewis, Stephen Guest, and Jeffrey Jowell, all of whom have been strong supporters of the Bentham edition and of the scholarship which it represents. Thanks are also due to Jonathan Wolff, the current Chair of the Bentham Committee, for all his support and good advice. The staff of University College London Library, particularly Gill Furlong and Susan Stead, have been tremendously helpful, responding efficiently and with good humour to a never-ending series of requests for access to manuscripts and rare books, and facilitating the editorial work of the Bentham Project to which this book owes so much.

An earlier version of Chapter 3 appeared as 'Jeremy Bentham's "Nonsense upon Stilts"', in *Utilitas*, 15 (2003), 1–26, and an earlier version of Chapter 4 as 'Jeremy Bentham, the French Revolution and Political Radicalism', in *History of European Ideas*, 30 (2004), 381–401. Echoes of Chapters 1 and 2 will be found in 'Jeremy Bentham, the Principle of Utility, and Legal Positivism', in M. D. A. Freeman (ed.), *Current Legal Problems 2003: Volume 56* (Oxford, 2004), 1–39; of Chapter 9 in 'Jeremy Bentham: Legislator of the World', in M. D. A Freeman (ed.), *Current Legal Problems 1998: Volume 51. Legal Theory at the End of the Millennium* (Oxford, 1998), 115–47; and still more distant echoes of Chapter 11 in 'The Constitutional Code of Jeremy Bentham', *The King's College Law*

Journal, 2 (1991–2), 40–62, and in 'Bentham on the Identification of Interests', *Utilitas*, 8 (1996), 223–34.

I would like to thank the following repositories for permission to quote from manuscripts in their possession: University College London Library; the British Library; the British Library of Political and Economic Science; the Bodleian Library, University of Oxford; the National Library of Ireland; University College Dublin Library; the Beinecke Rare Book and Manuscript Library, Yale University; Cornell University Library; and the University of Illinois at Urbana-Champaign Library.

Finally, I should thank my long-suffering family—my wife Kathryn, and our daughters Rebecca and Abigail—for enduring constant talk about Mr Bentham. Becky and Abbie find it difficult to understand what is so interesting about 'a man in a box', and wonder why their father is unable to find a better job (for instance, sweeping Preston Station). I am dedicating this book to them, and to my mother, for all her love and support.

Philip Schofield

University College London
29 September 2005

Contents

List of Abbreviations

Bowring	*The Works of Jeremy Bentham, published under the superintendence of his executor, John Bowring*, 11 vols. (Edinburgh, 1838–43)
Correspondence	*The Correspondence of Jeremy Bentham* (*The Collected Works of Jeremy Bentham*), 12 vols., various editors
Stark	*Jeremy Bentham's Economic Writings: Critical Edition Based on his Printed Works and Unprinted Manuscripts*, ed. W. Stark, 3 vols. (London, 1952–4)
UC	Bentham Papers, University College London Library (roman numerals refer to the boxes in which the papers are placed, arabic to the folios within each box)

1

Real and Fictitious Entities

I

Jeremy Bentham was afraid of ghosts. In his old age he reminisced that, when a child, his fears had been exploited by the servants at his grandmother's home at Barking. The servants had invented ghosts, including Tom Dark, Rawhead, and Bloody Bones, who lived in the 'houses of office', which Bentham had in consequence avoided, fleeing to the fields 'when suffering was intolerable'. A local innkeeper, Palethorp, had been transformed into a hobgoblin.[1] When 9 or 10 years old, Bentham had seen a puppet show, where the characters had included the devil and the devil's imp, who had then appeared in a nightmare: 'the devil and the imp', he confessed, 'dwelt in my waking thoughts for many a year afterwards'.[2] He recalled that, while at Westminster School, a portrait of Sulla, with his 'civic costume' and 'long flowing head of white hair', had 'wrought upon' his 'morbidly susceptible frame' and given him nightmares.[3] He had been frightened by the accounts of vampires in *Lettres Juives*,[4] by *Paradise Lost*, for '[t]here was the pandæmonium with all its flames',[5] and by the story of the goat in the cave in *Robinson Crusoe*, thinking it might be a devil.[6] He had discovered that 'the devil was everywhere' in *Pilgrim's Progress*,[7] 'and', he added, 'in me too'. He had seen a picture of the devil sowing tares, and wondered whether 'it was not a copy from the life?'[8] When Bentham, at the age of 12, had taken up residence at Queen's College, Oxford, in October 1760, he had been assigned to a 'very gloomy' chamber, which overlooked a graveyard. He had been plagued

[1] *The Works of Jeremy Bentham*, ed. J. Bowring, 11 vols. (Edinburgh, 1838–43) [hereafter Bowring], x. 18–19.
[2] Ibid. 19.
[3] Ibid. 20.
[4] See [Jean Baptiste de Boyer, Marquis d'Argens], *Lettres Juives, ou Correspondance Philosophique, Historique & Critique, Entre un Juif Voïageur en differens États de l'europe, & ses Correspondans en divers Endroits. Nouvelle Édition augmentée de XX Nouvelles Lettres, de Quantité de Remarques, & de plusieurs Figures*, 6 vols. (La Haye, 1738), Lettre CXXXVII, iv. 144–57.
[5] See John Milton, *Paradise Lost* (first published in 1667), i. 756–7, where Pandæmonium is described as 'the High Capital | Of Satan and his Peers'.
[6] See [Daniel Defoe], *The Life and Strange Surprizing Adventures of Robinson Crusoe, of York, Mariner* (London, 1719), 209–10.
[7] John Bunyan's *The Pilgrim's Progress* was first published in two parts in 1678 and 1684, respectively.
[8] Bowring, x. 11, 21.

with 'the visitations of spiritual beings', until he had managed to exchange rooms.[9] He continued to have nightmares when he slept alone,[10] and so, at least from the time when he moved into his home at Queen's Square Place, Westminster, on the death of his father in 1792, he had a boy sleep in his bedroom with him.[11] He understood that, though very real, his fear of ghosts was the product of his imagination:

> In no man's judgment can a stronger persuasion of the non-existence of these sources of terror have place than in mine; yet no sooner do I lay myself down to sleep in a dark room than, if no other person is in the room, and my eyes keep open, these instruments of terror obtrude themselves; and, to free myself from the annoyance, I feel myself under the necessity of substituting to those more or less pleasing ideas with which my mind would otherwise have been occupied, those reflections which are necessary to keep in my view the judgment by which the non-existence of these creatures of the imagination has so often been pronounced.[12]

His lifelong suffering from this source, he noted, was an apt illustration of the distinction between the judgment and the imagination.[13]

Bentham was, therefore, forced to confront the distinction between the real and the imaginary from his early childhood, and it is possible that, as C. K. Ogden has intimated, it was upon the 'grim foundation' of ghosts and spectres that he constructed one of his most important insights, namely his theory of real and fictitious entities.[14] If this was the case, some aspects at least of his theory of real and fictitious entities must pre-date his commitment to the principle of utility, and in particular his adoption of the phrase 'the greatest happiness of the greatest number'. Bentham later assigned his being 'set on the principle of utility' to the influence of Montesquieu, Barrington, Beccaria, and, 'most of all', Helvétius, and to the 'most interesting year' of 1769.[15] Bentham never did provide a systematic or detailed account of his intellectual development,[16] though,

[9] Bowring, x. 39. For Bentham's letter to his father Jeremiah of 21 April 1762 explaining his decision to exchange rooms see *The Correspondence of Jeremy Bentham* [hereafter *Correspondence*], vol. i, ed. T. L. S. Sprigge (London, 1968), 63–4.

[10] Bowring, x. 20.

[11] See Bentham to Jean Antoine Gauvain Gallois, Sept. 1814, *Correspondence*, vol. viii, ed. S. Conway (Oxford, 1988), 431.

[12] Bowring, xi. 84.

[13] Ibid. 64.

[14] C. K. Ogden, *Bentham's Theory of Fictions* (London, 1932), pp. xi–xvi. The use of the phrase 'theory of fictions' to refer to Bentham's thinking on ontology, logic, language, and grammar, though common in the secondary literature, is potentially confusing. Bentham did very occasionally use the term 'fiction' to represent what he meant by the term 'fictitious entity', but the two terms normally referred to two distinct, albeit related, ideas. The name of a fictitious entity, as we shall see, represented an entity which did not have physical existence, while a fiction was an erroneous proposition. Hence, it appears to be more accurate, as well as less confusing, when discussing Bentham's ontology, to speak of his theory of real and fictitious entities, rather than of his theory of fictions. Having said that, a fiction was erroneous just because it misrepresented the physical world. To borrow a phrase from M. P. Mack, *Jeremy Bentham: An Odyssey of Ideas 1748–92* (London, 1962), 1, a fiction was a proposition in which a claim was made 'that non-realities exist'.

[15] Bowring, x. 54.

[16] Bentham's relationship to Hume, Helvétius, Adam Smith, and the Epicurean tradition more generally is investigated in F. Rosen, *Classical Utilitarianism from Hume to Mill* (London, 2003).

from a number of scattered fragments, written at different times throughout his life (and not wholly consistent), several pertinent points do emerge. The figures whom Bentham mentioned most frequently were David Hume, Claude Adrien Helvétius, and Joseph Priestley, while John Locke, David Hartley, Cesare Beccaria, and Montesquieu also featured prominently. Bentham's attitude to Hume, as it was typically towards the other thinkers, was ambivalent. In *A Fragment on Government*, published in 1776, he remarked on the particular importance of Hume's account of utility in *A Treatise of Human Nature*:[17]

> That the foundations of all *virtue* are laid in *utility*, is there demonstrated, after a few exceptions made, with the strongest force of evidence: but I see not, any more than Helvetius saw, what need there was for the exceptions.
>
> For my own part, I well remember, no sooner had I read that part of the work which touches on this subject, than I felt as if scales had fallen from my eyes. I then, for the first time, learnt to call the cause of the people the cause of Virtue.[18]

Writing over fifty years later, Bentham complained that the notion of 'utility' as it had appeared in Hume's *Enquiry concerning the Principles of Morals*[19] was 'altogether vague'. Bentham identified a number of deficiencies in Hume's account. Hume had presented the notion of 'usefulness' as sometimes meaning 'conduciveness to happiness', but at other times as 'conduciveness to the end or purpose proposed', whatever that might happen to be, he had failed to show the way in which happiness was 'inseparably connected' with pleasure and pain; he had failed to explain the relationship between '[p]leasures, pains, desires, emotions, affections, passions, interests, virtues, vices, talents and other psychological entities'; he had furnished 'no criterion of right and wrong'; he had not properly distinguished between the virtues or explained their relationship to happiness; in the field of morals, as had been the case until Bentham's own work in the field of law, he had confounded what ought to be with what is; and nothing he had said in relation to good and evil had been applied to any practical use.[20]

If Hume had, in Bentham's view, provided at least some insight into the principle of utility, so had Hartley, who, in *Observations on Man*,[21] had connected happiness with pleasure and pain. Hartley, however, had failed to recognize the role of the principle of utility as 'an all-directing guide in the walks of public as well as private life'. Helvétius had been the first to describe clearly the connections between the key notions of utility, happiness, and pleasure and

[17] See David Hume, *A Treatise of Human Nature* (first published 1739–40), ed. L. A. Selby-Bigge, 2nd edn., revised by P. H. Nidditch (Oxford, 1978), Book III, 455–621.

[18] *A Comment on the Commentaries and A Fragment on Government*, ed. J. H. Burns and H. L. A. Hart (London, 1977), 440 n.

[19] See David Hume, *An Enquiry concerning the Principles of Morals* (first published 1751), ed. T. L. Beauchamp (Oxford, 1998).

[20] *Deontology together with A Table of the Springs of Action and Article on Utilitarianism*, ed. A. Goldworth (Oxford, 1983), 289–90, 322–4.

[21] David Hartley, *Observations on Man, his Frame, his Duty, and his Expectations*, 2 vols. (London, 1749).

pain. In *De l'esprit*[22] he had made 'a commencement . . . of the application of the principle of utility to practical uses', by linking the notion of utility to happiness, and happiness in turn with pleasure and pain.[23] Writing in the early 1770s, Bentham had remarked that Helvétius had 'established a standard of rectitude for actions', namely that an action was right 'when the tendency of it is to augment the mass of happiness in the community'.[24] Again, Bentham remarked that it had been Helvétius 'who first had discernment and courage to set up the principle of utility as the sole and universal standard of right and wrong' in matters of both morals and legislation, and had then been followed by Beccaria, in relation to legislation,[25] and by Priestley, the first writer in English to do so, though neither had acknowledged him.[26]

As far as Bentham himself was concerned, as we have seen, the critical moment was the 'most interesting year' of 1769, when he read Priestley's *An Essay on the First Principles of Government* (first published in 1768). He later claimed that it was in this work that he had discovered the phrase 'the greatest happiness of the greatest number', and that 'it was by that pamphlet and this phrase in it' that his 'principles on the subject of morality, public and private together, [had been] determined'.[27] Ironically, the phrase itself does not appear in Priestley's book, though his statement that 'the good and happiness of the members, that is the majority of the members of any state, is the great standard by which every thing relating to that state must finally be determined'[28] is perhaps close enough in terminology and sense to be the substantive source of the phrase adopted by Bentham.[29] When he published *A Fragment on*

22 Helvétius' *De l'esprit*, first published in French in 1758, appeared in English translation as *De L'Esprit: or, Essays on the Mind, and its several Faculties* (London, 1759).

23 *Deontology*, 290–1, 324–5; *Official Aptitude Maximized; Expense Minimized*, ed. P. Schofield (Oxford, 1993), 350–1.

24 Bowring, x. 70. Elsewhere (see Bentham to the Revd John Forster, Apr./May 1778, *Correspondence*, vol. ii, ed. T. L. S. Sprigge (London, 1968), 99), Bentham wrote: 'From [Helvétius] I learnt to look upon the tendency of any institution or pursuit to promote the happiness of society as the sole text and measure of its merit: and to regard the principle of utility as an oracle which if properly consulted would afford the only true solution that could be given to every question of right and wrong.'

25 Bentham, of course, had in mind Beccaria's *Dei delitti e delle peine*, first published in 1764, translated into French by Morellet in 1766, and into English in 1767. See A. J. Draper, 'Cesare Beccaria's Influence on English Discussions of Punishment, 1764–1789', *History of European Ideas*, 26 (2000), 177–99.

26 University College London Library, Bentham Papers [hereafter UC], Box clix, fo. 270. See also UC lxx. 23.

27 *Deontology*, 291–2, 325–6; *Official Aptitude Maximized; Expense Minimized*, 349–50.

28 Joseph Priestley, *An Essay on the First Principles of Government; and on the nature of Political, Civil, and Religious Liberty* (London, 1768), 17. Bowring certainly understood this work to be the source: see Bowring, x. 142 n. Priestley, however, unlike Helvétius, had not, in Bentham's view, made the connection between happiness on the one hand, and pleasure and pain on the other: see ibid. 567.

29 In his Commonplace Book of the early 1780s (see ibid. 142), Bentham was less certain about the source of the phrase: 'Priestley was the first (unless it was Beccaria) who taught my lips to pronounce this sacred truth:—That the greatest happiness of the greatest number is the foundation

Government in 1776, Bentham, according to his later account, adopted from Hume the phrase 'the principle of utility', and from Priestley (as he thought) the phrase 'the greatest happiness of the greatest number' in order to explicate the principle.[30] Although in *A Fragment on Government*, Bentham confessed, 'the language of *happiness* . . . is not *substituted* to that of utility, the word "utility" being employed as well as the word "happiness" ', nonetheless it was there that 'the two languages are translated into one another, and the two locutions represented as interconvertible', and the proper basis for a science of morals and legislation for the first time laid down.[31]

It seems clear that, in Bentham's mind, the discovery of the formulation 'the greatest happiness of the greatest number' in 1769 enabled him to bring together into a coherent account a number of the elements on which he had settled much earlier. He stated that, at the age of 6 or 7, he had been greatly impressed with Fénelon's *Telemachus*: 'That romance may be regarded as the foundation-stone of my whole character; the starting-post from whence my career of life commenced. The first dawning in my mind of the principles of utility, may, I think, be traced to it.' Of particular significance was the debate on the best form of government which took place as part of a trial to find a new king for Crete, and in which the answers of one of the contestants 'seemed . . . to border, at least, on the principles of utility; or, in other words, the greatest-happiness principle'. In this instance, Bentham had been disappointed with Telemachus, 'whose notions seemed to me a short but still too long a tissue of vague generalities, by which no clear impression was presented to my mind. . . . On every other occasion he was all perfection in my eyes: but on *this* occasion, I knew not well what to make of him.'[32] At the age of 12, when he had entered the University of Oxford and his father had forced him to translate Cicero's *Tusculan Disputations*, he had been repelled by the 'self-contradictory proposition' that 'Pain . . . was no evil' and that 'Virtue was, and is, of itself sufficient to confer happiness on any man who is disposed to possess it on those terms'.[33]

Most significantly, there is evidence that what would become Bentham's theory of real and fictitious entities was developing during these formative years.

of morals and legislation.' The related questions of the origin of the phrase, and the source from which Bentham might have taken it, are treated at length in R. Shackleton, 'The Greatest Happiness of the Greatest Number: The History of Bentham's Phrase', *Studies in Voltaire and the Eighteenth Century*, 90 (1972), 1461–82.

30 *Deontology*, 292. 31 Ibid. 326.

32 See Bowring, x. 10–11. For the Cretan debate see François de Fénelon, *Telemachus, son of Ulysses* (first published 1699), ed. and trans. P. Riley (Cambridge, 1994), Book V, 66–71, though it is not obvious that any of the briefly reported responses of Telemachus's rival contestants bordered on the greatest-happiness principle. In later life, Bentham said that he remembered reading *Telemachus* in the summer of 1754, when aged 6, 'as if it were but yesterday' (see Bentham to João Baptista Felgueiras, 5 June 1821, *Correspondence*, vol. x, ed. S. Conway (Oxford, 1994), 345), though a month earlier he had claimed that he had read it aged 7 (see Bentham to Toribio Núñez, 9? May 1821, ibid. 329–30).

33 *Deontology*, 300; *Correspondence*, i. 34–44, 53–5. Bentham perhaps had in mind *Tusculan Disputations*, v. 12–20.

As a young boy, even before entering Oxford, he had read Locke's *An Essay concerning Human Understanding*, and been 'puzzled by Locke's fictitious entities—such as *power*'.[34] Despite not having any 'clear notion of the principle of utility as the standard of merit of [moral] actions',[35] Locke had established 'a test of perspicuity for ideas', in that: 'The idea annexed to a word is a perspicuous one, when the simple ideas included under it are assignable.'[36] Bentham appears to have applied what he had learnt from Locke to his study of the political history of Britain. On reading Clarendon's *History of the Rebellion*,[37] Bentham's 'infant affections' had been enlisted 'on the side of despotism'. These 'affections' had then been reinforced at Oxford: 'The Genius of the place I dwelt in, the authority of the state, the voice of the Church in her solemn offices; all these had taught me to call Charles a Martyr, and his opponents rebels. . . . I saw strong countenance lent in the sacred writings to monarchic government: and none to any other. I saw *passive obedience* deep stamped with the seal of the Christian Virtues of humility and self-denial.' Bentham, however, became concerned that these doctrines were inconsistent with the Glorious Revolution of 1688. The lawyers who he had consulted had praised 'their Original Contract, as a recipe of sovereign efficacy for reconciling the accidental necessity of resistance with the general duty of submission', and had attempted to 'calm' his 'scruples' by administering to him '[t]his drug of theirs'. Bentham had asked them to show him 'that page of history' where the contract was recorded, whereupon they had been forced to 'confess the whole to be a fiction'.

This, methought, looked ill. It seemed to me the acknowledgment of a bad cause, the bringing a fiction to support it. 'To prove a fiction, indeed,' said I, 'there is need of fiction; but it is the characteristic of truth to need no proof but truth. Have you then really any such privilege as that of coining facts? You are spending argument to no purpose. Indulge yourselves in the licence of supporting that to be true which is not, and as well may you suppose that proposition itself to be true, which you wish to prove, as that other whereby you hope to prove it.' Thus continued I unsatisfying, and unsatisfied, till I learnt to see that *utility* was the text and measure of all virtue; of loyalty as much as any; and that the obligation to minister to general happiness, was an obligation paramount to and inclusive of every other.[38]

[34] Bowring, x. 22. For Locke's discussion of 'Power' see *An Essay concerning Human Understanding*, ed. P. H. Nidditch (Oxford, 1975), book I, ch. xxi, 233–87.

[35] UC lxx. 23 (*c*.1776).

[36] Bowring, x. 70. Bentham perhaps had in mind Locke's discussion 'Of Clear and Obscure, Distinct and Confused Ideas', in *An Essay concerning Human Understanding*, book II, ch. xxix, 362–72. The thought of Locke and that of Bentham on the subject of the definition of ideas is compared in R. Harrison, *Bentham* (London, 1983), 48–64.

[37] Edward Hyde, 1st Earl of Clarendon, *The History of the Rebellion and Civil Wars in England, begun in the Year 1641*, 3 vols. (Oxford, 1702–4).

[38] *A Fragment on Government*, 440–1 n. This passage may be read to suggest that Bentham read Clarendon's *History* at Oxford, but it appears from his account of his childhood reading at Bowring, x. 22, that he had read it before entering Oxford.

Elsewhere he stated that as early as 1764, when he had heard William Blackstone lecture at Oxford,[39] and Blackstone had 'lauded' the 'fiction' of the original contract, it had been 'an object of abhorrence'.[40] He also recalled that he had 'immediately detected [Blackstone's] fallacy respecting natural rights'.[41] On this account, Bentham had rejected the doctrine of the original contract, and apparently the doctrine of natural rights, before he had formulated the principle of utility. He must, presumably, have already had some inkling of his theory of real and fictitious entities, and its implications for the fictions so prevalent in the language of lawyers. If not, he would have had no reason to be dissatisfied with the original contract just because it was a fiction—in other words, because it had no basis in historical fact, and hence in the physical world. It is possible that reflection on his fear of ghosts and his reading of Locke had led him to important conclusions about the nature of the real and the imaginary even before he had gone to Oxford in 1760, and then while a student there in the early 1760s he had applied these insights to the law, politics, and religion. There would otherwise be no plausible explanation of the profound unease which he experienced when required to subscribe to the Thirty-nine Articles of the Church of England in order to take his degree in 1765.[42]

What is beyond dispute is that his thinking on these matters was well advanced when he wrote on mathematics, and geometry in particular, in the early 1770s, with the intention of furthering the education of his younger brother, Samuel, who was apprenticed to a shipwright, initially in Woolwich, and then in Chatham, between 1771 and 1778.[43] Bentham argued that it was necessary to show that mathematics was useful in order to encourage its study, otherwise a man had no motive 'for submitting to the fatigue that is necessary to enable him to apprehend it'.[44] Such a demonstration could only be achieved through a proper understanding of the subject-matter with which mathematics dealt, and this required an understanding of the distinction between real and

[39] For Bentham's engagement with Blackstone see J. H. Burns, 'Bentham and Blackstone: A Lifetime's Dialectic', *Utilitas: A Journal of Utilitarian Studies*, 1 (1989), 22–40.

[40] *Deontology*, 293. Cf. Bentham to Étienne Dumont, 14 May 1802, *Correspondence*, vol. vii, ed. J. R. Dinwiddy (Oxford, 1988), 25–6. Dumont, Bentham's Genevan friend and editor, produced five recensions of his writings between 1802 and 1828. For Dumont's relationship with Bentham see C. Blamires, 'Étienne Dumont: Genevan Apostle of Utility', *Utilitas: A Journal of Utilitarian Studies*, 2 (1990), 55–70.

[41] Bowring, x. 45.

[42] See pp.172–3 below.

[43] Much of this material (see UC cxxxiv and cxxxv), which appears to contain the earliest surviving text material composed by Bentham, is in Samuel's hand, and contains mathematical exercises undertaken by Samuel under Bentham's instruction. That which deals with real and fictitious entities is in Samuel's hand, but was dictated by Bentham. See the note, written by Bentham, at UC cxxxiv. 14: 'J.B. dictavit: S.B. scripsit.' It is perhaps not without significance that, when Bentham later began to write in detail on logic and language, he asked Samuel to send these papers to him: see Bentham to Samuel Bentham, 11 Aug. 1814, *Correspondence*, viii. 410–11.

[44] UC cxxxv. 1 (dated Wednesday 1 May, which points to the year 1771). At UC cxxxv. 46 (in Samuel's hand), Bentham recounts how, at some unspecified early age, he had been perplexed by the apparent lack of any practical use for the Euclidian geometry which he had been forced to study.

fictitious entities. A real entity was a body or a substance, that is 'anything which can be perceived by the senses'. Such a body was capable of exhibiting what were termed properties. While these properties could not be perceived one at a time, they were spoken of as though they could. Moreover, the names which were given to them were grammatically indistinguishable from the names of the substances of which they were predicated: 'to prevent their being confounded with real entities, with the bodies of which they are only, each of them, one of the constituents, that the names of them may be as opposite as possible, I have stiled these *fictitious* Entities in opposition to *Real* entities'. It had been the confounding of real with fictitious entities that had produced 'all the disputes among Geometricians and most others'. All the expressions in which fictitious entities occurred were 'metaphorical', and they were spoken of 'as if they did exist unconnected with others [i.e. other entities], when really they do not'.[45] Similarly, Bentham complained that geometers seemed to believe that 'what they assert concerning their fictitious Entities depends not on the existence of Real Entities'. However, fictitious entities only existed in real entities, and it was only from real entities that the idea of fictitious entities could be derived. Not only could a figure, such as a cube, not be shown to exist without being of a certain size, occupying a certain space, and being of a certain quantity, it could not even be conceived to exist: 'But even suppose one could conceive such a thing to exist as a line without breadth or a point without parts, of what use would it be?'[46] Bentham had not only developed the central distinction, which he later called 'the comprehensive and instructive distinction',[47] between real and fictitious entities, but had also concluded that the latter were incapable of definition *per genus et differentiam*, since they were of 'no genus', but were 'each of them a head itself under which substances may be classed according as they have that property'. The only way to expound them was 'by a paraphrasis', namely by as many sentences as was convenient to explain 'what appearances bodies exhibit' when the properties in question were said to exist.[48]

By the time that *A Fragment on Government* was published in 1776, Bentham's theory of real and fictitious entities was already in a mature form.

[45] UC cxxxv. 50 (in Samuel's hand). It is worth noting that Bentham had, at some point, studied James Harris's *Hermes: or, A Philosophical Inquiry concerning Language and Universal Grammar* (London, 1751) (see Bentham to Samuel Bentham, 9 Dec. 1774, *Correspondence*, i. 221), and that he was later excited by the appearance of John Horne Tooke's *A Letter to John Dunning, Esq.* (London, 1778), which, he remarked, 'contains an important discovery in Universal Grammar', by showing that most conjunctions were 'the imperatives of verbs' (see Bentham to Samuel Bentham, 27 Oct. 1778, *Correspondence*, ii. 181).

[46] UC cxxxv. 67 (in Samuel's hand).

[47] UC ci. 341 (7 August 1814) [Bowring, viii. 262]. Where works were not published by Bentham himself, rather than rely on the text which appears in the Bowring edition, I have, wherever possible, attempted to use my transcription of the original manuscript source. In these cases, for convenience, I have given the Bowring reference in square brackets. Exceptions are Bentham's essay on ontology, where I have given a reference to *De l'ontologie et autres texts sur les fictions*, ed. P. Schofield, J. P. Cléro, and C. Laval (Paris, 1997), and a portion of Bentham's writings on grammar, where I have given a reference to *Chrestomathia*, ed. M. J. Smith and W. H. Burston (Oxford, 1983).

[48] UC cxxxv. 59.

The principle of utility (a fictitious entity) was expounded in terms of its relationship to happiness (again a fictitious entity), which in turn was expounded in terms of its relationship to the real entities of pleasure and pain.[49] The writings on mathematics suggest that Bentham had already settled on the main features of his theory by the early 1770s. It is, furthermore, tempting to suggest that, even earlier than this, it had been the insights he had derived from his theory of real and fictitious entities that had led him in the first instance to identify what he regarded as the problems with Hume's account of the principle of utility, just as it had allowed him to appreciate the problems associated with the 'fiction' of the original contract, and then to recognize a solution to these problems by following Helvétius in linking utility, through happiness, to pleasure and pain, and by adopting what he took to be Priestley's phrase—'the greatest happiness of the greatest number'—as the appropriate formulation for the utilitarian criterion of right and wrong: hence, Bentham's later acknowledgment that it was by the works of Hume and Helvétius that the idea of 'utility' and of 'the greatest happiness principle' had been blended in his mind.[50] Just how Bentham combined the principle of utility with the sensations of pain and pleasure, and the phrase 'the greatest happiness of the greatest number', to create a ruling principle for the science of morals and legislation will be the subject of the next chapter. The task of the present chapter is to describe the foundation on which that science was laid, namely his theory of real and fictitious entities.

II

Bentham's most sustained period of writing on real and fictitious entities, in the context of works on education, logic, language, and grammar, took place in 1813–15. There was, nevertheless, an essential continuity between these writings and those of the 1770s. Bentham was, in effect, elaborating on the ontological insights which had underpinned his whole career as a thinker. The logical starting-point for his philosophy was the study of being, and in particular well-being. He gave the 'all comprehensive name' of 'eudæmonics' to the art which had for its object the attainment of well-being, and of which every other art was, more or less immediately, a branch or division.

> Directly or indirectly, *well-being*, in some shape or other, or in several shapes, or all shapes taken together, is the subject of every thought, and object of every action, on the part of every known *Being*, who is, at the same time a sensitive and thinking Being. Constantly and unpreventably it actually is so; nor can any intelligible reason be given for desiring that it should be otherwise.
>
> This being admitted, *Eudæmonics*, in some one or other of the divisions of which it is susceptible, or in all of them taken together, may be said to be the *object* of every branch

[49] The work also contains a classic example of the technique of paraphrasis: see p. 24 below.
[50] *Deontology*, 299.

of *art*, and the *subject* of every branch of *science*. *Eudæmonics*, the *art*, which has for the object of its endeavours, to contribute in some way or other to the attainment of *well-being*, and the *science* in virtue of which, in so far as it is possessed by him, a man knows in what manner he is to conduct himself in order to exercise that art with effect.

Given that well-being, in other words 'the existence of sensitive creatures—and that in a desirable state', was the object of eudæmonics, it followed that '*being* in some of its various shapes' was 'an indispensable *means*, without which the object of that art cannot in any instance be pursued and attained'. Sensitive being was 'the only *seat* of happiness', while being in general, including sensitive being, was 'the universal *instrument* of happiness'. In order to attain happiness, it was necessary to have 'an acquaintance, more or less considerable', with 'the *seat* of happiness' as well as with such beings as might form the instruments of happiness. The science which took being for its subject-matter was termed ontology. Hence, 'Eudæmonics is the art of *well-being*. Necessary to *well-being* is *being*. In every part, therefore, of the common field, concomitant and correspondent to *Eudæmonics* considered as an *art*, runs *Ontology*, considered as a *science*.'[51] In Bentham's view, every art had a correspondent science: it was a mistake to think that the field of thought and action could be divided into a series of distinct compartments, some containing an art, some a science, and some containing neither the one nor the other. The fact was that: 'Whatsoever spot is occupied by either, is occupied by both: it is occupied by them in *joint-tenancy*.' The distinction was founded on the distinction between practice and knowledge: '*Practice*, in proportion as *attention* and *exertion* are regarded as necessary to due *performance*, is termed *art: knowledge*, in proportion as *attention* and *exertion* are regarded as necessary to *attainment*, is termed *science*.' There was no 'determinate line of distinction' between an art and its correspondent science, but where 'that which is seen to be *done*' was regarded as being more prominent than 'that which is seen or supposed to be *known*', the more likely it was that it would be considered an art, and in the opposite case a science.[52] Ontology was, therefore, the art-and-science which comprehended all others, and from which all branches of art-and-science were derived. It followed that there was no other basis for knowledge, and for thought, than being—in other words, the physical world.

Bentham divided ontology into 'coenoscopic ontology', which dealt with 'properties or adjuncts common to all Beings',[53] and 'idioscopic ontology',

[51] *Chrestomathia*, Table V, 179–81. [52] Ibid. 59–60.

[53] Bentham noted that 'Metaphysics or Ontology in the common acceptation of the word' was the equivalent of coenoscopic ontology. In this context, Bentham rejected the possibility of knowledge derived from any source other than experience, and about any thing beyond experience. When he used the term 'metaphysics' to refer to a particular branch of knowledge, it was to refer to what he otherwise termed 'logic', a sub-branch, as we shall see, of idioscopic ontology. For instance, in the mid-1770s he defined '[t]he business of metaphysics' as being 'to examine what ideas we have belonging to the terms we use, and whether they are clear or no': see UC lxix. 152. Similarly, in his Memorandum Book for 1818–19 (Bowring, x. 510), he wrote: '*Logic*, alias *Metaphysics*, is the art and science whereby clearness, correctness, completeness, and connexity are given to ideas: its

which dealt with 'properties or adjuncts peculiar to different classes of Beings'. This latter branch of ontology was divided into somatology, which was concerned with the body, and pneumatology, which was concerned with the mind. The latter was then divided into pathoscopic pneumatology, which was concerned with the sensitive faculty, and nooscopic pneumatology, or noology, which was concerned with the intellect, and the latter in turn divided into coenonesioscopic, which was concerned with communication, and plasioscopic, which was logic, or '*the art of thinking*, with the correspondent matter of what belongs to the formation of the matter of thought'.[54] Bentham defined logic as 'the art, which has for its object or end in view, the giving to the best advantage, direction to the human mind and thence to the whole human frame, in its pursuit of any object or purpose, to the attainment of which it is capable of being applied'.[55] There were two main features of logic. First, no sphere of human activity was potentially outside its scope. There was no aspect of human knowledge (science) and activity (art) which might not be brought within the field of logic: 'As to its field or *subject*—the subject on which it is capable of operating—it is neither more nor less than the entire field of human thought and action.'[56] Second, logic was value-laden—only when the 'best advantage' resulted from the activity in question did it possess the property of logic. The 'ultimate end' of logic was well-being, just as it was of every other branch of art and science—whether ethics, medicine, or cookery—and not only the well-being of human beings but of all sentient creatures. Well-being existed 'directly as the magnitude of the aggregate of the pleasures of all sorts experienced' during the period of time in question, and inversely 'as the magnitude of the aggregate of pains of all sorts experienced'. It was only to the extent that logic was conducive to the increase of pleasure and diminution of pain that it was 'deserving of regard'.[57]

Logic was 'the art of thinking', but there could be no thought without language. Logic was a property of the operations of the human mind, insofar as these operations promoted well-being; and language was the instrument by which these operations were carried out. Language tended to be considered merely as an instrument of communication, but, observed Bentham, 'upon an attentive view, it will be found that when perception has been excepted, of all the several distinguishable faculties [of the human mind], there is scarcely one in the use of which it is not habitually employed—scarcely one which without it could be exercised with any considerable advantage or to any considerable extent'.[58] Language, or more generally discourse, composed of signs addressed to

usefulness is in the joint ratio of the importance of the ideas to which it applies itself—to the ideas themselves—and hence to the expressions whereby they are designated—since it is only by means of this sign that these qualities, or any qualities, can for any length of time be given to the ideas.'

[54] *Chrestomathia*, Table V, 183, 192, 198.
[55] UC ci. 92 (3 Aug. 1814) [Bowring, viii. 219].
[56] UC ci. 95 (25 July 1814) [Bowring, viii. 219].
[57] UC ci. 107–8 (25 Sept. 1814) [Bowring, viii. 222].
[58] UC ci. 289 (22 Aug. 1813) [Bowring, viii. 298].

the hearing, sight, or touch, was not only the means of communication, but also the instrument used in thought. The former case, where the discourse was addressed to the mind of some other person, represented the transitive use of discourse, and the latter case, where it was addressed just to the mind of the person employing it, represented its intransitive use. The crucial operation was 'designation', the giving of a proper name to an individual object, for without designation discourse could not take place. However, designation itself would not have taken place had it not been for the purpose of discourse, and in particular its transitive use. Discourse or language, therefore, owed its existence to its transitive use, but this should not lead one to underestimate the importance of its intransitive use: 'By its transitive use, the collections of these signs are only the vehicle of thought: by its intransitive use, it is an instrument employed in the creation and fixation of thought itself.' There was scarcely a mental operation in which, 'in respect of... its intransitive use,... in the character of a spring as well as a regulator of thoughts, language is not in an eminent degree subservient'. Without words, thoughts were like dreams or clouds, floating in and out of the mind: 'But for these fixt and fixative signs nothing that ever bore the name of *art* or *science* could ever have come into existence.' Well-being was in large measure dependent upon language, in that well-being depended upon thought, and thought depended upon language. For instance, man's 'superiority in the scale of perfection and intelligence' compared with other animals was due to his superior facility with language.[59]

There exists not that station in life be it ever so humble in which a man's well-being is not in some shape or other, in some degree or other, more or less dependent on the acquaintance he has with his own language. Language is not merely the instrument of discourse, it is moreover the instrument of thought. By language it is that a man not only discourses but thinks. The stock of a man's ideas is limited and determined by the stock of the words which he finds at his command—the words which he has to express them by.[60]

It was crucial, therefore, that a language possessed the quality of 'copiousness'—in other words, that it was 'capable of giving expression to all the ideas for the expression of which a demand is capable of having place'. In proportion as the copiousness of language was reduced, 'the place occupied by man on the scale of being' would descend 'from that of a member of the best governed and mannered community down to that of a barbarian, of a savage, of a beast'.[61] Yet language was also the source of error, either from the erroneous use of words, or from an erroneous combination of words when placed together in propositions.

[59] UC ci. 422–4 (29 July 1814) [Bowring, viii. 228–9].
[60] UC cii. 401 (24 Mar. 1814) [Bowring, viii. 319].
[61] UC cii. 344 (13 Aug. 1814); cii. 352 (16 Aug. 1814) [Bowring, viii. 309; 310]. For Bentham's optimism concerning the improvement of language, of which additions to its copiousness were of greatest importance, see UC cii. 392–4 (26 Aug. 1814) [Bowring, viii. 318].

The main purpose of the art-and-science of logic was to establish 'clear and determinate ideas', and thence to purge language of error.[62]

Given that thought could only be carried on by means of language, Bentham's central concern in his writings on logic was to understand the way in which language might be used both accurately to describe, and inaccurately or erroneously to misdescribe, the physical world. His argument was that language, in order to make sense, had to refer, either directly or indirectly, to physical objects. The basic unit of language was the proposition, which had to contain, whether explicitly or implicitly, at the very least four elements: namely the name of a subject, the name of some attribute or predicate, the name of a copula, and 'the sign by which existence is brought to view'. A single proposition always constituted a sentence, though a single sentence might contain any number of propositions.[63] Confusion arose, however, because the name of the subject, the noun substantive, was used in such a way as to suggest that it represented some physical object when, in fact, it did not always do so. The noun substantive might, for instance, represent a property of a physical object, or it might represent an abstraction. The grammatical structure failed to indicate to which of these classes of entities the noun substantive in question belonged. Within the context of a proposition, it made sense to talk about the property of a physical object, such as the ripeness or sweetness of an apple, or an abstraction, such as a law or a duty, just as it did to talk about a physical object, such as a person or a stone.[64] The way in which language was used unavoidably obscured the fundamental distinction between the two former categories, which, as we have seen, Bentham termed 'names of fictitious entities', and the latter category, which he termed 'names of real entities'. 'The only objects that really exist are substances—they are the only real entities. To convey any notion by words which are the names of any objects [other] than substances, we are obliged to attribute to such objects what in truth is attributable only to substances: in a word we are obliged to feign them to be substances. Those others in short are only fictitious entities.'[65] The mind was liable to be misled by the very language which it was compelled to use in order to describe the physical world because of the tendency, as in the case of qualities such as 'ripeness', but also in the case of

[62] UC ci. 103 (5 Aug. 1814) [Bowring, viii. 221].

[63] Bentham initially argued that a complete proposition need only contain the first three elements: see UC cii. 515 (13 Nov. 1815) and 503–6 (22 Nov. 1815) [*Chrestomathia*, 396–7, 399]. He then came to the view that a complete proposition contained four elements: 'to compleat the texture of the proposition, to the sign of the subject, the sign of the *quality*, and the sign of the *relation*, must be added the sign of existence: the sign by which existence is asserted to have or to have had place, viz. the existence of the relation between the subject and attribute.' See UC cii. 494 (30 Jan. 1816) [Bowring, viii. 337].

[64] UC cii. 451 (2 Dec. 1815) [Bowring, viii. 328].

[65] UC lxix. 241 (*c.*1776). It should be noted that Bentham distinguished fictitious entities themselves into physical or somatic fictitious entities (which included properties such as motion, quantity, quality, form, and relation); psychical, psychological, or noological fictitious entities (which included properties of the mind, such as desires and aversions); and ethical fictitious entities (which included abstractions such as powers and obligations): see UC ci. 323–30 (7–9 Aug. 1814) [Bowring, viii. 263–4], and UC cii. 508 (26 Nov. 1815) [*Chrestomathia*, 398].

abstractions such as power or obligation, to associate noun substantives with real entities, with objects existing in the physical world:

> Words, viz. words employed to serve as names, being the only instruments by which, in the absence of the *things*, viz. the *substances*, themselves, the ideas of them can be presented to the mind, hence, wheresoever a word is seen which to appearance is employed in the character of a *name*, a natural and abundantly extensive consequence is—a disposition and propensity to suppose the existence, the real existence, of a correspondent object—of a correspondent thing—of a thing to which it ministers in the character of a name.
>
> Yielded to without a sufficiently attentive caution, this disposition is a frequent source of confusion: of temporary confusion and perplexity: and not only so, but even of persisting error.[66]

Despite the fact that fictitious entities had been 'embodied as it were in names, and thus put upon a footing with real ones', and were 'so apt to be mistaken for real ones', they could not simply be annihilated: they were 'necessary fruits of the imagination without which, unreal as they are, *language* could not—scarcely could even *thought*, be carried on'.[67] A proper conception of language—more particularly of the relationship between language and human perception of the physical world—was the key to distinguishing between truth and error, between physical fact and mental fancy. A real entity was a 'corporeal substance'—an object which really had existence, whereas a fictitious entity was an object which 'must for the purposes of discourse be spoken of as existing'—an object to which one did not intend to ascribe real existence, but still an object which it made sense to talk about as though it had real existence.[68]

III

The radical distinction amongst noun substantives was that between the names of real entities and the names of fictitious entities—'under one or other of these denominations may be comprehended every object that ever was or ever can be present to any faculty of the human frame—to perception, memory, or imagination'.[69] The category of real entities was itself divided into two—perceptible real

[66] UC ci. 341 (7 Aug. 1814) [Bowring, viii. 262].

[67] UC ci. 95 (25 July 1814) [Bowring, viii. 219].

[68] UC cii. 24 (23 Sept. 1814) [*De l'ontologie*, 86]. Cf. UC cii. 16 (7 July 1821) [*De l'ontologie*, 164–5]: 'A real entity is an entity to which, on the occasion and for the purpose of discourse, existence is really meant to be ascribed.

'A fictitious entity is an entity to which, on the occasion and for the purpose of discourse employed in speaking of it existence is ascribed, yet in truth and reality existence is not meant to be ascribed.'

In short, language did not, in its ordinary use, convey the whole meaning intended to be conveyed by the discourser.

[69] UC cii. 21 (23 Sept. 1814) [*De l'ontologie*, 80].

entities and inferential real entities.[70] If a real entity was perceptible, then its existence was known through the senses: if it was inferential, then the senses gave no direct knowledge of its existence, but its existence was inferred through a chain of reasoning.[71] Bentham had in mind real entities which were simply incapable of being perceived, rather than real entities which the human mind would perceive were the entity in question brought before one or other of the organs of perception. For instance, a planet which was not itself observable from the Earth, but whose existence was inferred from its gravitational pull on another object which was observable, was not an inferential real entity, but a perceptible real entity whose existence was inferred. In this case the inference might be verified by the object in question being observed from a different vantage point. In contrast, the existence of an inferential real entity could never be verified by perception—such an entity could not be perceived by the human senses.

Bentham recognized that the relationship between the human mind and the physical world was not fully captured in the view that the human mind perceived directly the physical world, though such an account was sufficient for most practical purposes. His point was that what operated upon the mind were the perceptions of physical objects, and not the physical objects themselves. In strictness, if real entities were those which were directly perceptible, the only perceptible real entities would be the perceptions themselves, while physical objects would be inferential real entities.

Whatsoever claim an object belonging to the class of bodies may be considered as possessing to the attribute of reality, i.e. of existence, every object belonging to the class of *perceptions* will be found to possess a still better title—a title established by still more immediate evidence. Of the reality of perceptions, they are themselves their own evidence: it is only by the evidence afforded by perceptions that the reality of a body of any kind can be established.[72]

And again:

Of *ideas* our perception is still more direct and immediate than that which we have of corporeal substances—of their existence our persuasion more intense and irresistible than that which we have of the existence of corporeal substances.

Speaking of entities, ideas might perhaps be accordingly considered as the sole *perceptible* ones; substances, those of the corporeal class, being with reference and in contradistinction to them no other than *inferential* ones.[73]

[70] Bentham referred to a variety of other 'entities', most notably fabulous entities and non-entities. Such categories of entity were themselves expounded by reference to real and fictitious entities. See UC cii. 23 (23 Sept. 1814) [*De l'ontologie*, 84]: 'In language, the words which present themselves and are employed in the character of *names* are some of them names of real entities, others names of fictitious entities: and to one or the other of these classes may all words which are employed in the character of *names* be referred.' See pp. 17–18 below.

[71] UC cii. 7 (7 July 1821) [*De l'ontologie*, 162–4].

[72] UC cii. 14 (27 Sept. 1814) [*De l'ontologie*, 174].

[73] UC cii. 15 (25 Sept. 1814) [*De l'ontologie*, 180].

Bentham often referred to the perceptions received directly from physical objects as 'ideas', and in these instances his terminology differed from that developed by Hume, who had stated:

> ALL the perceptions of the human mind resolve themselves into two distinct kinds, which I shall call IMPRESSIONS and IDEAS. The difference betwixt these consists in the degrees of force and liveliness, with which they strike upon the mind, and make their way into our thought or consciousness. Those perceptions, which enter with most force and violence, we may name *impressions*; and under this name I comprehend all our sensations, passions and emotions, as they make their first appearance in the soul. By *ideas* I mean the faint images of these in thinking and reasoning. . . .[74]

On other occasions, Bentham adopted this distinction, and acknowledged Hume as the source of it.[75] He distinguished first, the 'impressions' produced by 'the application of sensible objects to the organs of sense'; second, the 'ideas' produced by 'the recollection of those same objects'; and third, the 'new ideas' produced by the imagination, through the 'decomposition and recomposition' of those impressions.[76] Having said that, both Hume's 'impressions' and 'ideas' would, in Bentham's terminology, be categorized as perceptible real entities.

When perceptions which had a physical object for their source were received, impressions were thereby made on one or more of the senses. What was immediately perceived by the perceptive faculty were the impressions, while the physical object, or corporeal entity, was perceived in only a secondary or comparatively remote way: 'of this supposed source of the perceptions that are experienced, the existence is, strictly speaking, rather a subject of *inference* than of perception: of inference, judgment, ratiocination, which is liable to be erroneous, and in experience is very frequently found to be so'.[77] In other words, perceptions might be misinterpreted in the course of inferring the existence of a physical object: for instance, an individual might be persuaded that a certain combination of shapes and colours represented a living person, when the object was actually a waxwork. While physical objects were presented to the mind by perceptions—whether impressions presented by the physical objects themselves, or ideas presented by the memory or imagination—the possibility existed that the inferences drawn by the mind as to the existence or nature of the physical objects which produced those impressions or ideas might be erroneous. Having pointed out that, in strictness, the only real entities were perceptions, Bentham noted that on most occasions it was more straightforward, when considering the 'bodies' or 'substances' which were taken to exist in the physical world, to use the term 'perceptible real entities' to refer to 'corporeal substances', and the term 'inferential real entities' to 'incorporeal ones'.[78]

74 Hume, *A Treatise of Human Nature*, 1.
75 See UC cii. 408 (27 Dec. 1815) [Bowring, viii. 320 n.]
76 UC cii. 13 (26 Sept. 1814) [*De l'ontologie*, 172].
77 UC ci. 118 (25 July 1814) [Bowring, viii. 224].
78 UC cii. 15 (25 Sept. 1814) [*De l'ontologie*, 180–2].

Amongst the category of inferential real entities, Bentham included 'the human soul considered as existing in a state of separation from the body' and '*God*, the almighty being, creator and preserver of all other real entities'. No one had ever perceived a human soul, at least 'no man who, upon due and apposite interrogation, would be able to obtain credence'. Such a thing was 'a ghost: and, at this time of day, *custom* scarcely does, *fashion* certainly does not, command us to believe in ghosts'. The reality of the human soul was not 'attested by *perception*' and could, therefore, only be inferred.[79] If one remained unconvinced by the inference which purported to establish the existence of a particular inferential real entity, then the noun substantive in question did not represent a real entity, but a non-entity. Given the 'imperfections of the human senses', God was not a perceptible entity, and, therefore, like the human soul, had to be assigned to the class of inferential real entities. Yet one might remain unconvinced by the reasoning on which the inference was grounded. In the case of the human soul, were one not prepared to consider it to be a real entity, one might consider it to be a fictitious entity—namely a combination of such 'psychical entities' as the understanding, the will, the perceptive faculty, the memory, and the imagination. In the case of God, were one not prepared to consider him to be a real entity, then there would be no option but to consider him to be not a fictitious entity, like the soul of man, but a non-entity.[80] A non-entity was like an inferential real entity in that it was imperceptible, but different in that one was not persuaded by the inference which purported to prove that it existed. The attribution of a particular noun substantive to one or other class of entity was ultimately, as we shall see, a matter of individual persuasion or belief.

A fictitious entity was not, of course, a non-entity or an inferential real entity, yet had this much in common with both: it was incapable of perception by the human mind. Bentham explained the distinction between the category of non-entities and that of fictitious entities by reference to a further category of entities, namely fabulous entities: 'Fabulous entities, whether persons or things, are supposed material objects, of which the separate existence is capable of becoming a subject of belief, and of which, accordingly, the same sort of picture is capable of being drawn in and preserved in the mind, as of any really existent object.' Examples of fabulous entities included 'Gods of different dynasties,[81]—kings, such as Brute and Fergus,—animals, such as dragons and chimæras,—countries, such as El Dorado,—seas, such as the Straits of Arrian,—fountains, such as the fountain of Jouvence'. The question as to whether a noun substantive represented a fabulous entity or a fictitious entity was settled by reference to

[79] UC cii. 9 (27 Sept. 1814) [*De l'ontologie*, 174–6].
[80] UC cii. 10–11 (27 Sept. 1814) [*De l'ontologie*, 176–8].
[81] Presumably Bentham had in mind deities which were supposed to have some perceptible presence, unlike the God of St Paul, 'whom no man hath seen, nor can see': see 1 Tim. 6: 16.

whether the noun substantive in question raised or did not raise in the mind an image of the 'corresponding' physical object:

> Of a *fabulous* object, whether person or thing, the idea, *i.e.* the *image* delineated in the mind by the name and accompanying description, may be just the same, whether a corresponding object had or had not been in existence, whether the object were a historical or a fabulous one.
>
> Fictitious entities . . . are such, of which, in a very ample proportion, the mention, and consequent fiction, requires to be introduced for the purpose of discourse; their names being employed in the same manner as names of substances are employed; hence the character in which they present themselves is that of so many names of substances. But these names of fictitious entities do not, as do the above-mentioned names of fabulous entities, raise up in the mind any correspondent images.[82]

Hence fabulous entities, like those purported inferential real entities of whose existence one was not persuaded, belonged to the class of non-entities rather than to that of real entities, even though the mental picture by which they were represented was created by combining a variety of real entities, albeit in a way in which they were not found combined in the physical world. Had the fabulous entity existed, it would have been perceptible, but the individual who assigned the object to the class of fabulous entities did so for the very reason that he did not believe it to exist in the physical world.

In contrast to a fabulous entity, a fictitious entity was not supposed to be perceptible. Bentham illustrated the point by means of a proposition which gave the address of the Devil, and described his physical characteristics—'having a head, body and limbs like a man's, horns like a goat's, wings like a bat's, and a tail like a monkey's'—and which was communicated with the intention of producing a persuasion that the Devil did exist. If one were persuaded of the truth of the assertion, believing the Devil to be a real entity, one would expect, if one went to the address in question, to see him. However, if one were not persuaded of its truth, believing the Devil to be not a real entity, but rather a non-entity, then one would not expect to see him. On the other hand, in the case of a proposition asserting the existence of a fictitious entity, such as an obligation imposed on a person, whether or not one were persuaded of the truth of the assertion, one would not expect the fictitious entity in question to possess 'for itself any separate, or strictly speaking any real existence'.[83]

It should be emphasized that Bentham recognized that persuasion or belief had a crucial role to play. A statement about what existed in the physical world could not be separated from a statement about what was believed to exist. As he explained, the 'immediate *subject*' of any discourse was necessarily 'the state of the communicator's mind: in other words of some one or more of the faculties belonging to it'. The human mind contained an active faculty, which itself

[82] UC ci. 342, 322 (7 Aug. 1814) [Bowring, viii. 262–3].
[83] See UC cii. 23–4 (23 Sept. 1814) [*De l'ontologie*, 84–7].

contained the will or volitional faculty, and a passive faculty or understanding, which included the perceptive faculty, the memory or retentive faculty, and the judgment or judicial faculty. An expression of the state of the perceptive faculty had to be made at the time that the 'exciting cause' was 'present and in action', otherwise the expression in question was an expression of the memory. However, it was almost without exception the case that a statement concerning the perception or memory also involved 'an act or exercise of the judicial faculty', and a declaration which concerned the state of the judgment was an expression of 'a persuasion in some shape or other, an opinion, a belief, in relation to some object or other'. Indeed, even when one reported the declaration of another person, this was also a persuasion, opinion, or belief—namely 'the persuasion of the existence of a recollection' that the person in question had made the declaration in question.[84] So no matter what the subject-matter, a discourse invariably involved a judgment, and hence a subjective element:

Opinion—an opinion entertained by the speaker—this is all of which in any instance communication can be made. Of an opinion thus expressed any imaginable matter of fact, real or supposed, may have been taken for the subject. But that to which expression is given, that of which communication is made, is always the man's opinion, i.e. in so far as the expression answers its intended purpose, that which he wishes should be taken for his opinion in relation to the subject in question—never any thing more.

Given that every portion of discourse, which was not the expression of a desire, included 'a communication made of the state of the judicial department of the speaker's mind',[85] even the most simple proposition concerning a matter of fact was complex. What was asserted by the proposition 'Eurybiades struck Themistocles' was that, 'It is my opinion that Eurybiades struck Themistocles.' Again, by the proposition 'He is there',

what is expressed is my opinion that *he* (the person spoken of) is in the place alluded to by the word *there*.

The consequence is—that in saying *He is there*,—the *proposition*, simple as it is in appearance, is in its imports complex—and if it be considered as designating, expressing, communicating the whole of the object of which it is employed as a sign, viz. the mode of *being* of my mind, it is *elliptical*. That to which it gives expression is the supposed matter of fact which (supposing me to speak truly) was the object of my thought: that of which it does not contain the expression is that *thought* itself: the only matter of fact of which the discourse in question is strictly and immediately the assertion is left to be inferred from the context: from such words as are actually uttered.[86]

It was irrelevant whether the subject of discourse was the state of one's own body, or the state of a body exterior to one's own body. In both cases 'the immediate

[84] UC cii. 298–300 (1–2 Aug. 1814) [Bowring, viii. 299–300].

[85] It should be pointed out that in this particular passage Bentham suggested that statements concerning simple perceptions internal to the person of the speaker (e.g. 'I am hungry') did not involve the judicial faculty, but this seems to be at odds with what he says elsewhere.

[86] UC cii. 410–12 (27 Dec. 1815) [Bowring, viii. 321].

subject is no other than the state of my own mind—an opinion entertained by me in relation to the ulterior object or subject'. The tendency to error was greater in the former case than in the latter. When expressing an opinion concerning his own sensations, the speaker was 'scarcely liable to be deceived or in error', but matters were different as soon as he attempted 'to pronounce an opinion relative to the cause of any of those sensations'. From this point he launched himself 'into the ocean of art and science': from this point he became 'physician; and, in the field of the physician the dominion of error is but too severely felt'. The 'practical inferences' from 'these speculative observations' were: '1. Avoid dogmativeness. 2. Still more avoid intolerance. In both cases never cease to bear in mind how slippery and hollow the ground on which your opinion, and consequently the utmost value of any expression which you can give to it, rests.'[87] However, for the purpose of his discussion, Bentham would ignore this complexity:

> The sort of infirmity just noticed being common to all discourse in the composition of which an assertion of the state of the speaker's mind precedes, introduces, and weakens the ulterior assertion which lies beyond it, the consideration of the intervening assertion may in every case but the present, in which, for the purpose of explanation, it has been necessary thus for once to bring it to view, be dropped, and the subject of the discourse may be stated as being, except in the particular case where it is the state of the speaker's body, the state of some exterior *entity* or assemblage of entities.[88]

Nevertheless, the point was that opinion or belief on the part of the speaker could not be disentangled from discourse. Bentham himself believed, on the basis of his experience and observation of the physical world, both that no person had ever perceived a human soul, and that the human soul was incapable of being perceived, and, therefore, categorized the human soul as a non-entity. In contrast, a person who believed that he had perceived a human soul, or believed that another person had and, therefore, believed that the human soul was perceptible, would categorize the human soul as a real entity. This did not, however, mean that any one belief was as good as any other, for there existed a means of testing the rectitude of a belief: this test was the conduciveness of the belief to well-being. But a further point should be made. Bentham seems to have accepted that it was the consonance of the belief with the reality of the physical world which made it conducive to well-being. In this way, truth was reconciled with utility. Given that Bentham did not believe in the existence of the human soul, the question arises whether he believed in the existence of any inferential real entity, and, if not, whether this committed him to atheism.[89] As we have seen, Bentham argued that if God did exist, and if he had never been perceived, then he belonged to the class of inferential real entities. Yet if one were not persuaded

[87] UC cii. 459–60 (15 Dec. 1815) [Bowring, viii. 330 and n.]

[88] UC cii. 461 (15 Dec. 1815) [Bowring, viii. 330].

[89] It has been generally assumed that Bentham was an atheist, though he never avowed himself to be such. See pp. 174–5 n. below.

by the reasoning on which the inference was grounded, one would be forced to conclude that God was a non-entity. This did not, in itself, mean that Bentham was an atheist. He assumed that all knowledge was founded upon the experience of the senses. God might still have some sort of existence not accessible to human perception, though not a sort of existence which human beings would be capable of comprehending. However, what this did mean was that, in the only respect in which it mattered—namely the effect on well-being—a non-belief in the existence of God, or indeed in any other inferential real entity, did not in itself produce any evil consequence. (This point should not obscure the fact that, in Bentham's view, the requirement to make expressions of belief or non-belief did have practical consequences.)[90] Comparing the belief in the existence of physical bodies inferred from the existence of perceptions with the belief in the existence of inferential real entities, whether human souls or God, inferred from the existence of perceptible entities, Bentham noted that the inference in the former case was 'much stronger and more irresistible' than that in the latter:

> Suppose the non-existence of corporeal substances—of any hard corporeal substance that stands opposite to you—make this supposition and as soon as you have made it, act upon it, pain, the perception of pain, will at once bear witness against you, and be your punishment, your condign punishment. Suppose the non-existence of the above-mentioned inferential incorporeal substances [i.e. inferential real entities], of any of them, or of all of them, and the supposition made, act upon it accordingly—be the supposition conformable or not conformable to the truth of the case, at any rate no such immediate counter-evidence, no such immediate punishment, will follow.[91]

A belief that a wall did not exist would not lessen or remove the pain one felt upon striking it with one's head. A belief that God did not exist would not of itself result in the suffering of physical pain. From the perspective of his ontology, Bentham concluded that the human mind was incapable of gaining any knowledge of God. No one had ever perceived God, or any other supernatural being for that matter, and, therefore, no one could claim to have any knowledge of God. This meant that those people who did claim to have knowledge of God, and used such terms as grace, providence, or atonement, which were only explicable by relation to God, were talking nonsense.[92] Bentham deployed the same argument against those who claimed to have knowledge of natural law and natural rights, as we shall see.[93]

IV

While arguing that belief or persuasion was an essential element in the process by which human beings categorized or interpreted the perceptions they experienced,

[90] See Ch. 7 below. [91] UC cii. 15 (25 Sept. 1814) [*De l'ontologie*, 180–2].

[92] There are, of course, connections to be made here with the account of religious knowledge in A. J. Ayer, *Language, Truth and Logic* (London, 1936), 119–26. [93] See Ch. 3 below.

Bentham accepted that the physical world had an existence which was independent of the human mind: 'Down to this present time . . . whatsoever has existed has had existence; whatsoever has not existed has not had existence: at this present time, whatsoever does exist has existence; whatsoever does not exist has not existence: and so at any and every future point of time.'[94] Again, Bentham noted that 'no really existing object' corresponded to the quality of uncertainty attributed to an event or state of things 'other than the state of the mind by which that event or state of things is contemplated'. As for the event or state of things itself, 'either it exists or it does not exist—between existence and non-existence there is no medium. Suppose it to exist, all uncertainty is out of the question: suppose it not to exist, all uncertainty is equally out of the question.'[95] The knowledge which the human mind acquired about the physical world was derived from the perceptions which it received, and in turn those perceptions resulted from the contact which took place between 'the organs of sense' and real entities—objects existing in the physical world. In short, what was known could be known only of those things which had physical existence. Nevertheless, knowledge was not merely a product of perception, but also of reflection on or thought about those perceptions, and, as we have seen, both thought itself and the communication of thought were not possible without language: 'in the character of an instrument altogether indispensable [language] serves not only for the communication but in great measure also to the formation of ideas'. The logical 'operations' undertaken by the mind gave rise to various classes of words which did not correspond to any object which existed in the physical world. One class of such words was, of course, that of the names of fictitious entities: 'To language then—to language alone—it is that fictitious entities owe their existence—their impossible, yet indispensable existence.'[96]

The key operation performed by the human mind was 'methodization' or 'arrangement'. Physical objects might be methodized or arranged either physically—for instance, specimens of animals, plants, or minerals might be placed in a particular order in a museum—or psychically—for instance, the names of the specimens in question might be placed in a particular order in a book dealing with zoology, botany, or mineralogy. In this latter case, it was 'only the ideas of the things in question that are the subjects of the arrangement, not the things themselves', and the ideas themselves could be arranged only by names.[97] Those ideas, or 'psychical entities' as Bentham termed them, which did not correspond to a physical object could likewise only be arranged psychically, and thus by means of names. Ideas could not be 'communicated or so much as fixt and

[94] UC cii. 75 (3 Oct. 1814) [*De l'ontologie*, 152].

[95] UC cii. 558 (17 Dec. 1815) [Bowring, viii. 348–9 n.]. For a discussion of Bentham's views on the ontological status of probability see G. J. Postema, 'Fact, Fictions, and Law: Bentham on the Foundations of Evidence', in W. L. Twining (ed.), *Facts in Law* (Weisbaden, 1983), 37–64.

[96] UC cii. 22–3 (23 Sept. 1814) [*De l'ontologie*, 82–4].

[97] UC ci. 340–1 (7 Aug. 1814) [Bowring, viii. 262].

rendered determinate, otherwise than by the means of the words employed to serve as signs of them'. Any attempt to place ideas in any sort of order required the use of words.[98] The problem was that language was all too prone to be deceptive: the employment of the name of a fictitious entity, often unavoidable in even the most simple proposition, gave rise to fiction. Take the proposition: 'That apple is ripe.' The apple was a real entity, but the property or quality of ripeness, or any other quality for that matter, did not have an independent existence. If there were nothing in the world that was susceptible of being ripe, then, asked Bentham, 'where would be the quality of ripeness?' His answer: 'No where.' From the perspective of the human mind, the apple was the 'receptacle' in which the quality of ripeness was 'lodged'. A quality, such as ripeness, was not a real entity, but a fictitious entity: 'Thus it is that in the use made of language, fiction at the very first step that can be taken in the field of language, fiction in the simplest or almost the simplest case in which language can be employed, becomes a necessary resource.'[99] Without a proper conception of language, and more particularly of the relationship between language and human perception of the physical world, the mind would be led into confusion: it would fail to distinguish truth from error, physical fact from linguistic fiction. A real entity, as we have seen,[100] was a 'corporeal substance'—an object which really had existence—whereas a fictitious entity was an object which 'must for the purposes of discourse be spoken of as existing'—an object to which one did not intend to ascribe real existence, but still an object which it made sense to talk about as though it had real existence. The names of fictitious entities were not capable of exposition by means of representation, where a specific object was produced and its assigned name pronounced, for there was no such object to produce. Nor was it possible to employ the Aristotelian method of definition *per genus et differentiam*. Definition in this sense was possible where the object belonged to some nest of aggregates, and was not the highest object in the nest, but was not possible where the word had no superior genus.[101] Words such as duty, right, power, and title, which 'abound so much in ethics and jurisprudence', had no superior genus, and so could not be defined *per genus et differentiam*.[102] Some other method or methods had to be found.

Bentham's solution consisted in the complementary techniques of paraphrasis and phraseoplerosis, by which those noun substantives which represented fictitious entities were expounded by demonstrating their relationship to those which represented real entities, and the technique of archetypation, which revealed the way in which all language was rooted in some physical image. The operation of phraseoplerosis, the filling up of the phrase, was logically prior to

98 UC ci. 312 (5 Aug. 1814) [Bowring, viii. 260].
99 UC cii. 461–2 (15 Dec. 1815) [Bowring, viii. 330–1].
100 See p. 14 and n. above.
101 UC ci. 215–16 (17 Aug. 1814) [Bowring, viii. 245–6].
102 *A Fragment on Government*, 495 n.

that of paraphrasis.[103] Bentham recognized that words only made sense in the context of a proposition, and, as we have seen,[104] argued that a proposition, in order to make sense, had to contain at least four elements. Yet, in common discourse, as we have also seen,[105] it was often the case that not all these elements were explicitly represented by corresponding words. Discourse often contained ellipses. Before the discourse in question could be subjected to exposition by paraphrasis, such ellipses needed to be removed by inserting the omitted words.[106] Bentham explained as follows: 'Looking at my son whose name is John—I say to him, John. He hears me—What is it that he understands by this? The import, the full import, belonging to one or other of these two phrases: My desire is that you *attend* (viz. to what more I am about to say), or, My desire is that you *come*, i.e. come near to the place at which I am sitting.'[107] Once the sentence had been 'filled up', the operation of paraphrasis could then be undertaken:

A word may be said to be expounded by *paraphrasis*, when not that *word* alone is translated into other *words*, but some whole *sentence* of which it forms a part is translated into another *sentence*; the words of which latter are expressive of such ideas as are *simple*, or are more immediately resolvable into simple ones than those of the former. . . . This, in short, is the only method in which any abstract terms can, at the long run, be expounded to any instructive purpose: that is in terms calculated to raise *images* either of *substances* perceived, or of *emotions*;—sources, one or other of which every idea must be drawn from, to be a clear one.[108]

Bentham exemplified the operation of paraphrasis by expounding the word 'duty'. A person (X) had a political duty when another person (Y) had a right to have him (X) made to do it, in which case X had a duty towards Y, and Y a right against X; what Y had a political right to have X be made to do was that for which X was legally liable to be punished for not doing, upon a requisition made on Y's behalf; in turn, punishment was the notion of '*pain* annexed to an act, and accruing on a certain *account*, and from a certain *source*'.[109] The exposition had 'resolved' the notion of having a duty into its simple, or more simple, elements: namely the prospect of suffering a pain, inflicted by the agents of the law (a term which itself would require further exposition), upon the forbearance to perform some action (or alternatively, the performance of some action which should have been forborne) when required to do so by the person invested with the corresponding right.

The name of a fictitious entity, therefore, was expounded by showing its relationship to the names of the real entities of which it was ultimately composed, and this was done by means of translating a proposition which included

103 UC ci. 219 (23 Aug. 1814) [Bowring, viii. 247]. 104 See p. 13 above.
105 See pp. 19–20 above. 106 See UC ci. 219 (23 Aug. 1814) [Bowring, viii. 247].
107 UC cii. 415 (27 Dec. 1815) [Bowring, viii. 321–2].
108 *A Fragment on Government*, 495 n. 109 Ibid. 494–5 n.

the name of the fictitious entity into a correspondent proposition which included the names of real entities: 'By the word paraphrasis may be designated that sort of exposition which may be afforded by transmuting into a proposition having for its subject some real entity, a proposition which has not for its subject any other than a fictitious entity.' A fictitious entity was 'a mere nothing', and, therefore, had no properties, and any proposition which ascribed properties to it was not 'in itself and of itself a true one, nor therefore an instructive one: whatsoever of truth is capable of belonging to it can not belong to it in any other character than that of the representative of—the intended and supposed equivalent and adequate succedaneum of—some proposition having for its subject some real entity'.[110] The real entity with which 'the import' of the name of the fictitious entity was 'connected', and on which that import depended, Bentham termed 'the *real source, efficient cause*, or *connecting principle*'.[111] In contrast, if an exposition by paraphrasis proved to be impossible, then the fictitious entity in question belonged to the class of non-entities, and the noun substantive by which it was represented was merely a sound, and any proposition in which it occurred was nonsensical.

The successful exposition of a term would help to reveal its archetype—the physical image which lay at the root of, or behind, every idea:

> Necessary to give a compleat satisfaction to the mind with regard to the import of an improper substantive is another mode of exposition that may be termed Archetypation.
>
> The word Archetype, a Latin word of Greek extraction, signifies a pattern. By Archetypation then I mean the finding of that real appearance of real entities that served as a pattern for the appearance suggested by any of those sentences of which an improper substantive makes a part.[112]

In order for an idea to be clearly understood, some real entity—whether a physical object or an internal sensation—had to be brought before the mind, and recognized as the 'real source' from which the idea had been derived. Archetypation was the operation by which this emblematic image was indicated. Where a property was attributed to a fictitious entity, 'some sort of image—the image of some real action or state of things—is in every instance presented to the mind. This image may be termed the archetype, or archetypal image, appertaining to the fictitious proposition of which the name of the characteristic fictitious entity makes a part.'[113]

Bentham illustrated the technique of paraphrasis and the related techniques of exposition by means of 'the groupe of Ethical fictitious entities, viz. *Obligations*, rights, and the other *advantages* dependent on obligation'. The 'real source' of all

[110] UC ci. 217 (26 Aug. 1814) [Bowring, viii. 246].

[111] UC ci. 218 (23 Aug. 1814) [Bowring, viii. 246].

[112] UC lxix. 221 (*c*.1776). By 'improper substantive' Bentham here had in mind both names of fictitious and of fabulous entities. The latter had their archetype in the physical objects from which they were combined.

[113] UC ci. 218 (13 Oct. 1814) [Bowring, viii. 246–7].

these fictitious entities was '*sensation*: the word being taken in that sense in which it is significative not merely of perception, but of perception considered as productive either of pain, of pleasure, or of both'. In the first instance, the operation of phraseoplerosis was performed by placing the word 'obligation' in the proposition 'an obligation is incumbent on a man', consisting of a subject (obligation), a predicate (incumbent on a man), and a copula (is). The operation of paraphrasis might then be performed: 'An obligation (viz. the obligation of conducting himself in a certain manner) is incumbent on a man (i.e. is spoken of as incumbent on a man) in so far as, in the event of his failing to conduct himself in that same manner, pain or loss of pleasure is considered as about to be experienced by him.' The archetypal image of an obligation was 'that of a man lying down, with a heavy body pressing upon him, to wit in such sort as either to prevent him from acting at all, or so ordering matters that if so it be that he does act, it can not be in any other direction or manner than the direction or manner in question—the direction or manner requisite'. Once the operation of exposition had been performed upon the term 'obligation', it was then possible to proceed to the exposition of other terms, such as 'right', of which obligation formed the basis.[114]

V

The end to which logic itself was directed was well-being or happiness—it was only to the extent that logic was 'conducive to happiness', which included 'every thing that for its own sake is worth having—every thing that in itself is of any value', that it was 'worth knowing', that 'an acquaintance with it' was 'of any value'.[115] Again, in relation to the Aristotelian view that the end of logic was knowledge, Bentham commented: 'But except in so far as in some shape or other it leads to and is productive of well-being—a balance on the side of happiness—what is the value of all the knowledge in the world?—Just nothing.'[116] Given

114 UC ci. 221–4 (23 Aug. 1814) [Bowring, viii. 247–8]. In *Deontology*, 207, Bentham suggested a different archetype when he noted that 'obligation' was derived from the Latin *obligio*, 'to bind'. The archetype was often revealed through the etymology of the term in question: e.g. 'spirit' was derived from the Latin *spiritus*, 'breath' (UC cii. 452 (2 Dec. 1815) [Bowring, viii. 328–9]); 'cardinal' form the Latin *cardo*, 'hinge' (*Deontology*, 180); and 'sanction' from the Latin *sanctio*, 'the act of binding', itself said to be derived from *sanguis*, 'blood' (*An Introduction to the Principles of Morals and Legislation*, ed. J. H. Burns and H. L. A. Hart (London, 1970), 34 n.)

All this confirmed Bentham's view that, '[a]ll our psychological ideas are derived from physical ones; all mental from corporeal ones': see UC cii. 445 (9 July 1826) [Bowring, viii. 327].

115 UC ci. 156 (23 July 1814) [Bowring, viii. 232].

116 UC ci. 158 (31 July 1814) [Bowring, viii. 233]. Cf. UC ci. 199 (29 Oct. 1826) [Bowring, viii. 241]: 'only with reference to use—understand always to the augmentation of happiness in some shape or other—has knowledge, how consummate so ever, any claim to attention—only by its subserviency to practice has knowledge any use: only by its subserviency to art is science in any shape of any use.'

that belief was founded on knowledge, it followed that a belief in the existence of God, or in the existence of the human soul, or in the existence of the Devil, or in the existence of some physical object, only mattered to the extent that well-being was affected by the belief in question. If a person's well-being was increased by believing in the existence of God, such a belief was valuable for that person; if diminished, harmful.[117] To the extent, then, that the assigning of the names of various entities to the class of real, fictitious, or non-entities, was a matter of belief or opinion, Bentham's ontology had a subjectivist element; but to the extent that the value of holding such opinions was measured by their tendency to promote well-being—that is, to increase pleasure or to avert pain, which were entities which existed in the physical world—his ontology had a naturalistic foundation. Not seeing any evidence to the contrary, Bentham postulated that all human creatures, and indeed all sentient creatures, shared the same basic physiology (or 'pathology' as he termed it).[118] Each and every individual was motivated to pursue pleasure and to avoid pain, even though different individuals had different beliefs, founded on their experience and observation, as to which activities would, in the particular circumstances in question, lead to the production of pleasure and the avoidance of pain. This introduced a further level of subjectivity into Bentham's account. Just how Bentham constructed a universal ethical standard, the principle of utility or the greatest-happiness principle, given these differences in sensibility, as Bentham termed them, is the subject of the following chapter.

[117] As we shall see (pp. 189–91 below), Bentham argued that such a belief would tend to diminish happiness.

[118] See e.g. *Deontology*, 87, where Bentham noted that 'psychological dynamics', the 'science' which dealt with motives, was founded on 'psychological pathology'. The close connection in Bentham's thought between the methods of natural science and those of moral science is discussed in D. G. Long, *Bentham on Liberty: Jeremy Bentham's Idea of Liberty in Relation to his Utilitarianism* (Toronto, 1977), 13–25.

2

The Principle of Utility

I

The phrase 'the principle of utility', by which Bentham denominated his standard of morality, represented the name of a fictitious entity. If the notion represented by this name was to make sense, a proposition in which the name appeared had to be expounded, as in the case of other fictitious entities, by the technique of paraphrasis, whereby the proposition in question was translated into another proposition containing the names of real entities. According to Bentham's ontology, there was nothing in human experience which was not ultimately referable to some physical fact—and this was true of propositions making reference to a moral standard, as it was true of propositions making reference to any other fictitious entity. Propositions concerning the principle of utility made sense because, when properly expounded, they would be seen to be propositions about the existence, or probable existence, of pleasures and pains, themselves real entities. Indeed, propositions which purported to express moral value were meaningful only if they could be expounded in this way, and propositions which made reference to the principle of utility were the only ones which could be so expounded:

> Of an action that is conformable to the principle of utility, one may always say either that it is one that ought to be done, or at least that it is not one that ought not to be done. One may say also, that it is right it should be done; at least that it is not wrong it should be done: that it is a right action; at least that it is not a wrong action. When thus interpreted, the words *ought*, and *right* and *wrong*, and others of that stamp, have a meaning: when otherwise, they have none.[1]

Propositions which included such terms as right and wrong, ought and ought not, made sense only when translated into propositions concerning the utility of the action in question, while utility itself was explicable only in terms of pleasure and pain.

In his discussion of the principle of utility in *An Introduction to the Principles of Morals and Legislation*, Bentham did not explicitly refer to paraphrasis or his

[1] *An Introduction to the Principles of Morals and Legislation*, 13. This work was printed in 1780 and published, with additional material, in 1789. A second edition, again with some additions, was published in 1823. Unless noted otherwise, the passages quoted or referred to appear in the printed version of 1780.

other methods of exposition, yet they form the foundation upon which the whole account is constructed. In the famous opening passage he announced that the perceptions of pain and pleasure constituted the 'real source' both of the principle of utility and of human motivation:

Nature has placed mankind under the governance of two sovereign masters, *pain* and *pleasure*. It is for them alone to point out what we ought to do, as well as to determine what we shall do. On the one hand the standard of right and wrong, on the other the chain of causes and effects, are fastened to their throne. They govern us in all we do, in all we say, in all we think: every effort we can make to throw off our subjection, will serve but to demonstrate and confirm it. In words a man may pretend to abjure their empire: but in reality he will remain subject to it all the while. The *principle of utility* recognises this subjection, and assumes it for the foundation of that system, the object of which is to rear the fabric of felicity by the hands of reason and of law. Systems which attempt to question it, deal in sounds instead of sense, in caprice instead of reason, in darkness instead of light.[2]

The 'sovereign masters' of pain and pleasure, more precisely an aversion to pain and a desire for pleasure, not only provided the motives for human action, 'govern[ing] us in all we do, in all we say, in all we think', but also constituted 'the standard of right and wrong'. They were the foundation not only of human psychology, determining what individuals actually did, but also of morality, pointing out what individuals ought to do. This 'subjection' to pain and pleasure was 'recognised' by the principle of utility, and it was on the basis of this 'subjection' that Bentham would 'rear the fabric of felicity'. In short, psychology and morality shared a common foundation in the perceptions of pleasure and pain, and unless discourse concerning psychology and morality could be expounded by reference to these real entities, such discourse was nonsense.

Bentham gave only a relatively brief account of human psychology in *An Introduction to the Principles of Morals and Legislation*, but more details of his thinking can be gleaned from his writings elsewhere, particularly on logic, language, and education in the mid-1810s. It was here that Bentham pointed out that, were it not for the existence of the perceptions of pain and pleasure, human existence would be devoid of any value. Pain and pleasure, like other perceptions, were physical experiences, and although almost always associated with other perceptions, were distinguishable from them. Bentham divided perceptions into apathematic perceptions, which did not consist of, or were not accompanied by, feelings of pain or pleasure, and pathematic perceptions, which did consist of, or were accompanied by, such feelings.[3] He gave two reasons why apathematic perceptions might be ignored: first, because they were of no consequence; and

[2] *An Introduction to the Principles of Morals and Legislation*, 11.

[3] UC ci. 406 (25 Jan. 1816) [Bowring, viii. 279]. Bentham elsewhere distinguished between 'simple perceptions' and '*sensation*, i.e. perception attended with pain or pleasure': see UC cii. 408 (27 Dec. 1815) [Bowring, viii. 320]. The former would constitute apathematic perceptions, and the latter pathematic.

second, because they were extremely rare. In relation to the first point, Bentham argued that since 'the only objects possessed of intrinsic and independent value' were pleasure and pain, apathematic perceptions, being 'altogether unconnected with either pleasure or pain', were of no significance and, as such, 'would not be comprehended within any part of the field of art and science'. In relation to the second point, Bentham noted that, in general, pleasure and pain on the one hand, and simple perceptions on the other, were 'experienced together'—in other words they were 'simultaneously concomitant'. In many instances a simple perception, which had neither pleasure nor pain for its 'contemporary adjunct', might, through mental processes such as 'attention, reflection, volition and transitive action', come to 'reckon feelings of both sorts in abundance among its consequences'. It was, therefore, highly unlikely that, in practice, a perception would not have some connection, immediate or remote, with pleasure or pain, 'and hence it is that, except for clearness of intellection, the distinction between pathematic and apathematic perception becomes void of practical use'.[4]

The perception of pleasure and pain was all that mattered. Moreover, the terms used to describe human psychology, such as motives, desires and aversions, intentions and dispositions, and interests, and which represented 'psychological entities', were intelligible only when expounded in relation to pleasure and pain:

> Among all the several species of psychological entities . . . the two which are as it were the *roots*, the main pillars or *foundations* of all the rest, the *matter* of which all the rest are composed—or the *receptacles* of that matter, which soever may be the *physical image*, employed to give *aid*, if not *existence* to conception, will be, it is believed . . . seen to be, PLEASURES and PAINS. Of *these*, the existence is matter of universal and constant experience. Without any of the rest, *these* are susceptible of,—and as often as they come *unlooked* for, do actually come into, *existence*: without these, no one of all those others ever had, or ever could have had, existence.

It was only by reference to the real entities of pleasure and pain that it was possible to form a clear idea of a motive, and the related notion of an interest. Each motive had for its 'basis' the 'eventual expectation' of some pleasure or pain. Where a motive existed, there also existed the following: first, a corresponding desire or aversion; second, the idea of a corresponding pleasure or pain; and third, the idea and belief of the existence of a corresponding interest.[5] To put this another way, a pleasurable interest produced a desire (conversely a painful interest produced an aversion), which in turn produced a motive. Without the existence of a motive, there would be no action: 'on every occasion, *conduct*—the *course* taken by a man's conduct—is at the absolute command of—is the never-failing result of—the *motives*, and thence, in so far as the corresponding interests are perceived and understood, of the corresponding *interests*, to the action of which, his mind—his will—has, on that same occasion, stood exposed.'[6]

[4] UC ci. 454 (19 Feb. 1815) [Bowring, viii. 288].
[5] *Deontology*, 87, 98–9.
[6] Ibid. 112.

A person was said to have an interest in a subject, whether a person or a thing, or in an event or state of affairs, to the extent that the subject or event was expected to be a source of pleasure or pain, and it was said to be his interest that a particular event took place if it was expected that '*good*, to a greater *value*, will be possessed by him than in the contrary case'.[7] In other words, where an agent expected to receive a sensation of pleasure (or avoid a sensation of pain) from some state of affairs which the action in question would bring about, he had an interest in performing that action.

Expectation played a crucial role in motivation, and the formation of expectation depended in turn on the faculty of the imagination, one of the sources of 'derivative' pleasures and pains. The pleasures and pains which a person experienced were either 'original' or 'derivative'. Original pleasures and pains were 'the immediate and simultaneous accompaniments of *perception*: viz. *physical*, i.e. *corporeal*, or merely *psychological*, i.e. *mental*'; while derivative pleasures and pains were derived from past perception, and thus the product of either memory or imagination. The imagination, which rearranged and abstracted the 'pictures' recollected in the memory, gave rise to pleasures of expectation:

> Derived from *imagination*, if the conception of them be accompanied with a *judgement* more or less *decided*—a *persuasion* more or less intense—of the future realization of the pictures so composed, the *imagination* is styled 'expectation'. And the pleasure, if there be any, which is the immediate accompaniment of such persuasion, is styled 'a pleasure of expectation', or a 'pleasure of hope'; if not so accompanied, a 'pleasure of imagination', and nothing more.

It was only through the intervention of the imagination, which 'brought to view' the original pleasure or pain enjoyed in the past, that a pleasure or pain of expectation could be formed.[8] A pleasure of the imagination did not necessarily give rise to expectation, and an expectation did not necessarily give rise to a motive, but a motive was necessarily founded on an expectation. A pleasure which did not 'operate as a spring of action' was 'inert', and such pleasures included those of 'mere recollection' and 'mere imagination'. Even a pleasure of expectation might be inert, for instance where the expected pleasure was regarded as certain and incapable of being brought nearer or increased by any action which might be performed. It was possible that an inert pleasure might lead to action, but only in an indirect way 'by means of some different pleasure, which it happens to bring to view'. For instance, the pleasurable recollection of a landscape might lead to a man returning to view, and enjoy, the landscape again. In this case 'the actuating motive' was not the pleasurable recollection, but 'the pleasurable idea of the pleasurable sensation *expected* from that *other* view'. Pleasure itself did not operate as a spring of action, except in the sense that the action in question was 'regarded as a means of *obtaining* it'.[9]

[7] Ibid. 91–2. [8] Ibid. 90. [9] Ibid. 89–90.

The will or volitional faculty was the faculty of the mind on which the motive operated and thereby produced action. Such action might be produced directly without reference to any other faculty of the mind, or else by reference to the faculty of the understanding.[10]

To the *will* it is that the idea of a pleasure or an exemption [from pain] applies itself in the *first* instance; in *that* stage its effect, if not conclusive, is *velleity*. By velleity, reference is made to the *understanding*, viz.: 1. for striking a *balance* between the *value* of this *good*, and that of the *pain* or *loss*, if any, which present themselves as eventually about to stand associated with it; 2. then, if the balance appear to be in its favour, for the choice of *means*: thereupon, if *action* be the result, *velleity* is perfected into *volition*, of which the correspondent *action* is the immediate consequence. For the process that has place, this description may serve alike in *all* cases: *time* occupied by it may be of any length; from a minute fraction of a *second* as in ordinary cases, to any number of years.[11]

Bentham distinguished between a motive to the will, which was a desire, and a motive to the understanding, which was 'any consideration, the apparent tendency of which is to give increase to the efficiency of the desire, in the character of a motive to the *will*'. The 'corresponding considerations' which might operate as motives to the understanding, and included the potential means of achieving an already desired end, were so great in number that 'no book could comprise the catalogue'. Once the desire had been formed, anything which appeared likely to be a means of attaining the pleasure or averting the pain in question 'operates in the character of an *incentive*, i.e. a *motive*: viz. by giving increase to the apparent *value* of the good in respect of *certainty*'. But just as desire might be influenced by judgment, so might judgment be influenced by desire. Where the judgment influenced the desire, the influence was 'regular and salutary, *rightly* instructive and *directive*', but in the opposite case the influence was 'irregular, and naturally *sinister*, deceptious, and *seductive*'. In other words, a strong desire would, if founded on some 'interest-begotten prejudice', tend to pervert the judgment.[12] It was, of course, possible for an individual to possess an interest without realizing that he did so, and therefore not to realize that he had a corresponding motive. Moreover, it was possible for an individual to be mistaken in relation to what constituted his interest, and therefore to possess a corresponding motive which, if acted upon, would result in the experience of sensations of pain, rather than the expected sensations of pleasure.

II

Just as the terms used in psychology were expounded by reference to the real entities of pleasure and pain, so were the terms used in morality, including the

[10] For a perspicuous account of Bentham's view of the relationship between the will and the understanding see Harrison, *Bentham*, 202–6.

[11] *Deontology*, 94.

[12] Ibid. 92–3. For interest-begotten prejudice see pp. 264–6 below.

criterion of right and wrong—the principle of utility. In *An Introduction to the Principles of Morals and Legislation*, Bentham expounded the principle of utility through a series of intermediate relationships: namely, between the principle of utility and utility; between utility and happiness; between happiness on the one hand and pleasure and pain on the other; and finally between pleasure and pain on the one hand and good and evil on the other. He could then show that a morally right action was one that produced pleasure, and a morally wrong action one that produced pain. First, to be a 'partisan' of the principle of utility meant that one bestowed approval on any action which increased utility. The principle of utility, stated Bentham, might be regarded as 'an act of the mind; a sentiment; a sentiment of approbation; a sentiment which, when applied to an action, approves of its utility, as that quality of it by which the measure of approbation or disapprobation bestowed upon it ought to be governed'. Second, to say that an action possessed utility was to say that it tended to promote the happiness of, or to prevent mischief occurring to, the persons affected, whether an individual or a community consisting of an aggregate of individuals. Bentham also linked the principle of utility directly to happiness: it was 'that principle which approves or disapproves of every action whatsoever, according to the tendency which it appears to have to augment or diminish the happiness of the party whose interest is in question'.[13] 'An action then', explained Bentham, 'may be said to be conformable to the principle of utility, or, for shortness sake, to utility, (meaning with respect to the community at large), when the tendency it has to augment the happiness of the community is greater than any it has to diminish it.' A 'partisan' of the principle of utility would approve of any action which in his view promoted the happiness of the community, and disapprove of any which in his view diminished it.[14] Third, as we have seen,[15] happiness, or well-being, consisted in 'enjoyment of pleasures, security from pains'.[16] Fourth, pleasure constituted what was morally good, and pain what was morally evil, as Bentham asserted in *A Table of the Springs of Action* (published in 1817):

> *Positive good* (understand *pathological* good) is either pleasure itself, or a cause of pleasure; *negative* good, either *exemption from pain*, or a cause of such exemption.
>
> In like manner, positive evil is either pain itself or a cause of pain; negative evil, either loss of pleasure, or a cause of such loss. . . .
>
> *Moral good* is, as above, *pathological* good, in so far as *human will* is considered as instrumental in the production of it: in so far as any thing else is made of it, either the *word* is without meaning or the thing is without *value*. And so in regard to *evil*.

Bentham went on to explain that the term 'physical' might have been used instead of 'pathological', except that such a term might be understood to include merely 'those pleasures and pains, the seat of which is . . . in the *body*', and to

[13] *An Introduction to the Principles of Morals and Legislation*, 12 and n. [14] Ibid. 12–13.
[15] See p. 11 above. [16] *An Introduction to the Principles of Morals and Legislation*, 74.

exclude those which had their seat 'only in the *mind*'.[17] He reiterated the point in 'Codification Proposal' (printed in 1822):

Good is pleasure or exemption from pain: or a cause or instrument of either, considered in so far as it is a cause or instrument of either.

Evil is pain or loss of pleasure; or a cause or instrument of either; considered in so far as it is a cause or instrument of either.

Happiness is the sum of pleasures, deduction made or not made of the sum of pains.[18]

Bentham equated moral good with the physical sensation of pleasure, and moral evil with the physical sensation of pain. The quality of utility referred to the tendency of the object in question to produce happiness, which in turn consisted in a balance of pleasure over pain. An adherent of the principle of utility approved of those actions which increased pleasure and disapproved of those which diminished it. Pleasure and pain were the real entities into which any statement concerning the principle of utility, the criterion of right and wrong, was resolved in order to render it meaningful.

Bentham's concern in *An Introduction to the Principles of Morals and Legislation* was to explain to the legislator how the task of promoting the greatest happiness of the community subject to him might be accomplished. The actions of the legislator should, of course, be guided by the principle of utility: 'the happiness of the individuals, of whom a community is composed, that is their pleasures and their security,[19] is the end and the sole end which the legislator ought to have in view: the sole standard, in conformity to which each individual ought, as far as depends upon the legislator, to be *made* to fashion his behaviour'.[20] It was essential to understand the nature both of morality and of psychology, in other words, both of the proper object of human action, and of the basis of human motivation. The legislator had to recognize that pleasure and exemption from pain constituted both the ends of action as well as the motives to action.[21] In 'Article on Utilitarianism' (written in 1829) Bentham stated:

In the several pleasures, and in exemption from the several pains, he [i.e. Bentham himself] saw the elements of which happiness is composed, and of which, in number and value taken together, it was to be a constant object of his endeavours to shew how the greatest quantity possible may be made to have place. In the several pleasures and exemptions from pain operating in the character of motives, he saw so many *means* adapted to the purpose of attaining or, say, of accomplishing, those same ends.[22]

In order to produce the greatest happiness, that is the maximum of pleasure and the minimum of pain (the end), it was necessary to produce appropriate

[17] *Deontology*, 88–9.

[18] *'Legislator of the World': Writings on Codification, Law, and Education*, ed. P. Schofield and J. Harris (Oxford, 1998), 256.

[19] By 'security' Bentham meant the absence of pain. Cf. *'Legislator of the World'*, 251: 'An instrument of political security in any shape is an instrument of exemption from certain pains.'

[20] *An Introduction to the Principles of Morals and Legislation*, 34.

[21] *Deontology*, 87.

[22] Ibid. 320–1.

interests, which would in turn constitute motives—themselves composed of pleasure and pain—for individuals to pursue the end in question. Whatever it was that was to be done, stated Bentham, 'there is nothing by which a man can ultimately be *made* to do it, but either pain or pleasure'. Pain and pleasure might, therefore, be considered either 'in the character of *final* causes' or 'in the character of *efficient* causes or means'.[23] Once the legislator recognized the 'subjection' of human beings to the 'two sovereign masters', he would understand not only how to produce action, but how to produce action of the right kind: in other words, pain and pleasure, operating as motives to action, would direct individuals in order to bring about, as the ends of their action, the avoidance of pain and the production of pleasure.

In *An Introduction to the Principles of Morals and Legislation* Bentham identified 'four distinguishable sources from which pleasure and pain are in use to flow'—namely the physical, political, moral or popular, and religious sanctions—which the legislator might make use of to produce appropriate motives, and thence to produce appropriate action. They were termed 'sanctions' insofar as the pleasures and pains arising from these sources were 'capable of giving a binding force to any law or rule of conduct'. The physical sanction was the source of those motives which arose from 'the ordinary course of nature' without human or supernatural intervention. The political sanction, which Bentham termed more fully 'the political, including the legal, sanction', had its source in the commands of the judge, acting according to the will of the supreme ruling power in the state. The moral or popular sanction had its source in the opinion of significant individuals: 'If [the pleasure or pain takes place or is expected] at the hands of such *chance* persons in the community, as the party in question may happen in the course of his life to have concerns with, according to each man's spontaneous disposition, and not according to any settled or concerted rule, it may be said to issue from the *moral* or *popular* sanction.' While the pleasures and pains which had their source in these three sanctions would be experienced in the present life, the pleasures and pains which had their source in the religious sanction, and were expected to be distributed by a supernatural being, might be experienced either in the present life or in some future life. The various sanctions represented the source from which pleasures and pains arose or were expected to arise, and did not indicate any variation in the pleasures and pains themselves. For instance, a man might experience the same pain even though it had its source in any one of the sanctions:

A suffering which befalls a man in the natural and spontaneous course of things, shall be styled, for instance, a *calamity*; in which case, if it be supposed to befall him through any imprudence of his, it may be styled a punishment issuing from the *physical* sanction. Now this same suffering, if inflicted by the law, will be what is commonly called a *punishment*; if incurred for want of any friendly assistance, which the misconduct, or supposed

[23] *An Introduction to the Principles of Morals and Legislation*, 34.

misconduct, of the sufferer has occasioned to be withholden, a punishment issuing from the *moral* sanction; if by an immediate act of *God's* displeasure, manifested on account of some *sin* committed by him, or through any distraction of mind, occasioned by the dread of such displeasure, a punishment of the *religious* sanction.

None of the three other sanctions (with the exception of the religious sanction operating in a future life) could operate except by means of the physical sanction, which, therefore, formed the 'ground-work' of the others, though the physical sanction could of course operate independently of the others: 'In a word, the powers of nature may operate of themselves; but neither the magistrate, nor men at large, *can* operate, nor is God in the case in question *supposed* to operate, but through the powers of nature.'[24]

Bentham later revised his account of the sanctions, adding the sympathetic, antipathetic, and retributive sanctions to the four identified in *An Introduction to the Principles of Morals and Legislation*.[25] While the force of the popular or moral sanction was applied by 'an unassignable number of individuals all the world over', the force of the sympathetic and antipathetic sanctions was derived from 'the acts of *assignable* individuals'. For instance, if a man's friend was harmed by 'the frolics of a drunkard', then his sympathy for his friend would produce antipathy towards the drunkard, resulting in 'a propensity to bestow good offices—services upon your sober friend', and to 'withhold them from his drunken adversary'.[26] The sympathetic sanction was grounded on the fact that few men could 'contemplate altogether without uneasiness . . . pain suffered or supposed to be suffered by a fellow creature'. Such uneasiness was the pain of sympathy, and such pain constituted 'the force with which the sympathetic sanction tends on every occasion to restrain the person in question from engaging in any act the tendency of which appears to him to be the giving birth to the sense of pain in the breast of a fellow creature'.[27] In short, the pain a man anticipated another person would suffer as a consequence of his action would be a restraint upon his acting in that way. The antipathetic sanction no doubt operated in an analogous way, though here the anticipated pain would operate as a stimulus to the action. It was, however, Bentham's view that 'as age and experience advance', the affection of sympathy, and thence the force of the sympathetic sanction, would increase, both in terms of its strength in the case of particular individuals, and its extent as it came to be applied by a wider range of individuals.[28] The force of the retributive sanction was also derived from assignable individuals, since it consisted in the pain or pleasure a man might receive from a person who had been affected by his actions. For instance, where a

[24] *An Introduction to the Principles of Morals and Legislation*, 34–7. See also *A Fragment on Government*, 496 n.

[25] Bentham to Dumont, 29 Nov. 1821, *Correspondence*, x. 444.

[26] Bentham to Dumont, 26 May 1822, *Correspondence*, vol. xi, ed. C. Fuller (Oxford, 2000), 86–7.

[27] *Deontology*, 201.

[28] Ibid. 202–3. The point is explored in A. Dube, *The Theme of Acquisitiveness in Bentham's Political Thought* (New York, 1991).

drunk inflicted injury on another person, and the latter retaliated in response to the injury sustained, the action in question emanated from the retributive sanction.[29]

In explaining that the avoidance of pain and the production of pleasure were not only the ends which the legislator had in view, but also the means or instruments with which he had to operate, Bentham commented that, 'it behoves [the legislator] . . . to understand their force, which is again, in another point of view, their value'.[30] The equating of 'force' with 'value' illustrated the connection between psychology and morality. The 'force' with which a pleasure operated was a matter of psychological fact, while the 'value' of that pleasure was a matter of moral worth, yet this was only to say the same thing from a different perspective. By both the 'force' and the 'value' of a pleasure Bentham had in mind a quantitative measure: a more forceful or more valuable pleasure was a pleasure of greater quantity, and, as such, not only operated with greater strength as a motive, but was more desirable as an end. Bentham outlined the various 'circumstances'—which he also termed 'elements' or 'dimensions'—on which 'the value of a pleasure or pain considered *by itself*' to 'a person considered *by himself*' depended: namely its intensity, duration, certainty or uncertainty, and propinquity or remoteness. Two further circumstances, fecundity and purity, were not strictly properties of a pleasure or pain, but of the act by which the pleasure or pain had been produced. An act which had produced pleasure had the quality of fecundity insofar as it was likely to be followed by further sensations of pleasure; it had the quality of purity insofar as it was unlikely to be followed by sensations of pain. Conversely, in relation to an act which produced pain, it had the quality of fecundity insofar as it was likely to be followed by further sensations of pain; it had the quality of purity insofar as it was unlikely to be followed by sensations of pleasure. Where the value of a pleasure or pain was considered in relation to more than one person, a further circumstance had to be taken into consideration, namely the circumstance of extent, that is the number of persons affected by the action in question. In order to draw up 'an exact account . . . of the general tendency of any act, by which the interests of a community are affected', the balance of the value of the pleasures and pains produced in the instance of a single individual was calculated, the process repeated for each individual affected, and finally the results aggregated: 'Take the *balance*; which, if on the side of *pleasure*, will give the general *good tendency* of the act, with respect to the total number or community of individuals concerned; if on the side of pain, the general *evil tendency*, with respect to the same

[29] Grote Papers, British Library Add. MS 29,809, fo. 67 (17 Feb. 1819). For Bentham's revised account of the sanctions see *Deontology*, 176–7. He had also by this time (11 Sept. 1823) divided the political sanction into the legal or judicial sanction and the administrative sanction, depending upon whether the source of the sanction was an official exercising judicial power or an official exercising some other branch of political power. On Bentham's typography of power see pp. 223–7 below.

[30] *An Introduction to the Principles of Morals and Legislation*, 38.

community.'[31] The circumstance of extent was, therefore, central to Bentham's exposition of the principle of utility:

> On the occasion of any proposed act, to make application of the principle of utility is to take one account of the feelings of the two opposite kinds—of the pleasures of all sorts on the one side, of the pains of all sorts on the other side—which, in all breasts that seem likely to be in any way affected by it, seem liable and likely, in the two opposite cases of the act's being done and of its being left undone, to take place.[32]

A moral judgment was produced by taking into account all the pleasures and pains expected to be produced 'in all breasts that seem likely to be in any way affected' by the act in question. Once the final 'circumstance' by which the quantity or value of a pain or pleasure was to be measured—namely that of extent—had been taken into account, a statement of psychological fact was transformed into a statement of moral value.

The importance of the circumstance of extent in this context was confirmed when, in the second edition of *An Introduction to the Principles of Morals and Legislation* which appeared in 1823, Bentham recommended that the phrase 'the principle of utility' be replaced by either 'the greatest happiness principle' or 'the greatest felicity principle'. The term 'utility' did not, in his view, sufficiently convey the idea of happiness. Moreover, the new formulation, unlike the original one, gave an indication, stated Bentham, of 'the *number*, of the interests affected', for it was 'the *number*' which was 'the circumstance, which contributes, in the largest proportion, to the formation of the standard here in question; the *standard of right and wrong* by which alone the propriety of human conduct, in every situation, can with propriety be tried'.[33] Consideration of extent was, therefore, crucial not only in terms of transforming a statement of psychological fact into a statement of moral value, but was also the most important element in the calculation of utility.

Related to this change of terminology is the question as to whether Bentham would have sanctioned the sacrifice of the interests of a minority to those of a majority. There is no lack of evidence that Bentham did accept the need to sacrifice the interests of some—and it might be the interests of a majority and not merely those of a minority—if such a sacrifice was conducive to an overall increase in happiness. Having said that, he cautioned that not every sacrifice of the interest of a minority would be justified by the principle of utility. In a passage probably written towards the end of 1792 he remarked:

> The part ought to yield to the whole: the minority to the majority:—the proposition is very true: but if ill applied, it may do great mischief: it may be the source of great illusion.

[31] *An Introduction to the Principles of Morals and Legislation*, 38–40.

[32] *Deontology*, 168.

[33] *An Introduction to the Principles of Morals and Legislation*, 11 n. This note was written in July 1822. Bentham, soon afterwards, announced to Dumont that the '*Principle of Utility*—is dead and gone. Greatest happiness principle has succeeded to it': see Bentham to Dumont, 6 Sept. 1822, *Correspondence*, xi. 149.

The minority must yield to the majority: true: but what is the whole the better for it if what the minority suffers by the sacrifice is more than what the majority gain by it? Consider that parts are what the whole is made of. If one after the other all the parts suffer, how fares it with the whole?[34]

In another passage written in June 1828 he noted that he had 'till very lately' regarded the phrase 'the greatest happiness' to be merely an abridgement of 'the greatest happiness of the greatest number'. He had realized, however, that 'by this mode of expression, if applied to practice, effects widely different from those intended—in a word mischief to an almost indefinite extent—might be produced', namely by simply ignoring the interest of the minority:

Bring to view in supposition two communities. Number of the individuals—in the one, 1,000: in the other, 1,001: of both together, 2,001. By the greatest happiness, the arrangement prescribed would be that by which the greatest happiness of all together would be produced. But wide indeed from this effect might be the effect of the application of the principle, if the arrangement productive of the greatest happiness of the greatest number—no regard being shewn to the happiness of the smaller number—were understood to be the arrangement prescribed by that same principle.

So long as the greatest number—the 1,001—were in the enjoyment of the greatest degree of comfort, the greatest possible degree of torment might be the lot of the smallest of the two numbers—the 1,000: and still the principle stating as the proper object of endeavour the greatest happiness of the greatest number be actually conformed to—not contravened.[35]

In both the passage of 1792 and that of 1828 Bentham's point was not that the interest of the minority should never be sacrificed to that of the majority, but that the interest of the majority would not necessarily outweigh the interest of the minority. Nevertheless, where the interest of a minority did not outweigh that of a majority, the interest of the minority would have to give way.[36] This is not to say that Bentham did not impose a high threshold for such a sacrifice,[37] or that he did not have considerable resources within his utilitarianism for improving the standing of those disadvantaged by traditional social relations,[38]

[34] UC cxlvi. 241. [35] *Official Aptitude Maximized; Expense Minimized*, 352.

[36] Cf '*Legislator of the World*', 250: 'If, on the ground of delinquency, in the name of punishment, it be right that any man should be rendered unhappy, it is not that his happiness has less claim to regard than another man's, but that it is necessary to the greatest happiness of the greatest number, that a portion of the happiness of that one be sacrificed.'

[37] The need, given great emphasis by Bentham, to avoid the disappointment of expectations, discussed in detail by P. J. Kelly, *Utilitarianism and Distributive Justice: Jeremy Bentham and the Civil Law* (Oxford, 1990), 168–206, contributed to the threshold in question. See p. 326 below.

[38] This issue is explored in F. Rosen, 'Majorities and Minorities: A Classical Utilitarian View', in J. W. Chapman and A. Wertheimer (eds.), *Majorities and Minorities: Nomos XXXII* (New York, 1990), 24–43; and L. C. Boralevi, *Bentham and the Oppressed* (Berlin, 1984). Moreover, as J. R. Dinwiddy, *Bentham* (Oxford, 1989), 26–7, points out, 'Bentham believed that the *optimal* goal included "the provision of an equal quantity of happiness for every one"', even though where this was '"impossible"', it would still be '"matter of necessity, to make sacrifice of a portion of the happiness of a few, to the greater happiness of the rest"'. The quotations are from *Parliamentary*

but without the potential for such a sacrifice, Bentham's whole utilitarian project would have ground to a halt. If he had not been prepared to sacrifice the interests of the minority, he would not, for instance, have been able to advocate the establishment of a representative democracy at the expense of the interests of monarch and aristocracy.

III

Bentham's position might be summarized as follows. A 'partisan' of the principle of utility was concerned with calculating the balance of pleasure and pain produced by an action. Such a 'partisan' would approve of any action which increased happiness (understood in terms of a preponderance of pleasure over pain), and disapprove of any action which increased suffering (understood in terms of a preponderance of pain over pleasure). He would take into account each and every individual affected by the action in question. Where only one person was affected, the extent would be equal to one, but where more than one person was affected, then the extent would be equal to the total number of those affected. Once extent had been taken into account, the 'partisan' of the principle of utility would then judge whether the action in question was deserving of approval or disapproval, or, to put this another way, judge whether the action was morally right or morally wrong. This judgment, therefore, was determined by a question of fact—namely the quantity of pleasure and pain which had been brought into existence by the action in question.

Bentham was quite explicit that an appeal to the principle of utility constituted an appeal to matters of fact. In *A Fragment on Government*, for instance, he stated that disagreements 'between the defenders of a law and the opposers of it' would be much more likely to be settled 'were they but explicitly and constantly referred at once to the principle of UTILITY. The footing on which this principle rests every dispute, is that of matter of fact; that is, future fact—the probability of future certain contingencies.'[39] Around the same time he wrote: 'Utility will reign sole and sovereign arbitress of all disputes. The only evidences admitted will be matters of fact: facts conjectured from facts experienced: against opinion, under every other guise than that of mere opinion, the door will be shut inexorably.'[40] In the autumn of 1789, when discussing the use of the words 'can not' in declarations of rights in order to assert moral claims, and the obstacles such usage placed in the way of rational discussion, he stated:

Change the language and instead of can not put ought not, the case is widely [different]. The moderate expression of opinion and will intimated by this phrase leads naturally to

Candidate's proposed Declaration of Principles: or say, A Test proposed for Parliamentary Candidates (London, 1831), 7.

[39] *A Fragment on Government*, 491. [40] UC lxix. 232 (*c.*1776).

the inquiry after a reason: and this reason, if there be any at bottom that deserves [the name], is always a proposition of fact relative to the question of utility. Such a law *ought not* to be established, because it is not consistent with the general welfare: its tendency is not to add to the general stock of happiness. . . . Now the question is put as every political and moral question ought to be, upon the issue of fact; and mankind are directed to the only true track of investigation which can afford instruction or hope of rational agreement, the track of experiment and observation.[41]

The facts in question were the feelings of human beings, or, it might be added, where appropriate, sentient creatures generally.[42] Addressing the proposal to appropriate the property of the clergy in France in the autumn of 1789, Bentham stated: 'The question of utility is a question not of sounds but of sensations: it depends not upon your choosing to allow or to refuse to this or that class of occupants this or that name, but upon the feelings of men of all classes.'[43] In 'Nonsense upon Stilts', written in 1795, he noted that regulations were to be judged 'by their effect on the feelings of those whom they concern'.[44] The principle of utility was a fictitious entity, and like other fictitious entities, if it was to make any sense, had to be expounded in terms of real entities. The real entities in question—the 'real source' of the principle of utility—were the feelings experienced by sentient creatures. And, as we have seen,[45] the only feelings which mattered in this respect were those of pleasure and pain.

P. J. Kelly has cast doubt on the view that Bentham seriously intended the legislator to engage in calculations of the sort in question. While Kelly admits that Bentham advocated such a procedure for the individual when determining the course of action he thought would contribute most to his own happiness, he claims that this was not how Bentham intended the legislator to operate when determining how to maximize the happiness of the community in general. In contrast, the legislator was to adopt a set of general rules, adherence to which would advance utility. While the individual was to adopt an act-utilitarian decision procedure, the legislator was to be a rule utilitarian.[46] However satisfactory as a reconstruction of Bentham's utilitarianism, the distinction between public and private decision-making was expressly rejected by Bentham himself:

Note that, to be at once appropriate and all-comprehensive, a deontological principle designed for giving direction to human conduct should apply alike to conduct in public and private life.

41 *Rights, Representation, and Reform: Nonsense upon Stilts and other writings on the French Revolution*, ed. P. Schofield, C. Pease-Watkin, and C. Blamires (Oxford, 2002), 188–9.

42 See *An Introduction to the Principles of Morals and Legislation*, 282–3 n.

43 *Rights, Representation, and Reform*, 216. 44 Ibid. 375. 45 See pp. 29–30 above.

46 Kelly, *Utilitarianism and Distributive Justice*, 34–6. Cf. F. Rosen, 'Individual Sacrifice and the Greatest Happiness: Bentham on Utility and Rights', *Utilitas*, 10 (1998), 129–43, at 135: 'The legislator has the difficult task of determining what general laws and policies increase happiness for all concerned, a task which cannot be achieved simply by calculating and adding up pleasures. Instead, he or she must look for secondary principles shared by most people and justify these in terms of their advancing human happiness.'

This does the greatest happiness principle:—*original contract*, not.
Original contract, if good for any thing, would have been applicable to private life.[47]

Now there seems little reason to dispute Kelly's statement that Bentham 'was acutely aware of the difficulty of providing an objective measure of subjective experience'[48]—the calculations would not be mathematically precise, or indeed anything other than subjective—but this does not mean that Bentham did not consider such calculations to have a mathematical basis.[49] Writing in the mid-1770s, Bentham noted that in order to compare the total amount of mischief produced by one act with that produced by another, one had to consider the 'ingredients in the value of every sensation', namely intensity, duration, extent, propinquity, and probability (what he later termed 'certainty'):

Let us see with what degree of accuracy each of these quantities is capable according to the nature of things of being measured.

That which is the least capable of all is Intensity. For this there is no common standard. Duration is a quantity that may be measured out and divided with great exactness: with the same exactness that time is measured on any other occasion.

Extent is a matter of numeration.

The value that it loses on the score of want of *propinquity* or in other words by *remoteness*, depends upon the measurement of time.

Probability is matter of calculation, and is measured by calculation: which is managed by guessing at the number of the past instances in which the event in question has failed on the one hand, and those in which it has taken place on the other hand, and viewing the proportion of the number of the one set of instances to that of the other.[50]

Almost half a century later Bentham's conviction of both the need for, and the limitations to, calculation in morals, and thence in legislation, remained unaltered. In a discussion dealing with the desirability of producing a code of law in which the enactive provisions would be accompanied with reasons which, insofar as they had any 'claim to regard', would 'show the conduciveness of the several arrangements' to happiness, he commented:

Reasons, indicative of this conduciveness, are reasons derived from the principle known by the name of the *principle of utility*: more expressively say *the greatest-happiness principle*. To exhibit these reasons is to draw up the account between law and happiness: to apply arithmetical calculations to the elements of happiness. *Political arithmetic*—a name that has by some been given to *political economy*—is an application, though but a particular and far short of an all-comprehensive one, of arithmetic and its calculations, to happiness and its elements.

[47] *Official Aptitude Maximized; Expense Minimized*, 352 n.

[48] Kelly, *Utilitarianism and Distributive Justice*, 32.

[49] T. Warke, 'Multi-Dimensional Utility and the Index Number Problem: Jeremy Bentham, J. S. Mill, and Qualitative Hedonism', *Utilitas*, 12 (2000), 176–203, convincingly argues that, in the parlance of contemporary economics, Bentham saw the question of the commensurability of pleasures as an index-number problem.

[50] UC lxix. 19.

The elements of happiness were, of course, pleasures and exemptions from pains. The magnitude of a pleasure consisted in its intensity, multiplied by 'the moments or atoms of time contained in its duration'. The magnitude of a pleasure being given, its value would be diminished insofar as it was either further away in time or less certain to take place, or, it might be added, both further away and less certain. Such a diminution in the value of a more distant pleasure was comparable to the diminution experienced in the value of a sum of money which would not be received until some specific time in the future, because of the loss of the interest which would have accrued in the meantime if the sum had come into immediate possession. Again, the value of an uncertain pleasure would diminish in the ratio of the uncertainty of acquiring it, just as the value of a sum of money would diminish by half if the probability of acquiring it was 'but as 1 to 2'. On the other hand, the value of a pleasure was increased in proportion to the number of persons by whom it was experienced.[51] There were two insuperable difficulties in making precise calculations. The first was that the intensity of pleasure could not be measured, though there was no such difficulty with the other four 'dimensions'—duration, propinquity, certainty, and extent. The second was that there was no scale against which pleasure might be measured: 'Weight, extent, heat, light,—for quantities of all these articles, we have perceptible and expressible measures: unhappily or happily, for quantities of pleasure or pain, we have no such measures.'[52] Although pleasure itself was not 'ponderable or measurable', money, as we have seen, might be used as the 'representative' of pleasure. Even though the calculation might not be absolutely perfect, 'the application thus made of arithmetic to questions of utility' was greatly superior to

> every form of argumentation, in which every idea is afloat, no degree of precision being ever attained, because none is ever so much as aimed at. Till the principle of utility, as explained by the phrase *the greatest happiness of the greatest number*, is, on each occasion, if not explicitly, implicitly referred to, as the source of all reasoning,—and arithmetic . . . employed in making application of it,—every thing that, in the field of legislation, calls itself *reasoning* or *argument* will—say who can in what large proportion—be a compound of nonsense and falsehood.

The principle of utility, as well as being 'the only true and defensible footing' upon which moral reasoning could be placed, was, moreover, the only one 'on which any tolerable degree of precision can have place'; and 'the degree of precision' was capable of being made 'near to mathematical'.[53]

Bentham appears to have believed that the human mind was, so to speak, programmed to operate as a calculating device for pleasure and pain. For instance, in answering the objection that 'passion does not calculate' when

[51] '*Legislator of the World*', 250–2, 253.

[52] In the mid-1770s Bentham had written: 'There is no marking out by any description a determinate lot to serve as a common measure of pain or pleasure: nor were such an aliquot marked out is there any way of knowing whether it subsists or not in a given subject.' See UC lxix. 41.

[53] '*Legislator of the World*', 253–5.

outlining the principles which should govern the proportionality between punishments and offences, he stated: 'When matters of such importance as pain and pleasure are at stake, and these in the highest degree (the only matters, in short, that can be of importance) who is there that does not calculate? Men calculate, some with less exactness, indeed, some with more: but all men calculate. I would not say, that even a madman does not calculate.'[54] Neither the madman nor the legislator could avoid calculation. That the legislator's calculations might be imprecise did not mean that he pursued a different methodology from that adopted by the individual. Indeed, as we shall see,[55] Bentham believed that the legislator would generally fare better in his calculations than the individual. But the point was that the legislator, like every other human being, was subject to the 'two sovereign masters', with all that implied.

IV

Bentham appreciated that any statement of value, whether true or false, like every other expression of opinion, necessarily involved a subjective element,[56] but that a true statement of value included, in addition, an objective element—or to put this another way, the opinion in question corresponded to facts in the physical world.[57] To say that an action was right, or that it ought to be done, implied approval, and to say that an action was wrong, or ought not to be done, implied disapproval. The approval or disapproval was only implied, since the expression of approval or disapproval might be insincere.[58] Leaving aside the question of sincerity, when a person asserted that an action ought to be done, all that he asserted was that he approved of the action in question—it was no more than an expression of opinion, and there was no guarantee that, as such, it coincided with the dictates of the principle of utility:

As often as, speaking of any man, I say he ought to do so and so or he ought not to do so and so, what accordingly I know and acknowledge myself to be doing is neither more nor

[54] *An Introduction to the Principles of Morals and Legislation*, 173–4.

[55] See pp. 47–50 below. [56] See pp. 18–21 above.

[57] D. Baumgardt, *Bentham and the Ethics of Today* (Princeton, 1952), 528 and n., helpfully distinguishes between 'the subjective feelings on which Bentham's hedonism is based', which were 'neutral, objective, and not arbitrarily changeable facts', and 'subjectivism' or 'relativism of judgment', namely 'a judgment without any objective validity'.

[58] More generally, Bentham regarded any attempt to discern the motives of an individual as both futile and unnecessary. He distinguished between the 'motive or cause' which produced an action, and the 'ground or reason which warrants a legislator, or other by-stander, in regarding that act with an eye of approbation'. While the only right ground of action was the principle of utility, the act might in fact be caused by any number of other principles or motives. However, it was the principle of utility alone 'that can be the reason why it might or ought to have been done'. In short, the legislator was not concerned whether an action was performed for the right reasons, but whether the right action was performed. See *An Introduction to the Principles of Morals and Legislation*, 32–3. Having said that, Bentham wished to encourage social motives on the grounds that they were more likely than dissocial motives to lead to the right action being performed.

less than endeavour[ing] to bring to view the state of my own mind, of my own opinion, of my own affections in relation to the line of conduct which on the occasion in question is stated as pursued by him—this much and nothing more.[59]

The writer on morals, the 'self-constituted legislator of the popular or moral sanction', used the words 'ought' and 'ought not' when laying down his 'laws':

When it is his will and pleasure that you should do the act in question, he tells you that you ought to do it, you are under an obligation to do it, and the obligation you are under is a positive one. When it is his will and pleasure [that] you shall not do it, he informs you that you ought not to do it, and then the obligation you are under is a negative one.[60]

The term 'virtuous' was to be understood in a similar way: it reflected the approval with which a person viewed an act, habit, disposition, or propensity. But what, asked Bentham, was the cause or ground of the sentiment of approval? 'My answer is: in different states of society, in different individuals belonging to the same society, the ground has every where, as yet, been very considerably different. Therefore, to this question no single answer can be given and be at the same time a true one.' As far as Bentham himself was concerned, his approval was grounded on the principle of utility: 'The efficient cause, or say ground, for whatever sentiment of approbation stands in [my] mind associated with the idea of any act, habit, disposition, or propensity, is its tendency to give a net increase to the aggregate quantity of happiness in all its shapes taken together, about to have place in the community, whatsoever it be, that is in question.'[61]

However, not everyone was a partisan of the principle of utility, and when the non-partisan used the words right and wrong, ought and ought not, their approval rested on some other ground. The terms in this case were to be understood by reference to some alternative standard of right and wrong. In Bentham's view, every such alternative, with the exception of the principle of asceticism,[62] resolved itself into 'the mere averment' of a man's 'own unfounded sentiments'—what he termed the principle of caprice, or the principle of sympathy and antipathy (Bentham preferred the latter phrase 'on account of its impartiality').[63] If a man's own caprice, his own approval or disapproval of an act 'without any regard to its consequences', was a sufficient standard, either this standard would apply to every other man, in which case it would be despotic, or each man would set his own sentiment as the standard, in which case it would be anarchic.[64] The principle of sympathy and antipathy failed to point out 'some external consideration, as a means of warranting and guiding the internal sentiments of approbation and disapprobation'. Apart from the principle of

[59] *Deontology*, 148–9. [60] Ibid. 206–7. [61] Ibid. 209.

[62] An adherent of the principle of asceticism would approve of any action which increased pain and diminished pleasure: 'Let but one part of the inhabitants of the earth pursue it consistently, and in a day's time they will have turned it into a hell.' See *An Introduction to the Principles of Morals and Legislation*, 17–21. [63] Ibid. 24 n.

[64] Ibid. 15–16.

asceticism, which was the opposite of the principle of utility, all other standards of right and wrong were reducible to the principle of sympathy and antipathy, and consisted 'in so many contrivances for avoiding the obligation of appealing to any external standard, and for prevailing upon the reader to accept of the author's sentiment or opinion as a reason and that a sufficient one for itself'. These standards, whether termed the moral sense, common sense, rule of right, law of nature, or whatever else, would nevertheless frequently, if unintentionally, coincide with the dictates of utility.[65]

What, then, did the difference between the principle of utility and the principle of sympathy and antipathy amount to? The partisan of the principle of sympathy and antipathy took into consideration no more than his own interest, or at most the interests of some number less than the whole number of persons affected by the action in question. The adherent of the principle of utility took into consideration, at least insofar as he was able, the interests of all the persons affected by the action in question. As Bentham remarked, reflecting on his reading of *Telemachus* at the age of 6 (or 7), he had 'made a sort of vow, however indistinct, that whenever human beings and human feelings were concerned, the numeration table should be my guide'.[66] The difference between the perspective of the partisan of the principle of utility and that of the principle of sympathy and antipathy was simply that of extent. In *Deontology*, for instance, Bentham argued that the prescriptions of moralists had hitherto been simply a reflection of their own interests and prejudices. Such moralists had no difficulty in issuing laws or precepts: 'it is an operation to the performance of which every man who has power is competent—the foolish not less than the most wise'. In contrast, to give good reasons, clearly expressed and duly arranged, was a work of great difficulty. The traditional moralist, characterized by indolence, arrogance, and ignorance, had assumed 'a commanding attitude' and expressed himself in 'a commanding tone', and merely coupled the expressions 'ought' and 'ought not' with a description of the sorts of action which he himself wished to see performed or not performed. He gave no explanation as to why the action should or should not be done. To give such an explanation would, of course, have necessitated an appeal to the principle of utility, the only source from which relevant reasons could be produced.[67] The moralist was motivated not by the prospect of the happiness of the community, but by that of his own advantage, such as an increase in his wealth or an enhancement of his reputation. In order to heighten his reputation, he was likely to pander to popular morality, which was biased towards 'severity': 'Thus it is that without reason and almost without thought, taking for his instruments these craven words "ought" and "ought not",

[65] *An Introduction to the Principles of Morals and Legislation*, 25–9.

[66] Bentham to Felgueiras, 5 June 1821, *Correspondence*, x. 345. See also pp. 37–8 above.

[67] See also *A Fragment on Government*, 446, 448: 'The principle [of utility] furnishes us with that *reason*, which alone depends not upon any higher reason, but which is itself the sole and all-sufficient reason for every point of practice whatsoever.'

he goes on laying on commands and prohibitions—imposing on mankind in both shapes those fictitious and metaphysical but not the less heavy and afflictive chains and burthens.' Observation, enquiry, and reflection were 'as superfluous as they are laborious. Wheresoever a man's *ipsedixit* passes for argument he has no need of any other.' Pleasures were condemned, and pains recommended in their place.[68] In relation to 'ought' and ought not', Bentham remarked ironically: 'These words—if for this one purpose the use of them may be allowed—*ought* to be banished from the vocabulary of Ethics.'[69]

In contrast to the principle of sympathy and antipathy, the reason why the principle of utility formed an external or objective standard was because it could be expounded by reference to real entities—in other words, it had its 'real source' in the physical world. A proposition which purported to be consonant to the principle of utility was no different from a proposition derived from the principle of sympathy and antipathy in that it was necessarily an expression of opinion on the part of the speaker. However, a proposition grounded on sympathy and antipathy failed to satisfy an ontological condition, for the standard to which it purported to appeal had no 'real source' in the physical world. The proposition in question was, therefore, nonsense. Only propositions which were grounded on the principle of utility met this ontological condition; and only when such a judgment was accurate, that is reflected matters of fact existing in the physical world, was it true.

> No otherwise than by reference to the *greatest happiness* principle, can epithets such as *good* and *evil*, or *good* and *bad*, be expressive of any quality in the *act* or other *object* to which they are applied: say an act of an individual: say an act of government: a *law*, a *measure* of government, a *system* of government, a *form* of government. But for this reference, all they designate is—the *state of mind* on the part of him in whose discourse they are employed.
>
> When, and in proportion as, this standard is employed as the standard of reference,—then for the first time, and thenceforward for ever, will the import of those same perpetually employed and primarily important adjuncts, considered as indicative of qualities belonging to objects they are applied to, be determinate.[70]

A statement of morality grounded on the principle of utility had a basis in the physical world which consisted of real entities, and it was this basis which distinguished it from all other pretended moral standards.

In *An Introduction to the Principles of Morals and Legislation* Bentham took it for granted that the legislator would wish to promote the greatest happiness of the community over which he ruled: 'The business of government is to promote the happiness of the society, by punishing and rewarding.' Bentham here succinctly brought together the two perspectives from which he had considered 'the two sovereign masters' of pain and pleasure, namely as the ends and as the means of government. The legislator would attach punishment to an act insofar as its

[68] *Deontology*, 252–5. [69] Ibid. 253. [70] '*Legislator of the World*', 256–7.

consequences were considered to be pernicious or detrimental to the happiness of the community, that is produced more evil than good,[71] and attach reward to an act insofar as its consequences were beneficial.[72] Bentham later realized, as we shall see,[73] that the legislator himself was just as prone to the influence of the principle of sympathy and antipathy as any other individual in the community, and left to himself would tend to promote his own happiness, even if this resulted in greater unhappiness being produced in the community in general. But setting aside consideration of this problem for now, there was a further difficulty—a difficulty which was deeply embedded in human psychology—for the well-meaning legislator: namely, the problem of idiosyncrasy. In *Deontology* Bentham laid down a series of 'aphorisms': 'Every person is not only the most proper judge, but the only proper judge of what with reference to himself is pleasure: and so in regard to pain'; every sort of pleasure was 'good and fit to be pursued', and the fact that a person, having once experienced a pleasure, pursued it again was 'conclusive proof of its goodness—of its relative goodness, relation being had to the person himself and his particular well-being'; because one individual did not find a particular act pleasurable, it did not mean that some other individual would not find it pleasurable; and because one person or group of persons did not find a particular act pleasurable, it did not mean that another person should be prohibited from performing the act in question.[74] The point was that different individuals had different susceptibilities to different sorts of pleasure and pain:

> to each man what is pleasure? To every man what is the greatest pleasure? To every man what is pain? To every man what is the greatest pain? That which in his own judgment, assisted by his own memory, and through that printed upon his own feelings, is so. Reader, whoever you are, ask of yourself and answer to yourself these questions: Is there—can there be—that man who knows or who can know as well as yourself what it is that has given you pleasure or what it is that has given you most pleasure?
>
> Of these observations what is the most obvious practical conclusion? That, being the best judge for himself what line of conduct on each occasion will be the most conducive to his own well-being, every man, being of mature age and sound mind, ought on this subject to be left to judge and act for himself: and that every thing which by any other man can be said or done in the view of giving direction to the conduct of the first, is no better than folly and impertinence.[75]

The subjective nature of the feelings of pleasure and pain with which the legislator had to deal increased the complexity of his task. The legislator who was a partisan of the principle of utility could not have complete and certain knowledge of all the feelings of others, but he was called upon to take account of all those feelings—unlike the partisan of the principle of sympathy and antipathy,

[71] He also identified limitations on the sphere of the legislator's operations, namely such 'cases' as were 'unmeet for punishment', where punishment would be groundless, inefficacious, unprofitable, and needless: see *An Introduction to the Principles of Morals and Legislation*, 158–64.

[72] Ibid. 74.

[73] See pp. 131–6 below.

[74] *Deontology*, 150–1.

[75] Ibid. 250–1.

who merely took account of his own feelings or of those of some lesser group than the whole.

What, then, justified interference of any sort, on the part of either the moralist or the legislator, with the conduct of individuals? It was the function of the practical moralist or deontologist to provide guidance to individuals where their conduct affected only themselves (where extent was equal to one). In this case, Bentham pointed out that even though, in relation to present pleasure and exemption from pain, a man was the best judge of his own feelings, as the pleasure or pain in question became more remote in time, he possessed less and less advantage over another 'who, with the same natural talent and appropriate mental acquirements, has taken the connection between causes and effects in that portion of the field of action for the subject of a more attentive scrutiny'.[76] There were, then, exceptions to the rule that each man was the best judge of what was most conducive to his own well-being, and this gave rise to the characteristic task of the deontologist:

> For the use of each man to lay before his eyes a sketch of the probable future more correct and compleat than, without the benefit of such suggestion, inflamed by the view of present or speedy pleasure or pain, men's appetites and passions will be apt in general to suffer them to draw for their own use: to assist them in making reflections and drawing comparisons—in taking a correct and compleat account of the past—and from thence in drawing inferences and forming eventual calculations and eventual conjectures in relation to the future; thereby to assist them—in the first place in the choice of subordinate, i.e. particular, *ends*—in the next place of the *means* through which the obtainment of those pleasures respectively shall be aimed at. . . .

The 'private' deontologist was a 'scout' who searched out the particular consequences which had tended to result from particular courses of action in the past, and compiled an account of them for the use of anyone who wished to take advantage of his services.[77]

The legislator, presumably, was also capable of taking a more correct view of the future consequences of actions. But whereas the deontologist offered advice, the legislator was able to coerce; and whereas the deontologist dealt with those actions which affected only the individual actor himself, the legislator was primarily concerned with those actions which affected not only the actor himself, but other persons as well. There might never be certainty that a particular measure would promote the greatest happiness, but a utilitarian legislator would at least be prepared to provide reasons in justification of his measures. Such reasons would have their 'real source' in the expected pleasures and pains which would result. While appeal to the principle of utility did not rule out disagreement, at least the parties would be talking meaningfully to each other.

[76] Ibid. 196. See also UC cii. 211 (18 Sept. 1814) [*Deontology*, 195 n.]: 'Each man best judge of present pleasure or pain—but not every man of future [pleasure or pain]. Like a 3^{d} person his future contingent individual pleasure or pain can not be judged of by him otherwise than from the species it belongs to.'

[77] *Deontology*, 250–1.

Having said this, there remained a tension in Bentham's thought between the role of the legislator in promoting the greatest happiness of the community, and the insistence that each man was the best judge of his own interest. It was, arguably, only when Bentham came to advocate a democratic system of government that this tension was resolved.

3

Natural Law and Natural Rights

I

Bentham's recognition of the principle of utility, with its 'real source' in the feelings of pain and pleasure experienced by sentient creatures, as a critical standard of morality allowed him to draw a distinction between law as it is and law as it ought to be.[1] This distinction in turn provided the basis both for his strategy of reform, and for his attack on the Common Law and on natural law with its related doctrine of natural rights. In *A Fragment on Government*, which took Blackstone's *Commentaries on the Laws of England*[2] for its target, Bentham distinguished two possible approaches which the legal commentator might adopt, namely that of the expositor and that of the censor: 'To the province of the *Expositor* it belongs to explain to us what, as he supposes, the Law *is*: to that of the *Censor*, to observe to us what he thinks it *ought to be*. The former, therefore, is principally occupied in stating, or in enquiring after *facts*: the latter, in discussing *reasons*.' The task of the expositor was to show what had already been done by legislators and judges, while that of the censor was to show what they ought to do in future. Different countries had established very different laws, but what ought to have been established was in great measure the same.[3] In Bentham's view, Blackstone, instead of clearly distinguishing between the functions of censor and expositor, had confounded them. Blackstone's 'professed object' had been to describe the laws of England, in other words to perform the role of expositor, but he had gone beyond this and, taking on the role of censor, had attempted to justify the laws which he had found established. There appeared to be an assumption that it was inappropriate to condemn 'an old-fashioned law', perhaps on account of 'a kind of *personification*... as if the

[1] It should be noted that Bentham's distinction between law as it is and law as it ought to be did not entail the conceptual distinction between law and morality, and thence between factual and evaluative statements, which, following H. L. A. Hart, *Essays on Bentham: Studies in Jurisprudence and Political Theory* (Oxford, 1982), 105–268, is usually attributed to him. As we have seen, Bentham's ethics had a factual or, in philosophical terminology, a 'naturalistic' basis, and he regarded any ethical proposition which had no such basis as nonsense. See further P. Schofield, 'Jeremy Bentham, the Principle of Utility, and Legal Positivism', in M. D. A. Freeman (ed.), *Current Legal Problems 2003: Volume 56* (Oxford, 2004), 1–39.

[2] William Blackstone, *Commentaries on the Laws of England*, 4 vols. (Oxford, 1765–9).

[3] *A Fragment on Government*, 397–8.

Law were a living creature', or on account of 'the mechanical veneration for antiquity' or some 'other delusion of the fancy'. This was not an assumption that Bentham was prepared to accept. He could not see why 'the merit of justifying a law when right should be thought greater, than that of censuring it when wrong'. He added: 'Under a government of Laws, what is the motto of a good citizen? *To obey punctually; to censure freely.*' Bentham's concern was not merely that Blackstone had strayed beyond the province of the expositor into that of the censor, but that he had in effect subverted the role of the censor by failing 'to censure freely'—he had, in effect, approved of everything, and disapproved of nothing. The proper role of the censor was not only to approve those laws considered to be right, but also to condemn those considered to be wrong.

> Thus much is certain; that a system that is never to be censured, will never be improved: that if nothing is ever to be found fault with, nothing will ever be mended: and that a resolution to justify every thing at any rate, and to disapprove of nothing, is a resolution which, pursued in future, must stand as an effectual bar to all the *additional* happiness we can ever hope for; pursued hitherto would have robbed us of that share of happiness which we enjoy already.[4]

In the context of a discussion of heresy, Blackstone had remarked that, following certain legislative amendments, 'Every thing is now as it should be.'[5] Bentham took this phrase—which he usually rendered as 'every thing is as it should be'—implying, as he saw it, that all established law was justified, to be characteristic of Blackstone's whole approach.[6]

For Bentham the practical point of separating the roles of expositor and censor, and in distinguishing law as it is from law as it ought to be, was to bring about a fusion between law as it is and law as it ought to be. Jurisprudence, like any other science, might be organized according to either a 'natural arrangement' or a 'technical arrangement'. A natural arrangement was one which 'men in general are, by the common constitution of man's *nature*, disposed to attend to'. In the case of actions in general, and thus in the case of actions regulated by the law, the aspect which men were most 'disposed to attend to' was their utility—their tendency either to promote or to diminish happiness. A law was justified to the extent that it promoted happiness (or increased pleasure) and prevented misery or mischief (or provided security against pain). The principle of utility was the standard by which 'the several institutions or combinations of institutions that compose the matter of this science' should be governed, and given the universality of the principle, any 'arrangement' which was appropriate 'for the jurisprudence of any one country' would likewise be appropriate 'with little variation for that of any other'. Those actions which diminished utility, which produced mischief, should be constituted into offences. An arrangement of

[4] *A Fragment on Government*, 398–9.
[5] Blackstone, *Commentaries on the Laws of England*, iv. 49.
[6] *A Fragment on Government*, 400, 407 and n.

this sort, where the 'leading terms' would 'belong rather to Ethics than to Jurisprudence', would represent a union of expository and censorial jurisprudence, law as it is and law as it ought to be. In praising the laws of England, Blackstone had tried to show that such a union did in fact already exist. The laws of England, however, were not based on the 'clear' and 'satisfactory' qualities associated with a natural arrangement, but on a technical arrangement, which was 'confused' and 'unsatisfactory'. Under a natural arrangement, the 'mischievousness of a bad law would be detected, at least the utility of it would be rendered suspicious, by the difficulty of finding a place for it': but a technical arrangement was 'a sink that with equal facility will swallow any garbage that is thrown into it'. The process of reasoning which characterized a technical arrangement made sense only in the context of the art, science, or profession in question—in this case the art or profession of law—and would make sense only to a person trained in the profession in question. Hence the terminology of English law, with its 'misprisions, contempts, felonies, præmunires', failed to indicate any connection between the actions which appeared to be randomly assigned to these categories and the principle of utility.[7] The laws of England, contrary to Blackstone's claim, did not unite jurisprudence and ethics—did not represent a fusion of law as it is with law as it ought to be.

Although Blackstone, in Bentham's view, had confounded the roles of expositor and censor, his more fundamental criticism was that Blackstone had attempted to justify the laws of England without reference to the principle of utility, the only basis for any sort of justification. On the contrary, Blackstone was a partisan of the principle of sympathy and antipathy, in the guise of the doctrine of natural law. Indeed, it was Blackstone's adoption of this doctrine that, in Bentham's view, had inevitably led to his confusion of the roles of expositor and censor. In *Commentaries on the Laws of England* Blackstone had asserted that the law of nature took priority over all other law: 'This law of nature, being co-eval with mankind and dictated by God himself, is of course superior in obligation to any other. It is binding over all the globe, in all countries, and at all times: no human laws are of any validity, if contrary to this; and such of them as are valid derive all their force, and all their authority, mediately or immediately, from this original.' The law of nature was the will of God, and consisted in 'the eternal, immutable laws of good and evil'. The content of these laws could be discovered from 'the due exertion of right reason' and from divine revelation. The role of reason was to discover what promoted happiness, for the 'divine goodness' had so ordered matters that 'the laws of eternal justice' were in harmony with 'the happiness of each individual'. If an action promoted happiness, then this was proof that it was 'a part of the law of nature'. However, the fact that man's reason was 'corrupt' meant that it did not provide an adequate guide. In order to remedy this defect, the divine providence

[7] Ibid. 415–18.

had, at various times and by various means, made known the law of nature 'by an immediate and direct revelation'. On the one hand, asserted Blackstone, there were many areas in which the natural law was 'indifferent', and here the human legislator had 'scope and authority' to decree actions to be unlawful. On the other hand, 'no human laws should be suffered to contradict' the law of nature and the law of revelation, for the human legislator could not make right what God had willed to be wrong, and make wrong what he had willed to be right. For instance, the unlawfulness of murder arose from its prohibition by the divine and natural law, and 'if any human law should allow or injoin us to commit it, we are bound to transgress that human law, or else we must offend both the natural and the divine'.[8]

Bentham not only condemned Blackstone for linking legal validity to a particular substantive content,[9] but also for thinking that the natural law provided any sort of basis at all on which to ground the substantive content of human law. Blackstone's view that a human law which conflicted with the divine and natural law should be disobeyed was, argued Bentham, a 'dangerous maxim'. If the law of nature was 'nothing but a phrase', and if there was no really existing standard with which the positive law of the state could be compared, and if there was hardly a positive law which 'those who have not liked it' had not discovered 'to be repugnant to some text of scripture', then 'the natural tendency of such doctrine is to impel a man, by the force of conscience, to rise up in arms against any law whatever he happens not to like'. The point was that the law of nature did not exist—and something which did not exist could not be known. Hence, any appeal to the law of nature in order to invalidate a positive law was either nonsense or a reflection of 'bare unfounded disapprobation' on the part of the objector to the positive law in question. No sort of government could survive in these circumstances. Blackstone had stated that 'a law always supposes some superior who is to make it'.[10] Bentham drew out the corollary: if there was no maker, then there was no law. Paradoxically, Blackstone's conservatism rested on a doctrine which was, in essence, anarchic. Only the principle of utility, 'accurately apprehended and steadily applied', could resolve the question of when it was proper to resist government.[11]

Bentham's criticisms of Blackstone's doctrine of natural law were all ultimately related to its non-existence. The same problem bedevilled a further device

[8] Blackstone, *Commentaries on the Laws of England*, i. 39–43.

[9] Bentham would presumably have endorsed John Austin's later comment, also made in the context of a discussion which was aimed, amongst other targets, at refuting Blackstone's conception of natural law: 'The existence of law is one thing; its merit or demerit another. Whether it be or be not is one enquiry; whether it be or be not conformable to an assumed standard, is a different enquiry. A law, which actually exists, is a law, though we happen to dislike it, or though it vary from the text, by which we regulate our approbation and disapprobation.' See John Austin, *The Province of Jurisprudence Determined* (first published 1832), ed. W. E. Rumble (Cambridge, 1995), 157.

[10] Blackstone, *Commentaries on the Laws of England*, i. 43.

[11] *A Fragment on Government*, 482–3.

adopted by Blackstone—the original contract. In *Commentaries on the Laws of England* Blackstone had argued that even though an original contract had never had any historical existence, 'yet in nature and reason [an original contract] must always be understood and implied, in the very act of associating together'. On the one part, 'the community should guard the rights of each individual member', and on the other '(in return for this protection) each individual should submit to the laws of the community'.[12] Bentham had hoped 'that this chimera had been effectually demolished by Mr HUME',[13] but recognized that lawyers had found the original contract an attractive notion, since it constituted 'a recipe of sovereign efficacy for reconciling the accidental necessity of resistance with the general duty of submission'. Bentham had in mind the way in which the contractarian doctrine had been used to justify the Glorious Revolution of 1688–9, without thereby justifying resistance to government in general. For Bentham, however, the original contract was a fiction, and it was, to his mind, the sign of 'a bad cause' if it required 'a fiction to support it'.[14] The original contract had supposedly been entered into by King and people, with the people promising to obey, and the King promising to govern in such a way as to promote their happiness. Bentham admitted that the fiction might have had some 'momentary use' in that it might have been easier to judge when a promise had been broken than to judge when 'a King had acted so far in *opposition* to the happiness of his people, that it were better no longer to obey him'. But in the end this 'manœvre' or 'contrivance' gained nothing, since: 'It was still necessary to determine, whether the King in question had, or had not acted so far in *opposition* to the happiness of his people, that it were better no longer to obey him; in order to determine, whether the promise he was supposed to have made, had, or had not been broken.' In other words, the introduction of a promise into the argument was superfluous. The only reason why promises should be kept, and be made obligatory by the threat of punishment, was the advantage of society: 'Whether the dependence of *benefit* and *mischief* (that is, of *pleasure* and *pain*) upon men's conduct in this behalf, be as here stated, is a question of *fact*, to be decided, in the same manner that all other questions of fact are to be decided, by testimony, observation, and experience.' A promise was binding not merely on account of its being made, but on account of its utility. Despite any promise they might have made to the King, the people should obey '*so long as the probable mischiefs of obedience are less than the probable mischiefs of resistance*'. The people had a duty to obey to the extent that it was in their interest to do so.[15] The corollary was that an individual had both a duty and an interest to resist government 'when,

[12] Blackstone, *Commentaries on the Laws of England*, i. 47–8.

[13] See David Hume, 'Of the Original Contract' (first published 1748), in *Essays Moral, Political, and Literary*, rev. edn., ed. E. F. Miller (Indianapolis, 1985), 465–87.

[14] See p. 6 above.

[15] *A Fragment on Government*, 439–48. Bentham also pointed out that the original contract was a defective basis of political obligation, at least as far as succeeding generations were concerned, in that a promise made by one person could not be binding on a third party: see ibid. 446.

according to the best calculation he is able to make, *the probable mischiefs of resistance* (speaking with respect to the community in general) *appear less to him than the probable mischiefs of submission*'. This point was, for each individual, 'the *juncture for resistance*'. There was no '*sign*' or '*common* signal' by which the juncture for resistance could be known, but for each individual the 'particular sign' was 'his own internal persuasion of a balance of *utility* on the side of resistance'.[16]

A further feature of contractarian theories was the transition from a state of nature to a state of society, which the original contract was supposed to have brought about. In some versions of the theory there were two contracts, though each might be posited independently of the other: first, the contract of society consisted in an agreement between sovereign individuals living in a state of nature to join together in a state of civil society; and second, the contract of government consisted in an agreement between governors and subjects regarding the terms on which the latter would obey the former. Bentham did not distinguish explicitly between the two (nor had Blackstone), but his comments on the fictitiousness of the original contract appear to have been directed against the contract of government, while his exposure of the falsity of the distinction between a state of nature, or natural society, where no government existed, and a state of society, or political society, where government did exist, appear to have been directed against the contract of society. Bentham's argument in this latter case was that there existed no temporal division between a state of nature on the one hand and a state of society on the other, but rather that both existed together, to a greater or lesser degree, in every human society:

> The idea of a political society is a *positive* one. . . . When a number of persons (whom we may style *subjects*) are supposed to be in the *habit* of paying *obedience* to a person, or an assemblage of persons, of a known and certain description (whom we may call *governor* or *governors*) such persons altogether (*subjects* and *governors*) are said to be in a state of *political* SOCIETY.
>
> The idea of a state of natural SOCIETY is . . . a *negative* one. When a number of persons are supposed to be in the habit of *conversing* with each other, at the same time that they are not in any such habit as mentioned above, they are said to be in a state of *natural* SOCIETY.

The distinction between political society and natural society rested on the presence or absence of the habit of obedience on the part of subjects towards their rulers, but there were few, if any, instances of the habit being perfectly absent, and none of its being perfectly present. Not only that, but the same person might be in a habit of obedience to more than one superior at any particular time; he might be governor of one group of men, but subject to another; and among governors, some might be in a perfect state of nature with relation to others,

[16] *A Fragment on Government*, 483–4.

some in a state of perfect subjection, and some in a state of imperfect subjection.[17] Bentham's critique of Blackstone's account of the natural law and the original contract betokened a scathing attack on what became, in the second half of the eighteenth century, the most influential political theory of the age—the doctrine of natural rights.

II

The most prominent manifestations of the doctrines of natural law and natural rights were found in the various declarations of rights issued in the newly formed United States of America and in the French Declaration of the Rights of Man and the Citizen. In response to these declarations, Bentham pursued two related, but distinguishable, lines of argument. One was to criticize the attempt to restrain the legislative power by means of such declarations—Bentham argued that it was unwise at any time to impose restraints of any kind on a legislature. The other was to criticize the formulation of such restraints in terms of natural rights. His doubts concerning the theoretical basis of the American Revolution had appeared in print as early as May 1775 in a brief contribution to an anonymous pamphlet, *Remarks on the Principal Acts of the Thirteenth Parliament of Great Britain*, which was the work of his friend John Lind. Bentham argued that the proper issue was not whether the Crown and Parliament had violated some abstract right in their policies towards the American colonies, but whether they had the legal authority to proceed as they had.[18] He later recollected that he had thought that 'the Americans used sadly stupid arguments, and that there was no better reason for their breaking out than for the breaking out of any other part of the country';[19] and that: 'The American colonies really said nothing to justify their revolution. They thought not of *utility*, and *use* was against them.'[20] Bentham expanded on this point in his writings on the subject of parliamentary reform in 1818, where he explained that he had been opposed to the Americans on account of the inadequacy of the two arguments which had been employed in their support:

> One was the sort of argument of which the matter of all the instruments called Declarations of rights seemed exclusively to be composed: arguments which consisted in

[17] Ibid. 428–33. For a provocative reconstruction of Bentham's view of the relationship between the exercise of political power and the habit of obedience, with its implications for Bentham's theory of sovereignty, see O. Ben Dor, *Constitutional Limits and the Public Sphere: A Critical Study of Bentham's Constitutionalism* (Oxford, 2000), 49–94.

[18] See [John Lind], *Remarks on the Principal Acts of the Thirteenth Parliament of Great Britain. Vol. I. Containing Remarks on the Acts relating to the Colonies. With a Plan of Reconciliation* (London, 1775), pp. xv–xvi. The relevant passage from Lind's pamphlet is reproduced at Bowring, x. 63. For Bentham's early hostility to the American case for independence, and his later admiration of the United States as a functioning democracy, see Hart, *Essays on Bentham*, 53–78.

[19] Bowring, x. 87. [20] Ibid. 584.

nothing but an assertion, the unsupported assertion, of the existence of the right in question, and that assertion, such as it was, involved in a cloud of words. But when thus without support given to it from the principle of utility, of what avail assertions? Give what force you will to it, to its direct opposite belongs equal force: each destroys the other: and the question remains without argument on either side.

The second argument was that there should be no taxation without representation. Parliament, it was accepted, had the right to legislate for the American colonies, but no right to tax them, because they were not represented in it. This argument was fallacious in that taxation was merely one species of legislation, and not a distinct activity.[21]

In 1827, explaining the circumstances of his contribution to Lind's pamphlet, Bentham acknowledged that the Americans did have a legitimate basis for their demands for independence, but reiterated that, at the time of the American Revolution, his opinions were opposed to those of the Americans:

The turn they [i.e. his opinions] took was the result of the bad arguments which I observed that side supported, no use being made of the only good one, viz. the impossibility of good government at such a distance, and the advantage of separation to the interest and happiness of both parties. The Declaration of Rights [i.e. the American Declaration of Independence] presented itself to my conception from the first, as what it has always continued to be, a hodge-podge of confusion and absurdity, in which the thing to be proved is all along taken for granted. Some hints to this effect were, I believe, given towards the close, in a note of my introduction to the Principles of Morals and Legislation.[22]

It was in a passage added to *An Introduction to the Principles of Morals and Legislation* for its publication in 1789 that Bentham criticized the declarations of rights which had been issued by various of the United States as ill-considered attempts 'to restrain supreme representative assemblies, from making laws in such and such cases, or to such and such an effect'. The documents were poorly drafted, using 'loose and inadequate terms', which revealed a lack of understanding in relation to 'the science of law, considered in respect of its form', and faced the following dilemma: 'Keep to the letter, and in attempting to prevent the making of bad laws, you will find them prohibiting the making of the most necessary laws, perhaps even of all laws: quit the letter, and they express no more than if each man were to say, *Your laws shall become* ipso facto *void, as often as they contain any thing which is not to my mind.*'[23] Whichever alternative was chosen, law-making would become impossible, and in the first case stagnation, in the second case anarchy, would ensue. The Declaration of Rights issued by North Carolina in September 1788, for instance, had announced that men could not be deprived or divested of their natural rights, which included 'the enjoyment of life and liberty, with the means of acquiring, possessing, and protecting property, and pursuing and obtaining happiness and safety'. If every law or order

[21] UC cxxvii. 483–4 (26 Oct. 1818). [22] Bowring, x. 63.
[23] *An Introduction to the Principles of Morals and Legislation*, 308–9.

which divested a man of the enjoyment of life or liberty was void, then every coercive law, every order to pay taxes or debts, and every order to attack an armed enemy in time of war, would be void.[24] Similar statements were to be found in the Virginian Declaration of Rights of 12 June 1776, the Declaration of Independence, and the Massachusetts Constitution of 1780: 'Who can help lamenting, that so rational a cause should be rested upon reasons, so much fitter to beget objections, than to remove them?'[25] The dilemma, then, was that on the one hand the legislator was unable to enact the laws which circumstances might render necessary for the well-being of the community, and perhaps even to enact any laws at all, depending on how 'loose and inadequate' the language in which the declaration happened to be expressed, and on the other hand the validity of law would depend upon the feelings of sympathy and antipathy of those who were supposed to be subject to it.

III

The focus for Bentham's most sustained attack on the doctrine of natural rights was the French Declaration of the Rights of Man and the Citizen. In July 1789 the Constituent Assembly decided that the new French constitution should be preceded by a declaration of rights,[26] and in the course of the next few weeks a number of drafts were produced. In a letter to Brissot, written in mid-August 1789, Bentham expressed his concerns:

> I am sorry you have undertaken to publish a Declaration of Rights. It is a metaphysical work—the *ne plus ultra* of metaphysics. It may have been a necessary evil,—but it is nevertheless an evil. Political science is not far enough advanced for such a declaration. Let the articles be what they may, I will engage they must come under three heads—1. Unintelligible; 2. False; 3. A mixture of both. You will have no end that will not be contradicted or superseded by the laws of details which are to follow them.... What, then, will be the practical evil? Why this: you can never make a law against which it may not be averred, that by it you have abrogated the Declaration of Rights; and the averment will be unanswerable. Thus, you will be compelled either to withdraw a desirable act of legislation—or to give a false colouring (dangerous undertaking!) to the Declaration of Rights. The commentary will contradict the text.... The best thing that can happen to the Declaration of Rights will be, that it should become a dead letter; and that is the best wish I can breathe for it.

Bentham did concede that it would be 'some remedy if the declaration were made provisional, or temporary'. Nonetheless, Bentham's reading of some of the

[24] Ibid. 309–10.

[25] Ibid. 310–11 n. Cf. UC cxlvi. 222 (1795): 'The pursuit of happiness is certainly a propensity—is it a right?—that depends upon the mode of pursuit. The assassin pursues his happiness by assassination—has he a right to do? If not, why declare he has? what tendency is there to make men wiser or better in such a declaration?'

[26] *Archives parlementaires de 1787 à 1860, première série (1787 à 1799)* (Paris, 1879–1913), viii. 216 (9 July 1789).

draft declarations had done nothing to shake his opposition: 'My first impressions have been strongly confirmed by looking over all the "projects" which have hitherto had birth.'[27] Around this time, Bentham began to compose what he intended to be a detailed commentary on several of these draft declarations, namely 'Observations on the Draughts of Declarations-of-Rights presented to the Committee of the Constitution of the National Assembly of France'. In the event he wrote no more than a few pages of general introductory material, and a brief and incomplete commentary on the draft declaration prepared by Sieyès.[28] Nevertheless, several important themes, which he later developed in 'Nonsense upon Stilts'—his more extensive critique of the Declaration of Rights—were foreshadowed in 'Observations on Draughts of Declarations-of-Rights'.

Bentham identified four purposes for which a declaration of rights might be issued: to limit the authority of the Crown; to limit the authority of the National Assembly as the supreme legislative power; to guide the National Assembly in its detailed drafting of future legislation; and to afford 'a satisfaction to the people'. He then showed that a declaration of rights would not answer any of these purposes, except the last, which was of too 'local' a character to merit consideration. A declaration of rights would be superfluous in setting limits to the authority of the Crown, since that was the object of the constitution itself. The limitation of the legislative power of the National Assembly would be unnecessary, since the people, if they objected to a particular measure, would express their disapproval whether or not there existed any conflict between the measure and the declaration of rights. Moreover, Bentham identified a dilemma which faced every declaration of rights issued with the intention of binding the legislative power in a state. If the declaration authorized exceptions and modifications to be made to its provisions by subsequent laws, it would fail to set limits to the power of the legislature, which was its avowed purpose. If it did not list the exceptions, it would prove impossible to comply with its provisions, since the detailed law would inevitably conflict with them. 'Suppose a declaration to this effect: No man's liberty shall be abridged in any point.—This, it is evident, would be an useless extravagance which must be contradicted by every law that came to be made. Suppose it to say, No man's liberty shall be abridged but in such points as it shall be abridged in by the law. This, we see, is saying nothing: it leaves the law just as free and unfettered as it found it.' As a restraint upon a sovereign legislature, a declaration of rights was either incoherent or worthless.

Finally, the notion that a declaration of rights might guide the legislature in the drafting of future, detailed legislation was founded on a confusion between

[27] Bentham to Jacques Pierre Brissot de Warville, mid-Aug. 1789, *Correspondence*, vol. iv, ed. A. Taylor Milne (London, 1981), 84–5.

[28] 'Préliminaire de la Constitution. Reconnoissance et exposition raisonnée Des Droits de l'Homme et du Citoyen. Lu les 20 et 21 Juillet 1789, au Comité de Constitution. Par M. l'Abbé Sieyes', printed in *Procès-verbal de l'Assemblée Nationale*, vol. ii, no. 33 (27 July 1789). Emmanuel Joseph Sieyès was author of the famous *Qu'est-ce que le Tiers État?*, published in Paris in early 1789.

'what is first in the order of demonstration and what is first in the order of invention'. In demonstration, the logical order was to begin with the general proposition, and proceed to the particular propositions included within it. But this was 'not the order of conception, of investigation, of invention', for here 'particular propositions always precede general ones. The assent to the latter is preceded by and grounded on the assent to the former.' The plan of the National Assembly was to declare a number of general, fundamental laws, and from these to deduce the laws of detail. However, the proper method was to enact the laws of detail, and then declare the more general laws, which would be 'exact and fit for service' insofar as they were consistent with the particular laws from which they had been derived. 'What follows? That the proper order is first to digest the laws of detail: and when they are settled and found to be fit for use, then, and not till then, from them may be selected *in terminis* or deduced by abstraction such propositions as may be capable of being, without self-contradiction, given as fundamental laws.' The desire to enact fundamental laws was 'the old appetite of ruling posterity, the old recipe for enabling the dead to chain down the living'. It was absurd to bind succeeding legislators with a general law whose consequences could not be foreseen.[29]

These arguments were, in effect, an elaboration of the arguments he had deployed against the American declarations of rights. Moreover, just as he had commented briefly on the language in which the American declarations were expressed, he extended his objections to the French draft declarations beyond the futility and mischievousness of attempting to limit the legislative power to the delusive language in which such documents were typically expressed. If a man were to say that no law '*ought*' to be made which would diminish general happiness, this expressed the 'simple matter of fact . . . that a sentiment of dissatisfaction' was generated 'by the idea of any such law'. If he were to say that no law '*shall*' be made, this signified 'that the sentiment of dissatisfaction' was 'so strong' as to have produced a determination 'that no such law should ever pass', to the extent that he had resolved to oppose its enactment. If he were to say that no law '*could*' be made, this signified the same determination, but 'wrapped up in an absurd and insidious disguise' in order to persuade others that they should 'pay no more obedience' to a particular law 'than if it were the random command of a single unauthoritied individual'. In order to achieve this end, he made 'the absurd choice of a term expressive in its original and proper import of a physical impossibility in order to represent as impossible the very event' he feared. Knowing that the 'event' was not 'impossible', still he told the people that it was 'impossible', and he expected them to believe him 'and act in consequence'. And finally, if he were to say that the law was 'a violation of the

[29] *Rights, Representation, and Reform*, 181–6. Bentham commented in detail on 'the fallacy of irrevocable laws' and the related 'wisdom of our ancestors fallacy' in *The Book of Fallacies: from unfinished papers of Jeremy Bentham. By A Friend* (London, 1824) (see Bowring, ii. 375–487, at 398–408). The 'friend' was Peregrine Bingham.

natural and indefeasible rights of man', this was as much as to say that he would endeavour to kill the persons concerned in the enactment of it. The issuing of a declaration of rights was an indication of 'the violence of the passions', for such a declaration was a means of 'subduing opposition at any rate and giving the will of every man who embraces the proposition imported by the article a weight beyond what is its due, its just and intrinsic due'. A declaration of rights was, therefore, a powerful instrument in support of the partisan of the principle of sympathy and antipathy. Bentham concluded: 'These several contrivances for giving to an encrease in vehemence the effect of an encrease of reason, may be stiled *bawling* upon paper.'[30]

The use of the words 'can not' was particularly obfuscatory, since these words might be used to denote either physical, or moral, or legal impossibility. In a legal context, to say that a subordinate magistrate could not perform a certain action made sense, in that it implied that he lacked legal power to do so. However, when applied to the supreme legislature, 'clouds of ambiguity and confusion roll in in a torrent almost impossible to be withstood'. Instead of the matter being referred to utility—'the only just standard for trying all sorts of moral questions'—there would be irrational assertion, which would either produce irrational acquiescence or be answered by irrational denial: 'I say the law can not do so and so. You say, it can. When we have said thus much on each side, it is to no purpose to say more. There we are completely at a stand: argument, such as it is, can go no further on either side: [either] neither yields, or passion triumphs alone, the stronger sweeping away the weaker.' If, instead of saying that the law 'can not', we were to say 'ought not', this 'leads naturally to the inquiry after a reason: and this reason, if there be any at bottom that deserves [the name], is always a proposition of fact relative to the question of utility'. While there was no certainty that agreement would be reached, 'the track which of all others bids fairest for leading to agreement is pointed out'.[31]

Bentham made little progress with 'Observations on Draughts of Declarations-of-Rights'. He was, perhaps, overtaken by events. The text of the Declaration of Rights was settled by the Constituent Assembly on 26 August 1789, and Bentham, if his purpose had been to persuade the French not to issue such a declaration, may have decided that it was futile to continue the essay. Six years later he explained why he had not criticized the Declaration of Rights when it had first appeared:

> My opinion of the declaration of rights considered in itself was the same at the moment of its first issuing as now. But there seemed some thing generous and liberal in the intention of it. Willing to hope the best, I flattered myself it would slide quietly into neglect, and be even turned into a dead letter: that either no attempt at all would be made to give it execution, to carry it into practice, or that the first attempt of the kind that came to be made would present such a view of the mischievous tendency of it, as should unite

[30] *Rights, Representation, and Reform*, 186–7. [31] Ibid. 188–9.

all opinions of the sense of the necessity of laying it aside under the character of a collection of moral precepts, designed but to guide men only and not to bind them.[32]

In the event, the Declaration of Rights had neither been quietly neglected, nor interpreted as a series of moral claims, and so Bentham—stimulated by the appearance of the Declaration of the Rights and Duties of Man, prefixed to the new French Constitution of 1795, and approved by the National Convention on 22 August 1795—composed 'Nonsense upon Stilts'. This essay contains a critique of all seventeen articles of the Declaration of 1789 (or more precisely the virtually identical text reissued with the French Constitution of 1791), a partial critique of the Declaration of 1795, and the beginnings of a critique of the draft Declaration drawn up by Sieyès in July 1789.[33] Bentham stressed more forcefully than he had previously the anarchical tendencies which characterized the doctrine of natural rights, and claimed that the doctrine had been responsible for the mischiefs which had afflicted France since the beginning of the Revolution. His purpose was not merely to denounce the two French Declarations of Rights in particular, but such documents in general: 'The opinion I set out with declaring, the proposition I set out with, is, not that the Declaration of rights should not have existed[?] in this shape, but that nothing under any such name or with any such design should have been attempted.'[34] Again, Bentham announced, 'What I mean to attack is—not the subject or citizen of this or that country . . . but all *ante*-legal and *anti*-legal rights of man, all declarations of such rights. What I mean to attack is not the execution of such a design in this or that instance, but the design itself.' The French had not failed in the execution of the design because they had used ambiguous language, but rather the design could not be executed at all without an abuse of language: 'From this Declaration of Rights learn what all other Declarations of Rights—of Rights asserted as against government in general—must ever be—the Rights of anarchy—the Order of chaos.'[35] While a large proportion of 'Nonsense upon Stilts' was concerned with detailed criticisms of drafting, Bentham's point was that such difficulties were inseparable from such documents. Having said this much, circumstances did later arise in which Bentham found himself prepared to take advantage of these ambiguities, and to advocate the issuing of such a declaration.[36]

Bentham arranged his criticism of the French Declaration of Rights into five main points. First, the Declaration had a tendency to produce anarchy. He

[32] UC cxlvi. 223 (15 Nov. 1795).

[33] The work has until recently been known as 'Anarchical Fallacies', which was not, however, Bentham's title, but the title given to the essay by Dumont, albeit in French as 'Sophismes anarchiques', when he published a version in *Tactique des assemblées législatives, suivie d'un traité des sophismes politiques*, 2 vols. (Geneva and Paris, 1816), ii. 269–392, and adopted for the version which appeared in Bowring, ii. 490–534. For the authoritative version see *Rights, Representation, and Reform*, 317–401, and for a detailed history of the text see ibid., Editorial Introduction, pp. xlv–liii.

[34] *Rights, Representation, and Reform*, 358.

[35] UC cxlv. 182 (1795).

[36] See pp. 71–4 below.

identified a paradox which faced 'the penners and issuers of this declaration': in justifying the insurrection which had produced the Revolution, they could not avoid encouraging future insurrection. The people were informed of their rights, and told that if any single one of them were violated by government, they had not only a right but a sacred duty to resist. Consequently: 'They sow the seeds of anarchy broadcast: in justifying the demolition of existing authorities, they undermine all future ones; their own consequently in the number.'[37] Second, the Declaration incorporated fallacious argument. The more abstract or extensive the propositions which a declaration of rights contained, the more likely they were to involve the fallacy of begging the question, which consisted in 'the abuse of making the abstract proposition resorted to for proof, a cover for introducing, in the company of *other* propositions that are nothing to the purpose, the very proposition which is admitted to stand in need of proof'. In this particular instance, the proper question would have been whether a particular provision would constitute a suitable law for France. However, 'as often as the utility of a provision appeared . . . of a doubtful nature, the way taken to clear the doubt was to affirm it to be a provision fit to be made law for all men: for all Frenchmen, and for all Englishmen, for example, into the bargain'.[38] Third, echoing one of the arguments he had advanced in the autumn of 1789, the Declaration encouraged violent feelings. Instead of restraining 'the selfish and hostile passions', its object had been to add 'as much force as possible to these passions already but too strong'.[39] Fourth, again reiterating an argument he had advanced in the autumn of 1789, the Declaration imposed limitations on succeeding legislatures. It was impossible to predict what course of action a future government might need to take: 'what a curse to the country a legislator may be who, with the purest intentions, should set about settling the business to all eternity by inflexible and adamantine rules drawn from the sacred and inviolable and imprescriptible rights of man and the primæval and everlasting laws of nature!' Bentham would rather be subject to a set of laws, no matter how bad, drawn up by another person, providing that there was no such 'perpetuating clause', than to a set of laws drawn up by himself with such a clause. He was persuaded 'that there is not a single point with relation to which it can answer any good purpose to attempt to tie the hands of future legislators'.[40]

Fifth—and this was the criticism which Bentham elaborated in greatest detail, and again a theme which had characterized his earlier comments on the American and French declarations—the Declaration was characterized by the misuse of language. The language of the Declaration would have suited 'an oriental tale or an allegory for a magazine', but was inappropriate for 'a body of laws, especially of laws given as constitutional and fundamental ones', where 'an

[37] *Rights, Representation, and Reform*, 319–20.

[38] Ibid. 320. Bentham discussed the fallacy of begging the question in *The Book of Fallacies*: see Bowring, ii. 436–8.

[39] *Rights, Representation, and Reform*, 321.

[40] Ibid. 360–1.

improper word may be a national calamity: and civil war may be the consequence of it'. Ambiguous words were used unnecessarily; the same word was given several different meanings; improper words were substituted for proper ones; and no attempt was made to limit the application of 'words and propositions of the most unbounded signification'. The result was 'a perpetual vein of nonsense flowing from a perpetual abuse of words'.[41] In short, the language in which the propositions contained in the Declaration were expressed was either ambiguous or self-contradictory. If one attempted to make these propositions clear and consistent, one discovered in most cases that their meaning was either trivial or false. If the propositions in question were not understood as statements of fact, but reconstructed as moral claims, they turned out to be nonsense, since they were not grounded on the principle of utility, but on a non-existent standard. As Bentham remarked: 'The criticism is verbal: true—but what else can it be? Words—words without a meaning—or with a meaning too flatly false to be maintained by any body, are the stuff it's made of. Look to the letter, you find nonsense:—look beyond the letter, you find nothing.'[42] This inappropriate use of language was the product of a false ontology, and it was, therefore, the issue which lay at the root of Bentham's critique.

One difficulty was that certain propositions, put forward as propositions of fact, were obviously false. In the first part of Article 1, for instance, it was stated that: 'In respect of their rights men are born and remain free and equal.' On the contrary, the fact was that all men were 'born in subjection, and the most absolute subjection: the subjection of a helpless child to the parents on whom he depends every moment for his existence', a subjection which continued 'for a great number of years'. The Article implied that the rights in question existed prior to the establishment of government, but whether this was the case was irrelevant in those places where government now existed. Even setting aside the dependence of children on parents, no such equality would be found under any existing government.[43] Instances in which individuals were not treated equally 'appear sufficient to suggest a reasonable doubt whether . . . the smack smooth equality which rolls so glibly out of the lips of the rhetorician be altogether compatible with that conformity to every bend and turn in the line of utility which ought to be the object of the legislator'.[44] Men without hereditary dignities were not equal in rights to those who did possess them, apprentices to their masters, wards to their guardians, and wives to their husbands. Bentham recognized, however, that the proposition in question might not have been intended as a statement of fact, but as an attempt to proscribe the inequalities in question—to subvert the relationship between master and apprentice and to destroy the institution of marriage.[45] But this created a further difficulty, which was ambiguity. He had referred to this difficulty in 1789 when discussing the

[41] Ibid. 321–2. [42] Ibid. 322. [43] Ibid. 322–3. [44] Ibid. 346.
[45] Ibid. 325–6.

draft Declaration drawn up by Sieyès. He commented that it was unclear whether the Declaration was intended to be merely prospective or both retrospective and prospective, 'whether it means solely to declare what shall be the state of the law after the moment of the enactment of this declaration, or likewise what has been its state previous to that moment'. If the Declaration was intended, as Bentham believed it was, to be a retrospective declaration, it followed: '1. that it is notoriously untrue; 2. that the untruth of it is supposed by the very act of enacting the declaration, since if what is there established were established already, there would be no use for establishing it anew; 3. that the declaration of the past existence of the provisions in question would be of no use, though the matter of fact were true'.[46] This confusion of historical fact and moral claim was apparent, for instance, in Article 12, which stated that the public force was instituted for the advantage of all, and not for the private advantage of those to whom it was entrusted. This might have been true in some instances, remarked Bentham, but not in others. It was unlikely that the author of the Declaration believed that William the Conqueror, for instance, had in view the well-being of the whole community when sharing out England amongst his followers. It was more likely that the author had no clear conception of the difference between 'a declaration of what he supposes was or is the state of things with regard to this or that subject, and a declaration of what he conceives ought to have been or ought to be that state of things: and this being the case, it may be supposed that in saying such was the end in view upon the several occasions in question, what he meant was that such it ought to have been'.[47] In the same vein, Article 16 stated that every society in which rights were not secured, nor the separation of powers established, had no constitution. Bentham was aware of Thomas Paine's assertion that Britain had no constitution,[48] but countered that, 'if government depends upon obedience, the stability of government [upon] the permanence of the disposition to obedience, and the permanence of that disposition [upon] the duration of the habit of obedience', it seemed more plausible to argue that it was France which was without a constitution.[49]

A prominent example of the ambiguity of the language of the Declaration, noted Bentham, reiterating a point he had made in 1789, was in the use of the word 'can'. The second part of Article 1, for instance, stated that 'Social distinctions can not be founded but upon common utility.' Apart from flatly contradicting the first part of the article, which stated that such distinctions,

[46] UC cxlvi. 233 (1789). [47] *Rights, Representation, and Reform*, 364–6.

[48] See Thomas Paine, *Rights of Man: being an answer to Mr. Burke's attack on the French Revolution* (London, 1791), 54: 'I readily perceive the reason why Mr. Burke declined going into the comparison between the English and French constitutions, because he could not but perceive, when he sat down to talk, that no such thing as a constitution existed on his side [of] the question.' Paine's allusion was to Edmund Burke's *Reflections on the Revolution in France*, first published on 1 November 1790: see *The Writings and Speeches of Edmund Burke. Volume VIII: The French Revolution 1790–1794*, ed. L. G. Mitchell (Oxford, 1989), 53–293.

[49] *Rights, Representation, and Reform*, 372–4.

implying as they did inequality, could have no existence, it was unclear whether this meant

> that no social distinctions but those which it approves of as having the foundation in question *are* established any where, or simply that none such *ought to be* established any where, or that if the establishment or maintenance of such distinctions by the laws is attempted any where, such laws ought to be treated as void, and the attempt to execute them to be resisted? For such is the poison that lurks under such words as *can* and *can not* when set up as a check upon the laws. They present all these three so perfectly distinct and widely different meanings. In the first, the proposition they are inserted into referrs [*sic*]to practice, and makes appeal to observation:—to the observation of other men in regard to a matter of fact: in the second, it is an appeal to the approving faculty of others in regard to the same matter of fact: in the third, it is no appeal to any thing or any body, but a violent attempt upon liberty of speech and action on the part of others by the terrors of anarchical despotism rising up in opposition to laws.

The first meaning was innocent, even though palpably untrue, while the second was equally innocent, allowing one the liberty to agree or disagree, but the third was 'the ruffian-like or threatening import': '*Can* and *can not* when thus applied, *can* and *can not* when used instead of *ought* and *ought not, can* and *can not* when applied to the binding force and effect of laws—not of the acts of individuals, nor yet of the acts of subordinate authority, but of the acts of the supreme government itself, are the disguised cant of the Assassin: after them, there is nothing but *do him* betwixt the preparation for murder and the attempt.' There were many laws which Bentham wished to see altered or abolished, and he could conceive cases where he might approve of resistance:

> But to talk of what the law—the supreme legislature of the country, acknowledged as such—*can* not do! to talk of a *void* law, as you would of a void order or judgment!—the very act of bringing such words into conjunction is either the vilest of nonsense, or the worst of treasons:—treason—not against one branch of the sovereignty, but against the whole:—treason not against this or that government, but against all governments.[50]

This use of 'can' and 'can not', with the attendant ambiguity, was related to the supposition that natural rights existed both independently of and prior to the establishment of government, as opposed to legal rights, which were the product of government. The priority of natural rights was asserted in Article 2, where it was stated that the end in view of every political association was the preservation of the natural and imprescriptible rights of man, namely liberty, property, security, and resistance to oppression; that these natural rights could not be abrogated by government; and that governments originated from formal meetings or conventions. The purpose of establishing government, according to this view, was to protect pre-existing natural rights, and any government which failed to do so, and indeed any government which did not originate in a social

[50] Ibid. 326–8. Elsewhere, Bentham referred to 'the ambiguous and envenomed *can*': see ibid. 337.

contract (which was intended to guarantee and protect such rights), lacked legitimacy. Resistance to and subversion of such a government was lawful and commendable. In truth, noted Bentham, there were 'no such things as natural rights—no such things as rights anterior to the establishment of government—no such things as natural rights opposed to, in contradistinction to, legal'. The notion of a state of nature, where men lived without government, was perfectly comprehensible, but in such a state there were no rights, and consequently no property and no security. Bentham understood that such rights might be regarded as desirable, but pointed out that the assumption that because a certain thing was desirable, the thing in question existed, was fallacious: 'In proportion to the want of happiness resulting from the want of rights, a reason for wishing that there were such things as rights. But reasons for wishing there were such things as rights, are not rights: a reason for wishing that a certain right were established, is not that right: wants are not means: hunger is not bread.' Furthermore, if natural rights did not exist, they could not be abrogated. To say that they were imprescriptible was to mount one nonsensical statement upon another: 'Natural rights is simple nonsense: natural and imprescriptible rights, rhetorical nonsense, nonsense upon stilts.' The purpose of declaring the existence of imprescriptible rights and employing such vague terms as property and liberty was 'to excite and keep up a spirit of resistance to all laws, a spirit of insurrection against all governments. Against the governments of all other nations, instantly: against the government of their own nation, against the government they themselves were pretending to establish, soon: that is as soon as their own reign should be at an end.' It was also to claim infallibility and, thereby, to enchain all future governments and peoples: 'Our will shall consequently reign without controul and for ever: reign now we are living, reign when we are no more. All nations, all future ages, shall be, for they are predestined to be, our slaves.' To claim that no government could abrogate natural rights was 'Terrorist language', whereas those who spoke the 'language of reason and plain sense' judged whether a right should or should not be established or abrogated on the basis of whether or not it was for the advantage of society to do so.[51]

In declaring liberty to be an imprescriptible right, the authors of the Declaration had misunderstood the relationship between liberty and rights, since 'all rights are made at the expence of liberty'. In Bentham's view, liberty consisted simply in the absence of coercion, whether of constraint or restraint.[52] The existence of a right implied a correspondent obligation; in other words, a liberty enjoyed by one person was created by imposing coercion on another or others. Indeed, coercive laws (that is all laws except those laws which repealed already existing laws) were necessarily abrogative of liberty, and, therefore, according to Article 2 of the Declaration, were null and void, and should be

[51] *Rights, Representation, and Reform*, 328–31.
[52] See e.g. *Of Laws in General*, ed. H. L. A. Hart (London, 1970), 119–20, 253–4.

resisted.[53] There was further confusion in Article 4 where liberty was said to consist in doing what was not hurtful to another. This was a perversion of language, since the liberty of doing mischief was still liberty. Moreover, the statement that the bounds of liberty could only be determined by the laws was contradictory and confusing. On the one hand it was claimed that liberty was 'one of four rights that existed before laws and will exist in spite of all that laws can do', and on the other hand that the limits to liberty would be determined by the laws.[54]

There were similar difficulties with the other 'imprescriptible' rights. The right to property implied that every man had a right to everything, which would be tantamount to destroying all property.[55] The right to security seemed to refer to security for person, though one might speak of security for liberty and security for property. Again, such a right was too sweeping, since it would nullify any law which prescribed capital or corporal punishment, or which exposed a man to risk in military service against foreign enemies.[56] The right of resistance to oppression was superfluous in that any oppression to which a man might be subjected would be an infringement of some one of his rights to liberty, property, or security. This particular right, however, fulfilled a different purpose from the others. Whereas the rights to liberty, property, and security were intended to restrain the legislator, the right of resistance to oppression was intended to encourage insurrection: 'as often as any thing happens to a man to inflame his passions, this article, for fear his passions should not be sufficiently inflamed of themselves, sets to work to fan the flame, and urges him to resistance'.[57] The incitement to resistance was taken even further in Article 3, where it was stated that the act of any government which had not been appointed by popular election, and by the whole nation, was void: 'Consequently all the acts of every government in Europe, for example, are void, excepted perhaps, or rather not excepted, two or three of the Swiss Cantons: the persons exercising the powers of government in those countries, usurpers: resistance to them and insurrection against them, lawful and commendable.'[58] Furthermore, the assertion made in Article 5 that 'the law has no right' to forbid any actions other than those hurtful to society, and in particular the phrase 'the law has no right', preached 'constant insurrection', a call to every man forcefully to resist 'every law which he happens not to approve of'.[59]

On several occasions Bentham remarked that the Articles of the Declaration were either 'nugatory' or 'mischievous'. His point was that on the one hand, if the rights were limited by positive law, the Declaration was nugatory in that

[53] *Rights, Representation, and Reform*, 334. [54] Ibid. 338–40.

[55] Ibid. 334–5. Bentham attributed the doctrine that 'Nature has given to each man a right to every thing' to 'some of the interpreters of the pretended law of nature' (see ibid. 332). The view was famously expressed by Thomas Hobbes in *Leviathan* (first published 1651), ed. R. Tuck (Cambridge, 1991), Part I, Ch. xiv, 91 [64], but similar views were formulated by Hugo Grotius, Benedict de Spinoza, and Samuel Pufendorf. [56] *Rights, Representation, and Reform*, 335–6.

[57] Ibid. 336–7. [58] Ibid. 337–8. [59] Ibid. 341.

positive law, and not natural rights, was the source of the rights in question; and on the other hand, if the rights were not limited by positive law, then their tendency was mischievous in that they constituted an incitement to insurrection. For instance, in Article 7 it was stated that no one could be accused, arrested, or detained but in the cases determined by law, and in the forms prescribed by law. Taken at face value this Article was nugatory: it gave the citizen no security against arbitrary power, for if the existing law authorized arbitrary arrest, the Article did nothing to prevent it. However, if the Article was interpreted in the context of Article 6, where it was stated that the law was the expression of the general will, it was mischievous, for 'no arrest or detention can be legal till the ground and form of it has been pre-ordained by a law issuing from that source'.[60]

Bentham had, as early as 1776, remarked on the linguistic confusion engendered by the word 'right': 'The same word used adjectively or substantively has two very different meanings: I *have a right* to have such a thing done for me: It *is right* such a thing should be done for me. In the latter phrase the word *right* denotes nothing more than mere opinion: in the former it refers to a matter of fact; the establishment of punishment by Law, for him who by Law ought to do for me the thing in question, and does not.'[61] In 'Nonsense upon Stilts' he drew out the associations possessed by each of the two uses of the word 'right'. As an adjective the word 'right' was 'as innocent as a dove: it breathes nothing but morality and peace', being 'synonymous with desirable, proper, becoming, consonant to general utility, and the like'. But as a substantive, as employed, for instance, in the proposition, I have a right to equality, 'it plants the banner of insurrection and lawless violence'. While it was easier to fall into this linguistic confusion in the English language than in the French—in English the sense of 'right' might be changed from an adjective to a noun-substantive without changing the letters which spelled the word—the lack of an adjective 'right' composed of the same letters as the substantive had not hindered the French: 'Is, has been, ought to be, shall be, can, all are put for one another, all are pressed into the service, all made to answer the same purpose. By this inebriating compound we have seen all the elements of the understanding confounded, every fibre of the heart inflamed, the lips prepared for every folly, and the hand for every crime.' Real rights were the product of real laws, while imaginary rights were the product of imaginary laws:

> *Right*, the substantive *right*, is the child of law: and when once brought into the world, what more natural than for poets, for rhetoricians, for all dealers in moral and intellectual poisons, to give the child a spurious parentage, to lay it at Nature's door, and set it up in opposition against the real author of its birth. . . . And thus it is that from *legal rights*, the offspring of law and friends of peace, come *anti-legal rights*, the mortal enemies of law, the subverters of government and the assassins of security.[62]

[60] *Rights, Representation, and Reform*, 349–51. Bentham identified the same dilemma in Art. 11: see ibid. 361–2.

[61] UC lxix. 93 (*c*.1776).

[62] *Rights, Representation, and Reform*, 398–400.

Bentham's critique of the Declaration of Rights was intended to demystify the language of natural rights, and to halt the subversive schemes of those who employed such language. He posed himself the question: 'If, as you say, it is nonsense, why spend so much time and paper upon nonsense?' He made two points in response: first, 'If it is nonsense, it is nonsense with great pretensions, with the pretensions of governing the world. A part of the world, too large a part in point of number, at least betrays a disposition to be governed by it. If the sceptre of nonsense can be effectually broken, the time and paper will not be altogether thrown away'; and second, 'If the criticism is just, the indication of the errors will have its use. Hints will have been given tending to the improvement of the art and practice of legislature.'[63] The issue was whether his 'antidote to the second French disease'[64] would be effective. The problem was that 'connections between words and ideas'—connections which were 'coeval with the cradle'—had to be dissolved. Education, although slow, was 'the surest as well as earliest resource'. It was also a vitally important one: 'The recognition of the nothingness of the laws of nature, and of the rights of man that have been grounded on them, is a branch of knowledge of as much importance to an Englishman, though a negative one, as the most perfect acquaintance that can be formed with the existing laws of England.'[65]

IV

Despite his criticisms of the American and French declarations of rights, there were occasions when Bentham was prepared to acknowledge some merit in the issuing of such documents, whether in the form of constitutional charters or declarations of rights. In the late summer of 1789, around the same time that he was condemning the decision of the Constituent Assembly to draw up a declaration of rights, he composed 'Short Views of Economy for the use of the French Nation but not unapplicable to the English', in which he sketched out a number of principles of political economy, and dealt with their implementation. He explained that if the French extended the scope of the proposed declaration of rights 'to such part of the business of government as respects finance', then the form in which he had presented his principles would constitute an appropriate basis for such a declaration—in this form it would not do any mischief, and might be of some benefit.[66] In a rudiments sheet written in connection with 'Observations on Draughts of Declarations-of-Rights', he noted that a declaration should 'inform people of their rights', but also 'reconcile them to their obligations', adding the comment that: 'If it affords a stimulant on one side, it ought to afford a calmant on the other.' A declaration should also '[s]erve as a

63 UC cviii. 108 (1795). 64 The first 'French disease' was, of course, syphilis.
65 *Rights, Representation, and Reform*, 400. 66 See ibid. 193–203.

guide to the legislator in detail'.[67] The crucial point was that such declarations should not be issued as law. In 'Nonsense upon Stilts' he stated that if they were to have any value, it would be in the form of instructions or advice. Article 7 of the Declaration of Rights, for instance, purported to provide security against arbitrary orders. Had the purpose of the authors of the Declaration been not to set limitations on 'their more experienced and consequently more enlightened successors', and to 'keep their fellow-citizens in a state of constant readiness to cut their throats', but rather to provide for the security of individuals, they would have advised succeeding legislatures to state in detail the procedures by which the powers of justice were to be exercised: 'for instance, that no man should be arrested but for some one in the list of cases enumerated by the law as capable of warranting an arrest, nor without the specification of that case in an instrument executed for the purpose of warranting such arrest: nor unless such instrument were signed by an Officer of such a description; and so on'. Instead, they had attempted 'to exhibit a code of such importance and extent and nicety in the compass of a parenthesis'.[68]

A striking example of Bentham's willingness to countenance a declaration, albeit not of rights but of securities, was the constitutional charter which he proposed for Tripoli in 1822. Through his friendship with Hassuna D'Ghies, who had been sent to London on a diplomatic mission by the Pasha of Tripoli, Bentham devised a scheme to introduce political reform in Tripoli, which he hoped would extend, if necessary with military aid from the United States of America, to other North African states. He composed a document containing 'constitutional securities . . . against abuse of power, now and for ever', which the Pasha would grant to the people of Tripoli. The securities would be preceded by two addresses from the Pasha. In the first address, the Pasha would claim that he had beheld a vision of the Prophet Mohammed, who had instructed him to set up a representative assembly and a judicial establishment. In the second address, the Pasha would acknowledge the greatest happiness of the greatest number as his 'only right and proper end in view and object of pursuit', and proceed to grant 'rights and securities . . . the securities against misrule: securities against abuse of power on the part of the Sovereign or those in authority under him' to his 'beloved people'.[69] In these circumstances Bentham was prepared to take advantage of the very ambiguity involved in the word 'rights' which he had condemned in the French Declaration of Rights. He explained to D'Ghies that the recognition of the rights in question might be given two interpretations: first, that the sovereign was merely recognizing rights which already existed of themselves, and did not require any act of his to create them; and second, that the rights were granted by the sovereign, and that he and his successors, therefore, retained the power to revoke them. On the one hand, if the rights were

[67] UC clxx. 48 (1789). [68] *Rights, Representation, and Reform*, 351–2.

[69] *Securities against Misrule and other constitutional writings for Tripoli and Greece*, ed. P. Schofield (Oxford, 1990), 74–8.

regarded as existing independently of the sovereign's will, there was a danger that he would not agree voluntarily to sign the declaration in question. On the other hand, if the rights were regarded as depending on his will, there was a danger that he would revoke them, and that the people would accept this without complaint and without any perception of injustice.[70] Bentham seems to have hoped that the Pasha would be persuaded to acknowledge the rights on the grounds that they constituted his gift to the people and that he would retain the power to revoke them, but that the people would see them as existing independently of the sovereign's will and, once promulgated, would resist any attempt to revoke them.

Although Bentham was invoking what he elsewhere termed a counter-fallacy,[71] he did believe that his charter for Tripoli represented a significant improvement on any such documents issued in the past. He explained that 'the radical defect' in previous legislative attempts to provide security for the governed against governors—for instance the Petition of Right and the Bill of Rights in England, the American Declaration of Independence, and the French Declaration of Rights—was that they had failed to present any conception of their very purpose, that of 'affording to the governed security against misrule—i.e. bad government at the hands of their governors'. The words 'security' and 'misrule' were clear, but by adopting the language of rights, the measures in question had resulted in 'a cloud, and *that* of a black hue, [enveloping] the whole field'. A claim that a right had been violated only made sense where a legal right had been violated, for in that case there was a really existing law which created the right: however, 'from a merely imagined law' (Bentham presumably had in mind the natural law) 'nothing can come more substantial than a correspondently imagined right'. Yet it was not where a legal right had been violated that the demand for security was most urgent, but where 'the laws being altogether at the command of the rulers—the very work of their hands, no violation of law can be needed for the accomplishment of the misrule'.[72] Bentham recognized that a declaration of rights might at least provide some protection against a sovereign, and more effectively still against subordinate officials, who oppressed the people through and by means of the law. Nevertheless the same objective would be achieved, and without the ambiguity and confusion involved in the word 'rights', by employing the phrase 'securities against misrule', with the great advantage that it was, moreover, applicable to cases where misrule took place without any violation of law. It was applicable to every circumstance in which a society might find itself, whether 'employed by a sovereign representative body on the occasion of the establishment of the constitution of the State', or whether introduced under an absolute monarchy, in the latter case so long as the securities in question did not appear, in the eyes of the monarch, to limit his authority. In relation to Tripoli, Bentham believed that his proposed securities against misrule might operate effectively even though the form of government

[70] Ibid. 76–7 n. [71] See p. 159 below. [72] *Securities against Misrule*, 23–4 n.

would remain an absolute monarchy. An absolute monarch, while unlikely to agree voluntarily to limits being imposed on his own power, might be prepared to limit that of his agents, 'in which case matters may be so managed, as that without knowing it he may thus be made to throw obstacles in the way of his own steps in so far as they proceed in a sinister direction'.[73]

By 1822 there did appear to be a greater latitude in Bentham's approach to declarations of rights compared with his position in 1795, when he had said that what he intended to attack was 'not the execution of such a design in this or that instance, but the design itself'.[74] It was, to some extent at least, his recognition that a declaration issued by sovereign authority might contain a declaration of securities against misrule, rather than a declaration of natural rights, that led him to accept that such documents might, in certain circumstances, be of some value. By the 1820s he had become a political radical, committed to democratic reform in Britain and elsewhere. The problem as he saw it in the early 1820s was not the prevention of anarchy, but how to encourage resistance to oppression committed by and according to the letter of the law. This was a problem which he had solved on his own terms by means of securities against misrule, and not by appeal to what he regarded as non-existent natural rights. Of course, one should not underestimate Bentham's sensitivity to the context with which he was dealing, and he might have been prepared to advocate measures for Tripoli which he would not have thought appropriate for Britain and France: he might have seen an ambiguous constitutional charter issued by the ruler as of some value in the African despotism, but not in the more liberal European regimes. Having said that, Bentham's detailed constitutional code, intended 'for all nations professing liberal opinions',[75] and his brief constitutional charter for Tripoli had this much in common—their essential purpose was to prevent misrule.

V

In *A Fragment on Government* Bentham's concern was with the distinction between the expositor and the censor, while in 'Nonsense upon Stilts' it was with that between the censor and the anarchist. On the one hand, 'the good subject, the rational censor of the laws', recognized 'the existence of the law he disapproves of', while proposing its repeal. On the other hand, 'The anarchist, setting up his will and fancy for a law before which all mankind are called upon to bow down at the first word—the anarchist, trampling on truth and decency, denies the validity of the law in question, denies the existence of it in the character of a law, summoning all mankind to rise up in a mass and resist the execution of it.' The anarchist claimed that while men might be slaves in respect of 'the pretended human laws, which though called laws are no laws at all, as

[73] *Securities against Misrule*, 24 n. [74] See p. 63 above. [75] See p. 304 below.

being contrary to the laws of nature', they remained at the same time 'free in respect of the laws of nature'.[76] In Bentham's view, the anarchy of the French Revolution was closely related to the conservatism of Blackstone. Blackstone had confounded the role of the expositor with that of the censor: he had claimed to be describing the laws of England, but at the same time had attempted to justify those laws on no other ground than that they were already in existence. Blackstone's approach, encapsulated in the phrase 'every thing is as it should be', confused what existed with what ought to exist. The same confusion was characteristic of the anarchist, who, in claiming to describe the law of nature, was putting forward prescriptions. The difference between them was that while Blackstone assumed that existing law was consistent with the natural law, and therefore valid law, the anarchist assumed that existing law was inconsistent with the natural law, and therefore invalid law.[77] Given that both were appealing to a non-existent standard in justification of their respective claims, both were talking nonsense. From one point of view, what distinguished them and explained their difference of approach, the one conservative and the other anarchical, was their respective interests—namely whether or not they believed it would be of benefit to them to retain or to overthrow the existing laws and institutions of their society. From another point of view, what united them was that they were both adherents of the principle of sympathy and antipathy.

Bentham attributed the popularity of the doctrine of natural law to the fact that it gave apparent justification to the sentiments of the speaker. A man who disapproved of a particular activity simply had to state that it was against a law of nature. If there was any sense in this claim, then it was because the so-called law of nature happened to coincide with the dictates of the principle of utility, but otherwise his appeal was to an 'imaginary standard' which was 'neither more nor less . . . than his own opinion in disguise'. If the man claimed that a particular usage or law was detrimental to the happiness of the community, he would be called upon to explain why, which he might not be able to do. 'He says not that it is contrary to a dictate of utility: for a dictate of utility, it would be seen, is no more than his opinion of what is useful. But he says it is against a Law of Nature: and a Law of Nature being a sacred thing, which multitudes have concurred in magnifying, it is but crying out profanation, and this gives him a pretence to be angry, to indulge his spleen, and to run out into invectives.'[78] The appeal to the

[76] *Rights, Representation, and Reform*, 324.

[77] Bentham's position is neatly captured by W. Twining, 'The Contemporary Significance of Bentham's Anarchical Fallacies', *Archiv für Rechts- und Sozialphilosophie*, 61 (1975), 325–56, at 329: 'if the *validity* of a law is judged by conformity to some purported statement of Natural Law or Natural Rights, then the distinction between law as it is and law as it ought to be is rejected. When this happens the door is opened to two lines of fallacious argument, one justifying anarchy, the other extreme conservatism. For the anarchist argues: "This is bad, therefore it is not a (valid) law, therefore I have no duty to obey it." The reactionary argues: "This is a (valid) law, therefore it is good, therefore it is immune from criticism."'

[78] UC lxix. 102 (*c*.1776).

principle of utility had to be justified by reference to matters of fact, but the appeal to natural right was no more than an appeal to a sound:

Talk of *utility*, and of pains and pleasures, this is grounding your doctrine on matter of fact: and to enquire into and duly to collect the matter of fact, takes more *trouble* than they are *willing*, and perhaps more *sagacity* than they are *able* to bestow.—Talk of *right*:—say a man has a *right* to such a thing in such a case, we have no matter of fact to encumber ourselves with.—When you have said he has a right—insist upon it: it is a plain case, all proof is needless. The business is thus settled in a trice by the help of a convenient word or two, and without the pains of thinking.[79]

Bentham argued that an appeal to justice and injustice was similarly an appeal to passion, rather than to reason. The appeal to the 'cold appellative of utility', which was 'generally recognized to be matter of calculation, matter of figures', did not have the rhetorical power associated with an appeal to 'the burning and impassioned sounds ... of justice and injustice'. Moreover, by appealing to justice and injustice there was no need for argument, unlike the appeal to the principle of utility, which required proof. The appeal to justice and injustice was more attractive, therefore, 'in proportion to the force of [a man's] passions and the weakness of his understanding'. The same sort of man who appealed to justice and injustice would also appeal to

its quasi-conjugate,—*right* understood in the sense of the phrase natural right, and for the same purposes and the same views. With him, every question, every one at least in which his interests or his passions are concerned, is to be placed on the ground of right—*Give us our rights!* never on the ground of utility, of expediency. The same sort of man, if it suits his purpose to teach morality as a science, and write a book on it, talks of the *moral sense*.[80]

In Bentham's view, only the principle of utility provided any rational ground for resolving moral, and hence political and legal, disputes, while talk of justice, injustice, natural rights, or moral sense was merely a veneer to give respectability to, or to endow with persuasive force, the likes and dislikes of the speaker.

The doctrine of natural law and natural rights was grounded on the delusive properties of language, and in particular the confusion involved in taking the name of a fictitious entity to be the name of a real entity.

Unfortunate it is—howsoever necessary and indispensable—that for speaking of fictitious entities there is no other possible mode than that of speaking of them as if they were so many real entities. This blameless falshood being universally uttered, and remaining universally uncontradicted, is to a considerable extent taken for truth. With every *name* employed an entity stands associated in the minds of the hearers as well as speakers—and that entity, though in one half of the whole number of instances no other than a fictitious, is in all of them apt to be taken for a real one. To speak of an object by its name, by its universally known name, is to ascribe existence to it. Out of this error

[79] UC lxix. 6–7 (*c*.1776). [80] UC lix. 84–5 (19 May 1805).

misconception, obscurity, ambiguity, confusion, doubt, disagreement, angry passions and even discord and hostility have to no inconsiderable amount had place. Many a man who could not endure patiently to sit and hear contested the reality of those objects which he is in the habit of speaking of as being *his rights*. For the assertion of the existence of these fictitious objects no small degree of merit has been ascribed, no small degree of praise claimed and given: assertion has in this case been taken for proof: and the stronger and more numerous the sets of words thus employed, the more compleat and conclusive has that proof been esteemed.[81]

The use of the noun-substantive 'rights' had given rise to the opinion that rights as such did actually exist. Now to talk of rights established by law did make sense, since they might be shown to have their 'real source' in the will of a sovereign legislature. But to talk of natural rights, with their source in natural law, was to talk nonsense. Such talk might be the product of ignorance, but in the instance of those who understood that such talk was nonsense, it was an attempt to persuade others of the existence of the law or rights in question in order to gain some benefit for themselves. The best that might be said about a proposition which appealed to natural law or natural rights was that it amounted to an expression of opinion on the part of the speaker that such a law or such a right *ought to* exist—in other words, the statement was a moral claim ambiguously expressed:

To say that a thing ought not to be done because there is a Law of Nature against it's being done, is an obscure and roundabout way of saying one of two things. 'It ought not to be done, because it would be mischievous or dangerous to the community': or else 2$^{\text{dly.}}$ 'It ought not to be done, because I say it ought not.' The grand mischief of the expression is that most commonly when examined into, the only meaning which it is found to cover is the latter. Tis the common resource of those who either tremble to take for the standard of right and wrong the Principle of utility; or meaning in general to take that for their standard know not how to try by it the proposition they approve of.[82]

The techniques of exposition which Bentham had developed in his theory of logic and language—albeit not explicitly stated in detail until the 1810s—were at the root of his attack on natural law and natural rights, just as they were at the root of his defence of the principle of utility.

81 UC cii. 447 (9 July 1826) [Bowring, viii. 327–8].

82 UC lxix. 106 (*c.*1776).

4

The French Revolution

I

The principle of utility, with its 'real source' in the sensations of pain and pleasure, provided Bentham with the means to construct a new theory of politics, and with it a new blueprint for society. This theory of politics did not, however, like the principle of utility in the 'most interesting year' of 1769,[1] emerge, as it were, at once, but was the result of decades of experience and reflection. While, in its essentials, Bentham's theory of real and fictitious entities, and the utilitarianism which was grounded upon it, remained constant throughout his adult life, this was clearly not the case in relation to his political thought. By 1822, when he embarked on the monumental writings on codification which saw him make substantial progress on his constitutional, procedure, and penal codes, he was committed to republicanism, and fully involved in the movements to achieve democratic political reform and law reform which had gained momentum after the end of the Napoleonic Wars. But he had not always been a democrat, and the question of the timing and circumstances which led to what has been called Bentham's 'transition' or 'conversion' to democracy, and thus to political radicalism, has been long debated.[2] It is generally agreed that the early period of the French Revolution, roughly from 1788 to 1792, when Bentham appeared to justify equality of suffrage and thus to put forward the earliest-ever defence of political equality on utilitarian grounds, is an important episode in this narrative, but what is disputed is the nature of Bentham's commitment to democracy at this time. Most commentators accept that Bentham was initially attracted to democratic reform, in both France and Britain, but that from 1792 he became afraid of the increasing disorder and violence within France. Not only did he reject popular government, he also came to oppose any reform of the British Constitution. Apart from this brief flirtation with democratic politics, it is argued, Bentham's permanent 'conversion' to radicalism occurred in 1808

[1] See p. 2 above.

[2] See J. R. Dinwiddy, 'Bentham's Transition to Political Radicalism', *Journal of the History of Ideas*, 35 (1975), 683–700, which refers to Bentham's 'conversion', as well as to his 'transition', to political radicalism. In contrast, the question of Bentham's 'transition' or 'conversion' to republicanism has been largely ignored.

or 1809.[3] An alternative view is advanced by M. P. Mack, who argues that Bentham became intellectually committed to the cause of democracy once and for all in 1790. Following the September Massacres in 1792 and the outbreak of war between Britain and France in early 1793, he found it prudent to be politically quiescent, and so turned his attention to other projects. When he again began to compose material on parliamentary reform in 1809, he was expressing convictions which he had long held.[4]

The starting point for the debate is Elie Halévy's *The Growth of Philosophic Radicalism*.[5] Halévy remarks that, 'Bentham, at the beginning of the French Revolution, seems to have caught a momentary glimpse of the possibility of founding a justification of a purely democratic régime on the principle of utility'. The crucial evidence came from what Halévy called 'Essai sur la Représentation', written at the end of 1788 and beginning of 1789, in which Bentham offered advice to the French who were preparing for the meeting of the Estates-General.[6] He 'demanded universal suffrage... condemned the plural vote; wished all elections to be held the same day, and to be completed in a single day; and demanded secret voting'. He argued that since the happiness of any one individual had no more value than the equal happiness of another, and that all individuals had both an equal capacity for and an equal desire for happiness, then, assuming that all individuals had an equal capacity of judging the tendency of an action to increase happiness, the best form of government would be that in which everyone had a vote. Minors, lunatics, and women were, however, excluded on the grounds of this incapacity, but otherwise equal political rights should be extended to all. 'Thus', remarks Halévy, 'is brought about a kind of transformation of the theory of the rights of man into the language of utility.' Halévy, however, cautions against attaching too much significance to what he terms 'this logical exercise', since Bentham was merely attempting to place the fashionable 'equalitarianism' of Rousseau into a utilitarian guise.[7] Bentham soon

[3] Some scholars choose 1808 on the grounds that this was the date when Bentham met James Mill, who, it is suggested, was responsible for his 'conversion' to political radicalism; others choose 1809, the date when Bentham began to compose the text which was eventually published as *Plan of Parliamentary Reform* (London, 1817).

[4] Mack, *Bentham: Odyssey of Ideas*, 407–43.

[5] E. Halévy, *La formation du radicalisme philosophique*, 3 vols. (Paris, 1901–4). Citations to this work are taken from the English translation, *The Growth of Philosophic Radicalism* (first published 1928), trans. M. Morris, corrected edn (London, 1952).

[6] It was Halévy who first drew attention to Bentham's writings on political reform at the time of the French Revolution (Bentham did not print these writings himself, nor did they appear in the Bowring edition), publishing brief extracts from 'Essai sur la Représentation' in *La formation du radicalisme philosophique*, vol. i, appendice 4. Hence, no discussion of these writings appears in Leslie Stephen's biography of Bentham in the first volume of *The English Utilitarians*, 3 vols. (London, 1900), which relies almost exclusively on the Bowring edition. The extracts do not appear in Morris's translation of Halévy, but they are translated into English in Mack, *Bentham: An Odyssey of Ideas*, App. D, 448–53. Surprisingly, the material is not discussed by C. W. Everett in *Jeremy Bentham* (London, 1966). Both Stephen and Everett accept that Bentham first became a political radical in 1808, the date of his meeting with James Mill.

[7] Halévy, *Growth of Philosophic Radicalism*, 147–8.

became preoccupied with his panopticon prison scheme, to the extent that, in Halévy's estimation, 'From the year 1789 . . . there was as it were a pause in the history of Bentham's thought'.[8] This 'pause' was ended in 1808 when Bentham came into contact with James Mill, who 'converted Bentham to the cause of liberalism and then to political radicalism'.[9]

Halévy's interpretation is challenged by Mack. She argues that it was in 'the charged atmosphere' of the Bowood Circle (the group of advanced thinkers which the second Earl of Shelburne, later first Marquis of Lansdowne, gathered together at Bowood House, his country home)[10] that 'Bentham became a democrat'. The crucial influences were Étienne Dumont and Samuel Romilly, both of Genevan extraction, and therefore with practical experience of the political state which, before the independence of the United States, had been 'the best operating model of democracy', and both advancing a utilitarian justification for democracy.[11] Moreover, 'Bentham had been greatly impressed by the United States where revolution had led, not to anarchy, as he had feared, but to tranquillity and prosperity'.[12] Like Halévy, Mack emphasizes the significance of Bentham's 'Essai sur la Représentation', in which 'he called for universal manhood suffrage and the secret ballot'—since 'every man has an equal desire for happiness', then 'every man should have an equal vote, regardless of property qualifications'. She adds that 'had prejudice against women been less violent and universal, he would have granted them voting rights as well'. As far as Bentham was concerned, none of the institutions of the Bourbon monarchy were worth preserving, and only radical reform could save it from collapse. At first, Bentham believed that a similar reform was unnecessary for England, since everything that an equal representation in France was meant to achieve had already been achieved in England,[13] but as he considered in greater detail the issues facing France—the need for a new concept of sovereignty, a representative assembly, an efficient and responsible administration, and a new system of judicial procedure—he began to see 'glaring inadequacies' in English society. 'He was at last forced to calculate: how long would the benefits of English government continue to outweigh the rising evils? By 1790 he read the balance on the side of accumulated evil and called for parliamentary reform.'[14] Bentham 'now became a full-fledged radical English democrat'.[15] Even though, on Mack's interpretation, '[t]he climactic change in [Bentham's] thought . . . was his conversion to democracy in 1790', changing circumstances—the French declaration of war in February 1793 rendered the English Constitution 'sacrosanct' and criticism of the government 'treason'—made it 'dangerous to speak out'.

[8] Halévy, *Growth of Philosophic Radicalism*, 153. [9] Ibid. 154.

[10] Bentham's first visit to Bowood House took place in the late summer and early autumn of 1781.

[11] Mack, *Bentham: An Odyssey of Ideas*, 409. The view that Romilly and Dumont were democrats requires considerable qualification: in the English context, both aligned themselves with reform-minded Whigs, but this hardly made them democrats. [12] Ibid. 410.

[13] Ibid. 416. [14] Ibid. 420. [15] Ibid. 429.

Bentham remained a reformer, but 'for a time, he put his larger ambitions aside and settled for the possible'. He concentrated on the panopticon, a scheme which was 'practicable', instead of parliamentary reform, which was 'visionary'. Bentham undertook 'A Fabian Retreat', waiting 'patiently... for the right moment'. This moment arrived in 1809, when 'he began exactly where he had stopped in 1790'.[16]

J. H. Burns rejects Mack's view that Bentham was converted outright to democracy at the time of the French Revolution. He accepts that in 'Essai sur la Représentation' Bentham 'asserts quite sweepingly democratic principles derived from utilitarian assumptions', but cautions that 'it is important to emphasize that Bentham was consciously dealing with specific questions about French problems at a particular time, not developing a general theory'. Bentham, distinguishing sharply 'between the French and British situations', argued that the rejection of parliamentary reform in Britain earlier in the 1780s represented the will of the nation itself, and that she already enjoyed the benefits of the '[l]iberty of the press, the absence of arbitrary executive power, and the impartial administration of justice... which France could not hope to enjoy without a radically reshaped representative system'.[17] In Burns's view the crucial period in 'Bentham's attitude to revolutionary France' occurred between September 1792 and March 1793. In the autumn of 1792 'he remained somewhat detached', his position balanced between extremes—' "a royalist in London", as he said, "a republican in Paris" '.[18] By the later date he was praising the excellence of the British system of government, and rejecting parliamentary reform, and by 1795 planning a work entitled 'Rottenness no corruption, or a Defence of Rotten boroughs'. Referring to Mack's description of Bentham's position after the outbreak of war with Revolutionary France in February 1793 as 'a Fabian retreat', Burns states that '[t]his is to call Dunkirk a tactical withdrawal'. He points out that Bentham did not write anything in favour of parliamentary reform between 1790 and 1809. Although Bentham never abandoned 'the pursuit of reform, of legal, administrative, fiscal, and social improvement... he believed that no useful reforming purpose would be served by major political changes'. Burns concludes that '[w]hatever the source and character of

[16] Ibid. 440–1. Mack relies on what she describes as the 'hundreds of pages' of manuscript material on the topic of the jury written in 1790 (see ibid. 424) in order to substantiate her account. This material, at UC xxxv. 1–112, was composed for, but not printed in, 'Draught of a New Plan for the organisation of the Judicial Establishment in France: proposed as a Succedaneum to the Draught presented, for the same purpose, by the Committee of the Constitution, to the National Assembly, December 21st, 1789', printed in 1790 (reprinted in Bowring, iv. 285–406, but with an emended title). It is, however, important to distinguish Bentham's schemes for law reform from those for political reform: see pp. 114–17 below.

[17] J. H. Burns, 'Bentham and the French Revolution', *Transactions of the Royal Historical Society*, 5th ser., 16 (1966), 95–114, at 98. The sources on which Burns relies were composed in 1788–9, and so pre-date the 'conversion' date of 1790 identified by Mack.

[18] The quotation is from Bentham to Jean Marie Roland de Platière, *c.*16 Oct. 1792, *Correspondence*, iv. 401–2.

Bentham's eventual conversion to radical democracy, it was no return to a revolutionary faith, for such a faith Bentham had never held'.[19]

The prevailing view of subsequent scholars, who have tended to accept much of Burns's interpretation, is summarized by John Dinwiddy:

> at the outset of the French Revolution [Bentham] was briefly converted to democratic ideas. In 1788–9 he came to believe that the Bourbon regime was so riddled with abuses that it required drastic structural reform, and he wrote an essay arguing that the French should adopt a system of representation based on near-universal suffrage and the secret ballot. Within a year or so, he moved to the view that similar arguments were applicable to England, and he drafted a work in favour of parliamentary reform. After about 1792, however, he became deeply alarmed, like many others of his class, by the course of events in France, and especially by the threats to security of life and property that seemed to be developing there: and he reacted strongly against democracy.[20]

There are three areas, however, in which this account needs to be revised. First, there has been considerable misunderstanding concerning the detailed development of Bentham's political views, because of an over-reliance on the extract from the so-called 'Essai sur la Représentation', which was published by Halévy and translated by Mack. The extract constitutes but a fraction of the essay, and the essay itself but a part of the material which Bentham wrote for France in 1788–9.[21] Second, it is doubtful that the very question as to whether Bentham was or was not a sincere convert to democracy is particularly helpful. Bentham's writings at this time were, as Burns points out, closely wedded to his perception of developments in France. Any attempt to find consistency in Bentham's thought at the level of the measures of political reform which he advocated for

[19] Burns, 'Bentham and the French Revolution', 110–12.

[20] Dinwiddy, *Bentham*, 11–12. Other scholars who broadly accept this interpretation include M. James, 'Bentham's Political Writings 1788–95', *The Bentham Newsletter*, 4 (1980), 22–4, and J. Steintrager, *Bentham* (Ithaca, NY, 1977), 57–8. More sympathetic to Mack's thesis is J. E. Crimmins, 'Bentham's Political Radicalism Reexamined', *Journal of the History of Ideas*, 54 (1994), 259–81. An alternative account is presented by D. Long, 'Censorial Jurisprudence and Political Radicalism: A Reconsideration of the Early Bentham', *The Bentham Newsletter*, 12 (1988), 4–23. Long argues that Bentham had become a political radical upon reading Helvétius in 1769, and that the 'transition' which took place in 1809 or thereabouts was 'from one political strategy to another, not from one way of thinking about morals and politics *in toto* to another'. Long is correct to point to the radical implications of Bentham's censorial jurisprudence, but it is unclear why the transition 'from one political strategy to another' does not, in effect, amount to the transition to political radicalism which other scholars have identified.

[21] This other material included 'France' (see *Rights, Representation, and Reform*, 1–61), in which Bentham offered advice on the political management of the forthcoming Estates-General, and 'Observations d'un Anglois sur un écrit intitulé *Arrêté de la noblesse de Bretagne*' (ibid. 147–65), in which he argued against adherence to the forms of the Estates-General of 1614 in the forthcoming assembly. His most extensive work was 'Political Tactics' (see *Political Tactics*,. ed. M. H. James, C. Blamires, and C. Pease-Watkin (Oxford, 1999)), in which he offered advice on the procedural organization of the National Assembly.

Bentham wrote in French because he had little confidence in the accuracy of French translations from the English. He was later persuaded to write in English, and to have his work translated. See *Rights, Representation, and Reform*, Editorial Introduction, pp. xxix–xxxi

France and those he advocated for Britain must not overlook his sensitivity to the differences he perceived in their respective circumstances, and in the nature of the audiences he was addressing. It makes more sense to see Bentham's proposals, following David Lieberman's suggestion, as part of his attempt to 'secure public notice for his legislative programme',[22] in other words, as part of a strategy to encourage legislators to introduce utilitarian reform. On this account, his plans for the reconstruction of the French state were of a piece with his promotion of the panopticon prison scheme, and the latter did not, as Mack suggests it did, represent a decisive break with the former—indeed Bentham at one point had hopes that a panopticon would be constructed in Paris.[23] Third, insofar as Bentham did propose measures of political reform at the time of the French Revolution, his understanding of the nature of the problem which he was attempting to solve was very different from what it would become in the 1810s and 1820s.

II

The central text for the debate on Bentham's commitment to democratic principles during the early stages of the French Revolution has been a short extract from the so-called 'Essai sur la Représentation', written in late 1788 and early 1789. This title was not, however, Bentham's title, which was 'Considérations d'un Anglois sur la Composition des États-Généraux y compris Réponses aux questions proposées aux Notables &c. 1788'.[24] Jacques Necker, the French Controller General of Finances, had addressed a series of questions to the Assembly of Notables, which had met at Versailles on 6 November 1788 in order to discuss the composition of the forthcoming Estates-General. Bentham saw an English translation of Necker's questions in *The Times* of 15 November 1788, and took it upon himself to provide answers, which he presented in 'Considérations sur la Composition des États-Généraux'. Bentham's proposals for electoral reform put forward in this essay were not as radical as commentators relying on the extract published by Halévy and translated by Mack have assumed. Much of this extract was taken from an introduction to the essay entitled 'Termes Capitaux', containing a discussion of equality, where Bentham did indeed provide a rationale for equal political rights. He outlined three principles: first, the equality of right[25] to happiness; second, the equality of

[22] D. Lieberman, 'Jeremy Bentham: Biography and Intellectual Biography', *History of Political Thought*, 20 (1999), 187–204.

[23] J. E. Semple, *Bentham's Prison: A Study of the Panopticon Penitentiary* (Oxford, 1993), 107–8.

[24] See *Rights, Representation, and Reform*, Editorial Introduction, p. xxv. Halévy appears to have given the title 'Essai sur la Représentation' to the work on the grounds that the text sheets carry the short working heading 'Représentation', and that Bentham referred to it as 'an essay on Representation' in a letter to André Morellet, 25 Feb. 1789, *Correspondence*, iv. 31.

[25] The word translated here as 'right' appears as 'droit' in Bentham's original French. Bentham presumably understood 'droit' in this context to refer to a moral claim. Whether an equality of right

capacity to feel happiness; and third, the equality of desire for happiness.[26] He accepted that if any measurable inequalities did exist in any single one of these respects, then inequalities in the distribution of happiness would be justified. His argument was not that such inequalities did not exist, but that they could not be measured.

Bentham's first principle stipulated that each individual had an equal right to all the happiness to which his nature was susceptible. A superior being who took pleasure in the happiness of a group of men, and who had no reason to prefer any one man to any other, would take equal pleasure in contributing to the happiness of any one as to that of any other. The equal happiness of any one would not, in the conception of the superior, outweigh the equal happiness of any other, though the greater happiness of one would outweigh the lesser happiness of another. Bentham did not here have in mind a supernatural being, but Louis XVI, the King of France, who, said Bentham, had committed himself to promote the happiness of the whole nation. Such a commitment implied an equal concern for the happiness of each of his subjects. In short, there was no justification for favouring a particular individual or a particular class of individuals at the expense of others. Bentham's second principle stipulated that each individual had an equal capacity to experience happiness. If some individuals had the capacity to experience a greater quantity of happiness than others, this would justify their receiving a larger share of happiness. Individuals did indeed have different capacities in this respect, but it was impossible to measure such differences. Hence, it had to be assumed that each person possessed the same capacity as every other. This assumption provided the basis for some simple rules of arithmetic in relation to portions of happiness. First, the utility of an action was in exact proportion to the number of persons to whose happiness it would contribute, assuming that each person would benefit equally. An action which gave an equal portion of happiness to ten persons was worth twice that of an

to happiness is derivable from the principle of utility, or is an independent principle, has been a matter of philosophical debate, fuelled by what John Stuart Mill, in *Utilitarianism* (first published 1861), famously referred to as 'Bentham's dictum "everybody to count for one, nobody for more than one"': see *Essays on Ethics, Religion, and Society*, The Collected Works of John Stuart Mill, vol. X, ed. J. M. Robson (Toronto, 1969), 258. The source of the quotation was, no doubt, 'Every individual in the country tells for one; no individual for more than one', which appears in *Rationale of Judicial Evidence, specially applied to English practice*, ed. J. S. Mill, 5 vols. (London, 1827), iv. 475 (Bowring, vii. 334).

Having referred to Bentham's 'dictum', Mill went on to claim 'a *right* to equality of treatment' for 'all persons', unless 'some recognised social expediency requires the reverse' ('Utilitarianism', 258). Rosen, *Classical Utilitarianism*, 230, is incorrect to surmise that Bentham did not assert 'that "everybody has an equal right to happiness"', though the fact that he did so only reinforces Rosen's argument 'that Bentham would have accepted most of what Mill wrote on the place of equality and justice in the principle of utility'.

[26] These principles appear to have the status of what Bentham elsewhere termed 'axioms', which had 'their immediate basis' in 'universal experience', and were 'incapable of demonstration, and require only to be developed and illustrated, in order to be recognised as incontestable'. See *An Introduction to the Principles of Morals and Legislation*, 3 n.

action which gave the same portion of happiness to only five persons. Second, the utility of an action was in exact proportion to the size of the portions of happiness which it conferred. On the one hand, an action which conferred two portions of happiness to each person would be worth twice that which conferred only one portion. On the other hand, an action which conferred one portion of happiness on ten persons was worth the same as that which conferred two portions of happiness on five persons. Yet some caution was necessary in the application of these rules, since, in the production of happiness, the effect was not proportional to the cause: doubling the quantity of the cause of happiness—for instance, doubling the quantity of wealth possessed by an individual—would produce much less than double the quantity of happiness.[27] The third principle stipulated that each individual possessed an equal desire for happiness. If some individuals had a greater desire for happiness, again this would justify their receiving a larger share of happiness. And again, individuals did have differing desires in this respect, but it was impossible to measure such differences. The conclusion was the same: it had to be assumed that each person possessed the same desire as every other. Given that there was no justification for favouring one individual or class of individuals at the expense of the rest, Bentham concluded that the question of the best form of government was easily settled—all that was required was to give a vote to each person.[28]

Having said this much, Bentham went on to point out that a further assumption was necessary to complete the utilitarian argument for political equality, namely that each individual possessed an equal capacity to judge how far an action would contribute to happiness. It was obvious not only that individuals did have different capacities in this respect—just as they had different degrees of susceptibility to and desire for happiness—but also that there existed clear means of distinguishing those who enjoyed this capacity from those who did not.[29] In 'Considérations sur la Composition des États-Généraux'—not, however, in the extract which Halévy reproduced, but in a passage which was, therefore, apparently unknown to Mack—Bentham reckoned that around 90 per cent of the French population was incapacitated in this way, and so should not be enfranchised. Bentham believed that no one would dispute that two classes in which the capacity for judging whether an action accorded with happiness was lacking were minors and the insane. He went on to note that a number of arguments had been advanced to show that females constituted a third class who lacked this capacity, and should likewise be excluded from the vote: first, to give them the vote would distract them from other, more necessary tasks; second, they were dependent on males; third, their domestic duties made it difficult for them to acquire knowledge of politics; fourth, they already possessed sufficient influence over males by the greater need of the latter for sexual

27 Bentham accepted what would come to be known as the principle of diminishing marginal utility: see e.g. *'Legislator of the World'*, 252–3, and Dinwiddy, *Bentham*, 52–3.

28 *Rights, Representation, and Reform*, 68–9.

29 Ibid. 69.

gratification; and fifth, disputes over politics would lead to conflict within families. Bentham did not endorse any of these arguments, but neither was he prepared at this time to dispute them. Females, together with minors and the insane, were, therefore, to be excluded from the vote.[30] Two further classes were to be excluded. The first was the class of non-proprietors, by which Bentham meant not those who had absolutely no property, but those who might think they would benefit if all the property of the country were divided equally among everyone. While non-proprietors would not in fact benefit by such a division, the difficulty was convincing them of it. Bentham predicted that non-proprietors would use their votes to try to bring about a division of property, thereby producing resistance on the part of the propertied classes, and leading to civil war.[31] The second was the class of non-readers. A person who could not read, noted Bentham, was incapable of exercising the right to vote either to his own advantage or to that of the public.[32]

Having laid down these general principles, Bentham gave them a more specific application in his detailed answers to the questions raised by Necker in relation to the composition of the Estates-General. In response to a question regarding the property qualification required for an elector for the Third Estate, Bentham argued that it should be as small as possible, but should not be negligible. Such a qualification would exclude all non-proprietors, while admitting as many proprietors as possible. So long as a man had something to lose, there was no danger that he would ally himself with those who had nothing in order to bring about an equal division of property, which would be tantamount to destroying property.[33] A further point on which Necker asked for guidance was whether one might be an elector in more than one province. Bentham strongly rejected this idea, involving as it did the possibility that a man might have more than one vote. The question of whether a man's property was dispersed among several provinces, and therefore entitled the possessor to votes in each of the provinces, or whether it was all within a single province, was an irrelevance. The arbitrary distribution of a man's property was not a reasonable basis for granting him additional votes. The proper question, argued Bentham, was whether a man should enjoy an additional number of votes in proportion to his wealth. But even then, the crucial point was not that individuals possessed different amounts of property, and should, therefore, have different numbers of votes, but rather that

[30] *Rights, Representation, and Reform*, 69–70. Perhaps a more accurate reflection of Bentham's own position is provided in a fragment, probably written in late 1788, in which he stated that he had looked for reasons why females should be excluded from voting, but had not managed to find any which had convinced him: 'D'après les principes généraux d'égalité, nul être humain ne devroit exclus: aussi pour motiver leur exclusion, il faudroit trouver quelques raisons particulières.' ('According to the general principles of equality, no human being should be excluded: moreover in order to justify their exclusion, it is necessary to find particular reasons.') It appears that Bentham intended to go on to list these reasons, presumably with a view to refuting them, but abandoned the text before doing so. See UC clxx. 64, headed 'Etats-Généraux. Femmes'.

[31] *Rights, Representation, and Reform*, 73–4. [32] Ibid. 78. [33] Ibid. 80–1.

each person had only one, and not two, three, or more 'âmes pour sentir' and 'esprits pour juger'. In fact, it was precisely because of his wealth that a rich man should not be given additional votes. The more wealth a man had, the greater the means he enjoyed to influence the votes of others. On the contrary, there was a stronger case for giving additional votes to the man who only just met the relevant property qualification. It had been argued, continued Bentham, that a person with more property had more interest in the prosperity and security of the state.[34] This argument might have some force in the instance of an important post in government, but not in the case of the franchise. The richer proprietors did not need to have additional votes in order to defend themselves against non-proprietors, nor did they need additional votes to defend themselves against smaller proprietors, for both large and small proprietors had an interest in the security of property. Natural allies, their only natural enemy was the non-proprietor, who should not have the vote.[35] Bentham reckoned that, if his proposals were implemented, out of a population of about 25 million, there would be about 2.5 million voters.[36]

Bentham argued that each vote should be of the same value. In order to achieve this, there would need to be equal electoral districts, in the sense that each district should contain a roughly equal number of voters. The basic electoral unit should be the parish, where polling would take place. An appropriate number of parishes would be combined in order to constitute a single electoral district with the correct number of voters.[37] Voting should take place by secret ballot, which would ensure that electors were not subject to undue influence from any quarter.[38] In drafting detailed regulations to deal with the question of contested votes, Bentham suggested that in electoral districts where there were more than two candidates, and where no candidate possessed an overall majority, there should be a second election contested by the two candidates who had the greatest number of votes. He explained that, without this institution, a district might not elect the deputy whom the greater number of the voters preferred. For instance, assuming a total of 10,000 votes, Candidate A might receive 3,400, Candidate B 3,350, and Candidate C 3,250. In this case, if there were no further vote, Candidate A would be returned, even though all of Candidate C's voters would have preferred Candidate B to Candidate A. In a second election, Candidate B might then have received 6,600 votes, whereas Candidate A would still have received only 3,400.[39]

According to the ancient forms of the Estates-General, the representatives sat and voted as separate orders. Bentham, however, argued that the Estates-General

[34] This argument was to be famously advanced by Burke in *Reflections on the Revolution in France*: see e.g. *Writings and Speeches*, viii. 102–3.
[35] *Rights, Representation, and Reform*, 83–5.
[36] Ibid. 108.
[37] Ibid. 117–18.
[38] Ibid. 71.
[39] Ibid. 138. Given the fertility of his mind, it is surprising that Bentham did not investigate, in his later democratic writings, potential alternatives to a 'first-past-the-post' system of polling. Given his wish elsewhere to avoid undue complication, he may have thought that this system did, at least, have the merit of simplicity.

should consist of a single chamber, and that the number of deputies returned by each order should be proportional to its numerical strength in the population as a whole.[40] Bentham recommended direct elections to the Estates-General, and not indirect elections through a number of intermediary assemblies, as had traditionally been the case, and would be so again in 1789. The point of elections was to enable constituents to choose their own representative, not to choose an intermediate elector who would then choose 'un homme inconnu'. The existence of several stages of election undermined the responsibility of the deputy towards his constituents, and increased the complication and thence the expense of the electoral system.[41]

In 'Considérations sur la Composition des États-Généraux' Bentham did not, therefore, as Halévy and Mack both assume, advocate universal suffrage, or even universal manhood suffrage. Not only did he exclude from the vote minors and the insane, but also women and non-readers, and he advocated a property qualification. By his own reckoning, this would have enfranchised only 10 per cent of the population. It should be noted that at the very beginning of the essay Bentham briefly stated the principles—namely security, equality, liberty, tranquillity, simplicity, and incontestability—which would form the basis of his answers to Necker's questions to the Notables. He pointed out that security, by which he principally meant security for property, should take priority over equality. Without security of property, there would be no property and no subsistence, and thence no subject-matter for equality.[42] In short, Bentham sacrificed the equality of political influence because it appeared to threaten the security of property.

Bentham's proposals were, of course, addressed to the particular circumstances of France, and were specifically concerned with the elections to the Estates-General. While taking it as axiomatic that the happiness of each individual should receive equal consideration, his recommendations in relation to the franchise were not democratic, if that is understood as involving universal suffrage or even universal manhood suffrage. This is not to say that Bentham did not think that, at an abstract level, political equality was to be preferred to political inequality. He noted, for instance, that a system of political equality had the advantage of simplicity, and that every individual had some interest in it. In contrast, whatever system of inequality was instituted would require to be justified on grounds which not everyone might accept. Moreover, once political equality had been introduced, there was no other ideal to aim at, whereas under a system of inequality there would always be an imagined imperfection, if not a

[40] See *Rights, Representation, and Reform*, 123–4. In general, Bentham's strategy for the Estates-General was to minimize the distinctions between the three orders. To this end he argued that members of the nobility and the Third Estate should be eligible to be elected by any of the three orders. The clergy should be eligible to be elected only by their own order (ibid. 87–93). The voting qualification for the nobility should be exactly the same as that for the Third Estate, namely the possession of property of a certain value and the ability to read (ibid. 102).

[41] Ibid. 107–9.

[42] Ibid. 67.

real imperfection—for instance, inequality of right would be regarded as an inequality of dignity or consideration. It followed that a system of inequality would only be justified if it avoided dangers which would arise under a system of equality.[43] Yet in France in late 1788 and early 1789, in Bentham's view, there did exist such reasons, in particular the existence of a majority of non-proprietors who might regard it as being to their advantage to overturn existing property relations, and against whom the propertied needed to be guarded by excluding them from the franchise.

III

Within a few months the situation in France had been transformed. The Estates-General, constituted with a double representation from the Third Estate, had become the National Assembly; the three orders were sitting and voting together; the privileges of the nobility had been abolished; the Declaration of Rights had been issued; and a new constitution was being drafted. In or around October 1789 Bentham took it upon himself (now writing in English) to draft a constitution for France—'*Projet* of a Constitutional Code for France'—in which he adopted many of the recommendations put forward in 'Considérations sur la Composition des États-Généraux': France should be divided into equal electoral districts, with each district returning one deputy;[44] there should be no intermediate stages of election;[45] and no person should have more than one vote.[46] As well as reiterating points such as these, he developed a number of more wide-ranging proposals. In the earlier essay Bentham had tentatively suggested that elections to the Estates-General should take place every four years,[47] but now recommended that the National Assembly be elected annually. The greater frequency of elections would strengthen the dependence of the deputy on his constituents, while not in itself militating against his re-election. Moreover, by diminishing the value of the office of deputy, it would diminish 'the ferment to be apprehended from election'.[48] He also argued that deputies should be capable of being removed during their term of office. If a set of constituents lost confidence in their deputy, then there was no longer any reason for him to continue in that role. The power to remove deputies collectively at general elections, and

[43] Ibid. 72–3. [44] Ibid. 244. [45] Ibid. 244–5.

[46] A man should only be admitted to vote for two districts 'if he has two existences to take care of, and two reasoning faculties to judge': see ibid. 231 and n. Bentham reiterated his view that each person's interest was to be treated equally. The only justification for giving more votes to the wealthy might be on the grounds either that wealth was a test of intellectual fitness, or that it formed 'a preservative against corruption'. Wealth, however, was not a security against ignorance, while universal suffrage rendered corruption impossible. In any case, wealth of itself brought political influence, and to add to that influence by 'positive institutions' was 'an operation equally unjust and needless'. See ibid. 252.

[47] Ibid. 130.

[48] Ibid. 239–40.

individually between general elections, was necessary to maintain the good conduct of the Assembly towards the people.[49]

In relation to the franchise, Bentham's proposals were strikingly radical: 'The right of election shall be in every French citizen, male or female, being of full age, of sound mind, and able to read.'[50] He remained committed to the underlying principle of equality: 'Whatever benefit belongs to the right of suffrage, there is no reason *prima facie* why it should be refused to one more than to another.' Nor had he altered his view that the suffrage might reasonably be denied to those incapable of making use of it, either to their own advantage or to that of others. He continued to accept that the insane, minors, and non-readers should be excluded on these grounds.[51] As for non-readers, the ability to read was 'the only circumstance which can serve to draw a distinct line between the condition of those who may reasonably be deemed to have it in their power to exercise the right in question to the advantage of their community and those who can not'. In order to judge the conduct of their representative, constituents would have to read printed accounts of proceedings in the National Assembly. A man who wished to vote, but who was disbarred from doing so on this ground, merely had to learn to read. Such an exclusion had the added benefit of encouraging non-readers to learn to read, and would thereby 'operate as a spur to the desire of instruction and as an instrument of civilisation'. Finally, it was easy to test whether a person could or could not read.[52] However, where Bentham had changed his opinion was in relation to the suitability of admitting the non-propertied and females to the suffrage. In relation to the former, he now accepted that political equality was not a threat to the security of property:

> Equality in respect of this branch of government is free from the objection which is so fatal to equality in matters of property. Equality in property is destructive of the very principle of subsistence; it cuts up society by the roots. Nobody would labour if no one were secure of the fruits of his labour. Equality in respect of the right of voting is attended with no such inconvenience. Push it to the utmost, the motives for labour remain untouched.[53]

In relation to female suffrage, he was now prepared to argue against the objections which had been put forward. First, he doubted whether females were less intelligent than males, as had been claimed. In the exercise of political power, for instance, women had proved themselves better monarchs than men, and it seemed unlikely that much danger would arise from their exercise of the much smaller fragment of political power which the franchise would give to each of them. Even if it were true that females were intellectually inferior to males, it would be irrelevant unless the least intelligent male were superior in intelligence

[49] *Rights, Representation, and Reform*, 230, 241.

[50] Ibid. 231. Bentham envisaged that not only elections to the National Assembly would be conducted on this basis, but also those to his proposed Provincial and Sub-Provincial Assemblies. See ibid. 234, 235, 259–60.

[51] Ibid. 246.

[52] Ibid. 248–9.

[53] UC cxxvii. 19.

to the most intelligent female. Second, it had been objected that giving females the franchise would encourage them to neglect their domestic duties. Bentham pointed out that men also had their domestic duties, and there was no reason to think that the franchise would affect the one sex any more than the other. It would make more sense to ban women from 'visitings and assemblies of amusement': it took only a minute to cast a vote, whereas one play or ball occupied the same amount of time as the exercise of the right to vote would require in a lifetime. Third, it had been objected that the 'very idea' of women's 'interference' in politics was 'ridiculous'. Bentham responded that it was the idea of excluding them from the franchise which was 'ridiculous'. A thing was 'ridiculous' to a person if he were disposed to laugh at it: 'The cause of ridicule resides not in objects but in the mind.' It was 'ridiculous' to suppose that it was in the power of one person to destroy the rights of another by laughing at them. Furthermore, even if it were desirable, it was impossible to exclude women from political influence. The question was whether women should exercise that influence 'by law or contrary to law . . . whether one half of the species are to be subjected to a stigma for the purpose of preventing what it is as impossible to prevent as it is undesirable?'[54]

Having discussed the question of the eligibility to vote, Bentham went on to discuss the question of the eligibility to be elected, and here he recommended that there should be no limitations at all. To disbar anyone from the right of being elected was to infringe the right of the elector. It was unlikely that 'an ideot, a child in arms, a woman, a negro, or a convicted murderer' would be elected, but if they were, there would be no disastrous consequence. The idiot would remain in hospital, the child in arms would remain in arms, and the convicted murderer would be dealt with like other convicted murderers. As for the negro and the woman, continued Bentham, 'were they by some strange accident to overcome the body of prejudice which combats their admission with so much force, there could not be a stronger proof of a degree of merit superior to any that was to be found among whites and among men'. Bentham suggested that Catherine Macauley, the historian, would make a worthy member of the House of Commons. Nor was there any reason to prohibit the election of foreigners. Bentham pointed out that Necker, a Genevan, was 'not of all men the least deserving of the confidence of French men', and suggested that it might be of advantage to both Britain and France were their legislatures 'to interchange a few Members'.[55]

Bentham, then, did advocate democratic political reform at the time of the French Revolution, but in his draft constitution for France written in the autumn of 1789, and not in 'Considérations sur la Composition des États-Généraux' (the so-called 'Essai sur la Représentation') written several months earlier. Two points, however, should be emphasized. First, throughout this

[54] *Rights, Representation, and Reform*, 246–8. [55] Ibid. 250.

period Bentham assumed that France would retain its monarchy: he did not advocate a republic. Second, his most radical proposals were made at a time when the French themselves had, through the Declaration of Rights, committed themselves to liberty, equality, and fraternity. Bentham was attempting to make the best sense of principles already publicly adopted. This point is further evidenced in his proposal for the popular election of judges, put forward in 'Draught of a New Plan for the organisation of the Judicial Establishment in France', composed in the spring and summer of 1790, as a counter-proposal to that put forward by the Comité de Constitution of the National Assembly.[56] Bentham recommended the institution of four types of court. The parish courts and district courts would be the courts of immediate jurisdiction, with authority to hear every sort of cause, with the exception of those involving military and ecclesiastical discipline. Each district would also have a court of appeal, while a metropolitan or supreme court at Paris would deal with appeals from the district courts of appeal. The parochial judge would be the 'principal ecclesiastical minister' of the parish, the 'judge *natural*', unless the parish or district assembly appointed an '*instituted* judge' to supplant him. The judges natural would, of course, not be elected by the people; nor would the instituted judges, who would be appointed by the parish or district assembly; nor would the judges in the metropolitan court, who would be appointed by the National Assembly. There remained the judges who presided in the district courts, who would be elected 'by the electors chosen by the active citizens of the territory over which he is to be judge, in the same manner as a member of the administrative body of that territory'.[57] The category of active citizens had been introduced by a decree of the National Assembly of 29 October 1789. An active citizen was a man over 25 years of age, paying the equivalent of three days' unskilled labour in taxes. Active citizens were entitled to vote for electors, in the proportion of one to each hundred active citizens. The electors, who had to pay the equivalent of ten days' unskilled labour in taxes, met in departmental assemblies to choose deputies to the National Assembly.[58] It was these electors, operating at the district level, who, under Bentham's proposals, would elect the district judges. As well as the right of election, they would also enjoy the power of dismissing the judges from office by means of a majority vote.[59]

Bentham was concerned that the proposal of the Comité de Constitution that judges in the higher courts be appointed by the King, upon the presentation of two candidates chosen for each vacant office by the people, was 'neither consistent with utility in the abstract, nor with received principles'. This power, nominally granted to the King, would in effect be wielded by his ministers, and

[56] See 'Projet de l'organisation du pouvoir judiciaire' presented by the Comité de Constitution to the National Assembly on 21 December 1789, in *Procés-verbal de l'Assemblée Nationale*, vol. x, no. 157 (22 Dec. 1789).

[57] Bowring, iv. 289, 296, 300.

[58] See W. Doyle, *The Oxford History of the French Revolution* (Oxford, 1989), 124.

[59] Bowring, iv. 290.

any argument which went to show that the choice of the people ought to be outweighed by that of the King's ministers would also go to show that the people ought not to have any share at all in the appointment. In contrast, the Comité de Constitution had proposed to leave the choice of the people in the lower courts completely unfettered. Bentham commented:

To confess the truth . . . they have gone farther on the popular side than perhaps, without the encouragement of their example, I should have ventured to have gone. I have been distressed for years what to do with the appointment of judges: whether to give it to the people; or to *give* it (or as in England it would be, to *continue* it), to the king. . . . It is surely a bold experiment this of trusting the people at large with the choice of their judges: the boldest, perhaps, that ever was proposed on the popular side. My thoughts were divided betwixt the king and the representative assemblies. I could scarce think of looking so far down the pyramid, as to the body of the people. But now that the committee has given me courage to look the idea in the face, I have little fear of the success. My wish, however, is to see the experiment fairly tried, in its simplest form, and not clogged by a temperament in which I see the mischievous effects I have been stating, and in which I can descry no use.[60]

Bentham was taking as his starting point the proposal already made by the Comité de Constitution for the popular election of judges, and trying to work out its detailed application in a coherent and consistent manner. He later wrote that he had been unfairly represented as a Jacobin by the British Foreign Minister Grenville, 'merely because after it had been determined that Judges should be elected by the people, I wrote upon that ground, fully sensible of the mischief, and striving to counteract it in the best manner I could devise'.[61] What appeared on the surface as a commitment to democracy was in fact an attempt to mitigate what he regarded as the potential dangers of a democratic principle previously adopted by the French authorities. Similarly, Bentham had been forced to adopt the distinction between active citizens and electors—a distinction which, with its reliance on indirect elections, he had argued was deeply flawed. Just to emphasize the point, in 'Constitutional Code', when Bentham was fully committed to representative democracy and a republican form of government, he recommended that judges be appointed by the Justice Minister, not popularly elected, although they might be dismissed by a majority vote of the electors in their respective electoral districts.[62] Leaving aside the question of the nature of Bentham's commitment to political radicalism, if it is 'Considérations sur la Composition des États-Généraux' that contains Bentham's earliest justification of political equality, it is '*Projet* of a Constitutional Code for France' that contains his earliest proposal in favour of universal suffrage. Both

[60] Ibid. 307–9.

[61] Bentham to Samuel Bentham, 13 Oct. 1804, *Correspondence* vii. 285. See also Bentham to Dumont, 19 Oct. 1802, ibid. 153, where Bentham speaks of 'the adoption I then looked upon it as *necessary* to make (though even then against the grain, and even declaredly so) of the principle of popular election'.

[62] See p. 308 below.

works, however, like so many other of Bentham's productions, remained unpublished and unknown during Bentham's lifetime and beyond, and any impetus they might have given to the movement for political reform was lost.

IV

In addressing the political situation in France, and drawing on British experience in doing so, Bentham was led to reflect on the desirability of political reform at home. He was, of course, aware of the wide-ranging debate on the nature of political society in general, and on the nature of the British Constitution in particular, which was provoked in Britain by the French Revolution.[63] He did not, however, produce a systematic essay on British political reform, and his views have to be collected from passing references in the essays written for France, from a few sequences of fragmentary text, and from rough jottings. Moreover, Bentham's opinion not only as to the desirability of political reform in Britain, but also as to the nature of that reform, underwent considerable modification in the light of events. In late 1788 and early 1789 he held a generally positive attitude towards the British Constitution, drawing on the experience of Britain to provide advice for the French, and comparing British institutions favourably with those under the *ancien régime*. In the autumn of 1789 he put forward far-reaching proposals of parliamentary reform. From the autumn of 1792 he became increasingly opposed to any measure of political reform, and particularly to any extension of the franchise. Bentham's advocacy of electoral reform in the autumn of 1789 should not, however, obscure his acceptance of certain key aspects of Whig constitutional doctrine—for instance the place of King, Lords, and Commons as the central elements in the British polity, the primary place of the House of Commons in legislation, and the location of executive power (or administrative power, as he preferred to term it) in the King and his ministers—nor should it obscure the underlying continuities in his constitutional theory—in particular his rejection of the theories of the division of power and the separation of power, and his advocacy of the principle of the dependence of rulers on subjects.[64]

In the various essays written in late 1788 and early 1789 Bentham argued that, despite his wish for an equal representation in France, electoral reform in Britain was unnecessary. He noted that efforts made a few years earlier to widen the

[63] See e.g. H. T. Dickinson, *Liberty and Property: Political Ideology in Eighteenth-Century Britain* (London, 1977), 232–318; I. R. Christie, *Stress and Stability in Late Eighteenth-Century Britain: Reflections on the British Avoidance of Revolution* (Oxford, 1984); M. Philp (ed.), *The French Revolution and British Popular Politics* (Cambridge, 1991); M. Morris, *The British Monarchy and the French Revolution* (New Haven, 1998); and A. Goodrich, *Debating England's Aristocracy in the 1790s: Pamphlets, Polemics and Political Ideas* (Woodbridge, 2005).

[64] See pp. 232–40 below.

franchise had been abandoned because they had lacked popular support.[65] The desirable measures which it might otherwise have required an equal representation to implement—for instance the liberty of the press, the abolition of *lettres de cachet*, the impartial administration of justice, equitable taxation, economy in government expenditure, the subordination of the military to the civilian authorities, and the impossibility of embarking on unpopular wars—were already features of the British state. It was not clear that there would be sufficient benefits to offset the destruction of established rights which the introduction of an equal representation would entail in Britain.[66] Bentham even lavished praise on the English legal system, though this must have been intended for polemical effect, his purpose being to criticize the Parlement of Paris by contrasting its practices with those of the Common Law courts.[67] His main point was that, in contrast to their *parlementaire* equivalents, the English judges had not attempted to usurp the role of the legislator: if England was free, he said, it was because the legislator was the master of the judge. However, reverting to his more familiar role as critic of the English legal establishment, Bentham did finish the passage with a reference to 'ces abominations de détail dont fourmille notre législation et surtout notre procédure' ('those abominations of detail with which our legislation and above all our procedure are swarming').[68] Bentham was also prepared to defend the English constitutional principle that 'the King can do no wrong', or rather to defend one of the interpretations commonly given to it. According to Blackstone, this doctrine meant first that the King could not be held personally responsible for any act of government, and second that 'the prerogative of the crown extends not to do any injury'.[69] Bentham was impressed with the former of these interpretations, whereby ministers were made responsible

[65] For accounts of the attempts to introduce measures of parliamentary reform in the late 1770s and early 1780s, and the loss of impetus to the movement following the conclusion of the American War of Independence, see G. S. Veitch, *The Genesis of Parliamentary Reform* (first published 1913), Introduction by. I.R. Christie (London, 1964), 52–103; J. Cannon, *Parliamentary Reform 1640–1832* (Cambridge, 1973), 72–97; and I. R. Christie, *Wilkes, Wyvill and Reform: The Parliamentary Reform Movement in British Politics 1760–1785* (London, 1962).

[66] *Rights, Representation, and Reform*, 7. We have seen (pp. 85–7 above) that the 'perfectly equal' representative system which Bentham advocated at this time (late 1788–early 1789) for France involved considerable limitations to the suffrage.

[67] For Bentham's generally critical attitude towards the Common Law see G. J. Postema, *Bentham and the Common Law Tradition* (Oxford, 1986), 263–301; D. Lieberman, *The Province of Legislation Determined: Legal Theory in Eighteenth-century Britain* (Cambridge, 1989), 217–90; M. Lobban, *The Common Law and English Jurisprudence 1760–1850* (Oxford, 1991), 116–84; and p. 242 below.

[68] *Rights, Representation, and Reform*, 9–13. Soon afterwards Bentham was complaining of unauthorized judicial amendments to Acts of Parliament by the judges, of having to pay 'venal lawyers' for information about them, and of justice being sold to the rich while being denied to the poor: see 'Necessity of an Omnipotent Legislature', in ibid. 269–70. Moreover, in December 1792 Bentham composed *Truth versus Ashhurst; or Law as it is, contrasted with what it is said to be* (London, 1823) (Bowring, v. 231–7), incorporating a fierce attack on the English judges along similar lines: see pp. 114–16 below.

[69] Blackstone, *Commentaries on the Laws of England*, i. 238–9.

for every order issued under royal authority, while any order issued without the counter-signature of a minister was deemed invalid. The corollary of this was that the King's person was considered to be inviolable. In Bentham's view, the maxim of royal impeccability admirably combined the personal interest of the King with the interest of the nation. It was, said Bentham, 'peut-être de toutes les inventions politiques la plus ingénieuse et la plus heureuse' ('perhaps of all political inventions the most ingenious and the most happy'). It was relatively easy to change ministers without violence, whereas it was impossible to change kings without considerable bloodshed. A king could not do harm except by means of instruments, and when they were removed he was unable to act. The people had nothing to fear from the king, and the king had no fears in relation to his personal security.[70]

A further important and valuable feature of the British Constitution was the 'confusion of orders', in contrast to the situation in France, where the Estates had traditionally been rigidly demarcated. The political divisions which existed in Britain were not predicated upon the division between the House of Lords and the House of Commons. Rather, the two Houses enjoyed a harmonious relationship, due in part to the clear superiority of the House of Commons, but also due to the absence of any such demarcation between nobles and commoners as that which existed in France. For instance, a number of the sons of peers, as well as Irish peers, who were regarded as commoners for this purpose, sat in the House of Commons.[71] There was also considerable intermingling of nobles and commoners at the time of elections. When the English noble returned to the country, it was not to oppress the peasant, like his French counterpart, but rather to flatter him so as to obtain his vote at the next election.[72] In contrast to elections to the Estates-General in France, in elections to Parliament in Britain, nobles (though not the peers themselves, who were disqualified from the franchise), clergy, and commoners voted together. Peers, while lacking power in their collective capacity as members of the House of Lords, had a considerable influence over the composition of the House of Commons. Many counties or boroughs elected the candidate nominated by a local aristocratic patron, whom they regarded as their neighbour and benefactor. The son of a noble nominated in this way, remarked Bentham, would often be elected in preference to a non-noble candidate whose main recommendation was his superior wealth.[73] Although Bentham favoured a single-chamber legislature, the separate existence

[70] *Rights, Representation, and Reform*, 28–30. While supportive of the doctrine in the first of Blackstone's senses (which he interpreted to mean that while the King himself was not punishable for any act which he performed, his ministers were punishable for any wrong act which they performed), Bentham was extremely critical of the doctrine in the second: see e.g. *A Comment on the Commentaries*, 185–9, 304–7. Bentham adopted the doctrine in the first sense in '*Projet* of a Constitutional Code for France': see *Rights, Representation, and Reform*, 256–9. In his later constitutional writings he condemned the doctrine outright: see *First Principles preparatory to Constitutional Code*, ed. P. Schofield (Oxford, 1989), 54–5.

[71] *Rights, Representation, and Reform*, 88–9. [72] Ibid. 90. [73] Ibid. 126–7.

of the House of Lords was not, in his eyes, a matter of any great concern: 'Ils ne sont que pour figure. Ils n'existent que par tolérance: on les a trouvés: on les laisse.' ('They are only for appearance. They exist because they are tolerated: one found them: one leaves them.') It was easier just to retain the House of Lords than to attempt to abolish it. Real authority lay with the House of Commons, who controlled the nation's finances, initiated legislation, communicated with the people, and dominated the Lords as much as they, and as much as the people, wished.[74] On the other hand, the peers had no reason to fear a threat to their property from the House of Commons—no more than they feared such a threat from St Marino, or from any other community or class in England. A consequence of the confusion of interests was that all opposition of interests was extinguished.[75]

The reforms which Bentham advocated for Britain in late 1788 and early 1789 were modest. In 'Considérations sur la Composition des États-Généraux' he argued that the introduction of the secret ballot would be a means of removing the undue influence of patrons over voters.[76] He was critical of the fact that it was possible for electors to have more than one vote, depending on the geographical distribution of their property. Since the voting qualification within the counties was landed property worth 40 shillings,[77] a person who held 20,000 acres of land in one county would have only one vote (or more strictly two votes, since two MPs were returned from each county), whereas a person who held twenty acres worth forty shillings each, but distributed across twenty counties, would have twenty votes (or more strictly, forty votes).[78] He saw no benefit in the returning of two members for each electoral district. The arrangement had been established in a period of 'la plus crasse barbarie', when the members representing the Commons had wished to complete their business (which normally consisted in agreeing to give money to the King) and to return home as quickly as possible. Two members had been returned from each district in order to ensure that the district was not left without representation should one of the members fall ill. A much simpler solution to this problem, suggested Bentham,

[74] Ibid. 119–20.

[75] Ibid. 126. Bentham was even prepared to commend the influence of the Crown, a topic of considerable controversy in the political history of the period (see e.g. I. R. Christie, *Myth and Reality in Late-Eighteenth-Century British Politics and Other Papers* (Berkeley, 1970), 296–310), on the grounds that it helped to guarantee the quiescence of the House of Lords. Corruption applied to the Lords prevented them from hindering the passage of salutary legislation. See *Rights, Representation, and Reform*, 42–3.

[76] Ibid. 71–2.

[77] The voting qualification for the counties consisted in 'the possession of freehold property valued for the land tax at 40 shillings per annum', though '[f]or electoral purposes the term 40s. freehold was widely interpreted', and included 'leases for lives; annuities, rent charges, and mortgages based on freehold property; ecclesiastical benefices; and appointments in Government service': see J. Brooke, *The House of Commons 1754–1790: Introductory Survey* (Oxford, 1968), 1.

[78] *Rights, Representation, and Reform*, 86. Bentham recognized that the discrepancy was somewhat mitigated in that, during a general election, it was not physically possible to vote in more than three or four of those counties, even though polling might continue for several days, and might take place at slightly different times in different counties.

were it thought serious enough to warrant a remedy, would be to nominate a deputy who would attend the sittings, but would only have the right of voting or speaking in the absence of the principal.[79] But far from advocating any radical reform, Bentham was prepared to excuse these defects and inconsistencies, for what was important was 'l'heureux résultat général en fait de gouvernement bon ou au moins passable, que le hasard a tiré de ce chaos rempli de détails qui sembleroient si peu propres à produire de tels effets' ('the happy general result with respect to a good or at least a passable government, which chance has drawn from this chaos full of details which seemed so unlikely to produce such effects').[80] Bentham did not at this point advocate an extension of the franchise—indeed, his opposition to plural voting would, to a small extent, have had the effect of reducing the number of 'electors'.

In jottings probably written around the same time, in which Bentham drew up an account of the advantages and disadvantages of the British electoral system, together with proposals for reform, his caution is again revealed. His main recommendation was that voting should take place in parishes by means of the secret ballot, as he recommended for France in 'Considérations sur la Composition des États-Généraux'. This would obviate the expense, bribery, drunkenness, and general disorder which elections tended to produce, as well as liberate voters from the 'influence of will on will'; that is, from their dependence on patrons. He listed one particular advantage of the British system: 'fournir des sujets capables au moyen des nominations particulières' ('to supply able subjects by means of particular nominations'). Bentham probably had in mind the election of men of talent for pocket or rotten boroughs, under the patronage of some influential aristocrat or wealthy commoner. That he was, at this time, by no means committed to a democratic suffrage is confirmed by his willingness to consider both the advantages and disadvantages of 'the influence of the people'. Their influence was welcome in that it tended to secure the execution of the laws, to secure contentment and tranquillity, and to help produce useful reforms, but unwelcome in that it tended to subject the government to popular prejudices.[81]

Yet soon afterwards in the autumn of 1789, possibly stimulated by drafting '*Projet* of a Constitutional Code for France', Bentham advocated wide-ranging measures of electoral reform in Britain. In fragmentary material and notes under the general heading of 'Parliamentary Reform', he put forward the most extensive suggestions for political reform which he was to propose before 1809.[82] He stated that the British Constitution, though good in comparison with an

[79] *Rights, Representation, and Reform*, 120. Bentham made a similar point in '*Projet* of a Constitutional Code for France' (ibid. 244): 'In the English Representation where every thing has been decided by chance and nothing by reflection: every thing at some barbarous and unexperienced period, nothing in an enlightened and cultivated age, two Members come from the same district in all counties and in most Boroughs.' Bentham did, however, approve of the absence of any provincial restrictions on the choice of electors. He noted, for instance, that some of the best minds from Ireland, despite her legislative independence, were returned to the British House of Commons. See ibid. 92.

[80] Ibid. 86. [81] UC clxx. 46. [82] UC cxxvii. 6.

absolute monarchy or an absolute aristocracy, was bad in comparison with 'a well-organized commonwealth'. The problems centred on the electoral system. The suffrage was too narrow and too dependent on landed property, which aggravated inequality and strengthened 'the seductive power of wealth'. The enormous inequality between electoral districts, both in terms of the number of voters and geographical extent, meant that many men did not exercise their vote on account of the great expense in terms of money and time involved, while the crowds which gathered at the polls caused disorder, delay, quarrels, and tumults.[83] He continued to advocate the secret ballot and recommended that voting should take place on a single day in each parish. He further recommended that the voting qualification be simplified, small electoral districts be introduced, and canvassing be prohibited, thereby reducing the expense and disorder of elections. Bentham regarded the secret ballot as a measure of central importance. He noted that the practice of public voting had been defended on the grounds that every elector was a trustee for his co-electors as well as for himself, and his vote should be cast openly so that he would be influenced by their opinion, and punished by their censure in case of misconduct. He rejected this argument on the grounds that it was crucial that the elector voted according to what he thought best for his own personal interest, not for the interest of some other person or persons whose interest was not the public interest, but who had it in their power to make him suffer. The point was that the interest of the majority of persons could not be separated from the interest of the whole. So long as each person was free to vote for his own interest, the promotion of the public interest would result.[84] As he had for France, Bentham proposed annual elections. This measure 'would not be innovation but restoration', since parliaments had originally been called for some momentary purpose, and almost immediately dissolved. The relative permanency of Parliament had been brought about by the King, not by the constituents, and against the wishes of the delegates themselves. Mischief had never arisen from parliaments of short duration, but had from those of long duration.[85] Furthermore, the franchise should be extended to all who could read (though presumably not to females), and eligibility for election should be made equally extensive by the abolition of the property qualification for MPs.[86] These measures, Bentham promised, would prevent the election of 'unfit' MPs, and result in the election of men of probity and talent. Unsatisfactory MPs were returned under the existing system because the choice lay in the hands of ministers, or in the hands of a few individuals who either nominated

[83] UC cxxvii. 7. [84] *Rights, Representation, and Reform*, 428–31.

[85] UC cxxvii. 9–10. Bentham had in mind the Long Parliament, which had sat from 1640 until its forcible dissolution by Oliver Cromwell in 1653.

[86] Bentham criticized the property qualification for MPs as an aristocratical device 'to keep out low fellows, who wish to serve their country and know how', for the sake of 'young noblemen and gentlemen who know as little about the matter as they care': see UC clxx. 169. His own ambitions to be returned for Parliament (see pp. 104–6 below) were perhaps at the back of his mind.

their own connections without regard to their ability or sold their votes, and because electors tended to be unduly influenced by personal solicitation instead of public reputation (a problem which would be remedied by the prohibition of canvassing).[87] The parameters of radical political reform in Britain had been established by the programme of the Westminster Committee put forward in 1780, which called for universal manhood suffrage, annual parliaments, equal electoral districts, secret ballot, exclusion of placemen, payment of MPs, and abolition of the property qualification for MPs.[88] Bentham's advocacy of universal manhood suffrage subject to a literacy test, annual parliaments, the secret ballot, equal electoral districts, and the abolition of the property qualification for MPs, constituted, even by the standard of the programme of the Westminster Committee, a radical agenda.

Bentham's fragmentary writings recommending parliamentary reform, and in particular electoral reform, were restricted in terms of chronology to the autumn of 1789, amidst the excitement occasioned by the rapid and fundamental political change taking place in France. His flirtation with political reform which, by the standards of the time, was certainly radical (and, therefore, democratic) was also extremely brief. He had, perhaps, begun to doubt the desirability of any wide-ranging measure of reform by the autumn of 1791 when he wrote: 'One of the best as well as characteristic features of the English Constitution is its perfectibility: a constitution which has [been] travelling on the road to perfection for so many centuries.'[89] Thereafter, the increasing violence of events in France appears to have shocked Bentham, as it did many of his contemporaries, and produced both a reaction against the perceived dangers of democratic government, and a more acute appreciation of the advantages of the stable government enjoyed in Britain. In particular, the insurrection of 10 August 1792, when the Tuileries was attacked and the royal family forced to flee, the September Massacres (Bentham was particularly distressed by the stoning to death of La Rochefoucauld),[90] the success of the French armies in Europe following the Battle of Valmy on 20 September 1792, and the abolition of the monarchy two days later, extinguished most of whatever sympathy for the Revolution still remained in Britain. The execution of Louis XVI on 21 January 1793 was the prelude to the French declaration of war on Britain on 1 February 1793. It was in these circumstances that Bentham became, if anything, anti-democratic. He identified the 'characteristic properties' of democratic government as ignorance, violence, extravagance, discontent, frequent wars, and danger of violent revolution.[91] The feature which he criticized most severely was the

[87] *Rights, Representation, and Reform*, 428–9.

[88] See E. C. Black, *The Association: British Extraparliamentary Political Organization 1769–1793* (Cambridge, Mass., 1963), 60–1; Christie, *Wilkes, Wyvill, and Reform*, 80–4, 107–9; Cannon, *Parliamentary Reform*, 82; and Dickinson, *Liberty and Property*, 220–1.

[89] UC cxlvi. 17.

[90] See Bentham to Lansdowne, 10 Sep. 1792, *Correspondence*, iv. 394.

[91] UC xliv. 5. Anarchy and civil war were regarded by many as typical features of a democracy: see Dickinson, *Liberty and Property*, 289–90.

ignorance, or lack of intelligence, of the people to conduct the business of government. Democracy, and particularly direct democracy, obliterated the division of functions between legislators and other members of the community: 'You employ one man to make laws for you as you employ another man to make shoes.' Even amongst the well-educated there were few who were 'equal to the business of government'. Yet in a democracy everyone needed to take an interest in and understand public affairs: 'To choose men he must judge them—to judge them he must judge their measures—to judge their measures he must understand what are the measures that in every case ought to have been adopted.' Such intelligence was beyond the capacity of the people: 'The people are all *will*—they have no reason, no understanding.' They were capable of dealing only with simple propositions, and even then were dictated to by their feelings, and in particular by their attachments to personalities. The slogan 'Wilkes and Liberty' was a case in point.[92]

Bentham argued that the financial savings expected from a democratic government were illusory.[93] The waste under the most wasteful monarchical government would be defrayed by a few days' labour on the part of the working classes, whereas a democratic government would require the labour of all citizens of all classes to be employed in the business of government: 'Either the major part of the whole labour of the state must be thus bestowed or those who take time to understand the business must be governed and outvoted by those who do not and can not take time to understand it.'[94] He did not accept that the United States was an appropriate model of democratic government in the European context. Social conditions in the United States were so far different from France (and presumably Britain as well) that democratic government there produced very different effects from those it would produce in Europe. The population of the United States was composed mainly of farmers, whose 'business keeps them separate and quiet', and who were more interested in domestic concerns than in 'the feeble share which any one man can expect to get in government'. There were no very large towns with mobs large enough to influence the whole country, nor were there 'swarms of professional men out of practice—Lawyers—Players—Abbés—News-writers—Artists'.[95] He admitted that '[t]hat government which the people like best is best', but argued that the British people 'would not

[92] UC xliv. 2. John Wilkes had posed as a champion of popular liberty against the arbitrary power of government after he had been expelled from the House of Commons in January 1764, and, having fled to France, been convicted of blasphemy and seditious libel and then declared an outlaw. In 1768 he had returned to England and, having been elected to Parliament for the county of Middlesex on four occasions, had each time had his election declared invalid by the House of Commons. For a detailed study of Wilkes see P. D. G. Thomas, *John Wilkes: A Friend to Liberty* (Oxford, 1996).

[93] Bentham here disagreed with Thomas Paine, who had calculated in *The Rights of Man. Part the Second. Combining Principle and Practice* (London, 1792), that an enormous reduction in expense and thence taxation would ensue from the adoption of a republican form of government. Bentham would later change his mind.

[94] UC xliv. 5.

[95] UC xliv. 2.

be so easy' under a republican government as under their existing one, and indeed might not even like a republican government so much.[96] Finally, he suggested that in a popular government the vote was hardly worth having: the greater the extent of the suffrage, the less valuable the right, for each man's vote had less effect.[97]

Bentham now found much to say in defence of the British Constitution. First, he emphasized its capacity for improvement. The criticism that it had 'swerved from the design of its institution, from its first principles' was besides the point, since it had never had any first principles.[98] The Constitution had begun 'with a very bad system—bad in itself', but one which had been 'good only in as far as it involved the possibility of changing into the present'. Improvement had rendered it 'better now than it was yesterday' and 'better yesterday than the day before'. Bentham predicted 'that it will be better still tomorrow, and still better again the day after tomorrow', although he cautioned that 'the tomorrow and the after tomorrow may be a good while a-coming'.[99] Second, under the British Constitution, the opinion of the people was not ignored. Indeed, noted Bentham, it was the 'excellence' of the Constitution that 'it does all that can be wished for from the interference of the people with so little actual interference'.[100] For instance, the war which the British government had threatened to undertake against Russia over possession of the Black Sea fortress of Ochakov had been abandoned on account of 'a slight expression of dissatisfaction on the part of the people'. Indeed, this example pointed to an important argument against democratic reform. When war was 'mediated by a Royal Administration, the people have a negative upon it', but when war was demanded by the people, there was no one to restrain them.[101] Third, the electoral system, under which it was possible to be returned to Parliament by means other than the suffrage of the 'ill-informed classes', placed government in the hands of the 'well-informed classes', and thereby provided a security against anarchy and civil war. At the same time, security was provided against bad government: periodical elections to Parliament secured the responsibility of governors to the body of the people; the liberty of public assembly and petitioning allowed the people to communicate

[96] UC clxx. 176.

[97] UC clxx. 178. The theme is taken up by M. James, 'Bentham on Voter Rationality', *The Bentham Newsletter*, 10 (1982), 4–7.

[98] It was a commonplace amongst radicals to complain that Britain's 'ancient constitution', dating from Anglo-Saxon times, had been corrupted by the monarchy and aristocracy: see Dickinson, *Liberty and Property*, 298.

[99] UC clxx. 178.

[100] UC clxx. 173.

[101] UC clxx. 173. Bentham, no doubt, had in mind his own 'expression of dissatisfaction' with regard to the threatened war against Russia which had appeared in four letters, signed 'Anti-Machiavel', published in the *Public Advertiser*, 15, 16 June 1789 (Letter I); 3, 4 July 1789 (Letter II); 11 July 1789 (Letter III); and 23 July 1789 (Letter IV). See S. Conway, 'Bentham versus Pitt: Jeremy Bentham and British Foreign Policy 1789', *Historical Journal*, 30 (1987), 791–809. Bentham later argued that democracies were peace-loving, whereas monarchs treated war as 'a game': see e.g. *First Principles*, 129, 163.

their views to one another; and the King was unable to act without the concurrence of ministers, while all executive officers, except the King, were legally responsible for their actions (a consequence of the doctrine that 'the King can do no wrong').[102] Bentham even advanced positive reasons in support of the House of Lords, an institution which he had earlier been prepared merely to tolerate on the grounds that it did no harm. Its 'use' was to 'give elevation' to the King, by increasing the number of intermediate bodies between King and people. He was 'glad' that there were various ranks of aristocracy, and would not have been sorry to have seen 'Arch-Dukes' added to the list. While there was no cure for the ignorance inseparable from popular governments—'instruction' operated too slowly to count for anything in this respect—there was a cure for the lack of public spirit in aristocrats, namely connecting their interest with their duty, though he did not detail the particular measures by which this might be achieved.[103]

Although Bentham criticized the democrats, this by no means led him to identify himself with Burke's appeal to prejudice as a defence of the British polity. While he complained that '[t]he system of the democrats is absurd and dangerous: for it subjugates the well-informed to the ill-informed *classes* of mankind', he saw little to choose between the democrats on the one side and Burke on the other, for Burke's system 'subjugates the well-informed to the ill-informed *ages*'.[104] Bentham also noted that the consequence of Burke's views would be 'the legislature of a country enslaved for ever to a past Assembly of dead barbarians, without a possibility of emancipation'. He continued: 'Indefeasible obligations as absurd, and more revolting to the imagination and the passions, and highly mischievous though not quite so mischievous as indefeasible rights'.[105] Bentham did not abandon his commitment to reform in general, but argued that political reform was not advisable in the circumstances of the time:

> I am no enemy to improvement, or if the word please better to innovation. I am a projector—an avowed advocate for projectors: I am as far as wishes and endeavours go an innovator: my whole life has been, and what remains of it will be, devoted to the pursuit.
>
> The longer I live the less reason I expect to see any considerable part of my projects to take effect in my lifetime.
>
> It is with this way of thinking and turn of mind that I stand forth and say notwithstanding—No change in the constitution.

Indeed, given Bentham's 'turn of mind and way of thinking', he speculated that his opposition to 'the proposed change in government' might carry additional

[102] UC xliv. 4. This list echoes the characteristics of a free government which Bentham had identified in *A Fragment on Government*, 485: see pp. 250–1 below.

[103] UC clxx. 173, 176. Bentham later advocated the abolition of all titles of honour, or 'factitious dignities' as he termed them: see e.g. *First Principles*, 299–324.

[104] UC xliv. 5.

[105] UC cviii. 114. Bentham could not have been more in agreement with Paine (*Rights of Man*, 9), who stated: 'Every age and generation must be as free to act for itself, *in all cases*, as the ages and generations which preceded it. The vanity and presumption of governing beyond the grave, is the most ridiculous and insolent of all tyrannies.'

weight.[106] In similar vein, he commented: 'No man in the three kingdoms has a fuller comprehension of the imperfections of the law: no man a more painful and indignant sense of them: no man has been more assiduous in investigating them: no man less sanguine in his expectations of seeing them voluntarily amended. It is with this body of grievances before my eyes that I say notwithstanding—No change in the Constitution—no Reform in Parliament.'[107] Having considered what the best constitution for both Britain and France would be were it possible to start anew, he remained unconvinced that Britain would do better to adopt the new one: 'If such has been my opinion with regard to what appeared to me the best possible of all new ones, it may be imagined what it was with regard to any other less approaching to perfection: if such has been my opinion even of a work of my own, it may be imagined what I should expect beforehand from the work of any one else.'[108]

Bentham's title for a proposed essay, 'Rottenness no Corruption—or a Defence of Rotten Boroughs',[109] has been seen as an indication of the strength of his reaction to political reform.[110] Yet, even at the height of his enthusiasm for reform, he had never totally condemned the existence of such boroughs, for they provided men of talent with a potential route into Parliament.[111] Furthermore, in the general election of 1790 Bentham had entertained hopes of being returned by Lansdowne (as Shelburne had now become, following his advancement in the peerage) for one or other of the pocket boroughs of Calne or Chipping Wycombe.[112] When Bentham realized that Lansdowne was not prepared to return him, he wrote a long letter accusing the Marquis of breach of promise, and outlined his views concerning the proper relationship between an MP and his patron.[113] Having explained that all that he had 'coveted for these many years' had been 'the opportunity of trying whether I could make myself of any use to the country and to mankind in the track of *legislation*', he complained that the MPs whom Lansdowne had returned were 'three men who amongst them all neither possess nor pretend to possess a grain either of affection or of what we mean by *principle*... and whose principles, if they had any would be as opposite

[106] UC clxx. 176. He had 'avowed' his support for projectors in *Defence of Usury; Shewing the Impolicy of the Present Legal Restraints on the terms of Pecuniary Bargains. In a Series of Letters to a Friend. To which is added, A Letter to Adam Smith, Esq: LL,D. On the Discouragements opposed by the above Restraints to the Progress of Inventive Industry* (London, 1787) (Bowring, iii. 1–29).

[107] UC clxx. 173.

[108] UC clxx. 178. As for the French attempts at constitution-making, Bentham remarked: 'In legislation, how deep they have sunk below the profoundest ignorance, how much the maturest design that could be furnished by the united powers of the whole nation has proved inferior in wisdom and felicity in comparison of the chance-medley of the British Constitution.' See UC cxlvi. 178 (written in 1795 for 'Nonsense upon Stilts').

[109] UC xliv. 3 (8 July 1795).

[110] Burns, 'Bentham and the French Revolution', 110; and Dinwiddy, *Bentham*, 12.

[111] See *Rights, Representation, and Reform*, 434.

[112] Bentham's expectations had been raised by a conversation with Lansdowne on 27 June 1789: see UC ix. 92, printed in Bowring, x. 214.

[113] Bentham to Lansdowne, 24 Aug. 1790, *Correspondence*, iv. 145–70.

to your own as those of any three men you could meet with any where'.[114] It was the duty of MPs 'to speak the sentiments of their electors', or else those of 'the Borough-master who puts them in'. Lansdowne's MPs would neither speak his sentiments nor those of the people of Calne or Chipping Wycombe:

Children a man does not choose: he must take them such as God sends them, with such opinions as they have. But Members for his Boroughs surely a man might choose, and with them the sentiments which are to pass in the world for his. There are two ways of providing for the exactness of such a representation. One is, to take low-minded men of no principles or of opposite principles, and make them swallow your's: another is to look out for high-minded men whose principles agree with your's already. This last I humbly conceive to be not only the most dignified course but the surest. Parliament surely is not the only field in which work is better[115] done by freemen than by slaves. What is your course?—You take narrow-minded men and leave them in possession of their own no-principles without a hope or a thought of mending or changing them.[116]

In contrast to the candidates actually returned, Bentham claimed that he would have been of considerable value to Lansdowne, especially in the light of his publicly and privately acknowledged 'faculty of exhausting what can be said on either side of any question', his ability to devise 'expedients of all sorts', and his ability to distinguish right from wrong and a good measure from a bad. He envisaged that his presence in Parliament would facilitate Lansdowne's return to office.[117] Bentham concluded by asking Lansdowne to give him 'an absolute and unconditional promise that I *shall* sit in the *next* Parliament'.[118]

Lansdowne replied that he had never offered Bentham a seat in Parliament. He had indeed explored the possibility with him, but had concluded 'that the same reasons which made you decline the practice of your Profession applied in great measure to Parliament'. Lansdowne had had his conclusion confirmed many times in conversations where Bentham had insisted on maintaining his 'perfect Independence'. He was prepared to consider Bentham for one of his seats in the future, but stressed that he himself had little ambition to return to office: 'I wish well to what I call the New Principles, and will promote them as far as a Free Declaration of my own Sentiments in public or private will go. But Politics have given long since too much way to Philosophy, [for me] to give myself further trouble about them.'[119] It is worthy of remark that Lansdowne assumed that Bentham would, by being returned to Parliament on his interest,

[114] Ibid. 152, 155. The three members in question were John Jervis, Joseph Jekyll, and John Morris. The fourth member was Lord Wycombe, Lansdowne's elder son, upon whose return Bentham did not comment.

[115] The printed text reads 'is not better', but this appears to contradict the evident sense of the passage.

[116] *Correspondence*, iv. 160–2.

[117] Ibid. 167–8. Lansdowne had, of course, been leader of the administration in 1782–3.

[118] Ibid. 170.

[119] Lansdowne to Bentham, 27, 28 Aug. 1790, ibid. 180–1. Bentham, no doubt sadder and wiser, responded that 'parliament may go to the devil': see Bentham to Lansdowne, *c.*30 Aug. 1790, ibid. 183.

forfeit his 'Independence'. Moreover, Bentham himself admitted that the role of the MP was to represent the views of the patron, and criticized Lansdowne's choice of MPs on this very ground. It is true that Bentham did not think that he would be acting in an unprincipled manner given that his own principles were in accord with those of Lansdowne. Nevertheless, the fact still remained that Bentham was prepared to set himself to work on Lansdowne's agenda, and that less than a year after proposing his most wide-ranging measures of electoral reform, he was harbouring serious hopes of being returned for a pocket borough at the nomination of an aristocratic patron. However desirable he may have thought electoral reform, it seems that his priority was to work within the existing political system as a 'projector' of legislation.

V

Confirmation that Bentham did not remain a tacit democrat following a 'conversion' to democracy at the time of the French Revolution, as Mack suggests he did, comes from his proposals for the education of children in the pauper panopticons which he hoped to establish. In material written in 1797 or 1798 for his unfinished essay 'Pauper Management Improved', he listed the subjects which should form part of the curriculum. As well as natural history, chemistry, mechanics, mathematics, and medicine,[120] he recommended the teaching of 'Morality Public—Politics and Constitutional Law'. He admitted that the proposal to teach 'Law in general and Constitutional Law in particular . . . to the lowest class of the Poor' might at first glance appear 'full of absurdity and extravagance'. The proposal would, however, appear more reasonable when it was realized that the 'instruction' would consist in 'a sermon, and that a short one, on the text: study to be quiet and mind your own business'. The 'practical' point of the instruction would be to dispose the pupils 'to be contented with their lot', on the grounds that their 'condition' was 'as favourable to happiness as any other', and '[t]hat if it were not, no efforts which they could use by the display of their collective force would have any tendency to mend it'. The paupers would be told that they should be content because they were themselves incapable of improving the government under which they lived; that they should refrain from 'turbulence' because it was impossible for any more than a small part of the community to be exempt from the need to labour; and that more 'uneasiness' would result to the community as a whole if those who had not been 'born and bred to labour' were forced to exchange places with those who had. Bentham wished to emphasize the disadvantages which would attend any attempt forcibly to redistribute property: there would inevitably be a struggle, which would result in the loss of life and the destruction of property; even if the

[120] UC cliii. 121–31.

property of the country were equally distributed, it would be no more than six months before people were once again obliged to labour; an equal division of property could only persist for a very short time, since events would almost immediately re-create inequalities; and if property was to be redistributed again, this would in effect destroy property, for it was only if a man was confident of being able to retain the produce of his labour that he would 'put himself to the trouble'. The paupers would also be reminded of the enormity of the task which would face them in bringing about the redistribution in question: 'the task consists in nothing less than in taking to pieces the whole system of government as it exists at present, and putting together a new one', which would require new systems of civil, penal, financial, ecclesiastical, constitutional, military, and international law. They would then have to persuade 'the clear majority' of their fellow inhabitants to join in the scheme.[121] It appears that Bentham's fears about placing political power in the hands of the propertyless, which had led him to deny the vote to the vast majority of the population of France in his writings of late 1788 and early 1789, but which he had then put aside in the autumn of 1789, had re-emerged in full vigour.

Bentham's advocacy of electoral reform in Britain was, therefore, confined to a few fragmentary notes, and to a brief period in the autumn of 1789. He was tentatively exploring possibilities; he had not developed a systematic argument in favour of democratic reform, even though he was clearly aware that the principle of utility implied an equal right or claim to happiness. It is important to note that his reasons for wanting political reform underwent a profound change between 1789 and 1809, even if the content of many of the measures he later recommended in relation to electoral reform was anticipated in the autumn of 1789. At the time of the French Revolution he was committed to working within the existing political system to bring about reform; by 1809 he had come to recognize that the rulers of Britain, whether Whigs or Tories, had no interest in promoting reform, but rather a 'sinister interest' in maintaining the existing political, legal, and ecclesiastical establishments. If any of his projects were to be realized, it would only be in the wake of radical political reform. It was the emergence of sinister interest, a product of his own disappointing experiences as a 'projector' of reform, rather than the events of the French Revolution, which would ultimately be responsible for pushing him into a novel form of radical politics. To put this another way, it is generally recognized that the onset of the French Revolution led to a reaction against political reform, both in terms of the suppression of radical activity and the production of a robust intellectual defence of the British Constitution.[122] If it is the case that one of main influences

[121] UC cliii. 133–8. Bentham's views had much in common with the socially conservative sentiments expressed by William Paley in *Reasons for Contentment; addressed to the Labouring Part of the British Public* (London, 1793).

[122] See e.g. Dickinson, *Liberty and Property*, 270–318; H. T. Dickinson, *British Radicalism and the French Revolution 1789–1815* (Oxford, 1985), 25–42; and Christie, *Stress and Stability*.

bringing about political, legal, and ecclesiastical reform in Britain in the years following the Napoleonic Wars was that of philosophic radicalism, and if philosophic radicalism was in large part the creation of Bentham,[123] it might be argued that the impact of the French Revolution was to delay political reform in a further way, namely by delaying the creation and propagation of the utilitarian case for democracy. Bentham was edging towards the development of a democratic utilitarian politics until the excesses of the French Revolution persuaded him to abandon this course, and instead to defend the existing institutions of the British polity. The intellectual impetus which Bentham might have given to radical reform in the early 1790s had to await the publication of *Plan of Parliamentary Reform* over twenty-five years later. Bentham himself, as we shall see, made the 'transition', or underwent the 'conversion', to political radicalism somewhat earlier.

[123] It is arguable that W. Thomas, *The Philosophic Radicals: Nine Studies in Theory and Practice 1817–1841* (Oxford, 1979), underestimates the influence of utilitarian doctrine during this period, and that J. Hamburger, *Intellectuals in Politics: John Stuart Mill and the Philosophic Radicals* (New Haven, 1965), underestimates Bentham's importance to, and influence on, the philosophic radicals.

5

The Emergence of Sinister Interest

I

For a brief period in the autumn of 1789 Bentham had been prepared to advocate a democratic franchise for France, and to contemplate an extensive measure of electoral reform in Britain. As events in France had taken an increasingly extreme course, he had dropped his proposals for reform, and emphasized instead the benefits of the security and stability provided by the British Constitution. Bentham was clearly not permanently 'converted' to democracy at this time, and for more than a decade after the September Massacres and the death of La Rochefoucauld had so outraged him he showed no desire for major political change.[1] The critical development in Bentham's political thought was not brought about by the French Revolution, but by the emergence of the notion of sinister interest,[2] from which he eventually drew the conclusion that democracy was essential to the achievement of good government. Bentham used the phrase 'sinister interest' as early as 1797 in his writings on the poor laws, but he only began to use it regularly in 1804 in his writings on judicial evidence and procedure. The notion which the phrase represented may have been a product of his despair and disappointment at what he took to be the effective rejection of the panopticon prison scheme by the government.

By the summer of 1802 Bentham had become exasperated by the treatment he had received at the hands of the successive administrations of Pitt and Addington. He complained that, although the legislature had, by the Penitentiary Act of 1794,[3] authorized the construction of a panopticon prison, the executive, in defiance of Parliament's wishes, had deliberately blocked the scheme.[4] He

[1] See pp. 100–4 above.

[2] Bentham later explained his choice of the word 'sinister' in this context: 'Like *bad*, *sinister* is here employed for the expression of disapprobation. When *motive* is the name of the subject or the object marked for reprobation, *bad* is the adjunct most commonly, though *sinister* also is sometimes, employed for that purpose: when *interest* is the name given to the subject or object, *sinister* is the only one of the two names that is given to the adjunct. Of sinister *motives* we hear sometimes: of bad interests never.' See UC civ. 346 (29 May 1811).

[3] 34 Geo. III, c. 84.

[4] On the rivalry between executive and Parliament in the context of the panopticon affair see L. J. Hume, 'Bentham's Panopticon: An Administrative History', *Historical Studies*, 15 (1973), 703–21, and 16 (1974), 36–54.

complained of 'the eight years provocation' which he had 'endured',[5] 'the course of perfidy' which ministers had pursued and 'the variegated mass' of 'injury' which he had suffered,[6] and of being subjected to 'underhand practices—the system of long-spun and elaborate, yet always transparent treachery', 'transparent frauds', and 'barbarous oppressions'.[7] He was genuinely bitter, and particularly so towards the Home Secretary, Pelham.[8] He received confirmation of what he had long suspected, that the government was not prepared to proceed with the panopticon, in a letter of 15 June 1803 from Sir Charles Bunbury, who had met with Pelham to put the case for it. Having listened 'very patiently', Pelham had said 'that the Judges did not appear to wish it to be carried into effect, and he did not suppose Mr Addington would furnish the money necessary to proceed with it at present'.[9] Bentham was unconvinced that the scheme had been rejected on account of objections from the judges. In his view, the real reason was 'the force of the secret influence' of the Grosvenor family.[10] Bentham was alluding to the fact that the main difficulty which he had faced throughout the panopticon saga had been the acquisition of a suitable piece of land on which to build the prison. He had initially attempted to purchase land at Battersea Rise, but had been frustrated by the opposition of the leaseholder, Earl Spencer, who did not want the value of his land blighted. Bentham's attempt in the summer of 1796 to acquire a site at Hanging Wood, near Woolwich Dock Yard, had likewise been thwarted by local landholders. He had then turned to Tothill Fields, where he had been frustrated by the opposition of the Grosvenor family, whose residence, Belgrave House, was close by. In November 1799 Bentham did eventually purchase land at Millbank, but he always considered the site to be too small.[11] It was in November 1797, in the context of expressing his frustration at what he saw as the self-interested interference of the Grosvenor family, who had exploited their connections with ministers and blocked the building of the panopticon at Tothill Fields, that Bentham used the phrases 'sinister influence' and 'sinister interest'. Recommending the building of a series of pauper panopticons which would be managed by a joint-stock company, and referring to the difficulties which would be faced in procuring sites because of the opposition of local landowners, he noted that '[t]he claims of justice and utility' were likely to be sacrificed to those of 'favour and connection': 'I am no stranger to this subject. I have a privilege derived from experience—long and dear bought experience. I know that on this ground neither

5 Bentham to Sir Charles Bunbury, 9 Aug. 1802, *Correspondence*, vii. 72.
6 Bentham to Bunbury, Letter II of 9 Aug. 1802, ibid. 74.
7 Bentham to Charles Abbot, 3 Sept. 1802, ibid. 108, 111.
8 See e.g. Bentham to Bunbury, 21 Aug. 1802, ibid. 85–7.
9 Bunbury to Bentham, 15 June 1803, ibid. 240.
10 Bentham to Bunbury, 17 June 1803, ibid. 240–1.
11 The whole sorry story is recounted in Semple, *Bentham's Prison*, 166–253. It is worth noting that Bentham later became convinced that the failure of panopticon had been due to the personal opposition of George III: see e.g. Bentham to 3rd Marquis of Lansdowne, 11 Jan. 1828, *Correspondence*, vol. xii, ed. L. O'Sullivan and C. Fuller (Oxford, 2006), 437–8.

Acts of Parliament, nor acts of the 12 Judges, nor ministerial engagements, nor ministerial decisions, nor all together, can stand against sinister influence. I have acquired but too good a right to speak with precision on this subject.'[12] Earlier in the same sequence of material, in relation to company management, he had referred to the danger of 'sinister interests' acting 'in opposition to the *common* interest', though he later replaced the word 'sinister' with 'particular'.[13]

It seems plausible to suggest that Bentham's search for the reason why the panopticon scheme had failed led him to conclude that it was due to the influence of sinister interest. He went on to apply this insight in his writings on the law of evidence and procedure, on which he began work in 1803.[14] The sinister interest of the legal profession had brought the law into its present deplorable state. Bentham then came to realize that the notion of sinister interest was no less applicable to the political establishment than to the legal establishment. The only effective means of producing that dependence of rulers on subjects which was essential to good government, and thereby negate the influence of sinister interest, was a democratic franchise. Hence Bentham's 'transition' to democracy followed from the emergence of sinister interest in his thought. Having said that, his 'transition' to democracy did not entail a contemporaneous 'transition' to republicanism: that further step, as we shall see,[15] was related to developments in Bentham's writings on codification.

II

The emergence of sinister interest did not, of course, turn Bentham into an advocate of law reform. He had long been highly critical of the English legal system, and had long advocated far-reaching reform. In *A Fragment on Government* he had announced his desire to reform morals, and in particular the law, in a way which would be analogous to advances in the physical sciences: 'if there be room for making, and if there be use in publishing, *discoveries* in the *natural* world, surely there is not much less room for making, nor much less use in proposing, *reformation* in the *moral*'. Alluding to Priestley's experiments with air, he remarked: 'If it be of importance and use to us to know the principles of the element we breathe, surely it is not of much less importance nor of much less use to comprehend the principles, and endeavour at the improvement of those *laws*, by which alone we breathe it in security.' It was this context which

[12] UC cliii. 283. The corresponding marginal summary sheet, at UC cliv. 79, is dated 5 November 1797.

[13] The quoted passage appears in a marginal summary paragraph on UC cliii. 278, and also appears on the marginal summary sheet at UC cliv. 79, where it has been copied by Bentham.

[14] The earliest reference to Bentham's being engaged on such a subject appears in a letter of 31 May 1803 from Romilly to Dumont: see *Memoirs of the Life of Sir Samuel Romilly, written by himself; with a selection from his correspondence. Edited by his Sons*, 2nd edn., 3 vols. (London, 1840), ii. 106–7.

[15] See pp. 247–8 below.

gave his criticism of Blackstone its urgency. This 'Author of great name' had avowed himself 'a determined and persevering enemy' of reform, and so it was necessary to undermine the reputation and influence of his works.[16] Like Blackstone, the legal profession in general, having been taught 'to accept of any thing as reason, and to yield the same abject and indiscriminating homage to the Laws here, which is paid to the despot elsewhere', were 'impotent to every enterprize of improvement':

> A passive and enervate race, ready to swallow any thing, and to acquiesce in any thing: with intellects incapable of distinguishing right from wrong, and with affections alike indifferent to either: insensible, short-sighted, obstinate: lethargic, yet liable to be driven into convulsions by false terrors: deaf to the voice of reason and public utility: obsequious only to the whisper of interest, and to the beck of power.

Given that most men were reluctant to challenge 'the Colossus of authority', there was little justification for condemning, as Blackstone did, those few who were 'occupied in bringing rude establishments to the test of polished reason'.[17] In relation to Blackstone's criticism of the statute of 1730 by which legal proceedings were to be rendered in English rather than Law Latin,[18] Bentham retorted:

> The case is this. A large portion of the body of the Law was, by the bigotry or the artifice of Lawyers, locked up in an illegible character, and in a foreign tongue. The statute he mentions obliged them to give up their hieroglyphics, and to restore the native language to its rights.
>
> This was doing much; but it was not doing every thing. Fiction, tautology, technicality, circuity, irregularity, inconsistency remain. But above all the pestilential breath of Fiction poisons the sense of every instrument it comes near.
>
> The consequence is, that the Law, and especially that part of it which comes under the topic of Procedure, *still* wants much of being generally intelligible.

Blackstone had complained that the change had led to 'inconveniences', namely the inability of young lawyers to read the old records, and the increased cost of legal documents, English being more verbose than Latin. Bentham retorted: 'After all, what seems to be the real evil, notwithstanding [Blackstone's] unwillingness to believe it, is, that by means of this alteration, men at large are in a somewhat better way of knowing what their Lawyers are about: and that a disinterested and enterprising Legislator, should happily such an one arise, would now with somewhat less difficulty be able to see before him.'[19] Bentham's programme of reform consisted in the replacement of the 'technical arrangement' of English law, as described by Blackstone, with a 'natural arrangement'. As we have seen,[20] a natural arrangement of 'the materials of any science' was one which 'takes such properties to characterize them by, as men in general are, by

[16] *A Fragment on Government*, 393–4. [17] Ibid. 402–3.

[18] See Blackstone, *Commentaries on the Laws of England*, iii. 322–3. The statute in question was 4 Geo. II, c. 26. [19] *A Fragment on Government*, 411–12 n.

[20] See pp. 52–3 above.

the common constitution of man's *nature*, disposed to attend to: such, in other words, as *naturally*, that is readily, engage, and firmly fix the attention of any one to whom they are pointed out'. The science of law, just like any other science, should be governed by the principle of utility, since the property of an action which most readily engaged and firmly fixed the attention of an observer was its tendency to produce happiness or unhappiness. In a natural arrangement, laws would be classified according to the actions which they prohibited. Such actions would be constituted into offences, which would themselves be classified according to their mischievousness. The only reason for constituting an action into an offence was the mischief which it produced: a bad law was one which prohibited conduct which was not mischievous, and would be seen to be such from the difficulty of finding a place for it in a natural arrangement. A technical arrangement, in contrast, was 'a sink that with equal facility will swallow any garbage that is thrown into it'. Offences which existed under English law but which were purely technical, for instance 'offences . . . against prerogative, with misprisions, contempts, felonies, præmunires', would either disappear altogether in a natural arrangement, 'or if, in deference to attachments too inveterate to be all at once dissolved, they were still to be indulged a place, they would be stationed in the corners and bye-places of the Synopsis: stationed, not as now to *give* light, but to *receive* it'. Except where unduly influenced by religious prejudice or 'what is called *sentiment* or *feeling*', men in general, when deciding whether to praise or condemn a law or institution, judged by the standard of utility. In contrast, 'Men of Law, corrupted by interests, or seduced by illusions, . . . have deviated from it much more frequently, and with much less reserve. Hence it is that such reasons as pass with Lawyers, and with no one else, have got the name of *technical* reasons; reasons peculiar to the *art*, peculiar to the profession.' The only consequences of a law in which men had any interest were pain and pleasure, and no man needed to go to a lawyer to know the meaning of pain and pleasure.[21]

In *A Fragment on Government* Bentham proposed a major reform of English law, both in form and substance, and blamed the legal profession for its unsatisfactory state. In Blackstone's case, 'the involuntary errors of the understanding' had led him to undertake the role of expositor, and 'the sinister bias of the *affections*' the role of censor, in an unsatisfactory manner. The deficiency in the role of expositor might be ignored since it produced 'little to excite, or at least to justify, resentment', but the deficiency in the role of censor required 'rigid censure'. Indeed, given that 'the discernment which enables a man to perceive, and . . . the courage which enables him to avow, the defects of a system of institutions' was of the same nature as 'that accuracy of conception which enables him to give a clear account of it', it would not be surprising, if the censorial department were 'filled with imbecillity', to see 'symptoms of kindred weakness'

[21] *A Fragment on Government*, 415–18.

in the expository. In Blackstone's *Commentaries on the Laws of England* the censorial and expository parts were 'intimately, and indeed, undistinguishably blended', though it had been the former which had provoked the criticism which Bentham had bestowed 'indiscriminately on the whole'.[22] While Bentham was strongly impressed with the deplorable state of English jurisprudence, and the unsatisfactory nature of Blackstone's account of it, the central problem he identified was that of 'discernment' or 'accuracy of conception'. It was the ignorance, and allied to that the deference to authority, of English lawyers, together with their interest in maintaining their income, which was to blame. Bentham had not yet developed a systematic account which linked the interest of lawyers to the abuses which characterized the law.

III

While Bentham's attitude to political reform fluctuated during the period of the French Revolution, he maintained a highly critical attitude towards the legal establishment. In other words, he saw no contradiction in advocating reform of the law and opposing reform of the political system. Indeed, he wrote a particularly stringent attack on the English legal system, *Truth versus Ashhurst; or, Law as it is, contrasted with what it is said to be*, in which he denounced the expense of litigation, in December 1792,[23] at a time when he had turned decidedly against political reform. In a charge delivered to the Grand Jury of Middlesex on 19 November 1792, Sir William Henry Ashhurst, Justice of King's Bench, stated that 'no man [is] so low as not to be within [the law's] protection'.[24] Bentham pointed out that the cost of a lawsuit was so great that most of the population were in practice deprived of recourse to the law, and that the cause of this cost was 'extortion, monopoly, useless formalities, law-gibberish, and law-taxes'. The judges not only received fees, but also set them, and furthermore enjoyed the patronage of other fee-receiving offices, whose value increased with the level of the fees. Even so, the money received by the judges themselves was 'nothing in comparison of what they see shared among their brethren of the trade,—their patrons, and bottle-companions, and relations and dependents'. As if this were not enough, 'session after session, the king is made to load the proceedings with taxes, denying justice to all who have not withal to pay them'. A man could not escape these costs by representing himself, even where not prohibited from doing so, rather than by going to a lawyer: 'The lies and nonsense, the law is stuffed with, form so thick a mist, that a plain man, nay, even a man of sense and learning, who is not in the trade, can see neither

22 *A Fragment on Government*, 404–5.

23 The work was eventually published in 1823.

24 See *Mr. Justice Ashhurst's Charge to the Grand Jury for the County of Middlesex*, printed by order of The Society for preserving Liberty and Property against Republicans and Levellers. Numerous versions of the *Charge* were printed.

through nor into it.' Procedures such as the bill of Middlesex, interrogatories in equity, and barring an entail were replete with lies. The lawyers would not allow 'an atom of this rubbish . . . to be cleared away', since '[i]t serves them as a fence to keep out interlopers'.[25]

Ashhurst claimed that 'we are not bound by any laws but such as are ordained by the virtual consent of the whole kingdom, and which every man has the means of knowing'.[26] To this Bentham responded that 'virtual' consent meant imaginary consent. Half of the law consisted of statute law, made by Parliament, 'and how small a part of the whole kingdom has anything to do with choosing parliament, you all know', while the other half consisted of Common Law, made by 'Mr. Justice Ashhurst and Co. without king, parliament, or people'.[27] Ashhurst's claim that every man had the means of knowing all the laws to which he was subject was similarly false, since both statute law and Common Law were 'kept most happily and carefully from the knowledge of the people: statute law by its shape and bulk; common law by its very essence'. The judges made the Common Law in the same way that 'a man makes laws for his dog. When your dog does anything you want to break him of, you wait till he does it, and then beat him for it.' They refused to say in advance what a man should not do, but 'lie by till he has done something which they say he should not *have done*, and then they hang him for it'. To find out what the law was, a man had to observe their proceedings in particular cases, but even then they refused to publish their proceedings themselves, and anyone who did publish them was liable to be sent to jail for a contempt of court.[28] The whole host of lawyers, from Coke down to Blackstone, had praised Common Law as being superior to statute law, yet it lacked any determinate meaning. Indeed, it was this very feature which made it attractive to lawyers: 'It carries in its hand a rule of wax, which they twist about as they please—a hook to lead the people by the nose, and a pair of sheers to fleece them with.' The French, on the other hand, 'have had enough of this *dog-law*; they are turning it as fast as they can into *statute law*, that everybody may have a rule to go by: nor do they ever make a law without doing all they can think of to let every creature among them know of it'. Bentham recommended that the example of the French be followed to the extent that those parts of the Common Law worth retaining should be enacted as statute law. The laws applicable to everyone should be published in 'one great book (it need not be a very great one,)' and those applicable to particular classes of people in 'so many little books', so that each person 'should have what belongs to him apart, without being loaded with what does not belong to him'. The general law-book might be read in churches and taught in schools. The law should be written in sentences of moderate length, instead of sentences of inordinate length 'stuffed with repetitions and words that are of no use, that the lawyers who draw them may be the

[25] Bowring, v. 233–4. [26] *Mr. Justice Ashhurst's Charge.* [27] Bowring, v. 235.
[28] Ibid.

better paid for them'. The lawyers well understood 'the art of poisoning language in order to fleece their clients'.[29]

Bentham continued his criticisms of the administration of justice in *A Protest against Law-Taxes*,[30] where he argued that a tax on law proceedings was the worst of all taxes. To those who could afford to pay, it was 'a *tax upon distress*', and to those who could not, it was '*a denial of justice*':

> Justice is the security which the law provides us with, or professes to provide us with, for everything we value, or ought to value—for property, for liberty, for honour, and for life. It is that possession which is worth all others put together: for it includes all others. A denial of justice is the very quintessence of injury, the sum and substance of all sorts of injuries. It is not robbery only, enslavement only, insult only, homicide only—it is robbery, enslavement, insult, homicide, all in one.

The legislator who introduced a law-tax, merely to raise some revenue which might better be raised elsewhere, was effectively outlawing the poor.[31] If the rich were prevented from going to law, they had other resources by which they might protect themselves from injury, namely 'the natural influence of wealth, the influence of situation, the power of connexion, the advantages of education and intelligence'. The poor, however, had no means of protection outside the law, and were driven from the law by the imposition of taxation: 'The poor, on account of the ignorance and intellectual incapacity inseparably attached to poverty, are debarred generally—as perhaps it is necessary, were it only for their own sake, they should be universally—from the sweets of political power: but are not so many unavoidable inequalities enough, without being added to by unnecessary injustice?' Bentham accepted that the poor should not enjoy political influence, but argued that this inequality should not be compounded by denying them access to justice.[32]

Taxes on law proceedings had been imposed, noted Bentham, in part from a mistaken belief that, by checking litigation, their effect was beneficial,[33] and in part from a confusion of this sort of tax with taxes on consumption and taxes on property and the transfer of property, which had the virtue of falling where there was some ability to pay. But the most important cause of the imposition of law-taxes was 'the prospect of acquiescence', in that there tended to be no one to complain about them: 'The oppressed and ruined objects of the taxes on justice, weep in holes and corners, as rats die: no one voice finds any other to join with it.' There was no certainty that a particular man would have to pay law-taxes, since he might never be involved in litigation. As a result: 'Suitors for justice have

[29] Bowring, v. 236.

[30] *A Protest against Law-Taxes, shewing the peculiar mischievousness of all such impositions as add to the expense of an appeal to justice*, printed in 1793 and published at London in 1795 (Bowring, ii. 573–83).

[31] Bowring, ii. 573–4.

[32] Ibid. 574–5. See also ibid. ii. 578: 'That all men should have *equal rights*, not only would be politically pernicious, but is naturally impossible: but I hope this will not be said of *equal justice*.'

[33] See ibid. 576–9.

no common cause, and scarce a common name—they are every body and nobody—their business being everybody's is nobody's.' There was a common misconception that the existence of the grievance was 'natural' rather than 'artificial', and thus 'inevitable and incurable, and at any rate... no more the fault of lawyers or law-makers, than gout and stone are of physicians'. Moreover, the wealthy recognized that they benefited, in proportion to their wealth, from law-taxes, in that they gained '[t]he power of keeping down those who are to be kept down, the power of doing wrong, and the more generous pride of abstaining from the wrong' which it was in their power to do.[34] If taxes on justice were abolished, justice would remain inaccessible to a great number of persons, but at least there would be fewer of them than if the taxes remained.[35]

While Bentham stridently criticized the legal profession—in particular for the part it played in denying access to justice through the imposition of fees and for keeping the law both unknown and unknowable to the public at large—and demanded far-reaching reform of the substantive and procedural law, he did not regard this commitment to legal reform as entailing a commitment to political reform. In *Truth versus Ashhurst* and *A Protest against Law-Taxes* he did not suggest that the key to legal reform lay in democratic political reform, but on the contrary stated that the poor should be 'debarred... from the sweets of political power'. Bentham, as we have seen, had complained about the deficiencies of English jurisprudence as early as 1776 in *A Fragment on Government*,[36] but it was only when he discovered the notion of sinister interest that he saw more deeply into the nature of the problem, and saw that it also encompassed the political establishment.

IV

The notion of sinister interest first appears in systematic form in Bentham's voluminous writings on judicial procedure and evidence, on which he commenced work in 1803, and with which he remained preoccupied until 1809. In tracing the emergence of sinister interest, a convenient starting-point is *Scotch Reform*, printed in 1807 and published in the following year,[37] and which took the form of a series of letters addressed to Grenville, leader of the short-lived

[34] Ibid. 580–1. [35] Ibid. 581.

[36] Indeed, two years earlier, Bentham had, in jocular vein, criticized Blackstone and the complications of English legal procedure in the lengthy 'Preface' to *The White Bull, an Oriental History, from an Ancient Syrian Manuscript, communicated by Mr. Voltaire*, 2 vols. (London, 1774), which was an anonymous translation of Voltaire's *Le Taureau Blanc*, and constituted Bentham's first publication.

[37] *Scotch Reform; considered, with reference to the Plan, proposed in the Late Parliament, for the regulation of the Courts, and the Administration of Justice, in Scotland: with Illustrations from English Non-reform: in the course of which divers imperfections, abuses, and corruptions, in the Administration of Justice, with their causes, are now, for the first time, brought to light. In a series of Letters, addressed to the Right Hon. Lord Grenville* (London, 1808) (Bowring, v. 1–53).

Ministry of All the Talents of 1806–7, who had introduced proposals for the reform of the administration of civil justice in Scotland. This essay was the first of Bentham's printed works to emerge from the writings on judicial procedure and evidence, and the earliest to contain any reference to 'sinister interest', and to a 'law partnership' which possessed the sinister interest in question.[38] Bentham explained that he had been puzzled by the rules adopted by the English courts which placed exclusions upon evidence. He noted that there were certain circumstances in which the courts were prepared to ignore each and every one of these rules, and justified their practice in doing so on grounds which went to prove the impropriety of the rules under all circumstances. He confessed that he had originally attributed this inconsistency in the law to 'primeval blindness and imbecility', but had come to realize that it was to a much greater extent the result of 'sharp-sighted artifice'. In order to combine profit with ease, 'it was necessary for the founders, and successive supporters of the system, to give to it a direction, opposite at every turn to the ends of justice'. The central feature of the system was the exclusion of 'the most instructive and indispensable *sources* of evidence', and then, in relation to the sources of evidence which were admitted, to prefer the less trustworthy and artificial to the more trustworthy and natural. These rules were merely one part

of a numerous and complicated system of *devices*, all tending to the same altogether natural, but not the less sinister end: and that, in a word, on these points, as on all others, the reason why the system was and is so bad as men feel it rather than see it to be, is, that the *power* found itself in company with the *interest*, and consequently the *will*, to produce as bad a system as the people, with the legislature at their head, could in their primeval, and as yet but little ameliorated, state of relative ignorance and helplessness, be brought, by the utmost stretch of artifice, to endure.

Similarly, in the reform proposed for Scotland, Bentham had found 'the profit and ease of the man of law were as carefully provided for as ever, the interests of the people, in their character of suitors, as completely sacrificed as ever to those original, and, with reference to the man of law, so much nearer objects'.[39]

He proceeded from this insight to demonstrate what he believed to be the systematic corruption which characterized the English legal profession and English law. The actual ends of the English legal system were not the ends of justice, but the ends of judicature. The direct ends of justice were the prevention of misdecision, that is, decision inconsistent with the substantive law, and the prevention of failure of justice, that is, the absence of a decision when one should have been made. The collateral ends of justice were the prevention of delay, vexation, and expense. The interest of the people as suitors was that the substantive law—assuming its utility—be enforced, but the interest of the judges was to enjoy the 'maximum of *profit* and *ease*; profit, as much as could be extracted, with as much ease as was consistent with the extraction of it'. The ends

[38] See e.g. Bowring, v. 6–7. [39] Ibid. 4.

of justice and the ends of judicature were in a state of 'constant opposition'. This opposition had arisen because judges, instead of being paid by salaries, had enjoyed the power to reward themselves by fees. 'In Scotland, as in England, and elsewhere, the system of judicial procedure has been, in the main, the work, not of legislators but of judges: manufactured, chiefly in the form—not of real statutory law—but of jurisprudential law:—imaginary law consisting of general inferences deduced from particular decisions.' The profit made from fees was proportional to the occasions on which they were extracted. Such occasions had, therefore, been invented, producing both 'factitious complication, intricacy, obscurity, unintelligibility, uncognoscibility' and 'a sort of sham science', with the result that suitors were forced to have 'recourse to the members of a distinct class or fraternity' who were the 'sole professors of that science, and of the arts belonging to it'. The profit of the lawyers increased with the factitious delay, vexation, and expense: 'Hence the closest community and general identity of interests;—a virtual partnership, which may be called the *law partnership*—with the judges, as managing partners, at the head of it.'[40]

The lawyers were joined in this community of interests by *malâ fide* suitors, those who were conscious of being in the wrong. Such suitors had an interest in increasing the quantity of delay, vexation, and expense, as a means of avoiding compliance with just demands, and of enforcing compliance with unjust demands.[41] Since *malâ fide* suits, which arose from the propensity to injustice, were more profitable to the judges than *bonâ fide* suits, the partnership had an interest in encouraging this propensity among the people more generally. The interest of the lawyers in injustice had produced a perversion of their understanding, characterized by 'a general propensity and aptitude, to mistake for justice the injustice by which they profit'.[42] There was, nevertheless, a way forward. The interest of judges might be reconciled with that of the rest of the community by the substitution of salaries to fees. In relation to the professional lawyers, while their interest could never be completely reconciled to that of the rest of the community, a great deal might be achieved 'by cancelling the *mendacity-license*, granted at present to them, and their clients'.[43]

The mendacity-license was a central feature of the English law of procedure. Developing the contrast he had identified in *A Fragment on Government* between the natural and technical arrangement of law, in *Scotch Reform* Bentham contrasted the natural and technical system of procedure. The object of the natural, or domestic, system of procedure was the ends of justice, and took for its model 'the course naturally pursued for the discovery of truth and administration of justice, as towards children, servants, or other dependents, in the bosom of a private family', and was instituted by 'the legislator, the legitimate and

[40] Ibid. 5. In *Scotch Reform*, for the first time in a printed work, Bentham referred to the partnership as 'Judge and Co.': see Bowring, v. 35.
[41] Ibid. 5–6.
[42] Ibid. 6.
[43] Ibid.

acknowledged legislator, acting in pursuit of the interests of the community'.[44] The object of the technical system of procedure, a product of the sinister interest of the law partnership, and instituted by the judges, was the collection of fees.[45] The object of natural procedure was to discover the truth, whereas technical procedure was characterized by the use of fictions—a fiction being 'a wilful falsehood, uttered by a judge, for the purpose of giving to injustice the colour of justice'. Fiction was valuable to the law partnership in that it created the impression that 'the vice of mendacity' was 'a necessary instrument of justice', and thereby helped to corrupt the morals and understanding of the people. More particularly, fiction was useful in producing injustice on the specific occasions on which it was used. Fiction, along with 'foreign language, obsolete language, technical language undefined, nonsense, ... ordinary language perverted', constituted legal jargon, which was analogous to the jargon used in astrology, palmistry, and alchemy. Legal jargon made the law into a 'matter of sham science' of which both the non-lawyer and legislator were conscious of their ignorance, and led the former to seek advice from the lawyer, thus boosting the 'opinion-trade', and the latter to regard reform either as hopeless or undesirable. Finally, it secured the monopoly of judicial offices to the professional lawyer, 'as if a monopoly of the faculty of serving as boarding-schools to girls, were secured to brothels'.[46]

In *Scotch Reform* Bentham did not suggest that the British legislature was in league with the law partnership, sharing in the same sinister interest. He may have had tactical reasons for not doing so, given that the work was addressed to Grenville, and through him to Parliament, but it seems more likely that he accepted that the legislature had itself been misled by the lawyers and their 'sham-science'. For instance, he contrasted favourably statute or real law, which was the 'work of the legitimate legislator, pursuing, after appropriate and comprehensive inquiry, the interest of the people', with jurisprudential or imaginary law, 'the work of judges, pursuing the partnership interest'.[47] Furthermore, in unpublished manuscripts written for *Scotch Reform* in 1806–7, while recognizing that there would be political obstacles to reforming judicial procedure, he was not so much concerned whether Grenville himself would be able to persuade Parliament to introduce measures for the reform of Scottish law, 'but whether Parliament itself be strong enough against the lawyers'.[48] He lamented 'a practice which seems to have grown into a maxim in both Houses', whereby, upon the introduction of any measure dealing with the law, and in particular dealing with the law of procedure, MPs asked whether it had the approval of the lawyers. This was like asking whether a measure for the defence of London had the approval of Napoleon. If the lawyers approved, 'the plan goes on', but if there was 'silence or a negative ... no more is heard of it'.[49] His

44 On this topic see J. H. Burns, 'Nature and Natural Authority in Bentham', *Utilitas: A Journal of Utilitarian Studies*, 5 (1993), 209–19.

45 Bowring, v. 7.

46 Ibid. 13.

47 Ibid.

48 UC xci. 3 (19 Jan. 1807).

49 UC xci. 34 (31 July 1806).

description of the British government as 'the best, and, at the same time, the most improvable of all governments',[50] and his reference to 'the mixt constitution, the limited Monarchy that so much to the advantage of the community upon the whole has taken place in Britain',[51] tend to confirm that Bentham had yet to extend his dissatisfaction to Parliament.[52]

In this manuscript material, Bentham expanded on the opposition of interest which existed between lawyers and suitors. While it was the interest of lawyers that the system of judicial procedure was encumbered with as much delay, vexation, and expense as possible, it was the interest of suitors that there be as little as possible. It was the interest of the lawyer that the proceedings be as expensive as possible, for the greater the expense, the greater his profit from the fees. Delay was inseparably connected with the expense, in that as many stages as possible were introduced into the proceedings in order to create a pretext for the imposition of the fees. No profit was produced to the lawyer 'abstractedly considered' from vexation, 'any more than any enjoyment presses on immediately and in a direct line into the bosom of the butcher from the dying agonies of the lamb', but given that the vexation suffered by the suitor was in direct proportion to the profit of the lawyer, 'the best that can happen to the suitor, is that his vexation should, in the eyes of the lawyer, by whom his fate is disposed of, [be viewed] as an object of indifference'.[53] If the lawyer did not enjoy the power to increase or diminish the number of occasions on which fees were levied, or the amount of work required on each occasion, this 'mode of payment would be not only unexceptionable but eligible'. However, in ancient times lawyers had possessed the power both to increase the number of 'profit-yielding occasions', and to stipulate the quantity of service, or rather 'sham service', rendered on each occasion, while in modern times, though no longer able to increase 'the fertility of those sources of profit', they were at least able to protect it against decrease. Things were made worse because the lawyer received only a percentage of the fees extorted, so that 'for every shilling put into his own pocket he has been obliged to draw a pound with its attendant delays and vexations out of the pocket of his employer'.[54]

The solution was to remove the opposition of interests which existed between lawyer and suitor. Here it became necessary to distinguish the official from the

[50] Bowring, v. 47. This passage was added to the second edition of *Scotch Reform* which was published in 1811, but was written before May 1808, when Bentham stopped work on the essay.

[51] UC cvi. 188 (16 May 1807).

[52] See also the imaginary dialogue, at UC xci. 39 (18 Dec. 1806), between the Lawyer and Non-Lawyer. The Lawyer suggests that the Non-Lawyer, who has pointed out the opposition of interests between suitor and lawyer, is in favour of parliamentary reform. The Non-Lawyer replies: 'No: nor against it neither: I have never thought anything about the matter: and with your leave, for the present occasion at least, with which it has nothing to do, I should be glad to save myself the trouble. If you have any thing to say about Parliamentary Reform, there's Major Cartwright ready for you. . . . The question you and I are upon is—not who shall govern us? but to whose benefit we shall be governed?'

[53] UC xci. 23 (27 July 1806).

[54] UC xci. 26 (27 July 1806).

professional lawyer: the latter was 'an incurable and irreconcileable enemy' of the suitor, while the former was not. The official lawyer received income partly in the form of salary and partly in the form of fees, whereas the professional lawyer's only source of income was fees. The official lawyer would be prepared to relinquish his fees in exchange for compensation, but the professional lawyer would not.[55] Reform could not be instituted 'without taking the whole body of professional lawyers for its victims', and they would, therefore, form 'determined and irreconcileable opponents'. The choice lay between two evils: if the present system continued, suitors would continue to suffer; if it did not, the lawyers would suffer. The point was that for every law-family that suffered a reduction in its income, there would be twenty other families, 'each possessing an equal right to sympathy', saved from ruin. Moreover, while the evil suffered by the lawyers did not extend beyond their lives, 'the good composed of the evil saved . . . remains perhaps till the end of time'.[56]

Bentham now had no doubt that, in the main, the problems with English law were systematic in that they were embedded in the law itself. He was aware that injustice might arise from accident, or from misconduct on the part of the suitor or the judge, but even these sources of injustice were to a large degree the result of imperfections in the system itself, and would be remedied by its reform. For instance, a misdecision brought about by the death of a witness whose testimony would have prevented it was commonly attributed to 'pure accident', whereas without the factitious delay created by the technical system the witness might have testified before his death, and 'the disastrous effect' would thereby have been avoided.[57] Judicial misconduct might be remedied by 'the institution of a superordinate judicature, occupied in the superintendence and controul of the proceedings' of the courts of first instance. Systematic injustice, however, could only be remedied by systematic reform, in other words by the 'removal of the imperfections by which, whether by design, or negligence, or ignorance, it has been rendered or left incapable to the degree in question of fulfilling the ends of justice'. The eradication of such injustice would require the natural system of procedure to be substituted for the technical.[58] The problem was that systematic injustice was far more valuable to the law partnership than accidental injustice: '[t]he delay of which the profit to [the judges] is sure and the hazard none, is the delay worked up into the system itself'. Such delay could not be blamed on particular judges who might be held responsible for it. It had been established 'in dark ages before the superintendence of the second branch of the legislature [i.e. the House of Commons] had acquired any considerable degree of perspicacity or constancy', and had been 'fixed by precedent and consecrated by that sort of sanction so dear to hypocrites and impostors in government under the name of the wisdom of ages'. The judge had no interest in causing delay where it might

[55] UC xci. 27 (27 July 1806). [56] UC xci. 29 (27 July 1806).
[57] UC cvi. 132–3 (2?, 4 Mar. 1807). [58] UC cvi. 134–5 (4 Mar. 1807).

be attributed to his mental indolence, inaptitude, or corruption, since that would damage his reputation. He had still less interest in bribery, since he would thereby put himself in the power of the person giving the bribe. Indeed, the acceptance of bribes, with its attendant risks, was rendered unnecessary, since the regular course of judicature gave English judges 'a regular mass of emolument so much superior to any obtained elsewhere by the most corrupt Judges at the highest risk'.[59]

The lack of a responsible individual helped in part to explain the absence of reform. In a pure monarchy, for instance, it was the interest of the monarch to rectify any defects in the field of legislation, but in a limited monarchy, such as Britain, no such individual existed. An exception was the Chancellor of the Exchequer, who was regarded as specially responsible for financial legislation, but there was no corresponding individual responsible for the state of the criminal or the civil law. Instead: 'Both these portions of the domain of legislation are understood to appertain in common to the community of lawyers: to appertain to them, and to be possessed by them upon the most convenient of all terms—power without responsibility—power without obligation.' No matter how flagrant the abuse, no single lawyer was regarded as responsible. On the contrary, not only was it the interest of lawyers not to point out the abuses of the law and to propose reform, but also to try to ensure that the mischief produced by the judicial system remained generally unknown, or at least was not blamed on the corrupt state of the law: 'It is for this reason that the more forcibly impressed he [the lawyer] is with the mischievousness of it in any instance, the more active and resolute he is in the defence of it: the defence of it if complained of, and what is still better to prevent complaint by rendering it hopeless, to drown beforehand the voice of possible complaint by an unceasing and indefatigable concert of praise.'[60] The worse the state of the law, the more it would be praised by the lawyer.

V

In *Scotch Reform*, written between 1806 and 1808, Bentham attributed the deplorable state of the system of procedure to the sinister interest of the legal profession. As he explained, he had reached this conclusion during his investigation of the exclusionary rules of evidence found in English law. He had undertaken this latter investigation between 1803 and 1805, as part of a broader study of the law of procedure and evidence. Some of this material, together with material written between 1809 and 1812, eventually appeared in *Rationale of Judicial Evidence*, published in 1827. As the manuscripts on which *Rationale of Judicial Evidence* are based no longer exist, it is not possible to identify at what

59 UC clxviii. 169 (26 May 1807).

60 UC cvi. 187–92 (16 May 1807).

date the material in the published text was composed. This renders *Rationale of Judicial Evidence* problematic in terms of untangling the detailed historical development of Bentham's thinking on judicial procedure and evidence, and in particular the emergence of sinister interest. However, a large number of manuscripts not included in the published text, written between 1803 and 1805 under the headings of 'Evidence' and 'Procedure', do survive, and shed some light on this question. A great many of the points outlined and then developed for *Scotch Reform* appear to have been first worked out in this material.

The earliest reference to sinister interest which has been traced, with the exception of that in the poor law writings of November 1797,[61] appears in a passage dated 18 February 1804, where Bentham contrasted the prohibition usually laid on extraneous witnesses from giving false evidence with the permission given to litigants or parties to do so. The reason for this apparent contradiction was not difficult to discover, noted Bentham, when it was considered 'that men of law are but men—that their interest is on many occasions in direct opposition to that of the community at large, and that this sinister interest is supported by powers adequate to the accomplishment of all its purposes'. The point was that the lawyer profited from the expense which arose from the prosecution of an extraneous witness for making false statements, whereas in the instance of the party it was to the advantage of the lawyer that false statements be permitted, since 'every assertion the object or effect of which may be to protract the suit, and thereby add to the number of steps that require on both sides to be taken in it, is a source of profit to the men of law on both sides'. Whether the assertion was true or false was irrelevant, since the benefit to the lawyers would remain the same, or if there were any difference, 'the effect of falshood will be rather to encrease than diminish the advantage'. Wherever a distinct legal profession had been established, its members had a common interest:

> In some points this particular interest has coincided with the general interest of the community at large: and thus far, according to the psychological and pathological laws of human nature, the dictates of justice would be pursued; at least according to the measure of men's intelligence. In other points the particular has acted in opposition to the general interest: and thus far as to these points the general interest would of course be sacrificed to the particular, and the result would be an established system of regular injustice.
>
> Where falshood on the part of the suitor was a source of profit to the man of law, falshood of course, so far as decency would permitt, and pretences could be found, would be rewarded and encouraged. Men's morals have been corrupted that their purses might be drained.[62]

Bentham's claim that, where his interest was opposed to that of the people in general, the lawyer would strive to sacrifice the latter to the former, rested on 'the psychological and pathological laws of human nature'. In *An Introduction to the Principles of Morals and Legislation* he had, of course, emphasized the connection

[61] See pp. 110–11 above. [62] UC lxix. 159–60 (18 Feb. 1804).

between interest, motivation, and action:[63] he now applied these insights to the situation of the lawyer. He began in general terms, contrasting the proper end of legislation, the happiness of the whole community, with the sinister end, the happiness of some particular part of the community whose happiness could only be promoted at the expense of the greater happiness of the rest:

In every line of legislation, the true, the proper end—the only true, the only proper *end*—will at this time of day be generally—not to say universally—acknowledged to be the happiness—the well-being—the welfare—the prosperity—the interest—all these words mean the same thing, of the community: of the aggregate body of human beings under consideration.

In every line of legislation, the interest and so forth of any minor assemblage of individuals forming part of that aggregate will, if put in opposition to the general interest, be in alike manner recognized as being a false—an improper—a *sinister* end. The pursuit of the sinister end will, in so far as the result is considered as sure to be or likely to be the loss of a greater quantity of the happiness of the *whole* body taken together than is gained to the *part*, will accordingly be recognized as being an improper, a sinister pursuit: and the accomplishment of such sinister end, an undesirable result: undesirable, to wit to any person, who, considering himself on the occasion and for the purpose, as the representative, or guardian, or agent, or advocate of the whole community considers for that same purpose and on that same occasion its interests as coinciding with his own.

In one sense, continued Bentham, it was a truism that every man, on every occasion, pursued his own interest. His conduct would be governed by the preponderant motive or motives which operated on him. In another sense, however, it was not true, for a man might act against what was his interest, either from a lack of understanding as to what his interest required, or from considerations of generosity, sympathy, and antipathy. In contrast, it was not in any sense true that a man *ought* on every occasion to pursue his own interest. But what was true, in other words, in accordance with the principle of utility, was that every man on every occasion ought to pursue the line of conduct most conducive to the aggregate interest of the community. In practice he would do so only if motivated by 'actually predominant interests, rightly or wrongly understood'. It was pointless merely informing a man that he had a duty to act in a particular way if his interest made it certain he would act in some other way. 'The interest of this or that body of men is adverse in certain points to the general interest of the community.—What is the application here to be made of the terms ought and ought not? It ought (shall we say) to pursue that sinister interest? to speak thus would be to say what is at once *false* and nugatory: that it ought not?—For this time not false indeed, but as nugatory as before.' The situation of the legislator had to be distinguished from that of other men, in that it was his duty to protect the interest of the whole community from the sinister interests of particular

[63] See pp. 30–2 above.

individuals and groups. Furthermore, a particular individual might be disposed by a sense of moral obligation, in other words by consideration for the public interest, 'to regard the sinister private interest with the same jealous eye'. A group of men, however, insofar as they possessed a particular and sinister interest, would pursue it with more determination than an individual would pursue his interest, whether legitimate or sinister. The individual was much more effectively restrained by the sense of shame imposed by the force of the moral sanction, even when not restrained by the fear of legal punishment. The members of a group paid more attention to the opinion of the other members of the group, which operated in support of their sinister interest, than to that of 'the great public', which operated in support of the general interest.

Having shown that sinister interest operated most strongly on the members of a group, Bentham turned to the legal profession and its role in the creation of the law of procedure. Lawyers were no different from other groups of men in the state in possessing 'a partial, a sinister interest adverse to that of the community', but, in addition, they possessed the requisite knowledge and power to accomplish their sinister designs, in other words to promote effectively their own interest to the detriment of the community as a whole. The sinister interest of lawyers was the most important factor in producing the abuses which existed in the system of procedure:

> And so sufficient will this single cause be found to be to the task of accounting for the effect, that the just cause of wonder will be not so much how it should have happened that there should be so much that will be found amiss—but how it should have happened that any thing should have been right. To trust the interest of suitors, that is of all mankind in their occasional capacity of suitors, to the management of the man of law, would have been exactly the same sort of policy, had there been any choice, as the committing of the sheep to the guardianship of the wolf: or rather to a sort of animal who under the outer covering of the faithful defender of the fold, has under the change of circumstances found it necessary to change his nature from the open voracity of the wolf to the more subtle and disguised rapacity of the fox.

All men desired money, reputation, and ease. Lawyers in all civilized countries had enjoyed considerable success in securing these advantages, but nowhere more so than in England:

> England, if with any such propriety, it may be stiled a paradise for men, may be stiled a very heaven for men of law. What of old time priests were in Egypt (not to speak of so many other countries) lawyers will be found to be—to be even to this supposed enlightened hour—to England. What *priestcraft* with its hieroglyphics was in Egypt, *lawyercraft* with its fictions and technicalities will be seen to be in England: nor were devotees more unmercifully *ridden* by the long-robed cast in Egypt, than they will be found to be in England by men of law.

Had the benefit reaped by the lawyers been no greater than the detriment suffered by suitors, there would, of course, not have been any grievance, but the fact was that the detriment to the latter was 'deplorably vast' compared with the benefit to the former.[64]

Whether considered by 'the light of reason' or from 'the page of history', Bentham thought that no one should be surprised by the state of the law of procedure:

> The interests of the wolf are not more plainly and diametrically opposite to those of the sheep, than those of the professional lawyer have every where been to those of the suitor: and to expect that at the time when any of the several established plans of inquiry in the way of judicial procedure were instituted and brought to their present form, the interest of the suitors should have been the real object is exactly such an expectation as would be formed were any one to suppose that the security of the sheep would be the first object in a line of march prescribed by wolves.

The system of procedure would have been very different had it been instituted by a legislator who both understood how justice might be attained, and was uninfluenced by sinister interest. However, no such legislator had existed, and the system had been the product of judges who, deriving their profits from the suitors, and having the suitors at their mercy, took advantage of the situation in the way that any other class of men would naturally have taken advantage of it: 'In a word, the sheep having been every where without a shepherd, their lot has been every where determined upon by the wolves.'[65]

The interest of lawyers was, in a variety of ways, opposed to that of the people at large in their capacity of suitors. First, in relation to the cost of legal proceedings, the lawyer had a clear interest in the fees and other costs that went fully and directly into his own pocket, though his interest in the costs which he did not receive was more equivocal. In one respect he was a loser, in that the more a suitor was made to pay to other people, the less he could afford to pay to the lawyer. In another respect he benefited, in that '[t]he general principle and practice of imposing upon suitors factitious and unnecessary expence is sanctioned by it'. By taxes upon law proceedings the lawyer lost some clients, namely those unable to pay the tax and thereby denied access to justice, but in this loss of emolument he saw 'a premium by which he ensures the continuance of the rest': it was the price of an alliance with 'the man of finance', whose political position gave him the power to prevent reform. Second, while delay did not in itself serve the interest of the lawyer, in that the longer it took for a given quantity of emolument to be extracted the less its value, it nevertheless gave rise to 'incidents', each of which produced expense for the suitor and profit for the lawyer. Third, the ease of the lawyer was promoted by the institution of law terms and the corresponding vacations, which freed him from labour for large parts of the year, but without diminishing his income. This 'time of comfort and amusement' enjoyed by the lawyer produced injustice either to one party or to the

[64] UC lxix. 162–74 (13 Aug. 1804).

[65] UC lxix. 325–6 (14 June 1804).

other, or to both: 'While the time of the man of law is filled with amusement, the time of the injured suitor is filled with bitterness.'[66]

There were, however, areas in which the interest of the lawyer coincided to some degree with that of the community in general. For instance, the interest of the lawyer and suitor coincided in relation to reducing the cost of law proceedings where the cost of a cause was so expensive that it was not instigated, thus denying the lawyer the profit he would have reaped had it been instigated. The lawyer and the suitor also shared an interest in avoiding injustice in the form of an apparently wrong decision. Having said that, while the suitor was interested in the reality of justice, the lawyer was interested in the appearance, and only in the reality insofar as it was necessary to produce the appearance. Every category of lawyer, whether professional or official, and if official, whether a judge or a subordinate officer of the court, possessed a similar interest in relation to the appearance of justice. The judge had a personal interest not in justice, but in the reputation of justice. Indeed, providing he enjoyed the reputation of justice, it was 'a matter of indifference' to him whether his decisions were just or unjust. Yet his reputation would be affected by any actual injustice he committed to the extent of the publicity given to the proceedings of his court. Furthermore, where the parties had the option of taking the same cause to more than one court (for instance to the different Common Law courts in Westminster Hall), the income of the judge would depend to some degree upon his reputation. The judge, therefore, had an interest in maintaining a reputation for dispensing justice, and would compete with the judges of the other courts in this respect. As far as the subordinate officials were concerned, the abstract justice or injustice of the judge's decisions was a matter of indifference, but insofar as their income depended upon the quantity of business, and insofar as the general reputation of the court depended upon that of this or that subordinate office, the official would have an interest similar to that of the judge.

Similarly, the professional lawyer, and particularly the advocate, had an interest not in the abstract justice or injustice of the decisions, but in the reputation for justice possessed by the court in which he practised: 'Whatever serves to encrease the business of the Court in which the Advocate practices, produces thereby an additional chance for encrease of business to the Advocate.' But in another respect the interest of the professional lawyer had to be distinguished from that of the official lawyer. As far as the professional lawyer himself was concerned, his interest was promoted by the reputation of injustice rather than that of justice, so long as the decision was in his favour: 'In medicine the more desperate the case, the greater the glory to the physician who treats it with success and triumphs over the disease. In the practice of the law, the more desperate the case, the greater the glory of the lawyer who treats it with success and triumphs over justice.' Between real and apparent justice, between abstract

[66] UC lxix. 175–9 (14 Aug. 1804).

justice and the reputation of justice, there was a close connection: 'Whatever be the line of life, to act justly is the most effectual course that can be taken, the only general rule that can be given, for purchasing the advantage of being thought to do so.' However, in practice, 'spurious dictates of justice' had been established by judges, with the result that 'in the minds of men of law, and consequently of all others who borrow their opinions on questions of law from the known opinions of men of law, a decision conformable to these established rules . . . will never appear to be adverse to justice'. Once such 'spurious dictates of justice' had been established, the reputation of the judge would depend upon the conformity of his decisions to them, and not to the dictates of 'real and substantial justice'. In short, while the lawyer benefited from delay, expense, and vexation of law proceedings, and from the general uncertainty of the law, he had only a partial and equivocal interest in real justice.[67]

The legal profession had created the system of procedure, and then maintained it by bestowing extravagant praise upon it, and by refusing to undertake any critical investigation of it. All the books on the subject having been written by lawyers, the course of procedure established in every court in every country was presented as 'the work of the purest probity guided by the profoundest wisdom'. No one else ever attempted to investigate the law of procedure because 'the ingenuity and absurdity of men of law' had rendered the subject too obscure. Given that every account of the system of procedure which had appeared had been 'couched in terms of the most exalted panegyric', it was no surprise that 'universal delusion' had been the result. If the nonsense of the law was taken for science, 'every thing will appear admirable—every thing immutable—every thing inexplicable', but if it was recognized to be 'the work of fraud in confederacy with absurdity', everything became clear—'you have a key, and that a sure one, to whatever is abstruse and mysterious in jurisprudence'.[68] The so-called science of the law, accumulated over the centuries like the filth in the Augean stable, had been developed, if not invented, in order to confound the understanding of the suitor. The suitor was told by the lawyer that although the law appeared on the surface to be folly, it was, at bottom, the profoundest and purest wisdom, and if the suitor was unable to see this, the difficulty lay not in the absence of what he was looking for, but in the weakness of his eyes. There was, however, no reason why the science of the law had to be in such a 'deplorable and disgraceful state'. The unintelligibility of the law was not the product of necessity or wisdom, but of artifice coupled with absurdity, and it was in the highest degree pernicious. Reflecting on his own experience, Bentham commented: 'Such were the lights that flashed more than 40 years ago through the veil of accommodating sophistry in which the subject was involved by the ingenuity of Blackstone. Such was the suspicion that presented itself even to the timid and admiring eye of adolescence: such is the suspicion confirmed into

[67] UC lxix. 180–6 (14–15 Aug. 1804).

[68] UC lxix. 344 (12 June 1804).

assurance by the cold scrutiny of declining age.'[69] The key actor was the judge, for it was the judge who pronounced the decision, and who was thereby responsible for making law: 'From the sinister interest of no other species of lawyers can the body of the law undergo its modification in any shape otherwise than as their interests are adopted by him, and made to become his.' There was everywhere 'a very close community of interest' between judges and other classes of lawyers, either in the way of sympathy, whether professional or social, or in the way of pecuniary or other self-regarding interest. The closest ties of sympathy existed, as under the English system, where judges had risen through the subordinate ranks of lawyers, particularly that of advocates. In England, those who had not been advocates were prevented from being appointed to the principal judicial offices, though some minor judicial offices, such as that of Justice of the Peace, might be filled by men who had not been advocates: 'But for judicature extending over the whole or any considerable part of the field of law, especially in so far as the covering was by law in the shape of jurisprudential law . . . nothing like competence has for many ages past been ever expected to be found in any man that had not in the character of an Advocate been long and thoroughly exercised in that field.' Given that the interest of the professional advocate was so opposed to the ends of justice, it was unlikely that the judge, at least when first entering into office, would not regard the dictates of real justice as 'odious', and those of apparent justice as much more agreeable: 'In a man thus educated to look for a sincere friend to real justice, to the real welfare of mankind in any respect, would be to expect to find in the person of a Soldier of fortune or a War Contractor a sincere friend to peace:—to look for independency in the Courtier, to look for chastity and modesty in the stews.' Bentham conceded that economy and good government had reached such a level in England that, even though men would endure existing abuses, they would not tolerate any new ones. While the worst effect which could be produced by the prevalence of sinister interest in judges was to protect existing abuses from remedy, there could be no doubt that this was precisely what the judge would do.[70]

Bentham acknowledged that the lawyer needed the support of the legislator, who through lack of understanding or love of ease had allowed the establishment of the sinister practices of the lawyer, and had done nothing to prevent them continuing. Without the power of the state, the law would have no force, and without the sovereign enforcing his decisions, the judge would not be a judge.[71] Lawyers had on the one hand made it impossible for any one to possess an adequate knowledge of the law, yet on the other hand had adopted the maxim that ignorance of the law did not excuse any man from punishment. Bentham exclaimed:

how unfeeling, how barbarous, must the negligence of the legislator be seen to be . . . who suffers a whole people to live for ever under the gripe of so afflictive a dilemma! to be for

[69] UC lxix. 345–6 (12 June 1804).
[70] UC lxix. 192–8 (15–16 Aug. 1804).
[71] UC lxix. 302 (10? Apr. 1805).

ever, without an attempt or so much as a wish, to extricate them! who, regardless of his duty, trampling upon his trust, keeps his people in a state of bondage, or as the lawyer himself phrases it, *miserable slavery*, under his natural and inexorable tormentor and plunderer—the man of law![72]

In this material written in 1804, and in *Scotch Reform* written in 1806–8, Bentham did not link the interest of legislators with the sinister interest of lawyers, though he was critical of legislators for not extirpating that sinister interest. It was not long, however, before Bentham realized that the legal profession and legislators were bound together in a partnership of sinister interest.

VI

Bentham's recognition that not only the legal but also the political establishment embraced a common sinister interest is evident in *The Elements of the Art of Packing*, which was written in the first half of 1809.[73] He was prompted to write the work by what he conceived to be 'the utter destruction impending over the palladium of the English constitution, the liberty of the press'.[74] The immediate stimulus was the appearance of a letter in *The Times* of 20 February 1809 claiming that twenty-six printers and publishers were under threat of prosecution for slandering the Duke of York—one on account of the publication of, and the remainder on account of the reproduction of extracts from, a pamphlet published by Denis Hogan.[75] Bentham explained that for thirty or forty years he had held the view that, in English law, 'a *libel* is any paper in which he, who to the *will* adds the *power* of *punishing* for it, sees anything that he does not *like*'. If the libel law were to be 'consistently and completely executed', English liberties would be destroyed and the government transformed into a despotism. Only Parliament could provide 'a *radical* cure' by providing a definition of a libel, though the evil might receive 'a momentary *palliative*' from 'the intelligence and fortitude of a jury', through its refusal to bring in a guilty verdict. Indeed, it was possible for a single juryman to ensure that a guilty verdict was not returned, in consequence of the requirement for a verdict to be unanimous. Were such verdicts to be regularly returned in prosecutions for political libel, not only might oppression be avoided in the cases in question, but 'by a gentle and truly constitutional pressure, measures of complete and permanent relief might, as

[72] UC lxix. 116–17 (24 June 1805). The maxim to which Bentham refers is from 4 *Institutes* 246: 'misere servitus est, ubi jus est vagum, aut incognitum'.

[73] *The Elements of the Art of Packing, as applied to Special Juries, particularly in Cases of Libel Law*, first printed in 1810 (London, 1821) (Bowring, v. 61–186). For the date of the composition of the work see the surviving marginal summary sheets at UC xxvi. 68–136.

[74] Bowring, v. 171.

[75] *An Appeal to the Public, and a Farewell Address to the Army, by Brevet-Major Hogan, late a Captain in the Thirty-second Regiment of Infantry—in which he resigned his commission, in consequence of the treatment he experienced from the Duke of York, and the system that prevails in the Army respecting promotions; including some strictures upon the general conduct of our military force* (London, 1808).

from the *unjust* judge in the *parable*,[76] be extorted from the legislature'. Bentham had realized, however, upon reading Sir Richard Phillips's account of the office of sheriff in the City of London that such an eventuality would not take place, since the special jurymen, who were appointed for cases of political libel, were not 'really free to follow the dictates of *their own* judgment'.[77] The packing of special juries, he had been astonished to discover, 'had been moulded into a *system*, had become an established practice'.[78] Where a case was tried before a petty jury, it was relatively easy for the judge to prevent a verdict contrary to his wishes, but not so easy to obtain one in conformity with them. Where the latter was required, a special jury was resorted to:

When, therefore, in pursuance of a sinister interest, in whatsoever bosom it may have happened to it to originate,—*his own*, for example, that of the king, or that of any servant of the king's in any other department of the state, it has come to be an object with a judge to *obtain* at the hands of a jury a *verdict* in any way contrary to justice, a necessary endeavour has been to *obtain a jury*, so composed, as that the verdict pronounced by them may be depended upon as about to be conformable to his wishes....[79]

The judge had three potential instruments—intimidation, corruption, and deception—by which he might render the jury subservient to his will. Intimidation and the associated punishment would altogether destroy the power of juries: only corruption and deception, therefore, afforded 'any promise of being regularly and steadily applicable to this sinister service: *viz.* the securing of undue obsequiousness on the part of juries'. A jury might be corrupted either by appointing persons who were already disposed to be obsequious to the will of the judge, or by rendering obsequious the jurymen after they had been appointed. The former course of packing was by far the most simple, but it was the latter which had recently begun to be practised. A description of the general process was captured in what Bentham termed 'a fundamental axiom' in 'the science of *psychological* or *moral dynamics*':

Into the situation in question (it being a situation conferring power—legal power) cause to be placed the number of persons requisite (they being provided with the requisite legal qualifications)—you possessing in your hands, to a certain extent, the faculty of influencing their interest or welfare (that is, producing in their respective bosoms the sensation of pain or pleasure, or the eventual absence of either)—and no *preponderant* force acting on the same bosoms in an opposite direction: these things being done, the exercise of that power is thereafter at your command: and this, whatsoever be the name given to the act of power so exercised—such as *verdict, judgment, decree, sentence, vote, resolution, statute, law.*

While this axiom had perhaps not hitherto been 'reduced to any scientific form of words', no politician or official was unaware of its truth. The simplest

[76] See Luke 18: 1–8.

[77] For the passage on special juries see Sir Richard Phillips, *A Letter to the Livery of London, relative to the views of the writer in executing the Office of Sheriff*, 2nd edn. (London, 1808), 153–76.

[78] Bowring, v. 65–6.

[79] Ibid. 67–8.

application of it occurred when one person was dependent on the will of another for the receipt of some reward. In the instance in question, a juryman, who was paid for acting as such, was dependent upon the will of the person at whose hands he was liable to be dismissed, and to the extent that the verdict of the jury depended upon that juryman, the verdict was also dependent upon the will of that person. Each special juryman received a substantial emolument (one guinea per trial), and the juryman might be appointed time after time. The power of appointment and dismissal was in the hands of the judge, who, therefore, controlled the jurymen and their verdict. The system had been greatly improved by the introduction of permanent jurymen, which was contrary to the principle that each jury should constitute a panel of temporary judges in order to act as a security against sinister influence. In the case of 'simple package', new jurors had to be found for each trial, whereas under the principle of permanence tried and tested men were 'always at hand' and ready to do the bidding of the judge.[80]

The second of the instruments which the judge might use to produce a favourable verdict was deception. There was a danger that if the jury obtained a complete and correct conception of the case, their will, as expressed by their verdict, would contradict that of the judge. The point was to ensure that their conception was rendered in some way incomplete or incorrect so that their will coincided with that of the judge. The most advantageous method was to prevent the jurymen from forming a will of their own, and so force them to adopt that of the judge. There were two requisites for 'the system of deception': in the first place, the law had to be rendered as incomprehensible as possible to the jurymen; in the second place, the jurymen had to be convinced that the judge had a totally correct and complete knowledge of the subject. These objects were achieved by the use both of 'incorporeal instruments of deception'—namely 'jargon, nonsense, absurdity, surplusage, needless complication, falsehood—every kind of intellectual nuisance, in every imaginable form'—and of 'corporeal' ones, which might also be termed 'the instruments of fascination'—such as the elevation of the bench above the jury box, and the peculiar dress of the judge, which constituted the 'outward and visible signs of the inward and invisible graces and virtues, intellectual and moral, that dwell within'. The importance of the corporeal instruments was greater than the incorporeal, for without the fascination produced by them it might not be possible, given 'the stock of jargon, nonsense, absurdity, and so forth', to instil the belief that the judges possessed 'the stock of real knowledge' in question. Furthermore, the permanence of the jurymen allowed a friendship to develop between judge and jury, thereby reinforcing the influence of the judge: 'A sort of compact forms itself, under and in virtue of which the man of learning engages to afford direction, the child of simplicity to follow it: this compact once formed, the presumption, which on any particular occasion should presume to think and act for itself, would be an act not only of temerity, but of revolt and perfidy.'[81]

[80] Ibid. 70–3. [81] Ibid. 74–6.

The chief purpose of the packing system was to crush the liberty of the press, or rather to destroy whatever remained of it. It was here that the interests of the legal and political establishments were linked, and worked together to achieve the common goal. Bentham noted that in *Protest against Law Taxes* he had pointed out that a tax on law proceedings was the worst of all possible taxes.[82] Having said that, raising money by taxes as such did not produce anywhere near so much mischief as raising money by fees. Taxes as such were exacted by the man of finance, but he did not create the occasions on which they were exacted; fees were exacted by the man of law, and in particular the judge, and he did have the power to create the occasions on which they were exacted. The judges of the Westminster Hall courts, and in particular the Chief Justice of King's Bench, who was 'the master-manufacturer of *libel law*—and in effect the absolute master of *the press*', were linked by a 'community of sinister interest . . . linked with each other, and with some of the most influential members of those supreme assemblies [i.e. the Houses of Parliament], from which alone remedy to abuse, in this or any other shape, can come'. Some of the 'masses of emolument' produced by fees had been so great that they had been seized by some 'high-seated personage', leaving 'a *comparatively small* pittance' to 'the low-seated individual by whom the service was performed'. These masses of emolument had been shared between the judges and 'the vultures that hover about a court. And here we see a natural bond of the closest union between *Court* and *Bench*.'[83]

Bentham argued that all those who profited from abuse, whether in the legal profession or in government more generally, perceived that the greatest threat to their position came from the liberty of the press: 'Keeping the liberty of the press, as it were, in a state of constant *annihilation*' was 'among persons "in high situations" . . . the common object—the one, and almost the only one, in the attachment to which the agreement is among them constant and almost universal'.[84] The first object of the Chief Justice of King's Bench, 'the despot of the press', was to protect abuse in those instances in which he himself or his immediate connections benefited from it, but in order to do so he needed support from members of the political establishment: 'it would therefore be necessary for him to extend his protection without distinction to all established abuses from which any other man so situated as to be capable of giving him the needful support, derived or could conceive himself to derive in any shape a benefit: in a word, to act in the character of *protector-general* of all established abuse'. The special jury was the means of destroying the liberty of the press, wherever it existed, and, where it did not exist, of preventing it from coming into existence. Protection and encouragement were given to misrule by 'threatening with the vengeance of the law all such as shall do anything towards holding it [i.e. misrule] up to public view'. Nothing which judicial power was able to do towards this end had been left undone.[85] Under existing libel law, prosecution

[82] See pp. 116–17 above. [83] Bowring, v. 97–9. [84] Ibid. 101.
[85] Ibid. 99–101.

inevitably led to conviction, and when a political libel was the offence, the form of jury trial was 'but a melancholy farce'. The principles of libel law, as expressed by Ellenborough, Chief Justice of King's Bench, at the trial of William Cobbett on 24 May 1804, heard before a special jury, were as follows: punish whatever tended to bring a man in power into disesteem; punish whatever imputed unfitness to any man in office; punish whatever hurt anyone's 'feelings'; and punish whatever you disliked.[86]

In *Elements of the Art of Packing* Bentham suggested that members of the political establishment were motivated to pursue their sinister interest in exactly the same way as members of the legal establishment, and furthermore that there was an intimate bond of connection between them. It was not that the legal profession had hoodwinked the legislature—as he had suggested in the writings on judicial procedure in 1804 and in *Scotch Reform* a little later—but that they were acting in collaboration in order to promote their own interest, at whatever cost to the interest of the community in general. They both profited from abuses, and they both accepted that the major threat to their interest was the liberty of the press, which they aimed, therefore, to destroy.

Of the several departments of government, howsoever carved out and distinguished—judicial, financial, military, naval, and so forth—suppose that in all, or any of them, *abuses* exist—abuses, from which the persons, or some of the persons, by whom those departments are respectively filled, derive, each of them, in some shape or other, a sinister advantage. In this state of things, if there be any such thing as an instrument, by the operations of which all such abuses, without distinction, are liable to be exposed *to view*, the tendency of it is thereby to act with hostile effect against the several sinister interests of all these several public functionaries; whom thereupon, by necessary consequence, it finds engaged, all of them, by a common interest, to oppose themselves with all their means, and all their might, not only to its influence, but to its very existence. An instrument of this all-illuminating and all-preserving nature, is what the country supposes itself to possess in a free press; and would actually possess, if the press were free as it is supposed to be.[87]

The irony of the fact that the judges were using the jury, traditionally hailed as a guarantor of English liberties, in order to destroy liberty was no doubt not lost on Bentham.

It was in the interest of the governed that checks be applied to the power of the governors, on the condition 'that the *good* which, in the shape of *security against misrule*, is thus produced by the check, is not exceeded by the *evil* produced by the defalcation made by it from the quantity of power necessary to enable the holder of the power to render, in the highest degree of perfection, the service expected at his hands'. Governors, however, had no wish to see their power checked, just as the judge had no wish to see his power checked by a jury.[88]

[86] Ibid. 106. For Cobbett's trial see T. J. Howell, *A Complete Collection of State Trials and proceedings for High Treason and other Crimes and Misdemeanors*, Vol. XXIX (London, 1821), 1–54 (Ellenborough's summing up is at pp. 49–54).

[87] Bowring, v. 91.

[88] Ibid. 69–70.

Bentham now viewed the judge as just one category of official, all of whom had an interest opposite to that of the people:

> *Money*, *power*, *ease*, and *vengeance*, these, together with *reputation*, so far at least as the efficient cause of felicity in this shape may have the effect of serving as a security or means of increase for it in any of those others—reputation, how well or how ill soever deserved, may be set down as indicative of the several interests by which, when acting in the direction of *sinister interests*, the conduct of public functionaries in general, and of judges in particular, is, in a more particular degree, liable to be warped.[89]

Parliament provided no counterforce to 'the lawless power of the judge'. The judge might either give effect to or ignore the laws passed by the legislature, just as he pleased: 'In parliament, be his rebellion ever so flagrant, he beholds neither *inspector* nor *denunciator*, much less an *avenger*: two sorts of men alone does *he* behold there—*admirers*—ignorant and awe-struck admirers—or *accomplices* or *abettors*.'[90] Bentham recognized that just as corruption might operate on special jurymen to produce obsequiousness, so it might on 'any number of persons, in whatever situations placed, including members of the Commons and Lords'.[91] Of particular significance was the office of Lord Chancellor. Reform of the law would only be accomplished with his support, but were the law to be made subservient to the greatest happiness of the greatest number, it would be opposite to his interest in every respect—namely in terms of money, power, ease, reputation, and vengeance—and to that of his colleagues and friends.[92] The increasingly strident tone of Bentham's criticism of the legal and political establishments was accompanied by an awareness of a stark contrast between the privileged and non-privileged, between oppressors and oppressed: 'Two casts of men in this country: *men of family*, to whom, in case of delinquency, *impunity* is due: men of *no* family, to whom, in the like case, *punishment* is due. One cast, who have a right *to plunder*: another cast, who have a right to *be plundered*, and to be *punished* if they *complain* of it.'[93] These few scattered hints hardly represented a systematic attack on the political establishment of the country, but with the emergence in his thought of the notion of sinister interest, and the willingness to apply the insights which that brought to every aspect of the state, all that was wanting was the occasion. Such an occasion was not long in coming. The immediate cause of what was to become a sustained and detailed onslaught on the institutions of the English state was a speech delivered in the House of Commons by Charles Abbot, the Speaker, who also happened to be Bentham's stepbrother.[94]

[89] Bowring, v. 89. [90] Ibid. 178. [91] Ibid. 72 n. [92] Ibid. 143 n.
[93] Ibid. 117 n.
[94] Bentham's mother, Alicia, had died in 1759. In 1766, his father Jeremiah, had married Sarah Abbot (*née* Farr), the widow of John Abbot, Fellow of Balliol College, Oxford, and Rector of All Saints', Colchester. Sarah had two sons by her first marriage, John Farr and Charles.

6

Parliamentary Reform

I

The standard account of Bentham's 'conversion' or 'transition' to political radicalism is that provided by Dinwiddy. While accepting that in 1789–90 Bentham was 'briefly converted to democratic views', he points out 'that owing to the alarming course taken by the French Revolution the original conversion was very ephemeral', and argues that 'the fact surely remains that the really fruitful turning-point in the development of [Bentham's] political thought came in 1809, when he began the process of drafting and redrafting that was to culminate in the works on parliamentary reform published in 1817 and 1819'.[1] Dinwiddy agrees with Halévy and other scholars that James Mill, with whom Bentham came into contact in 1808, was 'a crucial factor in turning Bentham into a radical'. In articles published in the *Edinburgh Review* in October 1808 and January 1809 Mill had 'led the way in formulating, or reformulating, the basic argument on which the Utilitarian case for democracy was to be built'. Bentham began to write on the subject of parliamentary reform in August 1809, just after Mill and his family had joined Bentham at his summer retreat at Oxted. This 'notable coincidence of dates', according to Dinwiddy, 'tends to confirm the theory of Mill's influence'.[2] Having said that, Dinwiddy concedes that Bentham had already made 'jottings' on the question of reform in June and July 1809, and on 4 July 1809 had set out 'the grievances which in his view made political reform necessary'.[3] A further factor which 'may have been important in changing the character of Bentham's politics' was the sympathy generated for the liberal cause by the Spanish uprising against the French and the movement for independence in the Spanish colonies,[4] while an 'important background factor in facilitating [Bentham's] transition to radicalism was the example of the United States', where popular government had proved itself compatible with the security of property.[5] Dinwiddy plays down the significance for Bentham of the 'marked revival of radical feeling' in England in 1809, resulting from the indignation

[1] Dinwiddy, 'Bentham's Transition to Political Radicalism', 683. The works in question were *Plan of Parliamentary Reform* and *Bentham's Radical Reform Bill* (London, 1819) (Bowring, iii. 558–97).

[2] Dinwiddy, 'Bentham's Transition to Political Radicalism', 684–5.

[3] Ibid. 686.

[4] Ibid. 685–6.

[5] Ibid. 693–4.

caused by the acquittal of the Duke of York by the House of Commons from charges of corruption.[6] More important, however, was Parliament's behaviour towards the reform of civil justice in Scotland, which showed that it was not prepared to reform any aspect of the law without the sanction of the lawyers. Having previously accepted that 'the legislature had provided some check to the growth of legal abuses, [Bentham] now substituted the theory that abuses in the law and abuses in parliament were symbiotic'. Parliament and the legal profession formed a partnership to promote their sinister interest at the expense of the people: Parliament protected the lawyers in the enjoyment of their abuses, while the lawyers supported the political establishment in resisting reform.[7] Dinwiddy argues that John Plamenatz's view that it had been the failure of the panopticon scheme which had converted Bentham to democracy was 'an oversimplification', in that the scheme had fallen through several years earlier,[8] though he accepts L. J. Hume's view that Bentham's belief that the scheme 'had been killed by the personal influence of the king and of certain aristocrats', and that 'the executive had blatantly defied the authority of the legislative', did 'in some important respects prepare his mind for the reorientation'.[9]

Hume, in contrast to Dinwiddy, is sceptical about the influence of Mill in converting Bentham to political radicalism (indeed, on the available evidence, it might just as plausibly be argued that Bentham converted Mill to political radicalism, as that Mill converted Bentham),[10] and points to other circumstances which influenced Bentham in 1807–9. He finds an 'anticipation of democratic ideas' in Bentham's proposals for the election of judges by peers to the projected Court of Lords' Delegates,[11] and suggests that Bentham's disillusionment with the British political system was compounded by the fall of Grenville's Ministry of All the Talents in 1807, and the findings of the Select Committee on Public Expenditure, which had produced four reports by 1809 illustrating enormous expenditure of public money on pensions, sinecures, and other corrupt practices.[12] While Hume recognizes that between 1802 and 1822 the 'unifying element' in Bentham's thought was 'his ambition to track down, delineate and find antidotes to sinister influence within the political and social system', and that his disappointment in relation to panopticon had a profound impact,[13] he

[6] Dinwiddy, 'Bentham's Transition to Political Radicalism', 686–7. [7] Ibid. 687–9.

[8] Contrary to the impression given by Dinwiddy, Plamenatz ascribes Bentham's adoption of 'thorough-going radicalism' both to the failure of panopticon and to his meeting with James Mill, who 'helped Bentham to draw democratic inferences from his unfortunate experience over the *Panopticon*': see J. Plamenatz, *The English Utilitarians*, 2nd edn. (Oxford, 1958), 62–4, 82.

[9] Dinwiddy, 'Bentham's Transition to Political Radicalism', 690.

[10] Despite his detailed study of Mill's writings during the critical period, R. A. Fenn, *James Mill's Political Thought* (New York, 1987), 126–7 n., is unable to determine whether Bentham or Mill 'was a democrat first'.

[11] See 'Summary View of the Plan of a Judicatory, under the name of the Court of Lords' Delegates', dated 10 January 1808, and first published in Bowring, v. 55–60.

[12] L. J. Hume, *Bentham and Bureaucracy* (Cambridge, 1981), 175–8. [13] Ibid. 13.

fails to appreciate the significance of the emergence of sinister interest in the development of Bentham's political thought. In contrast, Dinwiddy does recognize the significance which Bentham ascribed to sinister interest in explaining the behaviour of the political and legal establishment, and the appearance of the notion in Bentham's writings on the reform of the Scottish legal system. He does not, however, appreciate the fact that Bentham first produced a detailed account of sinister interest around 1804, at a time when he was gravely disappointed at the rejection of the panopticon prison scheme by the government. The failure of panopticon, to the extent that it may have led Bentham to recognize the existence of sinister interest, deserves greater prominence in the account of the development of Bentham's political thought than Dinwiddy allows it.[14]

Further evidence that Bentham himself dated his commitment to radical political reform to a date prior to 1809 comes from *Plan of Parliamentary Reform* where, referring to the year 1809 when he had begun to compose the text, he noted that:

> For a long time past had the necessity,—and not only the necessity, but supposing it attainable, the undangerousness,—of a Parliamentary Reform, and that a radical one, presented itself to my mind, if not in a light as yet sufficiently clear for communication, at any rate in the strongest colours. Long had this sole possible remedy against the otherwise mortal disease of misrule, been regarded by me as the country's only hope.[15]

Bentham's claim that he had become convinced of the need for radical reform 'long' before he began writing on parliamentary reform in June 1809 needs qualification, as we have seen,[16] in that it was only in the first half of that year that he linked the sinister interest of lawyers with that of legislators. Furthermore, the very notion of a 'conversion', suggesting a sudden, revelatory moment, neglects the way in which the theoretical elements which produced Bentham's commitment to political radicalism had been developing since he had embarked on his life's work. The techniques of exposition which followed from his theory of real and fictitious entities, the principle of utility as a moral standard, and the development of a censorial jurisprudence, had all been in place by the mid-1770s at the latest and had all contributed to Bentham's critical outlook. He had originally attributed the corruption and irrationality of the law to a lack of knowledge and judgment on the part of legislators and practitioners, but from 1804 his increasing awareness of sinister interest had then alerted him to the real nature of the problem—namely the lack of any motive on the part of those he would later term 'the ruling and influential few' to promote the happiness of the community. Having attributed the unsatisfactory state of the law to the sinister interest of the legal profession, who had managed to dupe the legislature, he went on to recognize that the legislators shared the same sinister interest and were

[14] See pp. 109–11 above. [15] Bowring, iii. 535. [16] See pp. 131–6 above.

in alliance with the lawyers. When Bentham began to write on parliamentary reform in 1809 the foundations of his political radicalism were already in place: thereafter it was a question not so much of 'conversion' or 'transition', but of application.

The immediate cause which prompted Bentham to begin writing on parliamentary reform was a speech of his stepbrother Charles Abbot, Speaker of the House of Commons, delivered on 1 June 1809 during a debate on Curwen's Reform Bill, and published in *Cobbett's Weekly Political Register* of 10 June 1809. Curwen, a moderate Whig, had introduced a Bill which aimed to prevent the sale of seats by requiring MPs to take an oath that money had not changed hands in the course of their election.[17] Speaking in general support of the measure, Abbot warned the Commons that unless they 'proceed to brand and stigmatize' the sale of seats 'by a prohibitory Law . . . we shall see that Seats in this House are advertised for sale by Public Auction: And we shall have brought a greater scandal upon Parliament and the Nation, than this country has ever known since Parliaments have had an existence'. It was not the possession of money, but the possession of property, which should form the predominant title to a seat in Parliament, together with 'the virtuous and generous Motives of Friendship, Affection, and the fair preference of Talents and Integrity'.[18] Bentham's criticism of Abbot's speech formed the point of departure for an extensive essay entitled 'Influence', written in late 1809 and early 1810, in which he discussed a variety of issues relating to the conduct of MPs. As far as Bentham was concerned, 'of all the mischiefs resulting from the actual composition of Parliament', the selling of seats was 'one of the least mischievous'. The real problem lay in the dependence of a majority of MPs 'on the sinister will' of the monarch. Nor could Bentham see any difference between the sale of seats by private contract, as was the present practice, and public auction, except that by public auction the price would probably be higher.[19] He argued that if placing men in the House of Commons on 'the virtuous and generous motives of friendship and affection' was innoxious, as Abbot had claimed, then it was no less so if they were placed as a result of bargain and sale, and 'in short the same account may without much difference be given of every mode of appointment different from that which parliamentary reform supposes and requires'.[20]

[17] According to Cannon, *Parliamentary Reform*, 154, the proposal 'produced a series of debates that laid bare the working of the unreformed system'.

[18] See *Cobbett's Weekly Political Register*, vol. xv, no. 23 (10 June 1809), 865–72. The speech can also be found at *Parliamentary Debates*, xiv (1809), 837–43. Bentham did not explicitly state that it was Abbot's speech which was responsible for his embarking on his analysis of parliamentary reform in the summer of 1809, but the fact that the earliest manuscript on the subject (UC cxxvii. 114) dates from the same day, namely 10 June 1809, that the speech appeared in *Cobbett's Weekly Political Register*, and that it was given a prominent place in his subsequent writings on 'Influence', leave no doubt that this was the case.

[19] UC cxxx. 45–6 (31 Dec. 1809).

[20] UC cxxx. 185 (29 Dec. 1809).

II

When Bentham began to write on parliamentary reform in the summer of 1809, it appears that initially he drafted 'Parliamentary Reform Catechism'—which eventually appeared in the published text of *Plan of Parliamentary Reform*—and then went on in the autumn and winter of 1809–10 to draft a substantial quantity of 'explanatory material', of which the essay on 'Influence' was one part. Bentham had anonymously offered the 'Catechism' to 'one of the time-serving daily prints', but it had been turned down, and for several years thereafter 'despair of use' had kept it, 'together with so many other papers, upon the shelf'.[21] He had thereupon, amongst other projects, worked on two related themes—political fallacies and a critique of the established Church[22]—before returning to the subject of parliamentary reform in 1816. Being 'encouraged by the present posture of affairs' and 'vehemently urged on' by James Mill, he composed the 'Introduction', which superseded the earlier 'explanatory material'.[23] Hence when *Plan of Parliamentary Reform* was published in 1817, it consisted of an 'Introduction', written in 1816–17, followed by 'Parliamentary Reform Catechism', written in 1809. Bentham continued to draft new material, and in 1819 published *Bentham's Radical Reform Bill*, which consisted for the most part of a draft Act of Parliament, entitled 'Parliamentary Reform Act: being an Act for the more adequate Representation of the People in the Commons House of Parliament'. A further essay, 'Radicalism not Dangerous', written in 1819–20, did not appear in print until its publication in the Bowring edition.[24] While there was a great deal of continuity between the material written in 1809–10 and that written in 1816–19, there were some important developments in Bentham's thinking, particularly in relation to the notion of official aptitude, which he put forward as the antidote to sinister interest.[25]

In the 'Catechism' Bentham identified three objectives which would be achieved by parliamentary reform: first, securing the highest possible degree of aptitude on the part of MPs; second, removing or reducing to the smallest possible amount the inconveniences associated with elections; and third, removing or reducing to the smallest possible amount the inconveniences associated with election judicature.[26] The central problem was the existence of sinister interest, which manifested itself in corruption: 'Whatsoever is either *good* in itself, or thought to be so, is capable of being employed in the character of

[21] Bowring, iii. 435. In November 1810 Bentham had offered the 'Catechism' to Cobbett for publication in the *Weekly Political Register*: see Bentham to Cobbett, *Correspondence*, viii. 80–1.

[22] For *The Book of Fallacies* and *Church-of-Englandism and its Catechism Examined*, printed in 1817 (London, 1818), see pp. 155–62 and 176–86 below, respectively.

[23] Bentham to John Herbert Koe, 1 Jan. 1817, *Correspondence*, vol. ix, ed. S. Conway (Oxford, 1989), 3.

[24] See Bowring, iii. 599–622.

[25] The development of aptitude is considered in detail in Ch. 11 below.

[26] It appears that in 1809 Bentham had not yet coined the verbs 'to maximize' and 'to minimize', though he had done so by 1817: see p. 273 n. below.

matter of reward: and whatsoever is employed in the character of matter of reward, becomes *matter of corruption* when applied to a *sinister* purpose: when applied to a man, in such manner as to direct his endeavours to the doing *good* to the *one* or to the *few*, at the expense of preponderant *evil* to the *many*.' The bestowal of the 'matter of reward' by the King, or Corruptor-General as Bentham termed him,[27] was justified only when granted in recognition of some public service. If, on the contrary, it was granted 'as matter of *favour*', then not only did it amount to waste, but it also operated 'as matter of *corruption*, by the expectation of it'. The award of peerages to persons who had not performed any public service was 'a conspicuous example' of 'the matter of reward applied to the purpose of corruption'. The very wealthy, who would not be corrupted by other means, were corrupted by a peerage: those who sat in the Commons by the prospect of a peerage, and those already in the Lords by the prospect of an advancement in the peerage. It was necessary to remove or reduce the matter of corruption wherever it existed.[28]

The notion of aptitude formed the theoretical framework within which Bentham developed and elaborated his proposals for political reform. In the 'Catechism' Bentham explained that aptitude consisted in three elements: appropriate probity—the desire to promote the greatest happiness of the greatest number; appropriate intellectual aptitude—the capacity to form a correct judgment; and appropriate active talent—the capacity to perform the activities, such as introducing motions or delivering speeches, expected of a member of the House of Commons.[29] The standard against which all schemes for parliamentary reform were to be measured was whether they promoted the probity, intelligence, and active talent of members of the House of Commons. These were the principles, explained Bentham, on which his own measures had been grounded.[30] He recommended that 'placemen', that is officeholders appointed by the Crown, should be excluded from the House of Commons, though ministers should have the right to speak and propose motions; that elections should be held annually (with the King retaining the right to dissolve Parliament and call new elections at any point between the specified annual elections); that the proceedings of Parliament should be publicized; and that the attendance of MPs should be constant, punctual, and universal.

Bentham's proposals in relation to the exclusion of placemen reflected his strategy of rendering the executive subordinate to the legislative power. Officeholders, being dependent upon the pleasure of the King for the retention of the money, power, and reputation which they gained from their offices, would rather sacrifice the general interest than vote against the wishes of the King or his ministers. Excluding them from the Commons would promote probity. Granting ministers the right to speak and to propose motions, but without the

[27] The printer of the published text, fearing prosecution for seditious libel, substituted 'C—— G——' for 'Corruptor-General'.
[28] Bowring, iii. 545–6.
[29] Ibid. 539–40.
[30] Ibid. 552.

right to vote, would promote intellectual aptitude. The Commons would benefit from the intelligence possessed by ministers, and avoid the danger of 'having its decisions perpetually exposed to be turned aside into a sinister course, by the weight of so many dependent votes, expressive—not of any will of the voters, guided by any opinion of their *own* concerning the general interest, but of the will, guided by the particular and thence sinister interest, of the king, or of some minister, or of some private and unknown favourite of the king's. . . .' The King and his ministers would possess 'the only *honest* kind of influence, viz. *the influence of understanding on understanding*', freed from 'that *dishonest* kind of influence . . . viz. *the influence of will over will*'.[31] Distinguishing between the judgmental function of voting on the one hand, and the advocatory function of speaking and proposing motions on the other, would also obviate the problem of ministers and other officials avoiding scrutiny by sitting in the Lords rather than the Commons. Furthermore, instead of having to await written information, the Commons might demand immediate oral evidence from the relevant official, which might be followed up with appropriate questioning.[32] Being answerable to the Commons, ministers would have an incentive to be fully and accurately informed of the business of their respective departments, and this in turn would increase the aptitude of their subordinates, who would themselves be answerable to ministers.[33]

Annual elections, which, of course, would threaten MPs with the loss of their seats at intervals no greater than a year should they displease their constituents, would be a further means of securing probity. At the same time the maximum length of 'sinister service' which the King or his ministers might obtain from any one MP would be reduced from seven years (as had been the case since the Septennial Act of 1716) to one year, while a parliamentary candidate would be less likely to undertake an expensive electoral campaign in the hope of obtaining an office or other 'indemnification' from the Crown. Annual elections would also help to secure intellectual aptitude and active talent, since any perceived deficiency in the sitting MP would encourage potential rivals.[34] The publicity of parliamentary debates would secure probity by reminding the MP that he would be judged by the public in general, and by his constituents in particular, on the basis of his speeches and votes. While on the one hand publicity would help secure the intellectual aptitude of members by providing them with an accurate account of the information presented and arguments advanced on previous occasions, and thereby with the best grounds for their opinions, speeches, and votes, on the other hand they would be aware that any lack of intellectual

[31] Ibid. 541–2. [32] Ibid. 550–1.

[33] Ibid. 549–50. Bentham recommended that an official from every department from which information might be required should be present in the Commons. Distinctive uniforms might be provided for each of the officials, the choice of which, Bentham added sarcastically, would be 'an exercise—nor *that*, it is humbly supposed, altogether an unacceptable one—for the taste and talents of the *Prince Regent*'. See ibid. 490 and n.

[34] Ibid. 542–3.

aptitude revealed in their speeches would be fully exposed, and the influence of 'rhetorical *fallacies* and devices' counteracted. Those who, 'on the ground of experience . . . either in their own judgment, or that of their constitutional judges', had failed the test of publicity would not be re-elected.[35] The speedy, full, and accurate publication of debates in the Commons would, moreover, diminish the influence of the Lords, since if satisfactory arguments in favour of a measure had been advanced in the Commons, it would be difficult for the Lords to reject it, 'howsoever uncongenial it may be to particular interests or favourite prejudices'.[36]

The constant and punctual attendance of MPs would promote probity. An MP was capable of performing his duty only if he were physically in the House. If allowed to absent himself as he pleased, an MP obsequious to the will of the King might thereby fail to oppose a mischievous measure, and at the same time avoid the criticism he would otherwise have received had he directly supported the measure. By his absence, noted Bentham, he was able to do half the mischief which he would not have dared to do had he been present. Attendance would promote intellectual aptitude, in that the more frequently the MP attended, the greater his understanding of 'the nature of his business, whatsoever it be', and also promote active talent, in that the more he examined and managed the business, the greater his expertise in it would become. Bentham proposed the publication of a 'Daily-General-Attendance Table' and an 'Annual-Individual-Attendance Table', which would record the attendance, votes, and speeches of each MP, together with the excuse offered for any absence. If a stronger measure were considered necessary, MPs might be required to deposit a sum of money with the clerk of the House, receiving back a proportion on each day of attendance. The forfeited sums might be distributed amongst those who did attend, and thereby 'the force of *reward*' be 'added to that of *punishment*'. When considering whether to re-elect the MP in question, constituents could take into account whether or not attendance had, in their view, been satisfactory.[37]

In relation to the conduct of elections and the settling of election disputes, Bentham proposed a system of polling which, he argued, would be both inexpensive and uncomplicated, thereby reducing the opportunities for bribery and for litigation. The secret ballot would remove the incentive to bribery; the postal vote would obviate the need to convey voters to the polls, often undertaken at great expense; and a clear franchise qualification, consisting of the payment of a certain amount of taxes, and subject to a literacy test, would eliminate almost all causes of controverted elections.[38] Bentham believed that the secret ballot was vital in counteracting sinister influence. The standard objection to the secret ballot was that a majority of voters, if left free to vote from purely selfish considerations, would be bribed into choosing a 'less worthy' candidate, thus producing the 'sacrifice of public interest to private interest'. Bentham responded

[35] Bowring, iii. 543–4. [36] Ibid. 551. [37] Ibid. 544–5. [38] Ibid. 540, 547.

that, on the contrary, it was open voting which forced electors to vote against their consciences and in favour of the less worthy candidate, for instance where a tenant was forced to vote according to the wish of his landlord 'on pain of suffering . . . some personal inconvenience, to the magnitude of which there are no limits'. Under the secret ballot, the potential briber had no assurance that the voter would vote in his favour. Since the voter had no interest in choosing the less worthy candidate, it seemed reasonable to expect that he would vote for the more worthy.[39]

The franchise qualification—which would be the payment of direct taxes, and in effect the equivalent of householder suffrage—would be sufficiently wide to produce a uniformly large number of voters in each electoral district. Of the projected 600 seats in Parliament, two-thirds would be assigned on the basis of territory, and the remaining third on the basis of population. The territorial electoral districts would be formed by dividing Britain and Ireland into 400 districts, each returning one member, while the population electoral districts would be composed of towns whose population had surpassed a certain threshold (Bentham suggested around 10,000), with the seats then allocated according to the total size of population, so that larger towns would have a greater number of seats. Within certain limits, inequalities in the number of electors in each district would be tolerable in that they would be unlikely to diminish significantly the aptitude of a majority of MPs. By this system: 'The three capitals, London, Dublin, and Edinburgh, would thus possess that ascendency which is their due: due to them, not merely on the score of population, but also on the score of appropriate information and intelligence.' Persons who were traditionally excluded from the franchise, such as aliens, would not need to be disqualified, since they would be so outnumbered that no practical mischief would ensue from their admission. Even females might be allowed the vote 'with as little impropriety or danger' as they were in the election of directors of the East India Company, who governed 30 or 40 million people in British India.[40]

III

In the 'Introduction' to *Plan of Parliamentary Reform* Bentham put forward detailed reasons in support of the measures he had outlined several years earlier in the 'Catechism'. Apart from some modifications to his proposals—such as dropping the distinction between territorial and population electoral districts, and extending his proposed franchise (albeit not to females)—the overall scheme

[39] Ibid. 547–8.

[40] Ibid. 540–1. The Court of Directors, the executive body of the East India Company, was elected by the Proprietors, that is holders of the Company's stock, a number of whom were women: see C. H. Philips, *The East India Company 1784–1834*, 2nd edn. (Manchester, 1961), 2–8.

and its rationale were little altered, though Bentham appreciated that in the 'Introduction' there was an increased stridency in his tone or 'temper' compared with the 'Catechism' (or 'Plan' as Bentham referred to it): 'For *any* eyes that could find patience to look at it, was the *Plan* itself designed. A few exceptions excepted—(and those—alas! how few!)—for swinish eyes alone this melancholy *Introduction*,—not for honourable ones. Against interest—against a host of confederated interests—what can argument do? Exactly as much as against a line of musketry.'[41] While the increased stridency of the 'Introduction' might have been due to its being targeted at a different audience, it was also the case that by 1816–17 Bentham had come to believe that the need for radical reform was all the more urgent. He now claimed that Britain was 'at the very brink:—reform or convulsion, such is the alternative'. Habeas Corpus had been suspended, and further measures to prevent communication for the purpose of making complaint or obtaining remedy had been introduced or were in preparation.[42] English liberties would be destroyed, and the government, instead of a 'disguised despotism', would become a 'despotism in form, to which disguise is no longer necessary'. Unless radical reform was introduced, the result would be 'the destruction of everything by which the constitution of this country has been distinguished to its advantage'.[43]

In the 'Introduction' Bentham published a much more detailed and systematic account than he had hitherto of the operation of corruption in the English political establishment, drawing on a distinction between monarchical, aristocratical, and democratical interests. 'As early as the year 1809, and I forget how much earlier', remarked Bentham, he had realized that rulers followed a 'principle' to the effect that they were entitled to make fortunes at the expense of the people, a principle in which 'the road to national ruin might be but too clearly traced'.[44] An alliance of 'the two domineering interests—the monarchical and the aristocratical', extracted money from 'the every now and then struggling, but always vainly and feebly struggling, democratical'. The matter

[41] Bowring, iii. 536. Bentham often referred ironically to the people as 'the swinish multitude', alluding to a remark made by Burke in *Reflections on the Revolution in France* (see *Writings and Speeches*, viii. 130), in which Burke, it was claimed by radicals, had revealed his contempt for the people.

[42] Following an attack on the Prince Regent as he was returning to Carlton House after the opening of the parliamentary session on 28 January 1817, the government suspended the Habeas Corpus Act and passed the Seditious Meetings Act (57 Geo. III, c. 19), which placed public meetings under the control of magistrates. In the meantime, on 27 March 1817, the Home Secretary Sidmouth issued a Circular Letter to the Lords-Lieutenants, desiring them to remind Justices of the Peace in their respective counties that they had the authority to arrest persons selling seditious literature. See A. Aspinall, *Politics and the Press c. 1780–1850* (London, 1949), 45–56.

[43] Bowring, iii. 535.

[44] Bentham had exposed this principle, which, he claimed, had been avowed by Burke on behalf of the Whigs and George Rose on behalf of the Tories, in 'Defence of Economy against the late Mr. Burke' and 'Defence of Economy against the Right Hon. George Rose', written in 1810, but first published in *The Pamphleteer*, vol. ix, no. xvii (1817), 3–47 and vol. x, no. xx (1817), 281–332, respectively (see *Official Aptitude Maximized; Expense Minimized*, 39–94 and 95–155, respectively).

of good—composed of power, money, and factitious dignity—to the extent that it was sought by a member of the Commons or Lords from the King, operated as the matter of corruptive influence. The monarch endeavoured to acquire for himself as much of the matter of good as possible: 'And here we have one *partial*, one *separate*, one *sinister* interest, the *monarchical*—the interest of the ruling *one*—with which the *universal*, the *democratical* interest has to antagonize, and to which that all-comprehensive interest has all along been,—and unless the only possible remedy—even parliamentary reform, and that a radical one, should be applied,—is destined to be ever made a sacrifice....' Money had to be raised through Parliament, dominated by 'another partial, separate, and sinister interest—the *aristocratical* interest'. The universal or democratical interest had always been sacrificed to the 'conjunct yoke' of the monarchical and aristocratical interests. The desire to 'consummate' this sacrifice, in other words to establish despotism, had never been lacking, but the power to do so had never before 'swelled to a pitch approaching to that at which it stands at this moment'. This increase in power had been brought about by corruptive influence, operating through useless, needless, and overpaid offices, groundless pensions and sinecures, together with peerages, baronetages, and other honours. The King, by his very situation without the need of any overt act, was the Corruptor-General, disposing of power, money, and factitious dignity, for the benefit of the members of the Commons and Lords, and receiving their votes in return. The Corruptor-General, together with 'the corrupted and corrupting aristocracy', formed a partnership, Corruptor-General & Co., whose business was to drain 'the contents of all pockets into its own', the result being 'the *sacrifice* made... of the interest and comfort of the *subject-many*, to the overgrown felicity of the *ruling few*'. A community of interest between Corruptor-General and people did indeed exist, but it was analogous to that which existed between the slaveholder and his slaves, or the mail-coach contractor and his horses: 'While working them, and so long as they appear able to work, he accordingly allows them food. Yet, somehow or other, notwithstanding this community of interest, so it is, that but too often negro as well as horse are worked to the very death.' Having said that, it was recognized that the attempt to extract an infinite supply of money all at once would produce resistance on the part of the people, so a 'set of *drains*' had been established by which money was gradually 'drawn out of the pockets of the blinded, deluded, unsuspicious, uninquisitive, and ever too patient people'. These drains, or sources of expense, included wars (particularly involvement in European wars on the pretext of defending Hanover), the acquisition and retention of colonies, claims of supremacy over the sea, the maintenance of 'the splendour of the crown', and the erection of Hanover into a kingdom.[45] The solution lay in what Bentham termed 'democratic ascendancy', which would be

[45] The Electorate of Hanover, joined, of course, with the Crown of Great Britain, was erected into a kingdom at the Congress of Vienna in October 1814.

brought about by radical reform: indeed, there was no need to abolish the monarchy or peerage. He explained that his ruling principle 'in all matters of reform . . . in so far as it is not inconsistent with the very essence of the reform' was that of *uti possidetis*, 'that which you have, continue to have—and God bless you with it'. His aim was not to deprive the ruling few of the benefits which they enjoyed, but to extend them to the subject many.[46]

Misrule continued, noted Bentham, because government was in the hands of those whose interest it was that it should continue. He was content to leave the executive in the hands of the King and his ministers, but wanted the House of Commons, the controlling part of government, to be given to the people, whose interest it was (with the exception of those who would lose power and any money they expected to gain from the continuance of the misrule) that misrule should be replaced by good government.[47] Parliamentary reform was not itself the ultimate end, but the promotion of the universal interest:

> In the description of this end is included—*comprehension* of all distinguishable *particular interests*: viz. in such sort, that such of them, between which no repugnancy has place, may be provided for in conjunction, and *without defalcation*:—while, in regard to such of them, between which any such repugnancy has place, such defalcations, and such alone, shall be made, as, when taken all together, shall leave in the state of a *maximum* whatsoever residuum of comfort and security may be the result:—with exceptions to as *small* an extent as possible, interests *all* to be *advanced*: without *any* exception, all to be *considered*.[48]

The principles that every one had an equality of right to happiness, an equality of capacity for happiness, and equality of desire for happiness, which Bentham had iterated in 1788–9, once again appeared as the basis for the political equality which he championed in the 'Introduction'.[49] Underlying the claim that the happiness of any one member of the community was as much a part of the universal happiness as any other was the psychological axiom that everyone was susceptible of pain and pleasure. From the requirement to 'comprehend', or take into account, each and every particular interest—which meant the interest of each and every individual—Bentham derived the notion of political equality, which, he now claimed, implied virtual universality, practical equality, and freedom of suffrage. If it was right that one person should enjoy the franchise, it was right that every other person should do so, with the exception of those whose exclusion would for some specific reason be beneficial (hence 'virtual' rather than 'absolute' universality of suffrage). For instance, idiots and infants were incapable of exercising the suffrage either to their own advantage or to that of anyone else, and this justified their exclusion (though Bentham did, as we shall see, decide against the exclusion of lunatics). The principle that everyone should

[46] Bowring, iii. 438–42. [47] Ibid. 447–8. [48] Ibid. 452.

[49] See the passage at ibid. 459, which is reminiscent of the passage in 'Considérations sur la Composition des Etats-Généraux' discussed at p. 83–6 above.

possess a certain share in the franchise, while implying that each person should have a similar share, did not require each person's share to be absolutely equal to every other person's. In practice it would be impossible to create electoral districts with exactly the same number of voters, which absolute equality would require. Finally, there should be freedom of suffrage: each person should be free to vote according to his own judgment. A vote given in accordance with the will of some other person, from whom the voter hoped for some reward or feared some punishment, was not genuine, but spurious. Freedom of suffrage would be secured by the secret ballot, which remained, in Bentham's view, crucial to his whole scheme of reform. Even where there was a large electorate, universality and equality would not be sufficient without secrecy. Where voting was open, a very small sum would be enough to bribe each voter—Bentham confessed that a few shillings would have been enough to bribe him. Secrecy removed any temptation even to solicit a vote, still less to attempt to buy a vote.[50]

Bentham had always been prepared to exclude from the franchise those individuals clearly incapable of understanding what constituted their interest. Under what he termed the 'legitimate-defalcation principle', minors would be excluded from the vote, though the 'defalcation' would, of course, be temporary. Soldiers and sailors would be excluded, in order to prevent the Corruptor-General from quartering them in such a way that their votes would be decisive in a significant number of electoral districts. Non-readers would also be excluded. The exclusion was again temporary, albeit indefinite, and 'capable of being shortened by the exertions of the individual excluded'. In other words, the non-reader could learn to read.[51] In relation to female suffrage, Bentham thought that there was little at that moment that could be done. Measured against 'the interest-comprehension principle', justice had not hitherto been done to females in this area of law. There was inconsistency in excluding females from the franchise on the grounds of their intellectual incapacity when they had been allowed to hold the office of monarch, and to form part of an aristocracy when voting in elections of directors of the East India Company. While not prepared to give 'anything approaching to a decided opinion' on the grounds that to do so 'would in this place be altogether premature', Bentham recommended that the question of female suffrage be considered on the grounds of principle, rather than being dismissed with 'a *horse*-laugh, a sneer, an expression of scorn, or a common-place witticism'.[52] Writing after the publication of *Plan of Parliamentary Reform*, he pointed out that although not a single argument had since been advanced against female suffrage, he had been the object of 'contempt in abundance' for suggesting that there was 'no adequate reason on the ground of public utility, laying out of the case the current of general opinion', for their exclusion.[53] He did admit that one disadvantage of admitting females would be

[50] Bowring, iii. 452–4. [51] Ibid. 462–3, 464. [52] Ibid. 463.

[53] UC cxxvii. 261 (15 Sept. 1818). Bentham later remarked (see '*Legislator of the World*', 305): 'On the admission of females Mr. Bentham's plan [i.e. of parliamentary reform] forebore to lay

to double the delay, vexation, and expense associated with the election process. He also admitted that the exclusion of females would be justified if it could be shown that the interests of the male sex and the female sex were so closely connected that the former could not injure the interest of the latter without injuring its own, or if the injury done did not outweigh the evil produced in the shape of the additional delay, expense, and vexation. On the other hand, if it was ever shown that such a connection of interests did not exist, then there were no grounds for denying the suffrage to females.[54] Exceptions to 'the defalcation principle' were based on 'the simplification principle'. Various groups, such as foreigners, outlaws, convicts, vagrants, insolvents, bankrupts, and lunatics, might be regarded as unfit for the franchise on the grounds of possessing insufficient probity or intellectual aptitude. In practice, however, no real mischief would result from the admittance of these classes: each vote was only a fraction of a fraction of a power to establish laws and execute measures of administration, whereas any investigation into a person's right to vote would necessarily be attended with delay, vexation, and expense. On the grounds of simplicity, virtual universality of suffrage had a great advantage over householder suffrage.[55]

The advocacy of virtual universality of suffrage as opposed to householder suffrage, the qualification for which was taken to be the payment of direct taxes, marked a change in Bentham's position between the 'Catechism' and the 'Introduction'.[56] He had reached the conclusion that no danger to property would ensue from universality and annuality of suffrage. Before he had directed any '*purposed* attention' to the subject, he had regarded universal suffrage and annual elections 'as being in a general view inadmissible', but once the importance of the question had demanded 'attentive consideration and scrutiny' he had become more firmly convinced, 'on the one hand, of the undangerousness of the principle, taken in the utmost extent to which the application of it can ever reach,—on the other hand, of the facility and consistency with which, for the sake of *union* and *concord*, defalcation after defalcation might,—provisionally at any rate, and for the sake of experience—quiet and gradual experience,—be applied to it'.[57] It seems that Bentham had forgotten his advocacy of universal suffrage, including female suffrage, and annual elections, in his projected

much stress: because it found no grounds for any very determinate assurance, that in that case, the result would be materially different; and because no minds could be expected to be at present prepared for it. But it declared that it could find no reasons for exclusion, and that those who, in support of it gave a sneer or a laugh for a reason, because they could not find a better, had no objection to the vesting of absolute power in that sex and in a single hand: so that it was not without palpable inconsistency and self condemnation, that the exclusion they put upon this class could be brought forward.'

[54] UC cxxvii. 276–7 (25 Nov. 1818). [55] Bowring, iii. 464–5.

[56] See pp. 166–7 below for Bentham's criticism of schemes which linked the suffrage to the payment of taxation. He also came to the view that the extension of the franchise would be likely to produce an increase in the aggregate of appropriate aptitude on the part of the electorate: see pp. 282–4 below.

[57] Bowring, iii. 467–8 n.

constitutional code for France in the autumn of 1789.[58] Having said that, both shortly before and shortly after drawing up his projected constitution for France, he had rejected universal suffrage on the basis of the danger it posed to the security of property. No longer would the fear of the subversion of property stand in the way of Bentham's recommendation of a democratic franchise.

As for the secret ballot, Bentham explained that the question of whether voting should be secret or open, and, therefore, whether freely exercised or not, depended upon the relationship between the interest of the voter and the general interest. The point was that secrecy enabled the voter, and more generally any public trustee, to give effect to his own will, and to exclude the influence of that of every other person. Where the interest of the individual coincided with that of the public, secrecy was appropriate. An individual should only be permitted to promote his private interest insofar as doing so promoted the public interest. In contrast, where the interest of the individual was opposite to that of the public, giving publicity to his vote would prevent the sacrifice of the public interest. The public trustee, whose actions were exposed to publicity, did not enjoy the freedom to give effect to his own will, but only to the will of the public.[59] Freedom of will in a public trustee—and indeed freedom of will *per se*—was of no intrinsic worth, but only of value to the extent that its exercise was conducive to the general interest.

The central feature of existing political arrangements, according to Bentham, was that the private interest of MPs was opposed to that of the public. Rather than being dependent on the people, MPs were dependent on the King:

> Immediate cause of the mischief—on the part of the men acting as representatives of the people, coupled with adequate *power* a sinister *interest*, productive of a constant sacrifice made of the interest of the people.
>
> Causes of the above cause,—in the breasts of these same agents,—*undue independence*, coupled with *undue dependence*: independence as towards their princip[al]s; dependence as towards the C——r-General, by whose co——tive influence the above-mentioned sacrifice is produced.[60]

Democratic ascendancy, brought about by radical parliamentary reform, would at one and the same time render MPs independent of the King and dependent on the people. Corruptor-General & Co. had an immense mass of corruption at its disposal with which to tempt the MP. The solution did not lie in the futile attempt to prohibit the monarch from giving an office or factitious dignity to an MP or some person connected with him, but in giving his constituents the power to remove him from the Commons. While legal punishment could not be

[58] See pp. 89–91 above. This is confirmed by a comment which Bentham appended, almost certainly in 1809, to a rudiment sheet (UC xliv. 1) composed in the autumn of 1789 containing outline proposals for a radical reform of the parliamentary franchise. Surveying the proposals he had made at the time of the French Revolution, he commented incredulously: 'What could this be? Surely this was never *my* opinion.'

[59] Bowring, iii. 489–90.

[60] Ibid. 451–2.

inflicted on an MP where 'the matter of corruption' was given, not to the MP himself, but to a friend, relative, or some other connection of his, the people might 'rid themselves of the supposed betrayer of his trust' without the sort of evidence necessary for a conviction in a court of law. The power of constituents to remove their MP at an annual election would be supplemented by the exclusion of placemen from the Commons. Moreover, the short duration of parliaments would diminish the venal value of the office, both to the MP and the Corruptor-General. The benefit of corrupting an MP would be diminished still further if electors had the power to remove him at any time. Bentham was not, however, prepared to recommend this further measure, since the need to keep the electors in 'a state of almost continual attention and activity' would adversely affect their everyday occupations, and the inconvenience outweigh the likely benefit. It was enough that the date for the election be fixed, as electors would thereby be encouraged to prepare themselves for it. Constancy of attendance on the part of MPs operated as an additional security against undue dependence. An MP who, on the whole, was prepared to support the public good, but at the same time was under the sinister influence of the Corruptor-General, would absent himself when prompted by sinister interest to oppose a beneficial measure. If forced to attend, he might from sense of shame be induced to vote in favour of it.[61] If his programme for radical parliamentary reform, consisting in virtual universality, practical equality, and freedom of suffrage, together with annual elections and constant attendance, were implemented, Bentham claimed, it would be 'morally impossible' for open corruption to take place. Even under the existing system the will of Corruptor-General & Co. had occasionally met with resistance: 'how then could it ever be otherwise under a pure one?'[62]

In Bentham's view, 'the ultimate end—political salvation', could only be achieved by democratic ascendancy, which in turn could only be achieved by radical parliamentary reform. No doubt with a view to widening the appeal of his proposals, he emphasized their compatibility not only with other schemes of parliamentary reform, such as the plan of universal manhood suffrage and annual elections proposed by the Duke of Richmond in Parliament on 2 June 1780 and again in a pamphlet published in 1783,[63] but also with what he took to be ancient constitutional practice. In presenting the case for annuality of suffrage, he appealed to the experience of history, or usage, to support his argument from utility, on the grounds that, given the state of public opinion, the argument from usage might be more '*effectually persuasive*' than that from utility.

[61] Bowring, iii. 454–7. [62] Ibid. 457.

[63] See Richmond's letter to Lieutenant-Colonel Sharman, dated 15 Aug. 1783, which first appeared in *Proceedings relative to the Ulster Assembly of Volunteer Delegates: on the subject of a more equal representation of the people in the Parliament of Ireland. To which are annexed, Letters from the Duke of Richmond, Dr. Price, Mr. Wyvill, and others* (Belfast, 1783), 49–63, but was subsequently reprinted in several editions, most notably as *A Letter from His Grace the Duke of Richmond to Lieutenant Colonel Sharman . . . With Notes, By A Member of the Society for Constitutional Information* (London, 1792).

While usage was connected with utility 'through the medium of *experience*', it had the additional advantage of affording 'the means of defence... against adverse prejudices and fallacies'. In other words, the appeal to history would help to reconcile those who might oppose reform just because it was said to be 'innovation'. Radical parliamentary reform did not constitute an innovation: rather it called for the restoration of control over finance to 'the real representatives, the freely chosen deputies of the body of the people'. Such control had been enjoyed by the people from 1258 until the Wars of the Roses, and democratic ascendancy had been the result. Representatives, elected frequently and for a short time, had been dependent on the people, and independent towards the monarch. Bentham was even prepared to admit that talk of rights, for which he accused Richmond's scheme of indulging in '*ipse dixitism*', was not without value 'in point of persuasion'. He was not beyond turning to advantage here, as he would later in regard to Tripoli,[64] the ambiguity he associated with the word 'right', and for the use of which he had so stridently criticized the French Declaration of Rights. He admitted that 'the word *right*' might be used 'in a figurative and *moral* sense', in order 'that insensibly it may be taken and employed in a *legal sense*', hence producing the belief that long-continued usage had created a constitutional right which had only been superseded in its exercise, and not destroyed.[65] Bentham found another source of support in the recent experience of the United States, where 'all is regularity, tranquillity, prosperity, security', and which proved that there was nothing dangerous not only in democratic ascendancy, but also in pure democracy. The United States was 'the best government that is or ever has been', to which that of Britain formed 'so strong, not to say so complete, a contrast'. Nevertheless, he did not advocate pure democracy for Britain, but merely the ascendancy of the democratic interest 'under the existing forms of subjection'. Given that there was no danger in a pure democracy—'no diminution of security for property, reputation, condition in life, religious worship'—there was no reason to fear any danger to security in a partial democracy, which contained a monarchy and an aristocracy, supported by 'an irresistible standing army'.[66]

In comparing his plan with 'the original editions of Radical Reform', Bentham noted that, in relation to the elector, they coincided in regard to virtual universality and practical equality of suffrage, but differed on that of secrecy, and therefore freedom, of suffrage.[67] In a note, however, he conceded that the secret ballot had long before been advocated by John Cartwright, albeit in publications which he had not seen.[68] In relation to the representative, they coincided in regard to annual elections, due dependence as towards electors, and

[64] See pp. 72–4 above. [65] Bowring, iii. 446–7, 511–16. [66] Ibid. 447, 472.

[67] Bentham perhaps had in mind Richmond's plan. For Richmond's opposition to the secret ballot see *Letter to Lieutenant Colonel Sharman*, 13.

[68] Cartwright had first advocated the secret ballot in *The Legislative Rights of the Commonalty Vindicated; or, Take Your Choice! Representation and Respect: Imposition and Contempt. Annual Parliaments and Liberty: Long Parliaments and Slavery. The Second Edition* (London, 1777), 168–9.

due independence as towards Corruptor-General & Co. However, 'the original editions' had not included, as securities applicable to the final point, the exclusion of placemen from the right of voting, and universal constancy of attendance.[69] What Bentham did not emphasize was the different theoretical foundation of his plan and that of 'the original editions', namely his justification of political equality, and hence radical parliamentary reform, by reference to the principle of utility, rather than the ancient constitution or natural rights (though, as we have seen, he was prepared to appeal to 'usage' and to take advantage of the ambiguity of the word 'right' where it appeared to support his proposals). Bentham was, perhaps, concerned not to open divisions in the movement for radical reform, though his opposition to the theoretical basis of other plans did occasionally emerge. For instance, while admitting that the principle of 'Representation co-extensive with taxation' (a principle he had, as we have seen, earlier supported)[70] was in practice equivalent to the Duke of Richmond's demand for universal suffrage (since everyone was subject to taxation), he criticized it because it was a product of the imagination and paid no regard to '*universal interest* . . . to interest in any shape or to any extent—to human feelings in any shape or to any extent—to general utility—to utility in any shape or to any extent', but was 'a principle deaf, unyielding, and inflexible:—a principle which will hear of no *modification*—will look at no *calculation*:—a principle which, like that of the *rights of man*, is in its *temper* a principle of *despotism*, howsoever in its *application* applied to purposes so diametrically and beneficently opposite'. There was danger that adoption of the principle would lead to the destruction of liberty and property.[71]

Bentham was sceptical about the effects of, and the motivations behind, the proposals for moderate parliamentary reform advanced by the Whig-sponsored Association of the Friends of the People, which had been formed in 1792.[72] They had professed themselves favourable to reform, but their practice had belied their professions. The key to political conduct, Bentham reminded his readers, would be found in the state of interests, and not in professions and protestations. It was possible that a particular individual would not conform to the general rule, due to 'the unconjecturable play of individual idiosyncrasies', but there could be no doubt that a group of men, and particularly a political party 'the motives of which are in so great a degree open to universal observation', would act according to their interests. The Duke of Richmond, for instance, had advocated radical reform, yet it would never happen that all dukes,

[69] Bowring, iii. 458. To be fair, the programme of the Westminster Committee put forward in 1780 had anticipated virtually all of Bentham's proposals for electoral reform (see p. 100 above), constituting as it did the most radical by far of all the various schemes which had been discussed at the time.

[70] See p. 145 above.

[71] Bowring, iii. 467–8 n. Bentham was concerned that matters could be so arranged that no one would pay taxes, and, therefore, no one would be entitled to vote: see p. 167 n. below.

[72] See Veitch, *Genesis of Parliamentary Reform*, 196–200, and, more generally, F. O'Gorman, *The Whig Party and the French Revolution* (London, 1967).

or even a majority of them, would advocate radical reform, unless impelled to do so by fear. Similarly, an individual Whig might be prepared to support radical reform, but never the whole number or a majority of them, unless impelled to do so by fear, the same motive which would impel the Tories.[73] Whigs, characterized by their support for moderate reform, and Tories, characterized by their opposition to all reform, were united by the same sinister interest which was 'completely and unchangeably opposite to that of the whole uncorrupt portion of the people'. The Tories enjoyed the present possession of the corruptive gifts distributed by Corruptor-General & Co., while the Whigs looked forward to the future possession of them. It was, therefore, the interest of both Tories and Whigs that waste and corruption be as great as possible; both owed their parliamentary seats partly to their possession of property and partly to what Bentham termed 'terrorism', namely the influence of will upon will which they were able to exercise over electors; both had an interest in absenting themselves when they pleased from the Commons; both had an interest that the number of seats in their possession, and the value of those seats, should be undiminished, assuming they could not be increased; and both had an interest in ensuring that the patrons of seats had no obligation to return persons possessed of any degree of aptitude. Both Tories and Whigs were disposed to drive the country towards pure despotism, though the latter less forcefully than 'their naturally and almost constantly successful rivals'. If this process was to be stopped, it could only be 'by the energy of the people, headed and led by the few *people's men* by whom any place shall have been found in the House [of Commons]', together with any Whigs who viewed their share in the universal interest as exceeding in value their respective shares in their particular and separate interest. Bentham envisaged that his proposals for virtual universality, practical equality, and secrecy of suffrage would reduce the number of seats held by Tories and Whigs, while the annuality of elections, constant attendance, and the loss of the right of voting on the part of officials would reduce the value of all seats indiscriminately.[74]

IV

Bentham's writings on political fallacies, mainly composed between 1809 and 1811, complemented his work on parliamentary reform. He classified and described in detail the false arguments which had been and, he predicted, would be advanced by those opposed to reform or improvement, and related them to the sinister interests which prompted their proponents to deploy them. As

[73] Bowring, iii. 525–7. Cf. ibid. 507: 'On this occasion, as on all others, before you put yourself to any expense in the article of *argument*, look first to *the state of interests*:—think to overcome the force of interest by the force of argument? Think as well to take *Lisle* or *Mantua*, by peas blown out of a pea-shooter.'

[74] Ibid. 486, 527–9.

Bentham wrote to Francis Place, when trying to secure the services of John Cam Hobhouse to edit the work:

> While in name it will be *The Book of Fallacies*, in its effect, the work will include a defence of Parliamentary Reform against the most operative of the instruments of attack that are so continually employed against it: and, as Reform, in all other shapes whatsoever, is so compleatly dependent upon reform in the parliamentary shape, the use of the work, if it has any, in relation to parliamentary reform, will be its principal use—and *that* greater than all its other public uses put together.[75]

The link in Bentham's mind between his work on parliamentary reform and on political fallacies could not have been clearer. This close relationship has, however, been obscured by the way in which the material on fallacies was presented in the two versions of the work published in Bentham's lifetime, namely Dumont's edition of 'Traité des sophismes politiques', which appeared in *Tactique des assemblées législatives* published in 1816,[76] and Peregrine Bingham's edition of *The Book of Fallacies* published in 1824. Both editors aimed to present the work in a more abstract way than Bentham had conceived it, in order to widen its appeal. While incorporating material omitted by Dumont in which Bentham applied his principles to Britain,[77] Bingham followed Dumont in arranging the fallacies under the headings of fallacies of authority, delay, and confusion, though he added fallacies of danger. But this was, as Bingham recognized, to ignore Bentham's original arrangement of the material into fallacies liable to be employed by the 'Inns', that is by members and supporters of the ministry, those liable to be employed by the 'Outs', that is by the opposition, and those liable to be employed by 'Eithersides'.[78]

Bentham defined a fallacy as 'any argument that is considered as having been employed, or consideration suggested, for the purpose, or with a probability of producing the effect—of deception: of causing some erroneous opinion or opinions to be entertained by some person or persons to whose minds it is expected [it] will present itself'.[79] A fallacy was not merely a false opinion, but a discourse which, whether intended to do so or not, caused an erroneous opinion to be believed, or by means of an erroneous opinion already believed, brought about some mischievous course of action. A fallacy was distinguished in this respect from a 'vulgar error', a phrase coined by Sir Thomas Browne in the seventeenth century,[80] which denoted only the opinion, and not the consequences which it might produce. For instance, to believe that those who lived

[75] Bentham to Place, late 1820?, *Correspondence*, x. 251. In the event, the work was, of course, edited by Bingham rather than by Hobhouse.

[76] *Tactique des assemblées législatives*, ii. 1–267.

[77] Bowring, ii. 376.

[78] Ibid. 381–2. In his 'Memoirs and Correspondence' of Bentham, Bowring reproduced Bentham's own plan for the work: see Bowring, x. 519–21.

[79] UC ciii. 1 ([10 June] 1811) [Bowring, ii. 379].

[80] See Thomas Browne, *Pseudodoxia Epidemica: or, Enquiries into Very many received Tenents, And commonly presumed Truths* (London, 1646), the running title of which reads '*Enquiries into Vulgar and Common Errors*'.

in old times were, because they lived in those times, wiser or better than those who lived in modern times, was vulgar error; to appeal to that error in order to retain some mischievous practice or institution was fallacy.[81] Political fallacies were a particular class of fallacies which affected decision-making in government. By exposing their irrelevancy, the characteristic feature of fallacies, and thus destroying their persuasive force, Bentham hoped to facilitate the introduction and continuation of measures of good government.[82] The use of irrelevant arguments afforded a presumption either of the weakness of the arguments, or total absence of relevant arguments, in support of the cause in question. Fallacies were of use only to a bad cause, since a good cause had no need of them. A person who employed fallacies either suffered from intellectual weakness, or was contemptuous of the understandings of those to whom he addressed them. To be persuaded by them indicated intellectual weakness, while to pretend to be persuaded by them indicated improbity: 'The practical conclusion is—that in proportion as the acceptance, and thence in proportion as the utterance, of them can be prevented, the understanding of the public will be strengthened, the morals of the public will be purified, and the practice of government meliorated.'[83]

Fallacies were the product of either sinister interest, interest-begotten prejudice, authority-begotten prejudice, or self-defence against counter-fallacies. The ultimate cause of the employment of fallacies was sinister interest—if sinister interest did not exist, no one would have a motive to employ fallacies. In the ordinary course of things, the private interest of each 'public man' was in opposition to the interest of the community.[84] Every man with such a sinister interest had a common interest, and consequently 'a fellow-feeling', with every other man who had a similar interest. An attack on one of them was an attack on all of them—hence each man who had a share in this common interest would defend every other confederate's share with no less vigour than if it were his own. The only way in which abuse could be defended was by fallacy.[85] In this respect, the principle of passive obedience and non-resistance had at one time suited the purposes of the ruling few, capable as it was of giving unlimited increase to abuse. At the time he was writing, observed Bentham, it had almost lost its force. It was no longer feasible to create abuses, only to preserve those which already existed.[86] The favourite maxims of the defender of abuse were now 'whatever is, is right', and 'everything is as it should be',[87] appealing to usage, custom, and precedent. Good and bad institutions were defended together on the ground of custom, which was set up as the only proper, safe, and definable standard of

[81] UC ciii. 7–8 (4–5 Aug. 1811) [Bowring, ii. 380].
[82] UC ciii. 10–11 (6–7 Aug. 1811) [Bowring, ii. 380–1].
[83] UC ciii. 512–13 (7 Feb. 1811) [Bowring, ii. 474].
[84] UC ciii. 517–19 (29 May 1811) [Bowring, ii. 475].
[85] UC ciii. 525 (28 June 1810) [Bowring, ii. 476].
[86] UC ciii. 526–7 (4–5 Feb. 1811) [Bowring ii. 476].
[87] This was, of course, the sentiment which Bentham associated with Blackstone: see p. 52 above.

reference, while the principle of utility was represented as dangerous—which indeed, noted Bentham, it was to sinister interest.[88]

The second and third causes which led to the employment of fallacies were the closely related notions of interest-begotten prejudice and authority-begotten prejudice, which themselves were the product of sinister interest. A prejudice was an opinion which had been 'embraced without sufficient examination: it is a judgement which, being pronounced *before* evidence, is therefore pronounced without evidence'.[89] A fallacy was the product of interest-begotten prejudice when the person who accepted it did not perceive that sinister interest was his motive for so doing (had he perceived the motive, the fallacy would have simply been the product of sinister interest).[90] It was unavoidable that a man should take facts and opinions on trust, since the weakness of the human mind rendered it impossible for him to accept or reject, on the ground of his own examination, any more than a small proportion of his opinions. He was, therefore, forced to ground most of his opinions on judgments pronounced by others. The danger was that such judgments might be fallacious. In this case, the fallacy was the product of authority-begotten prejudice.[91] The legitimacy of the influence of a person who claimed authority, or was regarded as having authority, would depend partly upon his probity. The most usual and obvious deficiency in probity was a deficiency in sincerity, that is an opposition or discrepancy between the opinion declared and the opinion really entertained. A lack of probity was, of course, closely related to the existence of sinister interest, which might not only produce an insincere declaration of opinion, but also pervert the opinion itself. In other words, sinister interest might produce either misrepresentation of opinion or erroneous opinion. As far as the production of erroneous opinion was concerned, the effect of sinister interest would result either in the exclusion of relevant information from consideration, or in insufficient attention being paid to it. The correctness and completeness of the information, and thence the opinion grounded upon it, would depend on the adequacy of the means of collecting it, and the strength of a person's motives to employ those means. Taking correctness and completeness together, and assuming the absence of sinister interest, professional opinion or authority was most trustworthy, followed by authority derived from power (the greater the power, the greater the capacity to obtain relevant information), then authority derived from wealth (again, the greater the wealth, the greater the capacity to obtain information), and, lastly, authority derived from reputation. Of these, only the professional man possessed both the motives and means to procure correct information—indeed it was a result of his possessing the motives that led him to obtain the means. Whatever means were available to the others, they were

[88] UC ciii. 530–2 (28 June 1810) [Bowring, ii. 477].
[89] UC ciii. 540 (6 Aug. 1811) [Bowring, ii. 478].
[90] UC ciii. 535 (29 May 1810) [Bowring, ii. 477].
[91] UC ciii. 541–3 (28, 30 May 1811) [Bowring, ii. 478–9].

unlikely to possess the motives to obtain them. On the contrary, in proportion to the magnitude of power, a man tended to have less motive for exertion. In short, even where there was no sinister interest, the authority of the powerful and wealthy had little 'title to regard' on account of their lack of motivation to obtain accurate information. Matters stood even worse where a man's understanding was subject to the force of sinister influence: 'the more compleat as well as correct the mass of relative information is which he has present to his mind, the more compleatly destitute of all title to regard, i.e. to confidence, unless it be to the opposite purpose, will his opinion, pretended or real, be.'[92] In this case, the man would have every motive to misrepresent his opinion. Appeal to authority was fallacious when substituted to relevant arguments which were within the capacity of the debaters to understand, and more especially so when the authority in question was the opinion—real or pretended—of any person whose interest was opposed to that of the people.[93] To appeal to authority as the proper standard for judging a law or established practice was to accept either that the principle of utility was not the proper standard, or that the practice of earlier times or the opinion of other persons was the proper standard. To accept the former proposition was to acknowledge oneself to be an enemy of the community, and to accept the latter to acknowledge oneself incapable of reasoning. Those with some abuse to defend, but finding it indefensible on the ground of public interest, 'fly for refuge' to authority, 'the only sort of argument in which so much as the pretension of being sincere in error can find countenance'.[94]

The fourth cause which led to the employment of fallacies was self-defence against counter-fallacies. Fallacies might be employed in opposition to a pernicious measure on account of their utility in answering counter-fallacies. This was acceptable, stated Bentham, insofar as the fallacies were employed not as substitutes, but as supplements, to relevant and direct arguments.[95] Bentham himself, for instance, as we have seen,[96] supported his utilitarian arguments in favour of democratic ascendancy by reference to 'usage' and a pre-existing constitutional right, as well as taking advantage of the ambiguity involved in the word 'right'.

The demand for political fallacies, argued Bentham, was created by the state of interests. The proper end or object of every political arrangement was the greatest happiness of the greatest number. However, in every political community, with the exception of the United States of America, the interest of the many had been sacrificed to the particular interest of those by whom supreme power was exercised. Rulers were like other individuals, in that their self-regarding interest predominated over their regard for the interest of the community. Their self-regarding interest led them to maintain every abuse which

[92] UC ciii. 45–54 (22–4, 26–8 May 1811) [Bowring, ii. 388–90].
[93] UC ciii. 64–5 (18 July 1810) [Bowring, ii. 391].
[94] UC ciii. 66–7, 69 (17 Oct. 1810) [Bowring, ii. 391–2].
[95] UC ciii. 545 (4 Aug. 1809) [Bowring, ii. 479]. [96] See pp. 152–3 above.

they found established, whether or not they derived any profit from it, since to expose the mischievousness of an unprofitable abuse would at the same time expose that of the profitable. In Parliament both the 'ins' and the 'outs' were motivated by the same sinister interest, and both were prepared to employ whatever fallacies promoted that interest. The situation of the 'outs' was slightly more complex. Their object was to force the 'ins' from office, and thereby become the 'ins' themselves, by raising their political reputation against that of the 'ins'. They attempted to do this by promoting that portion of the universal interest which did not conflict with their sinister interest, and to diminish the reputation of the 'ins' by using fallacies to oppose any useful arrangements proposed by the latter. The 'outs' had to balance the advantage to their share in the universal interest from the establishment of a good measure proposed by the 'ins', against the rise in their own reputation in the event of successful opposition. In respect of bad arrangements by which the sinister interest of both 'ins' and 'outs' would be promoted, the 'outs' had to decide whether, in the event of successful opposition, the loss to their sinister interest would be outweighed by the gain in reputation.[97]

Under the British Constitution, there was a particular demand for fallacies on account of the fact that there existed a popular assembly with an effective role in government, where discussion was to a certain extent free, and accounts of its debates published. Under a despotism, there was no demand for fallacies: 'Fallacy is fraud, and fraud is useless on the part of a government where every thing is done, and any thing may be done, by force.'[98] For instance, in his writings on parliamentary reform, Bentham criticized as 'vague generalities' the objections to reform made by Charles Grey and Lord John Russell, the former claiming that it was absurd, visionary, and senseless, and the latter that it was wild and visionary.[99] These words, noted Bentham, were intended to appeal to the passions, and contained no argument.[100] He also remarked that debates in Parliament were characterized not so much by weakness of argument, but by utter lack of all argument. Speeches were composed of vituperation and fallacy, appealing to the passions and affections, particularly when parliamentary reform was being discussed. As much light was thrown upon the question '[b]y the barking of a dog—by the screaming of a parrot' as by many of the speeches delivered in the Commons and Lords. Moreover, the association of probity and wisdom with rank and opulence led the man of rank and opulence to expect other men to follow his opinion, which, on the same grounds of association, they did, and thus 'from the very causes of his inaptitude does he derive the

[97] UC ciii. 560–5 (3–4 Aug. 1819) [Bowring, ii. 482–4].

[98] UC ciii. 556 (14 July 1810) [Bowring, ii. 481].

[99] Russell, in the debate in the House of Commons of 1 July 1819 on the motion for parliamentary reform proposed by Sir Francis Burdett, had suggested that those who had advised Burdett to bring forward his motion of the previous year for annual elections and universal suffrage (the most important of whom was Bentham, as we shall see) were 'wild and visionary theorists': see *Parliamentary Debates*, xl (1819), 1496.

[100] Bowring, iii. 600–2.

assurance of his aptitude. Idiosyncrasies apart, a man of *twenty thousand* a-year will accordingly speak with twice the persuasive force of a man of but *ten thousand* a-year: a man which is everlastingly noble, with some number of times the force of one who is but honourable.'[101] This was a striking example of authority-begotten prejudice. Yet the truth was that men of rank and opulence were more likely to be deficient in intellectual aptitude and active talent, since they lacked any motive to undertake the hard labour necessary to acquire these endowments. They received their distinction from rank and opulence, and therefore had no need to acquire it through their actions. Bentham argued that intellectual aptitude and active talent were most likely to be found in MPs returned for pocket boroughs by patrons and in those who belonged to the professions. In the former case it was possible that a patron, 'on failure of all persons connected with him by natural relationship', would return a man who possessed the endowments in question. A country gentleman, in contrast, was a by-word for 'a sort of character, compounded of mental indolence, mental vacuity, and mental weakness'. There was, even then, no benefit to the universal interest from any intellectual aptitude possessed by MPs. The universal interest would still be sacrificed unless the intellectual endowments were combined with probity: 'But, the higher the degree in which, by the individual in question, they are possessed, the higher will be the price which, at the constantly *overt market* of which C——r-General is *clerk* they will fetch: the higher the price, the higher the temptation, and the less the probability of resistance.'[102] In other words, the more talented the MP, the more valuable he was to the King, and the more the King would be prepared to pay to secure his services.

By exposing, in *The Book of Fallacies*, the nature of fallacious argument, Bentham hoped to prevent its use. The more the public was convinced of the insincerity of the person who advanced such arguments, the greater the restraint imposed on his employment of them. The greater mischief, however, was not the employment of bad arguments, but the acceptance of them as influential or conclusive. It was, therefore, important not only that men were made ashamed to express them, but also made ashamed to accept them. One method of helping to extirpate fallacious argument would be to take a printed report of the debates of the House of Commons, and mark up the fallacies employed.[103] Bentham was optimistic that, as the world grew older and at the same time wiser, 'which it will do unless the period shall have arrived at which experience, the Mother of Wisdom, shall have past child-bearing', the influence of authority, particularly in Parliament, would diminish. In private morality, private law, and constitutional law, as 'the body of experience has encreased, authority has gradually been set

[101] Ibid. 498–500. [102] Ibid. 497–8.

[103] UC ciii. 578–82 (5 Feb. 1811) [Bowring, ii. 486]. Precisely such an attempt was undertaken by Bingham and Charles Austin in *Parliamentary History and Review; Containing Reports of the Proceedings of the Two Houses of Parliament. With Critical Remarks on the Principal Measures of Each Session*, 2 vols. (London, 1826) (see *Correspondence*, xii. 403 n.)

aside, and reasoning, drawn from facts and guided by reference to the end in view, true or false, has taken its place'. It was only in matters of law and religion that efforts were made to obstruct as far as possible the exercise of 'the right of private inquiry'. In every branch of physical art and science, the folly of appealing to authority instead of direct and specific evidence was universally acknowledged. In the moral branch of science, including religion, the folly would also be universally recognized were it not for the wealth, ease, and dignity which relied on authority for their support.[104]

V

According to Francis Place, the appearance of *Plan of Parliamentary Reform* in May 1817 produced 'a great sensation'.[105] A little over a year later Bentham's proposals were the subject of debate in Parliament itself, a result of an initiative which originated with Henry Bickersteth to combine the talents of Bentham and Sir Francis Burdett, the radical MP for Westminster. Bickersteth informed Burdett on 25 February 1818 that he was trying to persuade Bentham to draw up a plan of reform, which he hoped would then be publicized by Burdett. While a relatively brief set of resolutions would be presented to the Commons, a detailed Bill would be in readiness should the resolutions be adopted. A parliamentary debate, published with a commentary and the proposed Bill, would provide the most extensive publicity possible for the plan:

> If the names of Bentham and Burdett went together in this proceeding, we should not only have universal notoriety, but all the reflection and sagacity, as well as all the active zeal in the kingdom, would be called into immediate action on this subject; and it would be surprising indeed, if every succeeding year did not produce an increasing weight of petitions. The most profound philosophy cannot unite in vain with the greatest popularity of the time.

Bickersteth reported that Bentham was not prepared to 'engage in the work, unless he has some positive assurance that the labour he may devote to it will not be thrown away; and this assurance can only be given by Sir Francis Burdett'.[106] Burdett immediately agreed to bring before the Commons any resolutions on parliamentary reform which Bentham was willing to draft.[107] Despite Bickersteth's and Burdett's enthusiasm, Bentham was cautious: he was not sure whether he wished to give up his other projects at that moment, nor was he certain whether he would be able to draft a detailed Bill. No doubt aware of Burdett's ambivalence in

[104] UC ciii. 75–6 (24 May 1811) [Bowring, ii. 393].

[105] See Place to Thomas Hodgskin, 30 May 1817, reproduced in G. Wallas, *The Life of Francis Place 1771–1854*, 4th edn. (London, 1925), 127.

[106] See the 'document' of 25 February 1818 written by Henry Bickersteth and reproduced at Bowring, x. 492–3.

[107] Burdett to Bentham, 25 Feb. 1818, *Correspondence*, ix. 165–6.

relation to the secret ballot, he explained that he was not prepared to support a plan of parliamentary reform unless the suffrages were free, and could not see how they would be free without 'the safeguard of secresy'. He needed time to consider the matter, but did not envisage any great inconvenience from deferring any proposal until the next session of Parliament.[108] Having consulted Place, who assured him that 'Bickersteth is a very promissing fellow and as for Burdett, you may certainly rely on him, as far as he can rely upon himself',[109] he decided to go ahead with the collaboration. He did not expect the motion to make any impact on the Commons itself, but hoped it would do so on the people.[110]

There was, however, as Bentham had predicted, some disagreement with Burdett over the secret ballot. While having no objections himself to the ballot, Burdett thought there was no use in proposing it, 'and if not necessary even mischievous, because of prejudice to be surmounted'.[111] Thomas Northmore was another reformer who at this time tried to persuade Bentham to drop the secret ballot: 'It is not English. Montesquieu says, from Cicero, that the people's suffrage ought doubtless to be publick, and this shd. be considered as a fundamental law of democracy[112] . . . where there "is a demand for virtue" (to quote yourself) Englishmen obey the demand. *Try them* first, without your ballot, they will not be found wanting. Any bet you please.' Northmore thought that, if all other forms of influence other than '*Enthusiasm* for our country and its cause' were checked, there would be no need for the secret ballot, which might prove to be 'a cloak for deceits, and hypocricy'. In any case, it would not be possible to keep the votes secret.[113] Meanwhile, Bentham received support for his views on the ballot, and an indication of the impact of *Plan of Parliamentary Reform*, when Cartwright and Peter Walker, an Irish lawyer and radical reformer, communicated to Bentham a vote of thanks passed by a public meeting of Westminster householders on 23 March 1818:

> for the philosophical and unanswerable vindication in his 'Catechism on Parliamentary Reform', of the right of ALL the Commons of this Realm, *equally* to share, and *annually* to exercise, the franchise of choosing members to serve in Parliament; as well as their farther Right to a sure protection, by the application of the *ballot*, against injury or oppression, for having freely exercised that sacred franchise.[114]

Soon afterwards Bentham received an offer from Thomas Wooler to publish a new edition of *Plan of Parliamentary Reform* 'in a cheap way, for general circulation . . . making such alterations in the style as might render it more easy of comprehension

[108] Bentham to Burdett, 25 Feb. 1818, ibid. 166–7.

[109] Place to Bentham, 26 Feb. 1818, ibid. 168.

[110] Bentham to Burdett, 10 Mar. 1818. ibid. 177–8.

[111] Burdett to Bentham, 10 Mar. 1818, ibid. 179.

[112] For Northmore's quotation see Baron de Montesquieu, *The Spirit of the Laws*, trans. T. Nugent, introd. F. Neumann, 2 vols. (London, 1949), Book II, sec. 2, i. 12.

[113] Northmore to Bentham, 23 Mar. 1818, *Correspondence*, ix. 183–4.

[114] John Cartwright and Peter Walker to Bentham, 24 Mar. 1818, ibid. 185 and n. Bentham's work was given further publicity when the resolution appeared in *The Black Dwarf*, 8 Apr. 1818.

to the popular reader'. The new edition was published in instalments between 18 April and 11 July 1818, and then republished in book form.[115]

Bentham's ideas on parliamentary reform had, therefore, obtained an extensive circulation by the time Burdett presented his resolutions to the Commons on 2 June 1818. Bentham later claimed that the resolutions

> were employed as drawn, with the exception of 2 Resolutions which had been inserted for the purpose of completing the view given of the Constitution in all its parts, but without expectation of their being employed: the one bearing so hard on the Monarchical, the other the Aristocratical branch. In addition to the above important changes, a few of minor importance might perhaps be found. They were made, all of them, without concert with Mr. Bentham, he having given up the matter without reserve, to his friend, on whom alone all responsibility rested.[116]

Despite what Bentham says, Burdett appears to have made considerable alterations to the original draft, condensing some of the passages and merging some of the resolutions, reducing Bentham's forty-seven resolutions to just twenty-six.[117] Making use of apt quotations taken from speeches from the throne, the resolutions declared that the only adequate security for good government was a community of interest between governors and governed; that where conflict existed the interest of the few or the one ought to give way to that of the many; that such a state of affairs would exist only if ministers were made subject to the representatives of the people, themselves 'speaking and acting in conformity to the sense of the people'; and that this subjection would only be secured when the representatives were chosen and removable 'by the free suffrages of the great body of the people'. Virtual representation was pronounced to be a 'notorious fiction'; 'comprehensive, equal, and free suffrages' and annual elections were demanded; and the influence of the Crown on the Commons through 'the offices, commissions, and emoluments, the power, rank, dignities, and other advantages' at its disposal—and which, due to the increase in public debt and the standing army, had increased greatly since John Dunning's famous

[115] Thomas Wooler to Bentham, 31 Mar. 1818, *Correspondence*, ix. 186–7. All 750 copies of *Plan of Parliamentary Reform* had been 'disposed of' by this time: see Bentham to George Meadley, 9 Apr. 1818, *Correspondence*, ix. 189. The work was reviewed in the *Quarterly Review*, vol. xviii, no. xxxv (Oct. 1817), 128–35, and by Sir James Mackintosh in the *Edinburgh Review*, vol. xxxi, no. lxi (Dec. 1818), 165–203.

[116] *'Legislator of the World'*, 304–5.

[117] A copy of the resolutions as drafted by Bentham, in the hand of his amanuensis John Flowerdew Colls, dated 4 May 1818, is at UC cxxviii. 313–33; the resolutions actually debated on 2 June 1818 are printed in Bowring, x. 495–7. The resolution which concerned the monarchy was perhaps Resolution 7 (UC cxxviii. 313), where it was proposed that the King's signature of assent on Bills passed by the Lords and Commons should be countersigned by 'some official person, who . . . is responsible to Parliament', and that which concerned the aristocracy Resolution 8 (UC cxxviii. 313), where it was proposed that the House of Lords should not 'ultimately refuse its assent to any law or other measure, in respect of which it is become manifest, that it is perseveringly called for by the known wishes of the great body of the people'. This latter clause may have been directed towards ensuring that any measure of radical reform was not vetoed by the Lords, but its more general application would have rendered the Lords completely subordinate to the Commons.

resolution of 6 April 1780[118]—was condemned. Since no adequate diminution of influence was feasible at that time, 'the only resource which remains is to correct this influence by a counterforce, consisting of the influence of the people'. The final resolution stated that the House 'is resolved to make one great sacrifice of all separate and particular interests, and to proceed to establish a comprehensive and consistent plan of reform; in virtue whereof, the whole people of the United Kingdom may be fairly represented in this House', and called for universal male suffrage—the voters being resident householders or 'inmates' and of 'sound mind', the secret ballot, annual elections (with the Crown retaining the prerogative to dissolve Parliament at any time), equal electoral districts (divided where necessary into sub-districts) each returning one member, and polling to take place on a single day.[119] The resolutions were rejected by 106 votes to nil, the two tellers in favour being Burdett and his fellow member for Westminster, Thomas Cochrane. Since the division was on the order for the day, the resolutions were not entered upon the Journals of the House.[120] This had been no more than Bentham had expected, his plan 'being intended as a legacy and not as a *donatio inter vivos*',[121] and did nothing to dissuade him from pursuing the subject further.

VI

In December 1817 Cartwright had sent Bentham a copy of his *Bill of Rights and Liberties*,[122] in which, he told Bentham, 'all your principles are put into a practical and tangible shape'.[123] Bentham was not, however, happy with Cartwright's Bill, for in October 1819 he informed his brother Samuel that he was 'coming out with "Bentham's Radical Reform Bill" by particular desire: to supplant Cartwright's impracticable measure'.[124] *Bentham's Radical Reform Bill* consisted in the main of a draft 'Parliamentary Reform Act: being an Act for the more adequate Representation of the People in the Commons House of

[118] i.e. that the influence of the Crown 'has increased, is increasing, and ought to be diminished'. For the debate on Dunning's motion see *Parliamentary History*, xxi (1780–1), 340–74.

[119] Bowring, x. 495–7.

[120] *'Legislator of the World'*, 304. Burdett's speech was published as *The Substance of the Speech delivered by Sir Francis Burdett, Bart. in the House of Commons, on Tuesday, the 2d. of June, 1818, on moving a series of resolutions on the subject of Parliamentary Reform* (London, 1818).

[121] Bentham to John Bowring for the Conde de Toreno, 28 Nov. 1820, *Correspondence*, x. 195.

[122] *A Bill of Rights and Liberties; or, an Act for a Constitutional Reform of Parliament* (London, 1817). The copy sent by Cartwright to Bentham is at British Library shelf-mark C.T.86.(2.)

[123] Cartwright to Bentham, 17 Dec. 1817, *Correspondence*, ix. 134.

[124] Bentham to Samuel Bentham, 17 Oct. 1819, ibid. ix. 359. Bentham told Burdett that his letter of 25 February 1818, which had produced the resolutions of 2 June 1818, was 'the cause of its [i.e. *Bentham's Radical Reform Bill*] existence', which, in a more remote way, it was: see Bentham to Burdett, 6 Nov. 1819, ibid. 365.

Parliament'.[125] Bentham reiterated his call for secrecy, universality (subject to a literacy test), equality, and annuality of suffrage. Secrecy, which would secure 'genuineness', was 'of the very first importance'. Indeed, the introduction of the secret ballot would in itself be a significant step, while without it 'universality, equality, and annuality altogether, would be worse than nothing'.[126] Not only were tradesmen dependent on their wealthy customers, and labourers, servants, and journeymen on their masters, but paupers, who composed the great majority of the people, were dependent on magistrates for their very existence: 'The votes of the majority of the electors, and thence of the whole number of the representatives, would thus be at the command of magistrates:—of magistrates such as the Manchester magistrates! and through them, of ministers such as Lord Sidmouth, and monarchs such as his Prince Regent.'[127] If votes were not genuine, 'the supposed remedy would be but an aggravation of the disease'.[128] Under universality—or rather virtual universality—of suffrage, children and females would be excluded. There was no point in excluding the insane and criminals, since they would not be permitted to leave their places of confinement, nor in excluding foreigners, outlaws, bankrupts, insolvents, and peers, since their combined numbers would not be sufficient to return a single MP. As for the reading qualification, this was not in essence exclusionary, since every man who wished to qualify for the suffrage enjoyed the power to do so: an adult might learn to read in two or three months, using 'the hours of repose from work'.[129] It was important that literacy should be as widespread as possible, and to tie the franchise to reading would be a means of encouraging it: 'It is to reading that the people owe all their strength: that strength at which, even thus early, tyrants tremble.' On the other hand, a householder franchise, or qualification through payment of direct taxes, did constitute an exclusion, since not every man had the

[125] According to Bowring, iii. 599, it was published on 6 December 1819. At one point it had been Bentham's intention to provide an extensive rationale for the measures proposed, but he did not publish any of the material which he composed (see e.g. UC cxxvii. 216–545). Bentham also had in mind an ambitious compilation of his writings on the British political system, including material on political fallacies, on abuses in the law and the Church, as well as on parliamentary reform, with the projected title of 'Things as they are and ought to be: or, The System of Misrule briefly delineated': see UC cxxvii. 419–23 (18–19 Sept. 1818).

[126] Bowring, iii. 562–3.

[127] The 'Manchester magistrates' were those who had authorized the use of troops to disperse a reform meeting in St Peter's Fields, Manchester, giving rise to the so-called 'Peterloo Massacre' of 16 August 1819, where eleven people were said to have been killed and hundreds injured. In this context, Bentham's earlier proposals to distribute poor relief through the agency of the National Charity Company, removing paupers from the control of Justices of the Peace, takes on a political dimension. For accounts of Bentham's Poor Law proposals and the role of the National Charity Company see J. R. Poynter, *Society and Pauperism: English Ideas on Poor Relief, 1795–1834* (London, 1969), 117–44, and C. F. Bahmueller, *The National Charity Company: Jeremy Bentham's Silent Revolution* (Berkeley, 1981), though the latter is overly polemical.

[128] Bowring, iii. 558–9.

[129] Bentham drew inspiration from the work of Thaddeus Connellan, the Irish educator, who in three years, according to Bentham, had been responsible for teaching around 40,000 adults to read: see UC cxxvii. 334 (27 Apr. 1818), and Bentham to De Witt Clinton, 29 Sept. 1818, *Correspondence*, ix. 264–5.

means to pay rent and taxes for a house.[130] Qualification through payment of indirect taxes was not, however, an exclusion, but universality of suffrage in effect, in that everyone paid taxes on consumption.[131] The point was that neither the ownership of a house nor the payment of taxes was an adequate indication of appropriate aptitude, unlike the ability to read.[132] Equality of suffrage would ensure that each election district had a large enough electorate to render bribery and corruption impracticable. Exact equality was not an end in itself, so Bentham was not concerned if local circumstances produced some variation in the number of voters in each electoral district—he thought that from a half to double the average size would be an acceptable variation. Annuality of suffrage facilitated the removal of unfit representatives before they had time to produce any permanent mischief, and lessened their value to the Corruptor-General, who was less likely to attempt to bribe them.[133]

This was very much to reiterate the proposals first advanced in the 'Catechism' and justified in the 'Introduction', though there was perhaps an even greater emphasis on the secret ballot. Bentham did add some more detail to various aspects of his proposals. According to his proposed 'Parliamentary Reform Act', the country would be divided into 658 electoral districts (retaining the same number of seats as the existing House of Commons, as opposed to the 600 proposed in the 'Catechism'), as nearly equal to one another in population as local circumstances would permit, and each returning one MP. Since election districts were now conceived in terms of equality of population rather than equality of geographical extent, there was no need for the allocation of additional 'population seats' to the more populous districts. To obviate the need for long and expensive journeys to the poll, election districts would be divided into polling districts or sub-districts. Every male who had proved himself literate before three householders, and thereby secured a vote-making certificate, would be entitled to vote. Members of the armed forces would be excluded from the suffrage unless they were also householders. Any person might be nominated as a candidate for election on the recommendation of between six and twelve persons, and subject to the payment of indemnification money (Bentham suggested a sum of £120) to help defray election expenses.[134] Polling would take place on one and the same day in all the election districts, with an elaborate apparatus to ensure secrecy of voting.[135] The newly elected House would meet for the first time on the same day each year, though if 'by any accident' the new members were 'on that day prevented from forming a House competent to do

[130] Bentham also pointed out that if the 'mere accident' of paying direct taxes were to form the qualification for the franchise, then in a political state where no one was taxed, no one would have a vote. More generally, ministers would have the power to settle the franchise by taxing whom they pleased, while the need to fix a level of direct taxation as the qualification for the vote might lead to those close to that level enjoying the vote at one election, and being denied it at the next. See UC cxxvii. 388–90 (26–7 Oct. 1818).

[131] Bowring, iii. 559–60.

[132] UC cxxvii. 392 (26 Oct. 1818); cxxvii. 412 (5 Sept. 1818).

[133] Bowring, iii. 561.

[134] Ibid. 563–7.

[135] Ibid. 572–3.

business' the outgoing assembly would continue until the incoming assembly was competent. The House would not be dissolved by the death or disability of the monarch, and the business of the preceding Parliament would be continued by the succeeding one.[136] Bentham favoured limiting, or possibly prohibiting, the creation of peers. Elevation to the peerage was a bribe in the hands of monarch and minister, and gave additional strength to a body of men whose interests were distinct from and opposite to the universal interest. It was also wasteful, in that a large proportion of the peerage, as a result of 'increase of numbers and extravagance', was 'continually sliding down into a sort of elevated pauperism, which, according to an avowed maxim of Government, must be pampered at an expense proportioned to its factitious elevation', a principle avowed by both Whigs and Tories, as Bentham had shown in his 'Defences of Economy'.[137] He was in no doubt that the only good form of government was a representative democracy, and that 'Monarch and Aristocracy being... essentially and radically incompatible with good government', it would be best to 'exclude' the 'confederacy' from the British government. However, it was not possible to get rid of King and Lords without a civil war, the mischief of which would be greater than their continuance under democratic ascendancy, 'the representatives of the people legislating in effect, the Lords sleeping as at present under their coronets, the Monarch and his nominees carrying into effect the decrees emaning from the real Representatives of the people'.[138]

Even after the publication of *Bentham's Radical Reform Bill*, Bentham continued to compose material on parliamentary reform. In 'Radicalism not Dangerous', based on manuscripts written between November 1819 and the middle of April 1820, Bentham answered the charge that radical reform would prove dangerous to property. He reiterated his support for secrecy, virtual universality, practical equality, and annuality of suffrage, though he conceded that he would be prepared to accept householder and triennial suffrage.[139] In speeches from the throne of 13 July and 23 November 1819, it had been insinuated that the purpose of radical reform was 'the subversion of the constitution' and 'the subversion of the rights of property'. It was on the basis of these charges that 'those disastrous laws [i.e. the Six Acts], by which disaffection has been more abundantly propagated than by any of the writings which they are employed to repress' had been grounded. As for the former charge, it did not specify any determinate evil, and if it meant anything, could only mean that the reform would produce preponderant mischief. As for the latter charge, radical reform would produce preponderant benefit, and would not result in the

[136] Bowring, iii. 589.

[137] Ibid. 591 n. While Bentham had attempted to show that both Whigs and Tories were profuse in their distribution of public money for their own benefit, it was Rose who had specifically defended the 'provision for decayed nobility': see *Official Aptitude Maximized; Expense Minimized*, 103–9.

[138] UC cxxvii. 245 (7 Dec. 1818).

[139] Bowring, iii. 599–600.

subversion of property. Reformers, at least in any significant number, claimed Bentham, had never had any intention to subvert property.[140] In short, he argued that, as it would be impossible to level the property of the country, no one was capable of conceiving a design to attempt it.[141] The results of democratic ascendancy in Britain would be the same as they were in the United States of America, 'a region peopled with men of English race, bred up in English habits—with minds fraught with ideas, associated with all English ideas by English language'. Far from property being subverted in the United States, 'general tranquillity and felicity in other shapes' was superior to that in Britain. In New York and Pennsylvania there was not merely democratic ascendancy, that is 'representative democracy in conjunction with monarchy and aristocracy', but pure democracy, without the security which independent power in the hands of one, combined with independent power in the hands of the few, was supposed to give. Sedition and popular discontent had been unheard of in the near-forty years 'since the triple yoke of monarchy, aristocracy, and sham democracy, were cast off'. Economic distress had existed, but the people had recognized that it had been caused by a lack of demand. In Britain distress had in part been caused by a lack of demand, but also by the excessive taxation produced by a 'vicious constitution and misrule'. The 'misrulers' blamed the distress solely on the commercial situation, and not on the financial and constitutional causes, but 'it remains an undeniable truth, that if nothing will satisfy a man but the seeing the people quiet and content with their government while they are labouring in penury and distress, it is to pure democracy, or at least to democratic ascendancy, that he must look for it'.[142] Democratic ascendancy as it had existed in Ireland under the Volunteer Movement in the late 1770s and early 1780s had not led to the subversion of property or of the constitution, but on the contrary 'the average mass of felicity exalted to a pitch unknown before or since—public and private *felicity*; and, as at once a cause and consequence of it, public and private *virtue*'.[143] Bentham's point was that property was more secure under a democracy than under any other form of government—a startling conclusion given the received wisdom that democracy was prone to anarchy and civil war, and a considerable shift from the position he had adopted after his early enthusiasm for the French Revolution had subsided.[144]

140 Ibid. 602–4. 141 Ibid. 605–8. 142 Ibid. 612–13.

143 Ibid. 613. Bentham went on to argue that the monarchico-aristocratic ascendancy in Ireland had been willing to support the democratic element to the extent of commercial and parliamentary independence, since this was as much in their interest as that of the people, but had destroyed the Volunteer Movement when it came to demand parliamentary reform. Thereafter, it had been their policy to divide the Protestants, whose major grievance was 'the system of universal corruption and misrule', and the Catholics, who looked to emancipation, by offering concessions to the Catholics. See ibid. 613–20. For accounts of the Irish Volunteers see R. B. McDowell, *Ireland in the Age of Imperialism and Revolution 1760–1801* (Oxford, 1979), 255–74, and S. Small, *Political Thought in Ireland 1776–1798: Republicanism, Patriotism, and Radicalism* (Oxford, 2002), 83–154.

144 See pp. 106–7 above.

In an argument reminiscent of his attack on the French Declaration of Rights, Bentham stated that the phrase 'subversion of the Constitution' was 'one of those compounds of falsehood and nonsense, equally useful to, and equally employed by Tories and Whigs'. The falsehood lay in the implication that such a constitution existed, and the nonsense in claiming that a thing which had no existence could be subverted. In the United States of America, each of the twenty-two states did have a 'real constitution' of its own, while 'the Congressorial government... has a constitution in which all these others are included'. Each of these constitutions had been established 'by a convention chosen by the great body of the population—by that body out of whose obedience all power is composed, and by the interests of which all power ought in its exercise, in so far as it is not tyranny, to direct itself'. In contrast to those 'real constitutions', the British Constitution was 'a creature of the imagination—a sham—an imposture', whatever it suited the sinister interest of a man or a party to say it was.

> The Constitution you figure to yourselves,—tyrants, what is it? A collection of the pretences under which, and the written formularies in and by which, you have been in the habit of carrying on the incessant war for the sacrifice of the universal to your own particular interest—the carrying on in the most regular and commodious manner the work of oppression and depredation on the largest scale. This is what in your eyes is the Constitution. This is everything that you wish of it.[145]

Bentham's attitude towards the British Constitution had hardened considerably since he had written the 'Catechism' in 1809. In the meantime he had extended his criticism from the political establishment to the ecclesiastical establishment.

145 Bowring, iii. 622.

7

The Church

I

Bentham's assault on the English establishment, having begun with the law and progressed to parliamentary reform, was completed with an attack on the Church of England and its system of education, with the schools of the National Society[1] at its base and the universities of Oxford and Cambridge at its apex. As Bentham stated in the 'Preface' to *Church-of-Englandism and its Catechism Examined*, the work was very much a companion volume to *Plan of Parliamentary Reform*: 'In the Introduction to the work intituled *Plan of Parliamentary Reform*, &c., a sort of sketch was given of one of the two *natures*, of which our constitution, such as it is, is composed, viz. the *temporal* one. In the present work may be seen a portrait of the other nature, viz. the *spiritual* one.'[2] He explained that he had been brought up in a devout household, his father Jeremiah being a staunch Anglican. Under the instruction of one of his grandmothers, both of whom were daughters of Anglican clergymen, he had learnt the Catechism. When living at their respective houses during the school vacations, he had been 'an affectionate, reverential, and continual witness' at their daily devotions, which had been 'in every part accordant to the rites of the established Church'. He had been confirmed: 'I remembered [the Catechism] as well as I could—I understood as much as I could—I believed as hard as I could—and if any thing was wanting to belief, it was made up by trembling.'[3] His 'unfavourable opinions' and thence 'unfavourable affections' towards the Church had emerged while at Oxford, as a result of his reflection on two incidents.[4] One had been the

[1] The National Society for the Education of the Poor in the Principles of the Established Church had been founded in 1811 in order to promote the teaching of the theology of the Anglican Church by means of the 'monitorial' system of education, whereby the master taught the senior pupils and they taught the rest, which had been developed by Andrew Bell, an Anglican clergyman. The method had also been developed independently by the Quaker Joseph Lancaster, whose system had been promoted by the non-denominational Royal Lancasterian Society (later renamed the British and Foreign School Society), founded in 1808.

[2] *Church-of-Englandism*, Preface on Publication, pp. x–xi. See also Bentham to John Herbert Koe, 14 Jan. 1818, *Correspondence*, ix. 145: 'Church cat. follows up the blow given in Plan Cat.: it goes to the destroying of the whole mass of that matter of corruption which while the Tories feed upon in possession, the Whigs feed upon, and will continue feeding upon while they are any thing, in expectancy.'

[3] *Church-of-Englandism*, Preface, pp. xi–xiii.

[4] Ibid., p. xiii.

expelling of five Methodist students on account of 'heresy'. Their offence, according to Bentham, had been to interpret some of the Thirty-nine Articles of the Church of England in a different sense from the persons sent to question them, and to have attended 'conventicles', where they had studied the Bible: 'by the sentence, by which those readers of the Bible were thus expelled from the University, that affection which at its entrance had glowed with so sincere a fervor,—my reverence for the Church of England—her doctrine, her discipline, her Universities, her ordinances,—was expelled from my youthful breast.'[5] The other incident had taken place at his graduation, aged 16, when he had himself been required to subscribe to the Thirty-nine Articles. He had studied them:

> The examination was unfortunate. In some of them no meaning at all could I find: in others, no meaning but one which, in my eyes, was but too plainly irreconcilable either to reason or to Scripture. Communicating my distress to some of my fellow collegiates, I found them sharers in it. Upon inquiry it was found, that among the Fellows of the College [i.e. Queen's College] there was one, to whose office it belonged, among other things, to remove all such scruples. We repaired to him with fear and trembling. His answer was cold: and the substance of it was—that it was not for uninformed youths such as we, to presume to set up our private judgments against a public one, formed by some of the holiest, as well as best and wisest men that ever lived.

He had no one to turn to:

> Before my weak eyes stood no comforter. In *my* father, in whom in other cases I might have looked for a comforter, I saw nothing but a tormentor: by my ill-timed scruples, and the consequent public disgrace that would have been the consequence, his fondest hopes would have been blasted, the expenses he had bestowed on my education bestowed in vain. To him, I durst not so much as confess those scruples. I signed:—but, by the view I found myself forced to take of the whole business, such an impression was made, as will never depart from me but with life.[6]

He concluded that it was not only an effect of, but one of the purposes of, an English university education to produce mendacity and insincerity—'of mendacity, a forced *act* or two: and the object of it the securing of an *habit* of insincerity throughout life'. Moreover, it was an effect of, and again probably a purpose of, Anglican doctrine and discipline to produce 'humble docility' towards the rulers of the Church and their subordinates.[7] While Bentham's immediate reason for composing *Church-of-Englandism* had been to attack 'the exclusionary system' whereby 'all children whose parents will not force lies into their mouths' were excluded from the schools of the National Society, it had its

[5] *Church-of-Englandism*, Preface, pp. xv–xix. The incident in question was presumably the expulsion on 11 March 1768 of six students 'for holding Methodistical tenets, and taking upon them to pray, read, and expound the scriptures, and sing hymns in a private house', reported in the *St James Chronicle*, 17 Mar. 1768, and given notoriety by [John Macgowan], *Priestcraft Defended. A Sermon occasioned by the Expulsion of Six Young Gentlemen from the University of Oxford, for Praying, Reading and Expounding the Scriptures* (London, 1768).

[6] *Church-of-Englandism*, Preface, pp. xix–xxi.

[7] Ibid., pp. xxi–xxii.

origin in 'the witnessed expulsion of the Methodists, and the experience had of the forced injustice of the matter of the thirty-nine Articles'.[8] It also gave Bentham the opportunity to demonstrate that sinister interest pervaded not only the legal profession and Parliament, but also the Church.

Bentham seems to have perceived the episode in which he was forced to subscribe to the Thirty-nine Articles as the one occasion, or at least the most notable occasion, on which he had compromised his intellectual integrity. It was, perhaps, to avoid such compromises that he adopted a policy of not expressing his personal religious views, and not asking others to do so. In April 1820, for instance, when sending a contribution to Richard Carlile, the freethinker who had been convicted of blasphemous libel and sentenced on 16 November 1819 to three years' imprisonment and a fine of £1,500 for publishing Paine's *Age of Reason*,[9] he was careful to point out that his wish was to support the cause of religious liberty in general, and not to be associated with either Carlile's or any other person's doctrines: 'Whether your opinions be true or false, the dissemination of them beneficial or pernicious, I regard the cause for which you suffer as being the cause of whatever is good in religion or government: the cause of free enquiry, on which all truth, and consequently all useful truth depends.' He was neither ashamed of his religious opinions nor unable to defend them, but it was 'a fixt rule' with him never to express them. To do so 'spontaneously' in public might produce 'uneasiness in the mind of every reader with whose opinions they disagreed', while to do so in private when called upon might lead to 'persecution':

> In the hands of any one man who concerns himself to have another man in any degree in his power, a distinction of opinion, whether on the subject of religion or on the subject of politics, is an instrument capable of being employed in the exercising this power: and this power it has often happened to me to know, is but too apt to be most cruelly and ungenerously abused.
>
> Such, says the tyrant looking upon the man he has fastened on for his victim—such, says he looking him sternly and steadily in the face, is my opinion: so say the words, and to the words what the looks add is—and now, Sir, well and what are your's.
>
> Having had occasion to witness this tyranny, so have I had occasion to witness the fruits of it: and these fruits are no other than those which are sure to be the fruits of tyranny, in every shape, by whom, and on whom so ever exercised.

This was, explained Bentham, the most effectual course for alienating a father from a son.[10] He no doubt had in mind his own relationship with his father,

[8] Ibid., pp. xxv–xxvi. Bentham never overcame the resentment he felt at his being compelled, as he saw it, to subscribe to the Thirty-nine Articles, so much so that he described *Church-of-Englandism* as an 'expiation': see ibid., pp. xxiv–xxvi n. See also UC cxxvi. 50 (27 Sept. 1809), where, in reference to the expulsion of the Methodists and his own subscription to the Thirty-nine Articles, Bentham noted: 'From these acts of tyranny it was, that my mind received that impression the strength of which has not been abated by a lapse of five and forty years.'

[9] See J. H. Wiener, *Radicalism and Freethought in Nineteenth-Century Britain: The Life of Richard Carlile* (London, 1983), 33–54.

[10] The quotations reproduced from this letter are adapted from the rough draft reproduced in *Correspondence*, ix. 418–21.

which had been difficult.[11] There had been friction over money; over Jeremiah's second marriage; over potential marriage partners for Jeremy; over Jeremy's career; and, presumably, over religion. From early in his life Bentham had allied himself with those who were sceptical of religious belief and hostile to organized religion. There are several intriguing references in Bentham's correspondence with his brother, Samuel, in the 1770s to persons being 'one of us', with religion evidently in mind. When Bentham's anonymous translation of Voltaire's *The White Bull* appeared in 1774, he sent a copy to Samuel, who was apprenticed at Deptford. Informing Samuel that he was responsible for the translation, preface, and notes, he exclaimed: 'It's a sad wicked book you will perceive—You must keep it close; and not let it be seen by any body except in such an out of the way corner as your's you should chance to meet with one of us: and then you must use discretion . . . and whatever you do let it not be known for mine.'[12] In March 1776, upon the publication of the first volume of Edward Gibbon's *Decline and Fall of the Roman Empire*,[13] Bentham wrote to Samuel: 'There is just now come out by a Mr. Gibbons M.P. a history of the Roman Empire from Trojan to Constantine which is to be continued. I have a great account of it—He is quite one of us. . . .'[14] Upon meeting François-Xavier Schwediauer, Bentham remarked that 'he is one of us';[15] James Anderson, the Scottish writer on agriculture and economics, was 'quite one of us';[16] while Sambouski, the chaplain at the Russian Embassy in London, '[a]s far as I could judge from what I saw or heard of him in point of public affections, which is the main point, . . . seemed to be altogether one of us'.[17] The phrase 'one of us' was no doubt a code, intended to remain obscure to the rest of the world, but used by the brothers to refer to persons whom they conceived to be sympathetic to their own political and religious views, or to what Bentham on one occasion referred to as 'the cause'.[18] Whatever it meant to be 'one of us', it was not orthodox Anglicanism.

Irrespective of his personal religious views,[19] Bentham was a strident critic of religious establishments in general, and the Church of England in particular.

[11] See Bentham to Bowring, 30 Jan. 1827, *Correspondence*, xii. 303: 'Though a very affectionate father, he was, by a variety of infirmities, a very troublesome one, being too fond of looking out for occasions, and even pretences for giving exercise to paternal authority in the way of reproof.' For an account of their relationship see Mack, *Bentham: Odyssey of Ideas*, 48–55.

[12] Bentham to Samuel Bentham, July 1774, *Correspondence*, i. 187.

[13] Edward Gibbon, *The History of the Decline and Fall of the Roman Empire. Volume the First* (London, 1776).

[14] Bentham to Samuel Bentham, 5 Mar. 1776, *Correspondence*, i. 305. The passage continues, 'and attacks', but the following words have been crossed through and are illegible.

[15] Bentham to Samuel Bentham, 24 Oct. 1778, *Correspondence*, ii. 179.

[16] Bentham to Samuel Bentham, 30 Mar.–4 Apr. 1780, ibid. 404.

[17] Bentham to Samuel Bentham, 10–16 May 1780, ibid. 450.

[18] See Bentham to Samuel Bentham, 17 Mar. 1777, ibid. 38: 'There is a very short life of D. Hume come out, written by himself. I have just been reading it: it will do service to the cause.' See *The Life of David Hume, Esq. Written by himself* (London, 1777).

[19] It is often assumed that Bentham was an atheist (see e.g. J. Steintrager, 'Language and Politics: Bentham on Religion', *The Bentham Newsletter*, 4 (1980), 4–20, and J. E. Crimmins, *Secular*

In the mid-1770s, around the same time that he was using the phrase 'one of us', he was drawing attention to the potential mischiefs associated with the religious sanction, arguing that God's will could not provide a standard for temporal happiness, and denying the relevance of theology to morality and law. The expectation of a future state being the expectation of the future distribution of pains and pleasures, the question arose as to the way in which such pains and pleasures would be distributed. If they were to be distributed randomly, then the expectation of them could not have 'any tendency to incite to good, or to restrain from evil'. In fact, the mere expectation of the distribution of future pains and pleasures would be pernicious on the whole, since 'the fear of the pains is likely to make a more forcible impression on us than the hope of such pleasures', and thus produce more present pain than present pleasure. The doctrine would only be conducive to utility insofar as there was an assurance that the pains of the future state would be inflicted as a result of actions which were mischievous to society, and the pleasures as a result of actions which were beneficial. As far as the legislator was concerned, '[t]he mere inculcating the future existence of reward and punishment was doing nothing'; on the contrary, everything depended upon linking actions which appeared to be mischievous to society with future punishment, and actions which appeared to be beneficial to future reward. The 'great mischief' of the notion of future rewards, when linked to actions which were not beneficial to society, occurred when the pleasures of a future life were seen to so exceed in value those of the present life that it became a man's interest to do whatever was in his power, no matter what mischief resulted, 'to accelerate the period' when such pleasures would commence.[20]

Bentham came to the same conclusion when beginning, not with the expectation of future punishments and rewards, but with the nature of God. If God were benevolent, he could not consistently prohibit human beings from performing any action which promoted happiness. If God were not benevolent, there would be no reason to suppose that he would punish any act which he had declared he would punish, or reward any act which he had declared he would reward. In neither case did God's prohibition provide a motive for abstaining from any act which promoted happiness. This left 'the happiness of this life' as 'the standard of [the] rectitude [of an action]'. If divines, therefore, recommended any action which was not conducive to happiness in this life, this was an acknowledgment that 'their Religion' was 'at hostility to the state; the end which it has in view repugnant to the end which the state has in view'.[21] Since 'the idea of God' could not provide a guide to proper conduct, all that such an idea could

Utilitarianism: Social Science and the Critique of Religion in the Thought of Jeremy Bentham (Oxford, 1990), 282–92), but there does not appear to be any direct evidence for this view: see p. 20 above and P. Schofield, 'Political and Religious Radicalism in the Thought of Jeremy Bentham', *History of Political Thought*, 20 (1999), 272–91. Crimmins has restated his position in 'Bentham's Religious Radicalism Revisited: A Response to Schofield', *History of Political Thought*, 22 (2001), 494–500.

[20] UC cxl. 1–2. [21] UC lxx. 25.

do was 'to furnish a motive to the pursuing of such a mode of conduct as, from other considerations, shall have been previously determined to be a proper one. It is impossible therefore that Theology can throw any light upon either Morality or Jurisprudence.' It was nonsense to claim that God had commanded such or such a thing to be done, but then admit that no evidence for the existence of the command in question could be produced: 'In attempting to deduce moral duties or political regulations from the consideration of a Deity we turn about in a circle: but we advance not a single jot.' If the idea of God was the source of motives, but could not provide direction, it was better to ignore it: 'It can not instruct us: it can only serve to disturb, to fascinate, to terrify, to confound us.' Furthermore, mischief arose when authors presented their own opinions as the commands of God, and thereby gave their opinions a 'predominance' over those of others to which they were not entitled. Bentham was adamant that theology should not have any influence over legislation: 'In point of utility a book of Cookery might as well be interlarded with ejaculations, as a book of Jurisprudence with theological speculations. It might indeed better: for the devotions in a book of Cookery would only be useless: In a book of Jurisprudence it can certainly do no good, and it is a thousand to one but . . . it does mischief.'[22]

II

Bentham's central claim in *Church-of-Englandism* was that the inculcation of the Anglican Catechism into children, and particularly in the schools of the National Society, was purposely undertaken in order to produce moral and intellectual depravity. The ultimate object of the institution of the National Society had not been to advance either education or the religion of Jesus, but rather '*the preserving from reformation the abuses, with which the Church of England establishment is replete*'.[23] In the first place, the doctrines presented in the Catechism, together with the Thirty-nine Articles, were not those of Jesus, but constituted a substitute religion invented by the past rulers of the Church, and adopted by the present. The Catechism was taught to the child instead of 'the sacred original', and thus became 'the object of his faith'.[24] Subscription to 'any such pretended *Exposition*' as the Catechism or Thirty-nine Articles amounted not only to a renouncement of the religion of Jesus, 'but that renouncement a substantial and effectual one'.[25] The point of the Catechism was not to teach a 'true picture' of the religion of Jesus, but first to exclude one part of the poor

[22] UC lxix. 139.

[23] *Church-of-Englandism*, Introduction, 87. According to R. Hole, *Pulpits, Politics and Public Order in England 1760–1832* (Cambridge, 1989), 187–99, the aim of the Anglican promoters of the National Society was 'to enforce social control effectively and so defend the constitution in the state' and 'to strengthen the Church of England against the Dissenting challenge and so defend the constitution in the church'.

[24] *Church-of-Englandism*, Introduction, 43–6.

[25] Ibid. 51.

from the benefits of education, abandoning the children in question to 'ignorance, vice, and wretchedness', and second to undertake 'compulsory or seductive proselytism', whereby the other part was forced to come under the dominion of the Church.[26] As far as this latter group were concerned, the Catechism was employed

as an instrument of corruption, for corrupting altogether the intellectual part, and to a great extent the moral part, of the minds thus impregnated: the *intellectual*, through the medium of the *sensitive* part, that by weakness they might be rendered *unable*, because by terror they had been rendered *unwilling*, to discern the mischievousness of the dominion exercised at their expense: the *moral* part, that by their being themselves habituated to the practice of mendacity and insincerity in their own sphere, the spectacle of those vices, when practised at their expense in higher spheres, might in their eyes be rendered an object of indifference.[27]

That the purpose of the Catechism was to produce 'a prostration of intellectual strength' and 'a confirmed mental debility' had, in Bentham's view, been openly avowed by William Howley, the Bishop of London, who had remarked of the 'Unitarian system': 'Its influence has generally been confined to men of some education, whose thoughts have been little employed on the subject of religion; or who, loving rather to question than learn, have approached the oracles of divine truth without that humble docility, that prostration of the understanding and will, which are indispensable to proficiency in Christian instruction.'[28] The 'prostration' demanded was not towards the Bible, noted Bentham, but towards the Anglican clergy. The Bishop of London was endeavouring to establish 'a system of slavery;—of intellectual, and thence, as a necessary consequence, of moral and corporeal slavery'. The clergy were to be tyrants, members of the Church of England subjects, and non-members, in the character of 'enemies', slaves.[29]

In relation to what he termed the exclusionary system of education, Bentham suggested that the National Society, either on its own authority or better still on the authority of Parliament, should open its schools to all children whose parents were prepared to send them. The lesson books should be restricted to the teachings, parables, and miracles of Jesus as recorded in the Gospels, with the Anglican formularies and commentaries discarded. Non-Christians, such as Jews, as well as 'non-religionists', should be assured that the schools would accept their children, and that the children would be able to decide for themselves whether or not they wished to continue to profess 'the religion of their ancestors'. Schoolmasters, who would no longer be required to be Anglicans, should not attempt to persuade a child to relinquish its parents' religion. No scholar would

26 Ibid. 52. 27 Ibid. 20–1.

28 William [Howley], Lord Bishop of London, *A Charge delivered to the Clergy of the Diocese of London at the primary visitation of that Diocese in the year 1814* (London, 1814). Howley maintained that the Church of England was under attack from infidels and enthusiasts, and called for the clergy to support the schools of the National Society.

29 *Church-of-Englandism*, App., 87–91.

be made to declare what he himself believed, only what he understood was the belief of the Church or the government. Such a policy would, of course, avoid false declarations of belief, which led to the acceptance of insincerity and mendacity, and would ensure that no one suffered the torment which Bentham himself had experienced when subscribing to the Thirty-nine Articles at Oxford: 'Not less necessary is this expedient to the exclusion of insincerity out of the mouths and bosoms of the children of Church-of-Englandists themselves, than to the avoiding to exclude from the benefit of the instruction the children of heretics and unbelievers.' If the scholar accepted the official doctrines, then those in authority had what they wished. If the scholar did not accept them, then to force him to say that he did believe them would not make him believe them, but merely make him familiar with the habit of lying.[30]

Bentham recognized that 'the honest and thinking part of the English public mind' accepted government interference in religion in order to secure temporal happiness, but not for 'the salvation of souls'. However, in the case of the Catechism, government was interfering in 'the salvation of souls'. By employing the power of government to produce 'a *declaration of persuasion*', the result would be 'everlasting and universal tyranny', as the non-orthodox would be forced to conform to the established Church. Where the declaration was true, there was no need for any expense—whether in the form of reward or punishment—to produce it. Expense was necessary only where the declaration was untrue, and in that case the result was 'insincerity, mendacity, and mischievous obsequiousness'. The only way to produce a sincere belief was through argument. Even here, rulers were in an advantageous position in relation to subjects, since rulers were able to offer a greater quantity of reward than any one else for the production of argument. Argument, however, did not suit the purpose of rulers, since there were no good arguments on their side. Instead, they employed reward, and did not hesitate to employ punishment as well.[31]

The Catechism was peculiarly inapt in that it was aimed at children. At such an age, 'a declaration of persuasion in relation to a body of speculative religious doctrine' could only be 'an *untruth*', the habit of making such declarations 'an habitual course of *lying*', and the obligation of continuing on this course 'an *obligation* to enter upon and continue in a *course of lying*'. While the child stood exempted from guilt, this could not be said of 'the open-eyed, and deliberate, and determined teachers and suborners of immorality in this shape'. As in the case of 'every other characteristic part of Church of England discipline and doctrine', the reason for the existence of the Catechism was to be found 'in the situation of the rulers of the Church, and the sinister interest, that springs out of that source'. It was the interest of the ruling few that 'the intellectual, and thence the moral part of the public mind', should be as depraved as possible; that, on the part of the subject many, as the Bishop of London had expressed it, the

[30] *Church-of-Englandism*, App., 180–5. [31] Ibid. 59–64.

'"prostration of understanding and will" should be as abject and as universal as possible'; and that the subject many, being themselves in the habit of violating their duties, should be indifferent to the violation of duties on the part of the ruling few. Hence, if 'Church falsehood and Church sinecures' were seen 'not merely as objects of indifference, but as sacred', then 'State falsehoods and state sinecures' would be seen 'at the least . . . as objects of indifference'. These were the real terms of 'the so insolently trumpeted' alliance between Church and state. Christianity was merely 'a state engine . . . employed in the manufactory of the matter of corruption', providing 'a cement to the *Warburton Alliance* between *Church* and *State*: a cement for the wall of defence, built up for the protection of the whole stock of over-paid places, needless places, mischievous places, and sinecure places, sacred and profane'.[32]

In his *Charge* the Bishop of London had called for adherence to 'established laws of interpretation' of Scripture.[33] Bentham retorted that there were no such laws 'in the form of *written* or *statute* law', but only 'in the form of *unwritten*, *alias* Common Law'. While such laws could not be stated definitively, since it was their nature not to have any determinate form, their '*purport*' might be stated 'with sufficient accuracy'. One was 'the law of *virtual insertion*', by which any doctrine which benefited the temporal interests of the clergy was adopted; a second was 'the law of *omission*, or *virtual expunction*', by which, by means of silence, any doctrine of Scripture which opposed those interests was 'got rid of, and caused to be as if it never had been'; and a third was 'the rule of *virtual substitution*', a combination of the previous two, where an uncongenial doctrine was replaced by another which was not. The operation of the law of virtual omission had been applied to 'all those precepts of Jesus' which would result in 'any reduction in the articles of *opulence*, *power*, or *dignity*' on the part of the clergy. Jesus, for instance, had stated the difficulty, not to say impossibility, for those who trusted in riches to enter into the kingdom of God.[34] Yet it was by their riches, powers, and dignities that the clergy of an established church were distinguished from those of a non-established church. When the Anglican clergy spoke of the security of the Church and the danger of its subversion, it was the loss of their riches, powers, and dignities which they feared: 'Now if *this* be not *trusting in riches*, in what *other* shape, by what *other* tokens, can *trust in riches* be made manifest?'[35] Among the established clergy, 'attention to professional duties—any thing like constant and zealous attention' was 'a rare case', whereas among the sectarian clergy 'inattention' was 'an unexampled one'. This was because the sectarian clergy were dependent for respect, affection, and even

[32] Ibid. 99 n., 245–7. The classic exposition of the relationship between church and state in Hanoverian England was William Warburton, *The Alliance between Church and State, or, the Necessity and Equity of an Established Religion and a Test-Law Demonstrated, from the Essence and End of Civil Society, upon the fundamental principles of the Law of Nature and Nations* (London, 1736).

[33] See [Howley], *Charge to the Clergy of London*, 15.

[34] See Mark 10: 24.

[35] *Church-of-Englandism*, App., 96–102.

subsistence upon their good behaviour, whereas to the established clergy 'good behaviour is comparatively of no use'. On the contrary, it was 'their riches, their factitious dignities, their temporal power' which secured them 'respect—respect without desert, and independently of good behaviour'.[36]

The Anglican Church was, nevertheless, in danger, and from three sources. The first and most important source of danger lay in its 'doctrine and discipline', and particularly in 'the opulence, the power, the dignities, and the idleness' of the clergy. This was not only a source of danger, but a source of 'sure and inevitable destruction', given that it represented the 'very essence' of the Church, and constituted 'its own original sin' for which there was 'no means of redemption'. At the Reformation the Anglican Church had preserved as much of the doctrine and discipline of the Roman Church as possible, not for the benefit of the subject many, but for 'the private, personal, exclusive, and thereby sinister interest of the Monarch of that day [i.e. Henry VIII], in conjunction with his terror-struck and ever prostrate and prostitute instruments—the other members of the *unseen* and invisible, but not less severely *felt*, corporation of the *ruling few*'. The result had been a great inequality in clerical salaries, a large number of sinecures and pluralities, and the severing of any link between reward and the performance of service. The clergyman's only concern was with the money he received, while the human beings, 'in whose instance the difference between eternal felicity and eternal torment' was supposed to depend on him, were ignored. The clergyman measured the value of a benefice in the direct ratio of the quantity of pay attached to it, and insofar as the benefice required any, in the indirect ratio of the quantity of service to be performed. The people had no choice in the appointment of the clergyman who was supposed to instruct them, and no means of removing him should he become 'what in half the parishes of the kingdom he always is, a nullity, or what in so many of them he is—a nuisance'. Given that the task of the parish minister was to read formularies, any pay he received beyond that which would engage the lowest-paid clerk was money wasted, while the taxes imposed to raise this money constituted oppression. While the lay part of the official establishment was corrupt, it was 'purity itself' when compared with the ecclesiastical. It was only in the latter that 'the wilful neglect of duty—and with it obtainment of money on false pretences', was sanctioned by the legislature. The reason why the ecclesiastical establishment was regarded with 'so much inward affection and outward reverence' by those who profited from misrule was because abuses greater than those which existed in the political or legal establishments—'*Sinecures*, *Pluralities*, *Sale* or *Grant* of *Reversions*—Pay out of all proportion with service—pay without any service—pay without so much as pretence of service—factitious dignity, without merit or without use—shares in the sovereignty, without so much as the pretence of independence'—were 'protected not only from reformation but reproach:—all

[36] *Church-of-Englandism*, Introduction, 100–1 n.

these abominations not only *justified* but *sanctified*'.[37] The existence of abuses in the religious establishment acted as a bulwark against reform elsewhere.

The second source of danger to the Anglican Church lay 'in the sentiments and affections' of its own members. While money was extorted from both members and non-members of the Church on the pretence that services would be rendered, the non-members did not expect any benefit and, therefore, experienced no disappointment, 'whereas, with here and there a casual exception, by the Lay Members of the Church, whatsoever expectation of good is expected, has disappointment for its consequence'.[38] The third source of danger consisted 'in the style and character of those its *defences*, of which this *Charge* [i.e. that of the Bishop of London] may be set at the head'. There would come a time when men would no longer be prepared to prostrate their understanding, whereupon 'the open pulling off the mask—the unpalliated insult,—thus offered' by the *Charge* 'to all whose docility' might have led them to 'prostrate themselves' would do greater harm to the Church than any enemy could do.[39] The Bishop of London, who would not be satisfied with anything less than the system of passive obedience and non-resistance, had criticized the Puritans as exciters of trouble.[40] David Hume, despite his hatred of the Puritans, and 'in great measure for this very reason', had acknowledged that the country was indebted to them 'for whatsoever of those things called *liberties* are still, in practice, left to us, and for the advantage of having gold for a covering to the rods by which we are ruled'.[41] In Scotland, moreover, a system of church government had been established which was in stark contrast to that in England. Not only did the Scottish clergy inspect schools and manage the poor fund, but were free from 'abuses such as *Creeds*, *Unchangeable Formularies*, *Reading without thinking*, *Sinecures*, *Non-Residence*, *Pluralities*, *Surplice fees*, *Palaces*', and, furthermore, free from bishops, 'a set of puppets, invested each of them with a portion of the sovereignty, to no other purpose than that of giving, to a notoriously dependent assembly [i.e. the House of Lords], a mendacious colour of independence, covering interested servility with a thin cloak of gratitude'. If the Scottish system of church government had been the consequence of the troubles excited by the Puritans in Scotland, then the same troubles were needed in England.[42]

Bentham's programme for the reform of 'all religious and much political mischief' was captured in the slogan 'euthanasia of the Church'.[43] His positive object was '[t]o place the business of religious instruction and worship in

[37] Ibid., App., 121–9. [38] Ibid. 132–3. [39] Ibid. 133–4.

[40] See [Howley], *Charge to the Clergy of London*, 17.

[41] See David Hume, *The History of England from the Invasion of Julius Caesar to The Revolution in 1688* (first published 1754–62), 6 vols. (Indianapolis, 1983), iv. 145–6: 'So absolute, indeed, was the authority of the crown [during the reign of Elizabeth I], that the precious spark of liberty had been kindled, and was preserved, by the puritans alone; and it was to this sect, whose principles appear so frivolous and habits so ridiculous, that the English owe the whole freedom of their constitution.'

[42] *Church-of-Englandism*, App., 144–6.

[43] Ibid. 193.

England upon a footing as beneficial to the joint interests of piety, morality, and economy, as the nature of the case admits of', while his secondary or negative object was 'to produce as little disturbance as possible to established habits, expectations, and prepossessions'.[44] The 'dissolution' of the Church through 'euthanasia', or 'good death (to borrow a word from David Hume)',[45] was preferable to 'cacothanasia', or 'bad death'. There was no need for an order of priests to administer the liturgy of the Church of England, and still less for another distinct order consisting of bishops and archbishops to discipline them. These classes of men might be allowed 'to empty themselves by death without replenishment', and the bulk of the ecclesiastical income of England used to diminish taxation, but at the same time the teaching of its doctrine secured.[46] Reform would be undertaken on the *uti possidetis* principle. In international agreements terminating war, this was only one of a number of principles which might be adopted, but: 'In arrangements of internal national reform, in so far as concerns *money* and *factitious dignity*—in a word, as to every object of desire,—*power* excepted, which in this case can never be considered any otherwise than as held in *trust*,—the principle of *uti possidetis* admits of no other to stand in competition with it.' The *uti possidetis* principle, which required that every individual affected should be 'saved from the sensation of loss', might be applied advantageously to the clergy since their possessions were non-hereditary.[47] On the resignation, transfer, or death of any member of the clergy, the emolument would thereafter be paid to government, to be used 'in alleviation of the public burthens, or to any other more beneficial purpose, if any such purpose can be found'. Compensation would also be paid to the patrons of benefices, but there would be no difficulty here since the market value of the patronage was well known. Due regard would also be paid to the '*pretium affectionis*—the value of affection', though in relation to immovable objects this would only extend to a house that had been in the occupation of the present possessors for a considerable amount of time, together with any garden or adjacent field. Under this plan, although the benefit would only be realized gradually as the possessors died off, immediate suffering on their part would be reduced to its minimum, and consequently the provocation to resistance minimized and the probability of success maximized.[48]

The only duties which a priest might be compelled to perform were to recite parts of the liturgy and to read sermons. These duties, suggested Bentham, might be performed by the parish clerk or even a parish schoolboy, at little expense,

[44] *Church-of-Englandism*, App., 385.

[45] See David Hume, 'Whether the British Government inclines more to Absolute Monarchy, or to a Republic' (first published 1741), in *Essays Moral, Political, and Literary*, 53: 'Absolute monarchy . . . is the easiest death, the true *Euthanasia* of the British constitution.'

[46] *Church-of-Englandism*, App., 196–8.

[47] In 1789 Bentham had, for this same reason, supported the policy of the French National Assembly in appropriating the property of the clergy: see *Rights, Representation, and Reform*, 202–3, 214–17.

[48] *Church-of-Englandism*, App., 198–203.

especially if the boy had been '*Bell-taught*'.[49] In the place of 'home-made' sermons composed by the priest, a selection of sermons might be compiled, from which the Churchwardens might choose one to be read.[50] Only a small fraction of priests performed any duties beyond this, and thereby contributed in any way to the welfare of their parishioners. In order to perform these duties it was necessary to possess 'a correspondent stock of information in that line of appropriate science, which may be termed *Pastoral Statistics*', namely a knowledge of the circumstances of the parish, the dwellings it contained, and their respective inhabitants. The Church's practice of non-residence, which gave rise to '*anti-pastoral ignorance*', meant that it was impossible for most priests to acquire this knowledge. The practice of the Anglican Church again contrasted badly with the Church of Scotland, where Sir John Sinclair had obtained information on every one of its 895 parishes from their ministers.[51] Having said that, the fact that a priest was resident did not entail pastoral knowledge: he was more likely, suggested Bentham, to know the names of the local lord's hounds than those of the poor inhabitants of his parish.[52]

The Anglican Church, as an established Church, also compared badly to non-established churches in relation to the discipline exercised over the clergy. The Bishops, together with the Archbishops above them, and Archdeacons and other officials beneath them, were paid enormous sums on the pretence of maintaining discipline, but in fact they destroyed it. The Bishops were given seats in the legislature, which turned their attention away from spiritual duties, or at least would have done so had they performed any, and at the same time made them proud and ambitious. Instead of preventing their respective subordinates from receiving pay without performing the appointed service, they committed the same abuse themselves, converting cure of souls into sinecures for their own use. They exercised a corrupt despotism over their parish priests, by means of

> a separate and altogether useless body of *substantive law*,—with a correspondent system of *procedure* and *judicial establishment*—kept on foot, to no better purpose than that the patronage of the judicial establishment may be continued in the pre-eminently unfit hands of Bishops: complication, plainly useless, and palpably inexcusable,—and with it proportionable uncognoscibility,—thence to good purposes inefficiency, and to bad purposes efficiency,—being thus secured to the rule of action.[53]

In the non-established churches, discipline was maintained not by officials or coercive laws, but by the lay-members 'in their character of voluntary contributors to the expense'. If the minister did not perform his duties, or failed to perform

[49] An allusion to Andrew Bell: see p. 171 n. above.

[50] *Church-of-Englandism*, App., 206–16.

[51] See Sir John Sinclair, *The Statistical Account of Scotland. Drawn up from the communications of the Ministers of the different Parishes*, 21 vols. (Edinburgh, 1791–9). For the production of the survey see R. Mitchison, *Agricultural Sir John: The Life of Sir John Sinclair of Ulbster 1754–1835* (London, 1962), 120–36.

[52] *Church-of-Englandism*, App., 216–19.

[53] Ibid. 375–6.

them satisfactorily, each member could choose to stop attending the church and withdraw his financial support. This had the same effect as a legal sanction, but without the burden of the delay, vexation, and expense which accompanied litigation. As a result, the service was always performed, and sinecures did not exist. Under the established Church of Scotland, which stood between the non-established churches and the Anglican Church in this respect, there did exist a body of coercive laws for the maintenance of discipline (though there was no separate official establishment to execute them), and the form of procedure was natural, as opposed to the technical procedure of the Church of England, which was 'teeming with *factitious delay, vexation*, and *expense*,—all established and kept up for the sake of the lawyer's profit upon the expense'. Where the procedure was natural, actual litigation would reflect the number of transgressions, and the absence of litigation would indicate that no transgression had taken place. In contrast, 'under the system of *technical* procedure transgression may be universal, and still no application for execution ever have place'. Such was the state of things under the Church of England. It was notorious that in the Church of Scotland, where there was no separate official establishment for the purpose, the maintenance of discipline was 'at the *top* of the scale of perfection', whereas in the Anglican Church, with its Archbishops, Bishops, Archdeacons, and Rural Deans, it was 'at the very *bottom of it*'.[54] 'In respect of discipline, between the three species of Churches, the case may be thus briefly, nor yet incorrectly, stated. In the English Established Church may be seen the *forms* of discipline without the substance: in the Scottish, *form and substance* both: in the *Non-Established* Churches no form, but nevertheless the *substance*: and this but the better, for being *without* the forms.'[55]

Under Bentham's scheme, the government would not attempt to make any change in the doctrine of the Church, but it would abolish all forced declarations of belief concerning doctrine. On the death of any incumbent, the parish clerk or some other person appointed by the vestry would be paid to recite that part of the service traditionally recited by the priest, and to read the sermon. Surplice fees, which would be paid to the clerk, would be reduced to a nominal sum. The vestry would enjoy the power to choose a minister, whereupon they would have to contribute to his pay. The vestry would also enjoy the power to allow the parish church to be used by any Christian denomination. Where an incumbent died leaving a curate, the duty and pay of the curate would be continued, while the remainder of the pay of the incumbent would be paid into 'the Church-Reform fund'. Where a curate died leaving an incumbent, the pay of the curate would go to the fund, and the duty performed by the parish clerk or other appointee of the vestry. In regard to discipline, when a Bishop or Archbishop died or was removed, the Crown would have the power to nominate

[54] *Church-of-Englandism*, App., 289–93.

[55] Ibid. 299. For a comparative survey of the Episcopalian Anglican and Irish Churches and the Presbyterian Scottish Church see S. J. Brown, *The National Churches of England, Ireland, and Scotland 1801–1846* (Oxford, 2001), esp. 1–33.

an Archdeacon, with the title of Vice-Bishop, to execute all the powers of the office, but without a seat in the Lords. His salary, proportionate to the time and labour employed, would be paid out of the Church-Reform fund. As incumbents and curates died off, the Vice-Bishops' sees would be consolidated. On the death of an Archbishop or Bishop, or of any other sinecurist, including Deans and Canons, the lands and houses belonging to the province or see would be sold by auction, with the produce going to the Church-Reform fund. Any of these clerics would have the power at any time to sell the immovable property, or any part of it, and in lieu of his present income, accept for life a government annuity purchased with the produce of the sale, which in many instances would lead to 'very considerable additions to existing income'. On the death or removal of any member of a Chapter holding its property jointly, either his share would be paid to the Augmentation Office,[56] or the Crown would have the power to nominate to the vacant situation a wounded or superannuated army or naval officer, who would give up his half-pay and other allowance. Similarly, on the death or removal of any Scholar, the College, or in their default the Crown, would have the power to allow the gratuitous use of the vacated chamber to any such officer. The majority of a Chapter, and of the Fellows of University and other Colleges, would have the power to sell its property, and convert the whole property into government annuities. All tithes in kind would cease on the death or removal of an incumbent, with the occupants of the land paying a commutation tax in their place. The patron of the benefice would be compensated for the loss of the advowson and for the loss of the tithes where they had been appropriated. Where the patronage was in the hands of the Crown, no such compensation would be made: 'By this means that vast mass of the matter of wealth, operating in the hands of the [Lord] Chancellor, in the shape of matter of corruption, would be sunk, and the Constitution relieved from the pressure of it.'[57] The euthanasia of the Church, while not affecting its doctrines, and while securing the performance of the duties which its priests were supposed to perform, would remedy 'the mischief done by it to morality and good government . . . to morality, by the perpetual dominion which has been exercised by the above-mentioned confederacy of *vices* [i.e. in relation to doctrine, service, pay, and discipline]: to good government, by the support, which, through the medium of corrupt and corruptive influence, has been seen given to despotism'. Bentham proposed that the Church-Reform fund should be used to reduce taxation, and in particular to remove those 'taxes prohibitive of health, justice, communication: communication for supply of *commercial* wants—communication, for supply to the most crying of all wants—remedy against misrule'. Here was a source of revenue which government had never considered: 'But on this, as on every other quarter of the field of political

[56] The Court of Augmentations and Revenues had been established to administer the lands seized by the Crown upon the dissolution of the monasteries. The Court had been incorporated into the Exchequer in 1554 as the Augmentation Office, which continued to administer the estates of the Crown.

[57] *Church-of-Englandism*, App., 386–92.

abuse, where?—where, alas! are the hands, to which remedy can be looked for with any ray of hope?'[58] The answer was, of course, the people themselves.

III

After producing *Church-of-Englandism* Bentham went on to compose a substantial body of further material on religious doctrine and on religious belief more generally. His strategy, as he explained in a letter of 4 August 1823 to Jean Baptiste Say, had been first to undermine natural religion: 'Many there are in whose eyes Natural Religion, if separated from Revealed, is nothing worth: wanting as well utility as evidence. To those I should have so managed as to avoid giving offence: leaving for a time thus Revealed Religion to take refuge and fortify themselves in, as they became convinced how utterly untenable Natural Religion is.' Having done that, it had been his intention to have cast doubt on the truth of revealed religion, examining 'the religion of Jesus in particular, and [religion] established in the Romish, English and other Churches'.[59] Bentham's letter to Say had been prompted by the appearance of *Analysis of the Influence of Natural Religion on the Temporal Happiness of Mankind*, published under the pseudonym of Philip Beauchamp. The work had been edited from Bentham's manuscripts by George Grote, and represented the first part of Bentham's strategy in which he attempted to undermine natural religion.[60] The work,

[58] *Church-of-Englandism*, App., 395–9.

[59] Bentham to Say, 4 Aug. 1823, *Correspondence*, xi. 277.

[60] Philip Beauchamp, *Analysis of the Influence of Natural Religion on the Temporal Happiness of Mankind* (London, 1822). There is a question over the exact status of this work. M. L. Clarke, *George Grote: A Biography* (London, 1962), 30–1, and Crimmins, *Secular Utilitarianism*, 208–10, take the view that the substance of the work is Bentham's. In contrast, D. Berman, *A History of Atheism in Britain from Hobbes to Russell* (London, 1988), 191–2, argues that it is 'largely the work of Grote, although inspired by Bentham's point of view', and that it 'should be regarded as the work of both men, with Grote as the major and Bentham as the minor partner'.

In his letter to Say of 4 August 1822, Bentham claimed that he had never read the work, and was dissatisfied with the use in the title of 'that fine Greek word *Analysis*, which means any thing or nothing', was 'completely uncharacteristic', and 'would be sufficient to deter from meddling with it 999 out of 1,000' of its potential readers. He had loaned the relevant papers, with the title 'The usefulness of Religion examined', to Grote, but had then been informed by 'an intimate of his, that I must not be surprized, if I found in it a work, got up in a form considerably different from what I should myself have given to it: but that he had a mode of writing of his own, and either could not or would not put it into any other'. Bentham had intended to read the manuscript, but before he had been able to do so, and to his surprise, the work had been published, and his papers returned, 'of which a comparatively small part alone had been made use of'. Bentham was not, therefore, prepared to recommend the work as his own: 'if it is not so good as I should have made it, I should be sorry for my own sake it should be regarded as mine: if better, which may very well be, I could not without uneasiness, think of being, howsoever unintentionally the cause of his being robbed of the honor of it'. See *Correspondence*, x. 274–6.

The papers, having been left by Bentham in his will to the Grotes, are now in the Grote Papers at the British Library (British Library Add. MSS 29,806–9). A detailed textual study of the papers will eventually reveal how much of the work is Grote's, and how much Bentham's. Certainly my impression is that the style of the work, as Bentham's informant suggested, was quite different from

which was in effect an expansion and elaboration of the views Bentham had expressed in the mid-1770s,[61] dealt with the consequences to be expected from a belief in the existence of a God whose nature had to be inferred from the characteristics of a physical world which, it was assumed, God had himself created. Bentham defined religion as 'the belief in the existence of an almighty Being, by whom pains and pleasures will be dispensed to mankind, during an infinite and future state of existence'. Natural religion was characterized by the lack of any 'written and acknowledged declaration, from which an acquaintance with the will and attributes of this almighty Being may be gathered'.[62] It had been claimed that religion promoted happiness: 'It has been affirmed to be the leading bond of union between the different members of society—to be the most powerful curb on the immoral and unsocial passions of individuals—to form the consolation and support of misfortunes in declining life—in short it has been described as the most efficient prop both of inward happiness and of virtuous practice in this world.' This claim required investigation.[63] The question was whether a belief in an afterlife, where an all-powerful God distributed pains and pleasures, produced 'happiness or misery in the present life'.[64] If it turned out that natural religion not only stifled human happiness, but was also a positive source of misery, it would be self-contradictory to make natural religion the basis of the principle of utility. Yet this was precisely what had been attempted by previous exponents of the principle of utility, such as John Gay, John Brown, and most significantly William Paley, regarded by many of his contemporaries as the leading practical philosopher and theologian of his age. Paley's *The Principles of Moral and Political Philosophy*[65] dominated the teaching of the subject at both the universities of Oxford and Cambridge for many years after its publication in 1785.[66] Indeed, it is possible that the appearance of this work, which to Bentham's friend George Wilson had much in common with Bentham's own thinking, prompted Bentham to publish *An Introduction to the Principles of Morals and Legislation* in 1789, almost ten years after it had been first printed.[67] Twenty years later, Bentham had subjected Paley's defence of capital punishment, put forward in *Moral and Political Philosophy*, to a detailed critique.[68]

that which characterized the material which Bentham published himself. With this caution, however, it is not unreasonable in the meantime to treat at least the content of the essay as closely reflecting Bentham's own ideas, particularly as Grote does seem to have followed Bentham's advice to him in relation to the structure of the work: see Bentham to Grote, 9 Dec. 1821, *Correspondence*, x. 454–5.

61 See pp. 175–6 above. 62 *Analysis of the Influence of Natural Religion*, 3.

63 Ibid. 1. 64 Ibid. 3.

65 William Paley, *The Principles of Moral and Political Philosophy* (London, 1785).

66 See M. L. Clarke, *Paley: Evidences for the Man* (London, 1974), 126–9.

67 George Wilson to Bentham, 24 Sept. 1786 and 30 Nov. 1788, *Correspondence*, vol. iii, ed. I. R. Christie (London, 1971), 489–93, and ibid. iv. 15–17.

68 Bentham's essay, 'Law versus arbitrary power:—or, A Hatchet for Dr. Paley's Net', written mainly in January and February 1809, is at UC cvii. 199–266, with a copy at cvii. 278–343, and related manuscript at cvii. 183–8, 267–77.

There are passing references to Paley scattered through Bentham's works, usually suggesting that Paley had misunderstood or misused the principle of utility.[69] From one point of view *Analysis of the Influence of Natural Religion* was a further chapter in Bentham's engagement with Paley—a rebuttal of his system of utilitarianism, underpinned by natural religion—but it was also part of his broader onslaught on the Anglican Church, and thence on the English political, legal, and ecclesiastical establishment generally.

In *Moral and Political Philosophy* and his work on *Natural Theology*,[70] Paley aimed to show that the works of nature were not only evidence of, but also a reflection of, the divine will, and from this draw conclusions as to the nature of man and the obligations laid upon him. Just as the construction of a watch—where the passing of time was indicated by means of an application of the rules of mechanics—implied the existence of an intelligent being who had constructed it, so contrivance in nature implied the existence of a contriver, of a creator. For instance, the construction of an eye—with its ability to focus on objects near and far, the provision of muscles to turn it in one direction and then another, and the provision of lids for protection and glands for cleaning—was evidence of design. Where there was design, there must also be a designer. If contrivance existed, so did a superintending intelligence.[71] Observation of nature not only proved the existence of God, but also the divine goodness, for contrivance in nature was clearly intended to be beneficial. Everywhere one looked in the animal creation one found unbounded joy: 'The air, the earth, the water, teem with delighted existence.' Moreover, God had superadded pleasure to animal sensations when it was unnecessary for the purpose in question, or when the purpose, though necessary, might have been achieved by pain—for instance, God had added the pleasure of taste to the necessary function of eating. The fact that men had the capacity to feel pleasure directly from certain perceptions, and that there existed external objects to provide these perceptions, was too fortuitous to be the result of accident; it could only be explained by the pure benevolence of the creator.[72] There was no avoiding the conclusion 'that God wills and wishes the happiness of his creatures'.[73] However, the fact that God had endowed man with free will, giving him the capacity to cause pain and misery, and had not simply granted immediate and totally fulfilling pleasure to him, suggested that man had been placed in this world to prove his worth. The present world was 'a condition calculated for the production, exercise, and improvement of moral qualities, with a view to a future state, in which these qualities, after being so produced,

[69] See e.g. *Deontology*, 52–3, 328, and *Official Aptitude Maximized; Expense Minimized*, 351. For a comparison of the utilitarianism of Bentham and Paley see Rosen, *Classical Utilitarianism*, 131–43.

[70] William Paley, *Natural Theology: or, Evidences of the Existence and Attributes of the Deity, collected from the appearances of nature* (London, 1802).

[71] See *The Works of William Paley, D.D. with A Life, by Alexander Chalmers, Esq.*, 5 vols. (London, 1819), iv. 14–32.

[72] Ibid. iv. 355–84.

[73] Ibid. i. 53.

exercised, and improved, may, by a new and more favouring constitution of things, receive their reward, or become their own'. The man who proved himself virtuous would be rewarded with the pleasures of heaven, while the vicious man would suffer the pains of hell.[74] The standard for human conduct was the will of God, and the means of discovering 'the will of God, concerning any action, by the light of nature, is to enquire into the tendency of the action to promote or diminish the general happiness'. God willed the happiness of his creatures, hence that action was right which promoted human happiness. To say that a man acted right was to say that he acted consistently with the will of God, in other words that his action promoted the general happiness. Thus: 'Whatever is expedient, is right—It is the utility of any moral rule alone which constitutes the obligation of it.'[75]

According to Paley, utility and the will of God were one and the same. Bentham, in contrast, denied that the Deity posited by natural religion had the capacity to will human happiness. On the contrary, belief in such a Deity, and even more so any attempt to enforce such belief, produced positive misery. The central tenet of natural religion was the belief that the pains and pleasures human beings would experience in a future life were conditional upon their actions in this life, and that holding this belief promoted the happiness of the community. An immediate weakness in natural religion, suggested Bentham, echoing the argument he had advanced in the 1770s,[76] was its incapacity to lay down 'a *directive rule*, communicating the knowledge of the *right path*', and to provide '*a sanction* or inducement' for such a rule. All knowledge was founded on experience, but no one had any experience of the sort of conduct which would lead either to a future life of pleasure or to a future life of pain. The proponents of natural religion nevertheless assumed that God would reward those of whose behaviour he approved, and punish those of whose behaviour he disapproved. The sort of behaviour of which God would approve would depend, therefore, upon his nature. Were he benevolent, he would approve of actions which were beneficial to mankind; but were he malevolent, he would approve of actions which were mischievous. Paley had stated that nature revealed the benevolence of the Deity, and that the existence of evil was the result of man's free will in a world which was merely a state of probation. In Bentham's view, this was not an adequate solution to the problem of evil. Despite all the rhetoric to the contrary, there was no option but to regard the God of the advocates of natural religion, with his attributes of 'unlimited power' and 'incomprehensible agency', as being motivated by 'caprice and tyranny'. Those subject to unlimited power lived in a state of fear: they assumed that the holder of such power had a disposition to do harm, and lacked the means to protect themselves. A disposition to do harm, together with the power to effect it at pleasure, constituted 'the very essence of tyranny'. The notion of 'incomprehensible agency' translated into totally unpredictable behaviour, which, if the attribute of a human being, would be

[74] Ibid. iv. 385–417. [75] Ibid. i. 50. [76] See pp. 175–6 above.

condemned as capricious or even insane.[77] The existence in the world of both good and evil meant that God could not be understood as either consistently desiring good or consistently desiring evil, for, if he were consistent, his unlimited power would bring about the appropriate state of affairs: 'While there exists good in the universe, such a power cannot be wielded by perfect malevolence; while there exists evil, it cannot be directed by consummate benevolence.'[78]

Behaviour intended to please a God characterized by such 'caprice and tyranny', argued Bentham, would not promote, but diminish human happiness. A human despot, for instance, with his insatiable love of power, favoured those who contributed to his power, and hated those who threatened it. The despot had no regard for the happiness of any of those subject to him, with the exception of a few favourites. On the contrary, the despot aimed for the debasement and insecurity of everyone besides himself and his favourites. The consequence was that he approved of any qualities which tended to diminish human happiness, and detested those which tended to increase it.[79] By analogy, God would most favour the priesthood who 'disseminated his influence', and after the priesthood, those who debased themselves, performing actions which had no earthly benefit, in order to extol him. At the opposite end of the scale, God would most strongly disapprove of those who denied his very existence, and after them, those of independent mind who refused to abase themselves. These conclusions were entailed by a belief in a God who possessed unlimited power and who acted incomprehensibly.[80]

Bentham pointed out that the rewards and punishments of the religious sanction, at least in the present life, could not be shown to result from any supernatural agency, but arose from the actions of human beings.[81] Having catalogued the various ways in which natural religion was personally mischievous to the individual believer (for instance by 'inflicting unprofitable suffering' and 'imposing useless privations'),[82] he described the more extensive mischief produced in a community generally by belief in, and attempts to enforce, a system of natural religion. The crux of Bentham's argument was that natural religion subverted the capacity of the people to know and to promote their own interest. In particular, religion distorted public opinion and thereby undermined its effectiveness in preventing oppressive and mischievous acts:

To ensure on the part of every individual a preference of actions favourable to the happiness of the community, it is essentially requisite that that community should themselves be able to recognise what is conducive to their happiness—that they should manifest a judgment sufficiently precise and untainted to separate virtue from vice. The reason why the popular sanction is generally mentioned as an encouragement to good and a restraint upon bad conduct, is, because the major part of the society are supposed in most cases to know what benefits and what injures them—and that they are disposed

[77] *Analysis of the Influence of Natural Religion*, 9–17. [78] Ibid. 19–20.
[79] Ibid. 27–31. [80] Ibid. 31–2. [81] Ibid. 54–66. [82] Ibid. 68–75.

to love and recompense the former behaviour, to hate and punish the latter. Now the efficacy of the public hate, considered as a restraint upon mis-deeds, depends upon its being constantly and exclusively allied with the real injury of the public—upon its being uniformly called forth whenever their happiness is endangered, and never upon any mistaken or imaginary alarms. Whatever, therefore, tends to make men hate that which does not actually hurt them, contributes to distort or disarm public opinion, in its capacity of a restraint upon injurious acts—for the public sentiment is only the love or hatred of all or most of the individuals in the society.[83]

Religion led to the condemnation of practices which were not in fact harmful; it diverted popular criticism away from practices which were harmful; and it transformed the popular sanction from a safeguard for happiness into the instrument of evil.[84] The inappropriate bestowal of praise and blame perverted the science of morality, which had been 'cast into utter darkness and embarrassment' and enveloped 'in a cloud of perplexity and confusion'.[85] In practice, religion constituted an obstacle to human improvement—an obstacle which could only be overcome by the diffusion of knowledge.[86]

The mischievous effects of natural religion were intensified by a priesthood, whose interest was diametrically opposed to that of the people. Certain men, who were able to perform acts which appeared to others to have supernatural causes, were assumed to have a peculiar intimacy with God. Only they had knowledge of the divine will, and only through their mediation could God's power be harnessed. They were exalted into 'a station of supreme necessity and importance', and inundated with wealth and honours, which were diverted from useful purposes. Having enumerated a variety of ways in which the influence of the priesthood was hostile to human happiness, Bentham pointed out that the priesthood had a natural ally in the ruler of the state: 'He, as well as they, has an interest incurably at variance with that of the community, and all sinister interests have a natural tendency to combine together and co-operate, inasmuch as the object of each is thereby most completely and most easily secured.' The physical force which the ruler had at his disposal could be used to crush opposition on the part of the people, while the priesthood made such opposition unlikely by encouraging submission: 'They infuse the deepest reverence for temporal power, by considering the existing authorities as established and consecrated by the immaterial Autocrat above, and as identified with his divine majesty.' In return the priesthood was protected by the ruler, who responded with physical force to any dissent from its dogmas. In addition, the ruler extorted a large tribute from the people for the priesthood, 'in order to maintain them in affluence and in worldly credit; thus securing to them an additional purchase upon the public sentiment, and confirming his own safety from resistance'. Bentham concluded: 'Prostration and plunder of the community is indeed the common end of both.'[87]

83 Ibid. 84. 84 Ibid. 84–6. 85 Ibid. 86–7. 86 Ibid. 87–92.
87 Ibid. 137–40.

The more general perspective which Bentham adopted in *Analysis of the Influence of Natural Religion* overlapped at many points with the arguments developed in *Church-of-Englandism* in relation to the particular situation of the Anglican Church. Neither work was concerned overtly with the truth of religious belief,[88] but rather with the implications for human happiness of the propagation of religious doctrine by a priesthood, whose authority was sanctioned by the state. He reiterated his views when beginning work on the constitutional code, his blueprint for good government, in 1822.[89] He made two main points: first, the priest's most important contribution to misrule was delusion; and second, government should not provide reward for declarations of belief. First, in relation to the alliance of ruler and priest, Bentham observed that an absolute monarch had three groups of 'corporeal instruments'—namely soldiers, lawyers, and priests—to help him achieve his aim of maximizing his own happiness at whatever cost to the happiness of the community. Each had a distinctive means of operation: that of the soldier was force and intimidation; that of the lawyer force, intimidation, and delusion; and that of the priest, partly intimidation, but principally delusion. Delusion was a perversion of the understanding, or belief in an erroneous opinion or conception, which, in the context of government, encouraged people to give support to measures which were opposed to their interest. One source of delusion, for instance, was the association of superior virtue with superior wealth or rank. A second, and the means by which the priest operated, was fallacious argument. The priest invented a future life, 'a life which he fills with an all-comprehensive instrument of intimidation—a life filled with torments in intensity and duration infinite'. Having established a general rule that everyone was destined to suffer these eternal torments, he stated that certain persons would be excepted, and that to qualify as 'one of these exceptions, the first thing a man has to do is to do in all things, as far as lies in his power, the will of the Monarch, to the production of human misery in what quantity soever it may happen to it to be directed'.[90]

Second, Bentham argued that the power of government should not be used to establish any system of religious belief. If the system were true, there was no need to reward people for professing belief in it. Apart from being useless, the giving of reward, where a person asserted his belief in a dogma he regarded as untrue, was a corruption of morals—in effect subornation of perjury. The establishment of a priesthood to cause others, through the use of argument, to profess the belief in question was especially pernicious, since this vitiated both morals and intellect:

the individual hired to teach must, if he earns his hire, be continually brooding over whatever falshood he has committed: perpetually engaged in the endeavour to cause

[88] Bentham would, of course, have regarded theological discourse as just as nonsensical as discourse about natural rights: see Ch. 3 above. Cf. *Church-of-Englandism*, Catechism, 46: 'As to *grace*, on this occasion, as on so many others—not to say *all* others—it is a mere *expletive*; adding nothing to the sense.'

[89] See pp. 288–303 below.

[90] *First Principles*, 183–6, 261–2.

others to believe to be true that which he himself does not believe to be true but believes to be false: continually occupied in the endeavour to deceive. To the character of liar for hire, he adds the character of a deceiver for hire—or at least would-be deceiver for hire.

The teacher would exist in a state of distress if he did not himself believe the doctrine he was arguing to be true, so the only course open to him was 'the self-deceptive process', whereby he looked for arguments which supported the doctrine in question, and ignored those which contradicted it. The habit of partiality, from which the teacher 'derives a propensity to embrace falshood and error in preference to truth, whatsoever be the subject', was thereby established. The real reason, however, why religion was established was not to inculcate belief in the truth of its doctrines, but rather to enable the rulers to enjoy the patronage of the emoluments granted to the priests, and the priests themselves to enjoy their immediate use. The prospect of these emoluments constituted an inducement for the priests to obey the commands of the rulers and to support their authority: 'in no instance has a system in regard to Religion been ever established but for the purpose as well as with the effect of its being made an instrument of intimidation, corruption and delusion, for the support of depredation and oppression, in the hands of government'.[91] Religious belief, supported by an established priesthood, was one more weapon in the armoury of rulers to promote their sinister interest at the expense of that of the community generally. In order to promote political reform, the alliance between Church and state had to be dissolved, hence Bentham's proposals for the euthanasia of the Church. He did not, however, halt his attack on the Anglican Church with his critique of natural religion. He went on to undermine Anglican doctrine by associating it with the teachings of the Apostle Paul, and then showing that the teachings of Paul were at variance with those of Jesus. Paul, like other religious leaders, had used religion to further his own sinister ends. This attack on Paul's teachings belongs to the second part of Bentham's strategy, as he explained it in his letter to Say:[92] namely to undermine revealed religion.

IV

In *Church-of-Englandism* Bentham had been prepared to leave to one side the question of the truthfulness of the doctrine of the Anglican Church, provided that no attempt was made to coerce unwilling individuals either to declare their belief in any part of that doctrine or to contribute financially to the maintenance of the Church. In *Not Paul, but Jesus*,[93] he did attempt to subvert Anglican

[91] Ibid. 325–31. [92] See p. 186 above.

[93] *Not Paul, but Jesus* (London, 1823), was edited by Francis Place, and published under the pseudonym of Gamaliel Smith. No such controversy as that concerning the authorship of *Analysis of the Influence of Natural Religion* has arisen in relation to the status of this text. Place appears to have been extremely faithful to Bentham's manuscripts.

doctrine. He also went on to suggest that, whereas Paul supported monarchy, the form of government approved by Jesus was representative democracy. The Anglican Church had not restricted its canon to the teachings of Jesus, explained Bentham, but had also adopted those of Paul. Whatever his view as to the divine nature claimed for Jesus, Bentham expressed some sympathy for the secular content of parts of his teachings.[94] He regarded those of Paul as being of a very different cast altogether. In *Not Paul, but Jesus* Bentham subjected the Acts of the Apostles and Paul's Epistles to a detailed forensic scrutiny. At one level, the work belongs with Bentham's writings on evidence, in that the techniques adopted were those which he might have used in cross-examination in order to test the veracity of a narrative presented by a witness. At another level, however, the work was radical and subversive, in that the veracity of the narrative which it questioned constituted a significant part of the New Testament. Bentham noted that Conyers Middleton had cleared away from the religion of Jesus 'a heap of pernicious rubbish' with which it had been encumbered by the Church Fathers.[95] His own task would be to complete the task by clearing away the additions made by Paul. Indeed, Paul, the self-constituted apostle of Jesus, who preached in declared opposition to the eleven undisputed apostles of Jesus, had not merely added to the religion of Jesus, but had propagated a religion of his own. Paul's teachings had not only produced 'dissentions and mischiefs' among the followers of the religion of Jesus, but were also the source of the greatest part of the opposition which that religion, with its benevolent system of morals, had experienced. Whatever good had resulted from the combined religion was to be found in the religion of Jesus, and whatever mischief in that of Paul. Bentham concluded that Paul did not have the commission from Jesus which he claimed to have; that his enterprise was a scheme of personal ambition, and nothing more; that his system of doctrine was fraught with mischief; and that it had no warrant in anything said or done by Jesus.[96]

Bentham did not doubt the fact of Paul's outward conversion to the religion of Jesus, but claimed that there was no evidence that it was either caused by or resulted in either any supernatural intercourse with the Almighty or any belief in the supernatural character of Jesus himself. He inferred that any point of doctrine found in the Epistles of Paul but not in the Gospels belonged to Paul alone,

[94] Bentham's unpublished manuscripts on religion, however, reportedly contain material which is strongly critical of the teachings of Jesus: see e.g. Steintrager, 'Language and Politics: Bentham on Religion', 4–9. Certainly, Bentham did confess that he had a subversive purpose in relation to the title of the work: '*but* was the conjunction expressed: but it was that *not* might be the conjunction inferred: so at least the author [i.e. Bentham himself] informs me but of this there is no need to make any public mention: each man is master of his own inferences.' See Bentham to Say, 19 Oct. 1823, *Correspondence*, xi. 308.

[95] Conyers Middleton, *A Free Inquiry into the Miraculous Powers, Which are supposed to have subsisted in the Christian Church, from the Earliest Ages through several successive Centuries. By which it is shewn, That we have no sufficient Reason to believe, upon the Authority of the Primitive Fathers, That any such powers were continued to the Church, after the Days of the Apostles* (London, 1749).

[96] *Not Paul, but Jesus*, pp. iii–viii.

and formed no part of the religion of Jesus.[97] Paul's purpose in declaring himself a 'convert to the religion of Jesus' had been to make himself its leader, 'and, by means of the expertness he had acquired in the use of the Greek language, to preach, in the name of Jesus, that sort of religion, by the preaching of which, an empire over the minds of his converts, and, by that means, the power and opulence to which he aspired, might, with the fairest prospect of success, be aimed at'. He had found it necessary to form an alliance with the existing leaders of the new religion and their adherents—namely the Apostles, led by Peter, and the rest of their disciples.[98] A 'partition treaty' had been agreed by Paul and Peter. Precisely when this took place was unclear, but neither of the contracting parties had lacked adequate motives. Peter and the rest of the Apostles had gained security against persecution at the hands of Paul, while Paul's public recognition, rather than stigmatization as an impostor, by the Apostles, had been vital for the success of his schemes.[99] The terms of the partition treaty had been 'Paul to the Gentiles, Peter and his associates to the Jews'. The Apostles had retained their influence over that part of the world which they already possessed, namely Jerusalem and the Jewish world where Hebrew was 'the vernacular language'; all the rest had been left to Paul. However, in spite of the treaty, the Apostles had failed to prevent Paul preaching his own gospel, which had been different from theirs, and from that of Jesus, to persons within their sphere of influence: while in pretence and name an associate, Paul had been, in truth and effect, an adversary and opponent.[100]

The conflict had come to a head with Paul's fourth and final visit to Jerusalem. Though there was no direct evidence, it was clear from circumstantial evidence that Paul's motive for the visit consisted in a desire for '[t]he common objects of political concupiscence—money, power and vengeance': money in the form of the whole property of the Church; power in directing the consciences of the faithful; and vengeance for the repeated rebuffs he had received in his attempts to supplant the Apostles. Paul's ambition had, therefore, brought him to Jerusalem, the original metropolis of the Christian world; the Apostles had wished to keep him out of it.[101] Once at Jerusalem, Paul had been accused by the Elders of having encouraged Jews living amongst the Gentiles to forsake the Mosaic law. The accusation had been well founded, and Paul knew it was well founded, but he had lied by denying its truth. In order to prove the sincerity of his denial, the Apostles and Elders had proposed that Paul should perform a ceremony, whereby the sanction of an oath was attached to the denial in question. Paul had agreed to perform the ceremony. He had gone to the Temple, but before he had remained there for the requisite number of days, the Temple had been stormed by 'the indignant multitude', convinced that Paul was committing perjury.[102] Bentham did not blame Paul for teaching men to forsake Moses—this deserved

97 Ibid. 1–2. 98 Ibid. 73. 99 Ibid. 184–7. 100 Ibid. 203–5, 208.
101 Ibid. 210–11. 102 Ibid. 255–6. See Acts 21: 15–30.

positive praise—but for denying, rather than avowing and justifying, this teaching, and then aggravating the falsehood by a deliberate perjury:

And, to what purpose commit so flagrant a breach of the law of morality? Plainly, to no other, than the fixing himself in Jerusalem, and persevering in a project of insane and selfish ambition, which, in spite of the most urgent remonstrances that could be made by his most devoted adherents, had brought him thither: for, he had but to depart in peace, and the Apostles of Jesus would have remained unmolested, and the peace of Christendom undisturbed.[103]

As a result of what had taken place at the Temple, a great law case had commenced, *The Jews against Paul*, tried in the first instance before an irregular tribunal, and then before no less than four regular tribunals. For the execution of the definitive judgment, Paul had been sent to Rome. Having already laid the foundation of a spiritual kingdom in Rome, Paul had no objection to appearing there as a state prisoner, in order to impress the Roman Emperor with his eloquence.[104]

If Paul's supernatural intercourse with the Almighty had been a pretence—if his final visit to Jerusalem had been strongly opposed by the Apostles and their disciples—if not only the Apostles but also the whole population of Jerusalem had known him to be depraved, indulging not merely in habitual insincerity but in perjury in its most aggravated form—if it had only been by declaring himself a Roman citizen that he had escaped from the punishment, apparently capital, attached by the law of the land to the crimes of which he had been guilty—and if it had only been in places in which Jesus, his doctrines, and his Apostles had been unknown that he had been received as an Apostle of Jesus—if all, or even only some, of these points had been established, remarked Bentham, one could only conclude 'that whatever is in Paul, and is not to be found in any one of the four Gospels, is not Christianity, but Paulism'.[105] Moreover, Paul himself had avowed that he had received nothing from the Apostles, and that he had doctrines which were not theirs. If the Gospel had not been received by Paul by revelation of Jesus Christ, and had not been, as he himself claimed, 'of man', then 'it was made by him, out of his own head'.[106] For anyone who wanted an Antichrist, remarked Bentham, Paul was an undeniable one. He was an

[103] *Not Paul, but Jesus*, 266–7.

[104] Ibid. 347, 364. For the 'great law case' see Acts 21: 31–26: 32.

[105] *Not Paul, but Jesus*, 366–7.

[106] Ibid. 367–8. Bentham had in mind Gal. 1: 11–12: 'But I certify you, brethren, that the gospel which was preached of me is not after man. For I neither received it of man, neither was I taught *it*, but by the revelation of Jesus Christ.' James Mill, on reading this passage, commented: 'I think the meaning is that he *did* receive his gospel from Jesus, & in a more remarkable way than the rest of the apostles—they received it in the way of ordinary communication from Jesus—he by miraculous invitation' (Mill to Bentham, Aug. 1823, *Correspondence*, xi. 273). Bentham's point, however, was that while Paul had confessed that he had not received the gospel from the Apostles, he (Bentham) had shown that Paul's pretensions to a supernatural revelation were fraudulent.

opponent of the real Apostles of Christ, their disciples and followers, and of all that could in any intelligible sense be called Christ.[107]

Paul's teachings had perverted morality. All men who relied on supernatural terrors to support their authority regarded pleasure as their most formidable rival, and were proportionably hostile to it. Accordingly their morality and their law was characterized by a hatred of pleasure: 'Death is scarce severe enough, for a pleasure, which they either have, or would be thought to have, no relish for. So at least ways what they teach: but, teaching how to act is one thing; acting accordingly, another. Thus we all see it is, in so many instances: and thus, without much danger of injustice, we may venture to suppose it may have been, in that of the self-constituted Apostle.' Jesus, on the other hand, saw no harm in anything that gave pleasure. Jesus knew that happiness must be composed of pleasures, 'and, be the man who he may, of what it is that gives pleasure to him, he alone can be judge'.[108] In perverting the teachings of Jesus, Paul had also prepared the ground for the perversion of the form of government recommended by Jesus. The Apostles, in electing Matthias to their number,[109] had shown that in the Christian world, if government in any form was sanctioned by divine right, it was representative democracy, operating by universal suffrage. This method of filling offices had not been to the taste of Paul: 'He determined to open their eyes, and prove to them by experience, that monarchy,—himself the first monarch—was the only legitimate form of government.'[110] Bentham suggested that the early political organization of Christianity had been a representative democracy, echoing in important respects his own proposals which he was developing for his constitutional code:

As to the religion of Jesus, true it is, that so long as it continued the religion of Jesus, all was good government, all was equality, all was harmony: free church, the whole; established church, none: monarchy, none; constitution, democratical. Constitutive authority, the whole community: legislative, the Apostles of Jesus; executive, the Commissioners of the Treasury: not Lords Commissioners, appointed by a King Herod, but trustees or *stewards*; for such should have been the word, and not *deacons*,—agents elected by *universal suffrage*. In this felicitous state, how long it continued—we know not. What we do know, is—that, in the fourth century, despotism took possession of it, and made an instrument of it.[111] Becoming *established*, it became noxious,—preponderantly noxious. For, where *established* is the adjunct to it, what does *religion* mean? what but depredation, corruption, oppression, hypocrisy—these four: with delusion, in all its forms and trappings, for support.

Christian government had degenerated into a nuisance when it had been officially recognized by the Roman state.[112] By linking monarchical government with Paul, and representative democracy with Jesus, Bentham was attempting to

[107] *Not Paul, but Jesus*, 372. [108] Ibid. 393–4. [109] See Acts 1: 15–26.
[110] *Not Paul, but Jesus*, 217.
[111] Bentham had in mind the adoption of Christianity by the Roman Emperor Constantine.
[112] *Not Paul, but Jesus*, 391–2.

undermine the Christian basis for the alliance of Church and state in England. Having shown that natural religion could not provide a basis for good government of any sort, he had now shown that revealed religion, derived from the Gospel of Jesus, gave no support to the established form of English government, whether in Church or in state.

V

Bentham did not object to religious institutions as such, but rather to official religious establishments, funded by taxation which, by definition, was extracted by coercion. If individuals were willing to give their own money to support the clergy, and providing that no misrepresentation was employed to obtain it, and no injury done to any other person by the use of it, there was no reason why they should be prevented from doing so. Having said that, he was, on balance, prepared to recommend the imposition of taxation to support the provision of religious instruction, on account of the greater mischief which might ensue in the absence of such instruction.[113] In relation to the interference of government, religion was like trade:

> As for trade, so for religion,—different as they are in other respects, whatsoever may have been the case in the days of primæval barbarism,—the best thing that a government could *now* do, would be not to meddle with it, always excepted the purifying it from whatsoever portions of the *matter of wealth, power, or dignity*, in the shape of the *matter of corruption*, superstition has ever daubed with it. Revenue forces government to meddle with trade: but (witness America else), neither revenue nor any thing else forces government to meddle with religion. The perfection of all Church management is the absence of all Church government.[114]

But just as sinister interest impelled rulers to interfere in religion, so it impelled them to interfere in matters of trade, and particularly in the establishment of colonies.

[113] *Church-of-Englandism*, App., 231–2.

[114] Ibid. 149. Bentham presumably had in mind the First Amendment to the United States Constitution (1791), which provided that 'Congress shall make no law respecting the establishment of religion, or prohibiting the free exercise thereof'.

8

Colonies and Constitutional Law

I

In a letter written in or around April 1820 to the Argentine revolutionary and statesman Bernardino Rivadavia, Bentham stated that he had always been of the opinion 'that all colonies and distant dependencies, without exception, are essentially mischievous', or more precisely 'essentially and preponderantly mischievous to the great majority of the people on both sides'.[1] Bentham's claim to consistency has been challenged by Donald Winch, who points out that, while Bentham's reputation as an anti-imperialist is founded on his essay addressed to the National Convention of France,[2] he did not consistently maintain the views he expressed there:

Bentham spent most of his life in the process of revising and occasionally contradicting positions he had reached earlier... Bentham had great difficulty in maintaining a consistent anti-colonial position;... depending on the case under consideration, he

[1] Bentham to Rivadavia, April? 1820, *Correspondence*, ix. 428–9.

[2] Bentham's first major essay on the subject of colonies was 'Jeremy Bentham to the National Convention of France', written in late 1792, printed in early 1793, and published as *Emancipate Your Colonies! Addressed to the National Convention of France, A° 1793, shewing the uselessness and mischievousness of distant dependencies to an European state* (London, 1830). A few fragments dealing with colonies were written in 1801 for 'Institute of Political Economy', which remained unprinted during Bentham's lifetime (see *Jeremy Bentham's Economic Writings: Critical Edition based on his printed works and unpublished manuscripts*, ed. W. Stark, 3 vols. (London, 1952–4) [hereafter Stark], iii. 303–80). *Observations on the Restrictive and Prohibitory Commercial System; especially with a reference to the Decree of the Spanish Cortes of July 1820*, London, 1821 (Bowring, iii. 85–103), was edited from Bentham's manuscripts by Bowring, who added a considerable amount of material of his own. This essay was originally intended as an appendix to Bentham's most sustained essay on colonies, successively entitled 'Emancipation Spanish' and 'Rid Yourselves of Ultramaria', written for Spain and Spanish America between April 1820 and April 1822, and published for the first time, together with the *Observations*, in *Colonies, Commerce, and Constitutional Law: Rid Yourselves of Ultramaria and other writings on Spain and Spanish America*, ed. P. Schofield (Oxford, 1995). The chapter 'Des Colonies' which appeared in *Théorie des peines et des récompenses*, the second recension which Dumont prepared from Bentham's manuscripts, and published in 1811 (*Théorie des peines et des récompenses*, 2 vols. (London, 1811), ii. 314–32), was based on 'Jeremy Bentham to the National Convention of France', as Bentham himself explained: see *Colonies, Commerce, and Constitutional Law*, 22. Finally, in 'Colonization Society Proposal', an unpublished essay written in 1831, and inspired by Edward Gibbon Wakefield, Bentham described a scheme for the establishment of a new colony in South Australia: the relevant manuscripts are at UC viii. 149–97.

alternated between emphasis on the drawbacks of colonial rule and awareness of the opportunities presented by the existence of Britain's overseas possessions.[3]

Between the writing of 'Jeremy Bentham to the National Convention of France' in late 1792 and his death in 1832, 'Bentham modified his original position in accordance with changes in his interests and his political and economic ideas. At times these changes led to concessions being made in favour of colonies and colonization, while at others, they seemed to strengthen old criticisms. In so far as the story has any pattern, it is one of recurring ambivalence.' In his economic writings in the period 1801–4, notes Winch, Bentham approved of colonization on the grounds that emigration was beneficial where there was rising population pressure in the mother country, and even seems to have accepted that the export of capital to colonies might be beneficial when capital accumulation in the mother country outstripped investment opportunities at existing rates of profit—thus contradicting the view expressed in 'Jeremy Bentham to the National Convention of France' that capital was best employed at home. Winch points out, moreover, that in response to the events of the French Revolution, Bentham went through a 'patriotic-paternalistic' phase: 'Bentham's Toryism seems to have reasserted itself', and he was found 'indulging in patriotic sentiments which verge on jingoism about the prospects opened up by British overseas possessions'. At the beginning of the 1820s Bentham returned to anti-imperialism with 'Rid Yourselves of Ultramaria'. Winch, noting Bentham's claim that he had never departed from his earlier opinions on colonies, concludes that '[h]e appears to have forgotten his cautious statements about the dangers of granting independence to existing British colonies'. The final twist was Bentham's 'full support' in 1831 for Edward Gibbon Wakefield's project for the colonization of South Australia.[4]

In contrast, Lea Campos Boralevi argues that the inconsistency lies not in Bentham's attitude towards colonies, but rather 'in the attitude of his twentieth-century critics, who have applied the contemporary language of "imperialism" and "anti-imperialism" to Bentham's theory of "empire"'.[5] She points out that Bentham did not treat the problem of colonies as a single problem, but differentiated between English, Spanish, and French colonies in America; penal colonies in Australia; and British India. The key point was Bentham's sensitivity to the 'particular circumstances' of each case. She admits that changes in Bentham's political and economic thought did influence his colonial thought: for instance, the phase characterized by Winch as 'patriotic-paternalistic' coincided with the period of reaction against the French Revolution, while the anti-imperialism of the writings for Spain followed his conversion to political radicalism. Furthermore, his change in opinion around 1800 in regard to issues

[3] D. Winch, *Classical Political Economy and Colonies* (London, 1965), 25. Winch has restated his views in 'Bentham on Colonies and Empire', *Utilitas*, 9 (1997), 147–54.

[4] Winch, *Classical Political Economy*, 31–8.

[5] Boralevi, *Bentham and the Oppressed*, 134.

of population, namely that colonization might be a remedy for problems associated with population growth and excess of capital, accounts for his remarks in favour of colonization in 1801–4 and for his support of Wakefield's Australian project in 1831.[6] Boralevi emphasizes the distinction which Bentham drew between established colonies and the colonization of uncultivated land. Colonization was an economic issue—a possible source of relief for excess of population and capital—whereas colonies 'generated a series of problems, conditioned by their own political and socio-historical situations', and thus: 'Each case had its own problems, according to *circumstances* and to the people involved, and each had to be solved not in the name of abstract principles, but on the "solid foundation" of the principle of utility.' Bentham's general view was that the maintenance of colonies was economically expensive to the mother country and oppressive to the colonies, and that colonies with 'advanced societies'—characteristic of the French, English, and Spanish colonies in America—should be emancipated. However, emancipation was not the ultimate principle, but utility, and where overpopulation in the mother country would be relieved by the colonization of uninhabited or uncultivated land, as in Australia, the balance of utility was tipped in favour of colonization.[7] In the same way, Bentham supported the rule of the East India Company over India on the grounds that it was the best practicable government in the circumstances—the backwardness of the people of India was attributable to their legislation and religion, whereas British governors might better lead them on to welfare and progress. The oppression the Indians might suffer under British government would be less than that which they might suffer under their native rulers, while government through the East India Company would help to reduce the economic burden of the colonies to the mother country.[8] Rather than inconsistency, Boralevi sees 'a line of continuity in Bentham's attitude towards colonies which derives from the steadfast application of the principle of utility', which 'might on one occasion reinforce his conviction that colonies were not advantageous in themselves, or, on another, contradict it with evidence provided by other factors, which might make him decide in favour of "imperialism" '.[9] There is no doubt that Bentham's attitude towards colony-holding and colonization was complex, and there seems no reason to disagree with Jennifer Pitts's assessment that Bentham, despite his seeming inconsistency in certain respects, was in general sceptical about the benefits of colonial rule.[10] What needs to be added to these

[6] Ibid. 121–5. [7] Ibid. 127–9. [8] Ibid. 131–2.

[9] Ibid. 134. G. Hoogensen, *International Relations, Security, and Jeremy Bentham* (London, 2005), 130–60, while explicitly rejecting Boralevi's view that Bentham's support for either colonization or emancipation was determined by the differing dictates of the principle of utility in differing cases, implicitly accepts it by arguing that his support was determined by the differing dictates of security (which was, of course, a sub-end of the principle of utility).

[10] See J. Pitts, 'Legislator of the World? A Rereading of Bentham on Colonies', *Political Theory*, 31 (2003), 200–34, whose purpose is to distance Bentham's attitude towards colonialism from

accounts—though it is glimpsed at by Boralevi—is an assessment of the impact of the discovery of sinister interests, and the subsequent adoption of political radicalism, on Bentham's colonial thought. In his earlier writings on colonies, while aware of the potential for corruption, he emphasized the economic disadvantages of colony-holding; in his later writings, while never losing sight of the economic arguments, he highlighted the harmful constitutional ramifications of colony-holding. Indeed, it was the operation of sinister interest which explained the support for colony-holding manifested by rulers.

II

Bentham had briefly discussed the issue of colony-holding at the time of the American Declaration of Independence. He later recalled that he had written a paper on 'how the question between the mother-country and the colony ought to be determined', which he had leant to Lind, who had been in the midst of preparing *Remarks on the Principal Acts of the Thirteenth Parliament of Great Britain* for publication. To his surprise, Bentham had found his paper 'placed at the commencement of his work, and constituting the foundation of it'. He had supported the government because of 'the badness of the arguments used on behalf of the Americans'. Their whole case had been 'founded on the assumption of *natural rights*—claimed without the slightest evidence for their existence, and supported by vague and declamatory generalities', while 'no use' had been made of 'the only good [argument], viz. the impossibility of good Government at such a distance, and the advantage of separation to the interest and happiness of both parties'. He added: 'Little did I think at that time, that I was destined to write within 15 or 16 years thereafter, an address to the French Commonwealth for the express purpose of engaging them, by arguments, that applied to all mother countries, to emancipate their colonies.'[11] On his own account, and contrary to what he had written a few years earlier in his letter to Rivadavia in 1820, Bentham did alter his views on colonies between the time of the American Declaration of Independence and the French Revolution, when he put forward generally applicable arguments against colony-holding. This change of mind, however, was not brought about by the political arguments deployed in support

that of his pro-Imperialist successors in the utilitarian tradition, particularly James and John Stuart Mill, and to deny—*contra* Halévy, *Growth of Philosophic Radicalism*, 510–11, and E. Stokes, *The English Utilitarians and India* (Oxford, 1959)—that Bentham's utilitarianism, and therefore utilitarianism more generally, had some internal 'logic' which, in the context of India, resulted in the imposition of what were taken to be 'advanced' British laws and institutions on the 'backward' natives.

[11] Bentham to Bowring, 30 Jan. 1827, *Correspondence*, xii. 307–9. For Bentham's criticisms of the theoretical basis of the American Revolution, and his contribution to Lind's pamphlet, see pp. 57–9 above.

of American independence, but rather by economic considerations developed under the influence of Adam Smith's *Wealth of Nations*.[12]

The views which Bentham expressed in his first systematic anti-colonial treatise, 'Jeremy Bentham to the National Convention of France' composed in late 1792, were anticipated in 'Short Views of Economy', composed at the very commencement of the French Revolution.[13] In this latter essay Bentham offered advice to the National Assembly on means to overcome the fiscal crisis threatening France. The emancipation of the French colonies was a potential source of retrenchment, which would also help to lessen expenditure on the military and reduce the possibility of war, which constituted the 'most grievous of all profusion'.[14] Colonies were not only 'a plentiful source of expence', but the whole of the expense was 'waste'. This expense consisted in the permanent expense of governing and garrisoning the colonies, in providing fortifications and naval protection, and in the 'subsidies granted for Treaties of Alliance entered into for procuring assistance in case of wars of which quarrels about colonies may be the source', as well as the occasional expense of protecting them during wartime, together with the total expense of any war caused by quarrels about colonies. Moreover, the French colonies did not produce any clear revenue to offset the expense. The only profit which France derived from its colonies was the produce of the taxes imposed on the trade between France and the colonies, but such taxation was not dependent upon their status as colonies: 'The profit to be derived from Colonies as *markets* has nothing to do with the profit derivable from them as *possessions*.'[15] An independent America, for instance, was worth just as much to England as it had been when a possession, for its value was as a market. Indeed, losing the War of Independence had been 'a saving and a benefit' to England, for the English no longer had the expense of maintaining an establishment in America.[16]

Despite his emphasis on the economic loss sustained as a result of colony-holding, Bentham did not neglect the political perspective. Not only were colonies a source of expense, they were also a source of corruption: 'All public expence being an engine of corruption, all waste possesses in that character a malignity over and above what belongs to it in the character of waste. Waste in this manner begets and supports waste. The expence of each useless establishment is employ'd in bribing men to institute and support the others.' In anticipation of his later views, Bentham argued that while colony-holding was harmful to both the colonists and subjects in the mother country, it was beneficial to the ministers. No doubt Bentham had in mind the patronage

[12] For Smith's broadly anti-colonial views see *An Inquiry into the nature and causes of the Wealth of Nations* (first published 1776), 2 vols., ed. R. H. Campbell, A. S. Skinner, and W. B. Todd (Oxford, 1976), book IV, chs. vii–viii, ii. 556–662.

[13] For 'Short Views of Economy for the use of the French Nation but not unapplicable to the English', written in or around September 1789, see *Rights, Representation, and Reform*, 193–203.

[14] Ibid. 195. [15] Ibid. 199. [16] Ibid. 201.

which ministers derived from colonial appointments. For instance, continued Bentham, it had become clear that reform of the political and legal system in Quebec was necessary, and though a number of petitions had been received by Parliament from the province, the ministry had deferred putting forward any proposal.[17] Ministers were holding Canada 'in subjection', while preventing Parliament from listening to the grievances of the Canadians: 'The Canadians owe it as much to Great Britain as to themselves and to their brethren in bondage to slacken the yoke by the earliest opportunity. Their address should be to the body of the people who are their fellow-victims, not to those Ministers by whom and for whose interest the tyranny is kept up.' Colonies were also 'a source of complication', in that their affairs distracted attention from more pressing concerns. The French government would do well to find time enough to deal with the affairs of France, without having to find time to deal with those of the colonies as well.[18] Bentham recommended the '[e]nfranchisement of all the Colonies', both in order to save expense, and to reduce the potential for war. If colonies were not at issue, Britain and France would have no cause of quarrel.[19]

In material headed 'Colonies and Navy',[20] probably composed not long after 'Short Views of Economy', Bentham maintained that 'it is not the interest of Great Britain to have any foreign dependencies whatsoever', since, by increasing the potential subjects of dispute, they increased the possibility of war.[21] One of the main 'avowed reasons' for maintaining colonies was 'the benefit of trade'. Colonies did not, however, bring any economic advantages, since it was self-evident, as Adam Smith had recognized, that the trade of a nation was limited by the quantity of capital it possessed.[22] From this principle it followed that 'all laws and public measures whatsoever, for the pretended encouragement of trade: all prohibitions of rival foreign trade: bounties in every shape whatsoever: all non-importation agreements and engagements to consume home manufacture in preference to foreign in any other view than to afford temporary relief to temporary distress', were useless and mischievous. Trade with colonies could not be carried on without capital, and just so much capital as was employed in trade with colonies was so much kept or taken from other trades. The crucial point was to identify which mode of employing capital would produce the most profit. There was, however, no permanent solution to this problem, for as soon as one branch of trade was known to be more profitable than the rest, 'Men flock to it from all other branches: and the old equilibrium is presently restored'.[23] The

[17] When the issue had been raised in the House of Commons on 16 May 1788, the ministry had agreed to consider it 'early in the next Session' (see *Commons Journals*, xlii. 478–9, and *Parliamentary History*, xxvii (1788–9), 506–30). The Regency Crisis ensued, and, following further delays, a draft Bill was eventually presented to Parliament in February 1791.

[18] *Rights, Representation, and Reform*, 199–200.

[19] Ibid. 200, 201.

[20] A text reconstructed from Bentham's manuscripts is in Stark, i. 209–18, where it is dated to *c.*1790.

[21] Ibid. 211 and n.

[22] See Smith, *Wealth of Nations*, book IV, ch. ii, i. 453: 'The general industry of the society never can exceed what the capital of the society can employ.'

[23] Stark, i. 212–15.

holding of colonies was irrelevant in this respect. If the colonies were lost, and the trade to the colonies lost with them, the worst that could happen would be the redeployment of the capital in agriculture. There would not be 'any permanent loss to the nation'.[24] Britain should maintain a naval force no greater than was sufficient to defend its commerce against pirates, avoid treaties of alliance—whether offensive or defensive, and in particular those for the purpose of gaining some exclusive advantage in trade—and repeal any regulations, such as the Navigation Act and bounties on trade, intended to strengthen its naval force.[25] Britain, 'with or without Ireland, and without any other dependency', had no ground to fear injury from any other nation whatsoever. Nor did France have anything to fear from any other nation apart from Britain, and would have nothing to fear from Britain if she relinquished her foreign dependencies.[26]

In these writings Bentham anticipated the arguments, albeit specifically directed to the circumstances of France at the close of 1792, which he elaborated in 'Jeremy Bentham to the National Convention of France'. Here Bentham reiterated the economic arguments against colony-holding, as well as drawing attention to the political corruption which colonies engendered. France had never, and never would, gain any surplus revenue from her colonies. The revenue which France received was unlikely to meet the cost of defending them in time of peace, and certainly would not in time of war, particularly if Britain was the enemy. The expense of attempting to retain dominion over her colonies would be enormous. In short, the colonies were an enormous drain on the French finances, and contrary to popular opinion produced no revenue; they were a potential source of conflict with other nations, especially Britain; and they were a source of political corruption. In contrast, by emancipating her colonies, France would gain 'a vast resource'.[27]

First, emancipation would not result in the loss of the benefits which accrued to France from trade: there was no need to govern a people in order to trade with them. Even if the French colonies traded elsewhere, for instance taking corn from a third country, there would not be any diminution in total demand, and other countries would look to France to supply the corn previously supplied by the third country. The crucial point, as Bentham had previously pointed out, was that the quantity of trade in a country depended upon the quantity of capital which it had at its disposal, and not upon the extent of market:

> While you have no more capital employed in trade than you have, all the power on earth cannot give you more trade: while you have the capital you have, all the power upon earth cannot prevent your having the trade you have. It may take one shape or another shape; it may give you more foreign goods to consume, or more home goods; it may give you more of one sort of goods, or more of another; but the quantity and value of the goods of

[24] Ibid. 217–18. [25] Ibid. 211.

[26] Ibid. 212. Bentham expressed similar views in material composed about the same time for a proposed Preface to the second edition of *Defence of Usury*: see ibid. 202–4.

[27] *Rights, Representation, and Reform*, 291.

all sorts it gives you, will always be the same, without any difference which it is possible to ascertain, or worth while to think about.

The opening up of new markets, or the closing down of established ones, did not of itself affect the amount of trade. New markets were only advantageous to the extent that the profit made upon the capital employed in the new trade was greater than the profit made upon the established trade. It seemed unlikely that the distant markets represented by colonies would offer a higher rate of return than those closer to home.[28]

Second, it was misconceived to think that the control of colonies and the imposition of a monopoly on their produce was of financial advantage to the mother country. Taking the example of the monopoly imposed on the sugar trade, besides the need to raise money in the mother country to provide the means for enforcing it, and the injustice of preventing the colonists from selling their products in the markets where they could get the best price, the monopoly was in effect a tax on the poor to pay the rich for eating sugar: 'The burthen falls upon the rich and poor in common: the benefit is shared exclusively by the rich.' But even in the case of the sugar-eaters, the benefit was illusory, since a monopoly could not force the price of a commodity lower than the level to which it would be driven by competition, in other words lower than 'the price at which the commodity is kept by the average rate of profit on trade in general'. Furthermore, a monopoly could force no one into producing a commodity at a loss. Similar arguments applied to a monopoly requiring the colonists to receive only those goods produced in the mother country. Where the goods of the mother country were superior to those of any other country, internal competition would reduce the price to its natural level; where such goods were inferior, competition would still reduce the price, with the added disadvantage that the goods supplied would be of worse quality than they might otherwise be, and capital diverted from those areas in which it might otherwise be more advantageously employed. Moreover, monopoly caused variation in prices, since it usually involved a counter-monopoly. The French colonies were forced to sell all their sugar to France, and France was forced to buy all its sugar from her colonies. Hence, the failure of the sugar crop in the French colonies caused the price of sugar in France to rise, because the French were not allowed to trade with the colonies of other countries where the crop had not failed and the price remained relatively low.[29] As for the argument that revenue was raised from taxing trade with the colonies, Bentham pointed out that revenue could be, and was, raised upon goods exchanged with all other countries. The only means of raising additional revenue through trade was by taxing exports, and only then to the extent that smuggling was not made profitable—and such revenue might as easily be raised on trade with non-dependent as with dependent countries.[30]

[28] *Rights, Representation, and Reform*, 297–9. [29] Ibid. 299–303. [30] Ibid. 303–5.

Third, emancipation would remove a major military weakness. The French colonies drew fleets and soldiers away from the mother country, without contributing anything in return. Moreover, it would be impossible for France to defend her colonies against the naval strength of Britain. If France gave up her colonies, she would save herself the expense of her navy, whose only purpose was to guard her colonies.[31] Fourth, a further advantage of emancipation would be the removal of the issue of Negro slavery as a bone of controversy and contention within France.[32] Finally, justice demanded emancipation. The French had chosen their own government, and for the sake of consistency should not deny the same right to their colonies. It was no answer to say that the colonists would be allowed to send deputies to the National Assembly: 'To govern a million or two of people you don't care about, you admit half a dozen people who don't care about you. To govern a set of people whose business you know nothing about, you encumber yourselves with half a dozen [strangers] who know nothing about yours.' Open domination would be preferable to such masked tyranny. It was neither to the advantage of the French themselves nor the colonists that they be governed from France. The time required for communication between France and her colonies made effective government impossible: orders or instructions would not arrive in time to meet the emergency for which they were designed, while any information on which they were based would be incomplete and defective.[33]

Emancipation was easily done: 'it costs you but a word: and by that word you cover yourselves with the purest glory'.[34] France would set an example which other countries, including Britain, would be encouraged to follow: 'By reducing your own marine you may reduce our marine: by reducing our marine, you may reduce our taxes: by reducing our taxes, you may reduce our places: by reducing our places, you may reduce our corruptive influence. By emancipating our colonies, you may thus purify our parliament: you may purify our constitution.'[35] While colonies were an enormous source of expense to the nation as a whole, they did benefit ministers to the extent that they created offices of which they enjoyed the patronage. The acquisition and retention of colonies and the involvement in war were intimately related, the one leading to the other, but always with the consequence that more offices were created: 'Is it a secret to you any more than to ourselves, that they cost us much, that they yield us nothing—that our government makes us pay them for suffering it to govern them—and that all the use or purpose of this compact is to make places, and wars that breed more places?'[36] The point was ripe for development when Bentham came to think about the constitutional implications of colony-holding in his writings for Spain thirty years later.

[31] Ibid. 305–8. [32] Ibid. 310. [33] Ibid. 291–5. [34] Ibid. 313.
[35] Ibid. 310. [36] Ibid. 309.

III

On 1 January 1820 a Spanish expeditionary force assembled near Cadiz, which had been destined for South America, staged a revolt against the personal rule of Ferdinand VII, and declared in favour of the Constitution of 1812.[37] This Constitution, promulgated by the Cortes of Cadiz, and incorporating universal manhood suffrage, a representative legislature, and a responsible executive, had been drawn up when much of Spain had been occupied by French forces, and Ferdinand VII had been in captivity at Valençay in the South of France. Upon his return to Spain in March 1814, Ferdinand VII declared all the acts of the Cortes null and void, abolished the Constitution, and thereby restored royal absolutism. Such had become the dissatisfaction with Ferdinand VII's personal rule that the declaration of January 1820 in favour of the Constitution of 1812 met with little opposition, and on 6 March 1820 the King was obliged to summon the Cortes, and on the following day to agree to the restoration of the Constitution. As far as Bentham was concerned, not only did events in Spain present him with an opportunity to further his schemes for codification, but they allowed him to expound a number of new arguments against colony-holding. As he told Rivadavia, he now had more to add 'in point of argument' than before in support of his conclusion that colonies were 'essentially mischievous'. His opposition to colony-holding had been strengthened on account of his recognition of the operation of corruptive influence, which was

> necessarily exercised on the representatives of the people in the governing country by the patronage; I mean, by the power of nominating to situations, clothed in factitious dignity, and to offices, clothed with power and emolument, in the dependent country, as well as to offices in the military department by sea and land, and the civil department occupied in, or at least established for, the defence of the dependencies against foreign aggression, and keeping them in their dependent state.[38]

In one sense this was not a new development in that, as we have seen, at the time of the French Revolution Bentham had drawn attention to the political corruption engendered by colony-holding. In another sense it was new in that, through his awareness of the operation of sinister interest, he was now able to deepen his understanding of the relationship between government and colony-holding. Colony-holding was one more element in the system of misrule.

In his attempt to persuade Spain to relinquish dominion over her colonies (or her 'Ultramaria' as he termed it), and more pertinently, given that much of Spanish America was moving rapidly towards independence,[39] to relinquish any claim to exercise dominion over them, Bentham continued to emphasize the

[37] For an English translation see *The Political Constitution of the Spanish Monarchy. Proclaimed in Cadiz, 19th of March, 1812* (London, 1813).
[38] Bentham to Rivadavia, April? 1820, *Correspondence*, x. 429.
[39] See J. Lynch, *The Spanish American Revolutions 1808–1826*, 2nd edn. (London, 1986).

economic loss which was sustained by colony-holding. The Ultramarians, even if they possessed sufficient resources, would not willingly consent to be taxed in order to defray the expenses of the Spanish Peninsular government, while any benefit from commercial intercourse would only occur under conditions of free trade, and would be best encouraged if the colonies were independent. The only possible profit that could arise from the dominion would benefit a small section of Spain's rulers. To these economic considerations Bentham added arguments concerning the constitutional implications of the dominion. The dominion, and the war which would inevitably follow any attempt to enforce it, would provide an excuse for the creation of government offices—civil and military—of which the patronage would be placed in the hands of Spain's rulers, and in particular those of the King and his ministers. This would form a 'corruption fund' which would enable them to overturn the Constitution of 1812 and reimpose the old despotism. Bentham believed that the peoples, as opposed to the rulers, of Peninsular and Ultramarian Spain shared one all-embracing interest—namely, to be governed by their own separate governments, organized on the basis of representative democracy. Were Spain to liberate her colonies, she would then enjoy the same peaceful and prosperous relationship with them which Britain had in general enjoyed with the United States of America since the conclusion of the War of Independence.[40]

Bentham attempted to show that historically Spain had not benefited financially from her Ultramaria,[41] and then argued that even if the Ultramarians, rather than attempting to throw off Spanish rule, desired to remain part of the Spanish Empire, Spain would still derive no profit from them. In the first place, it was highly unlikely that the Ultramarians would willingly remit any money to Spain; yet if the money were to be collected by force, Spain would be faced with the enormous expense of maintaining an armed force in every province, and a fleet to transport it there. In the second place, none of the possible sources of revenue from Ultramaria were likely to be productive. A general tax could not be imposed on Ultramaria for the benefit of Spain without violating the principle of '*equal rights*, equal to all citizens of the state, as well on the one side of the sea as on the other', which ran through the Constitution. The Ultramarians would take the view that money raised in Ultramaria should be used to defer the expense of government in Ultramaria, not in Spain. The imposition of taxation on the importation of goods into Ultramaria would require the establishment of a chain of customs houses, an expense which would in itself be greater than the income generated. Similarly, trade prohibitions, forcing the Ultramarians to buy certain

[40] See 'Emancipation Spanish', 'Summary of Emancipate Your Colonies', and 'Rid Yourselves of Ultramaria', written between April 1820 and April 1822, in *Colonies, Commerce, and Constitutional Law*.

[41] Bentham drew on the various accounts of the Spanish finances collected in Joseph Townsend, *A Journey through Spain in the years 1786 and 1787*, 3 vols. (London, 1791), to show that politicians and commentators generally agreed that Spain had suffered financial loss on account of her overseas possessions: see *Colonies, Commerce, and Constitutional Law*, 10–20.

products from the Peninsula, would be regarded by them as a tax, and lead to even greater discontent when it was seen that the profits of the monopoly would be reaped by a few individual producers in the Peninsula. Moreover, the attempt to raise general taxation would be unwise given that it was this same grievance which had caused Britain's American colonies to revolt. The sale of lands in Ultramaria would produce no revenue for Spain: it had not been a customary source of revenue; no Ultramarian would regard purchase from the Peninsular government as a secure title; and any profit would be retained by the local authorities and not sent to Spain. Whatever emolument might be received by members of the ruling few in Spain from the holding of Ultramarian offices would not be offset against the taxes imposed upon, and therefore constitute no saving to, the people of Spain. Finally, men for military service might be obtained at a cheaper price in Europe than imported from Ultramaria.[42] All this assumed that Ultramaria would peaceably submit to Spanish dominion, but Bentham believed that such submission was beyond the realms of possibility. Judicial appeals to Spain, the entanglement in Spain's wars, the lack of local legislatures, the ineffectiveness of Ultramarian representation in the Cortes, and the injury suffered by the ruling class in Ultramaria from the presence of Peninsular officials, were some of the grievances which the Ultramarians would regard as intolerable.[43] In short, Spain would only benefit from Ultramaria if she engaged in free trade with them as independent communities.[44]

In Bentham's view, the economic implications of the claim to the dominion were bad enough, but the constitutional ones were worse still.[45] He identified a series of 'anti-constitutional evils', all of which would add greatly to the already-existing dangers from corruption, lead to the overthrow of the Constitution of 1812, with its declared end of the greatest happiness of the greatest number,[46] and the restoration of the absolute monarchy.[47] The key point here was the increase in corruptive influence which would result from the dominion. Corruptive influence operated where there existed an elected legislative body in conjunction with an unelected executive authority, which had 'any considerable mass of money or other of the sweets of government' at its disposal. The prospect of gaining a share of these 'sweets' led the members of the legislative body to

[42] *Colonies, Commerce, and Constitutional Law*, 53–61. [43] Ibid. 73–4, 154–94.

[44] Ibid. 61. This argument was developed in *Observations on the Restrictive and Prohibitory Commercial System.*

[45] See *Colonies, Commerce, and Constitutional Law*, 76: 'if the evil which attaches to [the claim to dominion] in a financial shape is great, the evil which attaches to it in a Constitutional shape . . . is perhaps still greater.'

[46] Such was the interpretation which Bentham gave to Arts. 4 and 13 of the Constitution (see ibid. 31), which were translated in *Political Constitution of the Spanish Monarchy* as follows:

'Art. 4. The Nation is obliged to preserve and protect, by wise and just laws, the civil liberty and the property, besides all other legitimate rights, of all individuals belonging to it.'

'Art. 13. The object of the Government is the happiness of the nation; since the end of all political society is nothing but the welfare of all individuals, of which it is composed.'

[47] *Colonies, Commerce, and Constitutional Law*, 23–4.

promote the particular and sinister interest of the executive to the detriment of the universal interest. The outcome was 'a virtual despotism' in which the universal interest would be no less sacrificed than under 'a despotism governing by force . . . and the people subjected to an all-comprehensive system of depredation and oppression'. In the Spanish context, the tendency of corruptive influence would be to give to the deputies in the Cortes 'a particular interest opposite to the universal interest, and to which, in consequence of the power attached to it, the universal interest will on every occasion of conflict be sure to be sacrificed'. Unless the new Spanish government was purified into a representative democracy, it was 'doomed to perish, and to perish by the means of corruptive influence'. While the claim to Ultramaria did not bring corruptive influence into existence, it did give 'addition to the quantity and efficiency of it, and acceleration to the destructive effect of it'.

The problem of corruption had been recognized by the drafters of the Constitution, but the arrangements they had proposed for dealing with it were patently inadequate. Under the Constitution (Art. 129), deputies were prohibited from accepting any employment conferred by the King during the period of their deputation. The deputies being elected for at most two years, there would be a maximum delay of two years, and possibly a delay of only two days, before they were permitted to accept such an employment. Further, an employment might be just as profitable to the deputy by being bestowed on a friend or relative as on the deputy himself. A further provision in the Constitution (Art. 130) prohibited deputies from obtaining a pension or dignity from the king for a year following their deputation. This prohibition, argued Bentham, was as ineffective as the previous one, for the same reasons: the delay was short, and the pension might be given to a relative. Moreover, since deputies who had received such pensions and dignities would be eligible for election to future Cortes, within a few years it might be difficult to find a deputy who was not a pensioner of the King. The seriousness of this lay in the fact that the Cortes was the body, and the sole body, which was supposed to act as a check upon royal despotism. The whole mass of patronage, whether in the shape of money, power, or factitious dignity, employed in the attempt to maintain the claim to the dominion and constituting an addition to the matter of corruptive influence, would be the means of restoring the old despotism. It was impossible to prevent completely the operation of corruptive influence, exercised by members of the executive on members of the legislative body, but what could be done was to reduce the number and value of 'beneficial official situations' to a minimum, to punish those in whose instance corruption had been legally proved, and to make public criticism effective in cases where corruption was suspected but not legally proved.[48]

Bentham identified a further group of 'anti-constitutional evils', the direct result of the dominion over Ultramaria, which undermined the ability of the

[48] Ibid. 85–92.

Cortes adequately to represent the interests of the Spanish people. The first of these was the potential domination of the Cortes by Ultramarian deputies. Under the Constitution (Art. 31), the number of deputies returned to the Cortes by each Spanish province, whether Peninsular or Ultramarian, was related to the size of its population. This, predicted Bentham, would not only produce two irreconcilably opposed parties in the Cortes, namely those from the Peninsula and those from Ultramaria, each with their own separate interests—'with the exception of that interest which is common to you and all Ultramarians, that is to say the being under the government of two different sets of rulers'—but also give a majority to the Ultramarians, since the population of Ultramaria was greater than that of the Peninsula. If it were retorted that the Ultramarian deputies would be kept in check by the corruptive influence exercised by the Spanish executive, this would not improve the situation of the people in the Peninsula: they would be placed 'under the dominion of a domestic interest still more constantly interfering with their own, and counteracting and overbearing it, than that foreign and distant interest can be'. In reality the situation was even worse. Since there had not been time enough to organize elections in Ultramaria, the Ultramarian deputies to the Cortes which had met in July 1820 had not been elected by any constituents in Ultramaria. Instead, until regularly elected deputies were able to arrive, thirty 'substitutes' had been elected by citizens of the overseas provinces resident in Madrid. The Spanish were to be legislated for and taxed by spurious Ultramarian deputies, with an interest opposite to theirs. These deputies had, moreover, been chosen by those who wished to maintain the claim to the dominion, and for the very purpose of maintaining that claim.[49]

A second 'anti-constitutional evil' was the substitution of biennial for annual elections to the Cortes. The Cortes had traditionally been appointed for one year, but under the new Constitution (Art. 108) it was to sit for two years, and this merely 'to give time for passage to and fro between Spain and Ultramaria'. Hence, the 'pursuit of this disastrous claim' to dominion had weakened 'whatever security' the Spanish otherwise had 'for the constitutional probity' of their deputies. The point was that the shorter the time for which the deputies sat, the less the evil that a corrupt deputy might perform before his constituents had the opportunity to remove him.[50] A third 'anti-constitutional evil' consisted in the waste of the Cortes' time. In Spain itself a whole range of issues were waiting to be settled by legislative provision. These in themselves, Bentham argued, required the Cortes to sit for the whole of the year. Yet under the Constitution (Arts. 106–7) the Cortes was to sit for only three months each year, except in special circumstances when its sitting might be extended to four months. Given that this amount of time was inadequate for the settling of Spain's own affairs, the situation would be disastrously compounded if the Cortes had to deal in addition with the affairs of Ultramaria. In fact, the affairs of

[49] *Colonies, Commerce, and Constitutional Law*, 76–85.

[50] Ibid. 93–4.

Ultramaria would demand more of the Cortes' time than those of Spain. The Constitution (Art. 373) gave citizens the right to make representations to the Cortes, and this was a right which the Ultramarians, given their innumerable grievances, would exercise profusely. Disputes concerning the taxation imposed on the Ultramarian provinces would have to come before the Cortes in order to be resolved, while all subordinate legislation passed in Ultramaria had also to come before the Cortes for approval.[51]

A final 'anti-constitutional evil' was the planting of a 'latent despotism' in Ultramaria, with the intention of transplanting it back in Spain. Bentham argued that the provisions of the Constitution (Arts. 326, 328, 335) whereby the Provincial Deputation of each province, dominated by members elected locally, was given responsibility for approving the taxes levied by the Cortes would preclude Spain receiving any money from Ultramaria. Should the elected members of the Provincial Deputation prove refractory, as they undoubtedly would, the only recourse lay in the Governor, who was appointed by the King, and who was President of the Provincial Deputation (Arts. 324–5). Providing the Governor had the necessary military force at his disposal, there was nothing in the Constitution to prevent him from using it to levy the taxes by whatever means he wished. The executive power, which the Constitution (Art. 170) lodged exclusively in the King, and by extension in the Governor, was given the authority to preserve public order in the interior, and to maintain the external security of the state. Moreover, the Provincial Deputation, and thence the Governor, was given the power 'to promote the prosperity of the province' (Art. 325), a power to which no limits could be set, and which was greater even than the emergency powers of the Roman dictators, which included absolute power over persons, lives, and property. It was unlikely that any judge, 'if either his fears or his hopes look to the peninsula', would raise any objection to the Governor's actions.[52]

The reintroduction of the old despotism, therefore, would result from any attempt to retain the claim to the dominion. On the other hand, there would be significant benefits from relinquishment. The historic connections between Spain and Ultramaria—language, religion, laws, and customs—would give her significant advantages over any other country in dealing with them. The Ultramarians, for instance, would be likely to prefer Spanish goods, unless they were hopelessly inferior to foreign productions, while commercial intercourse would be facilitated by the common language. The example of Britain and the United States was pertinent. After the American colonies had gained their independence from Britain, the amount of trade between the two countries had increased enormously. The colonies were worth more to the mother country when governed by rulers whom they had chosen themselves, than when they had been governed by foreigners, whether residing in the colonies or in the mother

[51] Ibid. 94–7. [52] Ibid. 101–2, 105–8, 111–12.

country. As well as being profitable, relinquishment would be honourable, in that to bestow self-government on the Ultramarian people would be an act 'of self-mastery and self-sacrifice', which could not but be admired by other nations, and would of course gain the gratitude of the Ultramarians themselves. Finally, Spain would no longer be implicated in the slave trade, 'this foulest of all political and moral leprosies'. She would find herself placed above England, France, and even the United States in this regard.[53]

While it was overwhelmingly the interest of the Spanish people to relinquish the claim to the dominion, the claim continued to be maintained because it benefited the Spanish 'ruling few', or at least a significant number of them. Some would benefit from the dominion insofar as it remained uncontested, but some would benefit even in the event of a war, and some because of the war. The dominion would be beneficial to those officials whose emolument or patronage would be increased by it, in particular the ministers of state, army and naval officers, the judiciary, the clergy, and the royal family, including the King, and to such merchants and manufacturers who hoped to gain through any trade restrictions imposed on Ultramaria. However, the situation was not quite so straightforward, nor so hopeless. Given that the expense of the dominion would have to be supported either by taxation or by retrenchment, and the prospect of raising additional revenue through increased taxation appeared remote, some of these classes of rulers were more vulnerable to retrenchment than others, and their particular interests were more likely to coincide with the universal interest. Bentham identified three such classes who were vulnerable to retrenchment: the King and his dependants; the clergy; and the public creditors. Even though government did not require a monarch, as the example of the United States proved, and the maintenance of the Catholic religion did not require an opulent clergy, as the example of Ireland proved, and even though the service rendered by the public creditors was real and beneficial service, it would be the public creditors who would be the first to suffer retrenchment, since they lacked the political power to defend themselves. Nevertheless, both the King and clergy had a particular interest which would coincide with the universal interest, and thus operate in opposition to the claim to dominion. Even those classes which regarded themselves as having most to gain from the claim also had an opposite share in the universal interest. The less the security which these classes believed to exist for their sinister and particular interests, the greater the value they would place upon their share in the universal interest. The present circumstances of Spain, having recently escaped from an intolerable despotism, provided an excellent opportunity for 'the friends of the universal interest' to make use of the assistance of 'their temporary allies' for ridding themselves of Ultramaria—'this endlessly and fruitlessly exhausting diarrhoea'.[54] Bentham's strategy, then, was to persuade one of the Spanish deputies to make a motion in the Cortes asking for

[53] *Colonies, Commerce, and Constitutional Law*, 118–31. [54] Ibid. 37–52.

a set of estimates to be produced by which the expense of attempting to maintain the dominion would be shown, including the expense of defending provinces still in peaceable possession and in reconquering those in a state of rebellion. This sum would be set against the revenue which might be extracted from those provinces, whether from taxation or from trade over and above what might be got if they were not dependent.[55] Bentham hoped that the transparent financial loss imposed upon Spain by attempting to maintain her colonies would lead to effective demands for relinquishment.

IV

There was certainly no lack of consistency between the views expressed in 'Jeremy Bentham to the National Convention of France' of 1792–3 and the writings for Spain and Spanish America of 1820–2. The emergence of sinister interest in Bentham's thought, while giving him a new perspective on the corruption engendered by colony-holding, had merely strengthened and confirmed his anti-colonial arguments. Yet, as Boralevi suggests,[56] Bentham was at the same time aware of circumstances in which the holding of colonies might be beneficial. Hence he approved of the colonization of vacant lands in response to the pressure of population growth in the mother country, and of colonial rule in countries where the native rulers were unfit to govern. Writing in 1801,[57] and therefore between his essay for France of 1792 and his essays for Spain of 1820–2, Bentham expressed a favourable attitude towards colony-holding and colonization: 'taking futurity into the scale,' he remarked, 'the well-being of mankind appears to have been promoted upon the whole by the establishment of colonies'.[58] He expressed this view before he had made his discovery of sinister interest, though he had of course identified colony-holding as a source of political corruption and as a source of war. He argued that while the holding of colonies was a burden to the mother country, this burden was outweighed by the benefit to the colonists themselves. In overall terms, the establishment of colonies resulted in an increase in wealth. Land, as well as labour, was necessary to the increase of wealth, and the land acquired by colonization was 'generally of a superior kind; rich even in raw materials which require nothing but extraction and conveyance to give them a value'. The benefit, however, accrued to the colonists, 'the individual occupiers of the fresh land', and not to the mother country. At first the colonists could not pay taxes to the mother country, and afterwards would not. On the other hand, the colonists required civil, military,

[55] Ibid. 114–16. [56] See p. 201 above.

[57] See the passage entitled 'Non-faciendum the fourth: Encreasing the quantity of land, viz. by colonization', in 'Institute of Political Economy', Stark, iii. 352–7. Stark has conflated several sequences of manuscript to produce the text of this passage. The bulk of the material, including that quoted here, dates from August and October 1801.

[58] Ibid. 355.

and naval establishments, the expense of which had to be borne by the mother country. As far as the mother country was concerned, the capital employed in establishing and maintaining colonies would have been more profitably employed at home. The only compensation to offset the loss of increase to national wealth was the diversification of produce through the introduction of novel commodities such as sugar, tea, coffee, chocolate, cochineal, and indigo: 'in so far as novelty and variety are sources of enjoyment, as these encrease, so does wealth, if not in *quantity*, yet (what is as good) in *value*'.[59]

As far as Britain was concerned, Bentham was worried that if the population continued to grow as rapidly in the new century as it had in the old, it would lead to 'great diminution of relative opulence, a severe sense of general poverty and distress', and eventually to the outstripping of the means of subsistence. Colonization of vacant lands would provide a solution.[60] Furthermore, colonization from Britain would have peculiar advantages:

It is desirable for mankind that offsets should be taken from the most flourishing and soundest root: that the races propagated every where in parts of the earth as yet vacant, should be races whose habits of thinking in matters of government should be taken from that constitution from which the greatest measure of security has been seen to flow, and whose habits of acting in the sphere of domestic economy and morals should be taken from that society which, in those respects, is in the most improved as well as improving state.

It was for the advantage of the colonies that they should continue under the government of the mother country, since their rulers, both in terms of law and moral conduct, would be 'men whose education has been derived from that most pure and elevated source':

men among whom are to be found some whom hereditary opulence has exempted from the necessity of binding down their minds to the exclusive pursuit of pecuniary gain: to whom it is possible at least to think chiefly for the public instead of acting and thinking exclusively for themselves: men who have leisure as well as money to bestow upon those more elevated pursuits by which the heart is softened and the understanding expanded and adorned. It is of advantage to the colonists to be regulated by minds such as those of the Hastings's, Teignmouths, Cornwallises, Wellesleys, Maccartneys, Hobarts, Norths, Dorchesters, Simeons, rather than those of the Tippoo's, the Wan Lan Yun's, the Scindias, or those of the disciples and associates of Thomas Payne.

It would, for instance, have been to the advantage of the United States to have remained in a state of subjection to Britain, and 'to have sent their children, such whose circumstances could have admitted of it, to that school of moral and

[59] Stark, iii. 353–4.

[60] The introduction of a demographic argument (missing from the earlier writings on colonies, and not utilized in the writings for Spain of the early 1820s) in 'Institute of Political Economy' perhaps reveals the impact of Malthus's pessimistic forecasts concerning the consequences of population growth outlined in *An Essay on the Principle of Population, as it affects the future improvement of society, with remarks on the speculations of Mr. Godwin, M. Condorcet, and other writers* (London, 1798).

intellectual virtue, and to have received from thence all their governors with a large proportion of their clergy, their military and naval officers, their professional men and artists'. They might then have 'escaped the exhibiting that unvaried scene of sordid selfishness, of political altercation, of discomfort, of ignorance, of drunkenness, which by the concurrent testimony of all travellers it presents at present'. However, the subjection would not have been advantageous to Britain. Indeed, '[h]ad wisdom prevailed over passion, the object of contention' in the American War of Independence 'would have been reversed', the Americans wishing to retain their subjection, Britain to renounce it. In the instance of Egypt, it would have been 'an advantage beyond all price to be under the government of Britain—that is, under a government of universal and perpetual security', or even under that of France,

> rather than under a government by which the very idea of security is banished, a government in which for want of that very imperfect degree of security which would be sufficient to maintain population in countries so richly favoured by nature, the numbers of mankind are seen condemned to a continual decline, a government rivetted to a religion of which incurable barbarity and ignorance seem to be inseparable features.[61]

It was not just that colonists who had emigrated to vacant lands were better off under the government of the mother country, but so were indigenous peoples whose own rulers lacked the education, and whose system of laws did not provide the security, of those of Britain and even those of France.[62]

Bentham advanced a similar argument in 'Defence of a Maximum', which was also written in 1801. Two conditions had to be fulfilled before colonization was desirable: first, the existence of scarcity caused by the growth of population; and second, an over-supply of capital. In these circumstances, the 'efflux' of population would mitigate the scarcity, and the 'efflux' of capital would mitigate the depreciation of capital. It was not that colonies did not continue to be 'a drain', but that, for that very reason, they constituted 'a relief'. If people and capital did have to emigrate, it was better that they emigrated 'to our own colonies', so long as the expense of governing and defending them did not increase. While no additional income would be extracted from the colonies, either from trade or from duties on trade, the future 'retribution' for the past expense would be 'a scene from *Paradise Lost*—a prospect such as the angel shewed to Adam: men spreading in distant climes, through distant ages, from the best stock, the earth

[61] Stark, iii. 355–7.

[62] Pitts points out that Bentham did not, unlike the Mills, equate backwardness in political affairs with non-European societies, and that Bentham supported British colonial rule in India on the grounds that the alternative was worse. She concludes: 'Although [John Stuart] Mill is often credited with exposing the narrowness of Bentham's vision, their writings on India and colonization demonstrate Bentham's greater flexibility on questions of social organization: his far greater willingness, for instance, to attribute value to non-British institutions and to respect the ability for and right to self-government on the part of non-Europeans . . . .' See Pitts, 'Legislator of the World? A Rereading of Bentham on Colonies', 210, 211, 221.

covered with British population, rich with British wealth, tranquil with British security, the fruit of British law'.[63]

In response to events in France, Bentham had come to look favourably on the security provided by the British Constitution, and at the same time had become suspicious of the emerging democratic governments in the United States. In his writings on the poor laws in 1797–8, as we have seen,[64] he had objected to the notion of popular participation in politics. It should not be surprising, therefore, that in 1801 he was prepared to express admiration for British political and legal institutions, and recommend their adoption in British colonies. Bentham's criticism of the United States at this time should not be seen as aberrant, but merely as an indication that he had not yet even begun to be convinced of the desirability of representative democracy, and, therefore, of the virtues of the American political system. Bentham did consistently maintain that colony-holding was economically disadvantageous to the mother country. Yet from the perspective of 'a citizen of the world', as Bentham liked to regard himself,[65] it was desirable that the mother country maintained her dominion insofar as she was more likely to promote the welfare of her colonies than rulers drawn from the inhabitants of the colonies themselves. In 'Jeremy Bentham to the National Convention of France' and the writings on Spain, Bentham argued that, in the instance of the established French and Spanish colonies, this was not the case. As he came to think the worse of the British government (following his discovery of sinister interest in the legal profession, and then in the political establishment more generally), and to think the better of the United States government, his view changed about the merits of American independence, and indeed of the merits of independence more generally. For instance, in 1827 Bentham drafted a petition for the emancipation of Canada from British rule. He suggested that the grievances suffered by Canada were attributable to its distance from the mother country, and recommended that the colony join the United States. He added, however, that emancipation for British India was inappropriate, since the inhabitants were unable to give themselves security for their property, and could only receive such security from the slow and gradual influence of European civilization.[66]

Bentham did not think that his attitude towards colonies was 'ambivalent', as Winch suggests it was. It seems unlikely that he would have authorized the publication of 'Jeremy Bentham to the National Convention of France' as *Emancipate Your Colonies!* in 1830 if he had recognized any serious lack of continuity in his thought. Indeed, in the reissued pamphlet, the anti-colonial and the pro-colonial views sit side by side. In the 'Postscript' (dated 24 June

[63] Stark, iii. 301–2. See Milton, *Paradise Lost*, books XI–XII, where the Angel Michael takes Adam to the top of a high hill and reveals visions of the future, from Cain's murder of Abel through to the second coming of Christ.

[64] See pp. 106–7 above.

[65] See e.g. Stark, i. 27, and *Colonies, Commerce, and Constitutional Law*, 204.

[66] UC viii. 137–8 (11, 14 Sept. 1827).

1829) added to the published work, while admitting that when he had written the tract he had not been aware of the danger of corruption arising from the patronage associated with colonial rule (though, as we have seen, he was not being entirely fair to himself), he stated that, as a citizen of Great Britain and Ireland, he wished for the emancipation of the British colonies:

> But, as a citizen of the British Empire, including the sixty millions already under its Government in British India, and the forty millions likely to be under its Government in the vicinity of British India, not to speak of the one hundred and fifty millions, as some say . . . of the contiguous Empire of China,—his opinions and consequent wishes are the *reverse*. So likewise, regard being had to the Colonization of *Australia* . . . .[67]

Even when Bentham had come to advocate political radicalism, he was not prepared to condemn colony-holding outright. In 'Constitutional Code', moreover, it was the duty of the Education Minister and Indigence Relief Minister to consider whether an excess of population might be relieved by sending orphans or the children of the indigent to colonize 'land unappropriated or unemployed, in this state or any friendly foreign State, near, adjacent, or in any degree remote'.[68] Bentham had not lost sight of the problems of population growth which he had considered in relation to colonization in 1801.

It was in the context of a crisis in the administration of the Poor Laws, characterized by high poor rates, agrarian unrest, and general pessimism about the effects of a growing population, that Bentham put forward his colonization scheme for South Australia in 1831. The views that he had expressed in 1801 on the benefits of the colonization of uninhabited lands re-emerged—but with a difference. His political radicalism meant that he could no longer endorse the transplantation of British institutions, nor anything but the most temporary period of British rule. The colonization scheme for South Australia would be administered by a chartered company, which would sell plots of land in the colony to those able to afford it, or hire the labour of those unable to buy a plot outright until they had earned enough money to do so. The colony would be governed in the first instance by a dictatorship appointed by the company, thereby ensuring that no patronage would be placed in the hands of the British government. Bentham envisaged that, after a few years, the colony would become an independent state. The colonial legislature and people of the colony would pay compensation to the company in London, with the British government guaranteeing the debt. Bentham advised the future colonists that, in relation to their form of government, they should avoid a monarchy, since there would not be enough money in the colony to support a monarch; and if there was no monarch, neither could there be a House of Lords. Instead, the government might be modelled either on that of the United States, though without the Senate, or on Bentham's own republican blueprint detailed in his constitutional code. A number of benefits would accrue from the establishment

[67] *Rights, Representation, and Reform*, 314. [68] Bowring, ix. 443.

of a colony: first, the emigrants would be transferred from a state of indigence to one of affluence; second, the remaining inhabitants of the mother country would be relieved from increasing indigence; third, the emigrants would be educated, in order to ensure their future well-being; fourth, the market for the produce of the mother country would be increased;[69] and fifth, stockholders in the company would receive an increasing rate of return on the capital advanced.[70] Bentham's scheme was, in important respects, consistent with his other writings on colonies: it made economic sense in the special circumstances in question; corruptive influence would be excluded; the colony would be emancipated as soon as was practicable; and a representative government of some sort would be established. In short, what commentators have tended to regard as inconsistent accounts of colony-holding—namely the anti-colonial writings for France and Spain on the one hand, and the pro-colonial writings of 1801—were here reconciled. The key was Bentham's ability to propose an acceptable form of government for the new colony, and a process by which it might be established, which avoided the creation of sinister interest. Rather than being a 'final twist' as Winch suggests,[71] the colonization society proposal was a culmination of Bentham's colonial thought.

Twenty years earlier Bentham had reminded Dumont, when discussing the subject of colonies, that he was in 'the constant habit . . . of looking out for the differences producible, be the subject what it may, by the circumstances of *place* and *time*'.[72] Bentham's underlying attitude towards colonies was captured in his phrase 'Emancipate Your Colonies!', but not where the mother country was more likely than the colony itself to govern it beneficially. While the mother country (or at least its subjects) usually fared badly from the establishment of colonies, in certain economic and demographic circumstances colonization might on the whole be advantageous. As far as the constitutional dimension was concerned, once Bentham had discovered sinister interest and embraced political radicalism, he identified colony-holding as one of the sources of misrule. Hence, in his colonization society proposals, he was careful to ensure that no additional patronage would fall into the hands of government. It may have been for the same reason that he was relatively sympathetic to maintaining British rule over India in the hands of the East India Company, rather than transferring it to the government. Bentham's attitude to colonies was not so much 'ambivalent', but rather, as Boralevi suggests, extremely sensitive to the particular circumstances of the case, within a general framework of economic and constitutional principles, but which themselves underwent modification as his thinking matured.

[69] Despite his earlier insistence, following Smith, that the amount of trade depended solely upon the amount of capital, Bentham appears here to have adopted the view that an increase in the extent of market would promote an increase in trade.

[70] UC viii. 150, 154, 171, 180–91 (5, 9, 13–14 Aug. 1831).

[71] See p. 200 above.

[72] Bentham to Dumont, 8 June 1811, *Correspondence*, viii. 165.

9

Codification, Constitutional Law, and Republicanism

I

By the time of the publication of *Plan of Parliamentary Reform* and the printing of 'Church-of-Englandism' in 1817, Bentham had for a number of years been committed to the radical reform of the English legal, political, and religious establishments. He had not yet, however, committed himself to republicanism, which meant, for Bentham, a political state which did not contain a monarchy or an aristocracy. This further development in his constitutional thought was related to developments in his theory of codification. Hitherto, he had tended to assume that a codified system of penal and civil law, based on the principle of utility and for that reason sensitive to local circumstances, might be introduced into any state, no matter what its form of government. He had, for instance, offered his services as codifier both to the President of the United States of America and to the Emperor of Russia in 1811 and 1814, respectively.[1] It was around 1817–18 that he came to the view that a utilitarian code of penal and civil law would not be introduced by rulers under any form of government except that of a representative democracy. Constitutional reform would have to precede all other legal reform: instead of being the last of the three major branches of substantive law[2] which required Bentham's detailed consideration, it became the first. Hence, when Bentham received an official letter from the Portuguese Cortes on 22 April 1822 accepting his offer to draw up penal, civil, and constitutional codes, it was the constitutional code on which he immediately began to work. In order to understand Bentham's eventual commitment to republicanism, it is necessary to consider the development of his theory of constitutional law.

Bentham established the framework for his later writings on constitutional law in his work on jurisprudence in the 1770s and 1780s. This point is easily overlooked because of Bentham's statement in *An Introduction to the Principles of Morals and Legislation* that he had made little progress at this time in relation to

[1] See '*Legislator of the World*', 5–35, 44–7.
[2] For Bentham's distinction between substantive and adjective law see p. 241 below.

constitutional law. In the version of the text printed in 1780, he wrote: 'that branch [of law] which concerns the method of dealing with offences, and which is termed sometimes the *criminal*, sometimes the *penal*, branch, is universally to be understood to be but one out of two branches which composed the whole subject of the art of legislation; that which is termed the *civil* being the other'. He went on to identify 'the whole business of legislation' with the 'civil and penal branches taken together'.[3] When he published the second edition in 1823 he added a footnote to this passage:

And the *constitutional* branch, what is become of it? Such is the question which many a reader will be apt to put. An answer that might be given is—that the matter of it might without much violence be distributed under the two other heads. But, as far as recollection serves, that branch, notwithstanding its importance, and its capacity of being lodged separately from the other matter, had at that time scarcely presented itself to my view in the character of a distinct one: the thread of my enquiries had not as yet reached it.

He did, nevertheless, refer readers to the final part of the 'Concluding Note' which he had added to the first edition of *An Introduction to the Principles of Morals and Legislation* published in 1789, in which 'the omission may be seen in some measure to be supplied'.[4] Here he had explained that the constitutional branch of law was 'chiefly employed in conferring on particular classes of persons, *powers*, to be exercised for the good of the whole society, or of considerable parts of it, and prescribing *duties* to the persons invested with those powers'. He had gone on to describe the combination of permissive and imperative laws, together with related 'expository matter' indicating the particular individuals invested with the powers and subject to the duties in question, which characterized constitutional law.[5]

Bentham's failure to deal with constitutional law in the original version of *An Introduction to the Principles of Morals and Legislation* had been pointed out to him by Shelburne, soon after they had met in July 1781. 'In the last conversation I was honoured with your Lordship' wrote Bentham, 'I well remember one question put to me by your Lordship was how it happen'd that I had not made the constitutional branch of the law the first object of my enquiry.' The criticism troubled Bentham, and he set about drafting a response. In this draft (which he did not send) he noted that even though the constitutional branch of law 'had hitherto occupied the smallest share of my attention', it had not been 'altogether unnoticed' by him; that he had referred to it in several passages, as well as in his writings on 'Indirect Legislation';[6] and 'that it could not have been [altogether unnoticed] will be sufficiently plain to anyone who considers how inextricably all

[3] *An Introduction to the Principles of Morals and Legislation*, 281. [4] Ibid. 281 n.

[5] Ibid. 308–9.

[6] In this material, Bentham discussed a number of measures, such as the division and distribution of power, the liberty of the press, and the right of association, which might be instituted in order to prevent the abuse of authority on the part of both supreme and subordinate rulers. The essay first appeared as 'Des moyens indirects de prévenir les Délits', in *Traités de législation civile et*

the several branches (into which the principles of government may be divided) are interwoven'. In any case, he continued, the constitutional branch of law was not as important as the other branches: 'The general end of government taken in all its branches being the happiness of the people . . . the laws which belong to the constitutional branch are those which . . . stand the farthest from that mark in the chain of causes and effects.'[7] In the letter which he actually sent to Shelburne, he was rather more contrite: 'Since I was at Shelburne-house [some days earlier], the nature of my design has led me to bestow upon the constitutional branch of law a share of attention which certainly has not been the less sollicitous for a hint which fell from your Lordship on that subject.'[8]

Yet despite his defensiveness in responding to Shelburne, and his remark that constitutional law stood most remote from human happiness, and his statement in the second edition of *An Introduction to the Principles of Morals and Legislation*, Bentham, as he had claimed in the draft of his unsent letter to Shelburne, had in fact developed important aspects of his constitutional theory in his early writings on jurisprudence. In one significant, albeit compressed, passage, which appeared in the 1780 and subsequent versions of *An Introduction to the Principles of Morals and Legislation*, he analysed the nature of sovereign power:

Sovereign power (which, upon the principle of utility, can never be other than fiduciary) is exercised either by rule or without rule: in the latter case it may be termed *autocratic*: in the former case it is divided into two branches, the *legislative* and the *executive*. In either case, where the designation of the person by whom the power is to be possessed, depends not solely upon mere physical events, such as that of natural succession, but in any sort upon the will of another person, the latter possesses an *investitive* power, or right of investiture, with regard to the power in question: in like manner may any person also possess a *divestitive* power.[9]

Several points are worthy of emphasis. First, Bentham did not say that sovereign power was always and necessarily a trust, but that 'upon the principle of utility' it could 'never be other than fiduciary'. In other words, sovereign power should be, or ought to be, exercised for the benefit of those subject to it, but would not necessarily be so exercised. Second, there might exist some person or persons with the power to invest the sovereign with its power, and the same or other persons with the power to divest the sovereign of its power. Third, the sovereign power, where exercised 'by rule', would be divided into legislative and executive branches. Bentham did not explain here the precise nature of this division,

pénale, ed. Étienne Dumont, 3 vols. (Paris, 1802), iii. 1–99, with the relevant chapter, entitled 'Précautions générales contra les abus d'autorité', at pp. 159–90. (For an English translation see Bowring, i. 533–80, esp. 570–8.)

[7] Bentham to Shelburne, 18 July 1781, *Correspondence*, iii. 28–9. [8] Ibid. 26.

[9] *An Introduction to the Principles of Morals and Legislation*, 263 n. The significance of this passage has been highlighted by J. H. Burns, 'Bentham on Sovereignty: An Exploration', in M. H. James (ed.), *Bentham and Legal Theory* (offprint from *Northern Ireland Legal Quarterly*, 24 (1973)), 133–51, at 138.

though he went on (in the 1780 and subsequent versions of *An Introduction to the Principles of Morals and Legislation*) to discuss the relationship between sovereign power and the other powers of government which were subordinate to it, and which might themselves be categorized as supreme and subordinate, and to show how such supremacy and subordination might be created:

Of sovereign power, whether autocratic, legislative, or executive, the several public trusts above-mentioned [in the previous paragraph he had referred to these as the 'judicial, prophylactic, military, and fiscal trusts'] form so many subordinate branches. Any of these powers may be placed, either, 1. in an individual; or, 2. in a body politic: who may be either supreme or subordinate. Subordination on the part of a magistrate is established, 1. By the person's being punishable: 2. By his being removable: 3. By the orders being reversible.

For the published edition of 1789, Bentham altered the final sentence, and added a fourth point:

Subordination on the part of a magistrate is established, 1. Where he is made punishable: 2. Where he is made removable: 3. When his orders are made reversible: 4. When the good or evil which he has it in his power to produce on the part of the common subordinate is less in value than the good or evil which the superior has it in his power to produce on the part of the same subordinate.[10]

Bentham had, then, by this time already developed his theory of supreme and subordinate power which would play a major role in his mature constitutional thought.

In *An Introduction to the Principles of Morals and Legislation* Bentham was drawing on ideas which he had developed even earlier in the fragmentary 'Preparatory Principles Inserenda' manuscripts written in the mid-1770s. Bentham's starting-point was an exposition of what was meant when someone was said to possess a power (a power being, of course, a fictitious entity). Power was attributed to a person when it was believed that once he had formed a wish in relation to some state of affairs, 'the physical effect would follow'.[11] To say that a man was in possession of power indicated his capacity to overcome any physical resistance which might otherwise be opposed to him: 'Give a man a new physical power, the sphere of his activity is enlarged: give him a legal power, the sphere of his activity is enlarged: in the first case by the encrease of force: in the other by the removal of resistance: viz: of that resistance that might otherwise

[10] *An Introduction to the Principles of Morals and Legislation*, 263–4 n. In this passage, Bentham appears to suggest that sovereign power may be either autocratic, or legislative, or executive. Taken together with the passage quoted at p. 223 above, where sovereign power is said to be either autocratic (exercised without rule) or legislative *and* executive (exercised with rule), the following conclusions can be drawn: first, that a state in which sovereign power is exercised without rule is one in which there is an executive power, but no legislative power; and second, where sovereign power is exercised by rule, and where there is both a legislative and an executive power, the sovereign may be either the legislative power or the executive power (or some combination of the two).

[11] UC lxix. 106.

arise from the activity or vis inertiae of the persons who are made the objects of restraint.'[12] The existence of power was necessary for the existence of a state. A state existed when, amongst certain persons, there existed 'a habit of submission to the punishments and obedience to the commands of persons of a certain description among them'.[13] The persons who were thus obeyed constituted the government, while 'that person in Government or that number of persons acting in a body which commands all the rest, and is commanded by none', constituted the supreme power. This definition of a state, remarked Bentham, was 'framed to include every state well-governed or ill-governed, and whether by Laws or without them'.[14] The supreme power was, in other words, the sovereign power.

Bentham did not, therefore, distinguish between the legislative and executive powers on the grounds that one was necessarily sovereign (or supreme) and the other was necessarily subject (or subordinate). Instead, the basis for his distinction was the subject-matters or 'modal objects' on which the respective powers operated. Furthermore, the legislative power itself was distinguishable into supreme and subordinate. These two distinctions produced 'three conceivable Powers' which might exist in a state:

> The Power that issues Commands concerning sorts of actions, without any Power above it to make null those Commands; the Power that issues Commands concerning sorts of actions, with a power above it that may make null those commands; and the Power that issues commands not concerning sorts of actions, but individual actions only. Call the two first of these both Legislative, the one supreme, the other subordinate, and the third executive, you have three names whereby to distinguish the three Powers. . . .[15]

On the one hand, the fact that legislative power was concerned with types of actions, and executive power with individual actions, did not mean that the two powers were necessarily exercised by different persons. On the other hand, the fact that the persons who most frequently exercised legislative power on occasion also exercised executive power, and the persons who most frequently exercised executive on occasion also exercised legislative, did not alter 'the nature of the two Powers'. In contrast, supreme legislative power was distinguishable from subordinate legislative power only by reference to the persons who respectively exercised them: the 'nature' of the power which they exercised was identical.[16] Nor, as we have seen, was the executive power necessarily subordinate to the legislative, although in England that was the case. If one understood the function of the executive power to be the 'executing on particular objects such general commands as are already issued by the Legislator', then the executive power would be deemed to be subordinate to the legislative. However, the distinction between commanding types of actions and commanding individual actions did

[12] UC lxix. 130. [13] UC lxix. 147.

[14] UC lxix. 89. Cf. UC lxix. 100: 'The Supreme power in a state is *that person*, or *those* persons *acting in a body*, whose commands touching any matter all the rest of the persons in the state are in the habit of observing or enforcing, himself or themselves being commanded by none.'

[15] UC lxix. 113. [16] UC lxix. 110.

not necessarily imply superiority in the former and inferiority in the latter. The function of the executive power was to issue commands concerning individual actions, and there was no more reason that it be inferior to the legislative power than the legislative to the executive (though having said that, wherever there was a legislative power, an executive power would be necessary in order to apply its general commands to the particular cases in question). Indeed, a state might not possess a legislative body, in which case the executive power, issuing particular commands, would be supreme (sovereign power would, presumably, be 'autocratic'). This was the case in 'many Mahometan Countries', where there were 'no Laws, or next to none'.[17] In short, it was a mistake to assume that the supreme power in a state must necessarily be the supreme legislative power.

In Bentham's view, the judicial power was not composed of a distinct type of power. There were, as we have seen, just three types of power—supreme legislative, subordinate legislative, and executive. Judicial power was a branch of the executive.[18] Both the judiciary and the legislature might exercise executive power, but there were two differences between the way in which they respectively exercised this power. First, the judiciary could act only under existing laws, whereas the legislature could act against such laws. Second, the judiciary could act only at the instigation and request of some determinate party, whereas the legislature could act from its 'own mere motion without the instance or request of any one'.[19] The fact that the legislature was capable of exercising judicial power demonstrated that the difference between the two powers was not that the legislature issued commands dealing only with types of actions, and the judiciary only with individual actions. It was true that the judiciary was always concerned with 'either one or more determinate persons or at least an assemblage of persons so cemented in a body as to constitute one *party*', but it was also the province of the legislature to command a 'single person to do an act which he was before free to do or not do'.[20]

The distinctions between the varieties of power which Bentham identified cut across the governmental institutions by which they were customarily exercised and with which they were customarily associated. This was also true of the investitive and divestitive powers. In further passages written in the mid-1770s Bentham distinguished between legislative, judicial, dispensatorial, and military powers, together with investitive and divestitive powers with respect to the persons invested with the other powers. Both legislative and judicial power were concerned with 'appointing what acts shall be deemed offences', and the same persons who held legislative and judicial power might also exercise

[17] UC lxix. 112.

[18] At UC lxix. 110 Bentham divided the executive power into military, fiscal, and judicial power, though he also referred to the 'dispensatorial' rather than the 'fiscal' power.

[19] Cf. UC lxix. 10: 'In Judiciary power, the *acts* and *circumstances* that are the *objects* of *command* are pre-determined: viz: by the Law. In Powers Legislative they are left at large.'

[20] UC lxix. 144–5.

dispensatorial, military, or investitive and divestitive powers. The investitive and divestitive powers were particularly associated with constitutional law, whose function it was to indicate to which 'sort of person' the various powers belonged, and to indicate which particular individual was entitled to exercise those powers: 'Constitutional Law is not made up so much of commands; portions of discourse designative of offences—marking out what shall be deemed offences, as of descriptions of those by whom commands shall be issued, and of the cases in which commands may and may not be issued by those persons.'[21] Investitive power was 'the power of appointing what individual persons or things shall be reputed to be of such and such sorts of persons and of things', and like any other power might be possessed by an individual or by a group of individuals. A person possessed investitive power 'when the minds of men whether by Law or custom are disposed, that upon his declaring it to be his will that any person shall be treated as being of the sort of persons or a thing of the sort of things over which his power extends, such person or such thing is accordingly reputed to be of such sort'. Investitive power was plainly not the same as legislative power:

> The acts of the Legislative power are commands: But an act of this investitive power is not a command. To every command belongs a modal object: the act or the forbearance of the person who is the personal object of the same command. But of an exertion of the investitive power there is no such modal object. To appoint a person to be an officer is one thing, to command that person to do or to forbear doing any act is another....

An act of investitive power influenced the conduct of the persons who were the objects of it by subjecting them 'to whatever commands are ad[d]ressed to sorts of persons distinguished by that specific name which those individuals are by that appointment made to bear'.[22] As Bentham recognized in *An Introduction to the Principles of Morals and Legislation*, the possessors of the sovereign power would themselves, except when 'mere physical events' were relied upon, be constituted such by the exercise of the investitive power. At this point he did not recommend any particular location for that power, or for any other of the powers which he identified.

In *An Introduction to the Principles of Morals and Legislation* Bentham said very little, if anything, on the question of the relationship between the sovereign and constitutional law. However, it was a question which he had begun to explore in *A Fragment on Government*, and which he would go on to develop in *Of Laws in General*.[23] There were two issues of importance in this respect: first, what form of government was best; and second, what was the nature of constitutional law. First, Bentham's theory of sovereignty did not in itself prescribe a particular

[21] UC lxix. 235. [22] UC lxix. 236.

[23] When writing *An Introduction to the Principles of Morals and Legislation*, and attempting to distinguish civil and penal law, Bentham realized that, in order to solve this problem, he needed to explain what was meant by an individual law: the result was *Of Laws in General*. See *Of Laws in General*, Editorial Introduction, pp. xxxi–xxxiv, and Hart, *Essays on Bentham*, 105–7.

constitutional structure: indeed, in order to be a convincing account of sovereignty it had to accommodate any number of institutional forms which sovereignty had taken in the past or might plausibly take in the future. It was only when he eventually came to consider what form of government would be most desirable that he needed to relate his theory of sovereignty to the constitutional structure in question.[24] Second, in *A Fragment on Government* Bentham had argued that it was an abuse of language to say that the sovereign or supreme power (whether an individual or a group of individuals) could act illegally. Nevertheless, it did make sense to say that the sovereign could be limited by 'express convention', which reflected limits to the people's disposition to obey. In other words, such an 'express convention', while it could not subject the sovereign to the force of the political sanction, did subject the sovereign to the force of the moral sanction, that is to the force of public opinion.[25] While composing *Of Laws in General* Bentham came to the view that such 'express conventions', in short constitutional law, while not fully imperative, amounted to more than subjection to the moral sanction. He distinguished between the 'ordinary sort of laws' addressed to the subject and those laws addressed to the sovereign himself:

> The business of the ordinary sort of laws is to prescribe to the people what *they* shall do: the business of this transcendent class of laws is to prescribe to the sovereign what *he* shall do: what mandates *he* may or may not address to *them*: and in general how he shall or may conduct himself towards them. Laws of this latter description may be termed, in consideration of the party who is their passible subject, laws *in principem*: in contradistinction to the ordinary mass of laws which in this view may be termed laws *in subditos* or *in populum*.

Laws *in principem* directed to the sovereign who himself issued them were *pacta regalia* or royal covenants, while those directed to any future sovereign or sovereigns were recommendatory mandates. Bentham argued that recommendatory mandates would tend to be implemented by the future sovereign partly on account of the expediency which had brought about their adoption in the first instance, and partly on account of the force of habit on the part of the people of seeing such conditions implemented. Particularly under a monarchy, noted Bentham, 'the exercise of the sovereignty and the observance of the covenants entered into by preceding sovereigns are looked upon as being in such a degree connected that upon taking upon him the former a man is universally

[24] But even before that, the utility of sovereign rule itself would have to be demonstrated: if the existence of a sovereign was itself detrimental to happiness, then no such institution ought to be established. Bentham had to show first that there ought to be government, before deciding what sort of government there ought to be. If bad government was better than no government, then the mere existence of a sovereign was entitled to some degree of approval. In this respect see e.g. p. 242 below, and *Rights, Representation, and Reform*, 329–30, where Bentham described a state without government as one where there would be 'no rights, consequently no property: no legal security, no legal liberty'.

[25] *A Fragment on Government*, 484–90, 496–8.

understood to have taken upon him the latter: understood, not only by the people, but by the sovereign himself'.[26] The nature of a law *in principem* seemed problematic in that it involved a man addressing a command to himself, and imposing an obligation upon himself. The point, however, was that the sovereign was capable of being bound to perform any obligations he imposed upon himself by 'an exterior force', by the assistance of which 'it is as easy for a sovereign to bind himself as to bind another'. A law *in principem* could not, as such, be enforced by the political sanction—'within the dominion of the sovereign there is no one who while the sovereignty subsists can judge so as to coerce the sovereign: to maintain the affirmative would be to maintain a contradiction'—but it might be enforced by the religious or the moral sanction. The moral sanction might be 'exerted by the subjects of the state in question acting without, and perhaps even against, the sanction of political obligations, acting in short as in a state of nature', or exerted by foreign states, for instance when engaged by express covenant to enforce the law in question. The moral and religious sanctions would probably not have the efficacy of the legal sanction:

> But to deny them all efficacy would be to go too far on the other side. It would be as much as to say that no privileges were ever respected, no capitulation ever observed. It would be as much as to say, that there is no such system in Europe as the Germanic body: that the inhabitants of Austrian Flanders are upon no other footing than the inhabitants of Prussia: those of the *pays d'états* in France than those of the *pays d'élection*: that no regard was ever paid to the American charters by the British Parliament: and that the Act of Union has never been anything but a dead letter.[27]

There was, then, a distinction to be made between the issuing of the law in question and its enforcement. While both laws *in populum* and laws *in principem* were issued by the sovereign, the former were enforced by the sovereign's subordinates acting through the legal sanction, and the latter by persons not sharing in the sovereign power, but acting through the popular sanction.

Bentham was aware that it might be said that there existed a certain person 'within the dominion of the sovereign . . . who . . . can judge so as to coerce the sovereign'. Such a proposition, however, involved a confusion in terminology, for it was impossible for a sovereign to be judged by anyone. This was not to say that the powers in a state might not be distributed in such a way that one person, who would in common speech be called the sovereign, possessed every power except, in the instance of a public accusation, the power exercised by a second

[26] *Of Laws in General*, 64–7. Technically, a law *in principem* was a prohibition addressed to the sovereign restraining him from interfering with the liberty of the people. Such a law, which might not be explicitly stated, was implied in certain 'undecisive mandates', that is permissions or non-permissions (as opposed to prohibitions or commands), addressed to the people, and which formed 'some of the most important laws that can enter into the code, laws in which the people found what are called their liberties'. See ibid. 99 and n. For commentary on Bentham's distinction between commands, prohibitions, permissions, and non-permissions, and their logical relationships, see L. J. Lysaght, 'Bentham on the Aspects of a Law', in James (ed.), *Bentham and Legal Theory*, 117–32, and Hart, *Essays on Bentham*, 111–18.

[27] *Of Laws in General*, 67–71.

person of judging him and of executing the judgment. In this case there was no one person who was sovereign: 'It is plain the sovereignty would not be exclusively in either: it would be conjunctively in both.' Bentham was not concerned with the desirability of such an arrangement, merely with its possibility: 'I consider here only what is possible: now it is possible: for every distribution as well as every limitation of power is possible that is conceivable.'[28] In other words, he did not deny that a legislature might be subject to the decisions of a judicatory: he merely wished to emphasize that, correctly speaking, in such a case the legislature and judicatory would share the supreme power.

It is worth emphasizing that Bentham did not simply equate sovereignty with either the supreme legislature or with the supreme legislative power more strictly conceived. His theory of sovereignty was intended to accommodate all conceivable constitutional structures, including those which incorporated a supreme or constitutional court. The point was that the theory began with the notion of power, which was the foundation of all government. Having said that, power would not exist on the one side without a disposition to obey on the other. It was, ultimately, the varieties which might be manifested in the disposition to obey which made possible the varieties in the form taken by the sovereign power:

> The power of the governor is constituted by the obedience of the governed: but the obedience of the governed is susceptible of every modification of which human conduct is susceptible: and the rules which mark it out, of every diversity which can be clearly described by words. Wheresoever one case can be distinguished from another, the same distinction may obtain in the disposition to obedience which may have established itself among the people. In the former case they may be disposed to pay it to one magistrate, in the latter to another: or in the former case they may be disposed to obey one of those magistrates, and in the latter nobody.[29]

Again, Bentham remarked:

> the efficient cause . . . of the power of the sovereign is neither more nor less than the disposition to obedience on the part of the people. Now this disposition it is obvious may admit of innumerable modifications—and that even while it is constant; besides that it may change from day to day. The people may be disposed to obey the commands of one man against all the world in relation to one sort of act, those of another man in relation to another sort of act . . . those of one man in one place, those of another man in another place . . . those of one man . . . at one time, those of another man or set of men . . . at another: they may be disposed to obey a man if he *commands* a given sort of act: they may be disposed not to obey him if he *forbids* it and vice versa.

The sovereign power might be limited by being divided, which would reflect a division in the habit of obedience. For instance, the Huguenot Protestants in France 'would have done anything else' for Louis XIV, 'but they would not go to mass', while '[t]he Catholics of Great Britain would obey any other law of the

[28] *Of Laws in General*, 68, 68–9 n. [29] Ibid. 68–9 n.

Parliament of Great Britain but will not stay away from mass'. The scope of, or limits to, the habit of obedience might be explicitly articulated in the legal arrangements of the state, but they might just as plausibly be marked 'by an inward determination which bids defiance to the law'.[30]

Bentham did not intend to recommend any particular form of government, but to show that there might be as many limitations on the power of government, and hence forms of government, as there were conceivable variations in the habit of obedience. Any limitations applied to sovereign power through laws *in principem* would depend, both in terms of their substance and their effectiveness, upon the nature of the habit of obedience in the community in question. For instance, in a discussion of declaratory laws, he pointed out that 'custom and disposition' might provide the basis for laws *in principem*. While declaratory laws *in populum* might refer to rights and obligations founded on pre-existing statute law, this was not the case with declaratory laws *in principem*, except in those few instances in which the sovereign had become such 'by an original contract between him and his subjects actually and expressly established'.

In other cases the authority of the sovereign is founded or at least in a great degree influenced by custom and disposition: on a habit of commanding on one side, accompanied by a habit of obeying on the other: and more immediately on the one part in a disposition... to expect obedience, on the other part in the disposition to pay it, according to the course of that custom from whence that disposition takes its rise. In such cases the force and efficacy of the [declaratory] law may depend in a considerable degree on the existence, real or supposed, of some customs to which it is or pretends to be conformable. When therefore a law *in principem* is established having custom for its foundation, the appealing to that custom is a sort of step taken towards the ensuring the observance of it.[31]

The implication of this, as Postema has pointed out, was that the relationship between sovereign and subject was dynamic. The disposition to obey had the potential to shift both its content and its object, and at the root of this dynamism lay changes in opinion.[32]

II

Bentham was prompted by the events of the French Revolution to confront the more concrete problems associated with the reconstruction of the French state. Having previously been content to discuss questions of sovereignty and constitutional law at a highly abstract level, and to describe the various sorts of

[30] Ibid. 18–19 n. [31] Ibid. 108–9.

[32] On the relationship between sovereignty and the habit of obedience see Postema, *Bentham and the Common Law Tradition*, 230–62.

powers which might exist in a political state, he now found it appropriate to recommend the institutional form which those powers might take in the specific circumstances of France, in order to promote such desirable ends as security and political equality. Of particular significance in this respect was his proposed constitutional code for France which, as we have seen,[33] was drafted in the autumn of 1789. He rejected the traditional doctrines of the separation of powers and the balance of powers, which he branded together under the term 'the division of power'.[34] The sovereign power, which 'comprehended every conceivable act of power' which was 'not refused or placed in other hands' by the code, would be placed in the National Assembly, subject to 'the consent of the King', while subordinate assemblies at the provincial and sub-provincial level would have authority to make laws for their localities.[35] The National Assembly, consisting of a unicameral body elected annually, would form the supreme legislature. The franchise would be given to 'every French citizen, male or female, being of full age, of sound mind, and able to read', voting by secret ballot in equal electoral districts. Individual members of the Assembly would be subject to removal at any time between the annual elections by a majority vote of the respective electors.[36] The executive power, which consisted in 'whatever political power is not either legislative or judicial', would be placed in the King. Bentham noted that the only quick way of defining the executive power was 'by speaking of it as comprising whatever branch of power is not included under one of the two other great divisions: the description they admitt of being much the most simple and precise'. In the construction of a constitution, 'the Royal authority' should be seen 'as a general magazine or repository out of which particular powers may be drawn, in proportion as a nearer research exhibits them as

[33] See pp. 89–91 above.

[34] The separation of powers was usually taken to refer to the distribution of legislative, executive, and judicial powers to relatively autonomous institutions, and the balance of powers to the sharing of power between different orders in the state. According to standard constitutional theory, the British Constitution exemplified both doctrines. The separation of powers was found in the allocation of the legislative power to the House of Commons, the executive to the King, and the judicial to the House of Lords (or more loosely in the association of these powers with the institutions in question), and the balance of powers in the sharing of legislative power by King, House of Lords, and House of Commons. The distinction between the separation of powers and the balance of powers had been recognized by Montesquieu: see F. T. H. Fletcher, *Montesquieu and English Politics* (*1750–1800*) (London, 1939), 117–18.

[35] *Rights, Representation, and Reform*, 229–30. Bentham pointed out, as he had in the 'Preparatory Principles Inserenda' manuscripts (see pp. 225–6 above), that legislative power was not synonymous with supreme power, a confusion which had 'probably arisen from the observation that the possessors of what is called legislative power controul and issue orders to the possessors of what is called the executive'. The distinction between supreme and subordinate power had nothing to do with that between legislative, executive, and judicial power. There was no need to preclude the subordinate assemblies from the exercise of legislation in order to maintain the supremacy of the National Assembly: 'To maintain its supremacy, controul is perfectly sufficient: monopoly is neither necessary nor so much as practicable. The effective power of the Supreme Assembly is no more curtailed by the power communicated to the subordinate ones than the power of a military Officer is by putting soldiers under his command.' See *Rights, Representation, and Reform*, 260–1.

[36] Ibid. 230–1.

requisite for such and such a particular purpose'. The King would merely retain those powers which could not be better placed elsewhere.[37] The executive power, however, would not include the powers of declaring war and making peace, of making treaties, and of 'burthening the Nation with debts', since these were branches of the legislative power. Moreover, it would be inadvisable to entrust the King with the power of declaring war, since war, besides the misery it created, was 'a well-known door to despotism and every mode of political abuse'. Reserving to the National Assembly the power of supply, or any other power, would not afford 'any tolerable security' against 'this most tremendous of all abuses', for once it had been commenced, its termination would not depend upon the National Assembly, but upon the enemy. If the National Assembly refused to supply the resources necessary to fight the war, this would be to place the country 'into the power of an exasperated enemy'. A declaration of war, or the signing of a treaty, had a whole range of legal implications—'it suspends a multitude of rights and powers and revives a multitude of others'.[38] It was, therefore, a power properly assigned to the legislature. Should the King object to a proposed law, he would have no power of veto, but would be able to exercise his power to dissolve the National Assembly. Such a dissolution would be in effect an appeal to the people, since the King would only exercise this power if he thought the electors would approve of his action. Should the new Assembly persist in its support of the law in question, and the King in his opposition to it, then appeal would be made to the Provincial Assemblies, and if necessary ultimately to the Sub-Provincial Assemblies, though Bentham considered such an outcome highly unlikely. (He did not specify the mechanism by which this appeal would take place.) No political act of the King would be valid unless countersigned by at least one of his ministers. The King would enjoy personal immunity for his actions, with responsibility attached to any person who assisted him in the commission of any crime. If he did commit any crime unaided, this would be taken as conclusive evidence of insanity.[39]

The structure of government envisaged by Bentham was not, therefore, characterized by a separation or balance of powers, but by a chain of subordination, with the National Assembly, wielding supreme legislative power, subordinate to the people as electors (the institutive power), and the King, wielding the executive power, subordinate to the National Assembly. In these circumstances there was no need to limit the sovereign power: 'From the total absence of all specific limitations to the sovereignty of the King and National Assembly no inconvenience can arise, so perfectly is the dependency of both upon the people insured by the power of revoking Deputies given to all classes of the people in their character of constituents, and by the unlimited right of making known their sentiments insured to them in quality of citizens.' So long as

37 Ibid. 252–3. 38 Ibid. 253–5.

39 Ibid. 232–3, 238–9. For Bentham's approval, at least at this period, of the maxim of English law that 'The King can do no wrong' see pp. 95–6 above.

the National Assembly remained dependent upon the people, 'every idea of specific limitation is big with absurdity and inconvenience'. Any limitation would abridge the power of the people; it would subject those more experienced to the pretended wisdom of the less experienced, and the living to the power of the dead; and it would give 'the preference to a general and therefore cursory and hasty view over the close and particular views of the same subject'.[40] Bentham's point was not that the notion of limitations on the sovereign power was incoherent, but that, under the constitutional structure he was proposing for France, they were undesirable.

At around the same time as drafting his proposed constitution for France, Bentham criticized the doctrine of the division of power. The 'current theory of government', as he called it, was 'hollow and delusive', consisting of '[a] confused division, an unintelligible nomenclature, and false maxims relative to the branches of power to which that nomenclature has provided names'. A confusion at the very outset was that some adherents of the theory divided power into two branches—legislative and executive, the latter including the judicial—and others into three branches—legislative, judicial, and executive. The different branches of power were then allocated to different individuals or institutions, on the grounds that despotism or arbitrary power would result if this were not done. According to the theory, 'division of power is the only safeguard of constitutional liberty, the only efficient cause of good government', and therefore '[t]he more the power is divided, the better the government and the more the liberty'. The liberty enjoyed under the British Constitution was ascribed to the division of legislative power between the two Houses of Parliament and the King. This theory had, however, been cast into doubt by the example of France, where the whole legislative power had been 'swallowed up' by the National Assembly, 'and the result is already the first constitution ever formed in which the many were not sacrificed to the few'. In Bentham's view, constitutional liberty (or what he regarded as equivalent to this term—good government) was secured not by 'the distribution of the general mass of power among three or any other number of bodies', nor by 'its division into three or any other number of branches', but through the dependence of 'the possessors of efficient public power' on 'the will of the body of the people, in virtue of the originative power they possess'.[41] The 'whole sovereign power'—consisting of the power 'of making laws in all cases, that of judging in dernier resort whether they have been disobey'd in any instance, and that of providing for their being executed *upon* those by whom they have been disobey'd: and therefore in so far judicial power and executive'—should rest in the hands of persons placed and displaceable by the body of the people. In other words, good government would result when the sovereign

[40] *Rights, Representation, and Reform*, 237.

[41] Bentham was presumably using the term 'originative power' as equivalent to the term 'investitive power' which he had used in *An Introduction to the Principles of Morals and Legislation*: see p. 223 above.

power—legislative, executive, and judicial—was dependent on the people. The effectiveness of popular control would itself depend upon the liberty of speech, the liberty of assembling, the liberty of writing and printing, and the liberty of communication, for it was through these channels that the people could make known their will. The ability of the people to make appropriate decisions depended in turn upon the publicity of all acts performed by public officials and 'the matters of fact and other documents of all sorts which those persons had or ought to have had in review for the purpose of forming a just ground in point of reason and utility for those acts'.[42]

Constitutional liberty was secured by the dependence of rulers upon the people through the power it gave the people to prevent the implementation of measures of which they did not approve. This power could not, of course, be possessed by every individual, since if one chose that a thing be done, and another that it not be done, 'only one of them can have his will'. For this reason, stated Bentham, it should be possessed 'by the *major part* of the whole number of individuals'. Even if all power in the state were vested in the hands of a single person, providing he had no option but to exercise his power in conformity to the will of the people, there would be no detriment to constitutional liberty. On the contrary, if the power were divided amongst three persons, and if they agreed to exercise their power in opposition to the will of the people, constitutional liberty would be destroyed. No matter in what way power were distributed, whether divided into three different branches with each body possessing a single branch (i.e. a separation of powers), or whether each body retained the whole power but the agreement of all three was required for its exercise (i.e. a balance of powers), the result was that the power, instead of being held by the majority, would be transferred to a minority, in that a majority in one body, though constituting a minority overall, might prevent the implementation of any measure. The point was that the will of a majority in a particular body was more likely to reflect the will of the majority of the whole people than the will of a minority of that body:

> Till some special cause of difference is assigned, the will of any part of the body of the people must in proportion to its numbers be taken for a fair sample of the will of the whole. If the chance of rectitude of decision is directly to be measured by the proportions *pro* and *con* in the whole body, there can be no reason why the reverse should be the case in any smaller body taken out of that whole. If numbers are a just measure of rectitude of decision in any one case, so untill some special reason can be assigned to the contrary, must they be deemed to be in every other.

On the one hand, when the three bodies failed to agree, 'the wheels of government are at a stand'; on the other hand, when they did agree, the division was pointless. In this latter case, they could do anything, no matter how detrimental to the people, provided four conditions were met: their proceedings were secret;

[42] *Rights, Representation, and Reform*, 405–9.

public meetings were suppressed; the press was subjected to control; and the freedom of communication was restricted. In contrast, a constitution in which the whole power of government was given to a single individual, who was able to make laws, issue orders, and appoint and dismiss ministers as he pleased, yet who was unable to prohibit 'the people from manifesting their sentiments to each other as well as to himself in all manner of ways and upon all occasions', would afford the greater security to the people against bad government—in other words would be more favourable to constitutional liberty—than one in which power was divided. This was because it was 'on the opportunities possessed by the people of manifesting their will that the freedom of a constitution depends, not upon any other circumstance such as that of the division of the general mass of power into three independent branches'. There was one situation in which the division of power did, but only fortuitously, promote liberty, namely where rulers were divided into two contending parties, and each was forced to appeal to the people in an attempt to overcome their adversary. In England, for instance, when the King had quarrelled with the two Houses of Parliament, or the House of Lords with the House of Commons, or the one House with the King supported by the other, the contending parties had appealed to the people, and 'as the appeal spread and the people availed themselves of it, the people gained liberty'. The division of the legislature into two Houses had otherwise produced 'enormous mischief', and given that the only 'good effect' to proceed from the division might be produced with more certainty by other means, it followed 'that the existence of that House which is under no direct dependence with regard to the body of the people is a mischief and a grievance'.[43] Bentham, at this point, would have been happy to see the abolition of the House of Lords, if it could have been achieved without creating conflict.[44]

Bentham's recommendations in relation to the British Constitution would not have led to the abolition of the office of King, but would have considerably revised its role. He accepted that the office should remain hereditary, and 'the person invested with it irremoveable and unaccountable as to every thing done in virtue of his office', though no act should be valid without the concurrence of some other person, appointed by the King, who would take responsibility for it. Neither the King nor anyone else who was 'unaccountable to the body of the people' should, however, enjoy any efficient share in legislation, though the King might possess a 'nominal share' consisting in an appeal from one set of deputies chosen by the people to a succeeding set (in other words, the King would have the power to prorogue Parliament, in the same way that Bentham envisaged the French King would have the power to prorogue the National Assembly). The King should not be allowed any share of judicial power, 'whether in the giving direction to the exercise of that power or in the appointment of the persons by whom it shall be exercised', nor any share in the executive power, 'for the

[43] *Rights, Representation, and Reform*, 409–14. [44] See p. 97 above.

executive, if it means any thing, means the power of providing for the execution of the laws *upon* those who fail in their obedience to them', and this power was 'a necessary appendage to, or more properly the essential substance of, all that is really power in the functions of judicature'. The King should command the military force, subject to 'the controul of the sovereign authority'. This power over the military, 'inasmuch as it consists in the administering of so much of the public property as is destined to that use, may in so far be termed *administrative*'. Indeed, the power of the King would be better denominated the administrative power rather than the executive power.[45]

It should be noted that this material was written during the short period in late 1789 when Bentham was willing to countenance political reform in both France and Britain. As we have seen,[46] he soon afterwards gave up such demands, and added his support to the existing institutions of the British Constitution, including the House of Lords. There is no reason to think that his disavowal of reform ever led him to retract his criticism of the theory of the division of power. When he later returned to the theme, his criticisms were deepened, as in other areas of his thought, by his recognition of the sinister purposes which were served by the theory. For instance, in his writings on political fallacies, and referring to the balance of powers associated with the British Constitution, he noted that each of the three branches between which the aggregate powers of the government were divided (King, Lords, and Commons) was able to prevent the two others from doing anything. This meant that any measure which any one of them considered to be contrary to its own sinister interest would not be carried into effect, but that any measure considered by them all to promote their aggregate interest would be, no matter how detrimental to the universal interest. The term 'balance' was nonsensical in this context, but thereby served its purpose all the better—namely to confuse the people.[47] In a passage written for *Bentham's Radical Reform Bill*, but incorporated by Bingham in *The Book of Fallacies*, Bentham explained that the notion of the balance of powers took on a more elaborate form when presented in terms of antagonizing forces, but it amounted to the same thing:

In plain language, here are two bodies of men, and one individual more powerful than the two bodies put together—say three powers—each pursuing its own interest—each interest a little different from each of the two others, [and] not only different from but opposite to that of the greatest number of the people. Of the substance of the people, each gets to itself and devours as much as it can. Each of them, were it alone, would be able to get more of that substance, & accordingly would get more of that substance, than

[45] *Rights, Representation, and Reform*, 407–8. In '*Projet* of a Constitutional Code for France' Bentham argued that the King should not be permitted to command troops, though he might appoint the commander-in-chief. The probability was that a King would make a worse commander than another man; his presence in an army would be a source of weakness; and given the likelihood that he would regard warfare as a pastime, it would add to his temptations to engage in unnecessary war. See ibid. 255–6.

[46] See pp. 100–4 above.

[47] UC cii. 370–1 (25 Aug. 1819) [Bowring, ii. 445–6].

it does at present. But in its endeavours to get that more, it w^{d} find itself counter-acted by the two others: each therefore permits the two others to get their respective shares, and thus it is that harmony is preserved.

The image of a 'balance of forces' was employed with some propriety in the case of international law and international relations, where the object, beneficial to all the interested parties, was 'rest, the absence of all hostile motion, together with the absence of all coercion exercised by one of the parties over another: that rest which was the fruit of mutual and universal independence'. However, 'in the forces of the body politick as in those of the body natural', to be at complete rest meant death. Government would cease to function, and anarchy would take its place.[48]

In the 'Introduction' to *Plan of Parliamentary Reform*, Bentham similarly pointed out that the received constitutional doctrine of a balanced government was 'an allusion' or 'an emblem' which had no meaning. When there existed a balance of forces in a machine, the machine was without motion. In the body politic, as in the body natural, when motion ceased, the body died. Much praise was bestowed on the mixed nature of the constitution, whereby power was said to be divided among three interests—namely those of the one (the monarchy, represented by the King), the few (the aristocracy, represented by the House of Lords), and the many (the democracy, represented by the House of Commons). Such a form of government, admitted Bentham, was better than one in which the people had no power at all, but not better than one in which the interest of the people was the only interest that mattered. The claim that the excellence of the form of government consisted in the mixture itself was likewise nonsense. Excellence would not result from adding to 'the *simple* substance', consisting in a power having for its object the support of the interest of the people, a power which had for its object the support of the interest of 'one *single* person' or the interest of 'a comparatively *small knot* of persons'. Bentham could see no advantage in the '*mixture*' when compared with 'the *simple* substance'.[49]

In the 1770s and early 1780s, despite the diffidence he had expressed in his letter to Shelburne, Bentham had done much to establish the place of constitutional law in his broader legal theory. He had also outlined the basic principle of constitutional design: that good government depended upon the responsibility of rulers towards subjects. In 'Preparatory Principles Inserenda' he put forward two circumstances which marked the 'excellency' of a system of constitutional law: '1$^{st.}$ In the means employ'd to connect the interests of the governors with the governed. 2$^{d.}$ On the facility given or rather left to the governed, in case of their interest being neglected, to resist and put power into

[48] UC ciii. 374–8 (14 Nov. 1818) [Bowring, ii. 446–7]. The manuscript is in the hand of an amanuensis.

[49] Bowring, iii. 450–1. Bentham had mocked the view, expressed amongst others by Blackstone, that the mixed form of government, and hence the British Constitution, simply because of the mixture, was the best possible form of government in *A Fragment on Government*, 461–73.

other hands.'[50] Around the same time, in *A Fragment on Government*, he noted that the difference between a free and despotic government consisted essentially in the different degree of responsibility of rulers.[51] He had, moreover, in *An Introduction to the Principles of Morals and Legislation* and *Of Laws in General*, pointed out the existence of the investitive and divestitive powers, which might, of course, be vested in the people. It was not until the time of the French Revolution that he considered how these insights might be developed in a more practical direction. In the autumn of 1789 he insisted that good government, which he equated with constitutional liberty or security, was a product of the dependence of rulers on subjects, which might take the form of the election of the legislature by the people. In his projected constitution for France he recommended a unicameral supreme legislature (the National Assembly), with the delegation of local legislation to subordinate provincial and sub-provincial assemblies, together with a wide-ranging reform of the franchise. A hereditary King would have the power to dissolve the supreme legislature, and exercise what Bentham had begun to term the administrative power, which included operational control over the military force, and the appointment and dismissal of ministers and other officials. For a brief period he had proposed similar reforms for Britain. (In both cases, the sovereign power was located jointly in the representative assembly and monarch.) He had not as yet, however, drawn any republican implications from his consideration of constitutional design. Nor did his engagement with constitutional issues at the time of the French Revolution lead on to any lasting preoccupation with political reform. Indeed, as we have seen,[52] it was not long before he had changed his mind regarding the desirability of political reform. He became submerged in his attempts to build a panopticon prison in London, in the crisis over the Poor Laws,[53] and in economic and financial policy more generally.[54] As we have seen,[55] it was the emergence of sinister interest in his writings on judicial procedure and evidence in 1804 that gave fresh impetus to his political and constitutional thought. The constitutional structure which Bentham envisaged when he began to draft materials on parliamentary reform in 1809 had much in common with that which he had envisaged for France and Britain in 1789. Just as in 1789 he had opposed the influence of the Crown over the House of Commons on the grounds that this would undermine the dependence of its members on their constituents,[56] so the measures he advocated in *Plan of Parliamentary Reform* were intended to secure the 'due dependence' of MPs upon the people, and to exclude their 'undue dependence' upon the Crown.[57] The emergence of sinister interest led to a deepening of Bentham's understanding of the causes of misrule, and hence of the

[50] UC lxix. 10. [51] *A Fragment on Government*, 485. [52] See pp. 100–4 above.
[53] See *Writings on the Poor Laws: Volume I*, ed. M. Quinn (Oxford, 2001).
[54] See e.g. T. Dome, *The Political Economy of Public Finance in Britain 1767–1873* (London, 2004), 66–91. [55] See Ch. 5 above.
[56] See pp. 234–7 above. [57] See Ch. 6 above.

potential remedies to it, but not to any major revision of his constitutional theory in the sense that the basic principle of good government was to secure the responsibility of rulers to those over whom they ruled. Nor did the emergence of sinister interest in itself drive him to republicanism, although he came increasingly to admire the republican government of the United States. His republicanism resulted from a reassessment of the means by which he might implement his scheme for codification, an issue to which he returned with serious intent in 1808.

III

In the 1770s and 1780s Bentham had produced voluminous writings on civil, penal, and procedural law, intended to form part of a complete code of law or pannomion. A systematic, albeit brief, account of his views on codification first appeared in print in *Traités de législation civile et pénale*, edited by Dumont and published in 1802. The pannomion would be characterized by its 'all-comprehensiveness', or logical completeness, and by its 'interwoven rationale', each provision being justified by accompanying reasons.[58] Bentham had harboured hopes of presenting his penal code to various European sovereigns, and in particular to Catherine the Great of Russia,[59] but the French Revolution intervened, and he had then become embroiled in other schemes, of which the panopticon prison figured most prominently. As he later acknowledged, the appearance of *Traités de législation civile et pénale* had made his name 'generally known in Europe to men in public situation', and had 'in the instance of some of them paved the way for acceptance more or less favorable' to his codification proposal.[60] It was only in 1808, as we shall see, that he began again to offer to draw up a code of laws based on this plan. He later explained that he was not, however, inclined to embark on such an arduous task unless he received some 'encouragement' in the form of an invitation from a 'competent authority' asking him to do so, thereby implying that the authority in question would give serious consideration to his draft code. Moreover, Bentham hoped that any government accepting his offer would furnish him with documents describing the particular circumstances of the country in question, allowing him to adapt the provisions of the draft code accordingly. Were he to commence work

[58] See 'Vue d'un Corps complet de Droit', in *Traités de législation civile et pénale*, i. 141–370. An English translation, which also draws on the original manuscripts, is at Bowring, iii. 155–210.

[59] When visiting his brother Samuel in Russia, Bentham had the opportunity to be presented to the Empress, but forbore to take advantage of it: see I. R. Christie, *The Benthams in Russia, 1780–1791* (Oxford, 1993), 176.

[60] UC xxiv. 188v (18 Nov. 1821). The generally favourable reactions to Bentham's thought are dealt with in J. R. Dinwiddy, 'Bentham and the Early Nineteenth Century', *The Bentham Newsletter*, 8 (1984), 15–33, and the unfavourable reactions in id., 'Early-Nineteenth-Century Reactions to Benthamism', *Transactions of the Royal Historical Society*, 5th ser., 34 (1984), 47–69.

without such an invitation, he would have to adapt the draft code to the circumstances of England, but, as he explained, 'in that country not any so much as the faintest expectation of finding any such acceptance could in his position be consistent with mental sanity'.[61] In order to support his pretensions as a codifier, he collected together and printed 'testimonials', consisting of correspondence and official documents, which he hoped would demonstrate the esteem in which he was held by sovereigns, statesmen, legislators, and officials around the world.[62]

At the apex of the pannomion was the civil code, concerned with the distribution of rights and duties, or more broadly with the distribution of benefits and burdens. The purpose of the civil law was to maximize the four sub-ends of utility—namely subsistence, abundance, security, and equality.[63] The purpose of the penal law—by which a sanction in the form of punishment was attached to certain acts which, on account of their tendency to diminish the greatest happiness, were classified as offences—was to give effect to the civil law. Instead of punishment, reward might be attached to an act in order to create a sanction, and thus give rise to a remuneratory code, but in practice such a code would probably be unnecessary and would certainly be expensive.[64] The constitutional code was likewise, at least in part, distributive in character, being concerned with the powers, rights, and duties of public officials, and their modes of appointment and dismissal.[65] It was again the purpose of the penal law to give effect to the relevant parts of the constitutional law. The penal, civil, and constitutional law together formed the substantive law, which was itself given effect by the adjective law, or the law of judicial procedure. The chain was completed by the law concerning the judicial establishment, the purpose of which was to give effect to the adjective law, and thence to the substantive law.[66] In other words, the civil code, together with part of the constitutional code, would contain the 'directive rules' by which rights and duties were

[61] UC lxxx. 29–31 (19, 22 Nov. 1821). Bentham did not think that such an expectation was insane in 1808, even if he did so by 1821.

[62] The testimonials and other relevant correspondence were printed in *Papers relative to Codification and Public Instruction: including correspondence with the Russian Emperor, and divers constituted authorities in the American United States* (London, 1817), and 'Codification Proposal, addressed by Jeremy Bentham to All Nations professing Liberal Opinions', printed in 1822, with Supplements added in 1827 and 1830: see '*Legislator of the World*', 1–185, 300–84, respectively.

[63] The role of the civil law in promoting the four sub-ends of utility is given detailed treatment in Kelly, *Utilitarianism and Distributive Justice*.

[64] Bentham did, however, think that the usefulness of reward in promoting good government had not been given sufficient consideration: for his discussion of the uses of reward see *The Rationale of Reward* (London, 1825) (Bowring, ii. 189–266).

[65] For Bentham's later preference for the terminology of 'location' and 'dislocation', instead of appointment and dismissal, see F. Rosen, *Jeremy Bentham and Representative Democracy: A Study of the Constitutional Code* (Oxford, 1983), 77–8.

[66] See 'First Lines of a proposed Code of Law for any Nation compleat and rationalized', written in 1821, in '*Legislator of the World*', 194–236.

distributed, while the penal code would contain the sanctions 'by which provision is made for the observance of those directive rules'. The penal code would, therefore, contain a statement of the sanctions attached to those acts which were classified as offences, while the civil code would contain an exposition of the terms which appeared in the penal code. For instance, the penal code would forbid and sanction any interference with property by anyone without title to do so, while the civil code would explain 'what belongs to the several *sorts of titles*'. In terms of promulgation, the penal code would take priority, though the civil code, being closer to the 'common end', the promotion of the greatest happiness, was of greater importance.[67]

Bentham's commitment to codification arose from a profound dissatisfaction with the Common Law. His desiderata for a body of law were '*Utility, notoriety, completeness, manifested reasonableness*'.[68] These were the features of an all-comprehensive, rationalized code. The Common Law, in contrast, was corrupt, unknowable, incomplete, and arbitrary. It could not perform the minimum purpose for which law was instituted—the guidance of conduct. Still less was it able to afford protection to those basic interests of the individual—person, property, reputation, and condition in life—which constituted security, and hence a major component of well-being. Security involved both present undisturbed possession and the future expectation of undisturbed possession of one's person, property, reputation, and condition in life. Without security, and thus the confidence to project oneself and one's plans into the future, there could be no civilized life. Security was a product of law, resulting from the imposition of rules on conduct. It mattered less which set of rules was imposed than that some set of rules was imposed, and that these rules were known and certain.[69] The crux of the problem with the Common Law was that those subject to it did not, and could not, know what it ordained, and this created uncertainty.[70] Expectations could either not be formed or were constantly liable to be disappointed.

The problem of uncertainty was avoided by 'real law', in other words statute law, where the will of the legislator, the person with a right to make law, was made known to the public. Making real law was not difficult; in fact, it was extremely easy. A body of law was 'not necessarily any thing more than a mere expression of *will*. . . . Give a man but the power, be his *will* ever so flagitious, be it ever so foolish, *words* may be found for the expression of it: and, no sooner are they found, than they become *words of law*: and no sooner does the law thus

[67] 'Papers relative to Codification and Public Instruction', in '*Legislator of the World*', 122 n.

[68] Ibid. 168.

[69] Bentham would, of course, have preferred a substantive law which was more consonant to the principle of utility than one less so, but his point here was that any system of law was better than none. For an extended discussion of the relationship between rules, expectations, security, and utility in Bentham's legal theory see Postema, *Bentham and the Common Law Tradition*, 147–90.

[70] '*Legislator of the World*', 128–36.

made become *law*, than knaves by thousands, and fools by millions, not content with submitting to it, fall down and worship it.'[71] The difficulty lay in producing a body of law which possessed the qualities of all-comprehensiveness and 'justifiedness': 'Not only the most important but the most difficult of all human works may be safely pronounced, an uniformly apt and all-comprehensive code of law, accompanied with a perpetually interwoven rationale, drawn from the *greatest happiness* principle....'[72] All-comprehensiveness, or logical completeness, was secured by the use of the most general terms which covered not only 'the whole field of legislation' but also 'the whole field of possible thought and action'—terms such as obligation, command, prohibition, permission, condition, right, punishment, and reward. Any specific term would be contained within its genus; there would, for instance, be no specific obligation which would not be contained in some more generic obligation, and which would, therefore, always find its logical place in the code.[73] An 'interwoven' rationale meant that the reasons appeared immediately after the respective provisions which they were intended to justify, and indicated the way in which the provisions were conducive to the greatest happiness. The reasons had to appear contiguous to the provisions, in order to ensure their relevance, rather than in a preliminary discourse such as that which preceded the French Civil Code of 1802, which was 'an *ignis fatuus*, consisting of vague-generality gas, twinkling aloft in a region or regions of unmeasurable altitude'.[74] The rationale would be useful in a whole variety of ways. For the citizen, it would make the law easier to remember, and operate as 'an instrument of *interpretation*' in resolving doubts about the true sense of the law. It would increase his sense of security, both by clarifying the law and by restraining the legislator and judge: 'What difficulties will not such an instrument be seen to throw in the way of arbitrary power, wheresoever seeking to intrude itself, whether in legislation or in judicature!' By not being merely directive, as other codes were, but by explaining the need for the rules, it would constitute 'a book of *instruction* in the art and science of *morals*'. In a representative democracy, it would provide a standard against which constituents might judge the suitability of potential candidates for election to the legislature. For the legislator, the rationale would indicate the 'right path' where he was 'well disposed', act as a barrier preventing him from 'swerving into any wrong path' where he was 'ill-disposed', and provide a 'support' justifying his actions should he be the subject of criticism. It acted in a similar way as both guide and restraint upon the judge, preventing arbitrary and corrupt decisions.[75]

[71] Ibid. 143–4. [72] Ibid. 260.

[73] Ibid. 247–8. For Bentham's attempt to produce a logically complete classification of offences see *An Introduction to the Principles of Morals and Legislation*, 187–280. The question of completeness is discussed in Postema, *Bentham and the Common Law Tradition*, 421–34.

[74] '*Legislator of the World*', 257–8; *First Principles*, 180.

[75] '*Legislator of the World*', 141–3, 248–50.

IV

In the spring of 1808, while working on *Scotch Reform*, Bentham revived his ambitions as a codifier by offering to draw up a code for Scotland. He hoped that his offer would be presented to the House of Commons by Francis Horner and Samuel Romilly, but to his great disappointment they refused to do so, on the grounds that he had not yet written the code, and that his proposal to work gratuitously would be met with derision.[76] In the autumn of 1810, at the request of Francisco de Miranda, Bentham drew up a press code for Venezuela, and even considered emigrating to Venezuela in order 'to do a little business in the way of my trade—to draw up a body of laws for the people there'.[77] He then launched a sustained campaign to secure an invitation to codify aimed at the United States of America. Between 1811 and 1817 he pursued three avenues of approach, appealing separately to the President, the Governors of the individual states, and the people. First, in October 1811 he wrote to President James Madison offering to draw up penal and civil codes. The new codes would, of course, be all-comprehensive, rationalized, and sweep away the Common Law.[78] Second, he contacted Simon Snyder, the Governor of Pennsylvania,[79] and soon afterwards made a systematic approach to all the state Governors, using as his intermediary the future President, John Quincy Adams, who had met Bentham while serving as American Minister in London, and who had returned to the United States in 1817 to take up office as Secretary of State. Third, Bentham appealed directly to the people of the United States, encouraging them to put pressure on their legislators to accept his offer. Hence he composed an essay addressed to the citizens of the United States, which he again commissioned Adams to circulate to newspaper editors with a view to their publishing it.[80] He explained that the Governors were about to receive his offer to codify, presented testimonials demonstrating his aptitude to carry out such an undertaking, and outlined the nature of his codification plan.[81]

When Madison replied to Bentham's letter in 1816 (war between the United States and Britain had delayed his response) he claimed that it would be beyond his 'proper functions' to accept Bentham's offer to draw up a code of laws, and cast doubt on the feasibility of replacing the Common Law.[82] Snyder, however,

[76] Bentham to Romilly, 14 May 1808; Romilly to Bentham, 20 May 1808; Bentham to Romilly, 20 May 1808; Bentham to Dumont, 21 May 1808; and Romilly to Bentham, late May? 1808, *Correspondence*, vii. 483–92, 503–4.

[77] Bentham to Joseph Blanco White, 25 Oct. 1810; and Bentham to John Mulford, 1 Nov. 1810, ibid. viii. 74–8.

[78] Bentham to Madison, 30 Oct. 1811, ibid. 182–215.

[79] Bentham to Gallatin, 16 June 1814, ibid. 379–81; Gallatin to Snyder, 18 June 1814, '*Legislator of the* World', 38–9; and Bentham to Aaron Burr, 23 Feb. 1816, *Correspondence*, viii. 510.

[80] Bentham to John Herbert Koe, 25–7 Aug. 1817; and Bentham to Francis Place, 17–18 Jan. 1818, *Correspondence*, ix. 148.

[81] See '*Legislator of the World*', 113–72.

[82] Madison to Bentham, 8 May 1816, *Correspondence*, viii. 521–2.

proved to be more sympathetic.[83] In December 1816 he presented Bentham's offer to the Pennsylvanian legislature,[84] though it then went no further. The only other state Governor to respond positively was William Plumer of New Hampshire, who presented Bentham's offer to the state legislature in June 1818, whereupon a committee was established to consider it.[85] However, as the Governor's son William Plumer Junior explained to Bentham, the committee, composed mainly of lawyers, was antagonistic, and recommended that consideration of the offer be postponed until the next meeting of the legislature, thus in effect rejecting it.[86] Bentham's hopes of being asked to codify for the United States therefore came to very little, although Edward Livingston, who drafted various codes for Louisiana and then the federal government in the 1820s, was very much influenced by Bentham, and opened a correspondence with him in 1829.[87]

In the meantime, Bentham turned his attention to the Emperor of Russia, Alexander I. His intermediary was the Polish patriot, Prince Adam Czartoryski, at this time one of the Emperor's most influential advisers. Bentham had met Czartoryski in 1791,[88] and renewed his acquaintance when Czartoryski, accompanying Alexander I, visited London in June 1814. Czartoryski, who was hoping to see the restoration of the kingdom of Poland, with Alexander as King and himself as Viceroy, called on Bentham and extracted a promise from him that he would assist in drawing up a constitutional code for Poland, in the event that one were needed.[89] Czartoryski, in return, took away a copy of a letter to the Emperor which Bentham had drafted the previous winter offering to draw up a penal code for Russia. Czartoryski eventually presented this letter to Alexander I in April 1815 during the Congress of Vienna. The Emperor wrote to Bentham, thanking him for his offer, and informing him that he would instruct the Commission for the Compilation of Laws, which he had established in 1801 to draw up a new code for the Russian Empire, to direct its questions to him. He also sent Bentham a ring, contained in a packet closed with the Imperial seal.[90] Bentham returned the packet unopened, pointing out that he did not seek any sort of payment for his services, and reiterated his wish to submit a complete penal code for Russia, and not merely the answers to whatever questions the Commission might deign to send to him. Nevertheless, should the Emperor

[83] Snyder to David Meade Randolph, 31 May 1816, '*Legislator of the World*', 40–2.

[84] Ibid. 43.

[85] *Journal of the House of Representatives, June Session, 1818*, 30–1, 42–3.

[86] Plumer Junior to Bentham, 2 Oct. 1818, *Correspondence*, ix. 273–9; *Journal of the House of Representatives, June Session, 1818*, 276.

[87] See '*Legislator of the World*', 382–4. On the influence of Bentham on law reform more generally in the United States see P. J. King, *Utilitarian Jurisprudence in America: The Influence of Bentham and Austin on American Legal Thought in the Nineteenth Century* (New York, 1986).

[88] See Bentham to Caroline Fox, late Feb. 1791?, *Correspondence*, iv. 256.

[89] Henry Brougham to Bentham, 27 June 1814, ibid. viii. 382 and n.; '*Legislator of the World*', 49 n.

[90] Alexander I to Bentham, 22 Apr. 1815, *Correspondence*, viii. 454–5.

direct, he was willing to undertake the more limited task of drawing up penal and civil codes for Poland.[91] To Czartoryski, Bentham confirmed his willingness to draw up penal, civil, and, though more reluctantly, constitutional codes for Poland.[92] After responding as he had to Alexander I, Bentham was not optimistic that his offer to codify for Russia would be accepted, but he still had hopes that Czartoryski, if appointed as Viceroy, would seek his assistance for Poland. However, even here Bentham was to be disappointed, for when Alexander I arrived in Warsaw in November 1815, and later that month approved a new constitution for Poland, he passed over Czartoryski and appointed General Joseph Zajonczek, a person whom Bentham admitted that he had never heard of, as Viceroy of the reconstituted kingdom.[93]

Bentham's contact with Alexander I and Czartoryski show that he had not yet come to the view that, in order to establish a rationalized code of penal and civil law on the lines he advocated, a representative democracy would first need to be established. In July 1817, addressing the citizens of the United States, he emphasized that his penal and civil codes might form a model for adoption under any system of constitutional law:

> On the ground of Constitutional law,—you who on that ground have so nobly shaken off the yoke of English law—the system you have is to all essentials, a model for all nations. Accept these my services, so shall it be on the ground of penal law, so shall it be on the ground of *civil* law: accept my services, at one lift you shall ease your necks of that degrading yoke. Without parliamentary Reform, Britain can not, without revolution or civil war, no other monarchy can, take for a model the essentials of your *Constitutional* law: but on the ground of *penal* law, and to no inconsiderable extent, even on the ground of *civil* law, might it—and without change in any part of the constitutional law-branch, be made use of as a model any where: in Russia, in Spain, in Morocco. Hence it was—and without any thought or need of betraying him, [nor] any act of self-denying beneficence, (for my views of the contagious influence of reason in the character of a precedent, were not at that time so clear as they have become since) hence it was that these my services were offered to the Alexander of these days.[94]

Although the constitutional position of existing rulers would not be threatened by the adoption of Bentham's penal and civil codes, 'the contagious influence of reason' would ensure that once an all-comprehensive, rationalized code had been adopted by one government, it would be difficult for other governments not to resist demands to reform their law upon similar principles. 'Join hands with me, you and I will govern the world': such was the prospect which in July 1814 Bentham had held out to Snyder, the Governor of Pennsylvania, and to any other legislator prepared to adopt a code of law drawn up according to the

[91] Bentham to Alexander I, June 1815, ibid. 464–87.
[92] Bentham to Czartoryski, 21 June 1815, ibid. 458–63.
[93] Bentham to Burr, 23 Feb. 1816, ibid. 512–13; '*Legislator of the World*', 50 n.
[94] Ibid. 121 n.

method he proposed. Bentham would become in effect, as the Guatemalan statesman José del Valle was later to proclaim him, 'the legislator of the world':[95]

seeing that neither to establish, any more than to pen, a Code, supported throughout by reason, is a thing impossible, government will, in this or that other state, become ashamed of giving out codes, altogether destitute of this support. But it is by the nature of things, that *reasons*, in so far as they are good ones, are made: made *they* can not be, as laws may be and are, by any man that has *power*—by any such man at pleasure. Giving *reasons* every where, rulers will not, every where, without giving such as they would be ashamed to give, be able to give *reasons*, nor therefore to give *laws*, altogether different from *ours*: and thus, you see, our empire spreads itself.[96]

At some point between the summer of 1817 and the spring of 1818 Bentham realized that a rationalized and all-comprehensive civil and penal code would not be instituted unless it was preceded by constitutional reform, and in particular by the establishment of a representative democracy, the only form of government under which rulers were prepared to promote the happiness of the community in general. In April 1818, in a passage intended for a postscript to a proposed second edition of *Plan of Parliamentary Reform*, Bentham admitted to a change of mind:

So lately as in 1802 Mr Dumont (it was in the Preface to the first of his [i.e. Bentham's] works that have been published in French—so lately as in 1802, that intelligent and faithful disciple of his found himself authorized in saying that in the eyes of Mr Bentham, there scarce existed a political Constitution, there scarce existed that form of Government, under which, in his view of the matter, a good system of laws in its other branches—a good system of law in penal and civil matters—might not, supposing good principles once laid down and presented to the eyes of rulers, be reasonably looked for at their hands.[97] But the more clearly he pried into all these several branches, the more hopeless in his eyes has been the existence of a good system of penal and civil under a bad system of constitutional law, till at last the impossibility became a point demonstrated.

As to this courage then, whence came it? to what cause shall it be referred? Is it that in old age there is more courage than in youth? Is it that even in this particular instance there is or can have been more probity? No: but that as age has advanced, attention has been gradually led to this final point, and as occasion called bent towards it with a steadier and intenser force, the more anxious and unremitting and more scrutinizing intensity.[98]

[95] Ibid. 370.

[96] Bentham to Snyder, 14 July 1814, *Correspondence*, viii. 400. Cf. UC lxxx. 36 (16 May 1821): 'Under any one Government—to look no further—under any one Government should any such rationalized body of law, to any considerable extent, be established, it will form an æra in the history of Governments. It will be an example to all nations. In that nation or political state at any rate, the reign of arbitrary power will be at an end: it will be closed, and for ever. For, where rationalized law has once made its appearance, very shame will suffice to exclude not only the establishment of any considerable body of *unrationalized*, which would be as much as to say *arbitrary* law, but even so much as the bare proposition, for substituting any such unjustified because unjustifiable rule of action, to a justifiable and actually justified one.'

[97] The passage was presumably *Traités de législation civile et pénale*, 'Discours Préliminaire', i. pp. xvii–xviii.

[98] UC cxxviii. 256–7 (20 Apr. 1818).

Bentham's account here implies a gradual realization that the key to reform of the law in general lay in the reform of constitutional law. Having said that, his letter to Snyder in July 1814, his dealings with Alexander I and Czartoryski in 1814–15, and his address to the citizens of the United States in July 1817 show that until only a few months before writing this passage he still accepted the feasibility of reforming penal and civil law prior to the reform of constitutional law, and, therefore, suggest that the decisive turning point had been relatively recent. It is possible that disappointment at not having received an acceptance of his codification offer from the Russian Emperor was significant in this respect. Whatever the precise timing, it was Bentham's realization that the reform of constitutional law was a necessary precondition of legal reform in general that marks his transition from an advocate of 'democratic ascendancy' to an advocate of representative democracy or, what to him meant the same thing, republicanism. He had not, of course, received any acceptance from the United States either, though in that case he did not attribute his failure to the form of government, but to the opposition of the common lawyers. Indeed, it was their hostility which, in his eyes, proved conclusively that acceptance of his offer would result in the promotion of the greatest happiness. The committee of the New Hampshire legislature to which his offer had been referred had been dominated by lawyers, and their reaction had been one of 'aversion, scorn, contempt etc.' The 'plague of despotism', in the form of English rule, had been driven out of the United States, but the 'plague of lawyers' remained. While 'aptitude . . . no less astonishing than felicitous' had been given to constitutional law, there was little prospect of seeing 'real, rational, cognoscible and home-made law substituted to fictitious, irrational, uncognoscible Judge-made and foreign-made law' in the other branches of law, and in seeing judicature 'free from factitious delay, vexation and expense' instead of being 'loaded to excess with all those abominations'. The cause was not difficult to identify: in the House of Representatives in the federal Congress there were a hundred lawyers and only eighty-six non-lawyers, and in the Senate thirty-three lawyers and only eleven non-lawyers.[99] Apart from the predominating influence of lawyers, Bentham recognized another difficulty he faced in disseminating his ideas in the United States. The works by which he was best known in the early nineteenth century were not those which he himself published in English—though a number, such as *Defence of Usury* and *Panopticon*,[100] did have some success—but Dumont's recensions. The difficulty in the United States, noted Bentham, was that very few people were able and willing to read French, or at least to read philosophical works in French.[101]

It was, perhaps, not without significance that it was after his recognition that constitutional reform was a prerequisite to legal reform more generally that he

[99] UC clviii. 334 (11 May 1821); '*Legislator of the World*', 330 n.
[100] *Panopticon: or, the Inspection-house*, 3 vols. (Dublin and London, 1791).
[101] Bentham to Plumer Junior, Dec. 1818, *Correspondence*, ix. 305–6.

addressed his writings on codification to 'nations professing liberal opinions', that is a people or government 'professing to take the greatest happiness of the greatest number for the object and end in view of all its arrangements'.[102] He believed that only a government or people 'professing liberal opinions' would take seriously his offer to codify. Bentham recommended that any such government intent on securing the best possible code should issue an open invitation to all potential codifiers, not just to himself, and be prepared to consider every code submitted to it.[103] In Spain, following the restoration in March 1820 of the Constitution of 1812, and then in Portugal, following the proclamation on 30 June 1821 of a Constitution based on the Spanish model, he believed that he had found two such nations.[104] Bentham made a formal offer to draw up penal, civil, and constitutional codes for Portugal,[105] which the Cortes resolved to accept on 26 November 1821. The official letter accepting his offer reached Bentham on 22 April 1822.[106] This was a moment of immense significance for Bentham, representing the successful culmination of his strategy to persuade a legislature to accept his codification offer. He did not begin to draft either the penal or civil codes, but turned to the constitutional code. As he explained to William Plumer Junior: 'Seeing how unavoidably dependent in principle & even in tenor, the non penal [i.e. civil] and penal Codes, are on the Constitutional, it is with that I have begun.'[107]

[102] UC lxxx. 52 (10 Mar. 1822).

[103] '*Legislator of the World*', 297.

[104] For Bentham's view that the Spanish Constitution recognized the greatest happiness principle as the foundation of government see p. 210 above.

[105] '*Legislator of the World*', 332–4.

[106] Ibid. 335–6.

[107] Bentham to William Plumer Junior, 15 Dec. 1823 and 3 Jan. 1824, *Correspondence*, xi. 334. When Bentham printed and finally published *Constitutional Code*, Volume I, in 1827 and 1830 respectively, a note to the heading (see *Constitutional Code*, Vol. I, ed. F. Rosen and J. H. Burns (Oxford, 1983), 11 n.) read: 'Of the whole *Pannomion*, the first part in the order of importance, thence in the order of appearance, is this Code.'

10

Publicity, Responsibility, and the Architecture of Government

I

By the time that Bentham began to draft his constitutional code in April 1822, he was convinced that the only form of government which would promote the interest of the people was a representative democracy. It was only under a representative democracy that means might be found to oppose effectively the sinister interest of rulers, and secure their responsibility to the people, and it was only under a representative democracy that a complete and rationalized code of laws would be introduced. The point was not that representative government was desirable in itself, but that the key to good government was publicity: 'those two intimately-connected liberties—the liberty of the press, and the liberty of public discussion by word of mouth' were 'indispensable, at all times and everywhere . . . to everything that can with any propriety be termed good government.'[1] As we have seen,[2] good government depended on the responsibility of rulers to subjects, and this depended in turn on publicity. And it was representative democracy which afforded the best security for publicity. As early as *A Fragment on Government* Bentham had drawn attention to the links between the freedom of the press and free government, and between subjection of the press and despotic government. He noted that the difference between a free and despotic government did not rest on the total amount of power which each form of government was able to exercise, but rather,

> on the *manner* in which that whole mass of power, which, taken together, is supreme, is, in a free state, *distributed* among the several ranks of persons that are sharers in it:—on the *source* from whence their titles to it are successively derived:—on the frequent and easy *changes* of condition between govern*ors* and govern*ed*; whereby the interests of the one class are more or less indistinguishably blended with those of the other:—on the *responsibility* of the governors; or the right which a subject has of having the reasons publicly assigned and canvassed of every act of power that is exerted over him:—on the *liberty of the press*; or the security with which every man, be he of the one class or the

[1] *On the Liberty of the Press, and Public Discussion*, written in September and October 1820, and published at London in July 1821, at Bowring, ii. 276.

[2] See pp. 238–40 above.

other, may make known his complaints and remonstrances to the whole community:—on the *liberty of public association*; or the security with which malecontents may communicate their sentiments, concert their plans, and practise every mode of opposition short of actual revolt, before the executive power can be legally justified in disturbing them.[3]

This list is not systematic, nor based on any detailed consideration of constitutional law, but it does reveal the importance which Bentham, even at this early stage in his career, gave to factors related to publicity and responsibility. It was a recurring theme, whatever Bentham's views on the desirability or otherwise of political reform. In *Political Tactics*, written in 1788–9, with the forthcoming meeting of the French Estates-General in mind, Bentham linked the existence of publicity and open discussion to a 'free country', and secrecy to 'despotic states'.[4] He made the same connection thirty years later in *On the Liberty of the Press, and Public Discussion*, where he pointed out that 'the distinction between a government that is despotic, and one that is not so' was that in the latter 'some *eventual faculty of effectual resistance*, and consequent change in government, is purposely left, or rather given, to the people'. There was more danger from the absence than from the presence of this faculty, given the tendency towards obsequiousness prevalent amongst the subject many. Only in extreme instances of misrule was this obsequiousness so far weakened as to produce revolution in government, or harm to the person or property of individuals: 'Of a government that is not despotic, it is therefore the essential character even to *cherish* the disposition to eventual resistance.' The production of such a disposition depended upon '*instruction, excitation, correspondence*'—instruction applied to the understanding, excitation applied to the will, and correspondence to bring together a sufficiently large number of individuals to produce the ultimate effect: 'Co-extensive with the instruction and excitation must be the correspondence: and therefore, as far as depends upon the government, under the government, if not a despotic one, will be the facility allowed and afforded to correspondence.' All three of these 'instruments' operating together were necessary to keep 'the national mind . . . in a state of appropriate preparation . . . for eventual resistance', and thus to effect a change of government if it became necessary, and to prevent or retard the necessity by constantly applying a check to misrule. Necessary to instruction and excitation, and thus to the state of preparation in question, was 'the perfectly unrestrained communication of ideas on every subject within the field of government', which included the liberty of the press and liberty of speech.

The characteristic, then, of *an undespotic* government—in a word, of every government that has any tenable claim to the appellation of a *good government—is*, the allowing, and giving facility to this communication; and this not only for instruction, but for excitation—not only for instruction and excitation, but also for correspondence; and this,

[3] *A Fragment on Government*, 485. [4] *Political Tactics*, 31–2.

again, for the purpose of affording and keeping on foot every facility for eventual resistance—for resistance to government, and thence should necessity require, for a change in government.

There was nothing new in this, claimed Bentham, either in theory or practice. In the American Declaration of Independence—not that Bentham approved of the '*logic*' of the document, even though 'there is *thus much* in it of *good politics*'—the right of the people to alter or abolish the form of government, should it become destructive of the ends specified, was expressly asserted.[5] Even in England, at the time of the Glorious Revolution, it was recognized that a state of things had arisen, and, therefore, might do so again, in which it was 'right that the people should take the government into their own hands: an operation which, of course, could not be performed without *resistance* to the government then in existence'. The logic was still worse than in the American case, in that the falsehood was asserted that the King had entered into a contract with the people. This was a lie fabricated by lawyers, 'for without a lie in his mouth, an English lawyer knows not how to open it'. Nevertheless, even though the antecedent was unable to support the consequent, 'the consequent was in itself good: and in *that* we have all that is to the present purpose'.[6]

Bentham had always recognized the potential force of public opinion operating through the popular or moral sanction. Moreover, as early as *A Fragment on Government* and again at the time of the French Revolution, he had made the link between publicity and good government, in that the responsibility of rulers towards subjects required that the actions of the former be openly discussed by the latter. What he had yet to do was to recognize that the only form of government in which the influence of public opinion could be made effective, and thereby the only form of government under which dependence of rulers on subjects could be secured, was a representative democracy. In order for public opinion to promote the greatest happiness, it was necessary that all the relevant information for forming a proper conception of their interest be available to the people, and for them to be able to discuss it openly. Hence, publicity lay at the foundation of good government. This recognition eventually followed from the emergence of sinister interest in his thought around 1804, and his acute awareness of the interest of rulers in suppressing the freedom of the press, and in conducting their activities in secret. In order to strengthen the moral sanction exercised by public opinion in its role as a counterforce to the sinister interest of rulers, Bentham gave it an institutional basis in the public opinion tribunal. Yet the reciprocal relationship between the form of government and publicity highlighted a problem. While it was only in a representative democracy that government would be fully open to public scrutiny, it was only through the

[5] According to the American Declaration of Independence of 4 July 1776, it was a 'self-evident' truth, 'That when any Form of Government becomes destructive of these ends [i.e. the unalienable rights with which men 'are endowed by their Creator'], it is the Right of the People to alter or to abolish it'.

[6] Bowring, ii. 286–8.

pressure exerted by a reformed public opinion that a representative democracy would be instituted. Bentham had to deal with the problem of enlightening public opinion under a regime which was strenuous in its attempts to ensure that the people remained ignorant of their true interests.

II

According to Bentham: 'On architecture good Government has more dependence than men have hitherto seemed to be aware of.'[7] Now the history of English legal and political thought is not without striking examples of the use of architectural metaphors.[8] Blackstone, discussing civil remedies under the Common Law, and in particular the abandonment of the feudal forms of action and the adaptation of the newer, personal actions in their stead, remarked: 'We inherit an old Gothic castle, erected in the days of chivalry, but fitted up for a modern inhabitant. The moated ramparts, the embattled towers, and the trophied halls, are magnificent and venerable, but useless. The inferior apartments, now converted into rooms of convenience, are chearful and commodious, though their approaches are winding and difficult.'[9] According to William Paley, in *The Principles of Moral and Political Philosophy*, the British Constitution was like

> one of those old mansions, which, instead of being built all at once, after a regular plan, and according to the rules of architecture at present established, has been reared in different ages of the art, has been altered from time to time, and has been continually receiving additions and repairs, suited to the taste, fortune, or conveniency, of its successive proprietors. In such a building, we look in vain for the elegance and proportion, for the just order and correspondence, of parts, which we expect in a modern edifice; and which external symmetry, after all, contributes much more perhaps to the amusement of the beholder than the accommodation of the inhabitant.[10]

Bentham himself was not averse to using similar imagery, though writing in 1822 with Tripoli in mind, he revealed his preference for a 'modern edifice', rather than a 'Gothic castle' or an 'old mansion': 'That which the people of Tripoli have need of is the building up of the social edifice: and happily good materials for it are not wanting: that which the people of England have need of is the pulling down of the edifice still in existence: an edifice which, in the state into which it has fallen, is a mere den of thieves.'[11] In stating that good government

[7] *Constitutional Code*, I. 55.

[8] Another commonly used image, of course, is that of the human body: see e.g. Sir John Fortescue, *On the Laws and Governance of England*, ed. S. Lockwood (Cambridge, 1997), 'In Praise of the Laws of England', ch. xiii, 20–1; and Hobbes, *Leviathan*, Introduction, 9–10 [1].

[9] Blackstone, *Commentaries on the Laws of England*, iii. 268.

[10] See 'Principles of Moral and Political Philosophy', book VI, ch. vii, in *Works of William Paley*, i. 413–14.

[11] *Securities against Misrule*, 117 n.

depended upon architecture, Bentham did not, however, mean to use architecture in a metaphorical way to refer to the way in which the political and legal institutions of a state were organized and related to each other, but rather in a practical way to refer to the physical space in which government activities were carried on. He did, of course, recognize that the way in which the edifice of the state was constructed would have a direct bearing on the effectiveness of the public opinion tribunal, but he also recognized that the architecture of the buildings in which government activities took place would determine the degree of openness or secrecy to which those activities would be subjected. In other words, it was not just the institutional structure of government which had to be adapted to secure the publicity of official actions, but also the physical dimensions of public buildings:

Those who wish not for absentation or untimely departure, from any *seat of business*, must not admit of multiplied or unobserved entrances and exits. Those who wish to exclude abuse from *prisons*, must not have a space in which either the behaviour of any prisoner, or the treatment he experiences, is not continually exposed to every desiring eye. Those Judges, whose wish it is to exclude inspectors from the seat of judicature, (and such of course, have ever been all English Judges) know well how powerless every other *veto* is, in comparison of that which the Architect alone can issue, and secure completely against non-observance.[12]

Yet, as Bentham acknowledged, there were occasions on which secrecy was desirable—albeit such occasions were considerably fewer in number than those on which publicity was desirable—and architecture was capable of serving this end as well.[13] He went further than merely pointing out that the purposes served by an institution were related to the physical environment in which its activities took place, but drew up more or less detailed architectural plans for the three institutions to which he alluded in the passage above—namely the minister's audience chamber, the panopticon prison, and the courtroom—as well as for the debating chamber of a political assembly.

The minister's office or audience chamber, which Bentham described in *Constitutional Code*, formed part of a more extensive design for the administrative offices of government. He envisaged a total of thirteen ministers,[14] most of whom would be appointed by a prime minister. The ministers' offices would be arranged in a crescent, with the prime minister's at the centre, and, therefore, close enough to facilitate 'instantaneous intercommunication'. The prime minister's office would be linked to all the ministers' offices, and each of the ministers' offices to every other, by 'conversation tubes'—constructed from thin,

[12] *Constitutional Code*, I. 55–6.

[13] Cf. ibid. 440: '*architectural arrangements* in particular may, in quality of *means*, be made subservient' both 'to publicity and secrecy,—in the several cases in which they are respectively productive of *good*'.

[14] Or rather ministries, since one person might be appointed to two or more ministries.

airtight pipes[15]—by means of which the 'promptitude of oral intercourse' would be 'maximized'. A system of boxes and pulleys would be used to send documents from one office to another, thereby ensuring that none were lost or stolen in transit.[16] Each minister would need to communicate not only with the prime minister, his ministerial colleagues, and his subordinate officials, but also with the public in their capacity as 'suitors', that is with persons who had business to do either with the minister himself or at his office. The minister's office would have a polygonal space at its centre, surrounded by waiting-boxes, rather like theatre boxes, where suitors would wait their turn to be interviewed. The minister himself, along with his clerks and other officials, would sit at a table in the centre of the polygon. The majority of waiting-boxes would be public waiting-boxes, and the remainder private waiting-boxes, with the polygon partitioned in such a way that the private waiting-boxes could not be seen, nor any conversation between occupants and the minister overheard, by occupants of the public waiting-boxes. On the one hand, suitors in the public waiting-boxes would see and hear all that took place in the public part of the office, and the openness of the proceedings would be a security for prompt attention and good behaviour on the part of officials. On the other hand, secrecy would be maintained where the suitor had good reason to wish for a private conversation with the minister—for instance, if the suitor were openly to inform the minister of some criminal act, the perpetrator, forewarned that he faced arrest, might take advantage of the opportunity to flee.[17]

The polygonal or circular design was also a key feature of the panopticon prison. The activities of the inmates would be open to constant scrutiny from the prison governor or inspector, and the activities of both to the scrutiny of the public at large, who would be encouraged to visit the panopticon.[18] The cells, occupying several storeys one above the other, would be placed around the circumference of the building. At the centre of the building would be the inspector's lodge, with an open space between the lodge and the cells. Each cell would have a window to the outside of the building, which would, from the perspective of the lodge, backlight the cell in daytime, while lamps, placed

[15] Bentham had experimented with conversation tubes in 1793, with the intention of incorporating them into the panopticon prison: see Charles[?] Wyatt to Bentham, 23 Sept. 1793, and Bentham to Evan Nepean, 10 Nov. 1793, in *Correspondence*, iv. 480, 485–90; *Constitutional Code*, I, 442–3 n.; and Bowring, iv. 41, 84–5.

[16] *Constitutional Code*, I, 441–4.

[17] Ibid. 445–50. Bentham's wish to prevent 'needless delay, vexation and expense', and 'haughty' and 'negligent demeanour' on the part of officials (ibid. 445) was perhaps not unrelated to his own bitter experience of dealing with officials when pursuing his panopticon prison scheme. See e.g. Bentham's account of his attempt in May 1799 to gain an audience with Charles Long, Secretary to the Treasury, in *Correspondence*, vol. vi, ed. J. R. Dinwiddy (Oxford, 1984), 151–2 n., and, more generally, Semple, *Bentham's Prison*, 218–53.

[18] Semple, *Bentham's Prison*, 140, points out that within the panopticon, 'Bentham's system of inspection had five different aspects; first, the prisoners were watched by authority to ensure discipline and good behaviour; secondly, the governor would watch the actions of his subordinates; thirdly, these subordinates would watch the governor; fourthly, the inmates would spy on each other; and fifthly, the whole structure would be thrown open to the public.'

outside the lodge with a reflector behind them, would light the cells at night. The lodge would be so constructed, with appropriate partitions and blinds, that the inspector would be able at all times to see into all the cells, while the prisoners would be unable to see whether they were being watched. Moreover, the lodge would be connected to each cell by means of a conversation tube, so that the inspector might communicate with any prisoner without the knowledge of any of the others.[19] The principle which underlay the design, explained Bentham, was the facilitation of inspection, an operation necessary not only in prisons, but also in mental asylums, hospitals, schools, poor-houses, and factories, and to which the panopticon design was also applicable:

> It is obvious that, in all these instances, the more constantly the persons to be inspected are under the eyes of the persons who should inspect them, the more perfectly will the purpose of the establishment have been attained. Ideal perfection, if that were the object, would require that each person should actually be in that predicament, during every instant of time. This being impossible, the next thing to be wished for is, that, at every instant, seeing reason to believe as much, and not being able to satisfy himself to the contrary, he should *conceive* himself to be so.[20]

The activities of the prisoners would be transparent to the inspector; his actions, insofar as the prisoners were concerned, were hid behind a veil of secrecy. Having said that, it was a cardinal feature of the design that the activities of the inspector and his officials should be laid open to the general scrutiny of the public, both official and unofficial. In the English context, the official inspectors of the prison would be judges or justices of the peace, who would be able to perform their task much more effectively than in a conventional prison, where a thorough inspection would require a visit to each individual cell, not an enticing prospect when disease was all too frequent.[21] In the panopticon, which would be clean and well-ventilated, everyone and everything could be inspected from the central tower. As for unofficial inspection, the prison would be open to any member of the public who wished to visit it for any reason whatsoever, whether to assure themselves that friends and relatives who had been sentenced to imprisonment were not being mistreated, or merely to satisfy their curiosity. Bentham took it for granted that 'the doors of these establishments will be, as, without very special reasons to the contrary, the doors of all public establishments ought to be, thrown wide open to the body of the curious at large—the great *open committee* of the tribunal of the world'.[22]

The courtroom was another scene of official activity to whose architectural arrangements Bentham gave consideration. In regard to judicial procedure,

[19] Bowring, iv. 40–1. Bentham later decided that cells would be shared by several prisoners, whereupon the secrecy of communication would not have been quite so absolute. For Bentham's abandonment of solitary confinement in the panopticon see Semple, *Bentham's Prison*, 129–33.

[20] Bowring, iv. 40.

[21] For the prevalence of 'jail fever' in eighteenth-century English prisons see J. M. Beattie, *Crime and the Courts in England* (Princeton, 1986), 301–6.

[22] Bowring, iv. 45–6.

Bentham acknowledged the competing demands of publicity and secrecy or privacy: publicity was 'the general rule, as being, in most cases, conducive to the direct ends of justice', whereas privacy was the exception. Rectitude of decision was the ultimate end of judicial procedure, to which the necessary means were the correctness and completeness of the evidence on which the decision was based. It was, however, not enough to give publicity to the evidence alone; it was also necessary to give publicity, amongst other things, to the arguments delivered by the parties or their lawyers upon the evidence, to the summing up of the evidence by the judge, and to the reasons on which the judge grounded his decision. The publicity of the proceedings had a number of beneficial effects: first, new witnesses might come forward when they realized the potential relevance of their testimony; second, existing witnesses might be prompted to give additional evidence; third, information would be conveyed to that part of the public which was either involved in the proceedings or took notice of them; and fourth, a proper basis would be created for the praise or blame, and hence the 'good or ill offices', which the public in general might wish to bestow on 'the several actors'.[23] The extent to which publicity was given to judicial proceedings would depend not only upon legal provisions—for instance, the absence of any prohibition on the reporting of trials—but also, and even more decisively, upon the physical characteristics of the location in which those proceedings took place—as Bentham remarked, 'there are prohibitions, and there are stone walls: the walls are of rather the firmer texture'. If judicial proceedings took place in the open air, the only limit to the number of persons capable of following the proceedings would be determined by strength of voice and capacity of hearing. But proceedings would usually take place in a room, and it was the nature of a room, in proportion to the smallness of its size, to enhance privacy rather than publicity. Even a large room was not itself a guarantee of publicity, and might be quite the reverse, as experience of the royal courts which sat in Westminster Hall proved. In the Court of King's Bench, the proceedings were purportedly held in public, yet the number of persons able 'to come, or (being come) to hear, is not worth thinking of'.[24] In general, however, when publicity was the object, 'the magnitude of the theatre is among the instruments employed for the attainment of it', and when privacy 'the smallness, if not necessarily of the apartment itself, at any rate of the company for which it is destined' was the pertinent factor.[25] In order to reconcile the general need for publicity with the more limited demand for privacy, Bentham suggested that every court should have 'a private chamber or withdrawing room', with access from behind the bench, to which the judge and the requisite persons might 'withdraw one minute, and return the next, the audience in the court remaining undisplaced'.[26]

[23] Ibid. vi. 352–3.

[24] For a description of the Westminster Hall courts see J. H. Baker, *An Introduction to English Legal History*, 3rd edn. (London, 1990), 44.

[25] Bowring, vi. 354, 377.

[26] Ibid. 369.

In *Political Tactics* Bentham put forward a design for a debating chamber for a political assembly. Given that the president and each member of the assembly should be able to hear what any other member was saying, the chamber would need to be 'nearly circular', with 'seats rising amphitheatrically above each other—the seat of the president so placed that he may see all the assembly—a central space for the secretaries and papers—contiguous rooms for committees—a gallery for auditors—a separate box for the reporters for the public papers'. Such a building 'would have more influence than would at first be suspected, in securing the assiduity of the members, and facilitating the exercise of their functions'.[27] A further feature of the chamber would be the provision of a 'Table of Motions' visible from every part of the chamber, and on which the motion under discussion would be displayed. Such a device would constitute a significant improvement over those proceedings (Bentham had in mind the British Parliament) in which the motion was merely read at the commencement of a debate, and where the exact terms of the motion were liable to be misrecollected or misconstrued by orators and listeners alike, or indeed never even known by them if they arrived after the motion had been read. Moreover, should an orator fall into irrelevance, the president might silently, unobtrusively, yet effectively bring him back to the point by directing a stick or wand to the appropriate part of the motion.[28] A second table, a 'Table of Regulations', likewise visible from all parts of the chamber, would be placed by the side of the president, who would point to the appropriate rule when an infraction took place. The very visibility of the rules would help to ensure that they were not transgressed: 'when the law which condemns is before your eyes, and the tribunal which judges you at the same moment, no one will be more tempted to violate it than he would be tempted to steal red-hot iron'.[29]

These measures ensured the publicity of proceedings inside the assembly, which was, of course, a necessary condition for the proceedings to be made known outside the assembly. Bentham devised a system of checks which would ensure accurate reporting of the proceedings to the people at large. First, the assembly would produce an official report of its proceedings, including verbatim accounts of speeches where the subject was considered to be of sufficient importance. Second, as we have seen, provision would be made for the accommodation of newspaper reporters, who would be free to produce unofficial records of the proceedings, and thereby 'prevent negligence and dishonesty on the part of the official reporters', and indeed even obviate the suspicion of it. Third, the public would be admitted to the chamber to 'inspire confidence in the reports of the journals': the public would be assured that the reports were

[27] *Political Tactics*, 44–5. [28] Ibid. 45–8.

[29] Ibid. 50–1. Bentham would later suggest that a 'Table of Fallacies' be added to the two other tables: see e.g. Bentham to Henry Addington, 24 July 1800, *Correspondence*, vi. 335–7; manuscripts written for 'Political Fallacies' at UC cii. 582 (5 Feb. 1811) and civ. 37 (31 Jan. 1821); and *First Principles*, 64–5.

truthful and that nothing had been suppressed.[30] As in the minister's audience chamber, panopticon prison, and courtroom, the architectural arrangements ensured that, where appropriate, each actor or set of actors was visible to the others: watching over each other, they would each ensure good behaviour in all.

III

The primary purpose of these architectural arrangements was to secure the publicity of official actions, whether those officials were ministers, prison governors, judges, or legislators. Architecture was a means of securing publicity, while publicity was a means of securing responsibility. Government was a trust, and its officials were trustees for the people, to whom they were—or if not, ought to be made—responsible.[31] In *Political Tactics* Bentham pointed out that the best means for 'securing the public confidence' in a political assembly, and for 'causing it constantly to advance towards the end of its institution', was to give publicity to its proceedings. He envisaged a dynamic process, whereby open communication or dialogue between legislators and people would benefit both parties. The people would have greater confidence in their legislators, having no reason to suspect them of pursuing any secret policy. Legislators would learn the real wishes of the people, who would themselves be better informed, and would even derive amusement from reading about the proceedings of the assembly. Electors would have more information on which to base their choice of representative, while the representatives would be able to draw on the knowledge and expertise of persons outside the assembly. Furthermore, and perhaps most importantly in Bentham's view, publicity would 'constrain the members of the assembly to perform their duty'. The most effective means for ensuring that those who possessed political power resisted the temptation to abuse it was 'the superintendence of the public':

> The public compose a tribunal, which is more powerful than all the other tribunals together. An individual may pretend to disregard its decrees—to represent them as formed of fluctuating and opposite opinions, which destroy one another; but every one feels, that though this tribunal may err, it is incorruptible; that it continually tends to become enlightened; that it unites all the wisdom and all the justice of the nation; that it

[30] *Political Tactics*, 40. In 'Economy as applied to Office', written in 1822, Bentham again made the point that the presence of members of the public at debates would act as 'a check upon such persons as, with or without commission from the constituted authorities, may happen to make a practice of taking minutes of the Debates': see *First Principles*, 120.

[31] In *An Introduction to the Principles of Morals and Legislation*, 263 n., Bentham stated that sovereign power 'upon the principle of utility, can never be other than fiduciary': see p. 223 above. The role of the notion of trust in Bentham's political thought is explored in Hume, *Bentham and Bureaucracy*, 78–9, 216–17. The theme is more pervasive in Bentham's later writings on constitutional law (see e.g. *First Principles*, 187, 270–2, 312; *Constitutional Code*, I. 412–17) than is suggested by Rosen, *Bentham and Representative Democracy*, 241–2.

always decides the destiny of public men; and that the punishments which it pronounces are inevitable.[32]

Bentham here summarized a number of themes which he developed—at various times and in various ways—throughout his career. Public opinion, properly informed, would always coincide with the interest of the community as a whole; as time went on, the public would become better and better informed; public opinion was all-inclusive, consisting of the opinions of everyone who took notice of an issue; its voice was the most powerful force in politics, even though it might be constituted by a number of discrete opinions; and its sanctions were inescapable.

The effectiveness of public opinion depended upon the force of the punishments and rewards, the pains and pleasures, which it could bring to bear. As we have seen, the moral or popular sanction was imposed 'at the hands of such *chance* persons in the community, as the party in question may happen in the course of his life to have concerns with, according to each man's spontaneous disposition, and not according to any settled or concerted rule'.[33] Just as the political and legal sanction was typically enforced by a judicial tribunal, so the moral sanction was enforced by the public opinion tribunal. This body was not formally constituted in the manner of a court of law; nor did it have particular, designated individuals as its judges or other officials; nor did it have agents to carry out its orders. Its decisions were likely, though not necessarily, to be pronounced in much less determinate terms, and the sanctions at its disposal were again likely, though not necessarily, to be administered more haphazardly. Nevertheless, there was a mechanism through which the public opinion tribunal functioned in a way that was analogous to that of a legal tribunal—namely, a newspaper. The procedure followed in a legal tribunal when a claim or accusation was brought forward by an injured party was similar to what occurred when an individual made, in a newspaper, an allegation of misconduct against a government official. The receipt by the newspaper editor of the allegation was the equivalent of the receipt by the legal tribunal of the claim or accusation. Just as the legal tribunal would then receive a defence from the accused, and receive, collect, and store evidence, both in support of and in opposition to the accusation, so the newspaper editor would receive information from correspondents, and publish a reply to the allegation from the official concerned—whether a confession, a denial, or a presentation of arguments in justification of his conduct. Both the legal tribunal and the newspaper would provide a forum in which arguments relating to the evidence would be rehearsed. The arguments would be concerned with establishing the probability that the alleged act took place, or with the existence of any alleged justificatory circumstances, or with the

[32] *Political Tactics*, 29–34.

[33] See p. 35 above. The quotation is from *An Introduction to the Principles of Morals and Legislation*, 35.

propriety or impropriety of the act. The judge in the legal tribunal would finally come to a decision, give expression to it, and make some order which would lead to the execution of the decision in question. In the case of the newspaper, the editor would form his own decision on the matter and publish it. If the editor concluded that the official in question had committed a disreputable act, this was equivalent to a judgment in favour of conviction. The judgment would be executed to the extent that the reputation of the official was lowered in the eyes of the other members of the public opinion tribunal, and they in consequence either deprived him of any benefits or favours they might otherwise have conferred on him, or subjected him to any burdens or disfavours they might not otherwise have inflicted on him.[34]

The force exerted by the popular or moral sanction depended upon 'notification'—namely making known both the decision pronounced by the public opinion tribunal and the grounds on which the decision was made. Bentham recognized that the decision could never be definitively ascertained, but it was possible for each individual to come to a view as to what the content of the decision might be. From the particular circumstances of the case, and from his knowledge of the interests and views of the other members, each individual formed a conclusion respecting the decision 'likely to be pronounced' by the other members of the public opinion tribunal. As for the rectitude of the decision, there could not be any certainty, but the decision pronounced by a majority would be more likely to be correct than that pronounced by a minority.[35] The decision of the majority, in other words, was more likely to be conducive to the greatest happiness and was, therefore, to be taken for that of the public opinion tribunal as a whole. Conduct would always be determined by interest, or to be more precise, by the actor's conception of his interest. The opinion acted upon by each member of the public opinion tribunal would be determined by his own interest. Where there was disagreement on a certain question, the public opinion tribunal would be divided into two groups—the majority constituting the democratical section, and the minority the aristocratical section: 'The interest of the Democratical Section is that of the majority of the Members of which the whole Tribunal taken in the aggregate is composed: it is consequently the interest of the subject many: the opinion on which it *acts* will be that which is in the highest degree contributory to the greatest happiness of the greatest number. . . . ' In contrast, the interest of the aristocratical section was that of the majority of the members of 'the ruling and otherwise influential few'—the highest ruling functionaries in the state and their allies. The interest of this section, and, therefore, the opinion pronounced by it, would in most cases be 'in direct opposition' to that of the democratical section. In practice the democratical section would attach 'disrepute' to those actions which its members considered to be detrimental to the universal interest, and

[34] *Securities against Misrule*, 54–5, 60–4. [35] *First Principles*, 57.

'good repute' to those actions considered to be contributory to it: expressions of disapprobation would be made towards the former, of approbation towards the latter. Similarly, the aristocratical section would attach 'good repute' to those actions which its members considered to be contributory to its own particular interest—but since 'in a great, not to say the greater, part of the whole field of legislation', its interest was diametrically opposed to the democratical, it would approve of actions which tended to be detrimental to the universal interest. As it was 'the interest of the majority of those who act as Members' which would determine the opinion acted upon by 'the Tribunal considered as a whole', the opinion of the democratical section would hold sway.[36]

The informality of the public opinion tribunal did not mean that it was any less effective than a legal tribunal; nor that its decisions were likely to be less correct; nor its sanctions less appropriate. In Bentham's view, the case was quite the opposite. For instance, the 'natural procedure' adopted by the public opinion tribunal, far from being inferior to the procedure adopted by a legal tribunal, was the model on which the proceedings of the legal tribunal should be based.[37] One of the obvious differences between a legal tribunal and the public opinion tribunal was that the former was established by the sovereign, whereas the latter was merely an unofficial assemblage of self-chosen individuals, whose power and influence were contingent on their social status, wealth, and reputation. Having said that, in *Constitutional Code* the sovereign itself was identified with the public opinion tribunal: 'The sovereignty is in *the people*. It is reserved by and to them. It is exercised, by the exercise of the Constitutive authority. . . .'[38] The constitutive authority was the body which elected, or in Bentham's terminology 'located', the members of the legislative authority, but since each of its members was also a member of the public opinion tribunal, the constitutive authority was thereby closely linked to the public opinion tribunal. The public opinion tribunal was, of course, not identical to the constitutive authority, but potentially more wide-ranging, for it might include all those persons within the community in question who were excluded from the constitutive authority (namely females, minors, and non-readers) as well as members of any other political community. It was formed by any group of people who associated together for any political purpose: for instance, the persons who attended the sittings of the legislature or of a judicatory, persons having business with administrative officials (for instance those in the public boxes in the minister's audience chamber), persons attending public meetings, and persons merely commenting on the actions of officials. The only qualification for belonging to the public opinion tribunal was that a person 'take

[36] *First Principles*, 68–70.

[37] For Bentham's preference for 'natural procedure' over 'technical procedure' see pp. 119–20 above.

[38] *Constitutional Code*, I. 25. For the institutional arrangements proposed in *Constitutional Code* see Rosen, *Bentham and Representative Democracy*, 130–67, and pp. 301–3 below.

cognizance of the question, whatever it may be'.[39] Bentham's constitutional code gave official recognition to the public opinion tribunal:

This constitution recognises the *Public Opinion Tribunal*, as an authority essentially belonging to it. Its power is judicial. A functionary belonging to the Judiciary, exercises his functions by express location—by commission. A member of the Public Opinion Tribunal exercises his functions without commission; he needs none. Dislocability and punibility of members excepted, the Public Opinion Tribunal is to the Supreme Constitutive, what the Judiciary is to the Supreme Legislative.[40]

Although the public opinion tribunal as such could not remove from office or subject to judicial punishment the members of the government, it was able to enforce the will of the people by means of the moral sanction. Hence, Bentham compared the decisions of the public opinion tribunal with those pronounced by judges operating under the Common Law:

Public Opinion may be considered as a system of law, emanating from the body of the people. If there be no individually assignable form of words in and by which it stands expressed, it is but upon a par in this particular with that rule of action which, emanating as it does from lawyers, official and professional, and not sanctioned by the Legislative authority otherwise than by tacit sufferance, is in England designated by the appellation of *Common Law*. To the pernicious exercise of the power of government it is the only check; to the beneficial, an indispensable supplement. Able rulers lead it; prudent rulers lead or follow it; foolish rulers disregard it. Even at the present stage in the career of civilization, its dictates coincide, on most points, with those of the *greatest happiness principle*; on some, however, it still deviates from them: but, as its deviations have all along been less and less numerous, and less wide, sooner or later they will cease to be discernible; aberration will vanish, coincidence will be complete.[41]

Bentham's views concerning the potential force and beneficial effects of public opinion had not wavered since the composition of *A Fragment on Government* and *Political Tactics* some fifty and thirty-five years earlier, respectively. Yet in *Constitutional Code* he went further in attempting to strengthen that force, not only by giving explicit constitutional recognition to the public opinion tribunal, but in providing it, as we shall see,[42] with an institutional role in the form of the Quasi-jury—a tribunal of public opinion sitting within a court of law.

IV

In *Constitutional Code* Bentham recognized that 'deviations' existed between the dictates of the public opinion tribunal and those of the greatest happiness principle, even if these were becoming 'less and less numerous, and less wide', and he was optimistic that eventually 'coincidence will be complete'.[43]

[39] *Constitutional Code*, I. 35–6. [40] Ibid. 35. [41] Ibid. 36.
[42] See p. 312 below. [43] See above.

Nevertheless, his strategy of promoting good government faced an obvious difficulty if the views of the public opinion tribunal were at variance with its true interests. Along with corruption, delusion was a major impediment to good government. Delusion—produced by fallacious argument but also by other means—was a perversion of the understanding. Individuals adopted 'some erroneous conception or opinion', and were thereby induced to 'give support to misrule: namely adding themselves to the number either of those over whom it is exercised or those by whom it is exercised'. Rulers wished to inculcate the belief that those who actually possessed the powers of government were also the best persons for exercising those powers, and that the more power, wealth, and titles of honour a man possessed, the greater the degree of talent and virtue he possessed.[44] This belief might be produced directly by means of fallacious argument, but also indirectly through an association of ideas. For instance, a monarch's crown and throne were implements intended to persuade the people that the person who wore the one and sat on the other was a being of 'superlative excellence'. It was 'to the disgrace and sad affliction of the species' that the dress and the furniture had such a delusive quality: 'Wherever they see the external instruments of felicity heaped upon one object, there they fancy they see excellence: excellence, moral or intellectual, or both together: and on this vitiated state of the people's visual organs is the dependence of their adversaries . . . for the success of the imposture. How long will men be gulled, or affect to be gulled, by such impostures?' Bentham took comfort from the fact that such impostures did not exist in the United States of America, where the people enjoyed much greater happiness than in 'all Monarch-ridden states'.[45] Again, he recognized that in certain areas of private morality, 'for want of sufficient maturity in the public judgment, or by the influence of some sinister interest', public opinion might condemn an act which was not pernicious. A community might be intolerant in matters of religious dogma and practice, and in consequence punish a person who expressed opinions contrary to the prevailing orthodoxy. A community might be hostile to homosexuality, and while sex between males produced no evil in itself, yet by its very disclosure 'a whole life may be filled with misery'. In these cases it was best to keep one's opinions or one's sexual preferences a matter of secrecy: disclosure, rather than secrecy, was harmful in such circumstances.[46]

In effect, delusion was the product of fallacy, and, therefore, like fallacy, had its source in sinister interest, interest-begotten prejudice, and authority-begotten prejudice. As far as delusion was concerned, Bentham now added a fourth source, namely intellectual weakness.[47] As we have seen,[48] sinister interest led rulers and other officials to employ fallacies in order to produce delusion, and thence to promote and defend the abuses from which they profited. As we have also seen,[49] a second source of fallacy, and thence delusion, was interest-begotten

[44] *First Principles*, 261–3. [45] Ibid. 211–12. [46] Ibid. 290. [47] Ibid. 151.
[48] See pp. 155–62 above. [49] See p. 158 above.

prejudice, which itself had its source in sinister interest. A prejudice was an opinion which had been 'embraced without sufficient examination: it is a judgement which, being pronounced *before* evidence, is therefore pronounced without evidence'.[50] Elsewhere, Bentham more succinctly defined prejudice as 'erroneous prepossession'.[51] Interest-begotten prejudice, though it had its source in sinister interest, was liable to be far more powerful and thence more mischievous than the sinister interest itself. There was a limit to the number of persons who could share in a sinister interest—if an interest were shared by a majority of persons it would, by definition, be no longer a sinister interest but the general interest. In contrast, there was no limit to the number of persons who might share a prejudice. Moreover, prejudice was often more difficult to overcome than simple sinister interest:

> Those who are engaged to [the] course in question by no other tie than that of sinister interest, may by sinister interest operating in an opposite direction be in a moment engaged in a course directly opposite: whereas when once the mind is engaged in the trammels of prejudice, although it may have had its origin in sinister interest, there is no saying with what pertinacity and for what length of time it may not persevere in that same course: persevere, in spite of the opposite action of ever so strong a force of interest—of interest in which ever direction operating.

It was often easier to change the allegiance of those motivated by sinister interest than of those motivated by prejudice.[52] Another source of prejudice, and the third source of delusion, lay in the adoption of opinions on the authority of another person. To a large extent this was inevitable, since any one individual did not have the time or expertise fully to consider the grounds for his opinions except in a small number of cases, and so he had to take his opinions mostly upon trust. He had to adopt the opinion of some other individual or individuals as his own. Yet the opinion of this 'authority' might itself be grounded in sinister interest or prejudice, and, therefore, be erroneous.[53] An example of authority-begotten prejudice was the establishment of the Senate in the United States of America. Instead of considering the question of whether to add a second chamber to the legislature from the point of view of the principle of utility, the Americans had looked at other countries, and in particular Britain, seen the existence of two or more chambers, and without further thought added the Senate to the House of Representatives.[54]

The fourth source of delusion was intellectual weakness, which consisted of 'ignorance in respect of every thing by which, whether in a beneficial way or a pernicious way' one's interest was affected, and which gave rise to misconception, and thence error.[55] For instance, the beliefs 'that happiness and exemption from misery in a future life depends on [the] degree of obsequiousness to

[50] UC cii. 540 (6 Aug. 1811) [Bowring, ii. 478].
[51] *First Principles*, 151.
[52] Ibid. 151, 180–2.
[53] See pp. 158–9 above.
[54] *First Principles*, 106–7.
[55] Ibid. 154–5.

Monarch and his sinister interest', and that there existed 'a natural association between aristocratical superiority and virtue', were errors which favoured the sinister interest of a monarch and associated sinister interests to the detriment of the interest of the people in general.[56] The quiet acceptance of legal fictions was also evidence of intellectual weakness.[57] Bentham remarked that, at the root of every 'anti-popular arrangement', there was 'honest intellectual weakness'. He asked: 'How can it be otherwise? since among the people at large notions fraught with absurdity are not without example, notions which being adverse to the interest of those by whom they are entertained can not have had for their cause sinister interest, at any rate can not have had correct conceptions of particular interest.'[58] Presumably, if people in general had not suffered from 'intellectual weakness', then the delusion which originated in sinister interest, interest-begotten prejudice, and authority-begotten prejudice, would not have been able to establish itself.

Rulers had an interest in suppressing criticism of both the form of government and of their activities under it. Every criticism either of 'the texture of government' or of 'the conduct of any person bearing a part in the exercise of the powers of government' conveyed an 'imputation' on the reputation of those at the head of the government. The imputation might be 'defamatory', that is, an accusation that an individual had committed some specific act which was legally punishable; or 'vituperative', that is, a more vague and general accusation. Governments had treated both sorts of accusation as offences, even where the person accused was a private individual, but in general had assumed that the offence was more mischievous where the accusation was made against a public functionary, particularly in his public capacity, and much more so if made against the whole government, especially those at the head of it. To deter criticism of public functionaries in this way was 'to destroy, or proportionably to weaken, that liberty, which, under the name of *the liberty of the press*, operates as a check upon the conduct of the ruling few; and in that character constitutes a controuling power, indispensably necessary to the maintenance of good government'. Bentham's view, 'confirmed by the practice of the United States' where no prosecution was possible for sedition or any restrictions laid on public meetings,[59] was that, in the case of a public functionary, it should not be possible to prosecute for vituperation, and only for defamation when 'the imputation' was 'false and groundless' and 'the result of wilful mendacity accompanied with the consciousness of its falsity, or else with culpable rashness'. Moreover, the truth of the imputation should constitute a legal defence against rashness and wilful falsehood. The security for good government resulting from the liberty of

[56] *First Principles*, 155 n. [57] Ibid. 267. [58] Ibid. 175.

[59] Bentham presumably had in mind the First Amendment to the United States Constitution (1791), which provided that 'Congress shall make no law ... abridging the freedom of speech, or of the press; or the right of the people peaceably to assemble, and to petition the government for a redress of grievances'.

the press far outweighed any evil which might be produced in the case of the particular individuals who were the subject of the imputations. Indeed, as far as officials were concerned, the more elevated the person in question, the greater the resources he could deploy to disprove and refute any accusation made against him, while the benefits of the situation itself abundantly compensated him for any evil which might befall him in this and any other respect.[60]

V

Despite the existence of these sources of delusion, Bentham was convinced that public opinion was becoming more and more enlightened. One of the grounds for his optimism was his view that the maintenance of falsehood and the suppression of truth required an enormous effort: 'It is the characteristic of error to possess only an accidental existence, which may terminate in a moment, whilst truth is indestructible.'[61] In a similar vein, in the 'Introduction' to *Plan of Parliamentary Reform*, Bentham noted that in order 'to produce any permanent and unremedied bad effect' a corrupt majority in the House of Commons would itself have to be permanent, 'for suppose it ever to cease, the majority of a single day would suffice to unravel the web of corruption, and devote the corruptionists, if not to punishment under forms of law, at any rate to universal indignation and abhorrence, with a certainty of never more being reappointed to the trust which, by the supposition, they had thus abused'.[62] Publicity, through the ever-increasing amount of information which it made available, was the means of overcoming delusion, and thence sinister interest and misrule. For instance, writing in 1822, Bentham claimed that, thanks to publicity, no one could doubt that anyone in England who acted in support of the political system did so with full knowledge of its nature: 'After such notice as for so many years past has been given in all newspapers, a man can no more contribute to the corruptiveness of the system, a man can no more contribute to the delusiveness of the system, without design, than without design he could go about picking pockets.'[63] Bentham had predicted in *Political Tactics* that an increase in publicity and the consequent increase of information would produce an improvement in the quality of the opinions held by the people.[64] There was a dynamic relationship between publicity and political reform, and the extension of the means of communication was central to this process.[65] One of the most important instruments in this respect was the printing press, and perhaps the

60 Bowring, ii. 277, 279–80.

61 *Political Tactics*, 36. The theme is elaborated, in the context of the trustworthiness of testimony, in *Rationale of Judicial Evidence*, book I, chs. ix–xi: see Bowring, vi. 247–76.

62 Bowring, iii. 457.

63 *First Principles*, 263–4.

64 *Political Tactics*, 34–6.

65 On Bentham's 'strategy of reform', supported by public opinion, see Rosen, *Bentham and Representative Democracy*, 18–40, and on the extension of the means of communication see Ben Dor, *Constitutional Limits and the Public Sphere*, 191–233.

most important production of the printing press was the newspaper. In his comparison of the public opinion tribunal with a legal tribunal, Bentham had shown that bringing to bear the force of public opinion was a complex process, including the presentation of information and the formation and publication of opinions, which in itself involved a series of operations—finding out, writing down, printing, and circulating the opinions in question.[66] He continued: 'For all these several operations, one and the same article presents itself as the effectual and only effectual instrument. This instrument is no other than a *News-paper* . . . .' The newspaper was a far more efficient instrument than pamphlets or books simply because of its 'regularity and constancy of attention'—it noticed incidents as they took place. In a representative democracy, the editor of a popular newspaper was second only in importance to the prime minister—the latter gave impulse 'to the machinery of the political sanction', and the former 'to that of the social sanction'.[67] The utility of the newspaper would, of course, depend upon the extent of its circulation, which would in turn depend upon such matters as the constancy and frequency of its appearance, the cheapness of its price, the variety of its content, its impartiality, and its moderation of language.[68]

If the press were to make any significant impact, then the question of literacy had to be addressed. In the 1820s, as he had throughout his career, Bentham argued that a person unable to read and sign his own name should not be admitted to the franchise. Such a person would be incapable of making a properly informed judgment about the competence of a potential representative.[69] On the other hand, this was not a permanent exclusion: Bentham was convinced that a labourer might learn to read in his spare time within two or three months.[70] In 1789, when proposing the exclusion of non-readers from the franchise in France, he pointed out that in order to judge the conduct of their representative, constituents would need to read the printed accounts of proceedings in the National Assembly. Not only was the exclusion of non-readers one 'which every man has it in his power to free himself from whenever he thinks proper', but it would also 'operate as a spur to the desire of instruction and as an instrument of civilisation'.[71] In other words, linking the franchise to literacy would encourage the non-literate to become literate, and thereby undermine the effectiveness of delusive influence. Moreover, the publicity of proceedings in official institutions would have an educative dimension. Such institutions would

[66] See pp. 260–1 above.

[67] *Securities against Misrule*, 44–6. The 'social sanction' was Bentham's alternative term for the moral or popular sanction.

[68] Ibid. 46–50. The role of publicity and the press in Bentham's thought is discussed in D. Lieberman, 'Economy and Polity in Bentham's Science of Legislation', in S. Collini, R. Whatmore, and B. Young (eds.), *Economy, Polity, and Society: British Intellectual History 1750–1950* (Cambridge, 2000), 107–34.

[69] *First Principles*, 96–7.

[70] See Bowring, iii. 560, and p. 166 above.

[71] See *Rights, Representation, and Reform*, 248–9, and p. 90 above.

become 'schools' in their relevant areas, for instance schools of justice or schools of legislation. The Quasi-jurors, as we shall see,[72] were to benefit from the education which they were to receive as scholars in a school of justice. When Bentham was attempting to persuade a nation or government 'professing liberal opinions' to accept his offer to draw up a complete code of law,[73] he suggested that it should be open to any other person whatsoever to present rival codes for the consideration of the legislature in question, and that all codes, expense permitting, should be published by authority. This was in stark contrast to the usual method of employing a specially appointed and secret commission. One of the beneficial effects of this procedure would be the creation of a school of legislation.[74]

As well as encouraging publicity and education, it was also important to remove or undermine those institutions and practices which hindered communication. It was, of course, in the interest of rulers either to prevent information from being conveyed to the public, or to ensure that the public received partial or false information.[75] One of the great instruments for deluding the people was a religious establishment. Priests, as we have seen,[76] were hired in order to inculcate beliefs in certain religious doctrines—beliefs which were subservient to the interest of the rulers. A corrupt relationship was established between rulers and priests, whereby the priests enjoyed the income and prestige which they derived from their offices, and the rulers benefited both from the patronage associated with the disposal of these offices and the subservience which the teachings of the priest inculcated in the people. The legal establishment likewise was an important source of delusion, in particular a legal establishment such as that in England which had created 'a sort of God or Goddess upon Earth, a sort of Divinity which [the lawyer] calls Common Law'. The Common Law, which was a figment of the lawyer's imagination, served its purpose 'in finding pretences for giving fulfilment to the Monarch's sinister will as evidenced by his sinister interest'—in other words, to extract wealth from the people for the benefit of the monarch in the first instance, and for the benefit of the legal profession in the second.[77] The replacement of the 'sham' Common Law with a rationalized code would, as well as all its other benefits, remove a source of delusion.

VI

In *Political Tactics* Bentham argued that publicity was the means of rendering officials responsible to the people for the way in which they conducted them-

[72] See p. 312 below. [73] See pp. 244–9 above.
[74] '*Legislator of the World*', 92–3, 265–6. [75] *First Principles*, 292–5.
[76] See pp. 191–3 above. [77] *First Principles*, 184–5.

selves. Indeed, it was because government was a trust, but one so liable to be abused, that rulers had to be distrusted:

Is it objected against the régime of publicity, that it is a system of *distrust?* This is true; and every good political institution is founded upon this base. Whom ought we to distrust, if not those to whom is committed great authority, with great temptations to abuse it? Consider the objects of their duties: they are not their own affairs, but the affairs of others, comparatively indifferent to them, very difficult, very complicated,—which indolence alone would lead them to neglect, and which require the most laborious application. Consider their personal interests: you will often find them in opposition to the interests confided to them. They also possess all the means of serving themselves at the expense of the public, without the possibility of being convicted of it. What remains, then, to overcome all these dangerous motives? what has created an interest of superior force? and what can this interest be, if it be not respect for public opinion—dread of its judgements—desire of glory?—in one word, everything which results from publicity?

The efficacy of this great instrument extends to everything—legislation, administration, judicature. Without publicity, no good is permanent; under the auspices of publicity, no evil can continue.[78]

There were exceptions to the rule of publicity, especially when public opinion was not fully enlightened or prejudiced in some way. Moreover, in relation to legislative procedure, there were occasions when publicity should be 'suspended', for instance when it would benefit the projects of an enemy power, unnecessarily injure innocent persons, or inflict too severe a punishment upon the guilty. Bentham explained: 'It is not proper to make the law of publicity absolute, because it is impossible to foresee all the circumstances in which an assembly may find itself placed. Rules are made for a state of calm and security: they cannot be formed for a state of trouble and peril.'[79] Thirty-five years or so later, in *Constitutional Code*, Bentham noted that of the three 'departments' of government, that in which the demand for secrecy was least extensive was the judiciary, that in which the demand was most extensive the constitutive, and that in which the demand was intermediate the administrative (Bentham's term for the executive). One factor to be taken into account was the expense of publicity: the benefits might not justify the cost. Otherwise, there were a limited number of areas in which secrecy would be the rule rather than the exception, for instance in military and diplomatic affairs.[80] In the case of the constitutive authority, Bentham advocated the secret ballot 'for the preservation of liberty of suffrage'. The elector's independence in casting his vote for the candidate which he considered most likely to promote his own interest was vital, and there would be no security against the influence of corruption if votes were given publicly.[81] Yet even here, Bentham revealed just how strongly he viewed the influence of publicity—in this instance, the individual had to be protected against it. When Bentham claimed, in his writings on the panopticon prison, that this '*simple idea*

[78] *Political Tactics*, 37. [79] Ibid. 39. [80] *Constitutional Code*, I. 162–5.
[81] Ibid. 439–40. See also pp. 144–5 above.

in Architecture' constituted '[a] new mode of obtaining power of mind over mind, in a quantity hitherto without example: and that, to a degree equally without example, secured by whoever chooses to have it so, against abuse',[82] he was only pointing to the means, and not the source of power. The actual source of power was public scrutiny. Although the emergence in his thought of sinister interest in 1804 gave Bentham a greater insight into the psychology of rulers and thence the need for radical measures of reform, this should not obscure his lifelong commitment to 'free' government, and in this context his recommendation of publicity as an effective means of securing responsibility on the part of officials. Having said that, once Bentham had come to see that the real problem was that of overcoming sinister interest, he also came to realize that adequate publicity would only be secured under a representative democracy. Rulers under other forms of government—whether monarchy, aristocracy, or any mixture of monarchy, aristocracy, and democracy—would attempt to obstruct the dissemination of information. The use of publicity was to secure responsibility on the part of officials, but this in turn was the means to the proper objective of all constitutional arrangements: namely to secure the maximization of appropriate official aptitude and the minimization of government expense.

[82] Bowring, iv. 39.

11

The Antidote to Sinister Interest: Official Aptitude

I

It has been generally accepted that Bentham, in his mature constitutional theory, recognized that there existed a natural opposition of interest between rulers and subjects, and that it was the purpose of constitutional law to replace this natural opposition with an artificial identification of interest, whereby it became the interest of rulers to promote the general interest.[1] Bentham succinctly explained his strategy in a passage written in August 1822 for the essay 'Constitutional Code Rationale'.[2] He commenced with the greatest happiness principle: 'The right and proper end of government in every political community is the greatest happiness of all the individuals of which it is composed.' This proposition required modification since there would inevitably be conflicts between the happiness of some and the happiness of others: hence, 'instead of saying the greatest happiness of all, it becomes necessary to say the greatest happiness of the greatest number'. He went on to enunciate a second principle, the rulers' object-indicating principle: 'The actual end of government is in every political community the greatest happiness of those, whether one or many, by whom the powers of government are exercised.' This 'position' could be verified by a study of the actions of past rulers, or else by reference to the inherent self-preference of human nature: 'In the general tenor of human life, in every human breast, self-regarding interest is predominant over all other interests put together.' The ruler, if left to himself, could not be expected to act otherwise than according to the self-preference principle—he would pursue his own particular and sinister interest at the expense of the general interest, the right and proper interest. The discrepancy which existed between the right and proper end of government and the sinister and actual end of government had to be removed: this was achieved

[1] See e.g. Halévy, *Growth of Philosophic Radicalism*, 404–6; Harrison, *Bentham*, 232–3; and Dinwiddy, *Bentham*, 79–80. In contrast, D. Lyons, *In the Interest of the Governed: A Study in Bentham's Philosophy of Utility and Law*, rev. edn. (Oxford, 1991), argues for a natural identity of interest, but this is more a product of his own, highly original, reconstruction of Bentham's principle of utility, rather than a position to which Bentham himself would have subscribed.

[2] See *First Principles*, 232–6. The passage was first published in Bowring, ix. 5–8.

by 'the bringing of the particular interest of rulers into accordance with the universal interest', and gave rise to a third principle—the means-prescribing or junction-of-interests prescribing principle. To effect this junction of interests, any sinister interest to which the ruler was exposed, that is, any desire he might feel to sacrifice the general interest to his own particular interest, had to be nullified: this would leave that part of his interest which coincided with the general interest as the only interest by which his conduct could be determined. Hence, 'The first [principle] declares what ought to be: the next, what is: the last, the means of bringing what is into accordance with what ought to be.' The first and third principles had been present in Bentham's thought in the 1770s, with the principle of utility being proclaimed in *A Fragment on Government* and the conjunction of duty and interest first appearing in 'A View of the Hard-Labour Bill'.[3] The second principle, while also present in more general form in the recognition of the predominance of self-interest in human motivation, took on a new political significance following the emergence of sinister interest in Bentham's thought in 1804.

If the purpose of constitutional law was to produce an identification of interests between rulers and subjects, then such an identification would be achieved by the maximization of official aptitude and the minimization of government expense, hence the motto 'official aptitude maximized; expense minimized'.[4] Aptitude was increased in proportion as an agent or set of agents was more likely to act in a way which promoted the greatest happiness, while any act which produced an increase in expense (which Bentham intended to be understood not merely as pecuniary expense but as evil generally) was equivalent to a diminution in the greatest happiness. To maximize aptitude and to minimize expense would result in the promotion of good and the diminution of evil. When discussing the possibility of establishing a public examination system, Bentham commented that the same measure would often promote both ends: 'On this occasion as on so many others, the interests of *appropriate aptitude* and the interests of *frugality* will be seen going hand in hand: the cheapest plan it will be seen is not only the cheapest but in every other respect the best.'[5]

[3] In 'A View of the Hard-Labour Bill; being an abstract of a pamphlet, intitutled, "Draught of a Bill, to punish by Imprisonment and Hard-Labour, certain Offenders; and to establish proper Places for their Reception." Interspersed with Observations relative to the subject of the above Draught in particular, and to Penal Jurisprudence in general', printed in 1778 (Bowring, iv. 1–35), Bentham expressed his approval of the provision in the Penitentiary Bill that the salary of the governor of each proposed hard-labour house should be proportioned to the quantity of labour therein performed, for it would then 'become the *interest* as well as the *duty* of each governor to see that all persons under his custody be regularly and profitably employed'. This principle, remarked Bentham, was 'an excellent lesson to legislators'. See Bowring, iv. 12. For Bentham's use of the duty and interest conjunction principle in the panopticon prison see Semple, *Bentham's Prison*, 149–52.

[4] The phrases 'maximizing official aptitude' and 'minimizing official pay' (and the verbs 'to minimize' and 'to maximize') had first appeared in print in the 'Advertisement' to 'Defence of Economy against Burke', dated November 1816, and published in *The Pamphleteer* in 1817: see *Official Aptitude Maximized; Expense Minimized*, 41–7, and p. 141 above.

[5] *First Principles*, 85.

Bentham's most detailed and systematic account of the notion of aptitude appeared in 'Economy as applied to Office', written in 1822.[6] Aptitude consisted of three branches or elements: moral aptitude; intellectual aptitude (which was divided into scientific aptitude or knowledge, and judicial aptitude or judgment); and active aptitude. Moral aptitude was 'a negative quality'—an absence of the motivation naturally predominant in man, the pursuit of self-interest to the detriment of all other interests. Although self-regard was the predominant propensity of human nature, Bentham did not deny the existence of social interest—the pleasure a person experienced in seeing someone else happy. Yet so far as constitutional law was concerned, the legislator had to assume the worst—'In the framing of laws, suspicion can not possibly be carried to too high a pitch'—he had to assume that the functionary would act according to his self-interest whatever the consequence for the general interest. The object was so to place rulers that while they had no prospect of pursuing their self-interest to the detriment of the universal interest—of increasing their own happiness at the expense of the greatest happiness—they did have the prospect of pursuing their own self-interest through their share in the universal interest—of increasing their own happiness by promoting the greatest happiness.[7] The existence of moral aptitude, a disposition to promote the universal interest, would be worthless if the functionary did not understand how to recognize both the end itself and the means to achieve it. Hence the need for intellectual aptitude, which consisted of two sub-branches, the scientific and the judicial, the former appertaining to the knowledge which the functionary required to perform his duty, and the latter to his capacity for making correct decisions.[8] Furthermore, disposition and understanding were together worthless without activity. Active aptitude consisted in the conscientious performance of the duty—being at the place of work at the appointed times and carrying out the tasks allotted to the office.[9] The promotion of aptitude in all its branches was central to Bentham's programme of reform: 'The goodness of the government will be as the aptitude of the portions of law enacted by it and the operations performed by it. . . . the aptitude of these same portions of law will be as the appropriate . . . aptitude of the persons bearing part respectively in the enactment of them: the aptitude of the operations will be as the aptitude of the operators.' The quality of what was done depended upon the aptitude of the functionaries responsible for doing it. The greater the aptitude of the functionaries, the better the general interest would be served. The arrangements incorporated into constitutional law in order to promote aptitude were termed securities for appropriate official aptitude. Appropriate meant simply relation to the end: if the greatest happiness were the end, then what was

[6] This was the essay which Bentham began to write upon receiving, on 22 April 1822, an official letter from the Portuguese Cortes accepting his offer to codify (see p. 249 above). It was intended to form an introduction to *Constitutional Code*, though in the event it remained unpublished during Bentham's lifetime.

[7] *First Principles*, 13–15.

[8] Ibid. 77–8.

[9] Ibid. 87–9.

appropriate was so with relation to the greatest happiness. These securities were in effect sanctions which provided motives for self-interested officials to act in the general interest.[10]

The notion of aptitude formed the link between Bentham's psychology and his constitutional theory. In *An Introduction to the Principles of Morals and Legislation* he had remarked that 'the action of a thinking being is the act either of the body, or only of the mind: and an act of the mind is an act either of the intellectual faculty, or of the will'.[11] Active aptitude was a property of the body, while moral aptitude was a property of the will, and intellectual aptitude a property of the intellectual faculty (in other words, the understanding). An action might be motivated by the will alone, or by the understanding through the medium of the will. Where the understanding was concerned in the motivation of an action, the action was likely to produce the desired result in proportion as knowledge was more complete and judgment more profound. Whether the understanding was involved or not, in order for an action to take place, the power to perform the action was necessary as well as the will to perform it: 'As in the case of every other act, so in the case of every act of government: add the power to the will, the act takes place: take away either, the act does not take place.'[12] From this perspective, a person would only possess active aptitude, or manifest the quality of active aptitude, in those instances where there existed such a combination of will and power. Hence, Bentham incorporated a further principle of constitutional design: the officials, or functionaries as he came to term them, had to be granted sufficient power to enable them to perform effectively the tasks, or functions, assigned to them.

II

The whole of Bentham's legal and political thought, underpinned by the principle of utility with its 'real source' in pleasure and pain, culminated in the notion of official aptitude. The notion of aptitude did not, however, appear suddenly in Bentham's thought in a fully developed form. The explicit terminology of aptitude first emerged, as we have seen,[13] in his writings on parliamentary reform of 1809–10. The notion underwent refinement in the material written for Spain in 1820–2, and reached maturity, as noted above, in 'Economy as applied to Office'. Having said that, the substantive content signified by the terminology of aptitude was foreshadowed in the notions of probity and talent which appeared much earlier in his thought, and which he applied in a political context in his writings for the French Revolution.[14] In 'Véracité avec

[10] Ibid. 4–5, 9. [11] *An Introduction to the Principles of Morals and Legislation*, 96.

[12] *First Principles*, 276. [13] See pp. 142–5 above.

[14] M. H. James, 'Bentham's Democratic Theory at the Time of the French Revolution', *The Bentham Newsletter*, 10 (1986), 5–16, at 10–12, attempts to read back the mature notion of

Fidelité', written in the autumn of 1788 with the forthcoming meeting of the Estates-General in mind, Bentham attempted to reconcile the 'fidelity' of the deputy in promoting the interest of his constituents with his 'sincerity' in expressing his genuine opinions by distinguishing between the function of casting a vote and that of presenting an argument. On the one hand, argued Bentham, the deputy should be free, even encouraged, to argue in favour of what he conceived to be the general interest, while on the other hand constrained to vote according to the particular interests of his constituents, in the event of their formally instructing him to do so. There was no need for the deputy's vote to be consistent with his speech: 'Par le premier j'exécute la volonté d'autrui, la volonté de mes commettans: par l'autre je déclare ma propre opinion, je suis, je mets au jour mes propres lumières.' ('By the first I execute the will of others, the will of my constituents: by the other I declare my own opinion, I follow, I bring to light my own understanding.') A declaration taken by the deputy compelling him to prefer the general interest of the nation to the particular interest of his constituents would help to secure his sincerity by encouraging him to present what was truly his own opinion, despite the fact that he might be obliged to vote in accordance with the duly declared will of his constituents. The point of this arrangement was not to ensure that some abstract notion of the general interest prevailed over every particular interest, for the general interest itself was no more than the aggregate of all particular interests, 'ainsi plus les intérêts particuliers sont libres [de] se développer, mieux la décision se trouvera d'accord avec l'intérêt général' ('thus the more that particular interests are free to develop themselves, the more the decision will be in accord with the general interest'). The point was rather to preserve the probity of the deputy, and to prevent his constituents from acting unjustly by removing him because of his probity. His constituents could not but recognize the impediment which the declaration created for the deputy should he attempt to argue in favour of their particular interest: such a course of action would amount to perjury on his part. By his vote, the deputy promoted the particular interest of the constituents who elected him, while by his speech, in which he explained the reasons why he regarded that particular interest as contrary to the general interest, he preserved his sincerity.[15] Probity, then, was linked with a duty to support the general interest, and was secured by protecting the sincerity of the deputy, particularly in those difficult circumstances where he perceived an opposition between the particular interest of his constituents and the general interest.

In relation to the members of a political assembly, argued Bentham in 'Considérations sur la Composition des États-Généraux', not only should they possess the quality of probity, but, more importantly, talent. Probity could easily

aptitude to the French Revolutionary period, but this is to overlook the developments detailed below.

[15] *Rights, Representation, and Reform*, 51–2.

be created by institutional arrangements, for instance in an assembly chosen and removable by the people: 'Établissez entre l'intérêt de l'emploié et son devoir une liaison manifeste et indissoluble, ou il sera vertueux, ou il agira tout de même comme s'il étoit.' ('Establish between the interest of the employee and his duty a clear and indissoluble link, either he will be virtuous, or he will act as if he were.')[16] Talent, in contrast, could not be easily created. In the House of Commons, for instance, probity was far more in evidence than talent. Indeed, the common opinion that probity was all that was required for good government was false: all the harm that arose and all the good that failed to occur was not due to a lack of probity, but to a lack of talent. Much of the talent that did exist was absorbed by the contention between political parties and by the legal profession, so that very little remained for the business of legislation. Bentham condemned an attempt to increase the property qualification for MPs, with the declared intention of increasing the amount of probity, as in effect an attack on talent.[17]

Bentham did not state explicitly what it meant to possess talent, but if his later work on parliamentary reform is any guide, it was related to 'wisdom'. This seems to be confirmed in a passage discussing the requisites for members of a representative assembly, where, instead of probity and talent, he referred to probity and wisdom. The question had arisen as to the number of deputies which the Estates-General should contain. Bentham believed that the general lack of experience on this point meant that any recommendation would be fairly arbitrary. On the one hand, it might be argued that a large assembly would tend to be less subject to the influence of public opinion, since it would form 'une espèce de petit public' ('a sort of little public') of its own, whose opinion would influence the members more than that of the public in general outside the assembly.[18] On the other hand, it might be argued that a larger number of deputies would tend to increase probity, since the less likely it would be that sufficient funds would be available to corrupt them. Bentham dismissed the latter argument. Although a larger number of deputies might act as a counter-force to corruption which had its source in royal or ministerial influence, it would not act in the same way to that which had its source in the interests of a class such as the nobility or clergy: 'Dans le cas de ces classes favorisées, la grande corruption ne vient pas du dehors: c'est un péché originel planté dans le cœur de chacun à l' instant de sa naissance.' ('In the case of these favoured classes, great

[16] Ibid. 91–2.

[17] Ibid. 76–7. In his later writings, far from arguing that there existed an abundance of probity, Bentham concluded that it was precisely probity (or moral aptitude) which was lacking in the House of Commons, not to mention everywhere else in the English establishment: see pp. 280–4 below.

[18] In *Political Tactics*, 30, Bentham made a similar point. Even the most numerous assembly would be unable 'to supply the place of the true public'. An assembly would most frequently be divided into two parties who would not possess, with reference to each other, 'the qualities necessary for properly exercising the function of judges'. In consequence of this lack of impartiality, '[t]he internal censure will not be sufficient to secure probity, without the assistance of external censure'.

corruption does not come from without: it is an original sin planted in the heart of each one at the moment of birth.') On the contrary, in the particular circumstances of France, royal influence might help to secure probity by providing an antidote to this inborn corruption. Yet this did not help the case, for there was little doubt that the lucrative offices at the disposal of the King would easily be sufficient to corrupt the Estates-General. And even if the resources available were not enough to corrupt a majority, they would merely be targeted against the leaders, with the same result. Another argument which might be put forward in favour of a larger number of members, noted Bentham, was that the wisdom of the assembly would be increased. He was similarly unconvinced. First, each member's opinions would become less influential as the number of members increased, hence the motives encouraging him to display his intellectual qualities would be diminished proportionately. Second, the likely existence of such qualities would be in direct proportion to the number of proposers and pleaders, and not judges—in other words, to the number of those capable of putting forward opinions and reasons, and not to the number of those with the formal right to vote. The first group should be unlimited in number, comprising not only all the inhabitants of France who wished to contribute, but all inhabitants of the civilized world. There were cases in which an increase in members might produce a greater degree of wisdom—for instance in secret assemblies, or in a time of ignorance, such as in ancient Athens or Rome, where writing was rare and printing unknown—but these were quite different from the case of the Estates-General.[19]

While Bentham remained uncommitted with regard to the ideal number of members in the instance of the Estates-General, in the more abstract discussion in *Political Tactics* he declared himself in favour of a larger rather than a smaller number of deputies. Given that 'legislative functions demand qualities and virtues which are not common'—echoing his plaints on the rarity of talent—they would be found only in a large assembly. Furthermore, the local knowledge necessary for legislation would likewise be obtained only 'in a numerous body of deputies chosen from all parts of the empire'. A small legislative assembly would easily be subjected to the influence of the executive, and introduce laws opposed to the general interest, whereas a larger assembly subject to periodical election would 'participate too strongly in the interest of the community to neglect it long. Oppressive laws would press upon themselves.' If the number of deputies were too small, 'the extent of the electoral district would render the elections embarrassing', and the value of the franchise would be reduced almost to nothing

[19] *Rights, Representation, and Reform*, 119–23. The importance of publicity as a means of providing the best information to legislators, and thus ensuring their access to 'all the national intelligence', especially in the light of the fact that Locke, Newton, Hume, Smith, 'and many other men of genius, never had a seat in parliament', is emphasized at *Political Tactics*, 33–4. Moreover, one of the reasons why any member, and not just the executive, should enjoy the right to propose motions to the assembly was, 'That the intelligence of the whole assembly may be improved for the general good': see ibid. 110.

at the same time that the relative value of being elected would be increased to the extent that elections would be exposed 'to the most violent contests and intrigues'.[20] The whole point of political tactics—the arrangements which should govern a political assembly, including the number of deputies—was 'the prevention of everything which might prevent the development of [the deputies'] liberty and their intelligence'.[21] And again: 'The more nearly [a system of tactics] approaches perfection, the more completely will it facilitate to all the co-operators the exercise of their intelligence and the enjoyment of their liberty.'[22] In this context, the notion of 'liberty' appears to be closely linked to that of probity, for what Bentham presumably had in mind was the liberty of deputies to decide for themselves, and liberty from subjection to the will of the executive. Moreover, Bentham referred explicitly both to probity and intelligence when discussing the qualities desirable in electors: 'The conditions required to constitute an elector, have for their object the exclusion from political power those who are considered incapable of exercising this power with intelligence or probity;—they are precautions against venality, ignorance, and intrigue.'[23]

Bentham had, therefore, in his writings for France in 1788–9 identified probity (the desire to promote the interest of the community) and talent (the possession of intelligence or wisdom) as requisites for members of a legislative assembly and, in a more limited degree, for electors. Bentham reiterated this point in relation to governors generally when he criticized the doctrine of the division of power in the autumn of 1789.[24] The advantage of the structure of government he recommended as an alternative to the division of power was that it would produce the qualities in governors which were necessary for good government:

> The accomplishment of good government, like the accomplishment of any other object to be accomplished by human faculties, depends upon the concurrence of the three requisites of intelligence, power and inclination. Government will be good in proportion as those who stand invested with the power possess inclination to render it so, and in addition the measure of intelligence to that purpose.
>
> The degree of inclination will be in exact proportion to the dependence of the governors on the governed: to the dependence of the persons intrusted with the power, on the persons by whose obedience the power is constituted: to the dependence of men in power on the body of the people: of those who exercise power on those on whom it is exercised. In as far as a man who has power is independent, his inclination will be [to] make use of it for his own benefit: in as far as he is dependent upon any one, he will find himself obliged to employ it for the benefit of him on whom he depends. In this there is no jargon, no obscurity. It is founded on the universal, necessary, undisputed and not even to be lamented, property in human nature—the predominance of self-regarding affections over the social. It is understood at once: and to him who once understands it, it can not be easy to avoid assenting to it.

[20] Ibid. 16 n. [21] Ibid. 15. [22] Ibid. 20. [23] Ibid.
[24] See pp. 232–7 above.

The inclination in question was precisely what Bentham referred to in his writings for France as probity and in later writings as moral aptitude, while intelligence was the equivalent of the later notion of intellectual aptitude. The possession of power, however, was not the equivalent of the later notion of active aptitude, though power was, of course, a prerequisite to any activity.[25] Again, anticipating what he would later say concerning the relationship between moral and intellectual aptitude,[26] he pointed out that 'inclination' was of greater importance than intelligence, for where it was lacking, the more intelligent the governors, the better able they would be to promote their own happiness to the detriment of the happiness of those subject to them. A division of power could promote inclination and intelligence only by accident. Where governors disagreed amongst themselves and, as a result, appealed to the people, the division of power might contribute to the inclination of governing well by making the governors in some degree dependent on the support of the people. Once the disagreement was resolved, the appeal to the people was ended, and the dependence and inclination disappeared. As to intelligence, there was no doubt that 'discussion and debate is favourable and that in the highest degree to intelligence', and to the extent that a division of power chanced to produce discussion and debate, it might be productive of intelligence. Yet a division of power on the one hand, and discussion and debate on the other, were capable of existing independently of each other. Moreover, in 'its natural effect . . . division of power is more favourable to ignorance than to intelligence'. In Britain, for instance, the arguments brought forward in support of a measure in one of the Houses of Parliament were not heard in the other, with the result that 'many a good law' was lost. The systematic means of securing good government—and that meant securing probity and talent in governors—was not through the division of power, but through the strict dependence of the governors on the governed.[27]

III

By the time that Bentham began writing on parliamentary reform in 1809–10, the notions of probity or inclination and of talent or intelligence had been incorporated into the notion of official aptitude, which was divided into three elements—appropriate probity, appropriate intellectual aptitude, and appropriate active talent.[28] The promotion of official aptitude was presented as the

[25] It is worth noting that in a related fragment (*Rights, Representation, and Reform*, 422) Bentham spoke of 'a relish for the function', a phrase he later used to characterize a quality which formed a significant component of active aptitude (see pp. 299–300 below). There are hints of the same idea at *Political Tactics*, 58: 'though inclination for an employment does not prove talent for its discharge, there is no better pledge of aptitude for the labour than the pleasure which accompanies it'.

[26] See p. 298 below.

[27] *Rights, Representation, and Reform*, 414–18.

[28] See Bowring, iii. 454, 539, 566, and p. 142 above.

antidote to sinister interest, the main source of misrule. Bentham asserted that 'the result of appropriate aptitude in all shapes on the part of the functionary' was '*good behaviour*',[29] and good behaviour meant acting in accordance with the principle of utility.[30] It will be recalled that *Plan of Parliamentary Reform*, published in 1817, consisted in a 'Catechism' written in 1809–10, and an 'Introduction' written in 1816–17. Bentham then went on to publish *Bentham's Radical Reform Bill* in 1819. In these works there is only one systematic consideration, and that a brief one, of official aptitude. This appears near the beginning of the 'Catechism', where Bentham noted that one of the ends of a parliamentary representation was '[s]ecuring, in the highest possible degree, on the part of members . . . the several *endowments* or *elements of aptitude*, necessary to fit them for the due discharge of such their trust'.[31] He continued:

> appropriate probity consists in [the representative's] pursuing that line of conduct, which, in his own sincere opinion, being not inconsistent with the rules of morality or the law of the land, is most conducive to the general good of the whole community for which he serves; that is to say, of the whole of the British empire:—forbearing, on each occasion, at the expense either of such general good, or of his duty in any shape, either to accept, or to seek to obtain, or preserve, in any shape whatsoever, for himself, or for any person or persons particularly connected with him, any advantage whatsoever, from whatsoever hands obtainable

—and in particular from the King and his ministers. Thus, an official who possessed probity would attempt to pursue the greatest happiness of the greatest number, and would be prepared to resist any attempt to corrupt him into pursuing a different course. Intellectual aptitude consisted in the ability of the representative to form

> a right judgment on the several propositions, which . . . are liable to come before him: and, to that end . . . forming a right conception, as well of the nature of each proposition, considered in itself, as of the *evidence* adduced or capable of being adduced, whether in support of it or in opposition to it, and the observations thereon made, or capable of being made, in the way of *argument for* it or *against* it . . . .

Intellectual aptitude, therefore, was concerned with the cultivation of the understanding, which Bentham divided into knowledge and judgment. Finally, active talent consisted in the possession of the '[t]alents suited to the due performance of the several *operations* which, in the course of his service, . . . it may happen to a member [of the House of Commons] to be duly called upon to perform, or bear a part in'. These 'operations' might include introducing a law, delivering a speech, proposing an amendment, writing a report, or chairing a committee.[32] If intellectual aptitude was concerned with the understanding as such, then it seems that active talent was concerned with the practical application

[29] Ibid. 513. [30] Ibid. 535–6.

[31] The two other ends identified were concerned with elections and election procedure: see p. 141 above.

[32] Bowring, iii. 539–40.

of knowledge and judgment:[33] a distinction which corresponded, to some degree at least, to that between science and art.[34]

While the published writings on parliamentary reform contain no other systematic account of the branches of aptitude, they do contain a number of scattered references. These, together with discussions in related unpublished manuscripts, help to elucidate Bentham's thinking. The central problem in the British political system, according to Bentham, was the sinister interest of MPs—their independence towards the people and their dependence on the Crown. MPs' subservience to the will of the monarch, rather than to the will of the people, had resulted from their having become 'obsequious to the influence of the matter of corruption', which amounted to 'a deficiency in the element of appropriate probity'.[35] The existence of probity was of little value unless it was accompanied with action: 'Be the place what it will, in which, if at all, the function, be it what it may, must be performed,—that function cannot be performed by a man who is not *there*. A maxim to this effect seems not to be very open to dispute.' Hence the importance of securing the constant attendance of all members in the House of Commons:

> And thus it appears, that, after everything which, for the securing of probity—appropriate probity—in the breasts of the individual members, each in his separate capacity, against the assaults of corruptive influence, can be done, has been done,—*universal constancy of attendance* remains, in the character of a supplement, necessary to the securing, on the part of the aggregate body, the same indispensable element of official aptitude.[36]

Bentham recognized that a complex interrelationship existed between the various elements of aptitude. In a manuscript written in 1809, dealing with the probity and intelligence required in the electorate, he put forward two extreme cases:

> Take of probity the utmost quantity ever known to be exemplified, with the least possible quantity of intelligence: all security would vanish presently. Take of intelligence the utmost known quantity, with the least known quantity of probity, people will not be so happy as under favour of a greater share of probity they would be, but the state will at the worst keep together, and individual security, howsoever pared away in this and that part, is in no danger of being destroyed.[37]

In other words, the worst possible case would occur when there was no intellectual aptitude whatsoever, since the state itself could not survive. Bentham was worried that a franchise which was too extensive might include a large number of people who were deficient in intelligence. A balance had to be struck between a franchise extensive enough 'to embrace all the different interests of the country in such sort as to preserve the interest of the majority, if not from being at any time sacrificed to that of the minority, at any rate from continuing so to be for any

[33] Bentham referred to 'the connected qualifications of appropriate intellectual aptitude, and appropriate active talent': see ibid. 506, and also 497.

[34] See p. 10 above.

[35] Bowring, iii. 455.

[36] Ibid. 457.

[37] UC cxxvii. 182 (14 Aug. 1809).

considerable length of time', and yet intelligent enough for electors to be capable of recognizing their true interest.

But if [. . . ?] for want of understanding what in matters of government his true interest is, each man, by the influence of some cause of deception, home-bred or imported, and thus the whole together, join in compelling the adoption of this or that measure prejudicial to the interest of the whole, here for want of due intelligence, the result may be some course of national conduct productive of effects more disastrous than any deficiency in the mere article of probity could have produced.[38]

For instance, the improbity of the legal profession had rendered justice inaccessible to the great body of the people. The abuse would not be remedied while the people were excluded from the franchise, but to admit them would result in the destruction of the lawyers in the same way that the two privileged orders of clergy and nobility had been destroyed in France at the time of the Revolution. The people would be pursuing the object demanded by probity in ridding themselves of the oppression, '[b]ut by employing, for want of due intelligence, for the effectuation of it such violent and unnecessarily destructive means, the mischief produced in and to the whole community would be far [from] preponderant over the good'.[39]

In 1809, as we have seen,[40] Bentham recommended householder suffrage, but by 1816–17 he had come to advocate virtually universal suffrage. His reasons for doing this were related to a change in his assessment of the danger to property which might result from such a franchise,[41] but also of the relative degree of intellectual aptitude possessed by the people of Britain. All three elements of appropriate aptitude were required to secure good behaviour on the part of an official: 'Only in so far as these two *intellectual* endowments [i.e. intellectual aptitude and active talent] are in the same breast united to the one moral one—only in so far as they are united to *appropriate probity*—will the *universal interest* receive from them any net benefit:—only on the terms of this auspicious union, will it so much as escape the being sacrificed.'[42] An abundance of active talent might in certain circumstances be not only not beneficial but positively harmful—an excessive desire to make speeches or write reports might give rise to a waste of 'disposable official time'. But no waste of time, or any other inconvenience, would be produced by an abundance of intellectual aptitude, while a lack of intellectual aptitude was only a '*theoretical*', and not a '*real*', inconvenience, providing the representatives, for whatever reason, voted on the right side.[43]

In manuscripts written in 1818 Bentham stressed more forcibly the view that the possession of intellectual aptitude was only subservient to the general interest insofar as it was accompanied with 'appropriate moral aptitude, appropriate

[38] UC cxxvii. 185 (25 Aug. 1809). [39] UC cxxvii. 186 (25 Aug. 1809).
[40] See p. 145 above. [41] See pp. 168–9 above. [42] Bowring, iii. 498.
[43] Ibid. 523 n.

probity, in the same breast', and that where a group of men were intent only on advancing their own interest, then 'the more strong, extensive and efficient their intellectual power, so far from promoting, they will disserve and injure the universal interest: they will render the sacrifice of it to their own narrower and sinister interest more easy, more extensive, more effectual'. Appropriate probity would not be found in a monarchy or aristocracy, whereas in 'a representative Commonwealth' it would increase in proportion to the extension of the franchise. Even if a representative democracy were significantly inferior to a monarchy and aristocracy in respect of intellectual aptitude, so far from being superior in respect of the aggregate of appropriate aptitude, the monarchy and aristocracy would possess none: 'the greater the quantity of intellectual power, the worse in all points in which the particular and universal interest were at variance—the worse the government'. Bentham believed that there were no grounds for supposing that a House of Commons elected by universal suffrage would in fact be inferior in intellectual aptitude to the House of Commons elected under the unreformed suffrage.[44] When Bentham in 1818, as he had in 1809, considered the balance between probity and intellectual aptitude, he no longer thought it reasonable to suppose that in practice an electorate based on the principle of virtually universal suffrage would be inferior in aptitude to the existing electorate. He admitted that, from a theoretical point of view, a case might be supposed in which one set of electors, who were superior in probity to a second set, were so deficient in intellectual aptitude that they would be inferior in respect of aggregate aptitude. Even if rulers were completely deficient in probity, it might be argued that it was better that there was bad government rather than no government at all. Another case might be supposed in which a more numerous set of electors, who, while not totally deficient in respect of intellectual aptitude, were superior in point of probity, would be inferior in aggregate aptitude to a less numerous set, who, though inferior in probity, were superior in intellectual aptitude. While not ruling out the theoretical possibility, it was Bentham's opinion that, in relation to his proposal to extend the franchise in Britain, the new electors would not be inferior, or so far inferior, to the existing electors that the reform would produce an overall diminution in aggregate aptitude.[45] The debate in Bentham's own mind as to whether probity or intelligence was the more important in terms of the promotion of the general happiness had been resolved in favour of the former.

IV

There is a sense in which the concept of aptitude moved from the periphery of Bentham's political thought to the very centre. In his parliamentary reform

[44] UC cxxvii. 458–60 (2 Sept. 1818). [45] UC cxxvii. 513–14 (26 Sept. 1818).

writings, Bentham's focus was on specific measures, such as reform of the electoral system, the exclusion of placemen, and the constant attendance of MPs, which would establish democratic ascendancy in Britain. In his constitutional code—which represented a move away from a consideration of the particular measures of reform desirable in the British House of Commons to a more general concern with the ideal principles and institutions of constitutional government—the securing of official aptitude was declared to be the very point of the arrangements of constitutional law. This greater emphasis on official aptitude was already evident in manuscripts written in the summer of 1820 for Spain on the subject of corruption and corruptive influence, where Bentham outlined the general theory of constitutional law which would afterwards be fully articulated in the writings for his constitutional code. The proper end of government was the greatest happiness of the greatest number; if the interests of rulers and subjects were in opposition, it was due to the natural predominance of self-interest in rulers; in order to bring the interest of rulers into coincidence with the interest of subjects, rulers had to be made dependent on subjects; in order to bring about such dependence, legislators were to be elected by the people; they were to be made legally punishable in the event of any breach of trust, but at the same time secured against any form of coercion or corruptive influence which might lead them into such a breach of trust; their pay was to be minimized; and their power was to be divided by having it exercised by a body acting by majority.[46] In another passage, he argued that the sole remedy to corruption was a representative democracy in which the legislators or the people could remove the administrators, and the people could remove the legislators. Furthermore, the value of lucrative offices had to be minimized, firstly by the annexation of a competent salary, and secondly by its sale through auction.[47] The point of these measures was to produce—to create securities for—official aptitude.[48] Having listed a series of measures intended to achieve this purpose which might be adopted in a government which contained a monarchy or an aristocracy, he noted:

> In relation to the functions of an office, all aptitude may be reduced to one or other of two modes: appropriate moral aptitude, and appropriate intellectual aptitude.
>
> Of moral aptitude, the most conspicuous and important mode or shape is *pecuniary trustworthiness*. A deficiency of it, manifested by an act of unlawful appropriation, is termed *peculation*, and is proved by, and in proportion to, the quantity of unallowed pecuniary emolument, which, by the powers or other means attached to the office, he contrives to possess himself.

Bentham suggested two securities for pecuniary trustworthiness: first, the provision of bondsmen for the monies in the possession of the functionary; and

[46] UC clxiv. 142–8 (3–4, 8 July 1820). [47] UC clxiv. 164 (20 June 1820).

[48] Bentham at some point coined the phrase 'securities for official aptitude', but probably not before 1822. Its appearance as a title at UC clxiv. 265 (22 Aug. 1820) was added when Bentham surveyed the manuscripts in 1822.

second, the reducing to a minimum the quantity of money in his hands.[49] There are a number of points to note here. First, the term 'moral probity' was in the process of being replaced with the term 'moral aptitude'. Second, moral aptitude was not concerned with the prevention of corruption in general, but merely with the prevention of one sort of corruption, that of financial irregularity, and at first glance appears to represent a narrowing of its content. However, it should be remembered that Bentham was here suggesting measures which might be introduced under a monarchy or an aristocracy, and applicable to the specific circumstances of officials in the administrative department of government. Third—and it is worth re-emphasizing—Bentham was discussing specific measures which would secure the aptitude of officials: his constitutional theory was firmly focused on the qualities possessed by the individuals who held offices of public trust, and only on the institutional structure of government to the extent that the institutions in question were themselves contributory to the production of the qualities in question, in other words, to the production of official aptitude. As for the remaining branches of aptitude, Bentham remarked that while he had sometimes treated active talent as distinct, in the case of officials it was included under the notion of intellectual aptitude, which could be secured only by public examination.[50] The use of examination as a security for intellectual aptitude had not featured in the parliamentary reform writings, but was a provision which Bentham elaborated in great detail for his constitutional code.[51]

In his other writings from this period on Spain and her colonies, Bentham made a number of passing references to aptitude and inaptitude, but did not develop the notion any further. For instance, in May 1820 he discussed the impact which the provision in the Spanish Constitution (Art. 110), rendering any member who had sat in the first Cortes elected in 1820 ineligible for the second due to meet in 1822, would have on the active talent of the members. Even though at first glance it appeared to be a mistake to exclude from an inexperienced assembly the benefit of what little experience did exist, the Cortes would be able to draw on the active talent of the administration which would remain in place, as well as seek the advice of the influential members of the preceding Cortes. No assistance could reasonably be expected from those members 'by whom nothing had been done to distinguish themselves—by whom no appropriate active talent had been manifested—by whom, in so far as depended upon such active talent, no influence had been obtained', so their being ineligible would be no loss.[52] In July 1820 Bentham discussed the admission of deputies from the Spanish overseas possessions into the Cortes in terms of their moral aptitude (he was at this time using the terms 'moral aptitude' and 'probity' interchangeably) and intellectual aptitude. There was no

[49] UC clxiv. 265 (22 Aug. 1820). [50] UC clxiv. 267 (22 Aug. 1820).

[51] See *Constitutional Code*, I. 310–37.

[52] *Colonies, Commerce, and Constitutional Law*, 268–9.

advantage to the Spanish people in having overseas representatives in the Cortes. The Spanish members themselves, 'in whatsoever degree be their moral aptitude', would at least have some local knowledge of their districts, and in comparison to members from overseas be 'in a greater or less degree . . . fit in respect of intellectual aptitude'. In relation to appropriate moral aptitude, the Spanish American members of the Cortes would become 'the creatures and instruments' of the executive.[53]

The earliest division of aptitude into the three branches, with the use of the corresponding terminology, of moral, intellectual, and active aptitude appears to be in a passage originally written in January 1821 for an appendix to 'Rid Yourselves of Ultramaria', and published in March 1821 in *Observations on the Restrictive and Prohibitory Commercial System*. This pamphlet, prepared for the press by Bowring, was described by Bentham as 'a partnership squib of Bowring's and mine'.[54] The original manuscripts for Bentham's draft reveal that Bowring took considerable liberties with the text, not only adding substantial passages of his own, but making significant emendations to Bentham's prose. The printed text, therefore, cannot be relied upon as a faithful rendition of Bentham's own words.[55] The original manuscript of the passage in which the three branches of aptitude are mentioned reads as follows:

> in a general point of view, extent and duration considered together, the prosperity of every branch of profit-seeking industry will encrease and decrease in the ratio of the degree of aptitude, in all elements of appropriate aptitude, moral, intellectual, and active taken together, of the persons engaged in it: on the degree, absolute and comparative, of prudence, vigilance, exertion, appropriate information and active talent possessed by them.[56]

In a second passage, for which the original manuscript does not appear to have survived, Bentham argued that the mischievous policy of commercial bounties owed its existence '[t]o the general causes of misrule; to the want of the necessary elements of good government; to a deficiency of appropriate probity, or intellectual aptitude, or active talent: in other words, to a want of honesty, or ability, or industry'.[57] By January 1821, therefore, Bentham had not yet settled decisively on the terminology for the branches of official aptitude which he would employ in April 1822 when he began work on 'Economy as applied to Office'. Nevertheless, the writings for Spain and Spanish America, dominated as they

[53] Ibid. 330–1.

[54] Bentham to Samuel Bentham, 28–30 Mar. 1821, *Correspondence*, x. 319.

[55] See *Colonies, Commerce, and Constitutional Law*, Editorial Introduction, pp. xlii–xliii.

[56] UC xxxvi. 139^{v}. The equivalent passage in the published text (see *Colonies, Commerce, and Constitutional Law*, 370) reads as follows: 'the general principle may be safely assumed and laid down, that the prosperity of every branch of industry will increase and decrease in the ratio of the degree of aptitude—of moral, intellectual, and active aptitude—on the part of the persons engaged in it; on the degree, absolute and comparative, of prudence, vigilance, exertion, appropriate information, and industrious talent, possessed by them.'

[57] *Colonies, Commerce, and Constitutional Law*, 377–8.

were by constitutional themes, represented a transition from the language of probity, intellectual aptitude, and active talent, to that of moral, intellectual, and active aptitude. While moral aptitude was the equivalent of probity, the change from active talent to active aptitude did involve a change of content, and in particular a division of the notion of active talent. In the writings for constitutional code, intellectual aptitude referred to the possession of knowledge and judgment, whereas active aptitude referred simply to the performance of action. The notion of active aptitude did not imply any particular form of action (such as introducing a law, delivering a speech, and so on), unlike the notion of active talent. In short, the expertise and skill associated with active talent was incorporated into intellectual aptitude, while what remained—the idea of performance—was captured in the revised notion of active aptitude.

V

Bentham's main concern in 'Economy as applied to Office', written in the spring and summer of 1822, was to produce a detailed and systematic account of official aptitude, which he divided into moral, intellectual, and active branches, and to show how the securing of official aptitude, and particularly moral aptitude, was related to the identification of interests. In short, the identification of interests described the situation which existed when the interest of an individual (or of the members of a group) coincided with that of the community as a whole, while moral aptitude was a quality possessed in that situation by that individual (or by the members of that group)—namely the desire to promote the interest of the community as a whole. To say that an identification of interests existed between an individual and the community was as much as to say that he possessed moral aptitude: 'As between each individual and the whole community, identification of interests has place, in so far as when in consequence of any act on his part, or any other event or state of things, good in any shape happens to him, good in the same or any other shape happens to the whole community; or in so far as evil happens, evil . . . .'[58] In the case of officials, where an identification of interests was absent, there was also an absence of moral aptitude, resulting in the sinister sacrifice: 'In so far as, in the instance of the functionary in question . . . identification fails to have place, the consequence is—on his part, in so far as depends on his endeavours, the sacrifice of the universal interest to his personal or other particular interest: say, for shortness, *the sinister sacrifice*.'[59] Securing the identification of interests, and thus the quality of moral aptitude in rulers, was at the very centre of the legislative arrangements recommended by Bentham:

By moral aptitude is . . . meant but practical innoxiousness; and such innoxiousness not having any other cause than impotence, in the station of each functionary to establish this

[58] *First Principles*, 125. [59] Ibid. 17.

impotence, leaving to him at the same time the necessary power—to render him unable to do wrong, yet sufficiently able to do right, is the great difficulty, and ought to be the constant object and endeavour of whatsoever labour is employed in the field of legislation.[60]

Bentham commenced 'Economy as applied to Office' by explaining the nature of government in terms of the powers of which it was composed, drawing on ideas which, as we have seen,[61] he had developed in the late 1770s and early 1780s:

Considered in respect of the nature of its functions, all power in Government is either *operative* or *constitutive*.

Operative power is that in the exercise of which the business [is] done: *Constitutive power* is that by the exercise of which it is determined who the person or persons are by whom the operative power shall be exercised. Constitutive is therefore such with relation to the operative.

Considering its rank in the scale of subordination, all power is either supreme or subordinate.

Bentham then divided supreme operative power into supreme legislative power and supreme executive power, with the latter subordinate to the former. The supreme legislative power was 'the power of imposing upon persons of all classes, obligations of all sorts, for purposes of all sorts, and with reference to things of all sorts: obligations such as are not capable of being annulled or varied by any other power in the State'. The supreme executive power was itself divided into administrative and judicial powers, exercised by the administrative and judicial departments, respectively. It was the function of both departments to apply the general rules sanctioned by the legislature to the particular persons and things to which they were intended to apply. The administrative department had a more particular function of disposing of the resources specially allocated to it for the use of the state itself, while the judicial department only applied the general rules in those instances where there had arisen 'a contest between two or more parties in respect to the point of right', and appeal had been made to specified legal procedures.[62] In a representative democracy, the electorate formed the constitutive power, and was superordinate in relation to the operative power, which included at its apex the legislative power. In *Constitutional Code*, as we have seen,[63] Bentham announced that '[t]he sovereignty is in *the people*. It is reserved by and to them. It is exercised, by the exercise of the Constitutive authority.'[64] While there was no substantive change in Bentham's theory of law between the earlier and later period, there was a change in terminology.[65] The investitive (or

60 Ibid. 15. 61 See pp. 223–7 above. 62 *First Principles*, 6–7.

63 See p. 262 above. 64 *Constitutional Code*, I. 25.

65 As Postema, *Bentham and the Common Law Tradition*, 260–2, points out, there seems little reason to accept Hart's view that Bentham's discussion of sovereignty and legally limited government in *Constitutional Code* involved 'a quite different theory of law' from that put forward in the late 1770s and early 1780s (see *Essays on Bentham*, 228–9), insofar as the content, rather than the terminology, of Bentham's theory of law is concerned. The difficulty for the 'continuity'

originative) and divestitive power had been renamed the constitutive power, while the legislature, executive, and judiciary together had become the operative power. Moreover, sovereignty, in the context of a representative democracy, was ascribed to the constitutive power: it was towards the people themselves that the disposition to obey would be directed. In *Constitutional Code* the legislature (or more precisely the supreme legislature, since Bentham allowed for local or sub-legislatures), instead of being sovereign, was said to be 'omnicompetent': 'Coextensive with the territory of the state is its local field of service; coextensive with the field of human action is its logical field of service.—To its power, there are no limits. In place of limits, it has checks. These checks are applied, by the securities, provided for good conduct on the part of the several members, individually operated upon . . . .' These checks were the securities for appropriate aptitude.[66]

Bentham recognized that the establishment of good government required the identification of the interests of two different sets of functionaries with the universal interest: in the first place, the interest of the supreme constitutive functionaries; and in the second place, the interest of the supreme operative functionaries, and in particular that of the legislators. Bentham's strategy, of course, was to place the constitutive power in the hands of those whose interest constituted the universal interest, and then to make the operative power subordinate to the constitutive power. The constitutive power, noted Bentham, 'can not be placed in any other set of individuals so aptly as in that set of individuals of the aggregate of whose several individual interests the universal interest is constituted'—in other words, it should be vested in the whole number of the members of the community, hence universal suffrage.[67] In this case the constitutive functionaries could not but possess moral aptitude, for their interest was the universal interest: to say that each member of the community, as a constitutive functionary, pursued his self-interest was merely another way of saying that the community as a whole pursued the universal interest.

interpretation is Bentham's statement that law was the product of the will of 'the *sovereign* in a state' (see *Of Laws in General*, 1). This might be taken to imply that in his early writings he assumed that the sovereign in a state was necessarily the legislator, and that to deny this, as he did in *Constitutional Code*, was indeed to put forward a different theory of law. He had, however, elsewhere in his early writings allowed for the possibility, for instance, that the executive or some combination of the legislature and judiciary might be sovereign (see pp. 229–30 above). He had, moreover, explained that legislative power might itself be supreme or subordinate: hence law might be the product of a subordinate legislature, which was not, by definition, 'the *sovereign* in a state' (see p. 225 above). Indeed, Bentham's fundamental point seems to have been that there was no predefined location for the sovereign power in a state—the sovereign was determined by the particular direction taken by the disposition to obey.

[66] *Constitutional Code*, I. 41–2.

[67] *First Principles*, 132–3. Cf. ibid. 71–3, where Bentham explained how the self-interest of each member of the 'subject many' naturally coincided with the universal interest, whereas that of the 'ruling few' naturally opposed it.

In relation to the operative power, the interests to be identified were those of rulers with those of subjects—in other words those of the supreme operative functionaries with those of the whole community. The problem arose, of course, from the self-preference inherent in human nature, which meant that, 'the particular interest of the ruling class is in a state of natural and diametrical opposition to that of the whole people considered in the correspondent character of subjects'.[68] The opposition of interests was manifested in political corruption, or the sinister sacrifice, which was the preference given to a particular interest to the detriment of a more general interest—in other words the promotion of the happiness of the few to the detriment of the happiness of the many. The process of corruption required the co-operation of two parties, the corrupter and the corruptee. The corruptee performed some act which benefited the corrupter, and in return received some reward (a bribe). There was no need for any explicit agreement or even communication between the two parties, merely two regular and known lines of conduct. The process was analogous to what took place in the instance of a householder, the householder's cat, and the cat's-meat barrow-woman. The cat, upon seeing the barrow-woman, knew that if he presented himself he would receive his dinner, paid for by the householder, despite never having entered into any agreement to that effect. In a state which contained a representative body, corruption might likewise be carried on without any explicit agreement or any explicit act, being instead a routine product of the constitutional arrangements there established—it was endemic to the system. The monarch, if the government were a mixed monarchy, would have offices and honours at his disposal which he might bestow on representatives in the legislative body; in order to receive these offices and honours, representatives would help to promote the interest of the monarch. No law was broken, yet political corruption took place. The sufferers were the subjects who in the end had to pay both for the offices which the monarch distributed as bribes and for the benefits bestowed in return on the monarch by the representatives. Though a representative democracy, like a mixed monarchy, contained a representative body which was equally liable to corruption, in this case by the president, the difference was that in the representative democracy effective securities against corruption were capable of being instituted. The crucial point was to render the legislature subject to the will of the electorate, in other words to make the deputies dependent on their constituents. If it was the will of the electorate that there should be no political corruption, such would be the will of the legislature.[69]

[68] Ibid. 16.

[69] Ibid. 19–26. Bentham preferred the term 'deputy' to 'representative': see *Constitutional Code*, I. 30–1n. The idea of a 'representative' was more ambiguous, and was often taken to imply that the representative should decide questions according to his own conscience, rather than following any 'instructions' which might be issued by his constituents. For the wider debate on this question see P. Kelly, 'Constituents' Instructions to Members of Parliament in the Eighteenth Century', in

The framework of representative democracy, by giving effective power to the will of the people, ensured that government officials would be motivated by the desire to promote the universal interest. The way in which Bentham envisaged that a truly representative system would translate the votes of individual constituents into a government dedicated to promoting the universal interest was as follows. The universal interest was the aggregate of all the individual interests in the community. The secret ballot allowed each individual to vote for the candidate he considered the most likely to promote his own self-interest. The candidate elected would be the one who most successfully appealed to the interests of the greatest number of individuals in his electoral district. In the legislative body, the deputy would genuinely seek to promote the general interest of his constituents, for he knew that if they came to believe he was not acting in their interest, they would remove him from office, or refuse to re-elect him at the next annual election, or even subject him to judicially administered punishment. Different sets of constituents might have different interests, but with each deputy voting according to the will of his respective constituents, the interest of the majority—the interest which, it had to be assumed, constituted the universal interest—would on each occasion prevail. The legislature was subject to the people, while the executive departments of government (the administration and judiciary) would be subject to the legislature. The rulers, with their particular interests, were made subject to the people, whose interests composed the universal interest: rulers could only promote their own individual interests through the share they had in the universal interest.[70]

A relationship of subordination existed when one individual had an 'adequate inducement' to submit his will to that of another, and make his conduct conform to that will: the superior was the superordinate, and the inferior the subordinate. Bentham identified three means by which one official might be rendered subordinate to another: first, subordination by dislocability, where the subordinate could be removed from his office at the command of the superordinate; second, subordination by declared punibility, where the subordinate was liable to be subjected to legal punishment by the superordinate; and third, subordination by undeclared punibility, where the subordinate was liable to be vexed—made to suffer in some way other than through due legal process—by the superordinate, with the result that the subordinate would prefer to resign the office rather than continue to suffer the vexation. In order for the subordination to be complete, the superordinate needed to be able both to dismiss the subordinate functionary from office and to subject him to legal punishment.[71] As

C. Jones (ed.), *Party and Management in Parliament, 1660–1784* (Leicester, 1984), 169–89. At the time of the French Revolution, Bentham had attempted to resolve the dilemma by distinguishing between the functions of debating and of voting: see p. 276 above.

[70] *First Principles*, 30–5, 135–6.

[71] Ibid. 8–9; see also *Constitutional Code*, I. 203. This analysis echoes that in *An Introduction to the Principles of Morals and Legislation*, 263–4 n., reproduced at p. 224 above.

well as being liable to dislocation by his superordinate, each functionary would be subject to legal responsibility—that is liable for trial and, if convicted, punished for any misdeed he might have committed. The combination of dislocation and punibility ensured the effectiveness of the subordination. It was because of the danger posed to the maintenance of the subordination of the legislature to the constitutive power that Bentham opposed the institution of a monarch or a second chamber of peers, or even of a second chamber of elected representatives.[72]

The structure of a representative democracy permitted the powers which it was necessary for government to exercise to be placed in appropriate relationships of superordination and subordination. The legislative power was supreme in relation to the administrative and judicial powers, which together formed the executive power. The legislative and executive powers together formed the operative power, by the exercise of which the business of government was carried on. The persons responsible for the exercise of the operative power was determined by the exercise of the constitutive power.

Thus we have already a chain of political subordination consisting of three links. [1.] Link the first or basis of the whole, the all-embracing constitutive power: subordinate to none; 2. link the second, the legislative or supreme legislative power: subordinate to the constitutive power and to that alone; 3. link the third, the supreme Executive power: subordinate to the legislative or supreme power, and thence to the supreme [constitutive] power, but not to any other: subordinate to the legislative to the end that it thus may be so to the all-embracing constitutive power, and not for any other purpose, for the sake of any other end.[73]

Of the two branches of the executive power, the administrative department would be headed by the Prime Minister, and the Judicial Department by the Justice Minister. The chains of subordination continued within each of these Departments. In the Administrative Department, for instance, the Ministers would be subordinate to the Prime Minister, and the functionaries within each Subdepartment (as Bentham termed the individual ministries) to the respective Minister. The application of the 'responsible-location-principle', whereby the subordinate official was 'located' by an 'effectually responsible superordinate',[74] meant that each and every official belonged to a clear and determinate chain of subordination. Hence the principle of subordination characterized not only the relationship between the electorate and legislature, but reached down through all the apparatus of government.

The chains of subordination had to be both brought into existence and made effective, which was the specific task of the securities for moral aptitude. In 'Economy as applied to Office', Bentham discussed six such securities, four of

[72] *First Principles*, 101–12. [73] *Securities against Misrule*, 269.
[74] *Constitutional Code*, I. 23.

which he termed *direct*, acting on the power of the functionary (albeit leaving him sufficient power to accomplish the functions assigned to him), and two of which he termed *indirect*, acting against the desire or the will of the functionary, to perform the sinister sacrifice.[75] The four securities which diminished the power of the functionary, by reducing the means at his command to corrupt others, were the minimization of his power, the minimization of public money at his disposal, the minimization of his pay, and the exclusion of factitious dignities or titles of honour. The two securities which lessened his desire to perform the sinister sacrifice were the maximization of legal responsibility, whereby he was made legally punishable for any misdeed he committed, and the maximization of moral responsibility, whereby his acts would be given maximum publicity so that in the event of his committing a misdeed or neglecting to perform a duty he would stand open to censure and loss of reputation in the eyes of the people acting as members of the public opinion tribunal.[76] These latter two securities depended, therefore, upon the effective operation of the political sanction and the moral sanction, respectively. Their aim was to secure the responsibility of the official in question, and to this end his actions had to be subject to publicity and to be identifiable as his. Hence, as we have seen,[77] Bentham had long regarded publicity as a key factor in securing good government, but now he showed the precise nature of its operation in this respect by showing its role in securing official aptitude. There could be no responsibility if the superordinate had no means of knowing what the subordinate was doing, hence the acts of the functionary were to be given maximum publicity so that in the event of his committing a misdeed or neglecting to perform a duty he would stand open to censure and loss of reputation in the eyes of the people. In this way moral responsibility was secured—the functionary was made subject to the moral or popular sanction applied by means of the public opinion tribunal. The public opinion tribunal, or at least the majority of its members, whose opinions were to count for that of the tribunal as a whole, would attach 'disrepute' to those actions which its members considered to be detrimental to the universal interest, and 'good repute' to those which they considered contributory to it: expressions of disapproval would be made towards the former, of approval towards the latter. The point about good repute, or public approval, was that it was the cause of respect. Respect was not only a source of pleasure in itself to the person who received it, but also the source of services, of good offices—the person to whom respect was paid could expect to receive favours at the hands of those by whom it was paid. In contrast, ill-repute, or public disapproval, was the cause of disrespect—not only a source of pain in itself, but also the source of disservices, of ill-offices. The functionary who acted in such a way as to promote the general interest would be praised by the public opinion tribunal and thereby earn the

[75] *First Principles*, 28. [76] Ibid. 30–76. [77] See Ch. 10 above.

respect of the people; the services which individuals would then perform for his benefit were both his inducement and reward for acting in that way. In contrast, the functionary who acted in such a way as to promote a sinister interest would find himself condemned by the public opinion tribunal and thereby earn the disrespect of the people; the disservices which individuals would perform to his disadvantage were both a discouragement to and a punishment for his acting in that way.[78] The political and moral sanctions would operate hand in hand: 'The efficiency of the popular or moral sanction, with its Public Opinion Tribunal, can not be strengthened, but the efficiency of the law, in so far as its force is employed in augmentation of the happiness of the people, is also strengthened.'[79] Both the legal and public opinion tribunals were able to apply punishments and rewards, and thus make the functionary in question responsible to them. Moreover, as we have seen, they operated in an analogous way. The difference between them lay not in the nature of the motives they respectively promoted, but in the source from which those motives arose: in the one case from the due deliberations of a judicatory established by the will of the sovereign; in the other from the opinions of any person who took notice of a matter.[80]

Publicity was of prime importance. Bentham recognized that there existed a dynamic relationship between publicity and representative democracy. The securing of publicity for official actions would not only help meliorate a bad government,[81] but would also be crucial to the implementation of democratic reform.[82] Moreover, once representative democracy was established, it would be in the interests of both rulers and subjects that publicity be secured. Provisions for the publicity of official decisions and actions permeated the detailed administrative arrangements of the constitutional code. Though the expense of publicity had to be taken into account as a counter-consideration, Bentham proclaimed that 'in every Subdepartment and Department, publicity will at all times be maximized'.[83] Thus the sittings of the legislature were, in the normal course of events, to be open to the public[84]—though Bentham's reason, as we have seen,[85] was not that the members of the public who attended the debates should act as a check upon their deputies, but rather to ensure that the debates were accurately reported. Each Department and Subdepartment was to keep a set of register books which would record the materials and money in its possession and the use made of them. The information would be available not only to other government officials, but also to the public at large. This system of accounting or recording would not only help to increase the efficiency of the Departments

[78] *First Principles*, 301–3, 306–9.

[79] Ibid. 291.

[80] See *Securities against Misrule*, 65, and pp. 260–1 above.

[81] In 'Securities against Misrule', written for Tripoli, he argued that the only remedy for misrule, assuming that the form of government would remain unchanged, was publicity: see *Securities against Misrule*, 23–111.

[82] See Ch. 10 above.

[83] *Constitutional Code*, I. 162–3.

[84] Ibid. 56–7.

[85] See pp. 258–9 above.

and Subdepartments in the performance of their routine functions, but would also allow the identification of any functionary engaging in misconduct, whether through wilfulness or negligence, and might form the ground of punishment—conversely, if the functionary performed with great merit, it might form the ground for additional reward.[86]

Related to responsibility was the notion of single-seatedness: 'In each official situation', said Bentham, 'functionaries no more than one.' He condemned the English practice of government boards: '*boards* make *skreens*: if any thing goes wrong, you don't know where to find the offender; it was the board that did it, not one of the members; always the *board*, the *board!*'[87] Instead, each function should be allocated to a single, designated official. It would then be obvious to the public opinion tribunal which functionary was responsible for each decision—there were no colleagues on whom he could attempt to shift the blame for any mischievous act he had committed, nor any colleagues who would aid and abet him in any conspiracy against the public interest. Not only did this help to secure aptitude in all its branches, but also to minimize expense, since pay had to be found for only one functionary, and not for several.[88] A problem which might arise from single-seatedness was the absence of the functionary through illness or some other legitimate cause. Bentham's solution lay in what he termed the self-suppletive function: each functionary would be required to supply a 'depute' or substitute to perform the functions of his office, and to pay his depute from his own resources.[89] There were exceptions to single-seatedness, including that of the legislature. If the whole legislative power were in the hands of one man, apart from the overwhelming amount of work it would involve, he would soon make himself despotic and secure the power for life—he would become a monarch. Moreover, each district of the state possessed its own interest, and so required its own deputy, acquainted with its peculiar circumstances, to represent it.[90]

Moral aptitude would be secured by these institutional arrangements—the individual was presumed to act on grounds of self-preference, and so arrangements were devised which allowed him to pursue his self-interest in no other way than through his share in the universal interest. The functionary, like other human agents, would calculate which course of action would best promote his interest: it was the object of the securities for moral aptitude to ensure that the functionary's own interest was identified with that of the community in general, so that he would not be tempted to commit the sinister sacrifice. Bentham was not prepared to rely on the traditional strategy of placing power in the hands of 'virtuous' men in order to produce good government. This view was encapsulated in Alexander Pope's oft-quoted couplet,

[86] *Constitutional Code*, I. 221–5.

[87] See Richard Rush, *A Residence at the Court of London* (London, 1833), 290, reporting Bentham's conversation.

[88] *Constitutional Code*, I. 173–6.

[89] Ibid. 215–17.

[90] *First Principles*, 36–7, 120–1.

> For forms of government let fools contest;
> Whate'er is best administer'd is best:[91]

which Bentham thought was '[o]ne of the most foolish couplets ever written'.[92] For Bentham, good administration was dependent upon the form of government. The point was to arrange matters in such a way that the functionary, when choosing which course of action to pursue, would find himself so constrained by the institutional arrangements put in place for the very purpose of securing moral aptitude that he would only be able to promote his self-interest through the promotion of the general interest. Bentham did not rely on the social motives of sympathy or benevolence. Referring both to the choice of deputies made by electors and the choice of measures made by those deputies in the legislative assembly, he noted:

> the universal good is the result of the continual conflict amongst the jarring elements of separate and sinister interests, desires and endeavours. To any imaginable amount self-sacrifice may in fact have place: but to the production of the greatest happiness of the greatest number not so much as a single instance of it is necessary in the general course of business.[93]

Again, in speaking of the 'superventitious inducements' by which moral aptitude could be produced, he stated that these inducements 'will principally be furnished' by the force of the moral and that of the political sanctions. He continued:

> In addition to the force of these sanctions may be added or set the force of the sympathetic sanction acting on a scale commensurate to that of the whole community and having for its object the happiness of the whole, and the force of the religious sanction. But as applied to the conduct of public functionaries the force of these two sanctions does not always exist in any perceptible quantity, and where it has place is not exposed to any such principle of measurement as has place in the case of the two sanctions abovementioned.[94]

Bentham refused to place any reliance on the social motives in the attempt to secure good behaviour on the part of rulers,[95] but rather relied on self-regarding motives. Each person by definition possessed a share in the universal interest (the universal interest was composed of the aggregate of individual interests). There were always actions the ruler could perform, strategies he could adopt, which would promote his own interest while at the same time promoting the universal interest. Bentham aimed to prevent only those self-regarding actions which would diminish the greatest happiness. Just as the penal law annexed punishment to certain acts in order to discourage subjects from committing them,

[91] An Essay on Man, III. 303–4.
[92] Bowring, x. 532.
[93] *Securities against Misrule*, 267.
[94] Ibid. 272–3.
[95] Cf. *First Principles*, 265: 'An abundant source of delusion is the conception or opinion by which, in men in general, greater degrees of strength are ascribed to the social affection than is generally capable of being possessed by it. Of this error, those by whom power is exercised and abused have all the benefit.'

Bentham wished to ensure that constitutional law operated on rulers in exactly the same way. It was on the supposition of 'the general predominance of self-regarding over social affection' that

> the ruling few actually and invariably proceed in every instance in which, for giving effect to the arrangements of penal and civil law, they make application of the matter of *good* and *evil*, in the shape of *reward* and *punishment*, in the exercise thus given by them to the power possessed by them over the *subject many*: and why, as applied to *themselves*, there should be less truth in it, is a question to which it rests with them, or any one who on this occasion may be disposed to speak for them, to find an answer.[96]

An artificial identification of interests would be substituted for the natural opposition of interests by counteracting that part of the self-interest of rulers which would otherwise conflict with the general interest. In other words, the appropriate moral aptitude of rulers would be maximized.

Good government required more than the securing of moral aptitude. It was possible that rulers might possess moral aptitude, but because of a deficiency in the other branches of aptitude, misrule would still result. In 'Constitutional Code Rationale', Bentham remarked that misrule was caused by the 'inaptitude' of rulers, that is 'relative inaptitude corresponding and opposite to appropriate aptitude in one, or more, or all, of its several branches'.[97] This left open the possibility, which he had identified in his writings on parliamentary reform,[98] of a situation in which moral aptitude was secured, yet due to a lack of intellectual or active aptitude, the individual was incapable (albeit not unwilling) of acting in the general interest. This is not to say that Bentham did not regard the absence of moral aptitude as the most serious problem. For instance, he argued that the objection that, under representative democracy, the people would lack the necessary intellectual aptitude to choose appropriate representatives was groundless, unless it could be shown that there was greater intellectual aptitude elsewhere, 'coupled with that equality in respect of moral aptitude without which superiority in intellectual aptitude is detrimental, and not contributory, to superiority in the aggregate of appropriate aptitude'.[99] Intellectual and active aptitude without moral aptitude was a positive evil rather than a good, since the talents of the functionary would be directed that much more effectually towards the promotion of his particular interest, whatever detriment this might produce to the universal interest.

Good government, therefore, required the maximization of aptitude in all its branches, and thus the institution of effective securities for intellectual and active aptitude. As we have seen, Bentham divided intellectual aptitude into a scientific branch—appropriate knowledge—and a judicial branch—appropriate

96 *Colonies, Commerce, and Constitutional Law*, 35–6.

97 *First Principles*, 270.

98 See pp. 282–3 above.

99 *First Principles*, 144. It had, of course, been precisely this objection to democracy which Bentham himself had made in the wake of the French Revolution: see pp. 100–1 above.

judgment. An ability to make correct judgments was an ability to weigh the interests which presented themselves and choose that course which would be most likely to promote the happiness of the persons affected. Each candidate for a particular office would be required to pass a public examination showing that he possessed the knowledge and judgment appropriate to the adequate performance of all its functions before he would be allowed to seek appointment to it. Not all offices required a special degree of intellectual aptitude—but many, including those of ministers, did. An examination judicatory would be established to supervise the examinations, which would be conducted *viva voce* and in public. The official examiners, members of the public, and the other candidates, would all have the right to interrogate the examinees. The results would be comparative, each candidate being ranked in each subject against his fellow candidates. The ranking would be decided by a series of votes: the examiners would vote both secretly and openly, while the candidates' instructors would also be allowed to vote, but only secretly. The overall result would be published in a 'ranking-table'. Provided the candidate had, in the opinion of the majority of judges, achieved a sufficient standard, his name would be inserted, at its appropriate rank, on the 'locable list' for the office in question. The locable list, therefore, contained the names of those individuals eligible for appointment to the office in question.[100] When an office became vacant, the patron or locator would be entitled to choose any candidate on the locable list—he would not be forced to appoint the person ranked highest. There would, however, be a further factor which he would need to take into account, namely the results of the economical auction, which was a security for active aptitude.

The purpose of the economical auction—or patriotic auction as Bentham had earlier termed it[101]—was to test the 'relish for the function' possessed by the respective candidates. Once a functionary was at his place of business, relish for the function—an expectation on his part that he would gain pleasure from the exercise of the power attached to the office—would improve his performance of it. The keener the official was to perform the function in question, the higher the standard of performance that could be expected.[102] Each office would have a certain amount of pay attached to it. When a vacancy arose, candidates entered on the relevant locable list who wished to apply for the office would enter bids for the pay, and hence engage in the economical auction. The candidate could either offer to accept a lower rate of pay for the office, or he could offer a lump sum in return for the pay, or he could do both. The advantage to the public was that the expense of government would be diminished in proportion to the amount of salary saved and the lump sums received.[103] The more a man desired to exercise the powers belonging to a particular office, in other words the greater his relish for the function, the more he would be prepared to pay for it, and the

[100] *Constitutional Code*, I. 313–23.
[101] See p. 307 below.
[102] See *First Principles*, 77–94.
[103] *Constitutional Code*, I. 337–8.

more likely he would be to perform well should he be appointed.[104] The patron—in the Subdepartments this would often be the respective Minister—would consider both the rankings in the locable list and the results of the economical auction before making his choice. Bentham believed that the patron would tend to give precedence to the ranking in the locable list, but where two candidates were virtually equal in intellectual aptitude, the economical auction would be decisive.[105] The patron retained a discretion to appoint the candidate of his choice, but would be responsible to the public opinion tribunal for his decision:

> To the members of [the Public Opinion Tribunal], it will be manifest in favour of which of the two Candidates the one indication operates, in favour of which of the two the other. The patron will judge which of the two is on the whole the most apt—affords the fairest promise—and the public will judge whether his judgment is apt. His reputation in respect of appropriate knowledge and judgment will in all cases be staked upon the result, and in some cases even in respect of appropriate moral aptitude.[106]

Active aptitude, as we have seen,[107] consisted in the physical performance of action. The securing of moral and intellectual aptitude in government functionaries would be fruitless if they were absent from their place of work, in other words the place where such performance had to take place. As well as economical auction, a further security for active aptitude—which Bentham had identified in his writings on parliamentary reform as a security for active talent—was constant and uninterrupted attendance.[108] It was obvious that if a function had to be performed in a particular place, it could not be performed if the functionary was not there. In order to ensure his attendance, his pay would be dependent upon his appearing at his appointed office at the appointed times: 'If no attendance, then no pay, such the rule for every day.' This rule would be applied to the highest as well as the lowest functionaries. Bentham pointed out that in existing governments there was a tendency to compel the attendance of the least important functionaries, such as privates in the army, whose lack of attendance had least impact, but not the most important functionaries, such as members of the legislature, whose absence might produce great suffering.[109] He proposed that deputies should be paid only when they attended the debating chamber:

> Each day, on entrance into the Assembly Chamber, each member receives that day's pay at the hands of the Doorkeeper. In his view, and in that of the company in the Assembly Chamber is a clock. On delivery of the pay, the Doorkeeper stamps, in the *Entrance and Departure Book*, on the page of that day, the member's name, adding the hour and minute.
>
> No member departs without leave of the President, who, on a sign made by the departer, rings, by a string within his reach, a bell hanging near the Doorkeeper, who,

[104] *First Principles*, 90–3. [105] *Constitutional Code*, I. 346–8.
[106] *First Principles*, 93. [107] See p. 288 above. [108] See p. 144 above.
[109] *First Principles*, 93.

after stamping in the Entrance and Departure Book, on the page of that day, the member's name, with the hour and the minute, lets him out....

Sick or well, for no day, on which he does not attend, vacation days excepted, does any *Legislator* receive his pay.[110]

All functionaries, of whatever rank, were to be subjected to the same discipline.[111]

VI

Bentham aimed to apply the securities for appropriate official aptitude to the different institutions of government in such a way that the various branches of aptitude were secured in each case to the degree necessary. While active aptitude was necessary to all functions, some required a greater degree of intellectual aptitude than others, and some, in proportion to the amount of power attached to the office, required stronger measures to secure moral aptitude. In other words, it was the requirement to maximize official aptitude, with its corollary of minimizing expense, which produced the distinctive institutional structure of the constitutional code. The territory of the state would be divided into equal electoral districts, each of which returned a single deputy to the legislature, thereby ensuring that each person's suffrage would be of roughly the same value. Each district would have a sub-legislature of its own to deal with local affairs. The electorate would be composed of all males above the age of 21 who had passed a literacy test.[112] Bentham was strongly in favour of female suffrage—females had as much an interest in legislation as males, for their happiness was as much affected by it—but he declined to propose female suffrage on tactical grounds. He feared that the 'contests and confusion produced by the proposal of this improvement would engross the public mind and throw improvement in all other shapes to a distance': it was, therefore, better to introduce reform in areas which would prove less contentious before proposing female suffrage.[113] The constitutive power would not only enjoy the power to elect deputies, but also the power to remove them from office. A petition calling for the dismissal of a particular deputy would need to be signed by a proportion (Bentham recommended one-fourth) of the whole number of electors of an election district. This would be followed by a ballot of all the electors of the district in question, with

[110] *Constitutional Code*, I. 50.

[111] The relationship between pay and service was a question to which Bentham devoted considerable attention throughout his career, but it has been largely ignored in the scholarly literature, an exception being N. Sigot, 'Jeremy Bentham on Private and Public Wages and Employment: The Civil Servants, the Poor, and the Indigent', in L. S. Moss (ed.), *Joseph A. Schumpeter, Historian of Economics: Perspectives on the History of Economic Thought* (London, 1996), 196–218.

[112] *Constitutional Code*, I. 11, 27, 30.

[113] *First Principles*, 99–100. For Bentham's earlier reflections on female suffrage see pp. 85–6, 90–1, 149–50 above.

the majority deciding whether the deputy should be retained or removed. The electors of one district could petition for the removal of a deputy from another district, but for the removal to be effected, a majority of the whole electorate would need to vote in favour. Several other functionaries, including the Prime Minister, the Ministers, the Justice Minister, certain judges, and a number of local officials, would be liable to removal in the same way.[114]

The legislature would be composed of a single chamber and elected annually. Being omnicompetent, it had the power to alter the constitutional code itself. The legislature was the hub of the system: on the one side, it was subject to the constitutive authority; on the other, the administrative and judicial powers were its instruments—they acted as its agents because it had neither the time nor the expertise to perform those functions itself.[115] The deputies would initially be subject to a period of non-relocability—they would not be permitted to sit in a succeeding assembly if they had served in the preceding one—until such time had elapsed that each district had a choice of candidates who had already served in the assembly.[116] Recognizing that temporary non-relocability and annual elections might lead to a loss of continuity between one legislature and the succeeding one, Bentham suggested that each legislature, before the end of its term, should appoint a Continuation Committee of some seven to twenty-one persons who would, 'under the direction of the Legislature, apply their endeavours, collectively or individually, in the next succeeding Legislature, to the carrying on of the designs and proceedings of the then next preceding Legislature, in an unbroken thread'. Any member of the outgoing legislature might be appointed to the Continuation Committee, and any of its serving members might be reappointed—there would be no limit to the length of time which a man might serve as a member of the Continuation Committee. Members would have the right to make motions and speak in the legislature, but not having been elected by the constitutive power, they would have no right to vote.[117]

The Prime Minister, at the head of the Administrative Department, would be elected by the legislature for a four-year term of office, but would be liable to be dismissed either by the legislature or, as we have seen, by a petition and vote of the constitutive power. He would be responsible for appointing Ministers, whom he could also dismiss, and would be commander-in-chief of the armed forces. He would, in the normal course of business, be excluded from the legislature, and would only correspond with it by letter: the legislature could, however, invite or order him to attend for a personal conference. He would not be re-eligible for office until there existed two or three ex-Prime Ministers from

[114] *Constitutional Code*, I. 31–3. [115] Ibid. 41–4.

[116] Ibid. 72–3. Bentham had considerable difficulty in deciding whether to adopt the principle of temporary non-relocability. In 1820 he had, as we have seen (p. 286 above), defended the temporary non-reeligibility clause in the Spanish Constitution, and in early 1823 recommended its application to the office of Prime Minister under his constitutional code (see *Securities against Misrule*, 279). Bowring claimed responsibility for persuading Bentham to change his mind: see Bowring, x. 528–30. [117] *Constitutional Code*, I. 67–8.

whom the legislature might choose.[118] There would be thirteen Subdepartments in the Administrative Department, each of which would be headed by a Minister, though any one person might be Minister at more than one Subdepartment.[119] Ministers would be appointed by the Prime Minister, who could choose any candidate from the relevant locable list. He would, of course, be responsible for his choice to the public opinion tribunal, informed as its members would be of the relative intellectual aptitude of the respective candidates and the results of the economical auction.[120] A Minister might retain his office for life, thereby allowing the public to benefit from the skill and expertise acquired from long experience,[121] but he might be removed from office by the Prime Minister, the legislature, or the constitutive authority by means of petition and vote.[122] Ministers were responsible for the appointment of subordinates in their respective Subdepartments, subject to a veto exercisable by the Prime Minister.[123] Ministers would be required to sit in the legislature, where they could take part in debates, propose motions, and answer questions put to them by deputies, but would not be allowed to vote.[124]

Bentham incorporated detailed proposals for the judicial establishment in the constitutional code. The point of these arrangements, which brought to a culmination ideas which he had been developing since the period of the French Revolution, was to secure the appropriate aptitude of judges and other officials involved in administering the pannomion. The subject, moreover, developed into one of immediate practical importance as demands for law reform became more widespread and insistent during the 1820s. Bentham's own profound dissatisfaction with the state of English law and the English legal profession came to manifest itself in a renewed enthusiasm for law reform at home, a project to which he was able to deploy all the resources he had developed over the previous fifty years.

[118] Ibid. 148–59. [119] Ibid. 171–2. [120] Ibid. 311. [121] Ibid. 295.
[122] Ibid. 365. [123] Ibid. 371–2. [124] Ibid. 417.

12

The Politics of Law Reform

I

It has been claimed, and not without reason, that '*Constitutional Code* represents the culmination of [Bentham's] long career as an advocate of reform and codification'.[1] This should not, however, obscure the fact that from the autumn of 1824 Bentham spent a great deal of time and energy promoting law reform in England, and in particular the reform of the judicial establishment. Bentham had, of course, committed himself to law reform at the beginning of his career, but his approach in the 1820s was distinguished by his appreciation of the existence of sinister interest and the need to counteract its operation with the securities for official aptitude which he had developed in his political thought in the 1810s and early 1820s. As we have seen,[2] in these years one of Bentham's primary objectives had been to receive an acceptance for his offer to codify, and in consequence his attention had been drawn overseas—to the United States of America, to Russia and Poland, to Spanish America, to the Iberian Peninsula, to Tripoli, and to Greece. The geographical extent of his ambitions was reflected in the sub-titles to 'Codification Proposal' and *Constitutional Code*, which respectively announced that they were 'addressed to all nations professing liberal opinions' and 'for the use of all nations and all governments professing liberal opinions'.[3] From the mid-1820s, while continuing to draft various parts of his pannomion or complete code of laws, in particular the penal and procedural codes as well as the constitutional code, he focused to a much greater extent on domestic issues, no doubt encouraged not only by the increasing support for political reform, but also by the widespread acceptance that some degree of law reform was necessary.[4] It was the latter which seemed to promise the greater chance of immediate success. While Bentham openly professed his republicanism and his radicalism, describing himself as the 'Leader of the new-born one

[1] *Constitutional Code*, I. Editorial Introduction, p. xi. [2] See Ch. 9 above.

[3] See '*Legislator of the World*', 243, and *Constitutional Code*, I. 1, respectively.

[4] M. Lobban, '"Old wine in new bottles": The Concept and Practice of Law Reform, *c.* 1780–1830', in A. Burns and J. Innes (eds.), *Rethinking the Age of Reform* (Cambridge, 2003), 114–35, points out that the increase in litigation which occurred in the early nineteenth century, and the inability of the courts to deal with it, had convinced many lawyers of the need for reform.

of the three parties—the *Radicals*',[5] and advocated an 'all-comprehensive' codification, he was still willing to suggest specific measures to deal with what were perceived to be pressing problems in the English legal system. His proposals included a new court to clear the backlog of cases which had built up in the Court of Chancery, a simplified system of bankruptcy procedure, and a codification of the law of real property. Having said that, Bentham had more in view than merely meeting the pressing needs of the moment: he intended his proposals to pave the way for further, wide-scale reform.

Bentham's renewed interest in English law reform was closely related to the emergence of the work eventually published in 1830 as *Official Aptitude Maximized; Expense Minimized*, a collection of eleven papers written at various times between 1810 and 1830 which Bentham referred to as the 'pasticcio', and which was intended to complement *Constitutional Code*.[6] A recurring theme in the work concerned the mischiefs associated with the payment of judges and other court officials by fees levied on suitors, rather than by salaries paid out of general taxation, and the power of judges to impose such fees at their own discretion. In 'Defence of Economy against Burke',[7] he had commented on the increase in fees sanctioned by an Order of the Court of Chancery issued on 26 February 1807 by Lord Chancellor Erskine and the Master of the Rolls, Sir William Grant. When he began to plan the pasticcio in 1824–5 he decided to look further into the practice of the Court of Chancery, and in particular into the patronage enjoyed by Lord Chancellor Eldon. What had been intended as a short preface to the volume expanded into a separate essay, eventually published in the summer of 1825 as *Indications respecting Lord Eldon*.[8] In the meantime, on a related theme, he composed a detailed commentary on a speech delivered by Robert Peel to the House of Commons on 21 March 1825 proposing to raise the salaries of metropolitan police magistrates to what Bentham regarded as an unacceptably high level.[9] As far as Bentham was concerned, the 'fee-gathering system' was the root of the problem. The solution lay in the substitution of salaries for fees, with the level of salary determined by economical auction.

[5] Bentham to the Marquis de La Fayette, 25 Mar. 1829, Cornell University Library, La Fayette Papers.

[6] See *Official Aptitude Maximized; Expense Minimized*, Editorial Introduction, pp. xv–xvii, xxviii–xl.

[7] This essay was written in 1810, and first published in *The Pamphleteer* in 1817: see p. 146 n. above.

[8] *Indications respecting Lord Eldon* (London, 1825). The essay was later reprinted in *The Pamphleteer*, vol. xxvi, no. li (1826), 1–55, and was republished in *Official Aptitude Maximized; Expense Minimized*.

[9] *Observations on Mr. Secretary Peel's House of Commons Speech, 21st March, 1825, introducing his Police Magistrates' Salary raising Bill. Date of Order for Printing, 24th March 1825. Also on the Announced Judges' Salary Raising Bill, and the Pending County Courts Bill* (London, 1825). The essay was later reprinted in *The Pamphleteer*, vol. xxv, no. 1 (1825), 405–43, and republished in *Official Aptitude Maximized; Expense Minimized*.

Bentham's attempts to promote law reform reflected his more general strategy for introducing utilitarian reform. In his view, as we have seen,[10] the most important resource was public opinion, informed by a free press. As well as printing and publishing his own works, Bentham established the *Westminster Review* in 1824 as a radical mouthpiece to rival the *Quarterly Review* of the Tories and the *Edinburgh Review* of the Whigs.[11] He made use of sympathetic newspapers, such as the *Morning Chronicle*, the *Morning Herald*, and the *Globe and Traveller*, and more specialized periodicals such as *The Jurist* and the *Law Magazine*. While publicly disseminating his ideas through the press, he worked privately to influence leading politicians, particularly those who had shown some degree of sympathy for reform. For instance, he corresponded with Peel, and met regularly with Henry Brougham. Bentham's relationship with both politicians was characterized by encouragement in private, and stringent criticism in public. He thought that the measures proposed by Peel and Brougham were too piecemeal, and on that account suspected that their true objective was to patch up the existing system, rather than to engage in the major reconstruction which he deemed to be necessary. He made contact with influential reforming lawyers such as James Humphreys, John Tyrrell, Henry Bickersteth, Thomas Denman, and Jabez Henry. He tried to encourage both the small group of radicals in the House of Commons, a group which included Joseph Hume and Francis Burdett, and the radical cause more generally, particularly through his friendship with Francis Place. Finally, a major element in his strategy was the motivation of the people themselves, through the presentation of petitions to the House of Commons, thereby demonstrating popular support for the radical agenda. In the end, it would be fear of revolt that would force the ruling few to concede reform.

II

Bentham's ultimate objective was, of course, the establishment of a pannomion grounded on the principle of utility. By the late 1820s one part of that pannomion, the constitutional code, had been drafted in detail, and printed in part, and much of the substance of the law reforms which he advocated at this time was taken from that part of the code which dealt with the judicial establishment. The main features of the judicial establishment which Bentham proposed in the 1820s had been anticipated in 'Draught of a New Plan for the organisation of the Judicial Establishment in France', which had formed part of his proposals for the reconstruction of the French state in the aftermath of the French Revolution.[12] There were some institutional differences between the two schemes—for instance

[10] See Ch. 10 above.

[11] See G. L. Nesbitt, *Benthamite Reviewing: The First Twelve Years of 'The Westminster Review' 1824–1836* (New York, 1934).

[12] See pp. 92–3 above.

in relation to the popular election of judges,[13] the number of stages of appeal, and the arrangements for judicial amendment of the pannomion—but otherwise, in most significant respects, the two plans were very similar. In the draft code for France, Bentham recommended the establishment of a uniform system of courts, with immediate jurisdiction in all but a few specialized matters lying with the Parish Court. Beyond that there would be a District Court, a District Court of Appeal, and a Metropolitan or Supreme Court, located at Paris. Bentham had initially included a Department Court between the District Court of Appeal and the Metropolitan Court, but later removed it from the proposed structure. A single judge would preside over each court, and the procedure would be summary: 'Expedition is the good to be aimed at: delay an evil to be submitted to through necessity, and only to the extent of that necessity.' Anticipating the notion of official aptitude, Bentham noted that the qualities requisite in a judge were '*probity*, *exertion*, and *intelligence*', all of which would be secured by the judge sitting singly. Unable to hide behind collective decisions or rely on the learning of his fellow judges, he would be fully responsible to public opinion for his decisions, he would not be able to neglect the business of his court, and he would have an incentive to improve his knowledge of the law. Still, it would be possible for a judge to make a mistake, and for this reason, as well as to guard against misconduct, it was necessary to institute a system of appeal.[14]

Justice would be administered without charge. Judges would be paid by salaries, and the taking of fees made illegal. Anticipating his later scheme of economical auction, Bentham proposed the patriotic auction, in order to ascertain the least amount of pay needed to fill judicial offices and the degree of liking of the candidates for performing their duties. Together with popular election, noted Bentham, the patriotic auction cemented 'the truly natural alliance between frugality and liberty'.[15] He recommended that each candidate should find a deposit as a guarantee of his good behaviour—this he termed 'the policy of pecuniary *qualifications*'. The less wealthy man was placed under the disadvantage of not having quite so good a chance of obtaining the office as the wealthier man; the advantage was that if he did obtain the office, his reputation would be enhanced accordingly. 'No other plan affords as illustrious an evidence of extraordinary merit', claimed Bentham, 'none so exact a measure.'[16]

Bentham was adamant that judges should not be permitted to legislate: 'Appointed for the express purpose of enforcing obedience to the laws, their duty is to be foremost in obedience. Any attempt on the part of the judge to frustrate or unnecessarily to retard the efficacy of *what he understands to have been* the decided meaning of the legislature, shall be punished with forfeiture of his office.' Yet he recognized that judges needed the power to suspend the law where they believed that its strict application would be 'unconformable to the

[13] Bentham had never been happy with the popular election of judges. He believed that he had had no alternative but to incorporate the measure into his draft code for France. See p. 93 above.

[14] Bowring, iv. 289, 322, 340–2. [15] Ibid. 372–4. [16] Ibid. 377–8.

principles manifested by the National Assembly, and especially to those contained in the declaration of rights'. The judge would report his use of the suspensive power to the National Assembly, and, if he wished, suggest an amendment to the law. The role of the judge was quite specific: 'The true and only proper object of inquiry in the exercise of this suspensive power, as far as it regards laws posterior to the convocation of the present National Assembly, is, not what *ought* to have been the intention of the legislature in the case in question, but only what would have been so, had the same been present to their view.' Bentham suggested that the National Assembly establish a committee of revision, which would monitor the way in which the courts interpreted legislation, and report any interpretations which appeared to be erroneous, thereby circumscribing any undue influence which they might otherwise have had.[17]

Many of the ideas Bentham had outlined in 'Draught of a New Plan for the organisation of the Judicial Establishment in France' reappeared, albeit with considerable elaboration, in the Constitutional Code, though he made a number of terminological changes. For instance, he used the term 'judicatory' instead of 'court', on account of the latter's association with monarchy,[18] and the term 'suit' instead of 'cause', thereby avoiding the ambiguities created by the use of the latter term in logic, and taking advantage of the conjugates—such as to sue, to pursue, suitor, pursuer, and pursuit—which the former possessed;[19] and he referred to the parties in a suit as the 'pursuer' and the 'defendant',[20] and to witnesses and others with relevant information as 'evidence-holders'.[21] One major difference, as noted above, was that instead of being popularly elected, judges were to be appointed—or located—by a Justice Minister, who himself was located for life by the legislature.[22] The Justice Minister was dislocable either by the legislature or by the constitutive authority, in the latter case following a petition and majority vote, in the same manner as the Prime Minister.[23] Furthermore, the measures to guarantee probity, exertion, and intelligence on the part of judges had been transformed into securities for their moral, intellectual, and active aptitude. The overall objective, however, had not changed: namely cheap and speedy justice. This would be achieved by the introduction of a summary or domestic system of procedure, the establishment of a pannomion consisting of 'real law', and the extirpation of 'the spurious substitute, sprung from necessity, nursed and kept on the throne by artifice—the chimera, called by such a multitude of names, of which *Common Law* is one'.[24]

The territory of the state would be divided into Districts, and these into Subdistricts. In each Subdistrict there would be an Immediate Judicatory, and in every District an Appellate Judicatory. Each Judicatory would be staffed by a single-seated Judge (who would appoint Deputes to sit in his absence or to preside over additional judicatories should the level of business demand it), a

[17] Bowring, iv. 287–8. [18] Ibid. ix. 458–9. [19] Ibid. 460 n. [20] Ibid. 460.
[21] Ibid. 473–4. [22] Ibid. 607. [23] Ibid. 610, and see p. 302 above.
[24] Ibid. 511.

Registrar to keep a record of the proceedings, a Government Advocate to represent the government in suits in which it had an interest, an Eleemosynary Advocate to represent any party unable to represent himself or secure assistance from elsewhere, and a number of minor functionaries, such as guards and jailors. A further feature of Bentham's proposed system was the Quasi-jury, the 'ever changing body of Assessors, convened from the body of the people at large, for the purpose of its serving ... as a *check* applied to the power of the *permanent* judges', and thus preventing the judges from promoting their own particular and sinister interest at the expense of the interest of the community at large. The Immediate Judicatory would be the court of first instance for all suits arising in its Subdistrict—in Bentham's terminology, the logical field of service of the Judge Immediate would be 'all-comprehensive'—with the exception of certain military and ecclesiastical suits, and in special circumstances when a suit might be transferred to a different Immediate Judicatory. The Immediate Judicatories would be distributed across the country in such a way that every individual would be able to travel to a Judicatory and return home again in a day. In accord with his aphorism, 'When sleeps Injustice, so may Justice too', Bentham insisted that at least one Judge should be sitting at all times of day and night in each Immediate Judicatory. The Appellate Judicatory would sit for eight hours each day. Once a suit had been heard in the Immediate Judicatory, initially before the Judge alone and then before the Judge sitting with a Quasi-jury, it would be possible, most commonly in consequence of a petition by a party, for the suit to be reconsidered in the Appellate Judicatory, where a Quasi-jury would attend all hearings.

As in the draft code for France, Bentham allowed the right of appeal, but reduced the levels of jurisdiction from four to two. The existence of the right of appeal, argued Bentham, would help both to secure moral aptitude, since a Judge Immediate would have no inducement to act corruptly unless he knew that the Judge Appellate would also act corruptly, and to secure intellectual aptitude, since a condition for the location of a Judge Appellate would be service for a specified period as a Judge Immediate. On the other hand, were it possible to appeal to a third court, the vast increase in delay, vexation, and expense would not be compensated by any significant increase in the appropriate aptitude of the Super-Appellate Judge over the Appellate Judge, and thence of the ultimate decision. The rationale for the geographical distribution of the Immediate Judicatories would not apply to the Appellate Judicatories. No suitor or evidence-holder would be required to attend an Appellate Judicatory, since the proceedings would consist in argument upon the record, which would be transmitted from the Immediate Judicatory. In England, for instance, all the Appellate Judicatories might be located in London, since communication with the rest of the country was good, and it was 'the seat of the best public', that is 'the spot in which the number of the most enlightened men capable of acting with more or less attention in the character of Judicial Inspectors' were situated.

The expense of appeal would be defrayed by the state, otherwise a denial of justice would result, since those unable to meet the expense would be subject to 'depredation and oppression, at the hands of all who *are* able'.[25] Guaranteeing universal access to justice was a prime concern for Bentham. In order to avoid justice being denied to the poor, for instance, an Equal Justice Fund would be established, supplied from the fines imposed on wrongdoers by the judicatories, and from monies provided by government and voluntary donations.[26] The proceedings would be held in public (except, for instance, where preponderant vexation would be produced by the disclosure of family or commercial secrets), and accommodation would be provided for suitors and witnesses awaiting their turn to be heard, as well as the officials, scribes, advocates, attornies, and Quasi-jurors (where called in).[27] Bentham was prepared to go so far as to force the inhabitants of the District, regular soldiers stationed nearby, and officers of the militia to attend by rotation, in order to provide an audience for the 'judicial theatre'.[28]

As he had throughout his career, Bentham emphasized the point that the primary duty of judges would be to enforce the law. He was aware, nevertheless, that he had to answer the stock objection that judicial discretion would be greatly increased, since many cases would arise which would not be covered by the provisions of the code itself.[29] Bentham's solution was to provide judges with an effective means for suggesting amendments to the pannomion. In short, judges would be able to propose changes in the law, but only the legislature would have the power to authorize them. Bentham was convinced that his scheme would obviate any future need for consolidation, and would prevent the growth of Common Law.[30] The judges would be given three main functions in this respect. First, the 'contested-interpretation-reporting function' would provide judges with the opportunity to propose amendments to the form, as opposed to the substance, of the law. When an appeal from an Immediate to an Appellate Judicatory rested on a ground of law, as opposed to a ground of fact, both the Judge Immediate and the appellant would submit their differing interpretations of the relevant provision in the pannomion, and, if appropriate, suggestions for amending its wording. The Judge Appellate would thereupon adopt the interpretation which he thought proper, or else add an interpretation of his own. A report containing these various interpretations would then be submitted to the Justice Minister, who might add his own interpretation, before submitting the whole to the Legislation Minister, who would transmit it to the Contested Interpretation Committee, a standing committee appointed by the Legislature. The Contested Interpretation Committee might then authorize or reject any amendment to the pannomion, but if it failed to act within a certain number of

[25] Bowring, ix. 464–70, 473–4, 515–16. [26] Ibid. 491–3.

[27] For the architectural arrangements see pp. 256–7 above. [28] Bowring, ix. 535–6.

[29] See e.g. Peel's comments in the House of Commons on 18 February 1830 (*Parliamentary Debates*, xxii (1830) 677).

[30] Bowring, ix. 512–13.

days, the interpretation sanctioned or proposed by the Justice Minister would be adopted.[31] Second, the 'eventually-emendative function' would provide judges with the opportunity to propose amendments to the substance of the law during the course of a suit. The Judge Immediate might draw up an amendment (possibly at the instigation of the parties, but possibly at the instigation of someone not directly involved in the suit), and, having consulted the Government and Eleemosynary Advocates, who might signify their approval, acquiescence, or disapproval, transmit an 'emendation-suggesting report' to the Judge Appellate of his District and thereupon to the Justice Minister, both of whom might in turn either approve, acquiesce in, or disapprove of the proposal. The report would then be passed on to the Legislation Minister, who would publicize the proposed emendation. If no action was taken by the Legislature within a certain number of days, the proposal would be rejected if disapproved by either the Appellate Judge or the Justice Minister, or adopted if not disapproved by either.[32] In the meantime the Judge Immediate would exercise his 'execution-staying function', thereby suspending the execution which would otherwise have been given to the law in question.[33] Bentham recognized that the issuing of an 'execution-staying decree' produced a dilemma. On the one hand, if the Judge Immediate executed the law as it stood, he committed what the Judge himself considered to be an injustice. On the other hand, if he refused to execute it, he likewise committed an injustice, and perhaps undermined the confidence of the people in the law. Having considered the respective utilities of each course of action, Bentham was in no doubt that the former course of action was the proper one:

> that which the people look to, at the hands of the Legislature and the Judiciary together is—the fulfilment of *salutary* ordinances, and no others: not the production of evil by admission or omission of this or that word in a law, through inadvertence or otherwise. What may, therefore, be reasonably looked for, is—that, by giving execution and effect to the imperfectly expressed portion of law in question, a severer shock would be given to the public confidence, than by forbearing so to do.[34]

Third, the 'preinterpretative function' would provide judges with the opportunity to propose amendments to the substance of the law without the need of litigation (or 'litiscontestation' as Bentham preferred to term it, thereby avoiding the unpleasant associations of the word 'litigation'). Any person would be permitted to appear before a Judge Immediate and ask him how he would interpret a particular legal provision. If the Judge was doubtful, and if it appeared to him that the ambiguity or obscurity might be removed by an amendment, he would draft an amendment exactly as he would when exercising the eventually-emendative function.[35] The advantage of the preinterpretative over the interpretative function was that certainty might be achieved without the need for litigation.[36]

[31] Ibid. 502–4. [32] Ibid. 435–7, 504–6. [33] Ibid. 508. [34] Ibid. 509.
[35] Ibid. 511. [36] Ibid. 512.

A further feature of Bentham's scheme, as we have seen, was the Quasi-jury, which had two main uses. The first was to act as a check upon the power of the Judge, and thus as a security for his appropriate aptitude. The second was to educate the members of the Quasi-jury themselves. One of the roles of a judicatory was to be 'a *school of justice*', and the Quasi-jurors would be amongst its 'scholars'. Hence the greater the number of the members of the community who served as Quasi-jurors, the greater the benefit to the universal interest.[37] Each Quasi-jury would be made up of three members, all of whom had to be electors,[38] but two of whom would be 'ordinary' members and one a 'select' member (individuals would have to apply to be entered on the list of select Quasi-jurors). The point of these arrangements was to secure the appropriate aptitude of the Quasi-jurors. Moral aptitude would be possessed by the ordinary members, whose interest would coincide with that of the greatest number, while intellectual aptitude would be possessed by the select member, who would be able to guide and instruct the ordinary members.[39] The Quasi-jury would not sit at trials of first instance, but only at what Bentham termed the Recapitulatory Inquiry, or Quasi-trial, which might be ordered by the original Judge or by either of the parties if they were dissatisfied with the decision, or definitive decree, reached by the Judge Immediate at the Original Inquiry. A Quasi-jury would also sit where it was claimed that the conduct of the Judge, in any other way than by a definitive decree, had produced misdecision. 'On both occasions', noted Bentham, 'petition for Quasi-trial, is in effect appeal from the Judge, acting *without* a Quasi-Jury, to the same Judge, or to another Judge, acting in that same judicatory, *with* a Quasi Jury.'[40] The Quasi-jury would not only listen to the proceedings, but also have the right to ask questions and express its opinion. Its comments would be entered on the record, as would any alterations which they proposed to the Judge's decision. The Judge was free to pay what regard he thought proper to the opinion of the Quasi-jury—otherwise his responsibility would be diminished—but any proposed amendment would be sent to the Judge Appellate for his adoption, rejection, or modification. In a wide variety of circumstances where they were dissatisfied with the decision of the Judge Immediate, the Quasi-jury had, at the instance of a party, the power to order a suit to be sent up to the Judge Appellate.[41]

III

The proposals for the judicial establishment which Bentham described in the constitutional code provided his blueprint for the reform of the judicial system

[37] Bowring, ix. 558.

[38] Ibid. 560. Details of exclusions (e.g. criminals and public officials) and exemptions (e.g. the infirm and members of the professions) from the list of potential Quasi-jurors appear at ibid. 563–6.

[39] Ibid. 559. [40] Ibid. 556–8. [41] Ibid. 556.

in England. They also indicate why he believed that the measures of legal reform proposed by Peel and Brougham, respectively, were seriously deficient. Bentham was not, however, content merely to criticize the reforms of Peel and Brougham, but made a serious attempt to persuade them to adopt the measures which he himself was advocating. In the House of Commons on 9 March 1826, Peel, having already undertaken a number of measures of law reform, notably consolidating the laws relative to juries and abolishing the death penalty for a number of petty offences, announced a plan to consolidate the criminal law and introduced a Bill to improve the administration of justice.[42] It was this latter measure which caught Bentham's attention, and led him to open a correspondence with Peel on 1 April 1826. However, the topic of this first letter was not law reform, but rather 'the distressed state of medical science'—namely the lack of bodies available for dissection in the medical schools. Bentham outlined a proposal for supplying the deficiency: by applying for admission into hospital, the patient would thereby consent, in the event of his death, that his body be 'examined and studied for the benefit of the public, by means of the instruction afforded to pupils in medical art and science'. He revealed to Peel that he considered this matter to be of such importance that he had directed, in his will, that his own body 'should be dissected in the completest as well as most public manner'.[43] In response, Peel assured Bentham that he had taken measures to deal with the problem, but questioned the prudence of legislating on the subject, and indeed of discussing it in public.[44] Bentham then sent Peel a copy of 'Draught of a New Plan for the organisation of the Judicial Establishment in France', which he thought might be relevant to Peel's proposed measure for improving the administration of justice.[45] Having read Humphreys' *Observations on the Actual State of the English Laws of Real Property; with the Outline of a Code*, he wrote again to Peel recommending the adoption of Humphreys' scheme for the reform of property law.[46] He warned Peel that if he stopped at consolidation of the law, and did not proceed to codification, 'the design' would be of use only to lawyers 'by somewhat alleviating their labours', and would leave the law 'as incomprehensible to non lawyers' as it had been before.[47]

[42] *Parliamentary Debates*, xiv (1826), 1214–44. For Peel's legal reforms see N. Gash, *Mr. Secretary Peel: The Life of Sir Robert Peel to 1830*, 2nd edn. (London, 1985), 308–43.

[43] Bentham to Peel, 1 Apr. 1826, *Correspondence*, xii. 205–8.

[44] Peel to Bentham, 4 Apr. 1826, ibid. 208–9. Bentham went on to draft a Body-providing Bill on 6 November 1826 (see UC xi. 220–4), which had some influence on the Anatomy Act of 1832: see R. Richardson, 'Bentham and "Bodies for Dissection"', *The Bentham Newsletter*, 10 (1986), 22–33, and, more generally, R. Richardson, *Death, Dissection and the Destitute* (London, 1987).

[45] Bentham to Peel, 13 Apr. 1826, *Correspondence*, xii. 210–11.

[46] Bentham was sufficiently impressed by Humphreys' *Observations on the Actual State of the English Laws of Real Property; with the Outline of a Code* (London, 1826), to write a favourable review article which appeared in the *Westminster Review*, vol. vi, no. xii (Oct. 1826), 446–507, and was republished as a separate pamphlet early in 1827 (see Bowring, v. 387–416).

[47] Bentham to Peel, 19 Aug. 1826, *Correspondence*, xii. 239–46. Peel was being encouraged to pursue quasi-Benthamite schemes of law reform by Anthony Hammond—schemes from which Peel felt the need to distance himself (see K. J. M. Smith, 'Anthony Hammond: "Mr Surface" Peel's

Thereafter, through to the spring of 1827, Bentham drafted and sent a series of letters to Peel on the subject of law reform, though he then seems to have decided that little progress would be made by this means. He went on to express his differences with Peel in a series of five letters which he published, under the pseudonym of Parcus, in the *Morning Herald* in April and May 1828.[48] Peel had not taken seriously the problems created by the payment of judges by means of fees, and indeed was not serious about reform at all, since his 'two intimately connected objects' were first, 'to swell, to the utmost possible amount, the expense of *things as they are*', and second, 'to stave off, to the most distant point of time possible, more particularly with regard to law reform, the bringing them to what they *ought to be*'.[49] The terms of reference of the two Royal Commissions (on Courts of Common Law and Real Property) which were being established as a result of Brougham's six-hour speech on law reform delivered to the House of Commons on 7 February 1828 were neither intelligible nor sufficiently wide-ranging. Peel had limited the scope of the Commissions in order to assuage the fears of 'the ballot-hating and vote-compelling Lords and 'Squires' that law reform would lead on to parliamentary reform. The proper way to proceed was not to wait for commissions composed of 'creatures' of government to report and then to propose laws, but to receive all-comprehensive codes from any individual willing to submit them, and to print them at public expense. Bentham complained: 'If you persevere, and give to two sets, of five men each, the commission to inquire whether, in an unintelligibly described portion of the field of law, any thing or nothing in the way of proposed law shall be commenced, what you will get is what you have so often got already, monopoly, trumpery, favouritism, and job.' Peel had three major aims in setting up the Commissions: the perpetuation of abuse; the production of jobs; and the obtainment of popularity. As for the jobs, Bentham estimated that the two Commissions would each cost around £10,000 per annum, with the patronage being distributed by Peel, Lord Chancellor Lyndhurst, and Lord Chief Justice Tenterden. Peel had looked for popularity from the lawyers, the 'bread-taxing class', and the people. As for the lawyers, Peel's measures of consolidation, by which statutes had been collected together into 'a moderate number of coops', would save them time in 'Statute-hunting'; he would increase the number of law situations open to them; and more importantly, 'by the putting in of the *consolidation*', he would achieve 'the keeping out of *codification*'. Consolidating

Persistent Codifier', *Journal of Legal History*, 20 (1999), 24–44). Bentham was aware of Hammond's advocacy of codification (see e.g. the extracts from Hammond's works at UC xi. 245 which Bentham sent to Peel on 3 February 1827), and had been in contact with him in early 1825 (see Joseph Hume to Bentham, 10 Jan. 1825, *Correspondence*, xii. 91).

[48] Letter I 'Peel, Bentham, and Judges' Salaries' (7 Apr. 1828); Letter II 'Peel and Munificence;—Bentham and Niggardliness' (15 Apr. 1828); Letter III 'Peel, Tenterden, Bentham, and Law Reform' (8 May 1828); Letter IV 'Written Pleadings Pickpocket Lies' (28 May 1828); and Letter V 'Inquiry-Splitting and Reform-Quashing Commission Jobs' (29 May 1828).

[49] *Morning Herald*, 15 Apr. 1828.

the statute law was futile unless the Common Law was abolished: 'so long as the nuisance called *Common*, alias *Unwritten*, alias *Judge-made* Law, continues unextirpated, the whole of the Statute Law might be enclosed in a nutshell, and men's rights and obligations remain as unknowable as ever—the needfulness, and, at the same time, the uselessness, of going to the Opinion-shop for guesses at what the Judges will do, as entire as ever'.[50] Instead of appointing two Commissions, in addition to the Commission which had been appointed in 1824 to investigate the Court of Chancery, just one commission authorized to investigate the whole of the law should have been appointed. The connection between the practice of the courts of Common Law, the courts of Equity, and the conveyancers of real property was as 'intimate' as the connection between the stomach, bowels, and head. It made no more sense to call in three physicians to look at each independently of the rest as it did to appoint three separate commissions to look at three aspects of the legal system. Moreover, it was in the interest of all the commissioners 'that the evils which furnished the alleged motives for the several Commissions should, so far from being lessened, receive every endurable increase'. The only exception would have been Humphreys had he been appointed to 'the Real-property Inquiry job'; he had, therefore, been excluded from the Commission.[51]

In the meantime, in September 1827, Bentham had contacted Brougham, who was at his country home near Penrith, in order to urge Bowring's claims to be appointed to the Chair of English Literature at the newly forming London University.[52] In response, Brougham explained that he disagreed strongly with Bowring's political principles, which he thought were too favourable to ministers, but promised his support for Bowring's appointment if he proved to be the best candidate, though warned that there was considerable antipathy towards Bowring on account of the latter's involvement in the Greek Loan scandal.[53] He took the opportunity to add that he intended, in the course of the next session, 'to reform our system . . . on a very large scale'.[54] Bentham, correctly assuming that the reform which Brougham had in mind was law reform rather than parliamentary reform, immediately offered to send Brougham copies of various

[50] Ibid., 8 May 1828.

[51] Ibid., 29 May 1828. Bentham became friendly with John Tyrrell in early 1829, who about this time was appointed to the Real Property Commission, and seems to have been responsible for ensuring that Bentham was consulted by it. Bentham's submission in relation to the registration of land was printed in the Commission's Third Report of 1832 (see *Commons Sessional Papers*, xxii (1831–2), and 'Outline of a Plan of a General Register of Real Property', Bowring, v. 417–35). For Bentham's involvement with Humphreys, Tyrrell, and the Real Property Commission see M. Sokol, 'Jeremy Bentham and the Real Property Commission of 1828', *Utilitas: A Journal of Utilitarian Studies*, 4 (1992), 225–45.

[52] Bentham to Brougham, 13 Sept. 1827, *Correspondence*, xii. 385–8.

[53] Brougham to Bentham, 16 Sept. 1827 and 22 Sept. 1827, ibid. 389–91, 394–6. For Bowring's role in the Greek Loan see F. Rosen, *Bentham, Byron, and Greece: Constitutionalism, Nationalism, and Early Liberal Political Thought* (Oxford, 1992), 103–22.

[54] Brougham to Bentham, 16 Sept. 1827, *Correspondence*, xii. 390.

works—including 'Codification Proposal', the first volume of 'Constitutional Code', and the fourth volume of *Rationale of Judicial Evidence*—invited him to dine at Queen's Square Place, and offered to show him his correspondence with Peel.[55] Brougham confirmed that he had been planning a major speech on law reform for about six months, but asked Bentham not to disclose his plan to anyone except James Mill. He explained that he did not intend to propose any particular measure, but rather to expose the absurdities of the Common Law, and to call for the establishment of a Commission of Inquiry.[56] Bentham was delighted, and promised his support, so long as Brougham remained a '*bonus puer*'.[57] It appears that Bentham and Brougham began to meet regularly upon Brougham's return to London in the middle of October 1827, and continued to do so until Brougham delivered his speech on 7 February 1828. Bentham's reaction to the speech, expressed in an anonymous letter which he drafted for a newspaper, was one of disappointment: 'Mr Brougham's mountain is delivered, and behold!—the mouse. The wisdom of the reformer could not overcome the craft of the lawyer. Mr Brougham, after all, is not the man to set up a simple, natural, and rational administration of justice against the entanglements and technicalities of our English law proceedings.' Brougham had joined with Peel in defending the system of special pleading, with the 'mendacity license' which it gave to lawyers, instead of recommending a summary system of justice, where the parties to a dispute would appear directly before the judge.[58]

Bentham, concerned that Brougham would oppose any effective measure of law reform, decided that it was 'matter of necessity' to undermine Brougham's influence. To this end he 'supplied' the 'matter'—'the *form*' being supplied by 'others'—for 'the greatest part' of an article which appeared under the title of 'Bentham, Brougham, and Law Reform' in the *Westminster Review* of October 1829,[59] and in which, according to Bentham, Brougham's speech on law reform was 'torn to rags and tatters'.[60] Bentham and Brougham were presented as 'the most intellectual representatives, the most able expositors' of the two great classes of law reformers: the former was a radical reformer of both constitutional and civil law, while the latter was 'a frequently declared anti-radical', opposing popular suffrage and the secret ballot. It was questionable whether Brougham, in the department of law, had 'brought any really beneficial change at all the nearer by his exertions, unless, indeed, by directing attention to abuses that exist, for which he has proposed to provide no efficacious, no adequate cure'. Brougham was 'not the Messiah of law-reform. Into the world of parliament came not he

[55] Bentham to Brougham, 20 Sept. 1827, ibid. 391–4.

[56] Brougham to Bentham, 22 Sept. 1827, ibid. 396–7.

[57] Bentham to Brougham, 24 Sept. 1827, ibid. 397–9.

[58] The letter, signed Misopseudo, is printed in Bowring, x. 588–9. For the 'mendacity license' see pp. 119–20 above.

[59] *Westminster Review*, vol. xi, no. xxii (Oct. 1829), 447–71.

[60] Bentham to Daniel O'Connell, 25 Aug. 1829 and 16 Oct. 1829, University College Dublin Library, P/12/3/205 and 207. Bentham later admitted his authorship to Brougham: see Bentham to Brougham, 19 Nov. 1830, Bowring, xi. 61.

that should come; the people must look for another.'[61] The proposals for law reform put forward by the two men were sharply contrasted: Bentham was an advocate of codification, whereas Brougham was not;[62] Bentham proposed the abolition of fees, whereas Brougham regarded them as a proper incentive;[63] Bentham proposed a summary mode of procedure and the abolition of written pleadings, whereas Brougham would retain the existing courts and the existing procedure which operated by means of written pleadings;[64] Bentham wished to introduce the Quasi-jury, whereas Brougham had praised the traditional jury;[65] and Bentham would not exclude any evidence except on the grounds of preponderant delay, vexation, and expense, whereas Brougham would not accept any evidence without a religious test.[66] The only measure which Brougham had suggested which had any merit was his proposal to revive the county courts, but even this appeared to be inadequate and expensive in comparison with Bentham's proposed system of local judicatories.[67] Little was to be expected from the two Royal Commissions appointed in the wake of Brougham's speech, and the very fact that two separate inquiries had been established, rather than a single one with authority to consider the law as a whole, would prove 'fatal to their extensive usefulness'. Brougham deserved credit for drawing attention to abuses and demonstrating the necessity of change, but he had lost the opportunity to lead the movement for law reform. Other eloquent advocates were emerging, and if Brougham would support them, 'abundant honours will yet attend him, and human nature will gain a splendid victory'.[68]

Bentham continued to express his dissatisfaction with Brougham's credentials as a law reformer in *Lord Brougham Displayed*,[69] written after Brougham's appointment as Lord Chancellor in 1830, and in response to his proposed reforms of the Court of Chancery and his Bankruptcy Court Bill. Bentham referred to Brougham as the 'Boa Constrictor, alias *Helluo Curiarum*', on account of his proposal 'to strangle and swallow up' the Vice-Chancellor's and Master of the Rolls' Courts into the Court of Chancery. The more he studied the proposal, confessed Bentham, the more convinced he became that Brougham was 'an adversary—and that an irreconcilable one', of law reform, 'to that all important undertaking, to which, from boyhood, the whole of my long life has been devoted'. There could be no hope of law reform while Brougham remained

[61] 'Bentham, Brougham, and Law Reform', 447–8. [62] Ibid. 448–9.

[63] Ibid. 449–50. [64] Ibid. 453–5. [65] Ibid. 455–8. [66] Ibid. 458–61.

[67] Ibid. 468–9.

[68] Ibid. 469–71. Bentham may have had good grounds for his disappointment with Brougham. According to M. Lobban, 'Henry Brougham and Law Reform', *English Historical Review*, 115 (2000), 1184–215, esp. 1186–91, Brougham never committed himself to the sort of radical legal and political reform advocated by Bentham, was 'only on the edge' of Bentham's 'group of followers', and in the period up to 1830 'tended . . . to turn to law reform only when it might further his political career'.

[69] *Lord Brougham Displayed: including I. Boa Constrictor, alias Helluo Curiarum; II. Observations on the Bankruptcy Court Bill, now ripened into an Act; III. Extracts from proposed Constitutional Code* (London, 1832) (Bowring, v. 549–612).

as Lord Chancellor.[70] Bentham was particularly critical of Brougham's address to the Chancery bar on 1 September 1831, reported in the *Morning Chronicle* of 2 September 1831, proposing that all three Chancery judges—the Lord Chancellor, Vice-Chancellor, and Master of the Rolls—should sit together in one judicatory, and criticizing, implicitly at least, Bentham's own preference for a system of single-seated judicatories.[71] In Bentham's view, Brougham had aligned himself with the legal profession and had, therefore, opposed himself to the suitors and to the people in general. The suitors wanted a system of procedure which would minimize delay, vexation, and expense, whereas the profession wanted a system which would maximize them, and thereby increase their own profit.[72] Bentham hoped that Brougham might be turned away from 'bit-by-bit, and ill-considered, unconcocted, incoherent, and unseasoned, supposed reforms or improvements in legislation', and would instead come to Queen's Square Place for advice. Brougham's proposal was 'inevitably doomed'. He would do better to confine himself to the functions of judicature, and leave the field of legislation 'to him, whose proficiency in that branch of art and science was recognized some years before the existing successor of Lord Bacon saw the light'.[73]

Bentham was equally scathing of Brougham's Bankruptcy Court Bill. Brougham had argued that, by the abolition of the seventy bankruptcy commissionerships, he would have less patronage at his disposal. Bentham countered that Brougham should give up all his patronage, and appoint to each office the man who, in his judgment, was most fit for it. Bentham did not want Brougham to lose any emolument, and proposed that he should be compensated for its loss by an addition to his salary:

> It would be against a fixed principle of mine—the disappointment-*preventing*, or (as far as prevention is impracticable) -*minimizing* principle:—that all-comforting principle—first-born of the *greatest-happiness* principle:—that principle which affords the only reason (nor can there be a more substantial one) for securing to every man his *own*, whatever it may be—black men and white men, in a state of slavery, excepted.[74]

It seemed to Bentham that ministers had consented to 'this job' in order to secure Brougham's support in the House of Lords. He would be prepared to forgive ministers, as would the people, only on condition of their 'throwing Jonas overboard, or making him into a scapegoat, and sacrificing on the altar of justice, him by whom justice herself is endeavoured to be sacrificed—sacrificed to his own sinister interest'.[75]

Bentham's alternative recommendation for reform of bankruptcy procedure was that three commissioners, with the possibility of more if business warranted

[70] Bowring, v. 553. [71] Ibid. 554. [72] Ibid. 560. [73] Ibid. 564.

[74] Ibid. 570. For the disappointment-prevention principle see 'On Remuneration' in *Official Aptitude Maximized; Expense Minimized*, 342–67; Kelly, *Utilitarianism and Distributive Justice*, 168–206; and p. 326 below.

[75] Bowring, v. 578. For the story of Jonah being cast overboard see Jonah 1: 4–16.

it, should be appointed by the King to sit singly at first instance, with appeal to a single-seated bankruptcy court judge, with no fees being taken by any official.[76] But this would only be a temporary arrangement, until 'the all-comprehensive local judicatory system' outlined in the constitutional code could be implemented, whereupon 'the business of this temporary and make-shift institution of a special judicatory for bankruptcy business, will then be absorbed and merged into the common mass of the business of those several judicatories'.[77]

IV

The true Messiah who was to come forward and promote Benthamic law reform in the House of Commons, and to whom Bentham alluded in the *Westminster Review* article of October 1829, was Daniel O'Connell. In a speech advocating parliamentary reform and law reform delivered at Dublin on 10 July 1828 following his return as MP for Clare, O'Connell proclaimed that, in relation to law reform, he was 'but an humble disciple of the immortal Bentham'. Bentham, seeing a report of the speech in the *Morning Herald* of 15 July 1828, immediately wrote to O'Connell expressing his delight with his commitment to reform. Having noted that law reform 'has been the occupation of by far the greatest part of my long life, and will be that of the small remainder', he emphasized his dissatisfaction with Peel's reforms: 'Mr Peel is for consolidation in contradistinction to codification: I for codification in contradistinction to consolidation.' Peel's object being to afford some relief to lawyers from the burdensome task of searching through the mass of Common Law cases, he had digested some parts of the Common Law into statute law. Bentham's own object, in contrast, was 'to render it possible to "lay gents" to pay obedience to all rules to which they are made punishable, and every day punished, for not obeying'.[78] In response, O'Connell expressed his support for codification, and his belief that Brougham's proposed reforms were 'but patches placed on a thread bare and rent coat, and cut out of an unused remnant of the original cloth'. He informed Bentham that he intended to come to London in March 1829,[79] and promised 'never to spend *one week* in the house unattended by some effort—to reform *the Law*—the parliament—Aye and the Church'. He continued: 'Give me all the assistance you conveniently can in the mean time—to qualify now for becoming in the house your mouth piece.'[80]

[76] Bowring, v. 578–80. [77] Ibid. 607.

[78] Bentham to O'Connell, 15 July 1828, ibid. x. 594–6.

[79] In the event, O'Connell arrived in London around 10 February 1829. He went back to Ireland in June 1829 in order to stand for re-election for Clare, where he was duly returned on 30 July 1829. He arrived again in London at the beginning of February 1830, and made his maiden speech in the House of Commons on 4 February 1830.

[80] O'Connell to Bentham, 3 Aug. 1828, *The Correspondence of Daniel O'Connell*, ed. M. R. O'Connell, 8 vols. (Dublin, 1972–80), viii. 198–200.

Despite O'Connell's enthusiasm, Bentham did not think that the making of speeches in Parliament—where 'the most brilliant and even effective speech that man ever made, or ever could make, would be a *flash in the pan* and nothing more'—would be effective in promoting law reform. Instead, he hoped 'to engage the people, one and all, to petition Parliament'.[81] To this end, from the late summer of 1828, and no doubt stimulated by the popular support which he expected from O'Connell's Catholic Association in Ireland,[82] Bentham drafted a 'Petition for Justice' and a 'Petition for Codification'. The two petitions had been printed by late February or early March 1829, by which time 'Petition for Justice' had grown to such a length that Bentham had decided to produce an 'Abridged Petition for Justice'.[83] The plan was that O'Connell would use the Catholic Association in Ireland to secure signatures for the petitions, which he would then present to the House of Commons,[84] together with what Bentham termed 'my plan for an all embracing regeneration of the law'.[85]

When *Justice and Codification Petitions*[86] was published later in 1829 it included the 'Full-length Petition for Justice' consisting of 207 pages, and the 'Abridged Petition for Justice' consisting of eighty-eight pages, but also a 'More Abridged Petition for Justice' consisting of fifteen pages, together with a 'Supplement' consisting of twenty-three pages (which could be added to any of the three petitions), and 'Petition for Codification' consisting of nine pages. Bentham, fearful that the 'Full-length Petition for Justice', given that it would have to be copied onto parchment, would prove both too bulky for 'its being carried about for signature', and too expensive to be engrossed, had, therefore, produced the 'Abridged Petition'. The 'Abridged Petition' had the further advantage that it was more likely to be read and signed by a greater number of persons than the 'Full-length Petition'.[87] The same considerations had then led him to produce the 'More Abridged Petition'.[88] As the subtitle to the work explained, the petitions were 'forms proposed for *signature* by all persons whose desire it is to see Justice no longer sold, delayed, or denied: and to obtain a possibility of that knowledge of the law, in proportion to the want of which they

[81] Bentham to O'Connell, 31 Aug. 1828, National Library of Ireland, MS 13,467 (27).

[82] O'Connell procured support for motions in favour of codification at meetings at Co. Kerry on 16 October 1828 and Kilkenny on 21 October 1828: see J. E. Crimmins, 'Jeremy Bentham and Daniel O'Connell: Their Correspondence and Radical Alliance, 1828–31', *Historical Journal*, 40 (1997), 359–87, at 370.

[83] Bentham to O'Connell, 25 Feb. 1829, Bowring, xi. 12; Bentham to Francis Place, 25 Feb. 1829, Rare Book and Special Collections Library, University of Illinois at Urbana-Champaign, Hollander 3954; and Bickersteth to Bentham, 2 Mar. 1829, Bentham Papers, British Library Add. MS 33,546, fos. 263–4.

[84] Bentham to O'Connell, 18 Nov. 1828, University College Dublin Library, P/12/3/196.

[85] Bentham to La Fayette, 25 Mar. 1829, Cornell University Library, La Fayette Papers.

[86] *Justice and Codification Petitions: being forms proposed for signature by all persons whose desire it is to see Justice no longer sold, delayed, or denied: and to obtain a possibility of that knowledge of the law, in proportion to the want of which they are subjected to unjust punishments, and deprived of the Benefit of their Rights* (London, 1829) (Bowring, v. 437–548).

[87] Bowring, v. 438–9.

[88] Ibid. 444.

are subjected to unjust punishments, and deprived of the Benefit of their Rights'. The allusion to the sale, delay, and denial of justice was a deliberate evocation of Magna Carta.[89] The 'Petition for Justice' demanded the abolition of the existing judicial establishment and its system of procedure, and its replacement by a system of procedure based on 'the *domestic* system', namely that 'pursued of course by every intelligent father of a family, without any such idea as that of its constituting the matter of an art or science'.[90] In effect, the work was a restatement of the proposals for the judicial establishment and its associated procedure which Bentham had elaborated in the constitutional code, with some amendments to render it compatible with the existing political system, together with illustrations of English practice drawn from *Rationale of Judicial Evidence.* The intelligibility and economy of Bentham's pannomion was contrasted with the complexity and expense of the Common Law. His overarching aim was to make justice accessible to all, instead of being denied to the many and sold to the privileged few. He once again identified the existence of fees as the key issue: the root cause of the oppression which characterized the current system, and which he had exposed in *Indications respecting Lord Eldon*,[91] was the power enjoyed by judges to pay themselves what they pleased by imposing taxes on suitors. This method of remuneration had created a sinister interest in judges, and in turn had led to the establishment of a technical system of procedure opposite to the ends of justice. The only effective remedy would be the substitution of the natural for the technical system of procedure, whereby the parties would be brought into the presence of the judge, and allowed to speak for themselves, without the intervention of 'middle men, whose interest it is that redress should be as expensive, and for the sake of their share in the expense, as tardy as possible', and without the exclusion of any evidence that might be relevant.[92]

Bentham's petitioners were to pray for the introduction of the judicial establishment which Bentham had described in 'Constitutional Code' (though adapted slightly to accommodate the Crown and House of Lords). All suits, whether criminal or civil, with the exception only of military and ecclesiastical suits, should be brought in the first instance before Judges Immediate, with the possibility of appeal to Judges Appellate. The existing courts should be abolished, as soon as the causes currently before them had been disposed of. Every individual should be able to travel to and from a judicatory in a single day. In order to secure responsibility, each judicatory should have a single judge. Every judicatory should sit continuously, throughout the day and night, every day of the year. The judges and other court officials should be remunerated by salary at public expense, and no one should receive any fee. The Quasi-jury (though Bentham did not here give it that name) should be instituted, and

[89] See Magna Carta, c. 40 (1215), c. 29 (1225), in *English Historical Documents 1189–1327*, ed. H. Rothwell (London, 1975), 320, 345: 'To no one will we sell, to no one will we refuse or delay right or justice.'

[90] Bowring, v. 438.

[91] See p. 305 above.

[92] Bowring, v. 444–6.

should sit at a second, recapitulatory hearing, when ordered by the judge at his own discretion or at the request of one or other of the parties.[93] Appeals should be heard by appellate judicatories, all single-seated, located in London, where public opinion was best-informed and most effective, and could provide the 'most influential and salutary check upon the conduct, and security for the good conduct, of these as well as all other public functionaries'. The only evidence received should be the record containing a transcript of the oral evidence received in the court below, thereby rendering attendance by parties and witnesses unnecessary. No person should be capable of serving as Judge Appellate who had not served for a certain amount of time as Judge Immediate. In every judicatory at both levels there should be a Government Advocate, who would officiate in suits in which government, on behalf of the public at large, was interested. There should also be an Eleemosynary Advocate, who would assist suitors either incapable of acting for themselves or too poor to purchase professional assistance. To defray the costs of those unable to pay them, the Helpless Litigant's Fund should be established. The fund would be supplied by the fines levied on parties judged to be in the wrong—with the abolition of all factitious costs it would be possible to impose heavier fines than under the present system.[94] No functionary should be allowed to transfer between the profession of advocate and that of judge, given that '*impartiality*' was 'the duty of the one', and '*partiality* the duty, and proposed misrepresentation the unavoidable practice, of the other'. A Justice Minister, responsible for appointing all other judges, should be placed at the head of the judiciary. The Justice Minister should not be permitted to sit in Parliament. The judicial authority of the House of Lords should be restricted to cases in which one of its own members was a defendant.[95]

Bentham's petitioners were, moreover, to pray that the power of judges to make law be subjected to the oversight of the legislature, to ensure that 'the field of legislation be preserved from being overspread by an overgrowth of *judge-made* law'. Judges should, however, by means of 'appropriate machinery', have the power to propose amendments to the law, subject to the approval of a Parliamentary committee.[96] Technical language should be abolished, being replaced throughout by

> such as shall be intelligible to all who have need to understand it: no word employed but what is already in familiar use, except in so far as need has place for a word on purpose: and that, to every such unavoidably-employed word, be attached an exposition, composed altogether of words in familiar use: and that, throughout, the *signs* thus employed be, of themselves, as characteristic as may be of the *things* signified.[97]

The petition concluded that the existing system was 'in every part repugnant to the ends of justice', and that the mischief it produced could only be removed 'by

[93] Bowring, v. 498–9. [94] Ibid. 503. [95] Ibid. 499–500. [96] Ibid. 500.
[97] Ibid. 503.

the entire abolition of it, coupled with the substitution of a system directed to those ends, and pure from all such corruptive tendency'.[98]

In the 'Supplement', Bentham outlined the way in which the sinister interest of legislators and lawyers would lead them to oppose the sort of reform he was proposing. While it was the moral duty of legislators to fulfil the main end of justice, which consisted in maximizing the execution and effect given to the laws, and thereby to prevent both mis-decision and non-decision, as well as to minimize delay, vexation, and expense, they were motivated by opposing interests which, 'being peculiar to the few', could only be promoted at the expense of the subject-many.[99] When any proposal for law reform was put forward, the legislators took advice from the lawyers, the only persons who had any knowledge of the existing law. It was, therefore, on their opinion that the decision to accept or reject the proposal was grounded. As it was in the interest of lawyers that the law should be 'in a state as opposite to the interest of the people, in respect of the ... ends of justice, as possible,—and, whatever it be, as little known as possible', they used their expertise not to promote but to prevent reform, whether 'in an open and direct way, or in a disguised and indirect way; in particular, by the promotion of such narrow improvements, apparent or even real, so they be—either by unadaptability, or by their narrowness and the consequent length of time requisite for their establishment,—obstructive of all adequate as well as beneficial change'. This explained why it was that almost all lawyers attempted to 'frustrate' any proposal to establish 'an all-comprehensive, uniform, and self-consistent rule of action,—conducive, in endeavour at least, in the highest degree possible, to the happiness of the whole community, taken together'. Silence had, in general, been the tactic adopted, since the lawyers recognized that overt opposition would draw attention to the proposal in question, and in turn to the weakness of their arguments against it.[100] There were, nevertheless, three classes of legislator who would support reform: those with a strong sense of moral duty; those whose interest was identified with the general interest; and those who feared that 'the subject-many should, in sufficient number, concur in doing for themselves what ought to have been done for them, and so doing cease to exhibit that compliance, by, and in proportion to which, all power is constituted'.[101]

In 'Petition for Codification' the petitioners were to complain of the difficulty of knowing what the law was, and therefore the impossibility of claiming their rights and fulfilling their duties, and of the contradiction involved in the claim that judges did not make the Common Law when it consisted in rules devised by judges. The people of England were subject to a worse tyranny than that to which slaves were subjected, since slaves were not punished for disobeying laws about which their masters had deliberately not informed them: 'That which, for this purpose, we have need of ... is a body of law, from the respective parts of

[98] Ibid. 507. [99] Ibid. 541. [100] Ibid. 541–2. [101] Ibid. 542–3.

which we may, each of us, by reading them or hearing them read, learn, and on each occasion know, what are his *rights*, and what his *duties*.' The framing of such a body of law would take time, but as a preparatory measure the petitioners called upon the House of Commons to invite all persons so disposed to submit in the first place a plan of an all-comprehensive code, and then the full text, in instalments if necessary. All such contributions, provided that they contained a rationale, should be printed at public expense; no one—for instance, foreigners—should be excluded from the invitation, and no remuneration should be given for any work submitted, beyond 'the eventual honour of distinction and public approbation' which the author might receive. The petitioners denied any intention of altering the political constitution of the country, and therefore prayed that the drafts should not contain any provision relative to the prerogative of the King, the privileges of the members of the two Houses of Parliament, and the electoral system.[102] Bentham was careful not to entangle the two issues of law reform and parliamentary reform.

V

In the course of writing *Petitions for Justice and Codification* Bentham was led to devise a scheme for clearing the backlog of business in the Court of Chancery. In the spring of 1829 he composed what he called a 'Supplement to the Petition for Justice', which, despite its title, was in fact a different work from the 'Supplement' eventually appended to *Petitions for Justice and Codification.*[103] This unpublished 'Supplement' included a section entitled 'Plan for the disposal of Equity suits in pendency',[104] which was the germ of the work published in 1830 as *Equity Dispatch Court Proposal*,[105] and the more detailed 'Equity Dispatch Court Bill', which remained unfinished at Bentham's death.[106] As far as the equity suitors were concerned, Bentham hoped to save them a great deal of time and money, and to render a correct judgment in their case more likely. A summary mode of procedure would be instituted, and a judicatory characterized by simplicity substituted 'to that complicated, diversified, entangled, extortious and purposely dilatory system of judicature' by which the current 'affliction' of

[102] Bowring, v. 546–8. [103] Bentham to Peel, 22 Apr. 1829, UC xi. 334–6.

[104] Bentham to O'Connell, 25 May 1829, University College Dublin Library, P/12/3/203.

[105] *Equity Dispatch Court Proposal; containing a plan for the speedy and unexpensive termination of the suits now depending in Equity Courts. With the form of a petition, and some account of a proposed Bill for that purpose*, London, 1830 (Bowring, iii. 297–317).

[106] 'Equity Dispatch Court Bill: being a Bill for the Institution of an experimental Judicatory under the name of the Court of Dispatch, for exemplifying in practice the manner in which the proposed Summary may be substituted to the so called Regular System of Procedure; and for clearing away by the Experiment, the arrear of Business in the Equity Courts', first published in Bowring, iii. 319–431. According to the editor's note, this work was 'the last upon which its Author was engaged: his career was closed whilst he was employed upon it': see ibid. 320.

suitors was 'produced'.[107] The Equity Dispatch Court was not merely intended to provide relief for equity suitors, but to point the way to more widespread reform. Bentham envisaged that, once introduced in the Equity Dispatch Court, its system of procedure would be adopted throughout the legal system. According to his plan, first, Parliament would pass appropriate legislation, drafted by Bentham himself; second, the King would commission the Dispatch Court Judge, who would have been previously elected by those suitors who had petitioned for relief; and third, the House of Commons would enquire into the benefits produced by the new procedure, with a view to extending it throughout the legal system.[108] The implementation of the plan would require a petition from existing suitors. The suitors were to go to the office of the *Westminster Review*, where they could sign a petition for relief without the knowledge of the professional lawyers who, Bentham recognized, would be harmed by every suit taken out of their hands, and whose resentment might lead them to injure or ruin the suitors in question. Bentham assured suitors that he had already drafted the petition and Bill, found an MP to move it, and secured support in the Commons. The motion would be made in the Commons when the number of suits petitioned for was, in the opinion of the mover of the Bill, sufficient 'to produce the requisite share of attention in the House'. A placard at the office would state the number of petitions received.[109]

The suitors' petition identified the payment of law fees as the cause of the delay, vexation, and expense which characterized the superior courts in general, and the equity courts in particular. Despite the clause in Magna Carta prohibiting the delay, sale, or denial of justice, in the equity courts justice was delayed, by artificial devices, to all; sold to the comparatively few able to pay the extortionate price; and denied to the vast majority who were unable to pay. The introduction, throughout the judicial system, of the summary mode of procedure, which would effectively exclude all factitious delay, vexation, and expense and would be more likely to produce rectitude of decision, would in the first instance require a considerable expenditure. It made sense to conduct an experiment to gauge the effects of substituting the summary system (which would require an all-comprehensive system of local judicatories) to the equity mode, and thereby test whether the projected improvement was practicable. Such a trial, the suitors pointed out, might be made by means of the judicatory described in Bentham's *Justice and Codification Petitions*. Given that, under the existing system, the interest of lawyers—and especially of those from among whom the King would have to choose a judge for the proposed new court—was for the most part irreconcilably adverse to that of the rest of the population, the proposed experiment would only succeed if the judge were elected by the suitors, subject to a veto on the part of the King.[110]

[107] Ibid. 299. [108] Ibid. 300. [109] Ibid. 300–2. [110] Ibid. 303–5.

The cases brought before the Equity Dispatch Court were not to be decided on the grounds of the existing law, which Bentham characterized as 'a set of general and *indiscriminating* enactments', but according to instructions which Bentham had drawn up for the judge, and which would allow him to adapt his decrees to the circumstances of each case.[111] The basis for the decisions of the Equity Dispatch Court judge would be the disappointment-preventive principle, which, 'next to the *Greatest Happiness* principle', was 'the main foundation' of the law of property, and which, 'in the genealogy of human feelings', was 'the immediate lineal descendant of that same parent principle'. Disappointment was always accompanied by a pain, of which the intensity, where money or money's-worth was the subject-matter, was in the direct ratio of its value in the eyes of the sufferer, and in the inverse ratio of his affluence. It was much more likely that disappointment would be prevented by aiming at that object directly, rather than by aiming at it through the existing rules of property on which the proceedings in question had been grounded, and which in many instances contradicted one another.[112] While the question of compensating lawyers for their loss was worthy of consideration, the suffering experienced by lawyers from ending the extortion would be small compared with the suffering experienced by suitors were it to continue: 'Refusal of summary procedure to you out of tenderness to lawyers—what would it be? It would be refusal of drainage to a pestilential marsh out of tenderness to apothecaries and undertakers.'[113]

[111] Bowring, iii. 300.

[112] Ibid. 312. It has been argued by Postema that *Equity Dispatch Court Proposal* provides compelling evidence that Bentham viewed the provisions of the pannomion as instructions which gave guidance to judges, rather than as binding laws which it was their duty to apply (see *Bentham and the Common Law Tradition*, 413–21). The point, however, is that Bentham intended to issue instructions to the proposed Equity Dispatch Court judge precisely because no pannomion was in existence. He regarded the existing law of property as unintelligible, and, therefore, as incapable of forming secure expectations. It was in these special circumstances that Bentham advocated a direct appeal to the principle of utility by means of the disappointment-preventive principle. Under the pannomion, the judge would be bound by the law, though, as we have seen (pp. 310–11 above), he would have the power to propose amendments. Bentham's position is rather the reverse of what Postema suggests it is. This does not settle the philosophical issue as to what might be the best way for a judge to proceed in a codified legal system based on the principle of utility, but appears to settle what Bentham himself thought. See further J. R. Dinwiddy, 'Adjudication under Bentham's Pannomion', *Utilitas: A Journal of Utilitarian Studies*, 1 (1989), 283–9.

[113] Bowring, iii. 314. It appears that in the event Bentham was unable to procure any signatures. Tyrrell reported the disappointing news that he had been unable to obtain any petitions for the Equity Dispatch Court Proposal: 'It is impossible (as you may suppose) to prevail upon the Attornies to recommend their Clients to become Petitioners. The Suitors (of whom I happen to know but very few) entertain a groundless fear that by petitioning they may prejudice their Cause or remove it to an unsatisfactory tribunal. I thought that I had induced two of them to send Petitions, but my advice was unbalanced by the influence of their Solicitors. My friends at the Chancery Bar, of whom many at my request have made application to the Suitors, have been equally unfortunate.' See Tyrrell to Bentham, 1 June 1830, British Library Add. MS 33,546, fos. 422–3.

VI

On 30 July 1829, the day on which O'Connell was returned for a second time as MP for Clare, he wrote to Bentham: 'I avowed myself on the Hustings this day to be "a Benthamite"—and explained the leading principles of your disciples—"the greatest happiness principle". Our sect *will* prosper.' He promised to act as Bentham's mouthpiece in the Commons: 'I begin my parliamentary career by tendering you my constant zealous and active services in the promotion of that principle. You have now one member of Parliament *your own*.' In the belief that 'the hour for successfully introducing a rational plan of procedure and a "Code"' was 'fast approaching',[114] O'Connell began to plan his campaign in the House of Commons: 'This session—now or never, for Law Reform.' On the first day of the session he would advocate the introduction of the Equity Dispatch Court, and afterwards make an address to procure a code: 'Every day I will have a petition on some one or more law-abuse.'[115] He hoped that Bentham's 'plan' for codification (it is not clear precisely what O'Connell had in mind, though it may have been extracts from 'Codification Proposal') would be printed by order of the Commons: 'You will live to see your work printed at the national expence—and I trust finally adopted.'[116] It was with the aim of supporting law reform in general, and of gaining support in Parliament for O'Connell's efforts in particular, that Bentham conceived of the Law Reform Association. He informed O'Connell that the idea for an association had occurred to him on the same day that a similar proposal had been published in the *Morning Chronicle*.[117] The proposal in question, headed 'Proposal for an Association for Promoting Legal Reform' and signed 'Unus', had appeared in the *Morning Chronicle* of 1 December 1829. Unus proposed the establishment of 'The British and Foreign Association for Promoting Legal Reform', which would organize public meetings and circulate printed works in order to draw attention to the defects of existing legal institutions and to point out the best remedies, present petitions to Parliament for reform, and hold correspondence with distinguished reformers abroad. Bentham proposed that his own Law Reform Association would undertake similar activities, but with a much clearer focus on pushing measures of reform through Parliament.

In the first instance Bentham appears to have consulted Bowring and Charles Sinclair Cullen, both of whom thereupon attempted to procure support for the Association. Joseph Hume, when approached, suggested a combined association for law reform and parliamentary reform. In a letter to Leicester Stanhope, Bentham explained that the effect of linking the two associations would be the

[114] O'Connell to Bentham, 30 July 1829, *Correspondence of O'Connell*, viii. 216–17.
[115] O'Connell to Bentham, 22 Oct. 1829, ibid. 219–21.
[116] O'Connell to Bentham, 4 Nov. 1829, ibid. 222–3.
[117] Bentham to O'Connell, 18 Dec. 1829, University College Dublin Library, P/12/3/209.

driving from each in indefinite number those who but for the conjunction would have joined in it.—I am for beginning with Law Reform, as that which would pave the way for the other—whereas the effect of pushing for Parliamentary Reform, which, if carried at all, could not be carried for this dozen or score years, would be to absorb the attention during the whole of that time, to the exclusion of the other—the only one of the two for which I could do any more than I have done already.

Bowring, Cullen, and Hume had drawn up 'a list of members and other influentials whom upon every occasion they intend to go on canvassing'. Burdett and John Abel Smith had expressed their support, while others were waiting 'to see who would engage likewise'. Henry Bickersteth, for instance, was awaiting the views of Tyrrell, but since Tyrrell had 'become an enthusiastic disciple of mine there can be little apprehension of the result'. Other potential recruits were Sir Alexander Johnston, Charles Strutt, who was writing for *The Jurist* and who Bentham described as 'a very clever young man', Robert Cutler Fergusson, 'the quondam Calcutta barrister', and Stanhope's brother-in-law, Lord Tavistock.[118] Bentham even tried to gain the support of the Duke of Wellington by offering him, in a letter which was characterized by a sustained military metaphor, the support of the Law Reform Association should he commit himself to law reform.[119] The approach to Wellington was, perhaps, part of Bentham's strategy to undermine Brougham, by showing that there were others in Parliament who were able and willing to carry forward law reform.

Over the next few months the efforts to recruit members continued.[120] At the beginning of March 1830 Bentham compiled a list of 'Members already engaged', consisting of nine MPs—Burdett (Westminster), John Smith (Midhurst), Hume (Aberdeen), Henry Warburton (Bridport), John Wood (Preston), Robert Otway-Cave (Leicester), John Berkeley Monck (Reading), John Marshall (Yorkshire), and William Marshall (Petersfield)—together with John Abel Smith (the son of John Smith), Leicester Stanhope, Thomas Perronet Thompson, and Cullen.[121] Meanwhile, Bentham, '[a]t the instance of some of the self-proposed members' drafted 'a Plan' for the Association,[122] which, under the title of 'Law Reform Association Proposal', was printed towards the end of March 1830,[123] and was being distributed by early April 1830.[124] The 'Proposal' contained an outline of Bentham's programme of law reform. It began by asserting that the law was in

118 Bentham to Stanhope, 11 Dec. 1829, University College London Library, Stanhope Collection, no. 31.

119 Bentham to Wellington, 12 Dec. 1829, Bowring, xi. 9–12 (where it is misdated 1828).

120 On 6 February 1830 Bentham drew up a list headed 'Members proposed for the Initiatory Association' (see UC lxxxv. 196), consisting of over thirty names.

121 UC lxxxv. 195 (2 Mar. 1830).

122 Bentham to O'Connell, 18 Dec. 1829, University College Dublin Library, P/12/3/209. See also Charles Sinclair Cullen to Bentham, 7 Jan. 1830, British Library Add. MS 33,546, fos. 360–1, who expressed himself 'anxious for a prospectus of our law-reform Association'.

123 Bentham to Cullen, 22 Mar. 1830, University College London Library, D. R. Bentham Collection, MS Add. A.1.53.

124 Bentham to Baron King, 4 Apr. 1830, ibid. A.1.47.

large part unknowable and unintelligible. The judicial establishment and system of procedure were repugnant to the ends of justice; the statute law was confused; and the Common Law was incomprehensible. Members of the Houses of Parliament 'in considerable number', in conjunction with others, had decided to form the Law Reform Association, in order to provide 'a nucleus' around which constituents and other members of the community were invited to gather.[125] The purpose was to achieve legislative reform either by supporting or cajoling ministers: 'in relation to the advisers of the Crown, in no state in which their minds can be, can an Association such as this fail to be of use: if evil-intentioned, it will be a *check* to them; if well-intentioned, but sluggish, a *spur*; if well-intentioned but timid, a *cordial* and encouragement'.[126] The issue of law reform was distinguished sharply from that of parliamentary reform. This distinction was not intended to imply any disapproval of the latter, but to avoid excluding any person from the Association who was prepared to support law reform but not parliamentary reform.[127]

As for the substance of the reform, this was to be nothing less than a pannomion, which would be effected through a series of proposed bills, each containing distinct or particular codes, relating, for instance, to particular conditions in life or occupations. Each code would be accompanied by 'an appropriate *rationale*: a sort of *perpetual commentary*, giving expression to the several considerations of utility, by which the several enactments, or groups of enactments, were suggested'. A new system of judicial procedure would be established, together with a judicial establishment consisting of local judicatories, each authorized to apply the whole of the law, with officials paid by salary. The Association would publish books and pamphlets illustrating the suffering and hardship produced by the existing system, and giving examples of 'remarkable deficiency in respect of appropriate aptitude, moral, intellectual, or active, on the part of individual judiciary functionaries'. It would encourage the dissemination of already-published works which aimed to improve the law, for instance through purchase or paying for advertisements; provide information about similar works dealing with English law published in other countries; and publish selections from periodicals.[128] The Association would cultivate support for the pannomion, in particular by obtaining petitions to Parliament praying for its introduction. Its members would make public speeches, cause '*lectures* to be delivered, in and by *circuits*, performed by men of appropriate attainments', encourage the establishment of similar associations elsewhere, and publish the 'Transactions of the Association'. Those members of the Association who were MPs were expected to vote, propose motions, and make speeches in Parliament.[129]

The officers of the Association would consist of a Treasurer and a Secretary,[130] and an apartment would be hired for holding meetings and housing a library.

[125] 'Law Reform Association Proposal', 1–2. [126] Ibid. 6. [127] Ibid. 7.

[128] Ibid. 7–10. [129] Ibid. 10–12.

[130] According to the list drawn up by Bentham on 6 February 1830 (UC lxxxv. 196), Thomas Perronet Thompson was earmarked for the role of Honorary Secretary.

The voting membership of the Society would consist of persons who made a donation of an as-yet unspecified sum, or paid an annual subscription of £2. Smaller sums would be accepted as donations, but to prevent the Society from being infiltrated by persons opposed to its aims, votes could not 'prudently be allowed, to persons contributing *less* sums than the above'.[131] At the first meeting a Committee would be appointed with the task of convening a General Meeting, at which Committees and sub-Committees would be appointed. The first meeting would be held at 2 Queen's Square Place, Westminster (Bentham's house), '*that* being the nearest place to the Houses of Parliament that can at present be obtained on gratuitous terms'.[132] Bentham concluded the 'Proposal' by stating that, although most of the founders of the Association were Englishmen, they would welcome the accession of natives of Scotland and Ireland:

For, of the numberless benefits producible by the contemplated all-comprehensive Code, not the least is—the prospect, which, taking for its leading principle the *greatest happiness principle*, it would afford—of producing an all-comprehensive *assimilation*, or rather, bating the unavoidable *diversification* of local circumstances, a perfect *identity*, of the rule of action,—throughout the three kingdoms, which compose the seat of the central government of the British Empire: not to speak of the so much more abundantly greater population of its distant dependencies.[133]

Echoing his remarks in his letter to Simon Snyder, Bentham envisaged that once utilitarian reform had been instituted in one country, there would be no bounds to its progress.[134]

Once the 'Proposal' had been printed, efforts were made to secure subscribers to the Society. Copies of the 'Proposal' were circulated, with Cullen particularly active in this respect.[135] Potential members were asked to sign a declaration appended to the 'Proposal': 'I hereby declare my accession to the Association the Proposal for which is in this paper contained.' Lord Radnor joined the Association and sent Bentham a subscription of £5.[136] Isaac Goldsmid, the Jewish leader and financier, agreed to subscribe anonymously. He feared that 'mischief' might result if he allowed his name to be publicly identified 'with any attempts at reform'.[137] Other positive responses were received from John Evans, the barrister, William Marshall, James Garth Marshall (the son of John Marshall, MP for Yorkshire), Daniel Sykes (MP for Hull), Richard Taylor the printer, Thomas Perronet Thompson, and Lord Weymouth.[138] It had, however, been

131 'Law Reform Association Proposal', 12–13. 132 Ibid. 14. 133 Ibid. 15.

134 See p. 247 above.

135 See the letters to Cullen from M. Taylor, declining to join the Association, and John Wood, sending his apologies for the first meeting, bound at British Library Chadwick Tracts, C.T.84.

136 Radnor to Bentham, 7 Apr. 1830, ibid.; and Radnor to Bentham, 18 Apr. 1830, British Library Add. MS 33,546, fos. 408–9.

137 Isaac Goldsmid to Bentham, 1 June 1830, British Library Chadwick Tracts, C.T.84.

138 Their signed 'Proposals' are collected at ibid.

decided not to ask practising lawyers to join the Association. The issue seems to have been thrown into relief by the position of Thomas Denman. Bentham was of the view that Denman's law-reform proposals, outlined in a pamphlet which he had sent to Bentham,[139] 'do not go to the root of the evil: if carried into effect, they wd. cut off no more than a comparatively minute portion of it, and give stability to the remainder'. Bentham continued:

> Be this as it may no call will on this occasion be made to him to declare himself. It is unanimously agreed, that partly for their own sakes partly for that of the public, no such call shall be made to any more of the lawyer class, official or professional, for this purpose. Not even Bickersteth, who is a most cordial friend to law refm. to its utmost extent... and has hitherto acceded without reserve to the letter as well as spirit of every thing proposed by me.

Bentham expected that Bickersteth would be appointed as 'one of the new Judges upon the Chancellor's [i.e. Lyndhurst's] sham-reform plan',[140] and did not want to 'place him in any such embarrassing situatn. as that of being obliged either to give or to decline giving his accession to a measure necessarily displeasing to the higher powers'.[141]

As the preparations for establishing the Law Reform Association were progressing, O'Connell, with whom Bentham was 'in constant communication',[142] was pressing ahead with his campaign in the House of Commons, which had opened its session on 5 February 1830. On 11 February 1830 O'Connell presented Bentham's 'Petition for Codification', praying that the law be rendered cheap, intelligible, and expeditious, read extracts from it, and secured an order for its printing.[143] In a debate on law reform on 18 February 1830 O'Connell argued that there should be one simple mode of procedure; that local tribunals should be established throughout the country; that the system of special pleading should be abolished; that fees should be abolished, and judges and other officials paid by salary; and that each court should have a single judge. These measures, he asserted, were preparatory to 'a thing necessary above all others—he meant the formation of a Code for England'.[144] On other occasions he called for a reform in the language of the law, 'so that all might understand it';[145] he called for the constant sitting of courts, echoing Bentham's aphorism 'when injustice sleeps so may justice' in his statement that, 'for as injustice never slept, so ought

139 Presumably *Every Man his own Attorney* (London, [1830?]).

140 On 22 March 1830 Lyndhurst had introduced a Bill for the reform of the administration of Equity, and had announced further proposals, including the addition of a puisne judge to each of the Common Law courts. The Bill was lost on the death of George IV on 26 June 1830 and the subsequent dissolution of Parliament. See J. B. Atlay, *The Victorian Chancellors*, 2 vols. (London, 1906–8), i. 69–71.

141 Bentham to John Smith, 21 Apr. 1830, British Library Add. MS 33,546, fos. 410–11.

142 Bentham to Edward Livingston, 23 Feb. 1830, ibid. fos. 373–8.

143 *Parliamentary Debates*, xxii (1830), 328–32; *Commons Journals*, lxxxv (1830), 26–7.

144 *Parliamentary Debates*, xxii (1830), 673–6.

145 Ibid. 919 (24 Feb. 1830).

justice never to slumber';[146] and he even called for the abolition of the usury laws, another measure recommended by Bentham.[147]

In the meantime Bentham was delighted to see that Peel, in the House of Commons on 9 March 1830 in a debate on the Welsh Judicature Bill, had announced an intention to abolish the taking of fees by officers of the courts. Peel had, in fact, moved for leave to bring in such a Bill on 18 February 1830, when he had argued that the existence of patent offices was one of the greatest obstacles to the improvement of the law, and that it was necessary, therefore, to end the creation of vested interests in courts of justice. The purpose of the measure was to convert the remuneration of existing officials from fees into salaries, with the fees thenceforward being received on public account, to compensate the officials concerned, and to ensure that no official appointed after a certain date would have any claim to compensation. 'The question of fees once set at rest,' remarked Peel, 'Parliament would be at liberty to deal with every question of legal reform in future according to its own merits, without being influenced by other considerations.' The policy of government was to make the administration of justice 'equal, impartial, expeditious, and as little expensive as possible'.[148] Bentham promised Peel all the assistance he was able to give, and informed O'Connell that he had proffered a 'right hand of fellowship' to Peel on account of 'the symptoms manifested in a late speech or two of his, in which he is coming round and attacking the army of Chicane in flank, at any rate, not to say in front, and, moreover, issuing a direct declaration of war against "*Technicalities*"'.[149] Indeed, it may have been Peel's remarks on 9 March 1830 which stimulated Bentham into preparing *Official Aptitude Maximized; Expense Minimized* for the press, focusing as it did on the theme of official remuneration.[150] In any event, here was official endorsement of Bentham's key recommendation.

At the end of April 1830 Bentham was optimistic about the prospects for the Law Reform Association: he believed that it was 'now organizing with no bad promise of success'.[151] A few days before the first meeting, which had been scheduled for 2 June 1830, Bentham encouraged James Mill to join the Association and to become one of the members of the management committee.

146 *Parliamentary Debates*, xxiii (1830), 63 (9 Mar 1830). For Bentham's aphorism see p. 309 above.

147 *Parliamentary Debates*, xxiv (1830), 60–1 (16 Apr. 1830). According to his nephew George Bentham (see *George Bentham: Autobiography 1800–1834*, ed. M. Filipiuk (Toronto, 1997), 327), Bentham around this time was 'in high spirits', enjoying the 'notice' which 'had been taken of him in the House of Commons'.

148 *Parliamentary Debates*, xxii (1830), 650–63. The Common Laws Fees Act (11 Geo. IV & 1 Wil. IV, c. 58) received the Royal Assent on 23 July 1830.

149 Bentham to Peel, 13 Mar. 1830, Peel Papers, British Library Add. MS 40,400, fos. 94–5; Bentham to O'Connell, 15 Mar. 1830, Bowring, xi. 37–8.

150 See *Official Aptitude Maximized; Expense Minimized*, Editorial Introduction, p. xvii, and p. 305 above.

151 Bentham to Adolphus Hauman, 30 Apr. 1830, Beinecke Rare Book and Manuscript Library, Yale University, James Marshall and Marie-Louise Osborn Collection, File B: item 1127.

He noted that John Smith, John Abel Smith, Burdett, Hume, Marshall (it is unclear which one of the three of those whose names had been linked with the Association), the Earl of Radnor, and Baron King would attend.[152] Presumably Cullen also attended, though it is unknown whether James Mill or indeed Bentham himself did so, since no record of the meeting appears to have survived. This first meeting, however, led to nothing. On 4 June 1830 James Silk Buckingham wrote to Bentham: 'I am sorry for the issue of your Meeting: but the indisposition to give money for the support of laudable objects seems to me the prevailing vice of the age: and I am sorry to say I find the most liberal professions rather more backward than the opposite side to promote what they profess to think desirable.'[153] This supports the account of the Association which Bowring gave in his 'Memoirs of Bentham':

[Bentham] thought, that many who would hesitate about lending their aid to the obtainment of Constitutional Reform, might not be unwilling to co-operate for the purpose of making justice more accessible to the whole community. For this purpose, he obtained the promised cooperation of many distinguished men: but the purpose never ripened to an efficient vitality. Names to ornament—reputations to attract, were easily found; but not so hands and heads to work. So the plan was abandoned, or deferred *sine die*. . . .[154]

Bentham and O'Connell were not immediately discouraged from continuing with their scheme to press for codification in the House of Commons. In mid-June 1830 Bentham sent a codification petition to Burdett, who had apparently expressed a willingness to present it to the Commons by reading it as part of a speech. 'Of course,' said Bentham, 'if you find it to such a degree grating to the aforesaid Honble ears that Honble Gentlemen run out of the House as they used to when Orator Burke was pouring forth the torrent of his eloquence,[155] you will stop in time.' He continued:

If ever there was a paper which, from the importance of the subject matter, as measured by it's extent, presented a prospect of experiencing this indulgence, it is this:—for the extent of it is neither more nor less than that of the whole field of legislation—a field which does not want much of being co-extensive with the whole field of thought & action: & this, with your unexampled brilliancy of imagination, you will deal with better than anybody else could do.

Burdett could be assured of support from Hume and O'Connell, but if he was not prepared to present it, then Hume would step in.[156] Bentham received a

[152] Bentham to James Mill, 31 May 1830, John Stuart Mill Papers, Manuscripts and Archives, Yale University Library.

[153] Buckingham to Bentham, 4 June 1830, British Library Add. MS 33,546, fos. 424–5. Bentham was, nevertheless, still distributing copies of 'Law Reform Association Proposal' in early August 1830: see Bentham to Stanhope, 3 Aug. 1830, University College London Library, Stanhope Collection, no. 12.

[154] Bowring, xi. 30.

[155] It was said that Burke became known as 'the Dinner Bell' because, when he rose to speak, many MPs would leave the chamber in search of mutton chops.

[156] Bentham to Burdett, 17 June 1830, Bodleian Library, University of Oxford, MS. Eng. Lett. d. 97, fos. 26–7.

non-committal response from Burdett, which he took to be a refusal, and asked O'Connell (rather than Hume) to move the petition, assuring him of support from Hume. He commented that his petition would take only fifty minutes to read, whereas 'Brougham's famously long speech, which did not touch upon the tenth part of the field occupied six hours & upwards'.[157]

In the event, Bentham's petition was not presented to the House of Commons. On 8 July 1830 O'Connell, who had earlier given notice of a motion proposing that measures be taken 'to have drafts or plans of a Code of Laws and procedure, either in the whole or in parts, to be laid before the House', withdrew the notice, on the grounds that it was too late in the session to embark on such an important subject. He revealed that the petition was 'from a man whose name was his highest eulogy—he meant Mr. Jeremy Bentham', and that it 'contained an offer to submit to the House the draft of a full Code of Laws and procedure, with reasons for every article, if the House would think proper to go to the expense of printing it'. Moreover, he had been 'instructed to say, that Mr. Bentham, in his plan, met the objection which had hitherto been made to all codes, that they were subject to misinterpretation'.[158] O'Connell's failure to present the petition appears to have marked the effective end of Bentham's direct attempts to introduce codification into the United Kingdom. O'Connell later apologized for his ineffectiveness: 'I am ashamed to call myself your disciple. I deem myself not worthy of your patronage or friendship; and I console myself only by working for useful objects in a lower grade, and endeavouring to make up by perseverance and moral energy, for the loss of the more brilliant prospect of usefulness which, I think, lay before me.'[159] Bentham responded sympathetically: 'You have cried *peccavi*, come up this day se'ennight and receive absolution.'[160] Nevertheless, there appears to be little doubt that Bentham was disappointed that O'Connell, despite having proclaimed himself to be Bentham's MP, had 'never been to be prevailed upon' to bring a Bill on law reform before Parliament.[161]

VII

Although the last few years of his life were devoted to codification and law reform, Bentham continued to support parliamentary reform, and continued to emphasize the importance of the secret ballot. In August 1828, for instance, he warned O'Connell that without radical political reform, there could be no security for codification and law reform. He identified the secret ballot as the central measure of radical reform, and on that basis doubted whether the Whigs,

[157] Bentham to O'Connell, 23 June 1830, National Library of Ireland, MS 13,468 (3).
[158] *Parliamentary Debates*, xxv (1830), 1114 (8 July 1830).
[159] O'Connell to Bentham, 22 Feb. 1831, *Correspondence of O'Connell*, viii. 229–30.
[160] Bentham to O'Connell, 26 Feb. 1831, Bowring, xi. 64.
[161] See Bentham's note on a copy of his letter to Peel of 7 Apr. 1827 at UC xi. 275.

who favoured moderate reform, would ever be induced to support the secret ballot: 'for, let but the ballot be established, away slips all the seats from under them. Some will be filled by Tories, some by Radicals, in proportions which, as things stand at present, it will not be possible to determine.' The introduction of the secret ballot was the key to obtaining 'a *good Government*, with the *faculty* of framing a *real constitution*, instead of, on every occasion, dreaming of an *imaginary* one'. He advised O'Connell to obtain petitions from Ireland calling for radical reform, or if that was not possible, calling for the secret ballot alone, and thereupon to introduce an appropriate motion in the House of Commons.[162] Less than a month later Bentham recommended that O'Connell begin with a motion for the ballot, on the grounds that he was aware of a number of MPs who would be prepared to support it, and it would engender less opposition than a complete programme of radical reform.[163] At the same time Bentham was attempting to reconcile O'Connell with Henry Hunt, with a view to their joining forces—the former with the support of Ireland and the latter with the support of London—to call for the introduction of the ballot.[164]

In March 1831 Bentham offered his support to the Parliamentary Candidate Society, established by Place in response to the first Reform Bill introduced by the Whig ministry.[165] The purpose of the Society was to promote reform by collecting together and publishing information 'respecting the character, talent, conduct, and connexions, of all persons who may be proposed as candidates for seats in the Legislature'.[166] Electors would then be in a position to make a correct choice of representative—a choice which would be all the more important 'when the manly, honest measures proposed by ministers, and sanctioned by the king, shall become the law of the land, and restore to the people the power of REALLY choosing their own representatives'.[167] The Society appears to have had its initial meeting on 14 March 1831,[168] and to have met regularly for a few weeks, but was soon disbanded.[169] It was probably as a result of this initiative that Bentham issued *Parliamentary Candidate's Proposed Declaration of Principles*, and wrote to Richard Potter and Reginald Prentice in favour of Bowring as a potential parliamentary candidate in Manchester.[170] Later in the year he

[162] Bentham to O'Connell, 31 Aug. 1828, National Library of Ireland, MS 13,467 (27).

[163] Bentham to O'Connell, 23 Sep. 1828, Bowring, x. 601.

[164] Bentham to O'Connell, 25 Sep. 1828, National Library of Ireland, MS 13,647 (27); Bentham to Henry Hunt, *c.*26 Sep. 1818, Bowring, xi. 5–7.

[165] Bentham to Place, 15 Mar. 1831, Place Papers, British Library Add. MS 35,149, fo. 42.

[166] 'Parliamentary Candidate Society, instituted to promote the return of Fit and Proper Members to Parliament', issued as a printed leaflet. A copy at UC cxxviii. 498, attached to a note from Robert Gouger, the Honorary Secretary, to Bentham, 25 Mar. 1831, lists Bentham as a member of the Committee.

[167] *Parliamentary Candidate Society, instituted to promote the return of Fit and Proper Members to Parliament* (London, 1831) (dated 31 March 1831), copy at UC cxxviii. 497.

[168] Place to Bentham, 18 Mar. 1831, UC cxxviii. 495–6.

[169] See Wallas, *Life of Francis Place*, 260–3.

[170] Bentham to Potter, Apr. 1831, British Library of Political and Economic Science, LSE Archives, COLL MISC 0146/12, fos. 251–2; Bentham to Prentice, 11 Apr. 1831, British Library

recommended Bowring to the 'future electors of Blackburn',[171] where Bowring was to be defeated by thirteen votes in the first election following the passing of the Great Reform Act. Bentham died on 6 June 1832, the day on which the Act received the Royal Assent. According to Bowring: 'The news of the Reform Bill having been carried greatly cheered [Bentham's] last hours.'[172] If so, it could only have been because he saw it as the thin edge of the wedge.

Add. MS 33,546, fos. 498–501. Bowring himself states that it was the occasion of the Parliamentary Candidate Society which led Bentham to write 'credentials for some of his acquaintance, many of whom, so recommended, found their way into Parliament on the passing of the Reform Bill': see Bowring, xi. 66.

[171] 'Jeremy Bentham to the Future Electors of Blackburn', London, [1831], dated Queen's Square Place, Westminster, 27 Oct. 1831.

[172] See Bowring's obituary in *The Times*, 7 June 1832, reproduced in J. E. Crimmins (ed.), *Bentham's Auto-Icon and Related Writings* (Bristol, 2002).

13

Last Things

I

In his 'Memoirs' of Bentham, Bowring described Bentham's death on 6 June 1832 as follows:

His head reposed on my bosom. It was an imperceptible dying. He became gradually colder, and his muscular powers were deprived of action. After he had ceased to speak, he smiled, and grasped my hand. He looked at me affectionately, and closed his eyes. There was no struggle,—no suffering,—life faded into death—as the twilight blends the day with darkness.

With a view to the advancement of anatomical science, he directed that his body should be dissected: and this direction was carried into effect.[1]

Bentham had left instructions in his will that his body should be used in a series of anatomical lectures. The bequest would not only promote education, but also undermine 'the primitive horror of dissection' which, he added, 'originates in nonsense & is kept up by misconception'. His intention was to show that 'the human body when dissected instead of being an object of disgust is as much more beautiful than any other piece of mechanism as it is more curious and wonderful'.[2] Moreover, given that there was a severe shortage of bodies available for dissection—in great part due to popular superstition about the consequences of dissection for bodily resurrection—Bentham hoped that his example would encourage others to do the same. His willingness to have his body dissected had been longstanding—in his first will drawn up in 1769, he had instructed that his body should be dissected should he 'chance to die of any such disease as that in the judgment of [his executor] the art of Surgery or science of Physic should be likely in any wise advanced by observations to be made on the opening of my body'.[3]

What Bowring did not mention was that in his will of 1832 Bentham not only ordered the dissection of his body, but left a series of further instructions.

[1] Bowring, xi. 76. The intimacy suggested by this account appears somewhat incongruous when set against that of George Bentham (*Autobiography*, 385): 'returning [i.e. to Queen's Square Place] in the afternoon, found him just expiring, and at half-past 5 he breathed his last, in the presence of Bowring, Doane, Chadwick and myself.'

[2] See 'Bentham's Last Will and Testament', in Crimmins (ed.), *Bentham's Auto-Icon and Related Writings*, 16.

[3] *Correspondence*, i. 136.

Once the anatomical lectures had been completed, he directed that his skeleton should 'be put together in such manner as that the whole figure may be seated in a Chair usually occupied by me when living in the attitude in which I am sitting when engaged in thought'. The skeleton was to be clothed in one of his black suits, and along with his walking stick (named 'Dapple' after Sancho Panza's donkey)[4] be placed in 'an appropriate box or case'. The operation was entrusted to Bentham's friend and physician, Thomas Southwood Smith. On 9 June 1832, three days after Bentham's death, an oration was delivered by Smith over Bentham's body at the Webb Street School of Anatomy and Medicine,[5] where the dissection subsequently took place. At some point the skeleton and other remains were taken by Smith, who proceeded to create Bentham's auto-icon, the combination of skeleton, wax head, clothes, and stuffing which now resides in University College London.[6] Bowring, as Bentham's literary executor, was charged with producing what became the eleven-volume edition of *The Works of Jeremy Bentham*. Not only did Bowring not mention Bentham's auto-icon in his 'Memoirs', he also suppressed Bentham's short essay entitled 'Auto-Icon; or, Of the Farther Uses of the Dead to the Living', despite its having been printed for inclusion in the *Works*.[7]

The tone of 'Auto-Icon'—which, according to the unidentified editor, Bentham referred to as his 'last work', and which 'occupied the last literary hours of his existence'—is highly satirical.[8] Betham noted that little thought had been given to 'any use of which the dead might become to the living', but rather dead bodies had tended to be regarded as something of a nuisance. They were a source of disease, hence means had to be found of disposing of them safely. Taking

[4] See Bowring, xi. 80; and Southwood Smith to William Munk, 14 June 1857, quoted in C. F. A. Marmoy, 'The "Auto-Icon" of Jeremy Bentham at University College, London', reprinted from *Medical History*, 2 (1958), 6. Confusingly, Bowring refers to Bentham's stick as 'Dobbin' at Bowring, x. 600.

[5] See T. Southwood Smith, *A Lecture delivered over the Remains of Jeremy Bentham Esq.* (London, 1832).

[6] The wax head was made by the French anatomical modeller Jacques Talrich. Bentham had intended that his own head would adorn the auto-icon. Smith had attempted to 'preserve the head untouched', but had decided that the result 'would not do for exhibition', and ordered the wax head instead. See Marmoy, '"Auto-Icon" of Jeremy Bentham', 5–6, and C. Fuller (ed.), *The Old Radical: Representations of Jeremy Bentham* (London, 1998), 51–2.

[7] Only twenty or thirty copies of the pamphlet were run off, and of these only three are known to survive. Nor do any of the corresponding manuscripts survive, though there is one sheet headed 'Auto-icon' at UC cxlix. 204 (26 June 1820). Bowring likewise excluded Bentham's major religious writings—namely *Church-of-Englandism, Analysis of the Influence of Natural Religion*, and *Not Paul, but Jesus*—from the *Works*.

[8] See 'Auto-Icon', Note by the Editor, 1. The title itself echoes Smith's 'Use of the Dead to the Living. An Appeal to the Public and the Legislature on the Necessity of affording Dead Bodies to the Schools of Anatomy by Legislative Enactment', which had first appeared in the *Westminster Review*, vol. ii, no. iii (July 1824), 59–97, and had then been published separately in 1828. Smith's point was that the advance of medical knowledge was being held back by the lack of bodies for dissection. In order to understand how the various organs in the body functioned, it was necessary to understand their structure, and hence the need for anatomical research. Elsewhere in the Bowring edition it is stated that 'Equity Dispatch Court Proposal' was Bentham's final work: see p. 324 n. above.

advantage of this fact, certain groups—namely undertakers, lawyers, and priests—had contrived ways of making money for themselves. Instead, argued Bentham, 'the mass of matter which death has created' should be 'disposed of with a view to the felicity of mankind', and thus 'the comparatively incorruptible part' should be made into an auto-icon, and 'the soft and corruptible parts employed for the purpose of anatomical instruction, in so far as there is a demand for them'.[9] Bentham envisaged a whole range of uses for auto-icons. They could, for instance, take part in theatrical performances, and would be particularly impressive if they were animated:

> By means of strings or wires, by persons under the stage, or if the Auto-Icon were clothed in a robe, by a boy stationed within, and hidden by the robe, . . . the eyelids might be made to move; and in so far as needful or conducive to keeping up the illusion, the hands and feet, one, more, or all. As to voice, by well-known contrivances, it may, without difficulty, be made to appear to proceed from the vocal organs of the figure; the body, if necessary, might, by obvious contrivances, be made to appear to breathe.[10]

Bentham suggested that the auto-icons might discuss a variety of philosophical topics: amongst the orators on morals would be Aristotle, Plato, Cicero, St Paul, and Helvétius; on politics Solon, Numa, Bacon, Locke, and Montesquieu; on jurisprudence Justinian, Theodosius, Glanville, Bracton, Coke, Blackstone, Eldon, Peel, Brougham, and, of course, Bentham.[11] On the topic of 'Law as it ought to be', with Bacon, Montesquieu, Dumont, and Bentham as the discussants, Bacon might address Bentham as follows:

> In regard to government and law, you first drew a clear line (and kept it in a conspicuous state throughout) between that which ought to be, and that which is. By Grotius, by Puffendorf, by their predecessors, by their successors the Burlamaquis, &c., that which ought to be, and that which is, were continually confounded: observing what had been the practice of men in power, they inferred, or rather took for granted, that it was right. Forming on any occasion their conception as to what was right, they took for granted that to this pattern the practice of men in power would be found to be conformable. But the complexion of their rules was commonly neither that of the one nor that of the other, but without indication given of any distinction, something neither the one nor the other. Thus so it is because it is right, or right this is, or has been, because thus it is, or has been.

Auto-icons would, therefore, be brought into service to educate the public in Benthamic principles of jurisprudence, as well as other advances in knowledge pioneered by Bentham.[12]

Auto-icons might be used for commemorational and genealogical purposes. For instance, 'a country gentleman' who had 'rows of trees leading to his dwelling' might place 'the Auto-Icons of his family' between the trees.[13] The auto-icons of members of the House of Lords 'should be disposed of in their own most Honourable House. Their robes on their back—their coronets on their

[9] 'Auto-Icon', 1–2. [10] Ibid. 13. [11] Ibid. 13–14. [12] Ibid. 14–15.
[13] Ibid. 3.

head—how rare a galanty-show!'[14] As an accompaniment to 'the document called a *pedigree*', the aristocrat might have 'the corresponding Auto-Icons': 'In their mansions opulent families might have an apartment as a receptacle for the Auto-Icons belonging to it, ranged like so many statues. If consecration be desired to sanctify the depository,—consecration might be obtained,—and such a depository be an advantageous substitute for a mausoleum or churchyard.' The auto-icons would possess the advantage of the likenesses being 'more perfect than painting or sculpture could furnish'.[15] This was to mock the practices of a hereditary aristocracy.

Bentham pointed out that one group who would benefit from the creation of auto-icons would be lawyers, and in particular property lawyers. 'A spick-and-span new subject-matter of property is brought for the first time into existence', noted Bentham, rather like the discovery of meteorites.[16] The first question which would need to be decided was whether auto-icons would be classified as corporeal or incorporeal property. 'No great room for doubt here', quipped Bentham. Next, it would need to be decided whether to classify them as real or personal property. Bentham presumed that they would be regarded as real property:

> But this being granted, in come the next of kin in any number, each claiming his or her share. But admitting it to be personal, might it not, by last will, be converted into a heirloom? What more appropriate, considering the use it might and would be of for the delineation of a pedigree!
>
> Passing in that character to co-heiresses, could it be made the subject-matter of a writ of partition?

Other questions would arise: 'In what manner would it pass by last will and testament?—devise or bequest,—which of those two modes of transfer would be applicable?' Which courts would have jurisdiction—the ecclesiastical courts or the Common Law courts? What number of years would be deemed valid in the leases which might be made of an auto-icon? 'Another riddle, Auto-Icon *in esse*—Auto-Icon in *posse*. Auto-Icon *in esse*, the body after it has undergone the conservative preparation: Auto-Icon *in posse*, the body while in its natural state waiting for the operation to be performed upon it. What a door opened to interesting and instructive pleadings!' Then there was the question of execution: 'Could an Auto-Icon be taken under a Fi. Fa. [i.e. *fieri-facias*], or an execution in aid, or under a commission of bankruptcy; or, as part and parcel of an insolvent's assets, could it be disposed of by an insolvency court?' If an auto-icon was taken

[14] 'Auto-Icon', 4. [15] Ibid. 5.

[16] It had only been after a shower of stones fell near L'Aigle, Normandy on 26 April 1803, and a subsequent paper on the subject by the French scientist Jean-Baptiste Biot, that it had been generally accepted that meteorites originated in space: see U. Marvin, 'Stones Which Fell From the Sky', in B. Zanda and M. Rotaru (eds), *Meteorites: Their Impact on Science and History* (Cambridge, 2001), 16–29, at 22–5.

for a pledge, would the Acts relating to pawnbrokers take effect? 'As to mortgage. The very word proclaims an Auto-Icon to be a still fitter subject-matter for the contract, than it is in the nature of any quantity or quality of land to be. Exists there anywhere a spot of ground of which it can with such propriety be said it is dead, as of an Auto-Icon it can be said to be?' There would also be questions in relation to auto-icons as treasure trove, whether they should be subject to tithes, and so on.[17] Bentham's point, of course, was to mock the practices of lawyers, by illustrating the unnecessary complexity of English law and the way in which that complexity gave rise to lawyers' fees.

Auto-icons would have religious uses, for instance becoming the objects of pilgrimage. Bentham imagined that his own auto-icon might become one such:

> Conceive the old philosopher preserved in some safe repository, to which the name of sacred might be applied, were it not so open to abuse, as well as already so much abused,—what might not be the pilgrimages made to him!
>
> Accompaniments to the *quasi* sacred Auto-Icon, (if by the adverb, the attribute sacred may be rendered endurable,) accompaniments of it, his unedited and unfinished manuscripts, lodged in an appropriate case of shelves. Why not to this monument, as well as to an old stone-coffin, or an old tombstone? In this far-famed receptacle, there would be no want of matter of wonder and admiration. Of miraculousness as well as of sanctity, it would repel with scorn the name.

The pilgrimage, or 'Quasi-hadji', would be made by 'the votaries of the greatest-happiness principle': 'Why not to this receptacle as well as to Mahomet's? Is not Bentham as good as Mahomet was? In this or that, however distant, age, will he not have done as much good as Mahomet will have done evil to mankind? But earlier than the last day of the earth, what will be the last day of the reign of the greatest-happiness principle?'[18] While 'the religion of Jesus' said nothing about the disposal of dead bodies, priests, in contrast, would be bitterly opposed to auto-iconization, since they would lose their surplice fees:

> From its birth to its death, the priest keeps his fixed predatory eye on the prey he covets, and this prey is everything human that either breathes or has breathed . . . . No sooner are you born, than priestcraft lays hold of you, and till you have paid toll to it, keeps shut against you the gate of the road which conducts you to your rights, and in return for the money, perhaps the 'uttermost farthing'[19] thus extorted from your friends, tells them that he has *christened* you; and unless this be done to you, and done by *him* to you, heaven, he informs them, has no comforts for you, nor will earth have any of which it is in his power to deprive you.[20]

Auto-iconization would save the expense of funeral rites, and particularly benefit the poor, who would no longer feel constrained to sacrifice their 'bodily comfort and enjoyment' in order to provide an 'ostentatious funeral' for their relatives. If the body was not auto-iconized, it could be inexpensively disposed of in a pit

[17] 'Auto-Icon', 10–12. [18] Ibid. 15. [19] Matt. 5: 26. [20] 'Auto-Icon', 16.

of lime.[21] Not only would the priesthood lose its fees, but religious sensibilities would be mocked by auto-iconization.

II

Bentham's 'Auto-Icon' continued the critique in which he had been engaged for almost thirty years. He targeted the three branches of the English state which had formed the main focus of his attack since the emergence in his thought of sinister interest in 1804: namely the legal establishment through his mockery of lawyers, the political establishment through his mockery of aristocracy, and the ecclesiastical establishment through his mockery of religion. It was this emergence of sinister interest which eventually produced Bentham's 'transition' to political radicalism, in that it gave him a deeper understanding of the psychology of rulers. Instead of ascribing the problems which, in his youth, he had identified in the law to a lack of knowledge or judgment on the part of legislators and lawyers, he realized that they were the product of deliberate policy. When, for instance, he had written *An Introduction to the Principles of Morals and Legislation*, he had assumed that it was the desire of rulers to promote the happiness of the communities over which they ruled. By the time that he began to draft material on parliamentary reform in 1809, he had come to appreciate that it was the desire of rulers to promote their own interest in whatever way they could, no matter how detrimental to the happiness of the community in general. Having recognized the true nature of the problem, he saw that the only effective solution lay in bringing about an identification of the interest of rulers with that of subjects. This was the task of constitutional law, a task which would be achieved by maximizing official aptitude and minimizing government expense. In other words, Bentham's movement 'from radical Enlightenment to philosophic radicalism', as Burns has described it,[22] was driven by his discovery of sinister interest and the working out of its implications..

The increasingly politicized and radicalized nature of Bentham's later work should not obscure the fact that the fundamental principles of his thought remained constant throughout his career. His starting point, both logically and chronologically, was his understanding of the distinction between the real and the imaginary, and his division of nouns substantive into the names of real entities and the names of fictitious entities. If any proposition, no matter how abstract it appeared, was to make sense, it had ultimately to be related to its 'real source', that is to some object or objects—to some 'substance'—which existed in the physical world. In this respect there was no distinction between a proposition which purported to be a factual one about the natural sciences, and a proposition which

[21] 'Auto-Icon', 9–10.

[22] See J. H. Burns, 'Jeremy Bentham: From Radical Enlightenment to Philosophical Radicalism', *The Bentham Newsletter*, 8 (1984), 4–14.

purported to be an evaluative one about what was valuable or desirable. When properly expounded, the latter proposition was just as much a factual one as the former, and morality was just as much a science as physics or chemistry. The entity represented by the phrase 'the principle of utility' was fictitious, but to talk about the principle of utility made sense because it could be expounded by reference to its 'real source' in the physical world—namely feelings of pain and pleasure experienced by sentient creatures. All other pretended foundations for the science of morality were either nonsensical because non-existent, or a camouflage for the selfish desires of the persons who articulated them. Hence, from an ontological point of view, the French Declaration of the Rights of Man consisted in a series of nonsensical propositions, because there was no really existing legislator who had created the rights in question. From a political point of view it was mischievous, because it was a camouflage for the selfish ambitions of those who had promulgated it. On the other hand, a declaration conceived as a series of moral claims, founded on the principle of utility, would have made sense and might have formed the basis for peaceful reform. The partisan of the principle of utility placed the question of the desirability of reform upon a factual basis. It was the mistake of the partisan of natural law, and of other non-utilitarian moral standards, to claim that he had knowledge of right and wrong without any reference to facts.

Bentham's theory of law, and thence his constitutional theory, had to make sense in terms of his theory of real and fictitious entities. The key was to provide an exposition of power and its corollary, obedience, since government existed where power was exercised. It is important, however, to distinguish between Bentham's exposition of power, with its different 'modifications', and his view as to the most appropriate way of distributing power amongst individuals and institutions. In his early jurisprudential writings he was concerned with identifying the 'modifications' or varieties of power which might exist—for instance whether it was applied generally or particularly, whether it was supreme or subordinate, and whether it was exercised by a particular sort of institution. The supreme power or sovereign in a state was the individual or institution which was ultimately able to enforce its will—in other words the individual or institution to which the other elements in society were disposed to pay obedience. The disposition to obey might, of course, be limited in an indefinite variety of ways, and such limitations represented limitations on the sovereign, whether or not these were formally recognized in legal provisions. It is worth emphasizing that Bentham did not equate the sovereign with the legislative power or with the legislature: the sovereign was that person or body of persons which was able ultimately to enforce its will, and that might be the executive or constitutive power rather than the legislative power, and it might be lodged not only in a legislature, but in a monarch, a judicatory, the people, or some combination of them. Bentham's exposition of sovereignty had both to make sense in terms of its 'real source'—that is, in terms of the real entities by which it was expounded—and to embrace the variety of constitutional arrangements which existed or which might plausibly exist. Bentham was not, in his early jurisprudential writings, prepared to recommend some particular constitutional arrangement as that which would best promote the greatest happiness of the greatest number.

The principle of utility, as conceived by Bentham, did, nevertheless, involve a commitment to a form of political equality. Bentham took it as axiomatic that one person's happiness was worth the same as an equal amount of happiness experienced by any other person. This was not, in itself, decisive in terms of justifying an equal right to participate in the political process—indeed, there were good reasons to the contrary, for instance where a person was incapable of judging for himself what would contribute to his own happiness. What it did justify was the right of everyone to have equal consideration given to their interest. A further argument was needed to justify democracy. Now, Bentham always accepted that the best form of government—and by this he meant that which best promoted the happiness of the community, and that in turn meant taking the interest of each individual in the community into account—was that in which the rulers were dependent on subjects. Hence, when he first turned his attention, albeit fleetingly, to constitutional design at the time of the French Revolution, he rejected the theory of the division of power (a term he used to include the theories both of the balance of powers and the separation of powers) on the grounds that it did not, except accidentally, secure such dependence. Bentham's proposed constitution for France, put forward in the autumn of 1789, was characterized not by a division of power, but by the dependence of the National Assembly, wielding supreme legislative power, on the people as electors. He rejected the need, in these circumstances, to impose any limitation on the legislative power of the National Assembly. This was, in essence, the structure of government which he would later adopt in the constitutional code. It was when Bentham recognized that the dependence of rulers on subjects, and thence the equal consideration of interests, would not be achieved except under a democratic form of government that the utilitarian justification for democracy was complete.

In the autumn of 1789, and in the wake of the Declaration of Rights which committed the French state to political equality, Bentham did propose a democratic franchise for France, including female suffrage, and was led to consider wide-ranging electoral reform for Britain. His enthusiasm for reform was short-lived. It was not long afterwards that Bentham was opposing any measure of political reform in Britain, and arguing against popular participation in politics—arguments which he continued to deploy until the late 1790s and possibly beyond. The crucial turning-point in Bentham's political thought was, as noted above, the emergence in his thought of sinister interest. Bentham became totally disenchanted with the successive ministries of Pitt and Addington following the effective rejection of his panopticon prison scheme in 1803. (The scheme was half-heartedly revived in 1810, but finally laid to rest in 1812.)[23]

[23] See Semple, *Bentham's Prison*, 254–81.

It seems plausible to suggest that his reflection on the causes of the rejection of the scheme—notably the self-interest of landowning aristocrats who did not want their estates blighted by a neighbouring prison—led him to discover the existence of sinister interest. A particular interest which was in opposition to the general interest was a sinister interest. From the perspective of his psychological theory, this discovery led to a deepening of his understanding of the motives of those who wielded power. Rather than possessing a desire to promote the interests of the community in general, rulers in fact possessed a desire to promote their own selfish or particular interests, whatever detriment this might cause to the general interest. Hitherto, Bentham had assumed that he could work within the existing political system in order to introduce the reforms he thought desirable. Henceforward, he recognized that since such reform would undermine the interests of rulers, they would bitterly oppose it, and stoutly defend all existing abuses.

Having given up hope of building the panopticon prison, in the late spring of 1803 Bentham had, turned his attention to the reform of judicial procedure and evidence. By the summer of 1804 he had worked out in detail the way in which sinister interest operated in this context. He argued that the appalling state of the English system of judicial procedure was not, as he had previously tended to assume, the result of intellectual deficiency on the part of lawyers, but the product of a steady and systematic policy on the part of the legal profession, and particularly the judges. The lawyers wished to maximize their income, which they primarily received in the form of fees, whatever the expense to suitors, and thence to the community in general. The lawyers had formed a 'law partnership' in order to extract the maximum amount of profit possible from suitors. The law partnership, and in particular the judges, had not only established the existing system of legal procedure in order to benefit themselves, they had also managed to convince legislators and the community generally that the system was excellent in all respects. By their use of technical language, they had prevented non-lawyers from investigating the state of the law, and thereby thwarted any attempts to introduce reform. In short, the existence of the sinister interest of the law partnership explained how things had got into the disastrous state in which they then existed, and why lawyers were adamantly opposed to reform.

Bentham's attribution of a sinister interest to the law partnership first appeared in print in *Scotch Reform* in 1807 (published in 1808), which drew on the more general material on judicial procedure and evidence on which he had been working since 1803. Bentham composed *Scotch Reform* in response to a proposal announced by government for the reform of the law of civil procedure in Scotland, and in the hope that he would be asked to codify for Scotland. In this work he was extremely critical of the law partnership, arguing that no meaningful reform would result if things were left to the lawyers. He did not, as yet, implicate Parliament in the partnership. The politicians, like the people, had been deluded by the lawyers on the question of the desirability and feasibility of law reform. He soon came to think differently. By the first half of 1809, when he composed the text later published as *Elements of the Art of Packing*, he had come to realize that sinister interest was a feature of both the legal and political establishments: it was Parliament which permitted the continuation of the fees which judges had imposed for the benefit of the law partnership. Bentham's immediate concern in the work was with the danger posed to the liberty of the press by prosecutions for libel, and by the appointment in these cases of special juries, which were packed with men subservient to the will of the judge. Both the legal and political establishments had an interest in destroying the liberty of the press, for it offered the greatest threat to their position. By exposing the abuses from which they profited, a free press would provide a check to misrule. So all who benefited from abuse—and this included all members of the legal and political establishments—were united in their desire to destroy the freedom of the press, for in achieving that end they safeguarded the abuses from which they derived so much profit.

With the insight that every aspect of the state was permeated by sinister interest, Bentham was in a position to launch a sustained and detailed attack on the English establishment—an onslaught which he carried on unremittingly until his death in 1832. It is clearly inappropriate to argue that he was 'converted' or underwent a 'transition' to political radicalism in 1809. The elements of his political radicalism were already in place when he began to write on parliamentary reform in the middle of 1809, stimulated as he was into doing so by a speech delivered by his stepbrother, Charles Abbot, to the House of Commons on 1 June 1809. It would not, however, be misleading to say that Bentham underwent a 'transition' to political radicalism between 1803 and 1809, as he applied his notion of sinister interest ever more generally to the English establishment. By June 1809, when he began to write on parliamentary reform, he was already a political radical. The work he eventually published as *Plan of Parliamentary Reform* in 1817 contained a 'Catechism' written in 1809–10, and a long 'Introduction' written in 1816–17. His aim in both was to secure 'democratic ascendancy' within the existing institutions of the British polity. The House of Commons would be made genuinely representative of the people, and it would be freed from any corruptive influence exercised by the King and the House of Lords. This would be achieved in large part by an extensive reform of the electoral system, which would be characterized by universal manhood suffrage, annual elections, equal electoral districts, and the secret ballot. The key proposal was the secret ballot. The secret ballot would enable each man to vote for the candidate whom he considered would best promote his own interest, for the universal interest was no more than the aggregate of the interests of the individuals who composed the community. The secret ballot would exclude the baleful effects of the influence traditionally exercised over voters by the wealthy and privileged within the local community. There would be no point, for instance, in offering a bribe, if the briber had no way of knowing whether the person he had bribed had voted as directed or not. Bentham never wavered from his commitment to the secret ballot, despite pressure on occasion to do so for tactical reasons. Without the secret ballot, the rest of the reforms would, in his view, have been ineffective; on the other hand, the introduction of the secret ballot alone would have paved the way to further reform.

Having recognized the existence of sinister interest in the legal and political establishments, Bentham extended his investigation to the ecclesiastical establishment. He had always argued that theology should not have any influence over morals and legislation, but had not hitherto attacked religious belief on the grounds of its pernicious effects on human happiness. He now saw that religious belief was used to further the sinister interest of the priesthood and those linked with it. As far as constitutional law was concerned, his main recommendation was that there should be no religious establishment. In Britain, the Anglican Church was merely another instrument in the hands of rulers to oppress and extort resources from subjects. The clergy extracted large sums of money from the population generally, in order to provide income for members of the ruling few, without having to provide any service or labour in return. The state supported the Church with its coercive force, while the Church manufactured delusive arguments in support of the state. Indeed, the scale of abuse in the Church was not only greater than that in the political and legal establishments, but acted as a bulwark against reform elsewhere. Bentham was particularly critical of the role of the Church in education, both in schools and in the universities of Oxford and Cambridge. In relation to the poor, its policy was to exclude from the benefits of education those unwilling to declare their belief in Anglican doctrine, and to pervert the morals and intellects of those who were willing. Bentham never overcame his resentment at being forced to subscribe to the Thirty-nine Articles while a student at Oxford, and it was this experience which led him to insist that the provision of education should not be linked to the profession of belief. As far as the Anglican Church in general was concerned, Bentham recommended its 'euthanasia', whereby, as livings and other offices became vacant, they would be abolished. The present possessors would retain their incomes and thereby not suffer the pain of disappointment, while the expense of the religious establishment to the state, and thus to the people generally, would gradually diminish, and the additional income derived from the sale of its assets would be used to reduce taxation. Those people who wished to receive religious instruction could continue to do so at their own expense.

Bentham's writings on parliamentary reform, while focusing on the reform of the House of Commons in order to render it dependent on the people, assumed the continuing existence of the King and the House of Lords. It was only in 1818 that Bentham appears to have committed himself to republicanism, by which he meant a representative democracy which did not include a monarchy or an aristocracy. This development in his thought was linked, perhaps, to his experience in attempting to persuade a 'constituted authority' to accept his services as a codifier. As stated above, he had first offered to draw up a code for Scotland in 1808, but his campaign had begun in earnest in 1811 when he had offered to draw up civil and penal codes for the United States of America. He had assumed that penal and civil codes of the sort he advocated might be introduced under any system of constitutional law. By 1818, perhaps because of the rejection of his offer by Alexander I of Russia, he had come to the view that it was only under a representative democracy that rulers would countenance the introduction of an all-comprehensive and rationalized code of law. It was necessary first to introduce a representative democracy in order to achieve utilitarian reform in other areas of law. Political reform was henceforward Bentham's central concern. When at last, in April 1822, he received an acceptance of his offer to draw up penal, civil, and constitutional codes from the Portuguese Cortes, it was to the constitutional code that he immediately turned his attention, and which dominated the final decade of his life.

As we have seen, for Bentham the key principle of constitutional design was to ensure the dependence of rulers on subjects, hence his rejection of the division of power, whether in the form of the balance of powers or the separation of powers, on account if its unsuitability in this respect. Instead he proposed chains of superordination and subordination, based on the capacity of the superior to appoint and dismiss (in Bentham's terminology to locate and dislocate) the inferior, and to subject the inferior to punishment and other forms of vexation. The supreme power or sovereignty in the state would be vested in the people, who would hold the constitutive power. Immediately subordinate to the people would be the legislature, elected by universal manhood suffrage, and subordinate to the legislature would be the administrative and judicial powers. The system of representative democracy was not an end in itself—the end was the greatest happiness—but it was an indispensable means to that end, in that it was only under such a system of government that effective measures could be implemented to secure the appropriate aptitude of officials and minimize the expense of government. The securities for official aptitude—otherwise termed securities against misrule—included the exclusion of factitious dignities (or titles of honour), the economical auction, subjection to punishment at the hands of the legal tribunals of the state, and the need to pass an examination, but the most important was publicity. Bentham went to great lengths to ensure that government would be open to public scrutiny, and thence subject to the force of the moral or popular sanction operating through the public opinion tribunal, which consisted of all those who commented on political matters, and of whom newspaper editors were the most important members. Bentham saw the freedom of the press as a vital bulwark against misrule, and therefore his attempt to encourage the diffusion of literacy by linking a reading and writing qualification to the suffrage. The main difficulty which had to be overcome was the propensity of rulers to make the sinister sacrifice, that is, to sacrifice the interest of the community to their own particular and sinister interest. All these measures would ensure that, instead of an opposition of interest between ruler and subject, there would be an identification of interest: in other words, the ruler would be placed in such a situation that the only way of promoting his own interest would be through the promotion of the general interest. Bentham's commitment to democratic government had a further consequence for his thought. The tension between the role of the legislator in promoting the happiness of the community and his insistence that the individual was, in general, the best judge of his own interest, was resolved by a representative democracy. With sovereignty placed in the people, those who were the best judge of their interests were given the power (through their deputies in the legislature) to pursue them effectively.

Bibliography

The following bibliography contains works referred to in the text and notes. For a comprehensive Bentham bibliography see http://www.ucl.ac.uk/Bentham-Project/info/bibliog.htm.

A. JEREMY BENTHAM

I. Volumes in *The Collected Works of Jeremy Bentham*, General Editors J. H. Burns (1961–79), J. R. Dinwiddy (1977–83), F. Rosen (1983–95), F. Rosen and P. Schofield (1995–2003), P. Schofield (2003–)

Chrestomathia, ed. M. J. Smith and W. H. Burston (Oxford, 1983).

Colonies, Commerce, and Constitutional Law: Rid Yourselves of Ultramaria and other writings on Spain and Spanish America, ed. P. Schofield (Oxford, 1995).

A Comment on the Commentaries and A Fragment on Government, ed. J. H. Burns and H. L. A. Hart (London, 1977).

Constitutional Code, Volume I, ed. F. Rosen and J. H. Burns (Oxford, 1983).

The Correspondence of Jeremy Bentham. Volume 1: 1752–76, ed. T. L. S. Sprigge (London, 1968).

—— *Volume 2: 1777–80*, ed. T. L. S. Sprigge (London, 1968).

—— *Volume 3: January 1781 to October 1788*, ed. I. R. Christie (London, 1971).

—— *Volume 4: October 1788 to December 1793*, ed. A. Taylor Milne (London, 1981).

—— *Volume 5: January 1794 to December 1797*, ed. A. Taylor Milne (London, 1981).

—— *Volume 6: January 1798 to December 1801*, ed. J. R. Dinwiddy (Oxford, 1984).

—— *Volume 7: January 1802 to December 1808*, ed. J. R. Dinwiddy (Oxford, 1988).

—— *Volume 8: January 1809 to December 1816*, ed. S. Conway (Oxford, 1988).

—— *Volume 9: January 1817 to June 1820*, ed. S. Conway (Oxford, 1989).

—— *Volume 10: July 1820 to December 1821*, ed. S. Conway (Oxford, 1994).

—— *Volume 11: January 1822 to June 1824*, ed. C. Fuller (Oxford, 2000).

—— *Volume 12: July 1824 to June 1828*, ed. L. O'Sullivan and C. Fuller (Oxford, 2006).

Deontology together with A Table of the Springs of Action and Article on Utilitarianism, ed. A. Goldworth (Oxford, 1983).

First Principles preparatory to Constitutional Code, ed. P. Schofield (Oxford, 1989).

An Introduction to the Principles of Morals and Legislation, ed. J. H. Burns and H. L. A. Hart (London, 1970).

'Legislator of the World': Writings on Codification, Law, and Education, ed. P. Schofield and J. Harris (Oxford, 1998).

Of Laws in General, ed. H. L. A. Hart (London, 1970).

Official Aptitude Maximized; Expense Minimized, ed. P. Schofield (Oxford, 1993).

Political Tactics, ed. M. H. James, C. Blamires, and C. Pease-Watkin (Oxford, 1999).

Rights, Representation, and Reform: Nonsense upon Stilts and other Writings on the French Revolution, ed. P. Schofield, C. Pease-Watkin, and C. Blamires (Oxford, 2002).

Securities against Misrule and other constitutional writings for Tripoli and Greece, ed. P. Schofield (Oxford, 1990).

Writings on the Poor Laws: Volume I, ed. M. Quinn (Oxford, 2001).

II. Other Collections and Editions of Bentham's Writings

Bentham's Auto-Icon and related writings, ed. J. E. Crimmins (Bristol, 2002).

De l'ontologie et autres texts sur les fictions, ed. P. Schofield, J. P. Cléro, and C. Laval (Paris, 1997).

Jeremy Bentham's Economic Writings: Critical Edition based on his printed works and unpublished manuscripts, ed. W. Stark, 3 vols. (London, 1952–4).

Tactique des assemblées législatives, suivie d'un traité des sophimses politiques, ed. Étienne Dumont, 2 vols. (Geneva and Paris, 1816).

Théorie des peines et des récompenses, ed. Étienne Dumont, 2 vols. (London, 1811).

Traités de législation civile et pénale, ed. Étienne Dumont, 3 vols. (Paris, 1802).

The Works of Jeremy Bentham, published under the superintendence of his executor, John Bowring, 11 vols. (Edinburgh, 1838–43).

III. Single Works

Analysis of the Influence of Natural Religion on the Temporal Happiness of Mankind (London, 1822).

'Anti-Machiavel' Letters, *Public Advertiser*: 15, 16 June 1789 (Letter I); 3, 4 July 1789 (Letter II); 11 July 1789 (Letter III); and 23 July 1789 (Letter IV).

'Art. VIII—Observations on the actual State of the English Law of Real Property, with the Outline of a Code. By James Humphreys, Esq. of Lincoln's Inn, Barrister. 8vo. London', *Westminster Review*, vol. vi, no. xii (Oct. 1826), 446–507.

'Auto-Icon; or, Of the Farther Uses of the Dead to the Living', printed for, but not published in, Bowring.

'Bentham, Brougham, and Law Reform', *Westminster Review*, vol. xi, no. xxii (Oct. 1829), 447–71.

Bentham's Radical Reform Bill (London, 1819).

The Book of Fallacies: from unfinished papers of Jeremy Bentham. By A Friend (London, 1824).

Church-of-Englandism and its Catechism Examined (London, 1818).

'Codification Proposal, addressed by Jeremy Bentham to All Nations professing Liberal Opinions', printed in 1822, with Supplements printed in 1827 and 1830.

'Colonies and Navy', *c.*1790, in Stark, i. 209–18.

'Colonization Society Proposal' (1831).

'Considérations d'un Anglois sur la Composition des États-Généraux y compris réponses aux questions proposées aux Notables &c. 1788' (1788–9), in *Rights, Representation, and Reform*, 63–146.

'Constitutional Code: matter occasioned by Greece' (1823), in *Securities against Misrule*, 257–76.

'Constitutional Code Rationale' (1822), in *First Principles*, 227–331.

'Defence of Economy against the late Mr. Burke', *The Pamphleteer*, vol. ix, no. xvii (1817), 3–47.

'Defence of Economy against the Right Hon. George Rose', *The Pamphleteer*, vol. x, no. xx (1817), 281–332.

Defence of Usury; Shewing the Impolicy of the Present Legal Restraints on the terms of Pecuniary Bargains. In a Series of Letters to a Friend. To which is added, A Letter to Adam Smith, Esq: LL,D. On the Discouragements opposed by the above Restraints to the Progress of Inventive Industry (London, 1787).

'Division of Power' (1789), in *Rights, Representation, and Reform*, 405–18.

'Draught of a New Plan for the organisation of the Judicial Establishment in France: proposed as a Succedaneum to the Draught presented, for the same purpose, by the Committee of the Constitution, to the National Assembly, December 21st, 1789', printed in 1790.

'Economy as applied to Office' (1822), in *First Principles*, 1–122.

The Elements of the Art of Packing, as applied to Special Juries, particularly in Cases of Libel Law (London, 1821).

Emancipate Your Colonies! Addressed to the National Convention of France, A° 1793, shewing the uselessness and mischievousness of distant dependencies to an European state (London, 1830).

'Emancipation Spanish' (1820), in *Colonies, Commerce, and Constitutional Law*, 195–276.

'Equity Dispatch Court Bill: being a Bill for the Institution of an experimental Judicatory under the name of the Court of Dispatch, for exemplifying in practice the manner in which the proposed Summary may be substituted to the so called Regular System of Procedure; and for clearing away by the Experiment, the arrear of Business in the Equity Courts' (1829–31), in Bowring, iii. 319–431.

Equity Dispatch Court Proposal; containing a plan for the speedy and unexpensive termination of the suits now depending in Equity Courts. With the form of a petition, and some account of a proposed Bill for that purpose (London, 1830).

'Essay on Language', in Bowring, viii. 295–338.

'Essay on Logic', in Bowring, viii. 213–93.

'First Lines of a proposed Code of Law for any Nation compleat and rationalized' (1821), in *'Legislator of the World'*, 187–239.

'A Fragment on Ontology', in Bowring, viii. 193–211.

'Fragments on Universal Grammar', in Bowring, viii. 339–57.

'France' (1788), in *Rights, Representation, and Reform*, 1–61.

'Greece: Principles of Legislation as to Constitutional Law' (1823), in *Securities against Misrule*, 181–90.

'Identification of Interests' (1822), in *First Principles*, 123–47.

Indications respecting Lord Eldon (London, 1825).

'Institute of Political Economy' (1801–4), in Stark, iii. 303–80.

'Jeremy Bentham to Greek Legislators' (1823), in *Securities against Misrule*, 191–205.

'Jeremy Bentham to the Future Electors of Blackburn' (London, [1831]).

Justice and Codification Petitions: being forms proposed for signature by all persons whose desire it is to see Justice no longer sold, delayed, or denied: and to obtain a possibility of that knowledge of the law, in proportion to the want of which they are subjected to unjust punishments, and deprived of the Benefit of their Rights (London, 1829).

'Law Reform Association Proposal', printed in 1830.

'Law versus arbitrary power:—or, A Hatchet for Dr. Paley's Net' (1809).

'Letters from Jeremy Bentham and Hassuna D'Ghies to John Quincy Adams' (1823), in *Securities against Misrule*, 143–80.

Lord Brougham Displayed: including I. Boa Constrictor, alias Helluo Curiarum; II. Observations on the Bankruptcy Court Bill, now ripened into an Act; III. Extracts from proposed Constitutional Code (London, 1832).

'Necessity of an Omnipotent Legislature' (1791), in *Rights, Representation, and Reform*, 263–88.

'Nonsense upon Stilts, or Pandora's Box Opened, or the French Declaration of Rights prefixed to the Constitution of 1791 laid open and exposed—with a comparative sketch of what has been done on the same subject in the Constitution of 1795, and a sample of Citizen Sieyès' (1795), in *Rights, Representation, and Reform*, 317–401.

Not Paul, but Jesus (London, 1823).

'Observations by an Englishman on a passage in Raffanel's *Histoire des événemens de la Grèce*, Paris, 1822' (1823), in *Securities against Misrule*, 207–56.

'Observations d'un Anglois sur un écrit intitulé *Arrête de la Noblesse de Bretagne*' (1788), in *Rights, Representation, and Reform*, 147–65.

Observations on Mr. Secretary Peel's House of Commons Speech, 21st March, 1825, introducing his Police Magistrates' Salary raising Bill. Date of Order for Printing, 24th March 1825. Also on the Announced Judges' Salary Raising Bill, and the Pending County Courts Bill (London, 1825).

'Observations on the Draughts of Declarations-of-Rights presented to the Committee of the Constitution of the National Assembly of France' (1789), in *Rights, Representation, and Reform*, 177–92.

Observations on the Restrictive and Prohibitory Commercial System; especially with a reference to the Decree of the Spanish Cortes of July 1820 (London, 1821).

'Of the Influence of the Administrative Power over the Legislative' (1789), in *Rights, Representation, and Reform*, 419–27.

'On Retrenchment' (1828), in *Official Aptitude Maximized; Expense Minimized*, 342–67.

On the Liberty of the Press, and Public Discussion (London, 1821).

'Outline of a Plan of a General Register of Real Property', dated 4 July 1831, in Bowring, v. 417–35.

Panopticon: or, the Inspection-house, 3 vols. (Dublin and London, 1791).

Papers relative to Codification and Public Instruction: including correspondence with the Russian Emperor, and divers constituted authorities in the American United States (London, 1817).

'Parcus' Letters, *Morning Herald*: Letter I 'Peel, Bentham, and Judges' Salaries' (7 Apr. 1828); Letter II 'Peel and Munificence;—Bentham and Niggardliness' (15 Apr. 1828); Letter III 'Peel, Tenterden, Bentham, and Law Reform' (8 May 1828); Letter IV 'Written Pleadings Pickpocket Lies' (28 May 1828); and Letter V 'Inquiry-Splitting and Reform-Quashing Commission Jobs' (29 May 1828).

Parliamentary Candidate's proposed Declaration of Principles: or say, A Test proposed for Parliamentary Candidates (London, 1831).

'Parliamentary Reform' (1789), in *Rights, Representation, and Reform*, 428–34.

Plan of Parliamentary Reform (London, 1817).

'*Projet* of a Constitutional Code for France' (1789), in *Rights, Representation, and Reform*, 227–61.

A Protest against Law-Taxes, shewing the peculiar mischievousness of all such impositions as add to the expense of an appeal to justice (London, 1795).

'Radicalism not Dangerous' (1819–20), in Bowring, iii. 599–622.

Rationale of Judicial Evidence, specially applied to English practice, ed. J. S. Mill, 5 vols. (London, 1827).

The Rationale of Reward (London, 1825).

'Rid Yourselves of Ultramaria being the advice of Jeremy Bentham as given in a series of letters to the Spanish people' (1820–2), in *Colonies, Commerce, and Constitutional Law*, 1–194.

Scotch Reform; considered, with reference to the Plan, proposed in the Late Parliament, for the regulation of the Courts, and the Administration of Justice, in Scotland: with Illustrations from English Non-reform: in the course of which divers imperfections, abuses, and corruptions, in the Administration of Justice, with their causes, are now, for the first time, brought to light. In a series of Letters, addressed to the Right Hon. Lord Grenville (London, 1808).

'Securities against Misrule' (1822), in *Securities against Misrule*, 23–141.

'Short Views of Economy for the use of the French Nation but not unapplicable to the English' (1789), in *Rights, Representation, and Reform*, 193–203.

'Summary of a Work intituled Emancipate Your Colonies in a letter from Philo-Hispanus to the Spanish people' (1820), in *Colonies, Commerce, and Constitutional Law*, 277–344.

'Summary View of the Plan of a Judicatory, under the name of the Court of Lords' Delegates', dated 10 Jan. 1808, in Bowring, v. 55–60.

'Supply—New Species Proposed' (1789), in *Rights, Representation, and Reform*, 205–26.

'Supreme Operative' (1821–2), in *First Principles*, 149–226.

A Table of the Springs of Action (London, 1817).

Truth versus Ashhurst; or Law as it is, contrasted with what it is said to be (London, 1823).

'A View of the Hard-Labour Bill; being an abstract of a pamphlet, intituled, "Draught of a Bill, to punish by Imprisonment and Hard-Labour, certain Offenders; and to establish proper Places for their Reception." Interspersed with Observations relative to the subject of the above Draught in particular, and to Penal Jurisprudence in general', printed in 1778.

The White Bull, an Oriental History, from an Ancient Syrian Manuscript, communicated by Mr. Voltaire, 2 vols. (London, 1774).

B. PRIMARY SOURCES

Anon., *Parliamentary Candidate Society, instituted to promote the return of Fit and Proper Members to Parliament* (London, 1831).

Anon., *The Political Constitution of the Spanish Monarchy. Proclaimed in Cadiz, 19th of March, 1812* (London, 1813).

Anon., *Proceedings relative to the Ulster Assembly of Volunteer Delegates: on the subject of a more equal representation of the people in the Parliament of Ireland. To which are annexed, Letters from the Duke of Richmond, Dr. Price, Mr. Wyvill, and others* (Belfast, 1783).

[ARGENS, JEAN BAPTISTE DE BOYER, Marquis D], *Lettres Juives, ou Correspondance Philosophique, Historique & Critique, Entre un Juif Voïageur en différens Etats de l'Europe,*

& ses Correspondans en divers Endroits. Nouvelle Edition augmentée de XX Nouvelles Lettres, de Quantité de Remarques, & de plusieurs Figures, 6 vols. (La Haye, 1738).

ASHHURST, WILLIAM, *Mr. Justice Ashhurst's Charge to the Grand Jury for the County of Middlesex*, printed by order of The Society for preserving Liberty and Property against Republicans and Levellers, [1792].

AUSTIN, JOHN, *The province of jurisprudence determined* (first published 1832), ed. W. E. Rumble (Cambridge, 1995).

BENTHAM, GEORGE, *George Bentham: Autobiography 1800–1834*, ed. M. Filipiuk (Toronto, 1997).

[BINGHAM, PEREGRINE and AUSTIN, CHARLES], *Parliamentary History and Review; Containing Reports of the Proceedings of the Two Houses of Parliament. With Critical Remarks on the Principal Measures of Each Session*, 2 vols (London, 1826).

BLACKSTONE, WILLIAM, *Commentaries on the Laws of England*, 4 vols (Oxford, 1765–9).

BROWNE, THOMAS, *Pseudodoxia Epidemica: or, Enquiries into Very many received Tenents, And commonly presumed Truths* (London, 1646).

BURDETT, FRANCIS, *The Substance of the Speech delivered by Sir Francis Burdett, Bart. in the House of Commons, on Tuesday, the 2d. of June, 1818, on moving a series of resolutions on the subject of Parliamentary Reform* (London, 1818).

BURKE, EDMUND, *The Writings and Speeches of Edmund Burke. Volume VIII: The French Revolution 1790–1794*, ed. L. G. Mitchell (Oxford, 1989).

CARTWRIGHT, JOHN, *The Legislative Rights of the Commonalty Vindicated; or, Take Your Choice! Representation and Respect: Imposition and Contempt. Annual Parliaments and Liberty: Long Parliaments and Slavery. The Second Edition* (London, 1777).

—— *A Bill of Rights and Liberties; or, an Act for a Constitutional Reform of Parliament* (London, 1817).

CLARENDON, EDWARD HYDE, 1st Earl of, *The History of the Rebellion and Civil Wars in England, begun in the Year 1641*, 3 vols. (Oxford, 1702–4).

[DEFOE, DANIEL], *The Life and Strange Surprizing Adventures of Robinson Crusoe, of York, Mariner* (London, 1719).

DENMAN, THOMAS, *Every Man his own Attorney* (London, [1830?]).

FÉNELON, FRANÇOIS DE, *Telemachus, son of Ulysses* (first published 1699), ed. and trans. P. Riley (Cambridge, 1994).

FORTESCUE, Sir JOHN, *On the Laws and Governance of England*, ed. S. Lockwood (Cambridge, 1997).

GIBBON, EDWARD, *The History of the Decline and Fall of the Roman Empire. Volume the First* (London, 1776).

HARRIS, JAMES, *Hermes: or, A Philosophical Inquiry concerning Language and Universal Grammar* (London, 1751).

HARTLEY, DAVID, *Observations on Man, his Frame, his Duty, and his Expectations*, 2 vols. (London, 1749).

HELVÉTIUS, CLAUDE ADRIEN, *De L'Esprit: or, Essays on the Mind, and its several Faculties* (London, 1759).

HOBBES, THOMAS, *Leviathan* (first published 1651), ed. R. Tuck (Cambridge, 1991).

HOGAN, DENIS, *An Appeal to the Public, and a Farewell Address to the Army, by Brevet-Major Hogan, late a Captain in the Thirty-second Regiment of Infantry—in which he resigned his commission, in consequence of the treatment he experienced from the Duke of*

York, and the system that prevails in the Army respecting promotions; including some strictures upon the general conduct of our military force (London, 1808).

HOWELL, T. J., *A Complete Collection of State Trials and proceedings for High Treason and other Crimes and Misdemeanors*, Vol. XXIX (London, 1821).

[HOWLEY], WILLIAM, Lord Bishop of London, *A Charge delivered to the Clergy of the Diocese of London at the primary visitation of that Diocese in the year 1814* (London, 1814).

HUME, DAVID, *The Life of David Hume, Esq. Written by himself* (London, 1777).

—— *A Treatise of Human Nature* (first published 1739–40), ed. L. A. Selby-Bigge, 2nd edn., revised by P. H. Nidditch (Oxford, 1978).

—— *The History of England from the Invasion of Julius Caesar to The Revolution in 1688* (first published 1754–62), 6 vols (Indianapolis, 1983).

—— *Essays Moral, Political, and Literary*, revised edn, ed. E. F. Miller (Indianapolis, 1985).

—— *An Enquiry concerning the Principles of Morals* (first published 1751), ed. T. L. Beauchamp (Oxford, 1998).

HUMPHREYS, JAMES, *Observations on the Actual State of the English Laws of Real Property; with the Outline of a Code* (London, 1826).

[LIND, JOHN], *Remarks on the Principal Acts of the Thirteenth Parliament of Great Britain. Vol. I. Containing Remarks on the Acts relating to the Colonies. With a Plan of Reconciliation* (London, 1775).

LOCKE, JOHN, *An Essay concerning Human Understanding* (first published 1689), ed. P. H. Nidditch (Oxford, 1975).

[MACGOWAN, JOHN], *Priestcraft Defended. A Sermon occasioned by the Expulsion of Six Young Gentlemen from the University of Oxford, for Praying, Reading and Expounding the Scriptures* (London, 1768).

MALTHUS, THOMAS, *An Essay on the Principle of Population, as it affects the future improvement of society, with remarks on the speculations of Mr. Godwin, M. Condorcet, and other writers* (London, 1798).

MIDDLETON, CONYERS, *A Free Inquiry into the Miraculous Powers, Which are supposed to have subsisted in the Christian Church, from the Earliest Ages through several successive Centuries. By which it is shewn, That we have no sufficient Reason to believe, upon the Authority of the Primitive Fathers, That any such powers were continued to the Church, after the Days of the Apostles* (London, 1749).

MILL, JOHN STUART, *Essays on Ethics, Religion, and Society*, The Collected Works of John Stuart Mill, vol. X, ed. J. M. Robson (Toronto, 1969).

MONTESQUIEU, Baron DE, *The Spirit of the Laws* (first published 1748), trans. T. Nugent, introd. F. Neumann, 2 vols. (London, 1949).

O'CONNELL, DANIEL, *The Correspondence of Daniel O'Connell*, ed. M. R. O'Connell, 8 vols. (Dublin, 1972–80).

PAINE, THOMAS, *Rights of Man: being an answer to Mr. Burke's attack on the French Revolution* (London, 1791).

—— *The Rights of Man. Part the Second. Combining Principle and Practice* (London, 1792).

PALEY WILLIAM, *The Principles of Moral and Political Philosophy* (London, 1785).

——*Reasons for Contentment; addressed to the Labouring Part of the British Public* (London, 1793).

——*Natural Theology: or, Evidences of the Existence and Attributes of the Deity, collected from the appearances of nature* (London, 1802).

——*The Works of William Paley, D.D. with A Life, by Alexander Chalmers, Esq.*, 5 vols. (London, 1819).

PHILLIPS, Sir RICHARD, *A Letter to the Livery of London, relative to the views of the writer in executing the Office of Sheriff*, 2nd edn. (London, 1808).

PRIESTLEY, JOSEPH, *An Essay on the First Principles of Government; and on the nature of Political, Civil, and Religious Liberty* (London, 1768).

[RICHMOND, CHARLES LENNOX, 3rd Duke of], *A Letter from His Grace the Duke of Richmond to Lieutenant Colonel Sharman ... With Notes, By A Member of the Society for Constitutional Information* (London, 1792).

ROMILLY, SAMUEL, *Memoirs of the Life of Sir Samuel Romilly, written by himself; with a selection from his correspondence. Edited by his Sons*, 2nd edn, 3 vols. (London, 1840).

RUSH, RICHARD, *A Residence at the Court of London* (London, 1833).

SINCLAIR, Sir JOHN, *The Statistical Account of Scotland. Drawn up from the communications of the Ministers of the different Parishes*, 21 vols (Edinburgh, 1791–9).

SMITH, ADAM, *An Inquiry into the nature and causes of the Wealth of Nations* (first published 1776), 2 vols., ed. R. H. Campbell, A. S. Skinner, and W. B. Todd (Oxford, 1976).

SMITH, THOMAS SOUTHWOOD, 'Use of the Dead to the Living. An Appeal to the Public and the Legislature on the Necessity of affording Dead Bodies to the Schools of Anatomy by Legislative Enactment', *Westminster Review*, vol. ii, no. iii (July 1824), 59–97.

——*A Lecture delivered over the Remains of Jeremy Bentham Esq.* (London, 1832).

TOOKE, JOHN HORNE, *A Letter to John Dunning, Esq.* (London, 1778).

TOWNSEND, JOSEPH, *A Journey through Spain in the years 1786 and 1787*, 3 vols. (London, 1791).

WARBURTON, WILLIAM, *The Alliance between Church and State, or, the Necessity and Equity of an Established Religion and a Test-Law Demonstrated, from the Essence and End of Civil Society, upon the fundamental principles of the Law of Nature and Nations* (London, 1736).

C. SECONDARY SOURCES

ASPINALL, A., *Politics and the Press c.1780–1850* (London, 1949).

ATLAY, J. B., *The Victorian Chancellors*, 2 vols. (London, 1906–8).

AYER, A. J., *Language, Truth and Logic* (London, 1936).

BAHMUELLER, C. F., *The National Charity Company: Jeremy Bentham's Silent Revolution* (Berkeley, 1981).

BAKER, J. H., *An Introduction to English Legal History*, 3rd edn. (London, 1990).

BAUMGARDT, D., *Bentham and the Ethics of Today* (Princeton, 1952).

BEATTIE, J. M., *Crime and the Courts in England* (Princeton, 1986).

BEN DOR, O., *Constitutional Limits and the Public Sphere: A Critical Study of Bentham's Constitutionalism* (Oxford, 2000).

BERMAN, D., *A History of Atheism in Britain from Hobbes to Russell* (London, 1988).

Black, E. C., *The Association: British Extraparliamentary Political Organization 1769–1793* (Cambridge, Mass., 1963).

Blamires, C., 'Étienne Dumont: Genevan Apostle of Utility', *Utilitas: A Journal of Utilitarian Studies*, 2 (1990), 55–70.

Boralevi, L. C., *Bentham and the Oppressed* (Berlin, 1984).

Brooke, J., *The House of Commons 1754–1790: Introductory Survey* (Oxford, 1968).

Brown, S. J., *The National Churches of England, Ireland, and Scotland 1801–1846* (Oxford, 2001).

Burns, J. H.,'Bentham and the French Revolution', *Transactions of the Royal Historical Society*, 5th ser., 16 (1966), 95–114.

—— 'Bentham on Sovereignty: An Exploration', in M. H. James (ed.), *Bentham and Legal Theory* (offprint from *Northern Ireland Legal Quarterly*, 24 1973), 133–51.

—— 'Jeremy Bentham: From Radical Enlightenment to Philosophical Radicalism', *The Bentham Newsletter*, 8 (1984), 4–14.

—— 'Bentham and Blackstone: A Lifetime's Dialectic', *Utilitas: A Journal of Utilitarian Studies*, 1 (1989), 22–40.

—— 'Nature and Natural Authority in Bentham', *Utilitas: A Journal of Utilitarian Studies*, 5 (1993), 209–19.

Cannon, J., *Parliamentary Reform 1640–1832* (Cambridge, 1973).

Christie, I. R., *Wilkes, Wyvill and Reform: The Parliamentary Reform Movement in British Politics 1760–1785* (London, 1962).

—— *Myth and Reality in Late-Eighteenth-Century British Politics and Other Papers* (Berkeley, 1970).

—— *Stress and Stability in Late Eighteenth-Century Britain: Reflections on the British Avoidance of Revolution* (Oxford, 1984).

—— *The Benthams in Russia, 1780–1791* (Oxford, 1993).

Clarke, M. L., *George Grote: A Biography* (London, 1962).

—— *Paley: Evidences for the Man* (London, 1974).

Conway, S., 'Bentham versus Pitt: Jeremy Bentham and British Foreign Policy 1789', *Historical Journal*, 30 (1987), 791–809.

Crimmins, J. E., *Secular Utilitarianism: Social Science and the Critique of Religion in the Thought of Jeremy Bentham* (Oxford, 1990).

—— 'Bentham's Political Radicalism Reexamined', *Journal of the History of Ideas*, 54 (1994), 259–81.

—— 'Jeremy Bentham and Daniel O'Connell: Their Correspondence and Radical Alliance, 1828–31', *Historical Journal*, 40 (1997), 359–87.

—— 'Bentham's Religious Radicalism Revisited: A Response to Schofield', *History of Political Thought*, 22 (2001), 494–500.

Dickinson, H. T., *Liberty and Property: Political Ideology in Eighteenth-Century Britain* (London, 1977).

—— *British Radicalism and the French Revolution 1789–1815* (Oxford, 1985).

Dinwiddy, J. R., 'Bentham's Transition to Political Radicalism', *Journal of the History of Ideas*, 35 (1975), 683–700.

—— 'Bentham and the Early Nineteenth Century', *The Bentham Newsletter*, 8 (1984), 15–33.

—— 'Early-Nineteenth-Century Reactions to Benthamism', *Transactions of the Royal Historical Society*, 5th ser., 34 (1984), 47–69.

——'Adjudication Under Bentham's Pannomion', *Utilitas: A Journal of Utilitarian Studies*, 1 (1989), 283–9.

——*Bentham*, (Oxford, 1989).

DOME, T., *The Political Economy of Public Finance in Britain 1767–1873* (London, 2004).

DOYLE, W., *The Oxford History of the French Revolution* (Oxford, 1989).

DRAPER, A. J., 'Cesare Beccaria's Influence on English Discussions of Punishment, 1764–1789', *History of European Ideas*, 26 (2000), 177–99.

DUBE, A., *The Theme of Acquisitiveness in Bentham's Political Thought* (New York, 1991).

EVERETT, C. W., *Jeremy Bentham* (London, 1966).

FENN, R. A., *James Mill's Political Thought* (New York, 1987).

FLETCHER, F. T. H., *Montesquieu and English Politics (1750–1800)* (London, 1939).

FULLER, C., (ed.), *The Old Radical: Representations of Jeremy Bentham* (London, 1998).

GASH, N., *Mr. Secretary Peel: The Life of Sir Robert Peel to 1830*, 2nd edn. (London, 1985).

GOODRICH, A., *Debating England's Aristocracy in the 1790s: Pamphlets, Polemics and Political Ideas* (Woodbridge, 2005).

HALÉVY, E, *The Growth of Philosophic Radicalism*, trans. M. Morris, corrected edn. (London, 1952).

HAMBURGER, J., *Intellectuals in Politics: John Stuart Mill and the Philosophic Radicals* (New Haven, 1965).

HARRISON, R., *Bentham* (London, 1983).

HART, H. L. A., *Essays on Bentham: Studies in Jurisprudence and Political Theory* (Oxford, 1982).

HOLE, R., *Pulpits, Politics and Public Order in England 1760–1832* (Cambridge, 1989).

HOOGENSEN, G., *International Relations, Security and Jeremy Bentham* (London, 2005).

HUME, L. J., 'Bentham's Panopticon: An Administrative History', *Historical Studies*, 15 (1973), 703–21, and 16 (1974), 36–54.

——*Bentham and Bureaucracy* (Cambridge, 1981).

JAMES, M.,'Bentham's Political Writings 1788–95', *The Bentham Newsletter*, 4 (1980), 22–4.

——'Bentham on Voter Rationality', *The Bentham Newsletter*, 10 (1982), 4–7.

——'Bentham's Democratic Theory at the Time of the French Revolution', *The Bentham Newsletter*, 10 (1986), 5–16.

KELLY, P., 'Constituents' Instructions to Members of Parliament in the Eighteenth Century', in C. Jones (ed.), *Party and Management in Parliament, 1660–1784*, (Leicester, 1984), 169–89.

KELLY, P. J., *Utilitarianism and Distributive Justice: Jeremy Bentham and the Civil Law* (Oxford, 1990).

KING, P. J., *Utilitarian Jurisprudence in America: The Influence of Bentham and Austin on American Legal Thought in the Nineteenth Century* (New York, 1986).

LIEBERMAN, D., *The Province of Legislation Determined: Legal Theory in Eighteenth-century Britain* (Cambridge, 1989).

——'Jeremy Bentham: Biography and Intellectual Biography', *History of Political Thought*, 20 (1999), 187–204.

—— 'Economy and Polity in Bentham's Science of Legislation', in S. Collini, R. Whatmore, and B. Young (eds.), *Economy, Polity, and Society: British Intellectual History 1750–1950* (Cambridge, 2000), 107–34.

LOBBAN, M., *The Common Law and English Jurisprudence 1760–1850* (Oxford, 1991).

—— 'Henry Brougham and Law Reform', *English Historical Review*, 115 (2000), 1184–215.

—— '"Old Wine in New Bottles": The Concept and Practice of Law Reform, *c.*1780–1830', in A. Burns and J. Innes (eds.), *Rethinking the Age of Reform* (Cambridge, 2003).

LONG, D. G., *Bentham on Liberty: Jeremy Bentham's Idea of Liberty in Relation to his Utilitarianism* (Toronto, 1977).

—— 'Censorial Jurisprudence and Political Radicalism: A Reconsideration of the Early Bentham', *The Bentham Newsletter*, 12 (1988), 4–23.

LYNCH, J., *The Spanish American Revolutions 1808–1826*, 2nd edn. (London, 1986).

LYONS, D., *In the Interest of the Governed: A Study in Bentham's Philosophy of Utility and Law*, revised edn. (Oxford, 1991).

LYSAGHT, L. J., 'Bentham on the Aspects of a Law', in M. H. James (ed.), *Bentham and Legal Theory* (offprint from *Northern Ireland Legal Quarterly*, 24 1973), 117–32.

MCDOWELL, R. B., *Ireland in the Age of Imperialism and Revolution 1760–1801* (Oxford, 1979).

MACK, M. P., *Jeremy Bentham: An Odyssey of Ideas 1748–92* (London, 1962).

MARMOY, C. F. A., 'The "Auto-Icon" of Jeremy Bentham at University College, London', reprinted from *Medical History*, 2 (1958).

MARVIN, U., 'Stones Which Fell From the Sky', in B. Zanda and M. Rotaru (eds.), *Meteorites: Their Impact on Science and History* (Cambridge, 2001), 16–29.

MITCHISON, R., *Agricultural Sir John: The Life of Sir John Sinclair of Ulbster 1754–1835* (London, 1962).

MORRIS, M., *The British Monarchy and the French Revolution* (New Haven, 1998).

NESBITT, G. L., *Benthamite Reviewing: The First Twelve Years of 'The Westminster Review' 1824–1836* (New York, 1934).

OGDEN, C. K., *Bentham's Theory of Fictions* (London, 1932).

O'GORMAN, F., *The Whig Party and the French Revolution* (London, 1967).

PHILIPS, C. H., *The East India Company 1784–1834*, 2nd edn. (Manchester, 1961).

PHILP, M. (ed.), *The French Revolution and British Popular Politics* (Cambridge, 1991).

PITTS, J., 'Legislator of the World? A Rereading of Bentham on Colonies', *Political Theory*, 31 (2003), 200–34.

PLAMENATZ, J., *The English Utilitarians*, 2nd edn. (Oxford, 1958).

POSTEMA, G. J.,'Fact, Fictions, and Law: Bentham on the Foundations of Evidence', in W. L. Twining (ed.), *Facts in Law* (Weisbaden, 1983).

—— *Bentham and the Common Law Tradition* (Oxford, 1986).

POYNTER, J. R., *Society and Pauperism: English Ideas on Poor Relief, 1795–1834* (London, 1969).

RICHARDSON, R., 'Bentham and "Bodies for Dissection"', *The Bentham Newsletter*, 10 (1986), 22–33.

—— *Death, Dissection and the Destitute* (London, 1987).

ROSEN, F., *Jeremy Bentham and Representative Democracy: A Study of the Constitutional Code* (Oxford, 1983).

——'Majorities and Minorities: a Classical Utilitarian View', in J. W. Chapman and A. Wertheimer (eds.), *Majorities and Minorities: Nomos XXXII* (New York, 1990), 24–43.

——*Bentham, Byron, and Greece: Constitutionalism, Nationalism, and Early Liberal Political Thought* (Oxford, 1992).

——'Individual Sacrifice and the Greatest Happiness: Bentham on Utility and Rights', *Utilitas*, 10 (1998), 129–43.

——*Classical Utilitarianism from Hume to Mill* (London, 2003).

SCHOFIELD, P.,'Political and Religious Radicalism in the Thought of Jeremy Bentham', *History of Political Thought*, 20 (1999), 272–91.

——'Jeremy Bentham, the Principle of Utility, and Legal Positivism', in M. D. A. Freeman (ed.), *Current Legal Problems 2003: Volume 56* (Oxford, 2004), 1–39.

SEMPLE, J. E., *Bentham's Prison: A Study of the Panopticon Penitentiary* (Oxford, 1993).

SHACKLETON, R., 'The Greatest Happiness of the Greatest Number: The History of Bentham's Phrase', *Studies in Voltaire and the Eighteenth Century*, 90 (1972), 1461–82.

SIGOT, N., 'Jeremy Bentham on Private and Public Wages and Employment: The Civil Servants, the Poor, and the Indigent', in L. S. Moss (ed.), *Joseph A. Schumpeter, Historian of Economics: Perspectives on the History of Economic Thought* (London, 1996), 196–218.

SMALL, S., *Political Thought in Ireland 1776–1798: Republicanism, Patriotism, and Radicalism* (Oxford, 2002).

SMITH, K. J. M., 'Anthony Hammond: "Mr Surface" Peel's Persistent Codifier', *Journal of Legal History*, 20 (1999), 24–44.

SOKOL, M., 'Jeremy Bentham and the Real Property Commission of 1828', *Utilitas: A Journal of Utilitarian Studies*, 4 (1992), 225–45.

STEINTRAGER, J., *Bentham* (Ithaca, NY, 1977).

——'Language and Politics: Bentham on Religion', *The Bentham Newsletter*, 4 (1980), 4–20.

STEPHEN, L., *The English Utilitarians*, 3 vols. (London, 1900).

STOKES, E., *The English Utilitarians and India* (Oxford, 1959).

THOMAS, P. D. G., *John Wilkes: A Friend to Liberty* (Oxford, 1996).

THOMAS, W., *The Philosophic Radicals: Nine Studies in Theory and Practice 1817–1841* (Oxford, 1979).

TWINING, W., 'The Contemporary Significance of Bentham's Anarchical Fallacies', *Archiv für Rechts- und Sozialphilosophie*, 61 (1975), 325–56.

VEITCH, G. S., *The Genesis of Parliamentary Reform* (first published 1913), Introduction by I. R. Christie (London, 1964).

WALLAS, G., *The Life of Francis Place 1771–1854*, 4th edn. (London, 1925).

WARKE, T., 'Multi-Dimensional Utility and the Index Number Problem: Jeremy Bentham, J. S. Mill, and Qualitative Hedonism', *Utilitas: A Journal of Utilitarian Studies*, 12 (2000), 176–203.

WIENER, J. H., *Radicalism and Freethought in Nineteenth-Century Britain: The Life of Richard Carlile* (London, 1983).

WINCH, D., *Classical Political Economy and Colonies* (London, 1965).

——'Bentham on Colonies and Empire', *Utilitas: A Journal of Utilitarian Studies*, 9 (1997), 147–54.

D. OTHER COLLECTIONS

A number of the articles listed above are available in the following collections:

DINWIDDY, J. R., *Radicalism and Reform in Britain, 1780–1850*, Introduction by H. T. Dickinson (London, 1992).

PAREKH, B. (ed.), *Jeremy Bentham: Critical Assessments*, 4 vols. (London, 1993).

POSTEMA, G. J. (ed.), *Bentham: Moral, Political and Legal Philosophy*, 2 vols. (Aldershot, 2002).

TWINING, W. (ed.), *Bentham: Selected Writings of John Dinwiddy* (Stanford, 2004).

Index